The Senate of Imperial Rome

Richard J.A. Talbert

THE SENATE OF IMPERIAL ROME

Princeton University Press
Princeton, New Jersey

Library of Congress Cataloging in Publication Data will be found on the last
printed page of this book

ISBN 0-691-05400-2

This book has been composed in Linotron Times Roman

Clothbound editions of Princeton University Press books are printed on acid-free
paper, and binding materials are chosen for strength and durability. Paperbacks, although
satisfactory for personal collections, are not usually suitable for library rebinding

Printed in the United States of America by Princeton University Press,
Princeton, New Jersey

To My Parents

CONTENTS

Part Three. Functions

LIST OF ILLUSTRATIONS

Figures

following page 99

Map. The meeting places of the senate and other locations of note in Rome, with enlargement of the central area

1. "Genius senatus" in bronze
2. Augustan coin with possible illustration of the Curia Julia
3. The restored Curia (front)
4. The restored Curia (side and rear)
5. The restored Curia (interior)
6. Reconstruction of the front of the Curia
7. Reconstruction of interior arrangements in the Curia
8. Coins

Acknowledgments

Figure 1 is reproduced from M. Almagro, *Guía de Mérida*, Madrid, 1979, plate X, with the author's permission. Figures 2 and 4 are reproduced from negatives F.U. 2979 F and 17 respectively, with the permission of the Fototeca Unione, Rome. Figure 3 is reproduced from Inst. Neg. 71.157, with the permission of the Istituto Archeologico Germanico, Rome. Figures 5, 6, and 7 are reproduced from A. Bartoli, *Curia Senatus: lo scavo e il restauro*, plates LIX, XCV and XCVI respectively, with the permission of the Istituto di Studi Romani. All the coins illustrated in Figure 8 are in the British Museum, and are reproduced with its permission.

PREFACE

No doubt many a topic for research emerges by unexpected means. In this instance, during the early 1970's when my study of Timoleon and Greek Sicily in the fourth century B.C. was nearing completion, it happened that I was directed to teach a substantial span of Roman history. It was thus that my interest was drawn to the potential value of studying the senate as a working assembly during the Principate. At an early stage it seemed that this might only duplicate research on the subject already planned by E. Badian. But he dispelled any such concern, and generously encouraged me to press ahead.

While it would be impossible to name every one of those to whom a debt is owed over many years, it is only right that certain individuals be singled out for thanks: among my colleagues here, A. E. Astin and R. P. Davis; elsewhere K. Hopkins and F. Millar, who both offered encouragement and commented upon certain chapters in draft; P. A. Brunt, A. Chastagnol, W. Eck, M. Grant, H. Halfmann, K. W. Harl, P. Herrmann, K. S. Morgan, J.K.B.M. Nicholas, J. Nicols, A. Ormanni, J. M. Reynolds, and A. G. Woodhead, all of whom furnished relevant material, both published and unpublished, or answered queries, or commented upon particular sections. Ian Alexander ably transformed my thumbnail sketch of the senate's meeting places into a lucid plan. The Armagh Planetarium supplied the times of sunrise and sunset at Rome and Carthage, and its staff were most courteous in explaining points raised in this connection. A visit to Rome in 1980 offered a welcome opportunity to examine the restored Curia and its surroundings at first hand.

The Queen's University has directly aided my researches through its substantial holdings of books and periodicals in the classical field, and through making grants toward some expenses of travel and research. However, its greatest service was to permit sabbatical leave for the academic year 1978-1979 which, with the help of a Fulbright-Hays travel award, I was privileged to spend at the Institute for Advanced Study, Princeton, New Jersey, as a member of the School of Historical Studies and Herodotus Fellow. Like many others, I found that it was a sustained period spent here, free from other responsibilities, which offered the stimulus to make really significant advances. The facilities placed at the disposal of the ancient historian by the Institute's own Historical Studies Library and by the Firestone Library, Princeton University, are of course unmatched. I could hardly have received better help from colleagues at the Institute either—especially C. Habicht among the faculty; J. Arce, D. van Berchem, G. W. Clarke, S. Lancel, and R. Syme among members and visitors. But it is to Ted Champlin of Princeton University that my greatest debt is owed. Having heard that he was then finishing his excellent monograph *Fronto and Antonine Rome* (now published by Harvard University Press), I did imagine that we were likely to share an area of common interest, and thus looked forward to making his acquaintance. What I had never expected was to gain such a firm friend, who would be so ready to discuss approaches, to share findings, and to comment painstakingly upon drafts, all with sympathy, enthusiasm, and formidable learning. His help and stimulus at that stage have been of lasting value.

Typing done by S. Lafferty in Princeton, and M. Bogie, J. Boyd, and P. Nolan in Belfast, deserves special thanks. It has been an honor to have this study accepted by the Princeton University Press, whose readers and staff have given every assistance toward its publication. Yet the last, and most heartfelt, word of thanks goes to my wife Zandra and our two sons. They have all patiently sustained the writing of this book, and will fully share the author's relief at its completion.

Belfast,
November 1982

ABBREVIATIONS

AE: *L' Année Epigraphique*
AJA: *American Journal of Archaeology*
AJAH: *American Journal of Ancient History*
AJP: *American Journal of Philology*
ANRW: *Aufstieg und Niedergang der römischen Welt*, ed. H. Temporini, Berlin and New York, 1972-
Arval Acta: A. Pasoli, *Acta Fratrum Arvalium*, Bologna, 1951 (note the comments by R. Syme, *Some Arval Brethren*, Oxford, 1980, p. 1)
B.A.R.: *British Archaeological Reports*
BCH: *Bulletin de Correspondance Hellénique*
BE: *Bulletin Epigraphique*
BGU: *Berliner griechische Urkunden*
BHAC: *Bonner-Historia-Augusta-Colloquium*
BICS: *Bulletin of the Institute of Classical Studies of the University of London*
BMC: H. Mattingly and R.A.G. Carson, *Coins of the Roman Empire in the British Museum*, 6 vols., London, 1923-1962
BMC followed by place name(s): *Catalogue of Greek Coins of . . . in the British Museum*
CIL: *Corpus Inscriptionum Latinarum*
CJ: *Codex Iustinianus*
CQ: *Classical Quarterly*
CR: *Classical Review*
CRAI: *Comptes rendus de l' Académie des Inscriptions et Belles-Lettres*
Diz. Epig.: E. de Ruggiero and others, *Dizionario epigrafico di antichità romane*, Rome, 1895-
EJ: V. Ehrenberg and A.H.M. Jones, *Documents illustrating the reigns of Augustus and Tiberius* (ed. 2 with addenda), Oxford, 1976
Fast. Ost.: L. Vidman, *Fasti Ostienses, Rozpravy Československé Akademie Věd*, vol. 67, sect. 6, 1957
FGrH: F. Jacoby, *Die Fragmente der griechischen Historiker*, Berlin and Leiden, 1923-
FIRA[2]: S. Riccobono and others, *Fontes Iuris Romani Antejustiniani*, 3 vols., Florence, 1940-1943
GRBS: *Greek, Roman and Byzantine Studies*
HA: *Historia Augusta*
HS: Sestertii
HSCP: *Harvard Studies in Classical Philology*
IG: *Inscriptiones Graecae*

IGRR: R. Cagnat and others, *Inscriptiones Graecae ad res Romanas pertinentes*, 4 vols., Paris, 1911-1927

ILAlg.: S. Gsell and others, *Inscriptions latines de l' Algérie*, 2 vols., Paris, 1922 and 1957

ILS: H. Dessau, *Inscriptiones Latinae Selectae*, 3 vols., Berlin, 1892-1916

Inscr. Ital.: *Inscriptiones Italiae*, Rome, 1931-

IOSPE²: B. Latyschev, *Inscriptiones Orae Septentrionalis Ponti Euxini* I (ed. 2), St. Petersburg, 1916

IRT: J. M. Reynolds and J. B. Ward Perkins, *The Inscriptions of Roman Tripolitania*, Rome, 1952

JHS: *Journal of Hellenic Studies*

JNG: *Jahrbuch für Numismatik und Geldgeschichte*

JÖAI: *Jahreshefte der Österreichischen Archäologischen Instituts*

JRS: *Journal of Roman Studies*

List. Fil.: *Listy Filologické*

MAAR: *Memoirs of the American Academy in Rome*

MAMA: W. M. Calder and others, *Monumenta Asiae Minoris Antiqua*, 8 vols., Manchester, 1928-1962

MEFR: *Mélanges d'Archéologie et d'Histoire de l'Ecole Française de Rome*

MGH: *Monumenta Germaniae Historica* (Auctores antiquissimi)

NC: *Numismatic Chronicle*

NSc: *Notizie degli Scavi di Antichità*

OGIS: W. Dittenberger, *Orientis Graecae Inscriptiones Selectae*, 2 vols., Leipzig, 1903-1905

Ox. Lat. Dict.: *Oxford Latin Dictionary*, Oxford, 1968-1982

Ox. Pap.: *Oxyrhynchus Papyri*

PBSR: *Papers of the British School at Rome*

PIR²: E. Groag, A. Stein, and others, *Prosopographia Imperii Romani saec. I. II. III* (ed. 2), Berlin and Leipzig, 1933-   (supersedes ed. 1 by E. Klebs, H. Dessau, P. de Rohden, 3 vols., Berlin, 1897-1898)

PLRE: A.H.M. Jones and others, *The Prosopography of the Later Roman Empire* 1, Cambridge, 1971

P. Ryl.: A. S. Hunt and others, *Catalogue of the Greek Papyri in the John Rylands Library Manchester*, Manchester, 1911-

PW: Pauly-Wissowa-Kroll, *Real Encyclopädie der classischen Altertumswissenschaft*

RG: *Res Gestae Divi Augusti*

RIB: R. G. Collingwood and R. P. Wright, *The Roman Inscriptions of Britain*, Oxford, 1965

RIC: H. Mattingly, E. A. Sydenham, and others, *The Roman Imperial Coinage*, 9 vols., London, 1923-1951

SDHI: *Studia et Documenta Historiae et Iuris*

SEG: *Supplementum Epigraphicum Graecum*

SIG³: W. Dittenberger, *Sylloge Inscriptionum Graecarum* (ed. 3), 4 vols., Leipzig, 1915-1921

St. R.: T. Mommsen, *Römisches Staatsrecht* (ed. 3), Leipzig, 1887-1888

TAPA: *Transactions and Proceedings of the American Philological Association*

ZNTW: *Zeitschrift für die Neutestamentliche Wissenschaft und die Kunde der älteren Kirche*

ZPE: *Zeitschrift für Papyrologie und Epigraphik*

ZSS: *Zeitschrift der Savigny-Stiftung für Rechtsgeschichte (Romanistische Abteilung)*

The titles of further works cited in brief should be self-explanatory. They appear in full in the bibliography.

For brevity and convenience most inscriptions which appear in *ILS, Inscr. Ital., AE,* or *SEG* are cited just by that reference, and earlier publication of them can be traced from there. However, for certain material of special significance, the relevant publication is cited direct.

All dates are A.D. unless otherwise stated.

The Senate of Imperial Rome

INTRODUCTION

The main aim of this study is to investigate the procedure and functions of the Roman senate as a corporate body during the Principate, that is, approximately between 30 B.C. and A.D. 238. By the former year Octavian (later to be named Augustus) had at last achieved undisputed victory in the long civil wars which followed the death of Julius Caesar: he was thus in a position to begin the revival of the shattered state. The latter year, A.D. 238, likewise marks a natural break. From this date adequate historical accounts in literary sources fade for a long period, and there ensues half a century of unprecedented instability for the empire. Its reconstitution in a new form thereafter is another story.

The changing composition of the senate during the Principate, the duties performed by individual senators in official posts, and the development of relations between senators and the emperor have engaged the attention of many modern scholars. All their studies make a valuable contribution, and they are drawn upon here with gratitude, especially in the two introductory chapters which seek to review who senators were, and what membership of their class might entail. But with interest in recent years drawn mainly to the aspects outlined, the work of the corporate body during the Principate, and the way in which it was done, have been overlooked. Such neglect is not new: indeed there has never been a book devoted to the topic. It is true that in the latter part of the last century T. Mommsen treated it in the course of his comprehensive discussion of the Roman constitution. But Mommsen, firm in his conviction that from the time of Julius Caesar the Roman system internally ". . . became . . . utterly withered and dead,"[1] concentrated for the most part upon the Republic. His bias was shared by C. Lécrivain in *Daremberg-Saglio* (1910), and by A. O'Brien Moore (of Princeton University) in *Pauly-Wissowa* (1935). Later encyclopaedia entries for the senate have proved either brief[2] or unsatisfactory,[3] so that a thorough investigation of senatorial procedure and functions during the Principate is still lacking.[4]

---

[1] *The History of Rome*, Everyman edition, London, 1868, vol. 4, p. 440.

[2] For example, A. Momigliano, s.v. senatus, *Oxford Classical Dictionary* (ed. 2), Oxford, 1970, pp. 973-975.

[3] For example, A. Nicoletti, s.v. senato (diritto romano), *Novissimo digesto italiano* XVI, Turin, 1969, pp. 1009-1016.

[4] Note the remarks of F. Millar, *The Emperor in the Roman World*, London, 1977, p. 350 in this connection.

The evident reluctance on the part of scholars to attempt such a study may readily be justified. Beyond question the old, sweeping authority of the senate was diminished during the Principate. This is not to overlook the earlier challenges mounted against it with growing success during the last century of the Republic. But now the reduction proved severe and permanent, so that the senate's role did remain a limited one. Moreover, most of the essential materials for research have perished, in particular the record of meetings in *acta senatus*, the *Lex Julia de senatu habendo* which governed procedure from 9 B.C., the overwhelming majority of *senatus consulta*, and all the commentaries written on this legislation by contemporary jurists. Hardly one full speech of any length made to the House survives verbatim either. And it is all the more disappointing that not so much as an outline of the entire business conducted at even a single meeting is preserved to convey some impression of the typical range and scope of the senate's work during the period.

Despite these obstacles an attempt to examine senatorial procedure and functions during the Principate may still not be a hopeless venture. Contrary to expectation, neither the loss of full authority nor the end of political freedom brought on a rapid decline into insignificance for the senate. This in itself is a paradox which merits explanation. Furthermore, with the scope of its business and the independence of its decisions restrained by powerful external forces, the senate during the Principate resembled a wide range of other assemblies in both the ancient and modern worlds, and as an institution may yet prove an instructive subject for study. Thus the hope is that this book will have an appeal not just to historians of any period, but equally to social and political scientists: for ease of reference the main technical terms used in the text are explained in a glossary.

As to evidence it is undeniable that there are yawning, irreparable gaps in our knowledge. But that said, they may not prove more serious than those regularly encountered by the ancient historian in almost all branches of the subject. In fact, it might be claimed that really we possess a deeper insight into the actual progress and conduct of senatorial sessions during the first and early second centuries A.D. than we do for this body, or any other, in the whole of Greek and Roman antiquity. Our knowledge of the Athenian assembly and council during the fifth and fourth centuries B.C., by contrast, lies mainly in their decisions, not their proceedings. In the case of the senate in Republican Rome, Livy is our best source. But the sessions for which his descriptions survive all took place at least a century and a half before his own day, and all at a time when in any event no regular, official record of proceedings was kept. For the late Republic, Cicero, as it happens, tells us less about actual sessions of the senate than we might hope for. For much of the first and early second centuries A.D., however, Tacitus and Pliny furnish astonishingly detailed, precise accounts, most of which—surprisingly enough—have not been exploited for the insights offered by them into the senate as a working assembly. Pliny described meetings which he had attended in person around 100. His contemporary Tacitus, as I shall argue, drew mainly, though not exclusively, on the full record supplied by *acta senatus* instituted from 59 B.C. Whatever its exact nature, which will be discussed below, this seems to have provided a fuller account of proceedings than we know to have been compiled for meetings of any other body in the ancient world. While the record is lost, in my view we may still gain a valuable impression of it through Tacitus, and this conclusion in turn may prompt some reappraisal of his approach to history and its importance. Three more members offer us a varied range of further relevant information from their own experience—Seneca in the mid first century, Fronto in the mid second century, and Dio Cassius in the late second and early third centuries. In addition, the emperor's attitude towards the senate and its members is a topic invariably treated in every imperial biography, both those by Suetonius written early in the second century, and later those in the so-called *Historia Augusta*.

Beside the literary evidence must be placed a diverse spread of other sources—coins, papyri, archaeological discoveries, inscriptions, legal texts. While all these have a significant contribution to make, the remarkable restoration of the Curia in Rome by Italian archaeologists in the 1930's might be specially singled out here. Otherwise it is the two latter types of source which merit particular attention.

First, the sheer range of epigraphic evidence for the senate and its work during the period is notable. Partly because the material is widely scattered and uneven in quality, it has never before been assembled with the present aim in view, let alone analyzed, so that its importance has yet to be appreciated. The continuing growth of such material is remarkable too. Certain especially valuable documents have come to light only in recent years, and it is perhaps reasonable to hope that others will follow.

Second, like inscriptions, relevant legal texts, too, have not been studied thoroughly in order to form a rounded impression of the senate's work during the Principate. While complete *senatus consulta* and jurists' commentaries upon them are indeed almost all lost, it is important to recall that the great majority of surviving Roman legal texts comprise excerpts from writers active between 100 and 250. Despite their truncation they convey an impressive amount of information about the scope and character of senatorial legislation during the Principate, as may be seen above all from the list in Chapter 15, which represents what—again, surprisingly—appears to be the first effort ever made to set out systematically all known legislative *senatus consulta* and *orationes* of the period, with an outline of the main provisions or purpose of each measure.

So while the major deficiencies in the evidence should not be overlooked, there do still seem to be grounds for believing that sufficient material already exists to embark upon the study presented here. In brief, the book is arranged to begin by introducing senators, their class and lifestyle. Then follow its two major parts, which consider at some length, first, the procedure of the senate, and then its functions, each very broadly defined. The final chapter aims to draw together certain themes and to reach some conclusions about the changing role of the senate.

Part One

THE CORPORATE BODY

1

THE SENATE

An understanding of the procedure and functions of the Roman senate during the Principate demands first a knowledge of its members. With such a purpose in mind this opening chapter gives some account of entry to the corporate body, senators' advancement thereafter, and the social composition of the membership. A short section on withdrawal and restoration is also included. This aspect excepted, the other three are all major topics in their own right. Within the limited compass here, therefore, no attempt can be made to cover certain relevant matters in depth, and a considerable debt throughout is owed to the detailed studies of earlier scholars.

1. Entry[1]

At all periods entry to the senate was restricted to Roman citizens of free birth and good standing. Thus, as Marcianus[2] says, conviction under the *Lex Julia de vi privata* barred a man from any position of honor or responsibility, including membership of the senate.[3] Sound health was also considered important. Ulpian[4] explains that a man who went blind could retain his senatorial rank, and could continue to hold any magistracy on which he had already entered. But in his view a blind man could not seek any further office, and he claimed to be able to support the point with many examples (none of which he cites). Certainly some, if not all, the

---

[1] See especially A. Chastagnol, "La naissance de l'*Ordo Senatorius*," *MEFR* 85. 1973. pp. 583-607; idem, " 'Latis Clavus' et 'Adlectio': l'accès des hommes nouveaux au sénat romain sous le haut-empire," *Rev. Hist. Droit* 53. 1975. pp. 375-394; C. Nicolet, "Le cens sénatorial sous la République et sous Auguste," *JRS* 66. 1976. pp. 20-38, discussed further by A. Guarino, "Il mestiere di senatore," *Labeo* 24. 1978. pp. 20-36.

[2] *Dig*. 48.7.1 pr.

[3] Equally, a member expelled from the senate was prohibited by law from acting as *iudex* (*Dig*. 5.1.12.2). Note the senate's own exceptional step in formally debarring the young *laticlavius* (?) Curtius Montanus from a public career (Tac. *Ann*. 16.33).

[4] *Dig*. 3.1.1.5.

members in our period known to have been blind[5] or deaf[6] may only have developed such disabilities in the course of their career, while we are told that in 13 B.C. Augustus would not consider anyone who was physically disabled for entry to the senate.[7]

In the Republic military service had been expected, and possession of the equestrian census rating (400,000 HS) also came to be required. Membership was made up of ex-magistrates, all of whom had a seat for life: insofar as a senatorial "order" was ever spoken of during the Republic, it meant simply the members themselves. Octavian evidently did not alter these qualifications in the course of his first review of the senatorial roll (*lectio senatus*) in 28 B.C. But we may gather that two changes were introduced either at the time of his second review in 18 B.C., or soon afterwards. First, possession of a higher census rating, one million HS, was now required. As Dio says in his first reference to these ratings (18 B.C.): "Augustus allowed all to stand for office who possessed property worth 400,000 HS and were legally eligible to hold office. This was the senatorial rating which he at first established; but later he raised it to one million HS. Upon some of those who lived upright lives, but possessed less than the 400,000 HS in the first instance, or the million in the second, he bestowed the amount lacking."[8]

Between 18 and 13 B.C. the new requirement evidently contributed to a drastic fall in senatorial recruitment. Dio says in his account of 13 B.C.:

After this there was another examination of senators. At first the rating of senators had been fixed at 400,000 HS, because many of them had been stripped of their ancestral property by the wars, and then, as time went on and men acquired wealth, it had been raised to one million HS. So no one was found any longer who would of his own choice become a senator: rather, even the sons and grandsons of senators, some of them really poor, others brought low by the misfortunes of their ancestors, not only would not lay claim to senatorial dignity, but also if chosen rejected it on oath. For this reason, earlier, while Augustus was still away, a decree had been passed that the so-called Vigintiviri should be appointed from the *equites*: but still none of them was enrolled in the senate without having held one of the other offices which led to it.[9]

Suetonius' figures differ from those of Dio. He says that Augustus "increased the senatorial census rating and fixed it at 1,200,000 HS instead

---

[5] Cerrinius (?) Gallus (Suet. *Aug.* 53; *PIR²* C 678); C. Cassius Longinus (Suet. *Nero* 37); Claudius Pompeianus (Dio 74.3.2).

[6] L. Sulla (Dio 60.12.3); Hadrianus (Galen, *De usu partium* 3. 895 Kühn) or Arrianus (II. p. 151 Helmreich) *consularis* (on the former reading, see *PIR²* H 6; on the latter, P. A. Stadter, *Arrian of Nicomedia*, Chapel Hill, 1980, p. 18 and notes 97 and 102).

[7] Dio 54.26.8.

[8] 54.17.3.

[9] 54.26.3-5.

of 800,000.''[10] The lower figure here is especially puzzling. It is otherwise unattested, and whether it represents a temporary, interim stage beyond 400,000 HS, or perhaps just a simple error by Suetonius, it is best set aside. The key to understanding the higher figure of 1,200,000 HS may lie in the context—a discussion of Augustus' generosity. Elsewhere more specifically Dio tells us that in A.D. 4 "since many young men, both of senatorial family and among the rest of the *equites*, were impoverished through no fault of their own, for most of them he made up the required census, and for eighty of them he increased it to 1,200,000 HS.''[11] Having noted this exceptional incident Suetonius has perhaps slipped into claiming that the higher amount was the required senatorial census, rather than one million HS which is almost certainly correct.[12]

Augustus' second change, probably introduced in 18 B.C. when a senatorial class was defined for the first time,[13] limited the wearing of the *latus clavus* (that is, the broad stripe on the tunic). Previously it had been worn not only by members themselves, but also by any young *eques* who aspired to a senatorial career. The links between senators and the upper range of the equestrian order were always close, and for young men of suitable standing a choice of career would be determined mainly by the degree of involvement in public life which they were prepared to undertake. Now, however, Augustus stipulated that the only non-members who might wear the *latus clavus* were to be the sons of senators.[14] All other *equites* were to wear just the narrow stripe. There was no diminution of their freedom to stand for the Vigintivirate and the senatorial magistracies[15]— among the latter usually the quaestorship, but sometimes the tribunate or aedileship,[16] and in the exceptional cases of Sejanus, Claudius, and perhaps L. Julius Ursus,[17] the consulship. Yet not until they had been elected to one such magistracy and entered office could they wear the *latus clavus*.[18]

[10] *Aug.* 41.

[11] 55.13.6.

[12] For gifts of one million HS to impoverished senators from Augustus and Tiberius, see Tac. *Ann.* 1.75; 2.37. For a reward of 1,200,000 HS to Ostorius Sabinus, equestrian accuser of Barea Soranus in 66, ibid. 16.33.

[13] See chap. 2 sect. 1.

[14] For discussion of legal difficulties which arose over inheritance of senatorial status, note *Dig.* 1.9.5-7.

[15] Note Strabo 5.1.11.

[16] Cf. Suet. *Aug.* 40; Dio 54.30.2; 56.27.1; 60.11.8; G. Alföldy, "Ein senatorischer Cursus Honorum aus Bracara Augusta," *Madrider Mitteilungen* 8. 1967. pp. 185-195 at pp. 193-194.

[17] A tantalizing *codicillus* of Domitian does not specify the mechanism which that emperor adopted to "transfer" L. Julius Ursus to the senate early in the reign, seemingly at the latter's own request. For a Praetorian Prefect mere adlection *inter praetorios* in the first instance might seem inadequate, not to say insulting; direct election to the consulship, as in Sejanus' case, appears more plausible, and is certainly the impression left by Dio's epitomator (67.4.2). See R. Cavenaile, *Corp. Pap. Lat.* no. 238 with *PIR*² I 630 and literature cited there, esp. R. Syme, *JRS* 44. 1954. p. 117.

[18] See Extended Note A.

Unlike Augustus' first change, this second, more formal one, did not last. The restriction imposed upon *equites* who aspired to a senatorial career was abandoned at the latest by Gaius' time. From then onwards it was possible for an *eques* to be granted the *latus clavus* by the emperor before actually gaining a senatorial magistracy.[19] We cannot trace the evolution of the development in any detail, but the sources do show that it soon became regular practice for the *latus clavus* to be sought from the emperor in the first instance by those who possessed the requisite qualifications and aspired to a senatorial career.[20] The support of an established senator, or of some influential figure in the emperor's circle, would normally be enlisted. Thus Pliny spoke for two or three men,[21] while the young Septimius Severus was supported by his relative C. Septimius Severus.[22] In contrast Livia helped the future emperor Otho's grandfather.[23]

We simply do not know how far a reasonable application could count on being successful. No case of a rejection can be cited, but that is hardly surprising: such a rebuff would be hushed up. There are two doubtful cases. Columella, the writer of an agricultural handbook, served a military tribunate, and implies sourly that he would have liked to seek higher rank: but possibly he never made the attempt. He remains vague on the point.[24] Griffin[25] deduces from the remarks of Seneca the Elder to his youngest son Mela (who, unlike his brothers, had no political ambition) that he himself would once have liked to become a senator: "But since your brothers care for ambitious goals and set themselves for the forum and a political career, where even what one hopes for is to be feared, even I, who otherwise am eager for such advancement and encourage and praise such efforts (their dangers do not matter, provided they are honorable), even I keep you in port while your two brothers voyage out."[26] Here there is no clear indication that Seneca went beyond contemplating advancement. Indeed when such alleged early ambitions hinge entirely on this passage, Griffin perhaps reads too much into the words. Seneca never indicates that

---

[19] For a clear example, cf. C. Julius Montanus (*PIR*² I 435).

[20] Not surprisingly, the actual grant of the *latus clavus* is seldom mentioned in the records of careers as set out on inscriptions: few men wished to have their non-senatorial backgrounds prominently advertised. But note, for example. *IGRR* III. 1422; *ILS* 1018 and 6857; *PIR*² I 427; *RIB* 1329; *AE* 1957. 238; cf. *SEG* 27. 1977. 723 with *BE* 1980 no. 443.

[21] See *Ep.* 2.9.2; 8.23.2; and perhaps 10.4.2 (cf. A. N. Sherwin-White, *The Letters of Pliny: A Historical and Social Commentary*, Oxford, 1966, ad loc. and R. Syme, *Historia* 9. 1960. pp. 365-367 = *Roman Papers* II, Oxford, 1979, pp. 480-483).

[22] See A. Chastagnol, "*Latus Clavus* et *Adlectio* dans l'Histoire Auguste," *BHAC* 1975/6. pp. 107-131 at pp. 111-113.

[23] Suet. *Otho* 1.

[24] Cf. *ILS* 2923; *De re rust.* I. praef. 9-10; *PIR*² I 779.

[25] M. Griffin, "The Elder Seneca and Spain," *JRS* 62. 1972. pp. 1-19 at p. 9; eadem, *Seneca: A Philosopher in Politics*, Oxford, 1976, pp. 33-34.

[26] *Controv.* 2. praef. 4.

he had been eager for his own sake in the past. He is simply expressing the eagerness in the present which any father would have for the advancement of his sons.

Emperors presumably differed in how selective they were, while at certain notorious periods the *latus clavus* could even be bought.[27] Again, we do not know to what extent emperors, when faced with a choice, sought to pitch the total of acceptances at or slightly above the likely number of vacancies. Without explaining the reason, Dio[28] does indicate that in 16 and certain other years fewer quaestors were elected than there were places available. But at least after the period 18-13 B.C. there is never any indication of another recruitment crisis sufficiently severe or sustained as to cause alarm. It is arguable that the unparalleled difficulty during these years was in part no more than the natural result of a uniquely low birth rate 20 to 25 years earlier amidst instability and civil war.[29]

By Gaius' time at the latest there is a very distinctive "senatorial class." *Laticlavii* are marked out even before they embark on their career. In holding military tribunates, as we shall see, it is true that they still overlap with *equites*. But they are now the exclusive occupants of the Vigintivirate. It was no doubt a mixture of logic and recruiting difficulties which had prompted Augustus to reduce the number of these junior offices from 26 to 20 early in his reign (perhaps between 20 and 13 B.C.). To hold one for a year became the essential preliminary to a senatorial career. All were bestowed by the emperor,[30] and demanded various token duties in Rome distributed among four posts. Patricians would expect the duty which rated highest, that of *triumviri monetales*. Men of noble background (that is, the sons of consuls) would expect at least to be *decemviri stlitibus iudicandis*, which rated second. The remaining seven places—*quattuorviri viarum curandarum*, followed by *triumviri capitales*—were left to the less distinguished.[31] A prospective senator would hope to occupy this office around the age of twenty, and apparently was not eligible to stand for the quaestorship without having done so. At least, in 20 Tiberius specially

---

[27] See chap. 2 sect. 3.

[28] 57.16.1; cf. 53.28.4 and see further chap. 4 sect. 1.

[29] For further discussion, see A. Chastagnol, "La crise de recrutement sénatorial des années 16-11 av. J.-C.," in *Miscellanea di studi classici in onore di Eugenio Manni* II, Rome, 1979, pp. 465-476.

[30] Cf. HA, *Did. Jul.* 1.4. The few known cases of appointment *ex s.c.* (all early in our period?) are exceptional: note *ILS* 915-916; perhaps *CIL* XI. 4359.

[31] For Augustan reform of the office, and for its duties, see H. Schaefer, *PW* 8 A s.v. Vigintiviri, cols. 2579-2587; note also *AE* 1967. 55. While the post a man held in the Vigintivirate is certainly a pointer to his standing within the senatorial class at the time, E. Birley goes too far in arguing that "the main lines of a man's career in the senatorial service were likely to be established by his grading in the vigintivirate" ("Senators in the emperors' service," *Proc. Brit. Acad.* 39. 1953. pp. 197-214 at p. 213).

asked the senate to exempt Nero Caesar from the duty of holding a post in the Vigintivirate, while in 41 Claudius stipulated that his sons-in-law should hold such posts in the ordinary way, and only later allowed them privileges in their tenure of higher offices.[32]

After the Vigintivirate a military tribunate might follow[33]—that is, an officership in a legion immediately subordinate to its *legatus*. It was awarded either by the emperor directly,[34] or by the governor of the province where the legion was stationed, subject perhaps to general imperial approval.[35] One such post out of the six available in each legion was commonly occupied by a *laticlavius* (the other five by *equites*), but proof is lacking that one and only one tribunate had always to be reserved thus. The intention was presumably that the post should offer young men some military experience; but of course only a limited number would see action, and for the rest there is no sign that formal training was organized. Normal length of tenure is uncertain, but around one year seems a fair conjecture.[36] A military tribunate was by no means an essential prerequisite for entry to the senate. *Novi homines* (that is, men from a non-senatorial background) did commonly hold one in fact, or in rare cases even more than one. Dio speaks of a young man in Domitian's time occupying the post "in the hope of becoming a senator."[37] But patricians, or members of long-established senatorial families, bothered with it much less.

For entry to the House it was necessary to secure one of the twenty quaestorships available each year. From 14, elections to this magistracy, and indeed to all others except the consulship, were left to the senate, subject to two provisos.[38] First, all candidates had to gain general approval from the emperor.[39] Second, he might support certain candidates, whose election was thus assured. But some degree of competition always remained, although for the quaestorship it is likely to have been slight once the vacancies in the Vigintivirate each year had been reduced to twenty.

Young men who sought entry to the senate in this way continued to form the overwhelming majority of its total membership. Alongside them, however, were others whom the emperor wished to introduce. They could be advanced by various means. Conceivably, no more than the *latus clavus*

[32] Tac. *Ann*. 3.29; Dio 60.5.7-8.

[33] Less commonly the order might be reversed.

[34] Cf. Suet. *Aug*. 38; Dio 53.15.2; Statius, *Silvae* 5.1.97; 5.2.165-167; Juvenal, *Sat*. 7. 88-89.

[35] Cf. Tac. *Ann*. 2.55; Plin. *Ep*. 2.13.

[36] For discussion of these points, see B. Campbell, *JRS* 65. 1975. pp. 18-19. A. R. Birley, *The* Fasti *of Roman Britain*, Oxford, 1981, p. 9, argues for longer tenure.

[37] 67.11.4.

[38] On elections see further chap. 10 below.

[39] Cf. for the tribunate, Plin. *Ep*. 2.9.2; in general *Paneg*. 69.1.

might be offered to them, so that they were still left to compete for office. This is how Gaius seems to have treated *equites* whom he enrolled in 38, according to Dio.[40] Marcus Aper is the only individual known to us who could have been treated likewise in the mid first century, although the outline which he gives of his career in Tacitus, *Dialogus* 7 remains ambiguous on whether he was ever supported by the emperor when standing for offices. The offer of *latus clavus cum quaestura* which Hadrian made to another Gaul, Q. Valerius Macedo, represents better treatment, but seems to be otherwise unheard of.[41] From our sources the means of advancement arranged by Claudius for certain entrants during his censorship remains obscure. We are told by Suetonius that he would not brook refusal from those he approached, a policy which may be illustrated by Dio's anecdote about Surdinius Gallus, whom the emperor "bound in golden chains" to serve in Rome as a senator.[42]

Even allowing for the evidence already cited, it is clear that the great majority of men introduced by the emperor were advanced by adlection, which conferred not a magistracy, but a rank within the senate. Allowing for many obvious differences, this method of entry recalled the pre-Sullan custom in the Republic whereby the censors might enroll such members of the senate as they pleased. Augustus took censorial powers rather than the censorship itself, but is not found using them for the enrollment of new senators. Claudius, however, was censor in 47/48, and he is the first emperor who is known to have adlected members. All the same, to judge from surviving inscriptions which alone document the point, the number of men advanced thus by him was small: only three are known for certain, all adlected *inter tribunicios* during the censorship. Thereafter no further adlections are known until the reign of Vespasian, when again most of the instances fall within the joint censorship of the emperor and Titus during 73/74, with a few earlier. Upwards of twenty men were advanced, not only *inter tribunicios*, but also *inter quaestorios, inter praetorios*, and one

---

[40] 59.9.5.

[41] *ILS* 6998; see further chap. 2 sect. 3 note 16. There might be a parallel in the case of M. Iul[ius] Ro[mu]lus, ". . . adlectus [tribunus p]lebis a divo Claudio," but there remains much dispute over his career (cf. *PIR²* I 523). For a further possibility (yet no more than that), see *RIB* 1329 with Herodian 3.15.1 and A. R. Birley, *The Fasti of Roman Britain*, pp. 140, 144. It would not be appropriate to treat here the vexed question of what the Gallic notables sought from Claudius in 48—*latus clavus, adlectio*, or office (cf. *FIRA²* I no. 43; Tac. *Ann*. 11.23-24). It should be added, however, that there seems insufficient evidence for the theory put forward by A. Chastagnol, "Les modes d'accèss au sénat romain au début de l'empire: remarques à propos de la table Claudienne de Lyon," *Bulletin de la société nationale des antiquaires de France* 1971. pp. 282-310. He relates the application to a *ius honorum* which provincials had to be voted before they could seek admission to the senate.

[42] Suet. *Claud*. 24; Dio 60.29.2; see further chap. 4 sect. 2 note 53. Fronto, *Ad M. Caes*. 2.9 = p. 31 van den Hout uses the same image of having to stay in Rome during his consulship.

inter aedilicios.[43] From Domitian's time we clearly find emperors adlecting new members at will during their reigns. Domitian, of course, was *censor perpetuus* from 84 or 85, and later emperors exercised censorial powers without the title. Before the Severan period the only instance of a non-senator being adlected direct to the highest rank, *inter consulares*, seems to be that of Tarrutenus Paternus, Praetorian Prefect under Commodus.[44] But in general it should be stressed that, so far as we can tell on present evidence, the number of adlections remained altogether small. No emperor ever used adlection, or any other means, to "pack" the House with his own men.

2. Advancement[1]

Election to the quaestorship made a man eligible to enter the senate. It is not clear whether there was a formal ceremony at which new members, say, signed the senatorial roll. Dio does refer to the occasion when the future emperor Septimius Severus was "enrolled in the senate,"[2] but of course he could be speaking figuratively rather than literally. At any rate, it was presumably to mark the memorable occasion of first entry that Rustius (or Ruscus) Caepio had required his heir to present a specified sum of money to every new member.[3] Suetonius, however, mentions it as a point in Domitian's favor that the emperor canceled this clause in the will, not least perhaps because it was drawn in favor of "incertae personae."[4] In certain circumstances, to be discussed below, a senator might later be deprived of membership, or might resign it. Yet otherwise, once enrolled, he was entitled to retain it for life.[5] His name would be included in the

---

[43] See further chap. 4 sect. 1.

[44] Dio 72.5.1.

[1] This section is again only an outline of a large topic. For detailed discussion, see J. Morris, "Leges Annales under the Principate, I. Legal and Constitutional," *List. Fil.* 87. 1964. pp. 316-337; "II. Political Effects," ibid. 88. 1965. pp. 22-31; W. Eck, "Sozialstruktur des römischen Senatorenstandes der hohen Kaiserzeit und statistische Methode," *Chiron* 3. 1973. pp. 375-394; idem, "Beförderungskriterien innerhalb der senatorischen Laufbahn, dargestellt an der Zeit von 69 bis 138 n. Chr.," *ANRW* II.i. 1974. pp. 158-228; B. Campbell, "Who were the 'viri militares'?" *JRS* 65. 1975. pp. 11-31; G. Alföldy, *Konsulat und Senatorenstand unter den Antoninen: Prosopographische Untersuchungen zur senatorischen Führungsschicht*, Bonn, 1977, the main findings of which were summarized in English by idem, "Consuls and Consulars under the Antonines: Prosopography and History," *Ancient Society* 7. 1976. pp. 263-299; A. R. Birley, *The Fasti of Roman Britain*, chap. I.

[2] 75.3.1; cf. 54.26.5.

[3] Suet. *Dom.* 9, "quotannis ingredientibus curiam senatoribus certam summam viritim praestaret heres suus." "Ingredi senatum" here must surely be taken in the sense of "to enter the House for the first time": cf. Tac. *Hist.* 4.40; HA, *Pert.* 3.2.

[4] Cf. Gaius, *Inst.* 2.238-243.

[5] For the "retirement age" beyond which there was no obligation to attend, see chap. 4 sect. 3.

list of all members posted up on a board, as stipulated by Augustus' *Lex Julia de senatu habendo* of 9 B.C. Dio[6] tells us how this practice still continued in the early third century, with annual revisions of the list. There is no evidence to indicate who was responsible for this updating, but since it was presumably just a routine task in normal circumstances, the *quaestores urbani* mentioned below are perhaps the most likely candidates. If the names were placed in order of seniority, such an *album senatorium*[7] must have been invaluable to presiding magistrates in calling upon members to speak.

Of the twenty quaestors regularly elected each year, about twelve would serve their magistracy stationed in Italy (until Claudius' time)[8] or as financial officer in a senatorial province; two would have administrative duties in the *aerarium Saturni* as *quaestores urbani*;[9] four would be attached to the consuls;[10] and two would be attached to the emperor as *quaestores Caesaris*.[11] Understandably, the position of the latter pair carried greatest prestige, so that patricians or those of noble background would expect to be chosen for this duty.

Except for the single post of the *ab actis senatus* from the late first century onwards,[12] there were no regular offices to which a senator below the rank of ex-praetor was appointed, although he might secure a position as legate to a governor.[13] For a short period, under Claudius' arrangements, junior senators superintended the *aerarium Saturni*,[14] and throughout the first century some were appointed to legionary legateships.[15] Otherwise at this stage of their careers they had only to be concerned with election to the next two magistracies.

During the Republic a man was allowed to be quaestor at 30 and praetor at 39 (or possibly 40). In all likelihood it was early in Augustus' reign

[6] 55.3.3. For a reference to the *album* in sixth century Constantinople, note Corippus, *In Laudem Justini* 4.142-143.

[7] For the term, Tac. *Ann.* 4.42. Note how at the fictitious meeting in Apuleius, *Metam.* 6.23, the divine president, Jupiter, addresses the gathering as ''dei conscripti Musarum albo.''

[8] Cf. Dio 55.4.4; 60.24.3; Tac. *Ann.* 4.27.

[9] See further chap. 9 sect. 3.

[10] See Plin. *Ep.* 4.15; 8.23.5, with Sherwin-White ad loc.; *ILS* 412; also chap. 3 sect. 3.

[11] See chap. 5 sect. 1. As A. R. Birley (*The* Fasti *of Roman Britain*, p. 13) argues, it may be that more than two were thus honored in certain years.

[12] See chap. 9 sect. 3. Note also Augustus' removal of *quaestorii* from the presidency of the Centumviral Court (Suet. *Aug.* 36).

[13] Exceptionally, a few men are known to have held legateships even before their first magistracy. See M. Dondin, ''Une anomalie du *cursus* sénatorial sous l'empire: les legations provinciales préquestoriennes,'' *Latomus* 37. 1978. pp. 148-172.

[14] Cf. Tac. *Ann.* 13.29.

[15] Cf. A. Passerini, *Diz. Epig.* IV. p. 567, s.v. legio; G. Alföldy, ''Die Legionslegaten der römischen Rheinarmeen,'' *Epig. Stud.* 3. 1967. pp. 103-105.

that these ages were lowered to 25 and 30 respectively.[16] In between, tenure of the aedileship or tribunate came to be required too.[17] Each magistracy was to be separated by a two-year interval (*biennium*). Yet quite apart from any special favors which the emperor might grant to individuals,[18] these rules were variously modified in practice. First, the quaestorship could be held in a man's twenty-fifth year, rather than strictly from his twenty-fifth birthday, on the principle that "a year begun counts as a full year."[19] The same applied to the praetorship, so that in effect a man could be quaestor at 24 and praetor at 29. Second, from Augustus' time a year's remission was allowed for each child.[20] Third, it is obvious that strict adherence to the sequence quaestorship/*biennium*/aedileship or tribunate/*biennium*/praetorship would require six years before entry to the latter office, so that it would not normally be possible for a man who was quaestor at, say, 25 to be praetor only five years later, at 30. However it seems that on the principle of "a year begun counts as a full year," one of the intervals between resignation from the quaestorship on 4 December or from the tribunate on 9 December, up to 31 December was regarded as a full year. So it was possible to hold the praetorship five years after the quaestorship. Many members would aim to achieve this, and at minimum age too.[21]

For the ten tribunates and six aedileships vacant each year, no more than slight competition might be expected. It is true that the few members adlected *inter quaestorios* would be seeking a magistracy for the first time at this stage. But patricians were debarred from the tribunate of the plebs, and excused tenure of an aedileship, so they would stand aside. Their numbers would fluctuate, while the earlier candidature allowed to fathers, along with other privileges specially granted by the emperor, would also cause the total of candidates to vary each year.[22] Both tribunes and aediles

[16] See J. Morris, *List. Fil.* 87. 1964. pp. 316-317. It is not known how the changes were introduced—whether at a stroke, or, say, by lowering the minimum ages by one year in each of five successive years. By rendering prospective holders eligible for office up to five years earlier than expected, the former arrangement is likely to have caused severe strains, especially in the competition for the fixed number of quaestorships.

[17] It was only civil war which allowed the *quaestorii* A. Caecina Alienus (*PIR*[2] C 99) and the future emperor Titus (*PIR*[2] F 399) to proceed direct to the consulship. Before 69 the latter had been expecting to pursue a normal career (cf. Tac. *Hist.* 2.1).

[18] Note, for example, *ILS* 1048 in honor of L. Aemilius Honoratus (*PIR*[2] A 350), "hos honores beneficio optumi princip(is) maturius quam per annos permitti solet, gessit."

[19] *Dig.* 50.4.8. Hadrian laid down the same age and principle for municipal magistracies (*Dig.* 36.1.76.1).

[20] Cf. *Dig.* 4.4.2.

[21] For these intervals and ages, cf. Dio 52.20.1-2. For age of entry to the quaestorship, see further G. V. Sumner, "Germanicus and Drusus Caesar," *Latomus* 26. 1967. pp. 413-435.

[22] Cf. Plin. *Ep.* 7.16.1-2 on how his early advancement proceeded in relation to that of his senatorial contemporary, Calestrius Tiro.

would spend their year of office in Rome. The traditional sweeping prerogatives of the former could hardly be invoked now,[23] and their work
comprised little beyond some minor judicial duties.[24] Aediles retained some
responsibility for the city and its markets, though major ancient functions
of their office, too, were now handled by imperial officials.[25]

Until the late first century competition for election to the praetorship
remained sharp, because this was the earliest stage at which the number
of candidates would significantly exceed the number of places available.
In the early part of his reign Augustus reduced the number of praetorships
to no more than eight each year, together with two *praetores aerarii*.[26]
Near the end of his life it was exceptional when he allowed all sixteen
candidates in A.D. 11 to be elected; otherwise he approved twelve vacancies
a year, and this number remained normal into Tiberius' reign.[27] In 16,
when rejecting Asinius Gallus' suggestion that the emperor designate magistrates five years in advance, Tiberius indicated his awareness of the strong
competition for the praetorship. Not surprisingly, when the death of one
praetor in 17 caused an unexpected vacancy, Germanicus and Drusus had
to fight hard to secure the election of their relative Haterius Agrippa, against
opponents with children who cited the preference due to them under the
Lex Papia Poppaea.[28] By the latter part of the reign, and under Gaius,
too, the number of praetors elected annually was around fifteen.[29] Under
Claudius it fluctuated between fourteen and eighteen, yet there was still
the risk of rejection.[30] In 60, when there were three more candidates than
places, Nero consoled the disappointed contenders for their "postponement
and delay" by appointing them to legionary legateships (that is, to posts
normally reserved for ex-praetors).[31] Two years later there were complaints
about fictitious adoptions on the part of candidates for election or ballot.
It is notable that Tacitus,[32] having first mentioned the practice in general
terms, then goes on to imply that the fraud was employed chiefly to secure
praetorships and proconsulships. Among magistracies this is indeed where
we should have expected rivalry to be fiercest. Thus there was point to

---

[23] See chap. 7 sects. 8 and 25.

[24] Cf. Tac. *Agr*. 6; Plin. *Ep*. 1.23; 6.8.3; HA, *Sev*. 3.1.

[25] Edict, *FIRA*[2] I no. 66; Dio 55.8.7. On the duties of tribunes and aediles, see
M. Hammond, *The Antonine Monarchy, Papers and Monographs of the American Academy
in Rome* 19. 1959. pp. 294-295.

[26] Vell. 2.89.3; Tac. *Ann*. 13.29; Dio 53.32.2.

[27] Dio 56.25.4; Tac. *Ann*. 1.14.

[28] Tac. *Ann*. 2.36 and 51.

[29] Dio 58.20.5; 59.20.5.

[30] Dio 60.10.4; Tac. *Ann*. 13.29.

[31] Tac. *Ann*. 14.28; Suet. *Nero* 15, perhaps generalizing from the single instance. The
total number of places allowed in this year remains unrecorded.

[32] *Ann*. 15.19. See further chap. 10 sect. 3.

the boastful description of L. Cornelius Marcellus (who must have been praetor in Nero's reign) as "designated praetor from many."[33]

Sharp competition for the praetorship was only eliminated from the Flavian period onwards, when eighteen places were regularly permitted. Disappointment and delay were now likely to be only slight,[34] and it is understandable that we never hear of any bitter contests again. In addition, from the censorship of Vespasian and Titus, adlection is used by emperors to promote to a higher rank men who were already senators.[35] Thus on this occasion Cornutus Tertullus[36] and L. Flavius Silva Nonius Bassus[37] were promoted *inter praetorios* from the rank of aedile. Not until the third century, however, do we find any promotion *inter consulares*. Praetors would remain in Rome during their year of office, assigned to various administrative and judicial duties.[38] They were also responsible for games.[39]

Under the Principate it was the opportunities opened up by magistracies, not the offices themselves, that were important. Above all, tenure of the praetorship qualified a senator to hold appointments in the service of emperor and senate. In the Julio-Claudian period a *novus homo* could feel pleased to have attained this rank, even if he rose no higher. But soon after that time, as we have seen, promotion to the praetorship became almost automatic for most members, and so it was only at this stage that wide differences would begin to appear between the careers of contemporaries. At one extreme, patricians would expect to hold the consulship very soon after the praetorship, around the age of 32 or 33, occupying no post between the two magistracies. Plebeians of senatorial background might expect to occupy only one or two posts as ex-praetors before proceeding to the consulship between the ages of 38 and 42. Their posts would all be in the imperial service: here the offices which in particular led up to the consulship were a legionary legateship, the governorship of a prov-

---

[33] *CIL* X. 7266, "pr(aetor) d[es(ignatus)] ex multis"; *PIR*² C 1403.

[34] Though other explanations are again possible, Attius, or Accius, Sura in whose support Pliny (*Ep*. 10.12) writes to Trajan when a praetorship comes unexpectedly vacant, could be a senator above the minimum age seeking the office, but not yet successful.

[35] Very remarkably an inscription in honor of A. Claudius Charax specifies the senate, not the emperor, as promoting him *inter aedilicios* from the rank of *quaestorius* in the mid second century (C. Habicht, *Istanb. Mitt.* 9/10. 1959/60. p. 110 lines 10-12). Though other sound evidence of the practice is lacking, it is conceivable that adlections were sometimes confirmed by the senate (cf. HA, *Sev. Alex.* 19.2, not necessarily in the House). But proposals can only ever have come from the emperor.

[36] H. Halfmann, *Die Senatoren aus dem östlichen Teil des Imperium Romanum bis zum Ende des 2. Jahrhunderts n. Chr.*, Hypomnemata 58, Göttingen, 1979, no. 22.

[37] W. Eck, *PW* Suppl. 14 s.v. Flavius no. 181, cols. 121-122.

[38] Note Dio 53.2.2 with *ILS* 914 (C. Propertius Postumus) "pr. ex s.c. pro aed. cur. ius dixit." See further M. Hammond, *The Antonine Monarchy*, pp. 292-294. For the value of praetors' functions, cf. Seneca, *De Tranq. Anim.* 3.4.

[39] See chap. 2 sect. 3.

ince, or a treasury prefecture. The more fortunate *novi homines* might expect to occupy at least three posts in the imperial service before gaining the consulship; the less fortunate would likewise need to occupy three posts, some of them in the service of the senate.[40]

The highest magistracy, the consulship, soon came to be bestowed exclusively by the emperor. The number to whom it was granted grew steadily during our period,[41] but even when emperors were at their most generous, no more than perhaps half those who embarked upon a senatorial career could hope to attain it. For much of the first century, of course, the proportion to be disappointed was even greater. From 5 B.C. Augustus doubled the number of consuls each year by replacing the traditional pair of "ordinary" consuls (who continued to open the year) with two "suffects" on 1 July. Thereafter the number of suffects came to be increased, and the terms of all holders progressively shorter. This continued the normal pattern to the end of Claudius' reign, except in certain years where the "ordinary" consuls resigned after only two months in favor of suffects who served for the next four months, giving way in turn to a further pair of suffects on 1 July. In such years, therefore, there were six consuls in all. But under Nero, nearly every pair of *ordinarii* did continue to remain in office for a full six months. However, that convention was finally broken from Vespasian's time onwards. During the Flavian period the number of consuls in each year varied between six and ten, each pair usually holding office for two, four, or six months. Trajan was content with six or eight consuls each year, Hadrian with eight. Antoninus chose eight or ten, M. Aurelius ten. Towards the end of the second century the numbers rose even higher, with an unprecedented maximum of twenty-four plus the emperor in 190 to satisfy a high total of adlected members at that stage.[42] But under the Severans the figure was stabilized at twelve. Thus Dio[43] speaks of two months as the normal maximum term for consuls in his own day. Many consular duties were taken over by imperial officials, while those which remained gradually became more formal as the term of office was curtailed.[44] But consuls always retained their presidency of the senate, exercised certain judicial functions, and celebrated games.[45] During an

---

[40] On these less prestigious posts, see W. Eck, "Über die prätorischen Prokonsulate in der Kaiserzeit. Eine quellenkritische Überlegung," *Zephyrus* 23/24. 1972/3. pp. 233-260.

[41] See most recently P. A. Gallivan, *Antichthon* 13. 1979. pp. 66-69 (reign of Gaius); *CQ* 28. 1978. pp. 407-426 (Claudius); ibid. 24. 1974. pp. 290-311 (Nero); ibid. 31. 1981. pp. 186-220 (Flavians); G. Alföldy, *Konsulat und Senatorenstand* (A.D. 138-180); otherwise A. Degrassi, *I fasti consolari dell' impero romano (30 a.c.-613 d.c.)*, Rome, 1952, with additions in *AE*.

[42] Dio 72.12.4.

[43] 43.46.5-6.

[44] See in general M. Hammond, *The Antonine Monarchy*, p. 292.

[45] See chap. 2 sect. 3.

emperor's absence from Rome they might act for him in the city,[46] and at his abdication or death they took over the leadership of the state.[47]

It is plain that attainment of the consulship normally demanded either high birth (above all, patrician status), or tenure of key posts in the emperor's service. In certain instances a claim might also be based on outstanding talent in oratory or jurisprudence. When choosing consuls Tiberius was not alone among emperors in weighing up "ancestral nobility, military distinction and civilian eminence."[48] Tacitus could write of the emperor Vitellius, son of Claudius' colleague in the censorship: "At the time of his death he was 57 years old, having won the consulship, various priesthoods and a name and place among the leading figures of Rome, all thanks to his father's eminence and without the slightest effort on his own part."[49] In a rhetorical vein Fronto asks M. Aurelius why he should be held in such affection by his pupil, and deprecatingly claims that he has performed none of those services which customarily bring high rewards from the emperor:

What benefit has your Fronto bestowed upon you so great that you should show him such affection? Has he given up his life for you or your parents? Has he braved your perils for you? Has he been the loyal governor of some province? Has he commanded an army? None of these things. Not even those everyday duties about your person does he discharge more than others; rather, if you want the truth, his attendance is sporadic enough. For he does not keep coming to your house at dawn, nor does he pay his respects to you daily, nor accompany you everywhere, nor keep you always in sight.[50]

Close attendance upon the emperor and his family was the service expected of patricians above all. After the consulship they were again unlikely to occupy official posts, except for the senatorial governorship of Asia or Africa, which was reserved for senior consulars and carried great prestige. Patricians might also look forward to a second consulship, often as *consul ordinarius* (that is, in the most privileged position of opening the year). Others whose progress from praetorship to consulship had been comparatively swift might expect to occupy more than one of the commands reserved for consulars, all of them in the imperial service. Outside Italy the governorships of Britain, Tarraconensis, and Syria, for example, rated very high,[51] while at Rome the City Prefecture was the summit of ambition.

---

[46] Cf. Suet. *Calig.* 18.

[47] Cf. Tac. *Ann.* 4.9; Herodian 2.12.4.

[48] Tac. *Ann.* 4.6.

[49] *Hist.* 3.86; cf. 1.52.

[50] *Ad M. Caes.* 1.3.4 = p. 3 H. For the view that Fronto did in fact merit the award of a consulship through tenure of two treasury prefectures, see E. J. Champlin, *Fronto and Antonine Rome*, Harvard, 1980, pp. 80-81.

[51] Cf. Tac. *Agr.* 40; A. R. Birley, *The Fasti of Roman Britain*, pp. 28-29.

Men of this caliber might hope for a second consulship.[52] To them, too, would fall priesthoods—distinctions conferred mainly at the emperor's behest upon patricians and other successful consulars. Velleius[53] was especially shocked that Iullus Antonius, son of the Triumvir, could commit adultery with Augustus' daughter Julia, even after the emperor had spared his life and honored him with priesthood, praetorship, consulship, and governorship of provinces, as well as linking him to the imperial house by marriage. These were the outstanding rewards. Men who had advanced slowly to the consulship were likely to be appointed only to the less splendid posts, if indeed they were invited to occupy any posts after the magistracy itself.

It is easy to assume that all senators wished to rise as high as possible in their careers. No doubt this was the ambition of the majority. But we do know of exceptions. Attention needs to be given to those members who either sought no further advancement, or even refused it when the chance was offered, in some instances withdrawing from public life altogether. As we have seen, at no time could more than perhaps half the eligible *praetorii* attain the consulship, and in the first century it was many fewer. Equally, up to the Flavian period, numbers of junior senators could reckon upon a long delay before they reached even the praetorship. It would be only natural, therefore, to expect some of those caught at these stages to abandon hope of further advancement. Individual cases are hard to identify, but we may believe that C. Bruttius Praesens L. Fulvius Rusticus, whom Pliny[54] encouraged to resume his activities as a senator, was one such *praetorius* who saw no hope of reaching the consulship. In fact, unforeseen circumstances later proved him wrong in his gloomy prognostications. Somehow he gained a legionary legateship in Trajan's Parthian campaigns, where brilliant service laid the foundation for a distinguished resumption of his career, culminating in a second consulship in 139.[55]

Two jurists of Augustus' day can be cited as members who refused advancement even when it was offered to them: Aulus Cascellius and Antistius Labeo both preferred to remain *praetorii* when Augustus held out the consulship.[56] We may gather from Tacitus[57] (who does not mention

[52] No wonder, therefore, that Gaius felt it "illegal" for him to have already been twice consul by the age of 27 (Dio 59.19.3)!

[53] 2.100.4.

[54] *Ep.* 7.3.

[55] See R. Hanslik, *PW* Suppl. 12 col. 133; W. Eck, ibid. 15, col. 77.

[56] *Dig.* 1.2.2.45 and 47. For all its firmness it is hard to accept Pomponius' claim here that Cascellius was only *quaestorius* when Augustus offered him the consulship. But see W. Kunkel, *Herkunft und soziale Stellung der römischen Juristen* (ed. 2), Graz, Vienna, Cologne, 1967, pp. 25-26; and A. Rodger, "A note on A. Cascellius," *CQ* 22. 1972. pp. 135-138.

[57] *Ann.* 3.75.

the offer of higher office) that dislike of Augustus was one of the reasons why Labeo never proceeded beyond the praetorship, but in the case of both jurists absorption in their legal work was no doubt another pressing cause.

Some senators sought advancement, or shunned it, as the political atmosphere changed. Pliny[58] praised Nerva for eventually advancing men who under Domitian had prayed that they should escape the emperor's memory and so avoid attention. It was the taint of friendship with Sejanus which had deterred Poppaea's father, T. Ollius, from seeking to proceed beyond the quaestorship,[59] while the "philosopher" Herennius Senecio was another who refrained from pursuing his advancement beyond an early stage.[60] According to Dio,[61] one of Domitian's grudges against him was that in the course of a long life he had never sought a magistracy higher than the quaestorship. We do not know whether there were really others, too, whose failure to hold offices was made a charge against them during the Flavian period, as Tacitus[62] alleges. Certainly two more "philosophers" tried with Herennius in 93, Helvidius Priscus the Younger and Q. Junius Arulenus Rusticus,[63] had risen to hold consulships.

Herennius' case highlights the dilemma widely felt in one form or another among the Roman upper classes. During our period, just as before it, philosophers continued to be much exercised by the problems of what service, if any, should be offered to the state, and how long those who did choose to serve should persevere when circumstances became intolerable—under a tyranny especially. This is a large topic which it would not be appropriate to treat here.[64] But we may note how at the end of the Republic Cicero and Sallust among senators had felt a strong need to justify their withdrawal from active participation in affairs.[65] Under the Empire

[58] *Paneg.* 90.6; cf. *Ep.* 8.14.7 and (of Nero's reign) Tac. *Agr.* 6.

[59] Suetonius (*Nero* 35) terms him *quaestorius*, while Tacitus (*Ann.* 13.45) describes him as "honoribus nondum functus" (which might agree with Suetonius if *honores* are taken to mean "higher magistracies").

[60] These two instances stand alone in the present state of our knowledge, so that in *Sat.* 1.6.130-131 Horace's choice of only the lowest magistracy to represent senatorial achievement does seem strange. Having explained why he is content to remain an *eques*, he concludes:

His me consolor victurum suavius ac si
quaestor avus pater atque meus patruusque fuerat.

Bücheler went so far as to conjecture "praetorque" for "patruusque." But it would be mistaken to argue that the passage must point to others who deliberately never proceeded beyond the quaestorship.

[61] 67.13.2.

[62] *Hist.* 1.2.

[63] *PIR*² H 60; I 730.

[64] See, for example, A. Grilli, *Il problema della vita contemplativa nel mondo greco-romano*, Milan and Rome, 1953, chap. 3; P. A. Brunt, "Stoicism and the Principate," *PBSR* 43. 1975. pp. 7-35; M. Griffin, *Seneca: A Philosopher in Politics*, chap. 10.

[65] Cf. Cic. *Brutus* 7-8; *De Off.* 2.2-3.3; *De Repub.* 1.9; Sallust, *BJ* 4.3-4.

a senator could at least look forward to the prospect of honorable withdrawal when he reached retirement age—a prospect which even Augustus reflected upon in a letter to the senate.[66]

Stoic beliefs were no doubt one influence among many which prompted Seneca's gradual withdrawal from public life,[67] and the same will be true of Thrasea Paetus' celebrated failure to attend the senate from 63. But Thrasea saw his action very much as a personal choice, and (despite the claim of his accusers) did not expect his example to be followed,[68] nor, apparently, was it.[69] We may fairly suggest a link between Stoic beliefs and the unexplained delays in the career of Helvidius Priscus the Elder[70]— quaestor under Claudius before 51, tribune in 56, praetor in 70. But once he had resolved on a more outspoken stance, his policy was to attend the senate punctiliously and use his right of speaking there to attack Vespasian. The emperor's tactful suggestion that he stay away, or remain silent, evidently went unheeded.[71] We hear from Philostratus[72] that in Domitian's time the senior consular of 66, C. Luccius Telesinus,[73] was so converted to philosophy that he willingly suffered exile rather than remain in Rome. Contemporary frustration felt in some circles at the refusal of such "philosophers" to participate in affairs perhaps helps to account for Quintilian's unexpected outburst against them: "But the man in public life who is truly wise devotes himself not to idle disputations, but to the administration of the state, from which those who are called philosophers have very far withdrawn themselves. . . ."[74]

It is impossible to determine whether or not Aelius Aristides' friend, the *praetorius* Sedatius, gave up his senatorial career irrevocably and turned to philosophy. Although we do find him in Asia in the summer and autumn of 145, and again in August 147, which could suggest a single visit, it may be only that he had received prolonged leave of absence for his health.[75] In the mid third century we hear that "not a few" senators were attracted by Plotinus' philosophical lectures in Rome, and even of one, Rogatianus, who under this influence

---

[66] Seneca, *De Brev. Vit.* 4.2-4.

[67] He must have reached the retirement age anyway in the early 60's. For discussion of his date of birth, see M. Griffin, *Seneca: A Philosopher in Politics*, pp. 35-36.

[68] Cf. his advice to Arulenus Rusticus (Tac. *Ann.* 16.26).

[69] Cf. Tac. *Ann.* 16.22.

[70] *PIR*² H 59.

[71] Epictetus 1.2.19-21.

[72] *Vit. Apoll.* 7.11.

[73] *PIR*² L 366.

[74] *Inst. Or.* 11.1.35; cf. 12.2.7.

[75] See Aelius Aristides, *Sacred Tales* 2.48; 4.16 and 43 with C. A. Behr, *Aelius Aristides and the Sacred Tales*, Amsterdam, 1968, p. 47. H. Halfmann, *Die Senatoren*, no. 78 indicates that an identification with M. Sedatius Severianus (cos. suff. 153) is no longer possible.

. . . advanced so far in renunciation of public life that he gave up all his property, dismissed all his servants, and resigned his rank. When he was on the point of appearing in public as praetor and the lictors were already there, he refused to appear or have anything to do with the office. He would not even keep his own house to live in, but went the round of his friends and acquaintances, dining at one house and sleeping at another (but he only ate every other day). As a result of this renunciation and indifference to the needs of life, though he had been so gouty that he had to be carried in a chair, he regained his health, and though he had not been able to stretch out his hands, he became able to use them much more easily than professional handicraftsmen.[76]

Here it is clear that ill health, too, may have prompted Rogatianus to give up his career. But the renunciation need not have been permanent: it remains an open question whether he is the same as C. Iulius Volusenna Rogatianus known to have been proconsul of Asia in 254.[77]

So far as we know, it was merely general dissatisfaction with alleged corruption in public life, rather than any philosophical influence, that prompted L. Calpurnius Piso (augur, cos. 1 B.C.) to threaten complete withdrawal to a remote spot at a meeting in 16, and then walk out of the House.[78] Suetonius[79] mentions the case of an otherwise unknown senator, Cerrinius Gallus, who was prompted by sudden blindness to starve himself to death, and was dissuaded from this course by Augustus, himself no stranger to such despair.[80] We may imagine that serious illness led other members to give up their careers, or to take more drastic action, but no individual case can be cited.[81]

In conclusion it should be stressed again that this section is intended as no more than an outline discussion of senatorial careers over two and a half centuries. By definition it must remain unsatisfactory and incomplete. There were few fixed elements in such ''system'' of advancement as existed, so that the temptation to generalize about any particular span or to formulate rigid rules must be resisted. We should remember that there was a long period of evolution during the first century, while the pressures and disorder of the late second century called for emergency action. The degree of ambition would have varied widely between individual senators. Not all started out ruthlessly ambitious; of those who did, some later modified their aspirations. Moreover, at all times advancement was affected not only by tradition and established practice, but also by different em-

[76] Porphyry, *Life of Plotinus* 7.
[77] *PIR²* I 629; cf. E. Fischer, *PW* Suppl. 15 col. 465.
[78] Tac. *Ann.* 2.34.
[79] *Aug.* 53.
[80] Plin. *NH* 7.149; cf. *Epit. de Caes.* 1.29.
[81] Ill health was of course one reason which induced Dio (80.5.2) to retire after his second consulship in 229, but he had reached retirement age anyway.

perors' appraisal of individuals, and by such unpredictable influences as a military crisis, say, or sheer luck.

3. Withdrawal and Restoration

As we have noted, once enrolled a senator was entitled to retain his membership of the corporate body for life. But there were circumstances in which he might resign it, or be formally deprived of it. Leaving aside the handful already discussed who withdrew on philosophical grounds, the few members said to have resigned voluntarily are all men in the Julio-Claudian period who maintained that they could no longer meet the minimum property qualification.[1] At the same time others, too, evidently responded to imperial pressure to resign under threat of otherwise facing expulsion, either because they also could not meet the minimum property qualification, or because the emperor considered them morally unfit to remain as members.[2] *Lectiones senatus* were liable to produce a spate of such withdrawals.[3] But in general, emperors, whether or not they actually held the office of censor, always claimed oversight of the morals of senators, and the right to expel them from the corporate body.[4] In 48 L. Vitellius, even as ex-censor, removed L. Junius Silanus Torquatus.[5] Such random evidence as survives for the removal of senators by the emperor on moral grounds is discussed further below.[6] Yet the arbitrary fashion in which certain rulers might exercise this prerogative may at least be noted here. Tiberius, for example, allegedly expelled a member just because he sought to economize by moving out of Rome to the country before 1 July.[7] When a letter from the same emperor in 32 attacked sycophantic proposals by Junius Gallio, the senate itself reacted with an immediate vote of expulsion. There was an identical response to denunciations of Rubellius Plautus and Faustus Cornelius Sulla Felix by Nero in 62.[8]

It was at least more understandable that Tiberius should deprive Apidius Merula of membership for the indictable offense of not taking the oath to the *acta* of Augustus.[9] This brings us to the general reason for many, if not most, withdrawals from the corporate body, namely, condemnation

[1] Tac. *Ann.* 12.52; cf. 1.75.
[2] Tac. *Ann.* 2.48.
[3] Note Tac. *Ann.* 11.25; Dio 60.29.1; see further chap. 4 sect. 1.
[4] Epictetus 1.2.19; Dio 53.17.7; Jerome, *Ep.* 52.7.3.
[5] Tac. *Ann.* 12.4.
[6] Chap. 2 sect. 6. Note also Tac. *Ann.* 14.17.
[7] Suet. *Tib.* 35, discussed in chap. 2 sect. 3 note 25 below.
[8] Tac. *Ann.* 6.3; 14.59.
[9] Tac. *Ann.* 4.42; cf. 16.22.

for an offense which carried with it the penalty of *infamia*. That meant loss of rank and exclusion from public life,[10] and would normally form part of the sentence passed against those convicted of any serious crime, *maiestas* and *repetundae* above all.[11] In the case of conviction for the former, *infamia* was often unimportant in itself, since many defendants were likely to receive a death sentence in any event. In the case of *repetundae*, where execution would be an extreme penalty, contemporaries saw sound practical reasons why convicted defendants should be deprived of their senatorial membership, in particular because of the unsuitability of allowing a senator condemned for this crime the right to sit in judgment later on one of his peers tried before the House for the same offense.[12] All the same, the senate was prepared to exercise the right which it claimed "both to reduce and to increase the severity of the law."[13] This could lead to certain defendants not being required to suffer *infamia*, who otherwise might have been expected to do so.

Infamia, as the word itself indicates, was public disgrace. But first it should not be too readily assumed that all convicted defendants upon whom the penalty was inflicted would thus by definition have to hide away as shunned outcasts for the rest of their days. In particular, those senators convicted of *repetundae* were likely to face no more than *relegatio*, a comparatively lenient form of banishment, where they would either be confined to a specified place (usually an island), or instead excluded from certain areas.[14] Normally they would retain their property, and in general would remain free to exercise the rights of a private citizen. According to Dio,[15] under A.D. 12, Augustus did try to introduce a range of notably more severe restrictions for all exiles, but there is little sign that these were ever enforced consistently. Altogether, therefore, in many instances exile was likely to offer to convicted senators a quiet, comfortable existence in a pleasant spot, with all the pressures, obligations, and fears faced by the working member conveniently removed. There was no secret about such an attractive prospect,[16] and understandably it might seem a welcome one to certain senators—for a spell at least—especially perhaps to those who had reached the praetorship and had held a proconsulship, but saw no good prospect of further advancement.

[10] Note Marcellus, *Dig.* 1.9.2; Paulus, ibid. 22.5.15, refuting Papinian, ibid. 22.5.13.
[11] For example, Tac. *Ann.* 3.17; 4.31; 6.48; 12.59; 13.11 (adultery with Messalina).
[12] Note Plin. *Ep.* 2.12.4; 4.9.19.
[13] Plin. *Ep.* 4.9.17, discussed in chap. 16 sect. 1 below.
[14] On exile and its different forms, see P. Garnsey, *Social Status and Legal Privilege in the Roman Empire*, Oxford, 1970, pp. 111-122. Note also Ulpian, *Dig.* 48.22.14 pr.-2; Paulus, ibid. 50.1.22.4.
[15] 56.27.2-3.
[16] Note Dio 58.18.4; Juvenal, *Sat.* 1.45-50.

Second, a sentence of *infamia* would not automatically impose lifelong loss of status. Restoration to the rank which the degraded member had occupied at the time of conviction was possible.[17] Either senate[18] or emperor could be approached. The latter might respond for a variety of reasons. For example, we know that Nero restored Plautius Lateranus from a desire to demonstrate clemency, and later Cossutianus Capito as a favor to Tigellinus.[19] In order to appear generous upon their accession both Galba and Otho were willing to see the restoration of members condemned under Claudius and Nero.[20] There were further restorations at the beginning of Vespasian's reign early in 70, though at the same time two convicted members who had been confident enough to leave their places of exile in anticipation of a pardon were both required to return.[21] Early in the third century Caracalla must have included exiled senators in a general amnesty aimed to win himself favor after the murder of Geta.[22] Domitian, by contrast, remained deaf even to unanimous pleading by the crowd at the Capitoline contest that he restore the talented orator, Palfurius Sura, removed from the senate by Vespasian.[23]

In brief, then, senatorial membership was lifelong. Voluntary resignation was rare, and expulsion confined to two small groups: those whose vices were flagrant enough to attract the emperor's disapproval, and those convicted of a serious offense. Even then, the latter group at least might hope for restoration later, if it suited the emperor's interest to show such generosity.

4. Composition

As we shall be seeing in more detail later,[1] Augustus reduced total membership of the senate to about 600, and it seems to have remained stable

---

[17] This clearly occurred in the case of Helvidius Priscus (*PIR*² H 59) and probably that of Tarquitius Priscus (below), for example. A similar type of concession may have been made to those senators removed by the *lectio* of 18 B.C. who wished to resume membership. Many did so, according to Dio (54.14.4-5). If they had all been forced to start their careers from the beginning again, there would hardly have been the recruitment crisis which ensued in the years immediately following the *lectio*.

[18] Note Suet. *Otho* 2 with Tac. *Ann.* 13.32 perhaps.

[19] Tac. *Ann.* 13.11; 14.48. Nero must also have restored Tarquitius Priscus (ibid. 12.59; 14.46).

[20] Tac. *Hist.* 1.77 (with *Ann.* 14.18); 2.86; cf. 4.6; Plut. *Otho* 1.

[21] Tac. *Hist.* 4.44.

[22] Dio 77.3.3; cf. 79.3.5. No doubt senators were specifically cited in P. M. Meyer, *Griechische Papyri im Museum der oberhessischen Geschichtsvereins zu Giessen*, Leipzig and Berlin, 1910, no. 40 col. II line 1. But it should be noted that this section of the document is far more badly damaged than is indicated, for example, in the translation of A. C. Johnson, P. R. Coleman-Norton, F. C. Bourne, *Ancient Roman Statutes*, Austin, 1961, p. 226.

[23] Suet. *Dom.* 13; Scholia on Juvenal 4.53.

[1] Chap. 4 sect. 1.

at that level for the rest of our period. Augustus also made senatorial status hereditary. With sons thus encouraged to follow their fathers into the House, we might expect the senate to have remained in large measure the self-perpetuating oligarchy which it had been in the Republic. Yet it is notorious that this did not happen. During the Principate, established senatorial families failed to continue supplying members for generation after generation. A detailed discussion of the reasons for the new trend is beyond the scope of this outline.[2] But at least we should not assume too readily (as some modern writers have done)[3] that the main cause necessarily lay in a natural inability or deliberate refusal of these families to perpetuate themselves. A wider range of possibilities must be canvassed. Execution and death on active service must be taken into account.[4] In other cases it is possible that financial embarrassment prevented sons embarking upon a senatorial career, or that, even when the opportunity was open, they shunned the hazards and drudgery of such a demanding life. In addition, by no means all the children who survived into adulthood will have been free of physical or mental weakness. Whatever the reason, there must have been many like the *laticlavius* of whom there was apparently nothing to record on his tombstone beyond the fact that he died aged one month under thirty.[5]

The patrician class had suffered most severely in the conflicts which followed the collapse of the Republic.[6] It continued to suffer under cruel emperors, Nero in particular. So far as we can tell, most Republican patrician families which did survive into the reign of Augustus were either extinct, or no longer represented in the senate, by the Flavian period. Both Augustus and Claudius elevated plebeian families to the patriciate: we know of around 20 thus honored by the former, and 17 by the latter. But less than half of the total of 37 are known to have had members in the senate by Trajan's time.[7] The continuing need to replenish the class is seen in upwards of 20 known elevations by Vespasian,[8] with further elevations

[2] See K. Hopkins, *Death and Renewal*, chap. 2 (forthcoming, Cambridge, 1983), with comment in chap. 2 sect. 1 below.

[3] Cf. M. Hammond, *JRS* 47. 1957. p. 75; G. Alföldy, *Ancient Society* 7. 1976. p. 290.

[4] For such casualties, soldiers and senior governors (who might already have children) spring to mind first: cf. R. Syme, *Tacitus*, Oxford, 1958, p. 69 notes 5-6, with Tac. *Ann.* 11.18, Plin. *Ep.* 7.27.2, and the case of Pliny himself. But among younger men note a quaestor (Plin. *Ep.* 5.21.3), a proconsul of Narbonensis who died aged 44 (*ILS* 950), two proconsuls of Achaea (Aelian, *Hist. Anim.* 13.21; *PIR*² I 719; E. Groag, *Die Reichsbeamten*, cols. 74-75 and 97-98), and a proconsul of Cyrene whose experiences in the post were a prime cause of his death not long afterwards (Josephus, *BJ* 7. 451-453; *PIR*² C 582).

[5] *CIL* VI. 1538; cf. *AE* 1978. 421.

[6] Note Dio 52.42.5.

[7] See in general H.-H. Pistor, "Prinzeps und Patriziat in der Zeit von Augustus bis Commodus," diss. Freiburg, 1965, esp. pp. 43-44.

[8] W. Eck, *Senatoren von Vespasian bis Hadrian. Prosopographische Untersuchungen mit Einschluss der Jahres- und Provinzialfasten der Statthalter, Vestigia* 13, Munich, 1970, pp. 108-109.

by all second-century emperors up to and including Septimius Severus.[9] In choosing new patricians a preference was commonly shown for the oldest Italian families represented in the senate; but from Vespasian's time onwards distinguished or promising provincials were also elevated.

Ancient plebeian families likewise faded swiftly from the senate. The tombstone of Sextus Appuleius, whose father and grandfather had both been consuls (in A.D. 14 and 29 B.C. respectively), must speak for many: in erecting the monument his mother describes him as "last of his line."[10] By late in Nero's reign there were perhaps no more than about fifteen families represented in the House who could claim ancestors sitting there in the second century B.C., and only a dozen others who could claim first-century ancestors in the same way. Thereafter the disappearance of the old families grew even more marked, so that by Caracalla's time it was a rare member who could trace senatorial ancestors back for more than one or two generations.

The surviving evidence does not enable us to trace the disappearance of the old families in detail. We are a little better informed, however, about the new senators, both Italians and provincials, who took their place. The latter are the most striking group. Julius Caesar had introduced a few provincials. Augustus and Tiberius continued the trend cautiously. Claudius' claim for their approach has a solid basis of truth, even if it is overstated: "By a new policy both my great-uncle, the divine Augustus, and my uncle, Tiberius Caesar, wished there to be in this House all the flower of the colonies and municipalities everywhere, that is, good men and rich."[11] In fact, during their reigns provincials came almost entirely from the West of the empire. Claudius continued along the same lines, so that from his time provincials became a notable group in the senate. As he himself argued in the speech just cited, his approach could be seen not so much as a novelty, but as a continuation of the tradition whereby selected outsiders had regularly been absorbed into Roman society.[12] Yet it was not until after the civil war of 69 and the accession of Vespasian that more than a handful of Greeks and Easterners felt ready and qualified to enter the House.[13]

Thereafter it is clear that the number of provincial recruits continued to grow, and that they became a significant proportion of the senate's mem-

---

[9] Pistor, op. cit. pp. 51ff.

[10] *ILS* 935; cf. *PIR*² A 961-963.

[11] *FIRA*² I no. 43 col. II lines 1-4.

[12] Note especially in this connection T. P. Wiseman, *New Men in the Roman Senate 139 B.C.-A.D. 14*, Oxford, 1971.

[13] For the argument that it was acquisition of suitable qualifications and contacts which delayed the entry of Easterners, more than any racial prejudice, see H. Halfmann, *Die Senatoren*, pp. 16-27.

bership. Yet the temptation to go further and to illustrate the trend in figures (as some scholars have attempted)[14] is best avoided. Our evidence is limited, and in many instances a man's origin cannot be identified with confidence from surviving sources, so that any totals for provincial entrants are liable to conceal an unacceptably high number of conjectures. Of course, even if greater precision were possible, we could still never tell what proportion of the senate's complete membership these men represented at a given time.

Any figures are robbed of value above all by the impossibility of securing a satisfactory definition of "provincial." It is true that contemporaries might draw a rough distinction between "Italian" and "provincial." It emerged starkly in the arguments put for and against Claudius' introduction of Gallic notables to the senate in 48, and Tacitus has Seneca refer to it in his bitterly ironic "retirement" speech: ". . . Accordingly I often ask myself: 'Is it I, son of a provincial *eques*, who am numbered with the leading men of the senate? Is mine the new name which has come to glitter among ancient and glorious pedigrees?' "[15] At the end of the Flavian period Statius protests of the young Septimius Severus, born in Leptis yet brought to Italy as a boy: "Your speech is not Punic, nor is your dress. Your mind is not that of a foreigner—you are Italian, Italian!"[16] At the races an *eques* sitting next to Tacitus asked "Are you an Italian or a provincial?"[17] He evidently saw value in framing such a question—which Tacitus chose not to answer directly.

It is doubtful, however, whether such a sweeping distinction between "Italian" and "provincial" is satisfactory for a modern student of the senate's membership. We must remember that neither group was truly representative or homogeneous. Within Italy there were sharp contrasts between the rich, more highly cultivated northern region of the peninsula, and the poorer, less populated south: as might be expected most Italian senators came from the north. Among provincials the contrasts were more varied, above all between Latin West and Greek East. But senatorial recruitment reflected further differences within each area too. To cite an extreme, long-romanized citizens from Baetica or Narbonensis would hardly have wished to be classed indiscriminately with Dalmatians or Britons. Men from the former two western provinces are among the earliest provincial recruits to the senate. Yet hardly a single Dalmatian is known to have entered before the second century, and only a handful entered from

---

[14] For example, M. Hammond, *JRS* 47. 1957. p. 77.
[15] *Ann.* 14.53.
[16] *Silvae* 4.5.45-46.
[17] Plin. *Ep.* 9.23.2.

that time up to the end of our period. Britain supplies no senator at all.[18] For the East, a count of 69 members known to have entered the House between the reigns of Augustus and Commodus shows as many as 55 coming from Roman colonies or places where settlements of Romans are attested.[19] There were further differences between Asia and all the other eastern provinces. A count of known senatorial families from the whole area in the first two centuries A.D. shows up to one-third (31 of 92) coming from Asia, and no other single province producing more than nine.[20] More generally, marriage ties are bound to complicate a definition of "provincial": how is the son of a mother from Italy and a father from Asia to be classified, for example? And finally in this connection, for how many generations are the descendants of a non-Italian entrant to the senate to be taken as provincial?[21]

For our purpose it is sufficient to appreciate that from the Flavian period onwards men who might loosely be described as "provincials" made up a significant proportion of the senate's membership. We may then proceed to the key question, which is not their numbers, but the nature of their impact upon the corporate body.

When Caesar admitted Gauls to membership, a current joke suggested they were so unsuitable that they would not even know the way to the House![22] More seriously, it could be argued that provincial newcomers might have a poorer sense of tradition than Italians, and a weaker grasp of procedure. Indeed their facility with Latin might even leave something to be desired, especially if they were from the East. Moreover, conscious of the prejudice against them in some quarters and of their debt to the emperor, they were liable never to consider adopting an independent approach to an issue, but merely to approve the wishes of the Princeps without question. Such an attitude was possibly to be expected in particular from

[18] I leave on one side the controversies over whether King Cogidubnus was Gaul or Briton by origin, and over whether or not he was granted senatorial rank. Without fresh evidence the latter notion remains only speculation. The fact that senatorial approval was gained for the dedication RIB 92 hardly affects the issue. See A. A. Barrett, "The career of Tiberius Claudius Cogidubnus," Britannia 10. 1979. pp. 227-242; P. Salway, Roman Britain, Oxford, 1981, Appendix 4; and literature cited by both.

[19] See C. Habicht, "Zwei neue Inschriften aus Pergamon," Istanb. Mitt. 9/10. 1959/60. pp. 109-127 at p. 122.

[20] See H. Halfmann, Die Senatoren, pp. 68-70.

[21] Presumably it is the future emperor Antoninus' Gallic descent which astonishingly leads P. Lambrechts (La composition du sénat romain de l'accession au trône d'Hadrien à la mort de Commode, Antwerp, 1936, p. 183) to categorize him as a "provincial" senator in the reign of Hadrian, even though M. Aurelius, of Spanish descent, is classified as an Italian member in the reign of Antoninus (ibid. p. 184). In appreciating the limitations of the figures produced by M. Hammond (note 14 above), it is as well to recall his reliance on Lambrechts' conclusions.

[22] Suet. DJ 80.

those *equites* in the emperor's service who came to be elevated to the
senate, especially at the end of our period.

These arguments can be accepted only with substantial modification. Of
course provincial entrants regularly encountered snobbery and prejudice.[23]
Yet it was not they alone, but all newcomers, who suffered thus in a
corporate body where birth traditionally commanded respect.[24] At the beginning of our period, Horace[25] speaks of marked snobbery towards new
senators, while Tacitus[26] notes the contempt shown by two nobles for their
colleague of lower birth when all three were commissioned to take a Gallic
census in 61. No doubt the representatives of established families were
among the loudest protestors against the admission of Gauls in 48,[27] but
so long as respect was still accorded to high birth in the pursuit of honors
(as we have seen that it was), they could have no complaint that their own
position was seriously in danger. Juvenal's caricature of the noble's attitude
is predictable:

> "You others are dirt," you say, "the dregs of our populace;
> Not one of you can point to his father's birthplace.
> But I am a person of the most ancient lineage."[28]

This is an extreme. Yet it was only natural that to the end of our period
feeling should persist against the suitability of certain first-generation senators or their conspicuous success. Pliny[29] mentions how it was in order
for a candidate on election day to cast aspersions upon an opponent's birth,
among other points; and in another context he does not fail to note that
the murdered *praetorius*, Larcius Macedo, was the son of a slave. Leading
members had boycotted Agrippa's funeral games in 12 B.C.[30] In the third
century Dio[31] was disgusted by Macrinus' elevation of Adventus, whose

---

[23] Note the peculiar criticism made by Alexandrian Greeks to Trajan that "his" συνέδριον
was full of Jews (H. A. Musurillo, *The Acts of the Pagan Martyrs*: Acta Alexandrinorum,
Oxford, 1954, no. 8 col. iii lines 42-43 and 47). As commentators have appreciated, this
term could be taken as either *consilium* or senate: for discussion, and support of the latter,
see E. M. Smallwood, *The Jews under Roman Rule* (corrected ed.), Leiden, 1981, p. 390
n. 7. But while rightly stressing that the document is not of a technical nature, she omits to
explain why the writer should first use συνκλητικοί for senators (col. ii lines 26-27), yet then
change to συνέδριον for the corporate body. Altogether *consilium* seems the more likely
interpretation, especially as the charge might then at least appear plausible, which it would
not in the case of the senate.

[24] Cf. Seneca, *De Benef.* 4.30.1; Plin. *Paneg.* 69.4-6.

[25] *Sat.* 1.6.27-44.

[26] *Ann.* 14.46.

[27] Cf. Tac. *Ann.* 11.23.

[28] *Sat.* 8.44-46; in the last of these lines, as again too in line 53, Juvenal's "Cecropides"
does not seem to have any narrowly Athenian connotation.

[29] *Ep.* 3.20.6; 3.14.1; cf. Tac. *Ann.* 11.21.

[30] Dio 54.29.6.

[31] 78.14.1-2.

background and education he considered not fitting for a senator. Clodius Albinus' allegedly distinguished birth brought him noble support against Septimius Severus.[32] But otherwise protests were not nearly so strong. According to Dio,[33] there had been displeasure expressed in some quarters at Pertinax's elevation to the consulship under M. Aurelius because of his low birth. And once proclaimed emperor, Pertinax was himself apprehensive about the reaction of "noble" senators, as the succession passed "to an upstart from a family without status and of humble origin." He at least made a show of offering the Principate to the most distinguished patrician of the time, M'. Acilius Glabrio.[34] Maximinus suffered similar embarrassment.[35]

While prejudice against provincials, and indeed against all new entrants, must be recognized, its significance should not be overrated. There were, after all, always many different causes of tension between members: this was only one, and not necessarily the most important. Virulent prejudice is likely to have been confined to the first century. Thereafter any displeasure on the part of old families can have counted for less and less, once their representatives in the senate had become a mere remnant. In the mid second century the newcomer Fronto had the temerity to suggest that *nobilitas* was dying,[36] while his contemporary Apuleius could write: "How few men among the unnumbered multitudes are senators, and among senators how few came from a noble line."[37] Certainly from the second century, if not even earlier, almost all members would be conscious of their non-senatorial origins. That consciousness was bound to persist, too, since the rapid turnover in membership, which might have seemed a temporary phenomenon during the first century, in fact turned out to be a permanent feature. Many families of new entrants during the Principate failed to produce members in later generations, and so faded from the House just as their Republican predecessors had done. The trend may be illustrated from an investigation of all recorded consuls between 18 and 235.[38] It shows how only about one quarter had a son known to have attained the same office, while only about one third had a direct descendant who likewise attained it in the next three generations. While recognizing that our knowledge of consuls during the period chosen is incomplete, the

[32] Herod. 3.5.2.

[33] 72.22.1.

[34] Herod. 2.3.1-4; see further E. J. Champlin, "Notes on the heirs of Commodus," *AJP* 100. 1979. pp. 288-306.

[35] Herod. 7.1.2.

[36] *Ad M. Caes.* 1.9.1 = p. 17 H, discussed by E. J. Champlin, *Fronto and Antonine Rome*, pp. 88-90.

[37] *Florida* 8. For comment, see T. D. Barnes, *Phoenix* 28. 1974. p. 448.

[38] See K. Hopkins, op. cit. in note 2 above.

rate of succession still seems remarkably low, especially when consuls by definition represent the most successful senators, and those therefore best placed to advance their sons in a senatorial career. But it appears that the low rate of succession in this group is typical, and that further recruits from non-senatorial families always continued to be needed.

It is questionable whether provincial newcomers to the senate would really have had a poorer sense of tradition than Italians, or a weaker grasp of procedure. In the first place we should recall the tremendous value they set upon membership. A stone says of Augustus' Italian contemporary, Q. Varius Geminus, "he was the first of all Paeligni to become a senator."[39] There is no doubt that certain provincials, too, were prepared to go to great lengths in seeking entry.[40] Not surprisingly, having secured it, they were likewise immensely proud of their new status, and of their successive advancement thereafter. Both literary and epigraphic evidence illustrates the point. A feeling that the senate is a special elite emerges time and again from Fronto's letters.[41] On stone, Publius Postumus Romulus, for example, is described as "first of the Thubursicitani to be awarded the *latus clavus*."[42] M. Arruntius Claudianus, adlected *inter aedilicios* by Domitian, was a Lycian from Xanthus, "the first man of the nation to become a senator of the Roman people," according to an inscription which he erected there himself.[43] An unknown senator describes himself with astonishing pride and precision on a stone found at Didyma as: "*laticlavius* of the Roman people, the fifth man ever to enter the senate from the whole of Asia, and from Miletus and the rest of Ionia the first and only one."[44] A boast of the same type may have been made by two men from Pannonia.[45] Certainly another senator is described as "first consul from Africa,"[46] while in the first half of the third century a stone at Ephesus calls Claudia Caninia Severa "daughter of Tiberius Claudius Severus, first Ephesian to be consul."[47]

[39] *ILS* 932.

[40] Cf., for example, Dio 72.12.3.

[41] See E. J. Champlin, *Fronto and Antonine Rome*, chap. VI, esp. p. 91.

[42] *AE* 1906. 6.

[43] See *ILS* 8821; D. Knibbe, *JÖAI* 49. 1968/71. Beiblatt 6. no. 1; C. Habicht, *ZPE* 13. 1974. pp. 1-4; H. Halfmann, *Die Senatoren*, no. 28.

[44] R. Harder, *Didyma* II, Berlin, 1958, no. 296 lines 6-11; for discussion of identity, H. Halfmann, *Die Senatoren*, no. 12.

[45] *CIL* III. 731 = 7395 with H. Halfmann, *Die Senatoren*, p. 212. Only a fragment of this inscription from Perinthus is preserved by Cyriacus of Ancona: "Tropaiophoro fratre ex provincia Pannonia in amplissimum ordinem adsumpto." In other words, might we conjecture that this man and his brother were the first (or some other number) to enter the senate from Pannonia? Halfmann's notion that the man honored here did not originate from Pannonia, but only happened to be stationed there, seems puzzling.

[46] *ILS* 1001. For identity, cf. T. D. Barnes, *CR* 21. 1971. p. 332.

[47] See *JÖAI* 45. 1960. Beiblatt 92. no. 19 = C. Börker and R. Merkelbach, *Die Inschriften von Ephesos* III, Bonn, 1980, no. 892 with C. Habicht, *ZPE* 13. 1974. pp. 4-6.

When provincials were keen to enter the senate and valued their membership so highly, it is unlikely that they would be careless of tradition and of procedure. We must remember that their educational background could hardly be very different from that of Italians. In practice no one would proceed into the senate without the training in language, literature, and rhetoric which was universal among the upper classes throughout the empire. In this crucial respect, therefore, there is no difference between the Italian and the provincial, and to draw distinctions is virtually meaningless. Links with native culture had to be severed.[48] Instead, all senators, whatever their geographical origin, were versed in a single heritage. It is true that occasional criticism of members' accents is heard,[49] but such carping remarks refer to Italians as well as provincials. As to procedure, we should reflect upon how much of our own knowledge is derived from the writings of provincial newcomers, who profited from what they were taught by more experienced members on entry, and in turn would themselves pass on this lore to others.[50] In the first century Seneca was a new entrant of Spanish descent, and Tacitus one from Gaul in all probability.[51] In the second century it is Fronto from Africa—that "Libyan of the Libyans," as he calls himself[52]—who discusses with M. Aurelius the fine question of words unsuitable for use in the House.[53] New entrants of provincial origin may well have contributed to the trend whereby the senate played less and less of an independent role, especially in its dealings with the emperor. But it should be stressed that this change was well on its way before they made up a notable proportion of the membership.

The two most striking developments in the composition of the senate during the Principate may be seen as the decline of a hereditary element, and the extension of membership to non-Italians. The majority of Republican senatorial families died out during the Julio-Claudian period. They were replaced by other Italians, and by a growing number of provincials, the latter at first drawn mainly from the West, but after 69 from the East too. Yet in many instances the families of these new entrants in turn failed to perpetuate their membership, so that further recruits were constantly required. Surprising though it may seem, however, neither the continuing

[48] Note the striking discussion of E. J. Champlin, *Fronto and Antonine Rome*, pp. 16-19, with reference to Africa.

[49] Cf. Suet. *Vesp.* 22; HA, *Hadr.* 3.1; *Sev.* 19.9. For Romans ridiculing an educated Greek's Latin accent, see Lucian, *On Salaried Posts* 24.

[50] For comment on the trend see R. P. Saller, *Personal Patronage Under the Early Empire*, Cambridge, 1982, pp. 142-143.

[51] R. Syme, *Tacitus*, chap. XLV; idem, *Ten Studies in Tacitus*, Oxford, 1970, pp. 140 and 145.

[52] *Ad M. Caes.* 1.10.5 = p. 23 H; cf. the prayer to one of his "dei patrii," Hammo Juppiter (*Ver. Imp.* 2.1.6 = p. 116 H).

[53] *Ant. Imp.* 1.2.5 = p. 90 H.

turnover in membership, nor the entry of provincials, can be shown to have weakened the corporate body in any significant way. In fact, the latter served to strengthen it. As a group the newcomers were proud of the status they had attained, while the provincials closely matched the Italians in wealth, education, and outlook. The senate remained a uniformly conservative institution, which upheld its tradition and its dignity.[54]

[54] The point is well made by A.H.M. Jones, *The Later Roman Empire*, Oxford, 1964, pp. 6-7.

2

SENATORS

Following our examination of the senator's position within the limited confines of the corporate body, this chapter proceeds to review his standing in a wider world. We begin by considering his legal position and his wealth. Then we examine the character and scope of demands laid upon him— financial, public, and private. In this context some attention is given to the reasons why certain *equites* declined to pursue a senatorial career, even when they were eligible. Finally, an attempt is made, insofar as the evidence permits, to gauge the nature of contemporary opinions and attitudes towards the senate as an institution, both on the part of members themselves, and of those of lower rank. Altogether, the purpose of the chapter is to afford an insight into the senator's obligations, and to assess the place in society occupied both by him and by the body which he represented.

1. Legal Position

During the Republic senators had always occupied an exalted place in Roman society. It was not only Augustus' wish that this position should be upheld; he also took the further step of defining a "senatorial class" for the first time in his marriage legislation of 18 B.C. Membership belonged to senators and agnatic descendants to the third generation and their wives.[1] As far as the evidence allows, we need therefore to examine the legal position of this class and its development.[2] The latter was a haphazard growth, not least because class-based rights and privileges, as well as restrictions, were never comprehensively defined. The fact that certain enactments evidently applied only to senators, yet others to their relatives as well, may have proved a further source of confusion. In any case, definition was hardly necessary, when in practice few men of lower rank would dare to question the wishes and actions of such lofty personages.

Toga, special sandals, and a broad stripe upon the tunic all made the

---

[1] *Dig.* 23.2.44 pr.
[2] For earlier treatment of some aspects, see Mommsen, *St. R.* III. 1. pp. 466-475.

senator in public instantly recognizable.[3] In addition consulars and senators' wives from Claudius' time had the right to be carried in covered chairs.[4] By definition, respect was always due to any senator. In the mid second century Gaius[5] noted that any injury to a senator by a person of low status was treated with special gravity as *iniuria atrox*. Perhaps as early as Augustus' time senators seem to have had some protection against certain civil charges (fraud in particular), which persons of low rank might seek to bring against them.[6] Certainly by the early second century senators and their wives sued for debt could enjoy the privilege of *distractio bonorum*, that is, individual items of their property could be sold off by a special agent in honorable fashion, while the accused themselves would suffer no loss of status (*infamia*).[7]

A senator's place of residence was considered to be Rome, and in general there were certain restrictions upon his free movement outside Italy.[8] For these reasons, and in virtue of the contribution which he was considered to be making to the government of the state, he was freed of the obligation to perform all local liturgies (*munera*).[9] But at the same time he retained a formal link with his place of origin, and he might still be called upon to hold office there.[10] Those senators who belonged to a municipal *ordo* would have their names inscribed first in its list of members.[11] It is striking how many of them, together with other members of their families, did respond to the tradition whereby persons of distinction in practice omitted to claim the exemption from local burdens to which they were technically entitled.[12] Rather they showed willing to shoulder the expense of acting variously as patron, magistrate, and priest, both in their own place of origin and elsewhere.[13] In the West they would act as patrons of

[3] See chap. 6 sect. 5.

[4] Dio 57.15.4; 60.2.3.

[5] *Inst.* 3.225. Cf. *Sent. Paul.* 5.4.10; *Dig.* 47.10.7.6-9.2.

[6] See *Dig.* 4.3.11.1 and P. Garnsey, *Social Status and Legal Privilege in the Roman Empire*, pp. 182-187.

[7] See *Dig.* 27.10.5 and 9; G. Wesener, *PW* Suppl. 9 s.v. distractio bonorum, cols. 27-32.

[8] See *Dig.* 1.9.11 and discussion in chap. 4 sect. 2 below. Similar restrictions imposed upon senators' sons by Julius Caesar are not heard of again (Suet. *DJ* 42).

[9] Cf. Tac. *Ann.* 2.33. There seem inadequate grounds for P. A. Brunt's speculation (*JRS* 71. 1981. p. 162) that consulars, or perhaps all senators, were exempt from payment of *tributum* in addition.

[10] *Dig.* 50.1.22.5 and 23 pr.

[11] Ulpian, *Dig.* 50.3.2; cf. *ILS* 6121.

[12] Note especially the tradition among sophists, discussed by G. W. Bowersock, *Greek Sophists in the Roman Empire*, Oxford, 1969, chap. 3.

[13] See W. Eck, "Die Präsenz senatorischer Familien in den Städten des Imperium Romanum bis zum späten 3. Jahrhundert," in *Studien zur antiken Sozialgeschichte: Festschrift F. Vittinghoff*, ed. W.Eck, H. Galsterer, H. Wolff, Cologne/Vienna, 1980, pp. 283-322, list I; L. Harmand, *Le patronat sur les collectivités publiques des origines au bas-empire*, Paris,

collegia,[14] and throughout the empire they contributed to municipal projects of all kinds.[15]

Considering the copious evidence for senators' public spirit, it is all the more remarkable that we now possess seven copies of *sacrae litterae* issued by Septimius Severus and Caracalla on 31 May 204: "It appears that you are ignorant of the decree of the senate. If you will consult with experienced persons, you will discover that it is not compulsory for a senator of the Roman people to receive public guests against his will."[16] Leaving aside one copy of unknown provenance, all the findspots for the others were at that date in the province of Asia: two examples were at Ephesus (both in Latin), two on Paros (in Greek and Latin), and one each in Phrygia and in Lydia (both in Latin).[17] It is likely that the same matter is also referred to in a letter sent to a senator by the emperors Valerian and Gallienus, and set up at Smyrna.[18] It would not be appropriate to discuss here the vexing problem of who exactly sought this "protection"—the governor of the province, or another senator, or his agent? Nor can we consider fully why the ruling was sought, or how it evidently came to be advertised on a number of senators' properties.

All the same, the special efforts made in these instances to claim one minor senatorial privilege may seem surprising. Yet strangely we find similar efforts made over another issue. According to Papinian, "freedmen of senators engaged in managing their patrons' affairs are excused the obligation to be guardian by decree of the senate."[19] Other evidence suggests that the privilege is stated too loosely here. The rescript of an unknown emperor is more precise: "A freedman engaged in managing the affairs of a senator of the Roman people is excused the obligation to be guardian; but since he also enjoys public benefits, he is not excused civic *munera*."[20] According to Ulpian,[21] the accepted ruling on this concession was for no

---

1957; J. Nicols, "Pliny and the patronage of communities," *Hermes* 108. 1980. pp. 365-385. The few senators known to have acted as patrons of provinces are treated by L. Harmand, op. cit. pp. 411-417, and A. R. Birley, *The Fasti of Roman Britain*, Appendix III. For discussion of the disputed dating of M. Nonius Balbus, patron of the *commune Cretensium*, see L. Schumacher, "Das Ehrendekret für M. Nonius Balbus aus Herculaneum (AE 1947, 53)," *Chiron* 6. 1976. pp. 165-184.

[14] See G. Clemente, "Il patronato nei collegia dell' impero romano," *Studi classici e orientali* 21. 1972. pp. 142-229. For a rare provincial instance, note *ILS* 5505 (Clemente, p. 209). For Ostia/Portus, see further R. Meiggs, *Roman Ostia* (ed. 2), Oxford, 1973, p. 316. *Collegia* were seldom permitted in the East.

[15] W. Eck, op. cit. in note 13, list II.

[16] In Latin: "Videris nobis senatus consultum ignorare quod si cum peritis contuleris scies senatori populi Romani necesse non esse invito hospitem suscipere."

[17] No. 164 in list, chap. 15 sect. 5.

[18] See W. Eck, *Chiron* 7. 1977. p. 367 n. 53.

[19] *Dig.* 50.1.17.1.

[20] Ulpian, *Frag. Vat.* 131.

[21] Ibid. 132-133.

more than one freedman of a senator, engaged in general management for him, to be so excused. This interpretation was reaffirmed by Gordian in 239.[22] The privilege was no doubt intended as a recognition of the long absences from home demanded of every senator, thus requiring him to lay heavy responsibilities upon the shoulders of others.[23] However it is plain from Gordian's rescript and from the jurists that all kinds of attempts were made to derive greater advantage from this limited privilege than the law allowed. Some members sought to gain exemption not just for a single freedman procurator, but for one in each of their houses.[24] Senators' wives claimed it for *their* freedmen procurators.[25] A man who had been a senator's freedman procurator, and remained so even after he had been granted *ius anulorum* (thereby ranking as freeborn), tried to continue to take advantage of the concession as well.[26] In this connection, too, it is worth noting the similar, though somewhat more sweeping, attempt by the freedman of a senator to be excused from other *tutelae* while acting as guardian for his patron's children.[27]

Surprising though they may seem at first sight, senators' attempts to take full advantage of these two minor privileges perhaps bear witness to the mounting pressure from army and government faced even by the highest class in society during the late second and early third centuries. Nonetheless, efforts to exploit the second privilege well beyond the legal limit were disturbing. Thus in another context it was possibly to guard against unjustified claims of special status that an *oratio* of M. Aurelius gave searchers for fugitive slaves the right of entry to any owner's property, including specifically that of the emperor and of senators.[28]

We hear of no disputes over the privileges enjoyed by senators in respect of their assignment as guardians. They were altogether exempt from such assignment while holding a magistracy at Rome. Furthermore, Severus and Caracalla ruled that they could never be required to act where the property to be administered lay more than 200 miles from the city.[29] Yet there was otherwise no objection to their being assigned as guardians to persons of lower rank, according to a rescript of M. Aurelius and Commodus. But apparently if a man were assigned as guardian of persons

---

[22] *CJ* 5.62.13.

[23] See, for example, *ILAlg.* 2.638 and *ILS* 1091 with comment by P.D.A. Garnsey, "Rome's African empire under the Principate," in P.D.A. Garnsey and C. R. Whittaker (eds.), *Imperialism in the Ancient World*, Cambridge, 1978, pp. 223-254 at p. 228.

[24] Ulpian, *Frag. Vat.* 132.

[25] Modestinus, *Dig.* 27.1.15.8.

[26] Tryphoninus, *Dig.* 27.1.44.3.

[27] Hermogenianus, *Dig.* 27.1.43.

[28] Ulpian, *Dig.* 11.4.1.2 and 4.3; no. 113 in list, chap. 15 sect. 5.

[29] Ulpian, *Frag. Vat.* 146-147; cf. *Dig.* 26.5.18. Marcianus (ibid. 27.1.21.3) mentions a limit of only 100 miles; cf. Callistratus, *Dig.* 5.1.36.

below senatorial rank, and he later became a senator himself, then he was to be discharged at once; on the other hand, if his wards were themselves of senatorial rank, there would be no such discharge.[30]

As the last of the privileges of the class, though not the least conspicuous, we may note the rule dating from Augustus' time that the first row at any show anywhere was to be reserved for senatorial spectators.[31] In Rome itself it had long been established that at the theater senators should sit together as a separate group in the orchestra,[32] where foreign envoys would be invited to join them.[33] Again, from Augustus' day, if not earlier, senators were likewise separately accommodated at the circus, and enjoyed fixed seating there from Claudius' reign.[34] The same arrangements applied in the amphitheater.[35]

Trial by peers has sometimes been taken to be a senatorial privilege. But as we shall see in chapter 16, it is impossible to determine the extent to which charges against members of the class would be laid before the senate in its capacity as a court. Certainly there was no legal obstacle to their standing trial elsewhere. In choosing which court to approach, it seems that a prosecutor would be swayed more by custom and by the nature of his charge than by the status of the accused. Thus in practice all cases of *maiestas* and *repetundae* would go to the senate or the emperor,[36] whereas it would be most unusual for the senate to hear any charge of *falsum*, for example, even though it was competent to do so. A prosecutor of the senatorial class, as much as one of lower rank, would be influenced by these considerations in his choice of court, although a senatorial prosecutor might persuade the House to hear a type of charge it did not normally accept, on the grounds that the case affected the honor or interests of the corporate body. At any hearing which did take place in the senate, defendants of the senatorial class could naturally expect a certain sympathy from their peers. But such bias should be not overestimated: the social class of the accused was only one factor among many likely to influence the attitude of the House. In particular, any defendant whose conduct had done damage to the senate or its interests would meet with hostility, whatever his or her standing. The senate claimed the right to fix sentences at its discretion, though both there and in other courts, convicted members

---

[30] Modestinus, *Dig.* 27.1.15.2-3.

[31] Suet. *Aug.* 44.

[32] Vitruvius, *De Arch.* 5.6.2; Suet. *Aug.* 35; *Nero* 12; Dio 54.14.4.

[33] Tac. *Ann.* 13.54; Suet. *Claud.* 25; Dio 68.15.2; cf. in general J. Reynolds, *Aphrodisias and Rome*, London, 1982, no. 8 lines 76-78 (39 B.C.).

[34] Suet. *Claud.* 21; Dio 55.22.4; 60.7.4; cf. Plin. *Ep.* 9.23.2, where a senator and an *eques* sit next to each other at the circus.

[35] Cf. Epictetus 1.25.26-27; Dio 72.21.

[36] Cases of *repetundae* against senators went only to the senate.

of the senatorial class would of course generally be punished according to the lenient scale of penalties reserved for the upper orders. Treason (*maiestas*) was almost the only crime for which they would be executed.[37]

If we move now to restrictions laid upon the senatorial class, one which clearly continued to exercise the legal writers may be considered first. Just how strictly it was always observed in practice, however, is obscure. By a *Lex Julia* of 18 B.C., which Paulus quotes,[38] members of the class were forbidden to marry freedmen, freedwomen, or others of low occupation. The ban was confirmed by the *Lex Papia Poppaea* in A.D. 9,[39] and at some stage the House added the stipulation that no senator might marry, or keep as a wife, any woman convicted by *iudicium publicum*.[40] A rescript of Antoninus Pius permitted an action to be brought against a freedwoman who had represented herself to a senator as freeborn and had married him.[41] The general ban was again affirmed by an imperial *oratio* and *senatus consultum* in the reign of M. Aurelius.[42] We happen to know that these later enactments referred only to marriage, not betrothal, and that they specifically declared void the marriage of a senator's daughter to a freedman. The latter point is again emphasized by Papinian,[43] while it was presumably in M. Aurelius' own time that the contemporary jurist Marcellus[44] explained how even if a freedman gave himself to be adopted into the family of a freeborn person, he would still not be qualified to marry the daughter of a senator, though he would enjoy other rights of the freeborn.

There is further evidence to suggest that the ban was discussed by jurists both before Marcus' time and after it. Among the former were Octavenus and Pomponius,[45] who are cited in Paulus' treatment immediately following his quotation of the *Lex Julia* mentioned above.[46] Later Ulpian discussed not only whether the marriage was dissolved when a man with a freedwoman wife was later made a senator, but also the converse, so to speak, namely, the standing of a freedwoman whose "husband" had been a senator, but was later removed from the order. In this latter instance, according to Ulpian,[47] the freedwoman did become the man's lawful wife

[37] Cf. Tac. *Ann.* 14.48; Dio 62.15.1ᵃ; P. Garnsey, *Social Status and Legal Privilege*, pp. 105-106.

[38] *Dig.* 23.2.44 pr.; cf. Dio 54.16.2 and discussion by S. Treggiari, *Roman Freedmen During the Late Republic*, Oxford, 1969, pp. 82-86.

[39] Celsus, *Dig.* 23.2.23.

[40] Ulpian, *Dig.* 23.2.43.10.

[41] Marcianus, *Dig.* 23.2.58.

[42] No. 129 in list, chap. 15 sect. 5.

[43] *Dig.* 1.9.9 = 23.2.34.3; cf. Ulpian, ibid. 24.1.3.1.

[44] *Dig.* 23.2.32.

[45] W. Kunkel, *Herkunft und soziale Stellung der römischen Juristen*, pp. 150-151 and 170-171.

[46] *Dig.* 23.2.44.1-8.

[47] *Dig.* 23.2.27; *CJ* 5.4.28.

on his demotion. Ulpian[48] further informs us that a senator could always approach the emperor to ask for a "wife" of freedwoman status to be made a lawful one.

Various further restrictions were placed upon the behavior and activities both of senators and in some instances of the whole senatorial class. No doubt the intention was always to uphold the dignity of the order, but the degree to which that aim was achieved must be placed in doubt by signs that some, if not all, the restrictions were infringed in practice. First, senators themselves were forbidden to act as *delatores*.[49] The date at which this ban was introduced is unknown (except that it was evidently later than Tiberius' reign), and it is hard to check how strictly it was observed. Though no source ever states the point, the ban cannot have applied to laying charges of *maiestas*. This was a crime of special significance for senators, and, as Paulus argued, "securing the emperor's safety and the maintenance of the state is everybody's concern."[50] It is well known how some members were ready enough to turn even against their own peers in bringing such charges, with tragic consequences under certain insecure emperors both for the corporate body and for the ruler himself.

Second, Paulus[51] cites as still current the Republican bans upon senators and their parents contracting to collect *vectigalia publica*, to own any ship for profit, or to supply horses for public games. All these activities were punishable under the *Lex Julia repetundarum* of 59 B.C. The ban upon the last of the three should not be seen as specially directed against senators, however, when the supply of horses for public games had traditionally been a privilege reserved for *equites* alone. In any case, according to Dio,[52] it was extended to senators by Augustus in 2 B.C., even if the extension may have turned out to be only temporary. The other two prohibitions were doubtless introduced to limit senators' commercial activities in certain respects, but there is no sign that they proved irksome during the Principate, or indeed earlier. Senators had always been able to pursue business interests through agents or intermediaries.[53] Perhaps the only remaining value of the ban upon ownership of ships was that it might afford a senator convenient exemption from having to undertake any liturgy which demanded conveyance by sea.[54] In other areas it is clear enough that during our period

[48] *Dig.* 23.2.31.

[49] Marcianus, *Dig.* 49.14.18.1; cf. Dio 58.21.6.

[50] *Sent. Paul. Frag. Leid.* 10.

[51] *Sent. Paul. Frag. Leid.* 3.

[52] 55.10.5.

[53] Note H. Pavis d'Escurac, "Aristocratie sénatoriale et profits commerciaux," *Ktema* 2. 1977. pp. 339-355; J. H. d'Arms, "Senators' involvement in commerce in the late Republic: some Ciceronian evidence," *MAAR* 36. 1980. pp. 77-89; and above all, J. H. d'Arms, *Commerce and Social Standing in Ancient Rome*, Harvard, 1981, esp. pp. 152-159.

[54] Cf. Scaevola, *Dig.* 50.5.3.

senators who owned clay districts near Rome, for example, were happy enough to have their names stamped on bricks as *domini*.[55] Senators must equally have lent[56] and borrowed[57] money on a large scale in common with other members of the upper classes. All the same, Tacitus' claim[58] that at the time of the financial crisis in 33 not one senator was innocent of the charge of lending out money above the legal rate of interest still seems exaggerated.[59]

Third, a set of wider measures concerning the behavior of the whole senatorial class did give some difficulty. Paulus explains: "The daughter of a senator who has prostituted herself, or has appeared on stage, or has been condemned by *iudicium publicum*, may marry a freedman: for no honorable standing remains to a woman who has so far degraded herself."[60] Likewise from 38 B.C. senators were forbidden to fight as gladiators, while in 22 B.C. appearances on stage or in shows were also prohibited to the whole class.[61] Later a senatorial decree of A.D. 19 laid down punishments for any member of the class who deliberately sought demotion in order to engage in prostitution, act, or appear in shows.[62] Whatever the success of this legislation, there is no doubt that senators continued to share the popular enthusiasm for entertainments. Ovid[63] represents them as present at mimes in large numbers, while in Tiberius' reign we find them forbidden even to enter the houses of *pantomimi*.[64]

Among emperors, the ban against appearances by senators on stage or elsewhere was first openly flouted by Gaius: he allegedly arranged races where the charioteers were all of senatorial rank.[65] At his various shows

[55] See P. Setälä, "Private domini in Roman brick stamps of the Empire: a historical and prosopographical study of landowners in the district of Rome," Ann. Acad. Scient. Fenn., Diss. Hum. Litt. 10, Helsinki, 1977, with a useful appreciation by G. Alföldy, *Erasmvs* 30. 1978. cols. 297-302. Senators seem to outnumber members of all other classes as *domini* here.

[56] See, for example, M. Griffin, *Seneca: A Philosopher in Politics*, pp. 232 and 291; Plin. *Ep*. 3.19.8 with R. Duncan-Jones, *The Economy of the Roman Empire: Quantitative Studies*, Cambridge, 1974, p. 21; HA, *Antoninus* 2.8.

[57] Note Tac. *Ann*. 2.27; Plin. *Ep*. 3.9.13.

[58] *Ann*. 6.16. See further in general C. Rodewald, *Money in the Age of Tiberius*, Manchester, 1976, chap. 1.

[59] It is perhaps appropriate to note here that there is no legal basis for the suggestion of E. Rawson in M. I. Finley (ed.), *Studies in Roman Property*, Cambridge, 1976, p. 91, followed by K. Hopkins, *Conquerors and Slaves*, Cambridge, 1978, p. 47 n. 65, that there had existed a ban on senatorial ownership of land outside Italy, which was only removed during the early Principate.

[60] *Dig*. 23.2.47.

[61] Dio 48.43.3; 54.2.5; cf. 51.22.4.

[62] No. 22 in list, chap. 15 sect. 5.

[63] *Tristia* 2. 502.

[64] Tac. *Ann*. 1.77.

[65] Suet. *Calig*. 18.

Nero was similarly contemptuous of the ban.[66] But it was reaffirmed by Vitellius,[67] thus giving Domitian grounds to expel a member from the senate for acting in pantomimes.[68] Yet there are signs that the ban continued to be infringed,[69] although Septimius Severus presumably had it in mind when he criticized the disgraceful lifestyle of certain senators at the end of the second century.[70]

Altogether it might be fair to conclude that both the legal privileges enjoyed by the senatorial class, and the restrictions laid upon it, were equally insignificant in practice. Among the former, exemption from certain local responsibilities carried the greatest potential value, but this was likely to be reduced when by custom leading citizens did not claim such rights in full. The point is perhaps not fully considered by Hopkins[71] when he speculates that one major reason why senators' sons did not follow their fathers into the House may have been their ability to claim the privileges of the class automatically. Among restrictions, the ban on marriage to persons of freed status was evidently the most irksome: but in time even this came to be circumvented by petition to the emperor, as Ulpian says. The high standing of the senatorial class was never derived from its legal privileges, nor much enhanced by them. Rather it was traditionally based upon members' offices, their wealth, and their leading position in society. It is these latter aspects that we should turn to now.

2. Wealth

Among other qualifications, membership of the senatorial class required wealth. In Claudius' words, Augustus and Tiberius "wished there to be in this House all the flower of the colonies and municipalities every-where"—with two significant qualifications—"that is, good men and rich."[1] It is important therefore that we should investigate the level of senators' fortunes.[2]

To most contemporaries in a society where there were extreme ine-qualities of wealth, even the minimum census qualification of one million HS was a colossal sum. To be an *eques* demanded 400,000 HS; to be a

[66] Tac. *Ann.* 14.14; *Hist.* 3.62; Suet. *Nero* 11; Epictetus 1.2.12-13; Dio 61.17.3.

[67] Dio 65.6.3.

[68] Suet. *Dom.* 8; Dio 67.13.1.

[69] Scholia on Juvenal 4.53 (Valla); Fronto, *Ad M. Caes.* 5.37 and 38 = p. 77 H; HA, *Marcus* 12.3.

[70] Dio 75.8.2.

[71] K. Hopkins, *Death and Renewal*, chap. 2 (forthcoming).

[1] *FIRA*² I no. 43 col. II lines 2-4.

[2] Unfortunately the useful work of I. Shatzman, *Senatorial Wealth and Roman Politics, Collection Latomus* 142, Brussels, 1975, deals only with the Republican period.

town councilor 100,000 HS. During the first century A.D. a legionary private was paid 900 HS a year, while his less privileged counterpart in the *auxilia* received 300 HS.[3] This pay was of course punctually forthcoming in full, and in that respect is hardly comparable to the meager, fluctuating earnings of the peasant, so dependent upon weather and harvest. Yet it is easy to see how the census qualification alone would exclude from the senate all but members of an extremely limited number of families, who made up a tiny proportion of the empire's population. In contemporary fiction, when the freedman Trimalchio explained how he was made his master's co-heir with the emperor, and thus gained "patrimonium laticlavium,"[4] his guests understood full well that he thereby gained wealth beyond the dreams of ordinary men.

Senators were perhaps the richest group in the Roman world, though their individual fortunes were still matched, and even outdistanced, by non-senators. Among themselves, as in other classes, there were wide differences in wealth. The surviving evidence hardly allows illustration of the point for more than the first and early second centuries, but there is no reason to doubt that disparities persisted. At the top end of the scale there were some of the richest men in the empire, members who numbered their fortunes in hundreds of millions[5] and, like Cn. Domitius Tullus, could hardly even recall all that they possessed.[6] There was a certain tasteless incongruity in Sextus Pompeius, with his townhouse in Rome occupying a prime site, his estates in Sicily, Macedonia, and Campania, and his name cited as a byword for wealth, attacking a fellow consular Manius Lepidus as "a lazy pauper of no credit to his ancestors."[7] Not surprisingly, the House sprang to the defence of Lepidus. In the mid second century, in his essays *Letter to Nigrinus* and *On Salaried Posts in Great Houses*, Lucian described with feeling the vulgarity and ostentation which he had found among the wealthy in Rome. Though he is careful enough never to name names, we can hardly doubt that he had some senatorial households in mind among others.

Yet by no means all members can have been so rich. In 47, when a consul designate attacked unscrupulous advocates like P. Suillius Rufus by demanding enforcement of the ancient *Lex Cincia*, which forbade acceptance of money or gifts for legal services, the latter claimed that they were "senators of moderate means, who in a peaceful state only seek

---

[3] See in general R. Duncan-Jones, *Economy*, pp. 3-5.

[4] Petronius, *Sat.* 76.2.

[5] See especially R. Duncan-Jones, *Economy*, Appendix 7. Note also a bequest of fifty million HS by Livia to the future emperor Galba—never paid! (Suet. *Galba* 5)

[6] See Plin. *Ep.* 8.18 with Sherwin-White ad loc.; *PIR*[2] D 167; R. Syme, *AJP* 100. 1979. pp. 253-255.

[7] See Tac. *Ann.* 3.32; R. Hanslik, *PW* 21 s.v. Pompeius no. 62, cols. 2265-2267.

peacetime incomes.''[8] Other senators, they argued, supported themselves by military service or agriculture. For their part, by giving attention to others' business, they neglected their own, and might reasonably claim some reward. Claudius was sufficiently moved by these pleas to allow fees up to a maximum of 10,000 HS.[9] For our present purpose, it is the level at which these senatorial advocates chose to describe their wealth that is of note, rather than the truth of their claim. In fact there is little question that Suillius had more than the "moderate means gained by hard work" which he mentions again at his trial in 58.[10]

The only senator whose financial circumstances are known to us in any detail is Pliny the Younger.[11] Despite some protestations about modest resources,[12] it is clear that he continued to live comfortably, while making lavish gifts both publicly and privately. He owned a number of estates in different parts of Italy, and perhaps six houses; from his will it is reasonable to infer that he possessed well over 500 slaves. Since the value of his Transpadane estates, in particular, is not known, it is difficult to estimate his total wealth, but a conjecture of around twenty million HS might be of the right order.

For inheriting and enjoying wealth, however, Pliny's situation was perhaps unusually advantageous.[13] There were apparently no other children to share the substantial fortunes left by his father, mother, and uncle. He married three times, and wives brought dowries which could be enjoyed in their lifetimes even if they had to be returned on death.[14] But most significant of all, he was himself childless. Inevitably, children imposed heavy financial burdens upon a senator. If daughters were to marry well, they would need to be equipped with sufficient dowries,[15] while sons who were to follow their fathers into the House must meet the census qualification. In recommending to Junius Mauricus a *praetorius* as husband for his niece, Pliny himself writes: "I am wondering whether to add that his father has ample means; for when I picture you and your brother for whom we are seeking a son-in-law, I feel nothing need be said about means; but in view of the prevailing habits of the day and the laws of the state which judge a man's wealth to be of primary importance, perhaps after all it is

[8] Tac. *Ann.* 11.7.

[9] Tac. *Ann.* 11.5-7.

[10] Tac. *Ann.* 13.42.

[11] For full discussion and documentation, see R. Duncan-Jones, *Economy*, pp. 17-32.

[12] See further sect. 4 below.

[13] Contrast in particular the situations of Aquillius Regulus (Tac. *Hist.* 4.42) and Gavius Clarus (below), and also the plight of Tarius Rufus' heir (Plin. *NH* 18.37).

[14] On dowries, see briefly J. Crook, *Law and Life of Rome*, London, 1967, pp. 104-105.

[15] Note how Livia is said to have helped many senators furnish their daughters with dowries (Dio 58.2.3); among the upper classes contributions were perhaps commonly made by a father's friends (cf. Cic. *De Off.* 2.55; Plin. *Ep.* 2.4.2; 6.32.2).

something which should not be omitted. Certainly if one thinks of the children of the marriage, and subsequent generations, the question of money must be taken into account as a factor influencing our choice."[16]

The young senator M. Hortalus, whose request for aid from Tiberius in 16 is so vividly portrayed by Tacitus,[17] may have been an incompetent spendthrift, but there is no question that he was faced by a formidable problem in equipping four sons for public life. Tiberius' gift of no more than 200,000 HS to each son can have been of limited value only. Hadrian appreciated a father's difficulty better. According to the *Historia Augusta*, "he supplemented the property of senators impoverished through no fault of their own, making the allowance in each case proportionate to the number of children, so that it might be enough for a senatorial career."[18] Thereby the plight of Calliodorus and his brother, about which Martial[19] composes a witty epigram, was avoided: there was sufficient property available in the family for one of them to meet the equestrian census, but not both! For a senatorial household the sums involved were larger, but the problem remained the same.[20]

We have little knowledge of "poorer" members. But we do hear how C. Sempronius Gracchus, with his father in exile, had had to scrape a living as a trader in Africa and Sicily.[21] Suetonius[22] says that after his governorship of Africa, Vespasian likewise was forced to engage in the mule trade in order to keep up his position. His conduct had been less typical perhaps than that of Quinctilius Varus, who, as governor of Syria, according to Velleius, "entered the rich province a poor man, but left it a rich man and the province poor."[23] Two other consuls of Augustus' time, L. Tarius Rufus[24] and P. Sulpicius Quirinius,[25] were said to have had extremely obscure beginnings. The former apparently never lost the parsimonious habits of his youth, even though he gained great riches later in life. The background of Curtius Rufus was likewise unmentionable.[26] Piso—Galba's choice for adoption—was considered a poor member of the senatorial class, while his contemporary Valens was a "poor" senator who gained sudden wealth in the civil war of 69.[27] Three members who later

---

[16] *Ep*. 1.14.9.

[17] *Ann*. 2.37-38.

[18] *Hadr*. 7.9.

[19] 5.38.

[20] For discussion of what might have constituted appropriate capital for a senator, see Appendix 2.

[21] Tac. *Ann*. 4.13.

[22] *Vesp*. 4; for Vespasian's financial straits, cf. *Tit*. 2 and *Dom*. 1.

[23] 2.117.2.

[24] Cos. 16 B.C.; Plin. *NH* 18.37.

[25] Cos. 12 B.C.; Tac. *Ann*. 3.23 and 48.

[26] Tac. *Ann*. 11.21; cf. Plin. *Ep*. 7.27.2, "tenuis adhuc et obscurus."

[27] Tac. *Hist*. 1.48 and 66.

achieved fame and fortune as *delatores* were also alleged to have risen from humble circumstances—Eprius Marcellus, Vibius Crispus, and Aquillius Regulus[28]—while another noted for informing, Cn. Domitius Afer, was for a long time poverty-stricken.[29] Tacitus[30] reflects the shock to rank and reputation caused by the financial crisis in 33 when large-scale debtors lost everything. Out of sympathy he later refrains from naming those nobles "made corruptible by poverty," who agreed to appear on stage for Nero.[31] Many senators would no doubt have agreed with the belief of their fellow member, M. Asinius Marcellus—against Tacitus[32]—that "poverty was the supreme misfortune."

It is again Tacitus who portrays some senators as alarmed by the application of leading Gauls to enter the House in 48. They despise the background and wealth of the Gauls, and ask "(if Gauls are admitted) what career would be left for our surviving *nobiles* or for a poor senator from Latium?"[33] It is attractive to guess that it was a senator who clasped Nero's freedman *a libellis*, Epaphroditus, by the knees and exclaimed in tears that he had only one and a half million HS left. To him such a sum represented misery.[34] Early in the second century Pliny recommends a friend for the praetorship, candidly describing him to Trajan as "poor."[35] Later, while L. Verus is in the East (163-166), Fronto tells him in more detail of the difficulties of Gavius Clarus:

Now, if my means were more ample, I would help him to the utmost of my power to enable him to discharge the duties of a senator with ease, nor should I ever allow him to cross the sea on this business. As it is, both the moderate nature of my means and his straitened circumstances have forced me to banish him against his will into Syria to secure the legacies which have come to him under the will of a very dear friend.

Such poverty has been the lot of my friend Clarus from no fault of his own, for he received no benefit from either his father's or his mother's estate; the only result of his being his father's heir was that he found difficulty in paying his father's creditors. But by economy and attention to duty and frugality he discharged all his obligations as quaestor, aedile, and praetor, and whereas your deified father paid out from your *fiscus* the expenses of his praetorship in his absence, as soon as ever Clarus recovered his health and came back to Rome he paid in the whole amount to your *fiscus*.[36]

[28] Tac. *Dial*. 8; *Hist*. 4.42; Plin. *Ep*. 2.20.13.

[29] Tac. *Ann*. 4.66; *PIR²* D 126.

[30] *Ann*. 6.16-17.

[31] *Ann*. 14.14; Dio 61.17.3-5.

[32] *Ann*. 14.40.

[33] *Ann*. 11.23.

[34] The story is told by Epictetus (1.26.11-12), who became Epaphroditus' slave. Cf. F. Millar, *JRS* 55. 1965. pp. 143-144.

[35] *Ep*. 10.12.2.

[36] *Ver. Imp*. 2.7.5-6 = pp. 127-128 H. On Fronto's level of wealth, see sect. 3 below.

For a time in the late second century Septimius Severus seems to have had very modest property in Italy—a tiny house in Rome and one farm at Veii—though of course we do not know what he owned abroad in addition.[37] Finally, the *Historia Augusta* can envisage many senators being in Rome with neither carriage nor slaves in Elagabalus' reign.[38]

While it can be seen how we have little enough knowledge of "poor" senators, frequent references to financial difficulties should also be taken into account. These would suggest in turn that many members attempted to pursue their careers with inadequate resources. It must be significant that in the mid second century Antoninus Pius specially removed the ban on legally valid gifts between husband and wife if the husband would thereby be enabled to seek the *latus clavus*, or enter the equestrian order, or celebrate games.[39] Loss of rank through poverty was no new phenomenon: it had occurred during the Republic.[40] But under the Principate the emperor could now be approached for aid, and he could win loyalty by bestowing it.[41] The friends and senators whose census qualifications Augustus had made up were beyond counting, according to the summary of the *Res Gestae*.[42] We may well believe it, judging by Dio's claim[43] that in A.D. 4 alone he helped over eighty young men. Among individuals whom we know to have gained such aid were Cn. Cornelius Lentulus,[44] and another senator whose debts were as high as four million HS according to Macrobius.[45] Of course some had lost their money through fecklessness, and it was for this reason that Tiberius required any senator seeking aid to explain his case to the House. He gave no help to those who had wasted their resources.[46] There is no sign that Claudius helped to make up the census qualification of senators in difficulties; rather he praised those who voluntarily resigned through poverty.[47] Nero was more generous:[48] in fact in 65 the Pisonian conspirators' plan was that the consul designate Plautius

[37] HA, *Sev.* 4.5, with A. R. Birley, *Septimius Severus*, London, 1971, p. 78 and references there.

[38] *Elagab.* 16.1.

[39] *Dig.* 24.1.42, reading with F. Millar, *Emperor*, p. 279 n. 1, "ut ecce si uxor viro lati petendi gratia donet vel ut equestris ordinis fiat vel ludorum gratia." Cf. Ulpian, *Reg.* 7.1.

[40] See C. Nicolet, *JRS* 66. 1976. pp. 27-28.

[41] Cf. Tac. *Ann.* 1.2 on Augustus' bestowal of wealth upon *nobiles*.

[42] Sect. 4.

[43] 55.13.6.

[44] Seneca, *De Benef.* 2.27.2; cf. Tac. *Ann.* 4.44; *PIR*² C 1379.

[45] *Sat.* 2.4.23. For the senator's ingratitude, see F. Millar, *Emperor*, p. 297 n. 55, and compare Seneca, *De Ira* 3.31.2.

[46] Tac. *Ann.* 1.75; 2.47; Suet. *Tib.* 47; Seneca, *De Benef.* 2.7.2; *Ep. Mor.* 122.10; Dio 57.10.3-4.

[47] Tac. *Ann.* 12.52; Dio 60.11.8 and 29.1.

[48] Tac. *Ann.* 13.34; Suet. *Nero* 10.

Lateranus, by ostensibly petitioning for aid, should clasp Nero and pin him down.[49] Vespasian, too, gave help.[50] Among later emperors, only Hadrian is explicitly attested as making up the census of senators,[51] though it may be that Nerva had also done so.[52] Rather, as we shall see, from the second century emperors came to help less wealthy senators with the expenses of office instead. But early in the third century Dio does have Maecenas advise Augustus about treatment of senators: "Do not get rid of any good man because of his poverty, but even give him the money he requires."[53]

We have no clear idea of whether a check was consistently kept on the level of senators' property, nor of how one might have been carried out. In the same speech written for Maecenas by Dio,[54] Augustus is recommended to appoint a senatorial officer who will supervise all matters concerning the families, property, and morals of senators and *equites*. At least by the time Dio was writing there evidently was an imperial official concerned with the census qualifications of senators and *equites*: according to Herodian,[55] Elagabalus appointed an actor to the post. Earlier we hear that in 13 B.C. when Augustus examined all members of the senatorial class aged under 35, he was content simply to accept sworn statements about their property.[56] If a remark by Seneca[57] be correctly interpreted thus, it would seem also that candidates for office were required to declare their debts. In most cases senators' resignations on the grounds of poverty appear to have been voluntary, though not always: Claudius resorted to compulsion in 52.[58]

In brief it would be fair to conclude that senators' wealth varied more widely than has sometimes been thought. In particular, it was by no means rare for a member to embark upon a senatorial career with resources which proved barely adequate at best. Altogether, as the following discussion of their obligations will show, many senators are likely to have suffered financial strain.[59]

---

[49] Tac. *Ann*. 15.53.
[50] Suet. *Vesp*. 17.
[51] HA, *Hadr*. 7.9, quoted above.
[52] Cf. Martial 12.6.9-11.
[53] 52.19.2.
[54] 52.21.3-5.
[55] 5.7.7.
[56] Dio 54.26.9.
[57] *De Benef*. 6.19.5.
[58] Tac. *Ann*. 12.52.
[59] Capital of 20 million HS, taken by K. Hopkins in P. Abrams and E. A. Wrigley (eds.), *Towns in Societies*, Cambridge, 1978, p. 49 note 36 as representative of a senatorial fortune in our period, is thus possibly rather a high estimate.

3. Financial Obligations

To maintain a position in public life was expensive, as Pliny did not hesitate to remind two of his beneficiaries.[1] We have noted already that many senators and their families bore the expense of holding local offices and priesthoods, and contributed to municipal projects of all kinds. But we need to consider in more detail the nature and extent of the financial obligations specifically laid upon members by their entry to the senate and advancement thereafter.

Among major expenses, the new aspirant to a senatorial career might find it costly to gain the *latus clavus* from the emperor in the first instance, if he had neither friend nor relative to support him. In 62, Fabricius Veiento was convicted of having offered to obtain the "ius adipiscendorum honorum," as Tacitus[2] puts it (that is, the *latus clavus*), for a fee. Around the same time Vespasian charged a young man 200,000 HS for the same service.[3] In the late second century Commodus' Praetorian Prefect, Cleander, must have levied a substantially larger sum. Dio quips: "In fact, some men became senators only after spending all they possessed, so that it was said of Julius Solon, a very obscure man, that he had been stripped of all his property and banished to the senate."[4]

Having gained the *latus clavus*, most aspirants to a senatorial career would incur election expenses at one stage or another. As we have noted above, election to the highest magistracy, the consulship, depended entirely on the emperor's recommendation. He would regularly support a proportion of the candidates for lesser magistracies, too, so that their election was certain and they were saved the trouble and expense of canvassing. Yet for the remaining places there was open competition. Tacitus says that when the elections were transferred from the popular assemblies to the senate itself in 14, senators were content with the change, "since it relieved them from the necessity of undignified canvassing and outlay."[5]

From Pliny's *Letters*, however, we can see how at the end of the first century sufficient competition still remained for elections to be taken seriously, so that canvassing among members was normal.[6] Significantly, in recommending a husband for the niece of Junius Mauricus, Pliny explains that the man has already risen to the rank of *praetorius*, "thus sparing you

---

[1] *Ep.* 2.4.3; 6.32.1. See further sect. 4 below.

[2] *Ann.* 14.50.

[3] Suet. *Vesp.* 4. Note the opposition of the father to his son's ambitions.

[4] 72.12.3.

[5] *Ann.* 1.15. An arrangement whereby the senate chose *praetores aerarii* from its own members was stopped as early as 23 B.C. because of improper canvassing (Tac. *Ann.* 13.29; Dio 53.32.2).

[6] Cf. Suet. *Vesp.* 2; Tac. *Ann.* 14.28.

the necessity of canvassing on his behalf.''[7] In particular, canvassing would involve the candidate and his supporters in the chore of approaching friends in person or by letter. As Pliny says of his own efforts in support of a candidate for the tribunate: "I am approaching all my friends to beg their support, and going the round of private houses and public places, testing what influence and popularity I have by my entreaties.''[8] He speaks likewise of his vigor on behalf of another candidate, probably seeking the quaestorship, and of the pains which a prematurely deceased friend had taken to gain an aedileship.[9]

These letters suggest that canvassing would demand time and effort rather than expenditure of money, and this was no doubt all that the *Lex Julia de ambitu* (18 B.C.) sanctioned. But in the mid first century, Columella, the disgruntled provincial from Gades, points perversely to the drawbacks of every occupation except agriculture, and shuns politics "because it is not with voluntary servitude, but with bribes, that office is bought.''[10] Pliny, too, shows that the law was commonly ignored in practice: "At the last elections the senate expressed the very proper opinion that 'candidates should not provide entertainments, distribute presents, or deposit money with agents.' The first two practices were employed without restraint or concealment, and the third was done secretly, but was well known.''[11] Later in the same letter he speaks of "candidates' scandalously gross expenditure." In the same way Epictetus, expressing his contempt for the demands of senatorial ambition, mentions canvassing expenses among other points: "If you wish to be consul, you must lose your sleep, run around, kiss hands, rot away at other men's doors, say and do many undignified things, send presents to many, and tokens to some every day.''[12]

We have no further knowledge of the expenses which a candidate for office would need to pay in practice, even if they were strictly forbidden by law. As Pliny explains in the letter quoted immediately above, Trajan attempted to eliminate expenditure on canvassing by a requirement that all candidates for office should invest one-third of their capital in Italian real estate. By then Augustus' demand of 8 B.C. that all candidates pay a deposit to be forfeit if they resorted to illegal methods, had evidently long fallen into abeyance.[13] Trajan's stipulation perhaps suffered the same fate

---

[7] *Ep.* 1.14.7.

[8] *Ep.* 2.9.5.

[9] *Ep.* 6.6; 8.23.5-6.

[10] *De re rust.* I. praef. 10.

[11] *Ep.* 6.19.1-2.

[12] 4.10.20; cf. Seneca, *De Brev. Vit.* 20.1, "mille indignitates." As Millar says (*Emperor*, p. 307), this canvassing mentioned by Epictetus must relate either to gaining the favor of persons close to the emperor (for the consulship), or to the earlier offices through which a man had to rise before attaining the highest magistracy.

[13] Dio 55.5.3.

in turn before being revived on a more modest scale by M. Aurelius, who demanded that senators of non-Italian origin should invest one quarter of their capital in Italy.[14] Again, this requirement, too, may soon have lapsed: certainly if it was maintained for any length of time, the amount of surviving evidence for ownership of Italian property by provincial senators is puzzlingly small.[15] At least while such rules did remain in force, they imposed a further burden on the non-Italian senator, or equally on the native Italian who had chosen to invest heavily in provincial estates. It is tempting to speculate that among the reasons which prompted Q. Valerius Macedo to decline Hadrian's offer of *latus clavus cum quaestura* was the unwelcome prospect of having to sell off many of his pleasant, profitable vineyards by the Rhone before his candidacy, in order to buy Italian estates.[16] By contrast, there must have been many provincial senators who removed altogether to Italy. Fronto surely did so,[17] while it is notable that his namesake, C. Caristanius Fronto, the first senator from Antioch in Pisidia (cos. suff. 90), is also the last member of his family to be mentioned there. Admittedly, haphazard destruction of epigraphical evidence may provide an equally plausible explanation in this latter instance.[18] More generally, however, Paulus[19] makes the striking point that a senator removed from the order is restored to his country of origin only by special request.

Once he had entered the senate a member would need to maintain a house in Rome.[20] In the Augustan period the architectural writer Vitruvius explains the style of residence suitable for a senator of standing: "For *nobiles*, who in holding offices and magistracies have obligations to fulfil to citizens, lofty regal vestibules must be built, and the most impressive atria and peristyle courts, with extensive groves and strolling-places in a style to add lustre to their dignity; moreover, libraries, picture-galleries and basilicas constructed with a magnificence to match those of public buildings, because these men's homes are so often the setting for meetings on public affairs and also private suits and arbitrations."[21]

---

[14] HA, *Marcus* 11.8.

[15] Cf. F. Millar, *A Study of Cassius Dio*, Oxford, 1964, p. 10; H. Halfmann, *Die Senatoren*, pp. 66-67. W. Eck announces preparation of a work on senators' properties in *Chiron* 7. 1977. p. 374 note 90.

[16] *ILS* 6998 with D. van Berchem, "Un banquier chez les Helvètes," *Ktema* 3. 1978. pp. 267-274 at p. 270 note 10. F. Millar (*Emperor*, p. 292) suggests that the offer may have been made when Hadrian visited Gaul in 121/122.

[17] E. J. Champlin, *Fronto and Antonine Rome*, p. 5. For the trend among leading Greeks, cf. Plut. *De Exilio* 14 (*Mor.* 605 B-C).

[18] See B. M. Levick, *Roman Colonies in Southern Asia Minor*, Oxford, 1967, p. 113.

[19] *Dig.* 50.1.22.4; cf. Modestinus, ibid. 1.9.3 and chap. 4 sect. 2 note 131 below.

[20] See in general B. W. Frier, *Landlords and Tenants in Imperial Rome*, Princeton, 1980, pp. 39-41.

[21] *De Arch.* 6.5.2.

No doubt this ideal was approached in the style of residence owned by outstanding *consulares* like Cn. Calpurnius Piso (ord. 7 B.C.), Sextus Pompeius (ord. 14), Arruntius Stella (suff. final months of 101), or Pedanius Secundus, *Praefectus Urbi*, whose town house had a staff of four hundred slaves at the time of his murder in 61.[22] But for the less wealthy senator, residence in Rome imposed a troublesome expense. As we might expect, the general cost of living there was higher than elsewhere, and property to buy or to rent was notoriously costly.[23] It was hard to economize: "I lack extravagant tastes," says Seneca apostrophizing, "but city life itself demands high expenditure."[24] Tiberius went so far as to degrade a senator who moved to his *horti* before 1 July, the day on which long-term urban leases were normally taken up. Thereby the latter might avoid the expense of retaining an establishment in the city throughout the year, and, whenever he did return later, could hope to secure at an artificially low rent accommodation which had remained vacant past the customary starting date.[25] Plainly the emperor considered such attempts to economize as undignified.

Unfortunately we do not possess figures to determine the outlay demanded of a senator for acquiring suitable staff and accommodation in Rome. Yet Horace[26] can insinuate that five slaves is far too small an escort for a *praetorius* making a journey in the vicinity of the city. And having explained how the severe censors of 125 B.C. reprimanded a senator for renting a house at 6,000 HS, Velleius comments: "This was 153 years ago. Nowadays, if anyone takes a residence at such a price, he is scarcely recognized as a senator."[27] All the same, less affluent members were hard pressed to find suitable accommodation. At the time of his son Titus' birth in 41 Vespasian was living near the Septizonium in a mean house with small, dark rooms.[28] And, as we have seen, Septimius Severus likewise only had a tiny house in Rome.

Typically, however, both Vespasian[29] and Severus did also own country

---

[22] Tac. *Ann.* 3.9; 14.43; Ovid, *Ex Ponto* 4.5.9-10; Martial 12.2.9-10. On large staffs in upper class households, see S. Treggiari, "Jobs in the household of Livia," *PBSR* 43. 1975. pp. 48-77.

[23] R. Duncan-Jones (*PBSR* 33. 1965. p. 225) conjectures from Suetonius, *DJ* 38 that basic rents in Rome were perhaps four times as high as they were in the rest of Italy during the mid first century B.C. Under the Empire the gap may have widened even further: see in general R. Duncan-Jones, *Economy*, Appendixes 8, 15.

[24] *Ep. Mor.* 50.3; cf. Apuleius, *Metam.* 11.28.

[25] Suet. *Tib.* 35 with B. W. Frier, *Landlords and Tenants in Imperial Rome*, pp. 34 and 39.

[26] *Sat.* 1.6.107-109. For the minimum needs of a *consularis vir*, note Plin. *Ep.* 3.16.8.

[27] 2.10.1; cf. Plin. *NH* 36.109.

[28] Suet. *Tit.* 2.

[29] Suet. *Vesp.* 5 ("in suburbano Flaviorum").

property nearby. In fact, every senator who could afford it would expect
to possess such property in addition to his establishment in the city.[30] In
his agricultural treatise of the mid first century Columella can only approve
in principle the advice of Mago the Carthaginian that the owner of an
estate should have no town house: "This precept, if it could be observed
today, I would not change. But as things are, since civic ambition often
calls most of us away, and even more frequently keeps us away when
called, as a result I rate it as most advantageous to have an estate near
town, which even the busy man may easily reach every day after his
business in the forum is done."[31] Pliny's villa seventeen miles from Rome
at Laurentum, near Ostia, came fairly close to Columella's recommendation: it could be reached by evening after a full day's work in the city.[32]
Pliny also owned a house on the Esquiline Hill in Rome.[33] Outside, Tibur,
Praeneste, and Tusculum were among the popular resorts.[34] Yet there is
every reason to believe that the price of property throughout the immediate
vicinity of Rome was high—though not, of course, as extortionate as prices
within the city.[35] Seneca[36] rightly sees ownership of great estates near the
city as one of the marks of a wealthy man. He himself had a "suburbanum
rus" at the fourth milestone, along with villas at Nomentum and Alba.[37]
Galba, among others, had a summer place at Tusculum[38] while the family
of Antoninus Pius possessed one at Lorium.[39] Pliny's much wealthier
contemporary M. Aquillius Regulus had gardens "across the Tiber" as
well as one country house ("rus") at the third milestone from Rome and
another at Tusculum.[40] Fronto likewise conformed to the pattern, with a
town house on the Esquiline, a suburban villa in the Aurelian district, and
seaside property at fashionable Surrentum on the Bay of Naples.[41]

In almost every magistracy which he held, a senator would be required
to make a substantial contribution for the cost of games and other purposes.
Taking the offices in order, first quaestors had to contribute towards paving

[30] For the general expectation that a senator would be likely to own more than one home,
note *Frag. Vat.* 132.
[31] *De re rust.* 1.1.19.
[32] Plin. *Ep.* 2.17.2; for what might have constituted a "full day," see chap. 6 sect. 2. It
would have been impossible to commute daily from Laurentum of course.
[33] See R. Duncan-Jones, *Economy*, p. 22.
[34] Cf. Plin. *Ep.* 5.6.45 with Sherwin-White ad loc.
[35] The only contradictory testimony—that prices around Rome were low—comes from
Pliny the Elder (*NH* 14.50), and is perhaps best set aside. See R. Duncan-Jones, *Economy*,
p. 52.
[36] *Ep. Mor.* 87.7.
[37] See M. Griffin, *Seneca: A Philosopher in Politics*, p. 287 and references there.
[38] Suet. *Galba* 4.
[39] HA, *Antonin.* 1.8.
[40] Plin. *Ep.* 4.2.5; Martial 7.31; cf. 1.12.
[41] See E. J. Champlin, *Fronto and Antonine Rome*, pp. 21-24.

roads (*stratura viarum*) until on the motion of P. Dolabella in 47 the "college" of quaestors designate each year was required to pay for a *gladiatorium munus* instead. Despite Agrippina's objection, this arrangement was abrogated soon after Nero's accession in 54.[42] It is puzzling therefore that Lucan's anonymous biographer describes him as having celebrated a show with his colleagues when quaestor in the 60's, "in the fashion then current":[43] but maybe those able to afford it still continued the customary entertainment even after the formal obligation had lapsed. According to Suetonius,[44] *quaestoria munera* were only reintroduced by Domitian; they were still celebrated in the time of Severus Alexander.[45]

So far as we know, tenure of the tribunate did not bring with it any substantial expenses. It was thus an exceptional occurrence—in honor of Augustus' tribunician power—when the tribunes' offer to celebrate the *Augustalia* in 14 was accepted by the senate. But even then the expense was borne by the state.[46] As we shall see, only at the very beginning of our period were aediles required to pay for games. Thereafter there were still expenses attached to the office, as Fronto indicates during the 160's in a letter to L. Verus about the career of Gavius Clarus, quoted above: perhaps these were connected with the aediles' *cura urbis*, but we have no evidence. At any rate the claim of the *Historia Augusta* that M. Aurelius "bestowed the rank of tribune or aedile on many senators who were poor, but honest,"[47] would certainly imply that both these offices were comparatively inexpensive to hold. Yet, like other magistrates, aediles might still give games voluntarily.[48]

However, the real burden of sponsoring games fell mainly upon praetors, and to a lesser degree upon consuls. For their trouble and expense both made a fine show.[49] From 22 B.C. Augustus arranged that the former should take over from the aediles the celebration of the ancient festivals. For the most part these were a mixture of circus races and theatrical performances. They comprised the *Ludi*:

1. *Megalenses*, 4-10 April (7 days)
2. *Ceriales*, 12-19 April (8 days)
3. *Florales*, 28 April-3 May (6 days)
4. *Apollinares*, 6-13 July (8 days)

[42] Tac. *Ann.* 11.22; 13.5; Suet. *Claud.* 24.
[43] *Vita Lucani*, p. 2 Endt, "more tunc usitato."
[44] *Dom.* 4.
[45] HA, *Sev. Alex.* 43.3-4; cf. *Fasti Filocali, Inscr. Ital.* XIII. 2. p. 261.
[46] Tac. *Ann.* 1.15; Dio 56.46.4-5 and 47.2.
[47] *Marcus* 10.4.
[48] Cf. Dio 54.8.5; HA, *Gord.* 3.5.
[49] Cf. Plin. *NH* 34.20; Plin. *Paneg.* 92.4-5; Juvenal, *Sat.* 10.36-46; 11.193-201. See further in general E. Habel, *PW* Suppl. 5 s.v. ludi publici, cols. 608-630.

5. *Romani* or *Magni*, 4-19 September (16 days)
6. *Plebeii*, 4-17 November (14 days)[50]

From 14 the *praetor peregrinus* had responsibility for the *Ludi Augustales* in addition (in October).[51] We hear once of a *praetor Parthicarius*, presumably in charge of games established to celebrate Parthian victories.[52] Until Claudius ended the practice, gladiatorial exhibitions, too, were commonly given by praetors.[53] In addition, voluntary celebrations of games might be sponsored by them from time to time,[54] and they would also bear some responsibility for *Ludi Saeculares* when these were performed.[55]

Consuls had a lesser responsibility for games, which is at the same time more difficult to discern. Yet, as we shall see, tenure of the office definitely involved expense, and it is perhaps right to assume that any consul would at least have to contribute towards the cost of games, whatever the time of year at which he held office.[56] It was specifically consuls who took charge of the games to commemorate Augustus' victory at Actium on 2-3 September,[57] and in honor of the emperor's birthday.[58] They might also give games on special occasions—in connection with triumphs, for example.[59]

Senators who were priests might be called upon to contribute towards games given by their colleges on special occasions,[60] but so far as we can tell, *summae honorariae* were not payable on entry to the colleges at Rome. Not only were the sums of eight or ten million HS which Gaius allegedly extracted from Claudius and others eager to serve as priests of his own cult wholly untypical; so also was the exaction itself.[61]

Our information on the actual cost of games and on the level of magistrates' contributions is thin. Yet in Tacitus' view the imposition of a *gladiatorium munus* upon quaestors would effectively have closed the office to candidates of modest means, and such a difficulty perhaps explains why

[50] For details, see *Inscr. Ital.* XIII. 2. p. 372.
[51] Tac. *Ann.* 1.15 and 54.
[52] Such games were founded by Trajan or Hadrian, but had lapsed by Dio's time (69.2.3). The one *praetor Parthicarius* known to us lived in the Severan period (*ILS* 2931 with J. Fitz, *Epigraphica* 23. 1961. pp. 84-94).
[53] Cf. Suet. *Nero* 4; Dio 54.2.4; 55.31.4; 56.25.8; 59.14.1-2; 60.5.6.
[54] Cf. Dio 54.26.2 and 34.1-2; 60.12.4-5 and 17.9.
[55] Cf. Tac. *Ann.* 11.11.
[56] For their celebration of games, cf. *RG* 9.1; 22.2; Suet. *Nero* 4; Epictetus 4.10.21; Fronto, *Ad M. Caes.* 2.1.1 = p. 24 H; Dio 56.46.4; 75.4.3.
[57] Cf. Dio 59.20.1-2.
[58] Plin. *Paneg.* 92.4-5; Tac. *Hist.* 2.95; Dio 56.46.4.
[59] Martial 8.78; Dio 56.1.1; 60.23.4.
[60] For example, Tac. *Ann.* 3.64; Dio 58.12.5. See further M.W.H. Lewis, *The Official Priests of Rome under the Julio-Claudians, Papers and Monographs of the American Academy in Rome* 16. 1955. p. 19.
[61] Suet. *Calig.* 22; *Claud.* 9; Dio 59.28.5.

the senate so quickly pressed to have the arrangement scrapped in its newfound freedom on Nero's accession.[62] Once the *munus* had been re-introduced, a senator of modest means like Gavius Clarus needed to exercise "economy, attention to duty and frugality" in order to discharge his obligations as quaestor and aedile.

It was above all responsibility for games which had once made the office of aedile an expensive one to undertake.[63] But as we have already noted, the burden was shifted by Augustus on to praetors from 22 B.C. At first he stipulated that all members of a college must contribute equal amounts to supplement any grants made by the state—an arrangement calculated to protect the less wealthy holders of the magistracy.[64] Yet in 18 B.C. he allowed praetors to spend three times the state grant, if they wished.[65] So far as we can tell, responsibility for the different festivals was regularly determined by the traditional method of the lot.[66] We hear how in his praetorship the future emperor Galba celebrated the *Floralia*.[67] Even if praetors were away during their term of office for some reason, they were still obliged to contribute towards the expenses, as Gavius Clarus and Septimius Severus both had to.[68]

The *Fasti Antiates Ministrorum Domus Augustae*[69] give some evidence for the level of the state grant made towards three festivals within the period A.D. 23 to 37: 380,000 HS for the *Ludi Apollinares* (1 day of circus races + 7 days of theatrical performances); 760,000 HS for the *Ludi Romani* (5 days circus + 7 days theater + 2 days feasts + 2 days horse trials); and 600,000 HS for the *Ludi Plebeii* (3 days circus + 7 days theater + 2 days feasts + 2 days horse trials). In addition, the token sum of 10,000 HS was granted for the *Ludi Augustales*. We do not know what size of grant was made towards other games, if any at all. It was commonplace that these state grants would not cover the full costs of the various celebrations. Republican aediles had been prepared to spend recklessly in order to increase their popularity and thus gain a better chance of election to the praetorship. Once responsibility was transferred to praetors, whose promotion to the consulship depended upon the emperor, this incentive disappeared. But of course, in contrast, parsimony would still excite popular disapproval. As we might expect from Tacitus' account, Agricola's

[62] Tac. *Ann*. 11.22 and 13.5.

[63] Cf. Dio 53.2.2 and 54.11.1 for resignations by holders who could not meet the expenses, the latter even in 19 B.C., after Augustus' changes.

[64] Dio 54.2.4.

[65] Dio 54.17.4.

[66] Cf. Dio 59.14.2; 60.31.7.

[67] Suet. *Galba* 6; cf. Dio 58.19.1-2.

[68] HA, *Sev*. 3.5; cf. Suet. *Aug*. 43.

[69] *Inscr. Ital*. XIII. 2. p. 206.

approach to the problem during his praetorship was judicious: "In sponsoring the games and other vanities of office he steered mid-way between cold reason and lavishness; on the one side he was far from extravagant, but at the same time he was sensitive to public opinion."[70]

Two of Martial's epigrams[71] can perhaps give some clue as to the amounts which a praetor might contribute from his own pocket. In one he speaks of a praetor spending over 100,000 HS on the races, in another of 100,000 HS being expected as a minimum contribution towards the *Ludi Megalenses*, as well as 20,000 HS for the *Ludi Plebeii*. The thought of these latter amounts prompted the prospective magistrate's wife to divorce him and take back her dowry at once![72] Yet it cannot have been outlay on this scale which had driven the contemporary *praetorius*, Caecilius Classicus, into debt to the tune of four million HS.[73] Equally we know that the sums indicated by Martial were well within Pliny's ability to furnish without trouble. He cheerfully gives away 300,000 HS to a friend from Comum, for example,[74] and his personal gifts were modest beside those of Cotta Messalinus (cos. 20),[75] who is thanked in verse on the tombstone of his freedman *accensus* for lavishing more than one equestrian census, as well as dowries, upon the children of this favorite.[76] Two senators of the Severan period were evidently able to show similar generosity to their concubines. The donations which the first, Pontius Paulinus, made to his freedwoman provoked a case in which they were alleged to be illegal under the law forbidding gifts between husband and wife: but Septimius Severus judged that the woman had been treated more as concubine than wife, and therefore allowed the gifts.[77] The second, Cocceius Cassianus, went so far as to make his concubine's daughter co-heir with his own granddaughter.[78]

While some members may have felt no strain, it is plain enough that the required contributions towards games did stretch the means of many

---

[70] *Agr.* 6.

[71] 4.67; 10.41.

[72] By contrast, the two million HS which Trajan gave Hadrian as praetor was plainly a quite exceptional sum, as was the lavish outlay of Gordian during his consulship (HA, *Hadr.* 3.8; *Gord.* 4).

[73] Plin. *Ep.* 3.9.13.

[74] *Ep.* 1.19. For Pliny's private gifts, see R. Duncan-Jones, *Economy*, pp. 28-29; for his celebration of games as praetor, *Ep.* 7.11.4.

[75] *PIR²* A 1488.

[76] *ILS* 1949. Unlike Pliny, Cotta had a son (*PIR²* A 1486), but it is no wonder that the latter needed Nero's help after his father's career of gourmandizing and reckless luxury. See Appendix 2.

[77] Ulpian, *Dig.* 24.1.3.1.

[78] Papinian, *Dig.* 34.9.16.1. By contrast, M. Otacilius Catulus (cos. suff. 88) only left 20,000 HS to a concubine (Celsus, *Dig.* 31.29 pr.).

others severely, or were even beyond them.[79] From a passage in Seneca,[80] we might gather that it was normal for the friends of a praetor to contribute towards his expenses. A gift of this type seems to be mentioned elsewhere only in a case formulated for discussion by Marcellus in the latter part of the second century, where a man's will had stipulated that his heirs should pay forty *aurei* to his sister's son "in honorem consulatus."[81] In general the practice was akin to that of contributing towards the dowries of friends' daughters, mentioned above, and sending gifts for the rebuilding and furnishing of a great man's house destroyed by fire, cited enviously by Juvenal.[82] All such presents naturally put the recipient under an obligation to return the kindness;[83] but they also illustrate the close-knit nature of the senatorial class.

Not surprisingly, emperors who extended games or increased the number of races hardly earned senators' thanks thereby,[84] while Commodus was bitterly hated for his demand that he be paid two *aurei* annually on his birthday by all senators, their wives, and their children.[85] Imperial efforts to reduce festival days came as a relief.[86] From 217, too, praetors evidently no longer had to distribute presents at the games they gave, except at the *Floralia*.[87]

Some magistrates simply could not meet their expenses, and thus had to resign.[88] Early in Nero's reign the praetor Fabricius Veiento considered the demands of the horsebreeders and charioteers intolerable, and so reduced his expenses by racing dogs instead.[89] As we have seen, it must

[79] It must be said that a level of perhaps 100,000 to 120,000 HS does not seem impossibly high when compared with the expenses envisaged in the *sententia prima de gladiatorum sumptibus minuendis* of c. 177, which amongst its various categories makes provision for *munera* costing 150,000 to 200,000 HS upwards at the top level (*Aes Italicense* lines 29-35, *Hesperia* 24. 1955. p. 332). All the same, the comparison should not be pressed. Eighty years or so separate Martial's figures from the *sententia prima*. It is not entirely clear whether one man alone would have to bear the entire cost of a *munus*, and anyway there is reason to think that the outlay on most *munera* would have been far more modest: see R. Duncan-Jones, *Economy*, pp. 245-246.

[80] *De Benef.* 2.21.5.

[81] *Dig.* 35.1.36 pr. The son evidently celebrated a *munus* while still *consul designatus*.

[82] *Sat.* 3.212-222, with *PIR²* A 1268 and F 51.

[83] Cf. Dio 57.8.6.

[84] See, for example, R. F. Newbold, "The spectacles as an issue between Gaius and the senate," *Proceedings of the African Classical Associations* 13. 1975. pp. 30-35; *Inscr. Ital.* XIII. 2. pp. 373-375.

[85] Dio 72.16.3.

[86] See, for example, Tac. *Ann.* 13.41; *Hist.* 4.40; Dio 60.17.1; 68.2.3; 78.17.1; HA, *Marcus* 10.10; *Pertinax* 15.5.

[87] Dio 78.22.1.

[88] See Dio 60.27.2 for resignation by consuls.

[89] Dio 61.6.2 and 8.2. For actors demanding higher pay, note Tac. *Ann.* 1.77; Dio 56.47.2.

have been to help overcome such difficulties in the mid second century that Antoninus Pius specially allowed wives to make their husbands gifts to cover the expenses of games. Among emperors, Augustus himself instituted the practice of helping magistrates (that is, mostly praetors presumably), who could not meet the cost of games. In *Res Gestae*[90] he claims to have celebrated games for others on twenty-three occasions—either because they were away, says Suetonius,[91] or because they lacked the means. Claudius likewise helped a praetor with his expenses.[92] From the second century this form of aid to consuls and praetors supersedes the previous custom of making up a census.[93] In the same way, aside from the honor, it may have been in order to save men the expenses of canvassing and holding office that emperors adlected some existing senators to higher rank. At least, it can hardly have been the prospect of stiff electoral competition that prompted adlection *inter aedilicios* of the two second-century *quaestorii*, C. Iulius Iulianus[94] and A. Claudius Charax,[95] for example. Plainly, no *quaestorius* should have faced special difficulty in gaining either an aedileship or a tribunate, its equivalent for purposes of advancement.[96]

Beyond possible help from friends or from the emperor, a senator would not receive much direct financial reward during those stages of his career when he needed it most. Attendance at the House was of course always unpaid.[97] The duties of magistrates in Rome carried no salary. At least, Dio[98] implies that it was exceptional for the *quaestores aerarii* instituted by Claudius to draw one. We may guess that quaestors on service abroad by contrast did regularly draw salaries. *Comites* of imperial *legati*, and no doubt of proconsuls too, certainly did so by the latter part of our period:[99]

---

[90] 22.2.

[91] *Aug.* 43.

[92] Dio 60.31.7.

[93] See Fronto, *Ver. Imp.* 2.7.6 = p. 128 H; Dio 80.5.1; HA, *Hadr.* 3.8; 7.10; *Antonin.* 8.4; *Marcus* 2.5; *Sev. Alex.* 43.3-4.

[94] *PIR²* I 366.

[95] See chap. 1 sect. 2 note 35.

[96] All the same, C. Claudius Severus, *adlectus inter quaestorios*, and C. Curtius Iustus, *quaestorius*, were both adlected *inter tribunicios* by Trajan(?) and Hadrian respectively: see *PIR²* C 1613; H. Halfmann, *Die Senatoren*, no. 39.

[97] For discussion of the curious clause in Rustius Caepio's will, which might have constituted an exception (Suet. *Dom.* 9), see chap. 1 sect. 2.

[98] 60.24.2. The payment of a salary to Salvius Julianus as quaestor Caesaris is a puzzle (*ILS* 8973, ". . . quaestori imp. Hadriani, cui divos Hadrianus soli salarium quaesturae duplicavit propter insignem doctrinam. . . ."). Is it relevant that he may have accompanied Hadrian in Egypt in 131, and thus have been paid like the quaestor of a province? On the difficult question of his career, including this point, see most recently D. Nörr, "Drei Miszellen zur Lebensgeschichte des Juristen Salvius Julianus," in A. Watson (ed.), *Daube Noster: Essays in Legal History for David Daube*, Edinburgh and London, 1974, pp. 233-252.

[99] Papinian, *Dig.* 1.22.4; cf. Modestinus, ibid. 4.6.32.

but of course comparatively few of them were lower in rank than *praetorius*,[100] and thus most would already have major outlays behind them. More generally, however, any senator on service abroad would always find available a variety of well-known avenues to make a profit on the side, if he were willing to take a slight risk.[101] At Rome, too, corrupt aediles and praetors could profit from their offices.[102] In the mid second century Venuleius Saturninus,[103] while mentioning that magistrates in the city were not to take bribes, nonetheless adds significantly that gifts should be limited to 10,000 HS in a year. Normally, all the same, it was not until after his praetorship that a senator would be eligible for really rewarding posts. And then more than ever of course, much would depend on chance and imperial favor. Any *praetorius*, except a patrician, who reached the consulship would first have occupied at least one salaried post for two or three years. This must be one reason why less is heard of consuls experiencing difficulty meeting their expenses in office than of praetors in this predicament. The emperor's payment of Dio's expenses during his second consulship in 229, for example, was presumably a mark of honor, not a relief of poverty.[104] Pliny[105] once portrays appointment to an official post as a reward ("praemium") for sound service in the praetorship and earlier magistracies. So when Hostilius Firminus, legate of the condemned governor of Africa, Marius Priscus, was made ineligible to draw lots for the governorship of any province, Pliny[106] pities his plight, even though the sentence appeared lenient: for thus, as he puts it, Hostilius was stripped of the privileges of senatorial rank, but was not rid of its toils and troubles.

Though our knowledge of this topic, like so many others, can unfortunately be built up only from random impressions, it seems plain enough that anyone who embarked upon a senatorial career was inescapably committed to a formidable outlay. Even with an eye to economy it was naturally very expensive just to acquire and maintain one or more establishments in Rome and nearby, to live in a suitable style, to canvass for office, and to make the necessary contributions towards games given by magistrates. New members who came from outside Italy would be likely to find their initial costs especially high, above all at those times in the second century when there was enforcement of the rules requiring a proportion of their property to be in Italy. Among all senators only a minority with luck and ability were destined to gain appointments which would handsomely repay

[100] See chap. 1 sect. 2 note 13.
[101] Cf. Tac. *Agr.* 6; Plin. *Ep.* 4.9.1 and 6.
[102] Cf. Tac. *Ann.* 14.41; Suet. *Dom.* 8; HA, *Marcus* 12.4.
[103] *Dig.* 48.11.6.2.
[104] Dio 80.5.1.
[105] *Ep.* 8.24.8.
[106] *Ep.* 2.12.3.

their expenditure, and even then a long interval would always ensue between outlay and reward. It is no wonder that in our period many senators became *delatores*, and that governors continued to extort money from provincials in order to pay off their debts, just as they had done during the Republic.

4. Other Demands

We have sought to gain some impression of the wealth required for a senatorial career, and of the expenditure which would unavoidably have to be incurred. Later we shall of course be considering in detail the sessions of the House, to which members were expected to devote much of their time. But it is important to appreciate that such attendance represented only one obligation among many. To form an accurate impression of a senator's life there is thus value in first reviewing the other demands, both formal and informal, made of him.

An unambitious man, set to enjoy a quiet life away from the public gaze, would hardly be suited to a senatorial career. Admittedly, once life membership of the House had been secured by election as quaestor, there was no compulsion to seek higher office: as Ulpian said, "a man can be a senator and yet not seek further honors."[1] We do know of two men who never tried to proceed beyond the quaestorship.[2] But it is hard to credit that many others became senators just to remain in the most junior position in the House. In any event, as we have seen, during the Principate advancement as far as the praetorship became progressively easier. Certainly there would have been serious repercussions for the filling of higher offices if widespread apathy had ever developed among junior members. But in fact the great majority did always respond to the general expectation that they should seek advancement, with all the effort and expense which such a quest entailed.

A senator therefore was set upon a career of honors and service. He had "public duties"[3] to fulfill. With these in mind, after describing to a correspondent how heartened he had been by a visit to the distinguished consular, Vestricius Spurinna, living in retirement, Pliny continues:

Meanwhile a thousand tasks fill my time, though here again Spurinna sets me a reassuring example, for he also accepted public offices, held magistracies, and

---

[1] *Dig.* 48.22.7.21.
[2] Chap. 1 sect. 2.
[3] For the expression, see Tac. *Ann.* 15.19; 16.27; Fronto, *Ad Ver. Imp.* 2.7.5 = p. 127 H; cf. Livy 27.34. Note how Pausanias (5.24.4) casually distinguishes between Roman citizens and senators—the latter plainly considered a group apart.

governed provinces as long as honor demanded, and thus his present retirement was earned by hard work. I have set myself the same race and goal, and I bind myself to it now with you as my witness. . . .[4]

Inevitably such a "race and goal" demanded a degree of ambition which was the despair of contemporary philosophers. Seneca,[5] himself a member, argues that no consul is to be envied since he will waste all his years in order to have one year named after him. And he caricatures the widespread refusal to be satisfied:

He gave me the praetorship, but I had hoped for the consulship; he gave me the twelve fasces, but he did not make me *consul ordinarius*; he was willing that my name should be attached to the year, but he disappointed me with respect to the priesthood; I was co-opted into a college, but why into one only? He brought me the highest honors, but he contributed nothing to my resources; what he gave me he had to give to somebody—he took nothing out of his own pocket.[6]

In similar vein Plutarch deplores the ambition of his fellow Greeks:

"But he was a Thasian," one may say. Yet there are others, Chians, Galatians or Bithynians, who are not content with whatever share of reputation or power among their own countrymen has fallen to them, but rather weep because they do not wear the shoes of a patrician; yet if they do wear them, they weep because they are not yet Roman praetors; if they are praetors, because they are not yet consuls; and if consuls, because they were proclaimed, not first, but later.[7]

We have already seen how tenure of magistracies demanded time and money. Such devotion to the affairs of others, with consequent neglect of one's own, was rightly singled out by Epictetus as one of the most striking demands made by a senatorial career: ". . . You are a senator for life. Do you not know that a man in such a post has to give only a little attention to the affairs of his own household, but for most of the time has to be away, in command, or under command, or serving in some official capacity, or in the army, or on the judge's bench?"[8]

Tacitus[9] pays tribute to the thirty-five years' public service of Vespasian's elder brother, Flavius Sabinus, while Caecina Severus claimed to have served as many as forty years in the provinces under Augustus and Tiberius.[10] Such notably long absence must always have been exceptional. But twelve or so quaestors out of the twenty each year would regularly

[4] *Ep.* 3.1.11-12; cf. 4.23.2.
[5] *De Brev. Vit.* 20.1.
[6] *De Ira* 3.31.2.
[7] *De Tranq. Anim.* 10 = *Mor.* 470 C.
[8] 3.24.36.
[9] *Hist.* 3.75.
[10] Tac. *Ann.* 1.64; 3.33.

spend their year of office abroad, while the mere fact that most posts available beyond the praetorship were commands in the provinces, rather than in Italy, meant that a spell abroad would sooner or later be required of those whose career had proceeded thus far.[11] Tacitus[12] himself laments how long absence from Rome as *praetorius* prevented him from ever seeing his father-in-law Agricola during the last four years of his life. Most painful of all, however, could be the predicament of those provincial senators who chose not to remove altogether to Italy: while there, or on service elsewhere, they might be forced to endure long periods of separation from wife and children left at home.[13]

In Rome a senator's formal obligations were by no means limited to attendance in the House. When the emperor was in residence, a regular appearance at his *salutatio* might be expected of all members, even if closer contact was reserved for a restricted circle. Thus when Vespasian gave offense by his lack of attention to Nero's performances during the emperor's tour of Greece in 66, he was excluded not just from *contubernium*, but even from the public *salutatio*.[14] According to a garbled anecdote in Plutarch,[15] it was towards the end of Augustus' reign, when Fabius Maximus attended a *salutatio* as usual, that the emperor broke off their friendship because Fabius betrayed confidences. Formal *renuntiatio amicitiae* by any emperor naturally involved exclusion from his house.[16]

From 12 B.C. Augustus had dispensed with the ceremony of *salutatio* on days when the senate met, so that sessions should not be delayed; and in extreme old age he asked for it to be dropped altogether.[17] Livia continued to receive the senate's greetings, however.[18] As emperor, Tiberius evidently tried to make the chore less troublesome, but for a period members found themselves having to wait upon both him and Sejanus.[19] Nero was praised for his ability to identify without prompting those who greeted him, but came to cause offense by the informal dress he wore to receive

---

[11] For exceptions, see R.J.A. Talbert, "Pliny the Younger as governor of Bithynia-Pontus," in C. Deroux (ed.), *Studies in Latin Literature and Roman History* II, *Collection Latomus* 168, Brussels, 1980, pp. 417-419. Dio (58.24.3) notes that Mamercus Aemilius Scaurus (*PIR*² A 404) had never governed a province: but the main reason in his case must be Tiberius' hostility.

[12] *Agr.* 45.

[13] For such children (Agricola and Dio Cassius among them), see W. Eck in *Festschrift F. Vittinghoff*, p. 284 note 11.

[14] Suet. *Vesp.* 4. For the more restricted circle in Vespasian's own reign, cf. ibid. 21; Plin. *Ep.* 3.5.9.

[15] *De Garull.* 11 = *Mor.* 508 A-B; cf. Tac. *Ann.* 1.5; *PIR*² F 47.

[16] See R. S. Rogers, "The emperor's displeasure—*amicitiam renuntiare*," *TAPA* 90. 1959. pp. 224-237.

[17] Suet. *Aug.* 53; Dio 54.30.1; 56.26.2-3; cf. 56.41.5.

[18] Dio 57.12.2.

[19] Dio 57.11.1 and 21.4; cf. Tac. *Ann.* 4.74.

senators.[20] During the interval between Nero's death and the arrival of Galba, when the Praetorian Prefect Nymphidius Sabinus sought to draw power into his own hands, Plutarch[21] notes significantly how the senate assembled daily at his door. In mid 69 there were long queues to greet Caecina and Valens, since the imperial authority exercised by Vitellius was thought to be slight.[22] Much later Plautianus was to be another Praetorian Prefect waited upon by senators.[23]

In his *Panegyricus* 48, Pliny contrasts the pain of Domitian's *salutatio* with the pleasure of greeting Trajan. Certainly Juvenal[24] portrays senators being excluded from audience with Domitian at his Alban villa, while the fisherman bearing the giant turbot is admitted! If we are to trust Pliny's testimony on the point, it would seem that under Domitian grades of admission had existed on a pattern common in great households. There may be an earlier hint of this practice in Seneca's mention of how Augustus made up "tota cohors primae admissionis" from his enemies.[25] According to Pliny the Elder,[26] Claudius issued those closest to him with gold rings allowing them access at any time, but Vespasian ended the practice. Pliny the Younger[27] claims that under Nerva and Trajan all grades of admission were abolished. They perhaps came to be reintroduced, however. At least we find the praetor L. Plotius Sabinus described on his funeral monument as "also enjoying the second *salutatio* of the emperor Antoninus Pius Augustus."[28]

At the same period Fronto marks out daily greeting and escort of M. Aurelius as services qualifying a senator for high office: the orator himself was arguably assiduous in this respect, despite his protestations to the contrary.[29] Dio[30] explains how Commodus would receive the senate's greetings dressed in the costume he wore for entering the amphitheater. Later, senators in a body—Dio himself among them—went to greet Didius Julianus on the morning after power had been conferred upon him as emperor.[31] We have evidence to show how the ceremony of *salutatio* was

[20] Suet. *Nero* 10; Dio 63.13.3.

[21] *Galba* 8.

[22] Tac. *Hist.* 2.92.

[23] Dio 76.5.3-4.

[24] *Sat.* 4.64.

[25] *De Clem.* 1.10.1. Note C. Caesius Niger, an *eques* who was "ex prima admissione" in the time of Augustus or Tiberius (*ILS* 1320).

[26] *NH* 33.41.

[27] *Paneg.* 47.4-5.

[28] *ILS* 1078.

[29] See *Ad M. Caes.* 1.3.4 = p. 3 H with E. J. Champlin, *Fronto and Antonine Rome*, chap. VII, esp. pp. 97-98. For Marcus' *salutatio* as Caesar, cf. Dio 71.35.4.

[30] 72.17.3.

[31] Dio 74.13.2; HA, *Did. Jul.* 4.1.

maintained when Caracalla spent the winter of 214/15 at Nicomedia, and in May 216 when he was at Antioch.[32] For the former instance Dio[33] describes (again from personal experience) how the emperor would keep senators waiting all day, and finally refuse to see them at all. In Rome, while Caracalla was away, Julia Domna had to be waited upon instead.[34] Finally Elagabalus offended members by reclining as he received their greetings.[35]

When senators were expected to pay respects to the emperor as part of their routine, it goes without saying that their presence was also looked for on great occasions. In the *senatus consultum* of which Augustus sent a copy to Cyrene in 4 B.C. it is striking that the senators selected to give a speedy hearing to provincials' cases of *repetundae* are exempted from all public duties, *except* public worship, until they have completed a hearing and delivered judgment.[36] In the same way, in the so-called *Tabula Hebana* of 19/20, all members of the senatorial class are expected (though not actually required) to attend the interment of Germanicus' bones, unless prevented by illness or a death in their own family.[37] This expectation that all fit senators should be present on great occasions may also be discerned in Pliny's letter about the senior consular Silius Italicus. The latter was well past retirement age, and living in Campania when Trajan first came to Rome as emperor in 99. Pliny writes: "He made his home in Campania, and did not stir from it even on the arrival of the new emperor: an incident which reflects great credit on the emperor for permitting this liberty, and on Italicus for venturing to avail himself of it."[38] If even Silius was expected to come to Rome on this occasion, how much more must the appearance of all active senators have been looked for. In the same connection, Pliny's view[39] of the sentence passed on Hostilius Firminus, legate of the condemned governor of Africa, Marius Priscus, is a notable one. It would have been better, he reflects, to adopt the proposal removing Hostilius from the order altogether. Instead, having merely been barred from eligibility to draw lots for provinces, he will be left as a member who cannot hide in retirement, but must expose himself as a marked man to the public gaze.

We glimpse senators most often, perhaps, at the emperor's entry to Rome (*adventus*) and departure (*profectio*). One or more members might

---

[32] *SEG* 17.759 col. I lines 2-3; cf. *CJ* 9.51.1.
[33] 77.17.3.
[34] Dio 77.18.3.
[35] Dio 79.14.4.
[36] *FIRA*[2] I no. 68 V lines 134-136.
[37] *EJ* 94a lines 54-57 with revisions by Oliver and Palmer.
[38] *Ep.* 3.7.6-7.
[39] *Ep.* 2.12.3.

be formally appointed to represent the House in this duty, but that was exceptional practice, to be considered elsewhere.[40] There was hardly need for such a step: every fit senator in the city was well aware that the arrival and departure of the emperor were among those occasions for which custom and respect required his presence anyway. We have numerous examples of the vows taken and fulfilled by the Arval Brethren for these occasions.[41] More specifically, a ceremonial reception greeted Tiberius on his return from Illyricum in 9.[42] Consuls, senate, and many others went out to meet Agrippina on her return to Rome in 20 after the death of Germanicus.[43] Senators are present in a body on Nero's first entry to Rome after his mother's death in 59, and on his return from Greece in 68.[44] In 64 it was during the ritual in the temple of Vesta that he took fright and abandoned his projected visit to Egypt the very day he was due to set sail, according to Suetonius.[45] Nero went as far as Naples to meet Tiridates in 66, and the king was received ceremoniously in Rome—a more tedious business than ever for senators and others whose presence was expected, because it had to be postponed due to bad weather.[46] Senators and *equites* came out to meet Vitellius as he approached Rome in 69;[47] later, after his attempt at abdication, it is notable that the "primores senatus" immediately went to the house of Vespasian's brother, T. Flavius Sabinus.[48] Some senators were among those who braved stormy seas to join Vespasian in Alexandria during winter 69/70, while other members later needed no prompting to proceed a long way out of Rome—even as far as Brundisium—to greet him on his return to Italy.[49] Martial[50] imagines the scene as the whole populace will turn out to greet Trajan on his first entry to Rome as emperor, while Dio[51] explains how later many were intending to meet him at a considerable distance from the city on his return from the East. Senators were certainly present at the arrival of Commodus in 180 and of Septimius Severus in 193—Dio among them on the latter occasion.[52]

Conversely, Gaius gave explicit orders that no senator was to meet him

---

[40] Chap. 14 sect. 1.

[41] See *Arval Acta*, para. 9c, lines 15-17; 26, lines 35-36; 34, I line 77; 35; 47, lines 14, 21-22, 40-41; 55, lines 26-30, 40ff.; 56, line 41; 60, II line 24. Cf. Tac. *Ann.* 3.47.

[42] Suet. *Tib.* 17; cf. Dio 56.1.1.

[43] Tac. *Ann.* 3.2.

[44] Tac. *Ann.* 14.13; Dio 63.20.5.

[45] *Nero* 19; cf. Tac. *Ann.* 15.36.

[46] Tac. *Ann.* 16.24; Suet. *Nero* 13; Dio 63.2 and 5.

[47] Tac. *Hist.* 2.87 and 89.

[48] Tac. *Hist.* 3.69.

[49] Tac. *Hist.* 4.51; Josephus, *BJ* 7.68-74; Dio 66.9.3.

[50] 10.6.5-8. Cf. Plin. *Ep.* 10.10.2.

[51] 68.29.3.

[52] Herodian 1.7.3; Dio 75.1.3-5.

on his return from campaign in 40,[53] while Nero caused offense by omitting to bestow the customary kisses upon members on his arrivals and departures—in sharp contrast to Trajan's more affable and more correct behavior in this regard in 99.[54] We have already seen his kindness in not expecting the aged consular Silius Italicus to come to Rome from Campania for the emperor's *adventus* in 99.[55]

The imperial *adventus* and *profectio* aside, senators are present in a body on other great occasions, too, in particular at triumphs, with their slow and tiresome processions,[56] as well as at funerals, games, and banquets.[57] When appropriate, a block of seats was reserved for them.[58] Altogether the explicit evidence for their attendance is thinner than we might hope for, but of course contemporary writers would largely take it for granted.[59] All the same, senators are invariably included in artistic representations of state functions, such as the consecration of the Ara Pacis on 4 July 13 B.C.[60] In connection with public religious ceremonial, it is entirely to be expected that the *collegium victimariorum* in Hadrian's time should claim service to "the emperor, priests, magistrates and senate."[61] Even the presence of children of *principes* was proposed for Augustus' funeral,[62] while at the *Ludi Saeculares* wives and children were definitely involved, as well as members themselves.[63] By contrast, it was a grave insult for

[53] Suet. *Calig.* 49.

[54] Suet. *Nero* 37; Plin. *Paneg.* 23.1.

[55] On *adventus* and *profectio*, note also Martial 8.65; HA, *Marcus* 8.10; and the Flavian reliefs from the Palazzo della Cancelleria in Rome, trenchantly discussed by J.M.C. Toynbee in a Charlton Lecture on Art of that title (Oxford, 1957). In both reliefs a personification of the senate appears. See further in general on the whole theme, for example, T.E.V. Pearce, *CQ* 20. 1970. pp. 313-316 (*adventus*); I. S. Ryberg, *Rites of the State Religion in Roman Art, MAAR* 22. 1955. chap. IX; T. Hölscher, *Victoria Romana*, Mainz, 1967, chap. II; G. Koeppel, "Profectio und Adventus," *Bonn. Jahrb.* 169. 1969. pp. 139-194, with treatment of copious evidence from monuments and coins not considered fully here.

[56] Suet. *Vesp.* 12.

[57] See, for example, Statius, *Silv.* 1.6.44; 4.2.32-3; Martial 8.50; Josephus, *AJ* 19.75; Suet. *Calig.* 17 and 58; *Dom.* 4 and 7; Dio 57.12.5; 59.11.3; 60.7.4; *Fast. Ost.*, kal. Mart. 112.

[58] See sect. 1 above.

[59] Note, however, Ovid, *Tristia* 4.2.15; *Consolatio ad Liviam* 202-204; [Seneca], *Octavia* 699-702; Suet. *Calig.* 16; *Epit. de Caes.* 13.11.

[60] J.M.C. Toynbee, "The Ara Pacis re-considered and historical art in Roman Italy," *Proc. Brit. Acad.* 39. 1953. pp. 67-95 at p. 72. See further G. Forni, *Enciclopedia dell' arte antica classica e orientale*, 7. 1966. s.v. senato, pp. 192-196; and in general, for example, R. Brilliant, *Gesture and Rank in Roman Art, Memoirs of the Connecticut Academy of Arts and Sciences* 14. 1963. From the late first century the senate is often represented by its *genius*: see H. Kunckel, *Der römische Genius*, Heidelberg, 1974.

[61] *ILS* 4963; cf. S. Weinstock, *PW* 8 A, s.v. victimarius, cols. 2483-2485.

[62] Suet. *Aug.* 100; cf. Herodian 4.2.4.

[63] G. B. Pighi, *De Ludis Saecularibus* (ed. 2), Amsterdam, 1965, pp. 237ff. and 292-294; for similar involvement of members' children, cf. Suet. *Calig.* 16. On the *Ludi Saeculares* in general, see G. B. Pighi, *Diz. Epig.* IV. pp. 2106-2125.

Nero twice to forbid Thrasea Paetus' presence, first when the whole senate went to Antium to congratulate the emperor on the birth of a daughter in 63, and next when Tiridates was ceremonially received in Rome in 66.[64] C. Cassius Longinus was similarly forbidden to attend the funeral of Poppaea in 65. Thrasea's absence on the same occasion was later made a cause of complaint.[65]

From personal experience Dio draws a vivid picture of the attendance at functions expected from members in the late second and early third centuries—"we senators," as he calls them, evoking the *esprit de corps* of a close-knit group. They were present when Commodus shot down wild beasts in the arena, and later he watched gladiatorial contests with them.[66] Dio explains how "when the emperor was fighting (as gladiator), we senators together with the *equites* always attended." Only Claudius Pompeianus was conspicuous by his absence. Otherwise the rest shouted out whatever acclamations they were ordered, and tried to conceal their mixed feelings of mirth and fear at the antics of Commodus in his madness.[67] Later those senators in Elagabalus' immediate entourage likewise had to attend the chariot "races" privately arranged by him.[68] In his description of the funeral of Pertinax arranged by Septimius Severus, Dio explains with care the role played by the senate, and lastly it is he who mentions how the whole senate was feasted by the emperor at the wedding of Caracalla to Plautianus' daughter in 202.[69]

It should hardly be necessary to underline again that there was an immense variety of public duties which senators might be called upon to fulfill both in Rome and elsewhere. We have already noted magistracies, priesthoods, and administrative and military posts. But a few others should also be mentioned briefly, together with two involving members' sons. Possibly the greatest honor was to be asked to sit on the emperor's private *consilium*—an invitation extended regularly to a small nucleus of senators, but seldom, if ever, to others. The size and composition of the *consilium* must have fluctuated constantly, depending not least upon where the emperor happened to be.[70] The only totals ever to emerge are 36 when Claudius heard a case,[71] and 11 on the occasion in Domitian's reign imagined by Juvenal in *Satire* 4.[72] Of course invitations to take part might not be confined

---

[64] Tac. *Ann.* 15.23; 16.24.
[65] Tac. *Ann.* 16.7 and 21.
[66] 72.18.2 and 19.5.
[67] 72.20.1-21.3.
[68] Dio 79.14.2.
[69] 75.4.4-5.5; 76.1.2.
[70] For some discussion, see J. Crook, *Consilium Principis*, Cambridge, 1955, p. 59.
[71] H. A. Musurillo, *The Acts of the Pagan Martyrs*, no. 4 col. ii lines 5-7.
[72] Compare how it was evidently 12 *amici* of the emperor who witnessed a grant of Roman citizenship in 177 (*AE* 1971. 534).

to senators, but there is little doubt that they would regularly make up the majority consulted. At least into the early second century senators were also being called to sit on the jury-courts (*quaestiones*) in Rome. How many were thus summoned is unknown, but there is reason to think that the total could have been a substantial proportion of active members.[73] In contrast, only 5 senators and 5 *equites*, appointed by the consuls, comprised the *consilium* at Rome which met on fixed days to hear certain applications for manumission.[74] Elsewhere, however, as we might expect, any senator abroad in the provinces for whatever reason would be a figure of sufficient note to be invited to take part in magistrates' hearings locally, as Modestinus[75] recommends. Last among miscellaneous senatorial duties we should note that four sons of members were regularly required for the Arval Brothers' ceremonial,[76] while it looks as if custom dictated that a senator's young son be chosen for the honorary post of *Praefectus Feriarum Latinarum* every year.[77]

A senator did not only have public duties and an obligation to the emperor. He in his turn was looked to by others. Naturally the distinguished member held his own *salutatio* and would expect to find it thronged. Contemporaries saw how hollow and tedious the whole practice could become—for the man who was greeted, as well as for those who greeted him.[78] Yet it was not all empty show. Claudius' prohibition on any soldier attending the *salutatio* at a senator's home was presumably intended to hamper subversive discussion.[79] Pliny says disingenuously of the senior consular Silius Italicus: "He ranked as one of our leading citizens without exercising influence or incurring ill-will; he was waited on and sought after, and regularly spent many hours on his couch in a room thronged with callers who had come with no thought of his rank."[80] It was at Pliny's own *salutatio* during a visit to his home town of Comum that he discovered how local parents were sending their sons to be educated in Mediolanum, and offered to support the opening of a school on the spot.[81] By contrast,

[73] See chap. 16 sect. 1 note 23.

[74] Gaius, *Inst.* 1.20; Ulpian, *Reg.* 1.13ª (using present tense); *Dig.* 1.10.1.2.

[75] *Dig.* 48.1.12 pr.

[76] Many references in *Arval Acta* (e.g. para. 41 lines 9-10); *Diz. Epig.* I. pp. 688-689.

[77] For list and discussion, see S. Panciera, "L. Pomponius L. F. Horatia Bassus Cascus Scribonianus," *Atti della Pontificia Accademia Romana di Archeologia*, Rendiconti 45. 1972/3. pp. 105-131. For discussion of whether the Prefect had the right to summon the senate—a purely academic question—note Gellius 14.8.1-2.

[78] Cf. Seneca, *Ep. Mor.* 19.11; Columella, *De re rust.* I. praef. 9; Plut. *de amic. mult.* 3 = *Mor.* 94 B; Lucian, *Nigrinus* 22-23.

[79] Suet. *Claud.* 25.

[80] *Ep.* 3.7.4.

[81] *Ep.* 4.13.3.

one of the ways in which Seneca indicated his retirement from public life in 62 was by no longer receiving the crowds who came to greet him.[82]

When he appeared in public, too, the distinguished senator might expect to be surrounded by an escort for protection and show.[83] Thus we hear of "familiae" and "comitum et servorum frequentia" who accompanied *primores* and their wives to a dinner given at the palace by Otho in 69.[84]

Again, like other prominent Romans, a senator could expect to be called upon for help by friends and clients of such varied social standing that they might even be graded into different categories.[85] Thrasea had caused offense by continuing to help his clients during the period when he would no longer attend the senate.[86] Entertainment, and even accommodation, of guests was important: it must have been for this purpose that the wealthy, long-lived consular and *Praefectus Urbi*, L. Volusius Saturninus, had a freedman *ab hospitis* in Rome.[87] So it was typical that when Pliny found himself placed next to Fadius Rufinus at dinner, the latter was accompanied by a man from his native town making his first visit to the capital.[88] Letters recommending subordinates, or supporting the applications of friends for posts or honors of one kind or another, are commonly found in the correspondence of Pliny and Fronto. Equally, both plead straitened circumstances and the high cost of maintaining a position in public life. In terms of financial resources alone it would be absurd to think that either was poor even by upper-class Roman standards. But their difficulty lay more perhaps in the sheer number of appeals made to them for help; to stop money being dissipated and too many applicants being disappointed, these appeals did have to be assessed carefully, and painful choices made. As an extreme, Pertinax is said to have greatly offended citizens of his home town once he became emperor: they flocked to him seeking appointments or help, and were disappointed when their expectations were not fulfilled.[89]

We may conclude with two passages by contemporaries which serve as an excellent summary of the varied and pressing daily demands made upon a senator in Rome. First, in verses written just before the opening of our period, Horace explains to Maecenas why he would not seek to become a senator even if the chance were offered him:

[82] Tac. *Ann.* 14.56.

[83] Cf. Suet. *Vesp.* 2, "anteambulo fratris"; Plin. *Ep.* 3.14.7; Lucian, *Nigrinus* 21 and 34.

[84] Tac. *Hist.* 1.80-81.

[85] Plin. *Ep.* 2.6.2; 7.3.2; cf. 9.5.3; 9.30. Suetonius (*Aug.* 74) comments upon Augustus' strict regard for rank at dinners.

[86] Tac. *Ann.* 16.22; cf. Seneca's recommendation in *De Tranq. Anim.* 3.3.

[87] *ILS* 7446; cf. *CIL* VI. 9474.

[88] *Ep.* 9.23.4. It is highly likely that Fadius was a senator (cf. Sherwin-White, *Pliny* ad loc.; *PIR²* F 99-100). On *hospitium*, see further the comments by R. P. Saller, *Personal Patronage under the Early Empire*, p. 185.

[89] HA, *Pert.* 13.6.

The masses would think me crazy, but you might think
I was wise to avoid a load of trouble which I've never been used to.
For then I should immediately have to acquire a larger establishment,
receive more callers, take one or two companions with me
to avoid being on my own when going off to the country
or traveling abroad; I should have to maintain more grooms and horses,
and take a convoy of wagons. As things are, I can
if I wish go all the way to Tarentum on a gelded mule
with his flanks chafed by the heavy saddle-bag and his withers by the rider.
No-one will call me stingy as they do you, Tillius,
when in spite of being praetor you have five servants behind you
carrying a commode and a wine-cask along the road to Tibur.
In this and a thousand other ways I've an easier life
than you, eminent senator.[90]

Next, early in the second century, Pliny addresses a letter to his fellow member, Bruttius Praesens, who has long been out of the city:

Are you ever coming back to Rome, back to your honors and official duties, your influential friendships and your clients' attentions? How much longer will you be your own master, stay up when you feel inclined, and sleep as long as you like? How long will your shoes go unworn and your toga stay on holiday, while all your day is your own? It is time you renewed acquaintance with our vexations, if only to prevent your pleasure diminishing through sheer surfeit. Come and pay your respects to us for a while, so as to be better pleased to receive other people's, and spend some time in the crowd here in order to appreciate your solitude the more.[91]

5. Avoidance of a Senatorial Career by Qualified *Equites*

As we have noted already, by no means all senators' sons followed their fathers into the House. Naturally enough there were also *equites* who could have looked to a senatorial career, but chose not to do so. It is worth considering briefly the motives of the few individuals in this group known to us, all of them from the first and early second centuries. They divide into two types.[1]

First may be mentioned those who lacked the zest for a competitive career in the public eye, and preferred another occupation. At the very

---

[90] *Sat.* 1.6.97-111 (translation slightly adapted from that of N. Rudd in Penguin Classics series, 1973). It is interesting that the regulations concerning the provision of transport for official use by Sagalassus in Pisidia early in Tiberius' reign stipulate an entitlement of up to ten wagons (*carra*) for "senator populi Romani"—the same as for the imperial procurator! See further chap. 4 sect. 2 note 36.

[91] *Ep.* 7.3.2-3; cf. Martial 12.29.

[1] For earlier discussion, note A. Stein, *Der römische Ritterstand*, Munich, 1927, pp. 195-202.

beginning of our period the poet Ovid is a clear example of an *eques* who began working towards entry to the senate, but then lost enthusiasm before he stood for the quaestorship. As he explains in later life:

Meanwhile the years slipped on with silent step. My brother and I put on the less restrictive toga, and our shoulders assumed the broad stripe of purple, while our interests remained as before. And now my brother's death when he reached twenty robbed me of part of myself. I took up the first office of tender youth as one of a board of three. The senate house awaited me, but I narrowed my stripe: that was too great a burden for my strength. My body would not stand up to the strain, nor was my mind suited to it. I shunned the uncertainties of ambition, and the Aonian sisters constantly urged me to seek the security of private life which had always appealed to my taste.[2]

It was perhaps for similar reasons that Ovid's contemporary, Vibius Viscus, whose two sons are mentioned by Horace, never aspired to senatorial rank at all. The scholiast explains: ". . . although he enjoyed both wealth and the friendship of Augustus, he still stayed in the equestrian order, even when he had made his sons senators."[3] In Tiberius' time Seneca and his elder brother Novatus seem to have been notably slow in taking up a senatorial career: not until the end of the reign, when they were in their late thirties, did they hold the quaestorship. Both were for long evidently disinclined to politics and suffered from poor health. Coming from a provincial background they may also have been discouraged by lack of powerful support, the taint of some family connection with Sejanus (even if only a remote one), and a general apathy during Tiberius' last years. In Seneca's own case absorption in philosophy and natural science further served to pull him away from public life.[4] Also in the latter part of Tiberius' reign, the future emperor Vespasian proved hesitant about taking up a senatorial career: in his case the reasons are unknown. His elder brother by contrast had pressed ahead.[5]

In the late first century Pliny's friend Maturus Arrianus evidently showed much interest in public affairs,[6] but lacked ambition. As Pliny says of him: "He is incapable of pushing himself forward, and for this reason has remained in the equestrian order, though he could easily rise to the highest rank."[7] By contrast, another friend, Minicius Macrinus, deliberately rejected a senatorial career. Rather he chose to remain a leading member of

---

[2] *Tristia* 4.10.27-40.

[3] Schol. in Horat. *Sat.* 1.10.78ff. (II p. 114 Keller).

[4] See the discussion by M. Griffin, *Seneca: A Philosopher in Politics*, pp. 43-51.

[5] Suet. *Vesp.* 2.

[6] *Ep.* 2.11 and 12, on the trials of Marius Priscus and Hostilius Firminus, are addressed to him.

[7] *Ep.* 3.2.4; cf. 2.11.1.

the equestrian order "because he desired nothing higher; the deified emperor Vespasian adlected him *inter praetorios*, but he has most steadfastly preferred an honorable life out of the public eye rather than our ambition— or should I say our dignity?"[8] From a fragmentary inscription set up at Athens in his honor during Domitian's reign we may fairly guess that Q. Trebellius Rufus of Tolosa (Narbonensis) had likewise been offered the chance of entering the senate, but had declined it because "he desired a quiet life."[9]

Of course members' sons just as much as *equites* might prefer other occupations to a senatorial career. For a time in his youth the pleasures of philosophy almost tempted Agricola to abandon his intention of following his father into the House,[10] while at the same age Cornelius Fuscus did actually go so far as to give up his membership of the senatorial class in order to find *quies*.[11]

But besides those *equites* who did not aspire to a public career, there were others with more ambition who weighed up the alternatives open to them. In this respect Augustus' employment of *equites* in positions of high responsibility, and the subsequent gradual development of an equestrian service by later emperors, were innovations of great significance. From the outset there were some men who shrewdly reckoned that by remaining as *equites* in the emperor's service they might still be able to gain influence and profit equal to those of a successful senator, without ever suffering the hazards and burdens of the latter's career. Two outstanding examples of Augustus' time are Maecenas and C. Sallustius Crispus. Tacitus writes of the latter: "He had easy access to an official career. But he rivaled Maecenas in that without senatorial rank he exceeded in power many *consulares* and winners of triumphs."[12] Though we know little of him

---

[8] *Ep.* 1.14.5. Terentius Iunior might have been another of Pliny's equestrian friends who shunned a senatorial career (*Ep.* 7.25.2), but Sherwin-White makes the assumption too readily. Terentius is merely described as "paratis honoribus" after his procuratorship in Narbonensis: "honores" could refer to any kind of office or distinction, in the senate or elsewhere (for similar looseness, cf. *CIL* VIII. 5770; Ulpian, *Dig.* 48.22.7.21-22).

[9] J. H. Oliver, *Hesperia* 10. 1941. pp. 74-75; ibid. 11. 1942. p. 80, note in line 39]καὶ συνκλητ[, in line 40 ἐ]πε[θ]ύμησεν ἡσυχίαν. For most recent comment, see M. Griffin, op. cit. in n. 4, p. 446. Around the beginning of the third century the writer Aelian (*PIR²* C 769) is another man who preferred a private life to an official career, as he explains in the epilogue to his treatise *On the Characteristics of Animals*. But whether he specifically shunned entry to the senate is not clear.

[10] Tac. *Agr.* 4.

[11] Tac. *Hist.* 2.86, ". . . vigens aetate, claris natalibus. Prima iuventa quietis cupidine senatorium ordinem exuerat." Despite its appeal, Grotius' suggestion "quaestus" for the manuscript reading "quietis" is best set aside: cf. R. Syme, "The colony of Cornelius Fuscus: an episode in the *Bellum Neronis*," *AJP* 58. 1937. pp. 7-18 at pp. 7-8 (= *Danubian Papers*, Bucharest, 1971, pp. 73-83).

[12] *Ann.* 3.30.

during the reign, C. Matius, described as "friend of the divine Augustus," may be another *eques* who remained content with the power he could exercise as a servant of the emperor in this rank.[13] Later in the first century, Annaeus Mela, according to his father[14] and brother,[15] at first lacked all ambition and shrank from holding office, as his older brothers eventually chose to do: instead of seeking "dignitas," he had the sense to prefer "quies," "otium," "tranquilla quietaque vita." But at some stage his attitude must have changed, because Tacitus—significantly describing him as "eques Romanus senatoria dignitate"—explains how: ". . . he had refrained from seeking office owing to his eccentric ambition to match a consul's influence while remaining an *eques*. He had also seen a shorter route to amassing wealth through service as a procurator handling the emperor's business."[16]

There need be no doubt that service as an imperial procurator would be profitable, although comparisons with the reward to be acquired from a senatorial career are not easily made. In all cases much depended on individual talent and good fortune, and on the extent to which the holder of a post was prepared to exploit it for personal gain. Though the salaries payable to holders of senatorial posts are not known except for the magnificent sum of one million HS drawn by the governor of Asia for his year's service in the early third century,[17] we may fairly guess that they were higher on average than those paid in the equestrian service. Yet, as we have seen, a senator's career brought with it many expenses, together with the prospect of holding posts (even if well paid) for only a limited number of years in the course of it. By contrast, a procurator had few such expenses, and could look forward to a salary over a longer stretch. The request which Fronto[18] makes of Antoninus Pius to grant a procuratorship to Appian (the historian) confirms how attractive the salary was. He assures the emperor that Appian wants the distinction only to enhance his dignity in old age, not out of ambition, nor for the money.

In the Julio-Claudian period, at any rate, when Mela made his apparently unusual choice, the real risk which such a man may have incurred was that he would not secure a place in the equestrian service at all, not to mention promotion thereafter. Here of course, as always, much would depend on the competition and on the individual and his relationship with the emperor. The same might naturally be said of a senator. But at least

[13] Cf. Tac. *Ann.* 12.60; Plin. *NH* 12.13.

[14] *Controv.* 2. pref. 3-4.

[15] *Ad Helv. de Cons.* 18.1-3.

[16] *Ann.* 16.17.

[17] Dio 78.22.5.

[18] *Ant. Pium* 9 = pp. 161-162 H with E. J. Champlin, *Fronto and Antonine Rome*, pp. 98-100.

there were regularly 20 vacancies in the senate each year, all carrying a good chance of some advancement. In the equestrian service, on the other hand, there were perhaps no more than 46 posts altogether even by the end of the Julio-Claudian period, a total built up gradually from 23 under Augustus. Almost all remained posts of substantial responsibility—not for young men.[19] At this time, therefore, it is likely that those fortunate youths who were in a position to contemplate a career in either the senate or the equestrian service would be influenced to choose the former not least by the far greater number of openings there.

While the equestrian service always remained modest in size by comparison with the senate, it is clear that the number of openings continued to rise steadily during the Flavian period and beyond, with an increase in opportunities at the junior level in particular. Though the trend cannot be documented, we might speculate that there was a corresponding increase in the number of suitable young men attracted by the equestrian service rather than the senate, especially once it became established practice for selected procurators of proven worth to be offered adlection into the senate, either when they were still fairly young (having shown promise in their early service), or once they were considerably more experienced. All the same, the potential effect of any such trend upon recruitment to the senate through the quaestorship would have been compensated for by the willingness already observed above to open membership more widely to Italians and provincials.

6. Estimates of the Senate and Senators

So far in this chapter we have considered the legal position of senators, the degree of wealth their career would demand, and other obligations laid upon them. The reasons which prompted certain qualified *equites* to eschew a senatorial career have also been treated briefly. But this limited aspect aside, no broader attempt has yet been made to assess contemporaries' estimates of the corporate body and its members. Naturally their opinions are hard to reconstruct, and too often we are forced to rely upon impression. But while a fully rounded picture will never emerge, there does exist relevant evidence from which conclusions may be drawn in respect of certain features. The aim of this section is to discuss that material.

The point does not need to be labored that from the most ancient times the senate had been an institution which formed an integral part of the fabric of the *respublica*. Predictably enough, in 47, when Corbulo as

---

[19] The growth of equestrian posts throughout our period is conveniently summarized in H.-G. Pflaum, *Abrégé des procurateurs équestres*, Paris, 1974, chaps. III, IV.

governor of Lower Germany settled the Frisii on land marked out by himself, he is said to have established their government along the Roman pattern—"senate, magistrates, laws."[1] At Roman religious ceremonies prayers were offered for the welfare of emperor, senate, and people.[2] Thus it was a grave insult for Nero to omit any mention of the senate from the prayer with which he inaugurated work on cutting a canal through the Isthmus of Corinth.[3] No doubt all Romans, however slight their feeling for history and tradition, had some notion of the position of the senate in the state and of its significance. But not surprisingly they seldom expressed it. It is ironic therefore that in our period the loftiest and most sustained appreciation of the senate's place should be put by Tacitus into the mouth of the emperor Otho, the short-lived ruler of 69 who came to be hated because, in Dio's words, "he had shown that the imperial office was for sale and had put the city in the power of the boldest men; also because he held the senate and people to be of no account, and had convinced the soldiers that they could both kill and create a Caesar."[4] While Otho was entertaining a large party of leading citizens and their wives, some Praetorians, nervous of treachery, had almost run amok in a misconceived attempt to protect him.[5] The following day he delivered a speech intended as a conciliatory rebuke. Understandably, his remarks about the senate were strongly influenced by the critical situation in which they were made, but they are striking nonetheless:

I hope that no army in the world hears the words you uttered against the senate. By heavens, not even those Germans whom Vitellius is making every effort to muster against us, would have the nerve to call for retribution against the cornerstone of the empire, the glory of every province. Can any son of Italy, any true Roman warrior, demand the bloody slaughter of an order whose radiance and glory enable us to blind the obscure and shabby following of Vitellius? True, he has gained hold of a few native tribes. He has some poor apology for an army. But on our side is the senate. So the state takes its stand here: there, over against us, are the enemies of the state. Do you really imagine that the splendor of this city stands or falls with mansions, buildings and piles of masonry? These are dumb, lifeless things—their collapse or restoration means nothing. But the survival of our empire, peace between the nations, and your life as well as mine find a firm support in the continued preservation of the senate. It was solemnly instituted by the patriarch and founder of our city. From the regal period up to the Principate it has survived in unbroken continuity. We received it from our fathers. Let us as

---

[1] Tac. *Ann.* 11.19.

[2] Note, for example, Dio 51.19.7; Apuleius, *Metam.* 11.17; Tertullian, *Apology* 30.4.

[3] Suet. *Nero* 37.

[4] 64.9.1-2.

[5] Cf. Suet. *Otho* 8; Plut. *Otho* 3; Dio 64.9.2-3.

surely hand it on to our sons. You are the source of new blood for the senate, and the senate in its turn supplies our emperors.[6]

The Praetorians' hostility towards the senate on this occasion contrasts strongly with the respect for it shown by the Fourth and Twenty-Second legions in Upper Germany on 1 January 69. There is room for speculation about the motives of the two senators, Julius Vindex and Verginius Rufus, governors of Lugdunensis and Upper Germany respectively, both of whom had insisted in 68 that "senate and people" must play a part in any steps taken after Nero's removal.[7] But the choice of an oath to "senate and people" on 1 January 69 by soldiers who were only dissatisfied with Galba, rather than disloyal to the state,[8] is striking in its simple devotion. Tacitus,[9] the sophisticated senatorial historian, may ridicule the shallowness of an ill-defined allegiance which officers soon persuaded the men to abandon in favor of supporting Vitellius. Yet the hastily formulated oath merely reflected a traditional concept of those institutions in the state which transcended individual emperors. So on the rare occasions when "the senate" is featured as a Roman coin type, stress is predictably laid upon its wise influence for stability and continuity in the state. In particular, the senate is portrayed as entrusting the empire successively to Galba,[10] Vespasian,[11] Nerva,[12] and Trajan.[13]

If we come now to consider in more detail how different sections of the population viewed the senate, it seems appropriate to begin with members' own opinion of their status and of the corporate body. But here a wide-ranging assessment is unfortunately made impossible by the unrepresentative character of contemporary senatorial authors whose work has survived. As we have noted already, all but one seem to be new entrants, whose sometimes touchy pride in their rank, and in the exclusive group they have joined, is never far from the surface. Predictably enough, each of them holds the senate, and its membership, in great esteem. Velleius[14] was happy to think that under Augustus dignity ("maiestas") was restored to it, and discord banished. Over a century later Fronto[15] similarly underlines the dignity of the senate house and of its membership. Seneca[16] in

---

[6] Tac. *Hist.* 1.84; cf. Josephus, *AJ* 19.265.

[7] Zonaras 11.13 (Dio, Loeb ed. vol. 8, p. 176); Dio 63.25.2-3.

[8] See R.J.A. Talbert, "Some causes of disorder in 68-69 A.D.," *AJAH* 2. 1977. pp. 69-85.

[9] *Hist.* 1.55 and 57.

[10] *BMC* I. p. 359 ("SENATUS PIETATI AUGUSTI").

[11] *BMC* II. p. 113 ("CONCORDIA SENATUI").

[12] *BMC* III. p. 21 ("PROVIDENTIA SENATUS").

[13] *BMC* III. pp. 38 and 157.

[14] 2.89.3 and 126.2; cf. Suet. *Aug.* 35.

[15] *Ant. Imp.* 1.2.5 = p. 90 H.

[16] *Ep. Mor.* 64.10; cf. Plut. *Quaest. Rom.* 81 = *Mor.* 283 C.

his turn insists that due respect be shown to senators, and especially to senior magistrates: he is passionately indignant at Gaius' senseless cruelty towards the class.[17] He cites a senate house as a place of special honor,[18] and regards attendance at meetings as a serious obligation. In illustrating the point that the best men often have to work while others idle, he explains how the House is often kept in session the whole day long, "at the very time when every worthless character is either happily relaxing out in the open, or lurking in an eating-house, or wasting his time in some group or other."[19] Whatever certain modern observers might feel, to Seneca the senate was clearly not a bunch of "worthless characters" wasting their time in "some group or other."

Tacitus' regard for the senate emerges in several ways, although seldom through direct personal comment. Yet in one striking passage he does openly express his own deep sense of senatorial tradition, when provincial deputations on the problem of asylum rights were to be heard in 22: "That day it was a splendid sight to see the senate investigating privileges conferred by its ancestors, treaties with allies, edicts of kings who had reigned before Rome was a power, even divine cults; and it was free, as of old, to confirm or amend."[20] His outburst about the innumerable sycophantic decrees of Nero's reign, which seemed to reach a climax after the discovery of the Pisonian conspiracy, reveals personal shame in the senate's degradation.[21] That shame is present, too, in a confession about the senate's enforced behavior at the end of Domitian's reign, when he was himself a member: "It was our hands which escorted Helvidius to his prison; the expressions of Mauricus and Rusticus wounded us; on us Senecio's innocent blood was spilt."[22]

Tacitus' regard for the senate emerges most strongly perhaps in the choice of material for his two principal works, Annals and Histories. Accounts of sessions based on detailed perusal of acta senatus are a major feature of both, but of Annals in particular, as we shall see later.[23] There are minor incidents selected for inclusion, or points made by speakers, which underline Tacitus' sense of pride and tradition. He would not omit an account of Domitius Corbulo's complaint in 21 that a young noble, L. Sulla, refused to give up his seat to his senior at a gladiatorial show. In the subsequent argument there was much citation of "ancestral precedent"; "age, traditional custom, and the support of older members" were

[17] De Ira 3.18.3-19.2; De Benef. 2.12.1-2.
[18] De Vita Beata 27.1.
[19] De Provid. 5.4.
[20] Ann. 3.60.
[21] Ann. 14.64.
[22] Agr. 45.
[23] Chap. 9 sect. 4II.

enlisted on Corbulo's side, while Sulla was defended by his aristocratic relatives, who eventually apologized for him.[24] In early 70 Tacitus records "an investigation conducted along lines which recalled the old days,"[25] after a senator, and indeed the whole senate, had been publicly insulted in the Italian town of Sena. It is always awkward to determine how far the opinions of others reported by Tacitus, or the words put into the mouths of speakers by him, represent his own views. But it is difficult to believe that he would not endorse Germanicus' rebuke to the mutineers in Germany for their contempt of the senate's authority and ill-treatment of its envoys, and also share in the universal derision felt at the farce of Rosius Regulus' one-day consulship at the end of October 69.[26]

Although Pliny[27] exaggerates the extent to which knowledge of traditional senatorial procedure was lost during Domitian's reign, his complaints are one indication among many of his high regard for the corporate body. He describes at length a number of its sessions under Nerva and Trajan, principally those in which he took an active part himself. Elsewhere, not only was his sense of rank outraged by the vote of honors to Claudius' freedman, Pallas, half a century earlier: he believed that the senate as an institution was degraded thereby.[28] Equally, even when assigned as prosecutor of a deceased proconsul whose crimes had been monstrous, his concern is still that "endangering a senator"[29] would have proved the most distressing aspect of the case, had the defendant lived. In general he approached the obligations of a senator with conspicuous seriousness. He shares the pride of an equestrian friend in the senate's handling of business worthy of it,[30] and during the period when votes at elections were recorded in writing, he is highly indignant at the way in which certain irresponsible members (who refuse to identify themselves) bring the whole experiment into disrepute by spoiling their ballot papers "in an important matter on a serious occasion."[31] Though he is aware that many consider the tribunate to be no more than an empty title, he would not agree himself: to him the office "really meant something," and he punctiliously refrained from practicing in the courts during his tenure of it.[32] In order to give his whole attention to the duties of *praefectus aerarii Saturni* he adopted the same policy when appointed to that post, and so agreed to act for the provinces

[24] *Ann.* 3.31.
[25] *Hist.* 4.45; see further below.
[26] *Ann.* 1.42; *Hist.* 3.37.
[27] *Ep.* 8.14.
[28] *Ep.* 7.29; 8.6.
[29] *Ep.* 3.4.7, "periculum senatoris."
[30] *Ep.* 2.11.1.
[31] *Ep.* 4.25.3.
[32] *Ep.* 1.23.

of Africa and Baetica in two trials for *repetundae* only with the special permission of senate and emperor.[33] It is notable that friends of the legal expert, Titius Aristo, found fault with Pliny's habit of composing verses and reading them in public because he was a senator, and that he took the trouble to defend this practice at some length.[34] Altogether he will not endorse extremes of behavior. He disapproves of class distinctions at dinner parties—a difficulty which he resolves by serving cheap wine to all![35] But at the same time he retains a firm conception of a senator's rank and place in a class-conscious society. In recommending a *praetorius* as bridegroom he can even praise his "senatorius decor," the bearing of a senator.[36]

Dio, as the son of a member, seems to be unique among surviving senatorial writers of our period. In his own day he shares the pride of earlier generations in the dignity and privileges of office,[37] and he expects the prerogatives of the corporate body to be upheld. His sympathy goes out to those members ashamed of having to take part in stage performances at Nero's command; he is appalled by Cleander's sale of senatorial membership and his appointment of unprecedented numbers of consuls.[38] Later it is a matter of genuine regret to him that Macrinus and Elagabalus used the imperial titles before the senate had voted them. No less painful were Macrinus' appointment of Adventus as *Praefectus Urbi* before the latter became a senator, and Elagabalus' usurpation of the consulship.[39]

Diverse though these surviving senatorial writers may be otherwise, they share a marked respect for the corporate body and the obligations of membership, together with high principles—by Roman standards at any rate. As such they are no doubt representative of a significant proportion of senators, perhaps even a majority. But it is important to recognize that not all members showed such respect, nor fulfilled their obligations with the same diligence and scruple. It is true that Augustus had made strenuous efforts to rid the senate of members whose behavior or morals he considered unsuitable,[40] and there can be no question that the numerous resignations which he either invited or compelled did serve to raise the moral tone of the corporate body.[41] His efforts were continued vigorously by Tiberius,[42]

[33] Cf. *Ep*. 3.4; 6.29; 10.3A-B.
[34] *Ep*. 5.3.
[35] *Ep*. 2.6.2-4. Other hosts reserved food and drink of good quality for the more highly esteemed guests.
[36] *Ep*. 1.14.8.
[37] See references to contemporary institutions and customs assembled by F. Millar, *A Study of Cassius Dio*, Appendix 4; note also 65.10.4.
[38] 61.19.3; 72.12.3.
[39] Dio 78.14.4 and 16.2; 79.2.2 and 8.1.
[40] Cf. chap. 4 sect. 1.
[41] Note Dio 57.10.4.
[42] Cf. Tac. *Ann*. 2.48; Suet. *Vitell*. 2; Dio 57.23.4.

Claudius,[43] and Vespasian.[44] Thereafter emperors always continued to claim a general oversight of the morals of senators and *equites*,[45] though much less is known about their exercise of the prerogative. We do happen to hear of a *quaestorius* expelled by Domitian for appearing on stage, for example.[46] And it is notable that in accordance with his philosophical views M. Aurelius chose from the senators as bridegrooms for his daughters, "not patricians of ancient lineage nor men noted for their accumulation of wealth, but those of orderly habits and sober lives."[47] Yet the same emperor was content to give nothing more than a mild warning to Vetrasinus, a senator of "detestable reputation," who was allowed to stand for the praetorship.[48] It remains hard to evaluate the charges of loose living leveled at nobles by Juvenal throughout *Satire* 8, as well as the tales of Commodus' excesses.

Other evidence confirms the point that not all senators took a solemn, high-principled attitude towards their rank and duties. At sessions, as we shall see,[49] altercations between members were commonplace, frequently accompanied by unrestrained personal abuse. Suetonius' picture[50] of senators and *equites* scrabbling for *tesserae* specially thrown into their seats at a show given by Domitian is not a dignified one, while at all times there were members willing, and occasionally able, to flout the legal ban against their appearance on stage or at shows. Above all, however, it is notorious that on service in the provinces many shamelessly exploited their positions for personal advantage, and met with little censure from their peers for so doing. In the unlikely event of a trial, they could expect general sympathy from the House, and at the worst a lenient sentence. When all our surviving senatorial authors reflect attitudes of seriousness and high principle, it is especially important to appreciate that alongside their kind there were always others less responsible and less scrupulous, none of whom have spoken to us in any writings. Their attitudes are not surprising: senators were human; on provincial service, in their positions of unassailable authority, the pressures and temptations which they encountered could be overwhelming; and their moral code was never ours. Indeed, in the East,

---

[43] Cf. Tac. *Ann.* 11.25; 12.52.

[44] Suet. *Vesp.* 9; Dio 67.13.1. Allegations that Vespasian knew L. Antonius Saturninus to be morally unfit when he adlected him to the senate may well have been fabricated after the rebellion of 89 (Aelian, frag. 112 Hercher; *PIR*² A 874 with R. Syme, *JRS* 68. 1978. p. 20).

[45] Dio 53.17.7.

[46] Suet. *Dom.* 8.

[47] Herodian 1.2.2.

[48] HA, *Marcus* 12.3.

[49] Chap. 7 sect. 22.

[50] *Dom.* 4.

bribery of officials was so established a practice that rigidly not to accept "presents" at all might even give offense.[51]

In varying degrees all senators were no doubt conscious of the paradoxical nature of their status. On the one hand they were supposedly exalted, independent leaders of the state; on the other, they were servants of the emperor, totally dependent upon his favor both for individual advancement, and for maintaining the position of the corporate body, indeed of their class as a whole.[52] All too often, of course, the emperor was far from sympathetic. The contradiction is most sharply exposed by Epictetus,[53] who tellingly reminds the great man who has been twice consul that even though he claims "freedom," he can still be ordered about by "Caesar, lord of all." Even Pliny[54] can quietly regret the lack of political business in the senate under Trajan: from his own descriptions at least, the impression emerges that the most notable sessions of the time were trials for *repetundae* in which the emperor scrupulously did not interfere.

If we turn now to consider the attitudes of non-members towards senators and their corporate body, we again meet an imbalance in the evidence, as well as the obvious problem of potentially wide contrasts in attitude between, say, an *eques* who at least had had some contact with senators, and a non-citizen provincial to whom any Roman in authority was a man to be obeyed unhesitatingly.

Without doubt the overwhelming majority of the empire's inhabitants regarded the status of senator as so lofty (if they ever thought about it at all) that it almost lay outside their imagination. When Martial's friend and fellow-townsman, the advocate Licinianus, returns to his native Bilbilis, the poet can assure him confidently that no senator will ever bother him there![55] Thus for the majority the wealth and position of a senator were beyond envy, and his wishes not to be trifled with. The "small matter" of the application to the senate in 105 by the *praetorius*, Sollers, for leave to hold a weekly market on his property near Vicetia may help to illustrate the point. The town council had the temerity to oppose the application, and engaged Tuscilius Nominatus (not himself a senator) to act as their advocate.[56] At the session where the dispute was to be heard, the latter had been alarmed by talking to his friends and had left the House in a panic just before he was due to speak. As he explained subsequently in a tearful plea: "They had advised him not to be too persistent in opposing

[51] Cf. *Dig.* 1.16.6.3.

[52] For imperial "protection" of the class, cf. Suet. *Vesp.* 9; *Dom.* 8; for gifts to poor senators, see sects. 2 and 3 above.

[53] 4.1.6-14.

[54] *Ep.* 3.20.10-12; 4.25.5.

[55] Martial 1.49.31-32; *PIR²* L 170.

[56] Plin. *Ep.* 5.4.

the wishes of a senator (and especially in the senate), who was no longer fighting the case on account of the proposed market, but because his influence, reputation and position were at stake; otherwise Nominatus would make himself more unpopular than on the last occasion."[57] Plainly, Tuscilius was not a bold man, but all the same the panic which unnerved even an educated advocate when he was called upon to oppose the "gratia," "fama," and "dignitas" of a *praetorius* perhaps gives some clue as to how the great majority of the population must have regarded senators.

In contrast to such defiance of Sollers, the deference displayed to the African senator, Strabo Aemilianus (cos. suff. 156), by the city council at Carthage, probably during the 160's, is no doubt understandable when there were those who were evidently mentioning him as a future proconsul of the province; but even so, the council's behavior must still be more typical.[58] Strabo made a point of being present when a motion was brought forward to honor his old friend and distinguished contemporary Apuleius with a statue, and in the course of declaring his support (a lead which all followed), stated his intention of erecting another statue privately at his own expense. As a result, the council's own motion was suspended until its next meeting, so that it might be seen as following Strabo in this project rather than in any sense competing with him. Similarly, in Claudius' time the whole province of Narbonensis somehow became noted for its outstanding deference towards senators,[59] while at a trial for provincial maladministration in which Pliny took part, the henchmen of a former proconsul reckoned that they had a watertight defense in claiming that "as provincials they were terrorized into carrying out any orders of their governors."[60]

In a remarkable inscription of the mid second century from the Italian *colonia* of Tergeste, the city council can express fulsome thanks to the senator, L. Fabius Severus, their fellow citizen, for all the services he has rendered the community, and the speaker of the *prima sententia* claims that: "he desired the dignity of senatorial rank for this reason above all, namely that he should both bestow benefits upon his native community, and render it safely defended against all harm."[61] Now when the whole tenor of the speech is laudatory, the claims do not have to be taken literally.

---

[57] Plin. *Ep.* 5.13.2.

[58] Apuleius, *Florida* 16; M. Fluss, *PW* 4A s.v. Strabo no. 2, cols. 75-76. It is not known whether Strabo actually came from Carthage itself, or whether he ever did become proconsul of Africa.

[59] Tac. *Ann.* 12.23.

[60] Plin. *Ep.* 3.9.15.

[61] *ILS* 6680, revised by A. Degrassi, *Inscr. Ital.* X. 4. no. 31. I lines 31-34, "ac senatoriam dignita[t]em hac maxime ex causa co[nc]upivisse, uti patriam suam cum orna[ta]m tum ab omnib[us] in[i]uriis tutam defensamque praestaret"; cf. II lines 32-33.

From other evidence, as we shall be seeing, the general impression must
be that diplomatic business in the senate was declining by this date, while
it may be doubted whether any man ever pursued a senatorial career
principally for the sake of his city (even if he would not mind being praised
in such terms). Yet the tribute paid here to the prestige and value of
senatorial rank in the eyes of non-members is impressive. Predictably
enough, however, when the speaker of the *prima sententia* comes to expand
upon the help given by Fabius, the examples cited, both in general and in
particular, are of cases before *iudices a Caesare dati* and the emperor
Antoninus Pius himself. None concerns the senate. The principal case was
a request that qualified men from two tribes "attributed" to the city be
allowed to take some part in its government:[62] naturally this matter, which
involved grants of Roman citizenship, was one strictly for the emperor,
not the senate. If a case involving Tergeste did come before the House,
admittedly Fabius could have acted as advocate. But in any debate the
influence likely to be exercised by him in his low rank of *quaestorius* must
have been slight. The special value of his senatorial rank, as his fellow
citizens appreciated, was the wider influence it would give him elsewhere.

Among individuals, it is no surprise to find that those who erected a
monument at Capena for the doctor C. Calpurnius Asclaepiades, who died
in 157, thought fit to mention how he was "respected by *viri clarissimi*
for his talents and character."[63] Early in the third century Aelian in his
treatise *On the Characteristics of Animals* does not just apologize for his
presumption in doubting certain features of Demostratus' account of the
mating habits of tortoises, but adds significantly "even though the latter
is a Roman senator,"[64] since Demostratus' rank deepened the offense.
Respect of this type is also reflected in two discussions by the contemporary
jurist Ulpian.[65] In the first he explains how in certain circumstances it may
be permissible for a *filius familias* to bring an action. If, for example, the
father was in a province, and the son was in Rome to pursue studies and
found that he had to recover by an action property which his father had
intended to cover his living expenses, then an action should be allowed.
And supposing the son were a senator, concludes Ulpian, would not this

---

[62] This is the aspect of the document concentrated upon by J. Gascou, "Le décret municipal
de Tergeste en l'honneur de Lucius Fabius Severus," *Annuaire de l'école pratique des hautes
études* (IVᵉ section, sciences historiques et philologiques) 99. 1966/7. pp. 511-520.

[63] *ILS* 7789 line 5, "studiorum et morum causa probatus a viris clarissimis."

[64] 15.19. Demostratus is difficult to date. It would certainly help if the author of this name
cited by Aelian were not the same as the one cited by Pliny the Elder—thus allowing him
to be a second-century figure, perhaps even C. Claudius Titianus Demostratus, as E. Groag
suggested (*Die Reichsbeamten von Achaia*, col. 75). See further *PIR*² C 1044; D 49;
H. Halfmann, *Die Senatoren*, no. 104.

[65] *Dig.* 4.8.3.3; 5.1.18.1.

action have all the more value because of his *dignitas*? Elsewhere he confirms that the praetor does have the right to compel an *arbiter* to complete the duties which he has undertaken, even if he be a *consularis*. Praetors, too, could be cowed by their seniors!

A negative indication of the high status of the senator in most people's eyes is the almost complete absence of evidence for usurpation of the status by non-members.[66] By contrast, it is well known that there were frequent accusations and rumors about freedmen, and others for some reason ineligible, posing as *equites*.[67] Yet hardly anyone posed as a senator. Juvenal's ambitious fantasies did not fly beyond acquiring equestrian rank. It is true that in Petronius' novel[68] the grotesque freedman millionaire, Trimalchio, has the *latus clavus* on his napkin, but otherwise his dreams, too, were clearly of joining the equestrian order, not the senate. Leaving aside those who falsely claimed to be a particular individual,[69] the only known instance where senatorial status as such was deliberately usurped in our period[70] seems to be the puzzling one of the schoolmaster, Numerianus, who set out from Rome and, posing as a senator, raised a highly successful volunteer force which he used in Septimius Severus' interest against Clodius Albinus during the civil war of 196.[71] Apparently, in the confusion of the time, even Severus himself believed Numerianus to be a genuine senator. He seems to have adopted the status for no reason beyond the prestige which, we should note, it unquestionably brought him. After the civil war he declined Severus' offer to bestow the rank in due form.

In more stable times, however, not only could a senator's name be checked against the *album senatorium*; the House was also so tight-knit a club that a few well chosen questions from any genuine senator would quickly unmask an impostor. Tacitus[72] reflects that closeness in suggesting that almost all members were likely to have some link through family or friendship with five distinguished senators put on trial as a group in 32. Admittedly when the senator Cassius Clemens was tried for supporting Pescennius Niger rather than Septimius Severus, he could claim to have

---

[66] For the offense in general, cf. *Sent. Paul.* 5.25.12; Modestinus, *Dig.* 48.10.27.2.

[67] See especially M. Reinhold, "Usurpation of status and status symbols in the Roman Empire," *Historia* 20. 1971. pp. 275-302. The incident of a tribune bringing his father, a freedman, to sit beside him on the magistrates' bench at the theater in 25 B.C., noted by Reinhold (p. 280), is hardly an instance of usurpation of senatorial status (Dio 53.27.6).

[68] *Sat.* 32.

[69] Note, for example, personation of Sextus Condianus (Dio 72.6.4-5; H. Halfmann, *Die Senatoren*, no. 108), and in general Valerius Maximus' section (9.15) "de iis qui infimo loco nati mendacio se clarissimis familiis inserere conati sunt."

[70] The story of a man who usurped praetorian *insignia* to gain transport and hospitality illegally, told by Valerius Maximus (7.3.9), relates to the Triumviral period.

[71] Dio 75.5.1-3.

[72] *Ann.* 6.9.

been acquainted with neither:[73] but this incident is of course another relating to the confusion of the civil wars at the end of the second century, and Cassius was struggling to escape execution. In place of posing as a member, a person of lower rank could always pretend instead to have honorary senatorial status, that is, the *ornamenta* of a magistrate. But not even one such case is known, and in practice the risk would have been equally great, because except in the latter part of the Julio-Claudian period the award of *ornamenta* was confined to individuals from certain well-defined categories, and even then was made most sparingly.[74] It was always safer to pose as an *eques*. The second order was infinitely larger, and lacked formal enrollment or common meeting-place. Equestrian rank was also quite sufficiently impressive to simple folk.

Leaving aside enmity towards individuals, it would only be natural that senatorial privilege and influence should provoke hatred against the entire class. Perhaps the most vehement hostility was that expressed by certain emperors.[75] Within Rome itself the populace no doubt for long retained that suspicion and distrust of the upper classes in general, and the senate in particular, which led it to support single rulers from Julius Caesar onwards.[76] Josephus[77] must be right in seeing the crowd as firmly opposed to any senatorial aspirations for a return of the Republic on Gaius' murder in 41. More widely among non-members, even allowing for contemporary expectation that a defendant's treatment would be determined by his status, we might still look for some resentment at the senate's notorious leniency towards its own members when sitting as a court. We do indeed find mention of it, but only once in passing. Pliny describes how after his attack upon Publicius Certus in 97, "almost the entire senate embraced me with open arms and overwhelmed me with enthusiastic congratulations for having revived the practice, long fallen into disuse, of bringing measures for the public good before the senate at the risk of incurring personal enmities; I had in fact freed the senate from the odium against it which raged among the other classes for showing severity to others while sparing its own members alone by a sort of mutual connivance."[78] Even though further testimony is lacking, this odium is likely to have been of long standing and widely felt. Neither will it have been fully satisfied by senatorial reaction to the attack on Publicius Certus, since we know that the House continued to show bias at trials during Trajan's reign.

[73] Dio 75.9.1.
[74] See chap. 11 sect. 6.
[75] See chap. 5 sect. 1.
[76] See Z. Yavetz, *Plebs and Princeps*, Oxford, 1969, especially pp. 53-54; 114-115; 136-137.
[77] *AJ* 19.228.
[78] *Ep*. 9.13.21.

More generally we need not be too surprised that so subversive a sentiment as plain hatred of the senate and senators rarely appears in writing. In his *Satire* 8 Juvenal is certainly scathing about the degenerate behavior of certain nobles; however, he condemns them, not for being senators, but rather because they believe that high birth permits them to behave as they please, without regard for effort or merit. Vatinius' hatred was more sharply directed, and as the friend of an emperor who came to share his view, he could afford to voice it freely. Dio claims to quote the actual words of his constant jibe which so pleased Nero: "I hate you, Caesar, because you are a senator."[79]

Yet most remarkable of all is the incident at the Italian town of Sena involving a senator who is otherwise unknown for certain. It presumably took place during the latter part of 69, and is recorded as follows by Tacitus: "A complaint was made by the member Manlius Patruinus to the effect that he had been roughly handled in the *colonia* of Sena by a rowdy mob, and indeed at the bidding of the local officials. Nor had the outrage stopped there. He had been cornered by a throng of groaning and wailing townsfolk who celebrated a mock funeral under his nose, and hurled insults and abuse at the entire senate."[80] This incident is unique, and we have no clue to the circumstances which provoked it. Sena may well have suffered from successive armies marching upon Rome during 69, but it is still puzzling that the passage of one not specially distinguished member through the town should have been the signal for a violent demonstration against the whole senate, which even local officials encouraged.

Just as we seldom find hatred of the senate openly expressed by non-members, so, too, it is rare to encounter a critical estimate of the corporate body and its functions. As we have already seen, in fairly conventional fashion the poets Horace and Martial can compare the wearisome obligations of an ambitious senator with the more leisured existence of a person of lower rank. We may regret not knowing more about the status or views of Titius Rufus, who committed suicide in Gaius' reign on being charged with having declared that the senate thought one way and voted another.[81] But it is the more penetrating opinions of Martial's contemporary, Epictetus, which are of special interest. The significance of his unconventional, even subversive, views about the imperial court and individuals who appeared there has already been brought out by others.[82] It must be recognized that this, and other, topics are introduced primarily to illustrate philo-

[79] 63.15.1.

[80] *Hist.* 4.45.

[81] Dio 59.18.5.

[82] C. G. Starr, Jr., "Epictetus and the tyrant," *Class. Phil.* 44. 1949. pp. 20-29; F. Millar, "Epictetus and the imperial court," *JRS* 55. 1965. pp. 141-148.

sophical arguments rather than for their own sake. Even so, the opinion which Epictetus formed about the senate under the Flavians, during his time in Rome as slave of Nero's freedman *a libellis*, Epaphroditus, is uniquely valuable in its turn. In arguing how we must accept our lot in life, he points to the demands of a senator's career, in which much time will need to be spent away from home attending to the affairs of others.[83] He claims that men will not find "freedom" by the commonly accepted method of rising high in society. Indeed, at the top, when a man becomes a senator, "then he becomes a slave as he enters the meeting, then he serves in the handsomest and sleekest slavery."[84] He continues in the same vein when urging that no man should say one thing and think another: "That is how a friend is condemned on the testimony of a philosopher, that is how a philosopher turns parasite, that is how he hires himself out for money, that is how in the senate a man does not say what he thinks, while within his breast his judgment shouts loudly, not a cold and miserable remnant suspended from idle argumentations as by a hair, but a strong and serviceable judgment and familiar with its business from training in action."[85]

He sets the boldness of Helvidius Priscus against the weakness of other senators. The former was so outspoken that Vespasian had advised him not to attend the House, or at least not to speak, but for the sake of his principles he was prepared to ignore the advice, even if it meant death.[86] By contrast, argues Epictetus, ". . . had Caesar told another man in such circumstances not to attend the senate, he would have said 'I thank you for excusing me.' A man like that Caesar would not even have tried to keep from attending but would have known that he would either sit like a jug, or, if he spoke, would say what he knew Caesar wanted said, and would pile up any amount on top of it."[87]

In common with other philosophers of our period Epictetus condemns worldly ambition. He is unimpressed by the congratulations generally offered to a man who has been elected to a magistracy,[88] and he deplores the way in which men become enslaved by their desire for a tribunate, praetorship, or consulship.[89] Predictably, he reserves his strongest disapprobation for the latter office: "This is how the situation stands: nothing is done except for a price. And why be surprised? If you wish to be consul,

---

[83] 3.24.36-37.
[84] 4.1.40. For the senator as slave, cf. Tiberius in Tac. *Ann.* 3.65.
[85] 4.1.138-140.
[86] For quotation, see chap. 4 sect. 2 note 5.
[87] 1.2.23-24.
[88] 1.19.24-25; cf. Tac. *Dial.* 7.
[89] 4.1.60.

you must lose your sleep, run around, kiss hands, rot away at other men's doors, say and do many undignified things, send gifts to many and daily tokens to some. And what is the result? Twelve bundles of rods, sitting three or four times on the tribunal, giving circus games, and distributing dinners in baskets. Or let someone show me what there is in it beyond this."[90]

At first sight it seems ironic that Epictetus' hostile opinions were recorded by Arrian, who himself later pursued a senatorial career and occupied the consulship about 129.[91] In his Preface he testifies to the persuasiveness of Epictetus' discourses, and it is understandable that he did not publish them until at some stage unauthorized versions began to circulate. Yet if the *Dissertations* reproduce Epictetus' teachings at Nicopolis around 108 (as seems likely), some of the illustrations perhaps reflect the plight of the House under Domitian rather than its greater freedom under Trajan, which we learn of from Pliny. It is also worth recalling that Epictetus fully acknowledged the need for the state to be administered:[92] what he objected to was dishonesty and self-seeking on the part of those who entered public life. Similarly, he sees nothing at all amiss with a senator's judgment;[93] it is just paralyzed in the House by a tyrannical emperor.

At any rate, Epictetus' criticisms of the senate did not discourage Arrian from making his career there. More generally, we may gather from an overwhelming body of epigraphic evidence that upper-class Greeks' estimates of the senate likewise remained unaffected by the criticism of philosophers or by members' sufferings at the hands of cruel emperors. To attain membership continued to be a supreme ambition for Greeks of suitable wealth, background, and education. Evidence cited earlier shows how they fulfilled their goal in increasing numbers from the mid first century onwards, and were proud of the achievement. Exaggerated pride is delightfully ridiculed in an anecdote recounted by Lucian, where a grandee, "who set great store by the breadth of his purple stripe," moved the second-century philosopher Demonax "to take hold of the garment and draw attention to it, while whispering in his ear: 'A sheep wore this before you, but it didn't make him anything more than just a sheep!' "[94] Even petty princes, by favor of Rome kings in their own right, did not disdain the

[90] 4.10.19-21; cf. 4.7.21-23; Juvenal, *Sat.* 10.33-46 (of praetors).

[91] H. Halfmann, *Die Senatoren*, no. 56; P. A. Stadter, *Arrian of Nicomedia*, chap. 2; A. B. Bosworth, *A Historical Commentary on Arrian's History of Alexander* I, Oxford, 1980, pp. 1-4. See further P. A. Brunt, "From Epictetus to Arrian," *Athenaeum* 55. 1977. pp. 19-48 at p. 31.

[92] Cf. 3.7.21.

[93] 4.1.140, quoted above.

[94] *Demonax* 41.

distinction of senatorial membership.[95] But the pride of relatives seems most intense of all. On inscriptions we commonly find both men and women described as father/grandfather/relative of senators, or preferably, consulars. Proud phrases of this type occur dozens upon dozens of times in Asia Minor, and to a lesser extent in Greece, so that a list becomes superfluous, and would in any event serve little purpose: the sheer quantity of instances is the important feature.[96]

By contrast, in other parts of the empire there was neither such intense rivalry to attain membership of the senate, nor the same widespread zeal to advertise success, so that relevant examples are few. They seldom approach the degree of flamboyance approved in the East, though in the late second century a dedication at Cirta (Africa) does set out Sosia Falconilla's relationship to four generations of consulars, while inscriptions of the same type citing three generations are found in Italy.[97] Equally, in the Antonine period, a lady whose only certain name is Fabia is described as "consularis [filia or uxor], senatoris soror, senatoris mater" by grateful recipients of *alimenta* at Hispalis in Baetica.[98] The description "pater senatoris," on the other hand, which P. Oppius Marcellinus used of himself on a monument he erected at Aeclanum in Italy, might seem subdued enough: but it is striking that these words occupy the most prominent position on the inscription, in between "d(is) m(anibus)" in the top line.[99] In the literary sources, Velleius' description of L. Aelius Sejanus as "connected on his mother's side with old, highly distinguished families noted for their honors, as well as having brothers, cousins, and an uncle who had attained the consulship,"[100] is quite outstandingly boastful. Tacitus[101] is more typical when he notes merely that the father and grandfather of M. Vinicius (coss. 30 and 45) had been *consulares*, while the *Life* of the poet A. Persius Flaccus, who died in 62, describes him as "a Roman *eques* born at Volaterrae in Etruria connected by blood and by marriage with gentlemen of the first order."[102] In inscriptions such descriptions are similarly restrained, and notable by their rarity.[103]

In the East, however, not only were leading citizens eager to take up a

[95] See H. Halfmann, *Die Senatoren*, nos. 25, 36, 96. It was common enough, of course, for other senators to draw attention to their descent from Eastern kings.

[96] Among notable examples, see *IGRR* III. 500; IV. 910; cf. Philostratus, *Vit. Soph.* 536. For some analysis, A. Stein, *Der römische Ritterstand*, pp. 293ff.

[97] *ILS* 1105; 1129-1134; *AE* 1978. 288-289.

[98] *CIL* II. 1174; *PIR*² F 73.

[99] *ILS* 6484.

[100] 2.127.3; cf. Tac. *Ann.* 15.48 of C. Calpurnius Piso.

[101] *Ann.* 6.15.

[102] *Vita* 2 Cartault.

[103] For examples note: Italy, *ILS* 2682, 2735, 6717, 8531; *CIL* IX. 1587. Sicily, *ILS* 6770. Lugdunum, *CIL* XIII. 1683 (early second century?). Africa, *ILS* 2956.

senatorial career seemingly regardless of fluctuations in the political situation at Rome; a wider and similarly unshakeable devotion to the senate was displayed in two further ways. First, very remarkably, the senate, described as ἱερὰ σύγκλητος (less commonly as θεὸς σύγκλητος or a similar term), is depicted on coins throughout our period and beyond, to the reign of Gallienus. Except for three in silver from Crete, all the issues were made in bronze by cities in the province of Asia. Altogether Forni[104] reckoned that there were about 500 issues made by just over 100 cities: during the third century such coins might be minted in substantial quantities. The senate is usually portrayed on the obverse in a guise notably different from that adopted by Romans.[105] On the corresponding reverse there appears most commonly either a local deity or other distinctive local emblem, or an emperor, or sometimes "dea Roma." Elsewhere in the East during the third century "S(enatus) R(omanus)" was featured on coins issued by Pisidian Antioch and Iconium, "SPQR" on some from Philomelium, and "SACRA SINATUS" (sic) on others from Mallus.[106]

Second, we have evidence for priests of the senate (either alone or with other deities) in Cyprus,[107] at Athens,[108] and in Asia Minor at Philadelphia,[109] Dorylaeum,[110] Tralles (or possibly Magnesia),[111] and Tmolus.[112] Beyond that, however, nothing at all is known of the cult. The testimony alleged for a similar priesthood at Ephesus should be set aside.[113] But Cn. Pedanius Fuscus Salinator, as proconsul of Asia in 99/100, is found dedicating one statue of the senate there,[114] while another in silver was among

[104] For his full study, see G. Forni, "ΙΕΡΑ e ΘΕΟΣ ΣΥΝΚΛΗΤΟΣ: un capitolo dimenticato nella storia del Senato Romano," Atti Accad. Naz. Lincei, Memorie (Classe sc. mor., stor., fil.) VIII. V. 3. (1953). See further J. and L. Robert, BE 1954, no. 54, pp. 111-113; L. Robert, Monnaies grecques, Geneva and Paris, 1967, pp. 75-78; and K. Kraft, Das System der kaiserzeitlichen Münzprägung in Kleinasien, Istanbuler Forschungen 29, Berlin, 1972, pp. 27-29.

[105] For designs, see Figure 8 (a) and (b) with chap. 6 sect. 5.

[106] See B. Levick, "The coinage of Pisidian Antioch in the third century A.D.," NC 6. 1966. pp. 47-59 at pp. 55-59, and references there.

[107] SEG 26. 1475 (strictly the point depends upon a conjecture, but it seems very certain).

[108] IG II² 3547, with restoration upheld by L. Robert, op. cit. p. 76 n. 2 and BE 1977. no. 76. p. 326, against the rejection of R. Mellor, ΘΕΑ ΡΩΜΗ, The Worship of the Goddess Roma in the Greek World, Hypomnemata 42. Göttingen, 1975, p. 102 n. 479.

[109] L. Robert, Monnaies grecques, chap. 13 (again strictly a conjecture, but a very convincing one).

[110] OGIS 479.

[111] AE 1894. 122; L. Robert, op. cit. p. 76 n. 4.

[112] J. Keil, "Die erste Kaiserneokorie von Ephesos," Num. Zeitschr. 52. 1919. pp. 115-120, p. 117 no. 2; L. Robert, op. cit. p. 76 (Domitianic date).

[113] Ancient Greek Inscriptions in the British Museum III. no. DC. line 24 = C. Börker and R. Merkelbach, Die Inschriften von Ephesos V. no. 1600, rejected by L. Robert, op. cit. p. 76 n. 4.

[114] ILS 8822 = C. Börker and R. Merkelbach, op. cit. V. no. 1499.

the gifts which C. Vibius Salutaris left to the city in 104.[115] It may be other such statues which we hear of in inscriptions from Comama (Pisidia) and Side (Pamphylia).[116] A statue was definitely erected by the people of Hierocaesarea (Asia), perhaps in thanks for confirmation of asylum rights in 22.[117]

The origin of these diverse forms of devotion to the senate is altogether uncertain. We might speculate that the senate's appearance on coins would follow the occasion in 23 when the cities of Asia voted a temple to Tiberius, Livia, and the senate, which Smyrna was permitted to erect in 26.[118] Yet in fact we know that such designs first occur earlier, and only reach their peak in the late second and early third centuries. Except for a rash of minting under Gordian III it would therefore be difficult to link this choice of obverse with political realities, for the most part. There is no question of the issues diminishing as the authority and role of the senate waned. Instead, paradoxically, they increase in this time of decline. Comparable devotion of the same type can be glimpsed in a private dedication of Severan date, inscribed beneath what was perhaps a statue of the Demos "of the glorious city of the Aphrodisians, devoted to the emperor, free and autonomous according to the decrees of the most sacred senate and the treaty and the divine (imperial) responses, with *asylia*."[119] The meticulous inclusion of a reference to the senate here, and its prominence, are both striking.

By contrast with the East, devotion of this type is almost unheard of in the West at any stage. We can only point to a few undated inscriptions from Africa which honor the "genius senatus" (mostly as protector),[120] and a series of Roman coins with the same legend issued under Antoninus Pius.[121] A bronze statue unearthed in the course of excavations in a temple consecrated to the imperial cult at Emerita in the imperial province of Lusitania, and plausibly identified as a "genius senatus," is therefore a

[115] *Forschungen in Ephesos* II. p. 127. no. 27. lines 160-161 = C. Börker and R. Merkelbach, op. cit. Ia. no. 27, with literature cited there.

[116] *AE* 1961. 23; *SEG* 6. 731 (third century?), with comment by G. F. Hill in *Anatolian Studies Presented to Sir W. M. Ramsay*, Manchester, 1923, p. 216.

[117] See Tac. *Ann.* 3.62-63 with L. Robert, *Hellenica* 6. 1948. pp. 50-52 no. 15. Note the unusual adjective, σύγκλητος ἐπιφανής. Its superlative may be used by a proconsul (?) writing to Pergamum in Trajan's time: [κατὰ δόγμα τῆς ἐπιφαν]εστάτης συνκλήτου (*IGRR* IV. 336 line 5).

[118] Tac. *Ann.* 4.15, 37, 55-56.

[119] J. Reynolds, *Aphrodisias and Rome*, no. 43. Since Asian devotion to the senate does not seem to have fluctuated with shifts in imperial attitudes at Rome, her suggestion (p. 170) that this inscription is most likely to have been set up during the reign of an emperor favorable to the corporate body may seem unduly restrictive.

[120] *CIL* VIII. 11017; *ILS* 3676; *AE* 1911. 10; 1917/18. 21; 1921. 27; cf. *CIL* VIII. 23604.

[121] *BMC* IV. pp. 31, 154, 181, 200, 214, 219. A similar coin of A.D. 213 (*BMC* V. p. 442) is said to be "quite doubtful."

really remarkable discovery, which at present remains unique and quite unexpected. It, too, may date from the mid second century.[122]

It might be said that this treatment of contemporary estimates of the corporate body and its members has proved impressionistic, and its conclusions predictable. In a society where the social pyramid was tall and steep, the tiny, proud circle of the highest class showed a natural concern for the preservation of its own position, while being variously regarded by those of lower rank with envy, hatred, deference, and awe, and just sometimes with indifference or even contempt. Arguably, this is all as we might expect. Yet two further points do stand out. First, the corporate body, for all its exclusiveness, was no closed elite. In our period entry could indeed be achieved by wealthy, educated citizens, suitably supported;[123] and willing candidates did continue to come forward, despite the manifest burdens and perils which a senatorial career might entail. Second, very remarkably, in the East the Roman senate came to stand as a symbol and an inspiration in a manner hardly to be expected when the scope and nature of its authority in affairs of state were really much reduced.

[122] See Figure 1 with J. M. Alvarez Martínez, "Una escultura en bronce del *genius senatus*, hallada en Merida," *Archivo Español de Arqueologia* 48. 1975. pp. 141-151, and more generally H. Kunckel, *Der römische Genius*, pp. 80-82.

[123] Even the son of a slave might rise so high in the right circumstances: cf. Suet. *Claud.* 24; *Nero* 15; *PIR*² H 73; L 97 with W. Eck, *ZPE* 42. 1981. pp. 245-246.

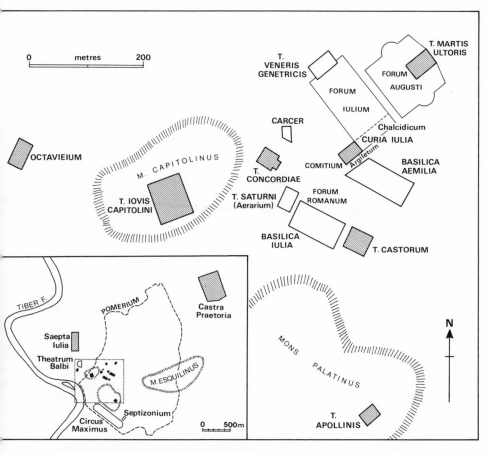

The meeting places of the senate (dotted) and other locations of note in Rome, with enlargement of the central area. The placing of the Chalcidicum is conjectural. See chap. 3 sect. 1 note 19.

This bronze statue, 55 cm high, was found in the course of excavations at the so-called "temple of Diana," Merida, Spain, and is now in the Museo Nacional de Arte Romano there. The temple was in fact consecrated to the imperial cult. The bearded male figure, wearing a toga and possibly the distinctive senatorial sandals, has been plausibly identified as a personification of the corporate body, a "genius senatus." As such a cult object it is unique in the present state of our knowledge. It symbolizes the age and wisdom with which the senate was popularly associated. A mid second century date is suggested. See further chap. 2 sect. 6 note 122 and chap. 6 sect. 5.

The dress is to be compared with that of the acephalous porphyry statue of early second century date (?) found in the area immediately behind the Curia in Rome in 1937, and now displayed in the Antiquarium Forense. See G. Calza, "Una statua di porfido trovata nel foro," *Atti della Pontificia Accademia Romana di Archeologia* (serie III) Rendiconti 22. 1946/7. pp. 185-191; A. Bartoli, "La statua porfiretica della curia (Roma)," *NSc* 1. 1947. pp. 85-100; with further illustration in idem, *Curia Senatus: lo scavo e il restauro*, plates LXII-LXIII.

Figure 1
"Genius senatus" in bronze

Figure 2
Augustan coin with possible illustration
of the Curia Julia

The building which features on coins issued between 29 and 27 B.C. (*BMC* I Aug. 631-632 and 643, plate 15.12-14) does bear a marked resemblance to the Curia Julia: apart from the general shape and elevation, note the central double doors above ground level; the three windows; the portico. Thus some scholars have plausibly considered the coins to depict the newly dedicated Curia. But the identification is by no means secure, so that certain radical suggestions made from it about the character and location of the Curia Julia rest on an insecure foundation: see chap. 3 sect. 1 note 13. Among alternative identifications proposed, the view that a Gallo-Roman shrine is represented hardly appeals. This was put forward by A. Voirol, "Die Darstellung eines Keltentempels auf einem Denar von Kaiser Augustus," *Jahrbuch der Schweizerischen Gesellschaft für Urgeschichte* 31. 1939. pp. 150-157, and is discussed by B. L. Trell, "Architectura Numismatica," *NC* 12. 1972. pp. 45-59 at pp. 55-57, and by B. L. Trell and M. J. Price, *Coins and Their Cities*, London, 1972, pp. 71-74. While certainty is impossible, Castagnoli is at least more persuasive when he views the building as one closely associated with the Princeps, namely, Augustus' house on the Palatine. See F. Castagnoli, "Note sulla topografia del Palatino e del Foro Romano," *Arch. Class.* 16. 1964. pp. 173-199 at pp. 193-195, with discussion of earlier suggestions. His view is supported by N. Degrassi, "La dimora di Augusto sul Palatino e la base di Sorrento," *Atti della Pontificia Accademia Romana di Archeologia* (serie III) Rendiconti 39. 1966/7. pp. 77-116 at pp. 96-97.

Figure 3
The restored Curia (front)

Figure 4
The restored Curia (side and rear)

Figure 5
The restored Curia (interior)

This view of the interior of the restored Curia today is taken from the front entrance looking towards the president's tribunal. Note the wide central aisle, with three raised steps on either side. The fine pavement is restored from the original design.

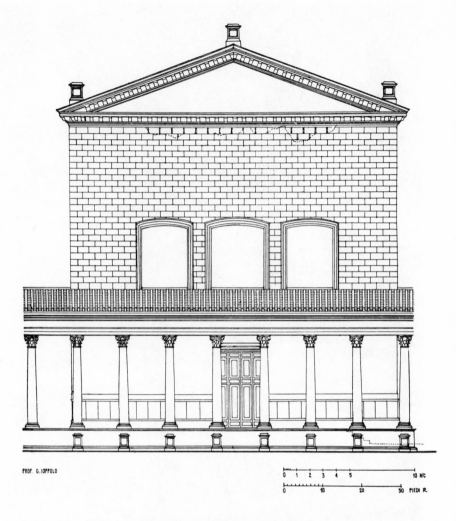

Figure 6
Reconstruction of the front of the Curia

G. Ioppolo's reconstruction of the front of the Curia, with a portico. The doors were approached by a flight of steps.

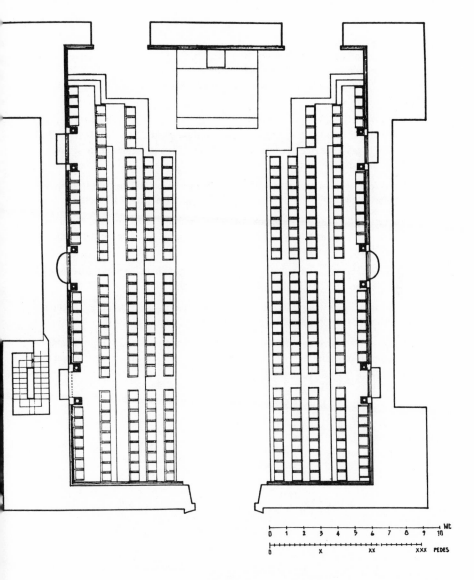

Figure 7
Reconstruction of interior arrangements
in the Curia

G. Ioppolo's reconstruction of interior arrangements in the Curia. For the argument that senators are likely to have occupied benches rather than individual seats as drawn here, see chap. 3 sect. 2.

(a) Obverse of early third-century bronze coin issued by Smyrna (Asia), with youthful female (?) bust of the senate and the legend ΙΕΡΑ ΣΥΝΚΛΗΤΟΣ (*BMC Ionia*, p. 262 no. 224). See further chap. 2 sect. 6 note 105 and chap. 6 sect. 5 note 21.

(b) Reverse of silver coin issued by Cydonia (Crete) during the reign of Tiberius, with veiled and bearded bust of the senate and the legend ΣΥΝΚΛΗΤΩ ΚΡΗΤΕΣ ΚΥ (*BMC Crete and Aegean Islands*, p. 32 no. 37). See further chap. 2 sect. 6 note 105 and chap. 6 sect. 5 note 21.

(c) Reverse of Roman bronze coin issued during the reign of Titus, illustrating the prominence typically given to the legend SC. See further chap. 12 sect. 3.

(d) Reverse of bronze coin issued by Antioch (Syria) during the reign of Domitian, illustrating the prominence typically given to the legend SC. See further chap. 12 sect. 3 note 5.

(e) Reverse of bronze coin issued by Philippopolis (Arabia) in the mid third century, with the legend SC. See further chap. 12 sect. 3 note 7.

(f) Obverse of silver coin issued in 68 by the usurper L. Clodius Macer, legate of Numidia, with the legend SC. See further chap. 12 sect. 3 note 10.

(g) Reverse of bronze coin issued by Laodicea (Asia) in the early third century, with a legend proclaiming that the city had been granted a neocorate "by decree of the senate," ΣΥΝ
KΛΗ
ΤΟΥ
ΔΟΓΜΑΤΙ

See further chap. 14 sect. 1 note 91.

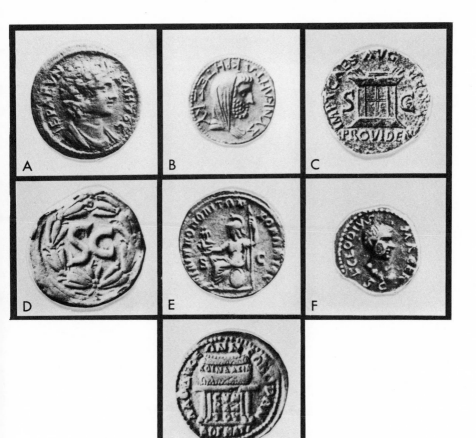

Figure 8
Coins

Part Two

SESSIONS

3

MEETING PLACES AND THE INTERIOR
OF THE CURIA JULIA

1. Meeting Places

In moving now to a full discussion of sessions the purpose of this opening chapter is twofold: first, to assemble and discuss such evidence as we possess for the meeting places of the senate during the Principate, and then to examine in more detail seating arrangements and the interior of the Curia Julia.

As Varro said in his handbook written for Pompey's entry to the House in 70 B.C., a decree of the senate was regular only if it was made in a place appointed by an augur and called a "temple."[1] This rule was always adhered to in the Republic, and the same seems to have applied in our period.[2] Thus the unknown speaker of the mid first century (Claudius?), whose words are preserved on papyrus, can harangue his fellow senators: "If these proposals meet with your approval, Conscript Fathers, say so plainly at once, in your own considered words. But if you disapprove, find other solutions, yet do so in this temple, or, if you perhaps want a more generous interval in which to think, take it, provided you remember that to whatever place you are called, you must give us your own opinion."[3]

This passage not only highlights the point that the senate would meet in a *templum*; it also indicates how it by no means felt confined to meeting in one place.[4] In this respect the senate differed from, say, the British Houses of Parliament which use the Palace of Westminster exclusively, and are closely associated with it. It is true that Parliament can meet

---

[1] Gell. 14.7.7. Cf. Servius, *ad Aen.* 11. 235. Technically, not all sacred edifices were temples, and a place appointed as a *templum* did not need to be consecrated to any particular divinity.

[2] As Dio (55.3.5) says, one of the occasions when the senate could do no more than formulate an *auctoritas* was when it met ἐν τόπῳ τινὶ μὴ νενομισμένῳ.

[3] *FIRA*[2] I no. 44 col. III lines 10-16.

[4] "Quoc[u]mque loci" in line 15 should be translated "to whatever place," not "in whatever order," as, for example, N. Lewis and M. Reinhold, *Roman Civilization* II. p. 119 render it.

elsewhere: after bombing in 1940, 1941, and 1944, removal was necessary. But this was an enforced, temporary evacuation. Certainly the senate was only convened within a fairly restricted area, the city of Rome and up to one mile beyond its *pomerium*.[5] But within that area it could meet in a variety of locations, and did so as a matter of course.

Having made this claim, it must be acknowledged that as far as we can tell from meager information, the senate in our period was most closely associated with the Curia Julia, and met most frequently there. Since this building was conveniently situated and enjoyed the unique distinction of being specifically designed for the sole purpose of accommodating the senate, it was only natural and sensible that meetings should come to be concentrated there. Indeed, as it happens, we never hear of any senatorial election or trial proceedings explicitly said to have been conducted elsewhere. The building occupied the traditional site for a senate house on the northern edge of the Comitium in the northwest corner of the Forum.[6] Throughout our period the structure was that known as Curia Julia, begun by Julius Caesar shortly before his assassination, and eventually dedicated by Octavian on 28 August 29 B.C.[7]

Not surprisingly public interest in the business of the senate ensured that this new meeting place—hailed by Propertius as "gleaming" and "lofty,"[8] and praised by Ovid as "now most worthy of so mighty an assembly"[9]—soon became one of the best known public buildings in Rome. The terrible omen of an eagle owl perched on its roof, both at the time of a meeting called during Augustus' final illness, and then as the first session was called after his death, came to be duly recorded in popular memory.[10] So, too, were the mingled laughter and barbarian clamor which mysteriously issued from there by night shortly before Boudicca's rebellion.[11] Not long afterwards the Curia Julia almost certainly escaped intact from the Great Fire of 64.[12] But according to a late source the *senatus* was among

---

[5] The tribunician veto extended no further. It is not clear what status or standing Galba intended to attach to the *senatus* which he set up in Spain at the beginning of his revolt in 68. In his description, Suetonius (*Galba* 10) tactfully refers to it as "velut instar senatus." See in general E. Gabba, "Senati in esilio," *Boll. Ist. Dir. Rom.* 63. 1960. pp. 221-232.

[6] For its situation "in comitio," see Pliny, *NH* 7.181; 35.27; and map above.

[7] Dio 44.5.1-2; *EJ* p. 51; *RG* 19.1; cf. 34.2. Figures 2-4.

[8] 4.1.11, "curia praetexto quae nunc nitet alta senatu."

[9] *Ars Amat.* 3.117, "curia consilio nunc est dignissima tanto."

[10] Dio 56.29.3 and 45.2. For the *bubo* as a terrible omen, see Plin. *NH* 10.34-35. According to Dio (73.24.1), the same bird hooted around the Capitol (rather than the senate house) shortly before Commodus' death.

[11] Dio 62.1.1-2.

[12] It is not listed by Tacitus (*Ann.* 15.40-41) among the buildings destroyed in the Fire. While the place of Thrasea Paetus' trial two years later is not known, the installation of a guard in the temple of Venus Genetrix certainly makes sense if the senate were meeting in the Curia Julia (Tac. *Ann.* 16.27).

many public works built by Domitian. It is perháps more likely to have been repaired or remodeled by him in some way, rather than completely rebuilt, but we have no further information on the point.[13] There may be a partial glimpse of it with a front portico on one of the reliefs from Trajan's arch at Beneventum,[14] though it is probably not represented (as some have claimed) on the alimentary relief of the "Anaglypha Traiani."[15] Thereafter we know only that it was burnt in 283 and rebuilt by Diocletian.[16] In the seventh century his structure was converted into the church of San Adriano, and only restored under the supervision of A. Bartoli in the 1930's.[17] It is the reasonable contention of modern experts that Diocletian had retained the size, site, orientation, and certain details of the previous building, so that an examination of his surviving structure may give us an accurate impression of the Curia Julia.

Two further structures were evidently associated with it, though almost nothing definite is known of their size and function. The first was variously called Chalcidicum, Atrium Minervae, Athenaeum.[18] It was either an actual part of the whole complex, or a separate building adjacent to the Curia.[19] It is a fair guess that it served as a record office for the senate, but no clear evidence on its function survives. The second structure was a *senaculum*. Varro writes of it as follows: "Above the Graecostasis was the *senaculum*, where the temple of Concord and the Basilica Opimia are; it was called *senaculum* as a place where the senate or the elders were to

[13] "Multae operae publicae fabricatae": Chronog. 354 (ed. T. Mommsen), *MGH* IX. Berlin, 1842, p. 146. For the more radical view that the Curia Julia originally stood to the north and west of Diocletian's Curia, and was only removed to the present site as a result of a complete rebuilding by Domitian, see L. Richardson, Jr., "The Curia Julia and the Janus Geminus," *Röm. Mitt.* 85. 1978. pp. 359-369, supported by J. C. Anderson, Jr., "Domitian, the Argiletum and the Temple of Peace," *AJA* 86. 1982. pp. 101-110. Their arguments should be treated with extreme caution. Undue weight is placed upon the Chronographer's sketchy record cited above; much also has to depend upon the belief (far from secure) that it is the Curia Julia, and not some other building, which features on coins issued between 29 and 27 B.C. (see Figure 2 above).

[14] See A. Bartoli, *Curia Senatus, lo scavo e il restauro*, Rome, 1963, p. 7 with Figure 6 above.

[15] See M. Hammond, "A statue of Trajan represented on the 'Anaglypha Traiani,' " *MAAR* 21. 1953. pp. 127-183 at pp. 137-138.

[16] Chronog. 354, *MGH* IX. p. 148, s. vv. Carinus and Diocletian.

[17] His account of the work, cited in note 14 above, is of primary importance; for an earlier, briefer record, see A. Bartoli, "Il monumento della perpetuità del senato," *Studi Romani* 2. 1954. pp. 129-137.

[18] Cf. Dio 51.22.1; the dedication to Minerva could date to Domitian's time, in view of his devotion to the goddess.

[19] Note *RG* 19.1, "Curiam et continens ei Chalcidicum," which is translated in the Greek version as βουλευτήριον καὶ τὸ πλησίον αὐτῶι Χαλκιδικόν. For discussion see F. Zevi, "Il calcidico della *Curia Iulia*," *Atti Accad. Lincei* (Classe sc. mor., storiche e filologiche) 26. 1971. pp. 237-251.

take their places.''[20] Valerius Maximus,[21] writing in Tiberius' reign, speaks of a place called *senaculum* in his own day, where senators could wait before meetings. Further information on it is lacking.

In the surviving evidence "Curia Julia" is seldom specified in full as the place of a session during our period. But it is named thus in a decree concerning Mytilene passed in June 25 B.C.[22] Ovid[23] refers to meetings here. The *SC de nundinis saltus Beguensis* of 138 was passed "in comitio in curia Iu[l(ia)]."[24] Here likewise the request for senatorial sponsorship of the Secular Games was made in 203, as it almost certainly had been in 17 B.C. too.[25] In most contemporary sources, however, "Curia Julia" is abbreviated to "Curia," even by Augustus himself.[26] Further support for the notion that most meetings came to be held here from an early stage in our period derives from Suetonius' account of events immediately after Caligula's assassination in 41. As he explains it: "The senate was so unanimously bent on asserting its liberty that the consuls first summoned it, not to the Curia, because it was called Julia, but to the Capitol."[27]

If we now turn to other meeting places,[28] it might indeed seem natural to place the Capitol first, not least because in the Republic meetings had often been held here, including the opening one of each year. But in fact there is no sign that the custom continued under the Principate. Dio[29] and Josephus in his *Jewish War*[30] do certainly concur with Suetonius in claiming that the senate met here after Caligula's assassination. Yet otherwise the Capitol is only once known to have been the place of a meeting in our period, in 238, on the death of the two Gordians. Herodian's account of the senate's action would strongly suggest that a symbolic purpose again lay behind the choice, as it had done in 41:

They were resolved to hold a meeting to discuss practical measures. . . . First, they must choose and elect for themselves emperors, whom they proposed should share the rule, to prevent power reverting to a tyranny in the hands of one man.

---

[20] *De Ling. Lat.* 5. 156; cf. Festus p. 470 Lindsay. The *Graecostasis*, a platform near the senate house on which foreign envoys waited before entering the chamber, is never mentioned again after the Republic, though there would long have been a use for such a structure: in addition to Varro, loc. cit., see Cicero, *Ad Q. Fr.* 2.1 = Shackleton Bailey 5.

[21] 2.2.6.

[22] R. K. Sherk, *Roman Documents from the Greek East: Senatus Consulta and Epistulae to the Age of Augustus*, Baltimore, 1969, no. 26 col. b line 39.

[23] *Ex Ponto* 4.5.21, "patres in Iulia templa vocati."

[24] *FIRA*[2] I no. 47 line 5.

[25] G. B. Pighi, *De Ludis Saecularibus*, p. 140 I line 5; p. 108 c; cf. p. 132 I line 8.

[26] *RG* 19.1.

[27] *Calig.* 60.

[28] See map.

[29] 60.1.1.

[30] 2.205.

The meeting therefore took place, not in their normal chamber, but in the temple of Jupiter Capitolinus, the god whom the Romans worship on their citadel. So they shut themselves up alone in the inner sanctuary, witnessed as it were by Jupiter as their fellow councillor and guardian of their acts. . . .[31]

The Capitol was abandoned as a meeting place partly perhaps because Augustus provided an alternative temple from 2 B.C. and prescribed that certain types of business must be discussed there. This was the temple of Mars Ultor, which dominated his new forum[32] and offered more spacious accommodation for a meeting than the Capitol, where there was no suitable chamber.[33] According to Dio,[34] it was in the temple of Mars Ultor that the senate had to take decisions about triumphs, while Suetonius mentions Augustus' instruction that "the senate should debate about wars or triumphs here."[35] All the same, we possess no record of a meeting in the temple for this purpose, beyond the bombastic instructions of Gaius during his German campaign in 39: "He sent a boastful despatch to Rome, having instructed the couriers that they should drive their vehicle right up to the Forum and the senate house, and that they should not hand the letter to the consuls except in the temple of Mars at a full meeting of the senate."[36] It is just conceivable that the temple fell out of use because its *cella*, while larger than any on the Capitol, still did not afford as much space as the Curia,[37] and therefore came to be found cramped for sessions at which the business attracted a high attendance.

Before our period there had seldom been sessions on the Palatine.[38] But under the Julio-Claudians meetings did come to be held for the convenience of the emperor in the library and portico of the temple of Apollo here, dedicated in 28 B.C.[39] These buildings formed part of a palace complex.

[31] 7.10.2-3. Most strangely, this meeting, specifically said to have been held in the *cella*, is barely noticed by L. R. Taylor and R. T. Scott, "Seating space in the Roman senate and the *senatores pedarii*," *TAPA* 100. 1969. pp. 529-582 at pp. 559-568 and 576 (only in note 67).

[32] For its dedication, see Dio 55.10.la and b; 60.5.3; Vell. 2.100.2.

[33] For the *cellae* on the Capitol, see Taylor and Scott, *TAPA* 100. 1969. pp. 563-564.

[34] 55.10.3.

[35] *Aug.* 29.

[36] *Calig.* 44.

[37] Approximately 21.5 × 15 meters within the columns, as opposed to the 25.6 × 17.7 of the Curia. Did Augustus perhaps approve the design of the temple at a stage when he was gloomy about his efforts to boost senatorial attendance? Cf. Macrobius, *Sat.* 2.4.9, for allegedly slow progress on the building work.

[38] For a notable instance in October 39 B.C., see J. Reynolds, *Aphrodisias and Rome*, no. 8 line 3 and discussion, p. 66.

[39] On the dedication, note, for example, Dio 53.1.3. We know that the two Jewish embassies of 4 B.C. (Josephus, *AJ* 17.301 and *BJ* 2.81) and an Alexandrian embassy of 12/13 (*Ox. Pap.* 2435 verso) were received here by Augustus. See further F. Castagnoli, "Sulla biblioteca del tempio di Apollo Palatino," *Accademia dei Lincei* (Classe di scienze morali), *Rendiconti* Ser. 8. 4. 1949. pp. 380-382; and D. L. Thompson, "The meetings of the Roman

Suetonius[40] records that sessions of the senate were often held here in Augustus' old age. It was at such a meeting in 16, with the statues of famous orators looking on, that the grandson of Q. Hortensius chose to beg Tiberius to help his family.[41] The text of a *senatus consultum* of 19 survives, passed "in Palatio, in porticu quae est ad Apollinis."[42] Likewise the *Tabula Hebana* of 19/20 specifies how *imagines* should be added "in the palace in the portico which is near the temple of Apollo, in which temple the senate customarily meets. . . ."[43] According to Dio,[44] the meeting at which Sejanus was denounced in 31 took place on the Palatine, while Josephus[45] records how Claudius summoned the senate here as soon as he grasped the imperial power in 41. The last record of a session on the Palatine is dated 54, early in Nero's reign, when doors had been built at the rear so that Agrippina could stand behind a curtain and listen unseen.[46] Having gone to this trouble she presumably hoped that sessions would be held here often, and it is possible that she did not hope in vain. At least it could be argued that on the death of Volusius Saturninus in 56 the senate would not have erected a statue to him "in the area belonging to Apollo, in sight of the senate,"[47] if it had not customarily met there in the past, and intended to continue so doing in the future. All the same, when relations between Nero and the senate came under strain as the reign progressed, it is understandable that this meeting place fell out of use. In all likelihood it was engulfed by the Great Fire of 64, and although the buildings were later restored by Domitian, the custom of convening the senate here was never revived.[48]

It has been claimed by some scholars[49] that the temple of Concord, in the northwest corner of the Forum close to the Curia Julia, was frequently used for meetings of the senate in the Principate. This temple was dedicated

---

senate on the Palatine," *AJA* 85. 1981. pp. 335-339, who must be right to argue that there was no other place where the senate met there during the Principate, despite the contrary impression which certain references might give (for example, Servius, *ad Aen.* 11. 235, "etiam in Palatii atrio . . . apud maiores consulebatur senatus").

[40] *Aug.* 29; cf. an undated occasion, ibid. 28.

[41] Tac. *Ann.* 2.37.

[42] No. 22 in list, chap. 15 sect. 5.

[43] *EJ* 94a line 1.

[44] 58.9.4.

[45] *AJ* 19.266.

[46] Tac. *Ann.* 13.5.

[47] *AE* 1972. 174 line 10, "i]ṇ aria [A]poḷ[inis] iṇ conspectum ç[uriae]," with comment by W. Eck, *Hermes* 100. 1972. pp. 471-472. For use of *curia* as "the senate" (wherever it was meeting) see, for example, Tac. *Ann.* 2.37.

[48] See Tac. *Ann.* 15.39; Dio 62.18.2; Suet. *Dom.* 20; and the discussions cited in note 39 above.

[49] For example, S. B. Platner and T. Ashby, *A Topographical Dictionary of Ancient Rome*, Oxford, 1929, p. 139; Taylor and Scott, *TAPA* 100. 1969. p. 559 n. 67.

on 16 January 10;[50] it incorporated a *cella* of unusual proportions (45
meters wide, 24 deep), which was indeed suitably spacious for a large
gathering. But Pliny the Elder's testimony about the works of art housed
in the temple[51] would suggest that the *cella* was hardly free from obstacles,
while the actual record of meetings here is thin. Dio[52] does tell us that
after the fateful session on the Palatine early on 18 October 31, the senate
reassembled in the temple of Concord later the same day. The dedication
of the temple was significant, and it was close to the jail, so that the
sentence of execution could be transmitted quickly. Learned members
might have further reflected upon the curious appropriateness of this apparently unusual setting for the session in question. The temple was erected
by L. Opimius, the consul responsible for the death of C. Gracchus; it
was used for debates on the Catilinarian conspiracy, and was later restored
by Tiberius himself.[53] Thereafter we have no reference to any meeting
here until the night of 31 December 192 when, according to the *Historia
Augusta*,[54] Pertinax was invested with the imperial power here because the
attendant to open the senate house could not be found. In the morning
Pertinax seems to have moved to the Curia Julia, and Dio[55] speaks of him
there. In our period the *Historia Augusta* does mention two further sessions
in the temple of Concord, but both are doubtful. The first was said to occur
on the day of Severus Alexander's accession in 222, according to a fictitious
quotation from *acta urbis*;[56] the second, on the death of the two Gordians
in 238, was a meeting which Herodian locates more plausibly on the
Capitol.[57]

   In the Republic the senate would sometimes meet outside the *pomerium*,
for example to hear a request for a triumph from a pro-magistrate who
would forfeit his chance of one by crossing the boundary, or to receive
foreign ambassadors who were not permitted to cross because their states
had no treaty with Rome. During the Principate meetings might still be
held outside the *pomerium* for reasons of this nature, though there was
much less frequent need than in the Republic. As consul on 1 January 7
B.C., however, Tiberius summoned the senate outside the *pomerium* so
that he would not have crossed it before celebrating a triumph. This meeting
was held in what Dio[58] describes as the 'Οκταουίειον. There is no evidence

[50] *EJ* p. 45.
[51] See Platner-Ashby, p. 139.
[52] 58.11.4.
[53] Dio 55.8.2.
[54] *Pert.* 4.9.
[55] 74.1.4.
[56] *Sev. Alex.* 6.2.
[57] Cf. HA, *Max. Balb.* 1.1 with Herodian 7.10.2-3 and Whittaker's notes ad loc.
[58] 55.8.1.

for further meetings there in our period, but it seems to have formed part of a complex including a *Curia Octaviae* mentioned once by Pliny the Elder.[59] Foreign envoys whose states had no treaty with Rome might still be received by the senate,[60] though we have no record of where any such meeting took place. Other meetings held outside the *pomerium* in our period are one on 23 May 17 B.C. in the *Saepta Julia*, when decrees were passed in connection with the *Ludi Saeculares*,[61] and (if Dio[62] can be credited) the astonishing occasion in June 68 when the senate allegedly entered the Praetorian camp to declare Nero an enemy and choose Galba as emperor.

There are single references to three further meeting places within our period. The first is the Athenaeum, a building erected by Hadrian for cultural and educational activities.[63] According to Dio,[64] the meeting in 193 at which Didius Julianus was condemned to death and Septimius Severus proclaimed emperor was held here, and there seems every reason to accept his eye-witness account.[65] However, it is less easy to believe Josephus' testimony[66] that after Gaius' assassination in 41 the senate met in the temple of Jupiter Victor: elsewhere in fact Josephus himself agrees with other sources in locating this meeting on the Capitol.[67] The temple of Castor and Pollux is mentioned by the *Historia Augusta*[68] in an unreliable passage as the place where the senate met to pronounce Maximinus and his son enemies of the state in 238. Sited conveniently close to the Forum, it had been used for meetings in the Republic, and had been maintained by a succession of emperors; but no other instance occurs of its use for sessions of the senate during the Principate.

Finally, if there is any truth in the *Historia Augusta's* story[69] about the unique combined meeting of senate and people to deify Marcus Aurelius just after his death in 180, it would be interesting to know where the gathering took place.

[59] See Platner-Ashby, s.v. Porticus Octaviae; Plin. *NH* 36.28.

[60] See chap. 14 sect. 3.

[61] G. B. Pighi, *De Ludis Saecularibus*, p. 111 line 50. For the Saepta as a duly consecrated structure, see L. R. Taylor, *Roman Voting Assemblies*, Ann Arbor, 1966, p. 49.

[62] 63.27.2ᵇ. Compare the way in which early in 69 Galba and his advisers considered whether the adoption of Piso should be announced "pro rostris an in senatu an in castris." The last was chosen, with a meeting of the senate soon to follow (Tac. *Hist.* 1.17 and 19).

[63] Platner-Ashby, s.v. Its site is unknown, though Philostratus, *Vit. Soph.* 589, could imply that it was some distance from the senate house. See in general H. Braunert, "Das Athenaeum zu Rom bei den Scriptores Historiae Augustae," *BHAC* 2. 1963. pp. 9-41.

[64] 74.17.4.

[65] Herodian (2.12.4) says that the meeting was in the senate house.

[66] *AJ* 19.248. For the temple, which may possibly have been on the Palatine, see Platner-Ashby, s.v.

[67] See note 30 above.

[68] *Maximin.* 16.1.

[69] HA, *Marcus* 18.3, part of the interpolated section.

2. Seating Arrangements and the Interior of the Curia Julia

Information on seating arrangements at sessions in our period is disappointingly thin, and we really have no knowledge for meeting places other than the Curia Julia. In fact this is not too severe a blow since, as we have seen, most sessions seem to have been held here, and only in this one purpose-built meeting place is there likely to have been any regularity in the seating arrangements. Elsewhere greater variety might be expected, together with considerable improvisation.

The interior dimensions of Diocletian's building are described as follows by Taylor and Scott:

The interior is 25.63 × 17.73 meters with an entrance from the Comitium about 4 meters wide. The central aisle measures 5.40m. in width and about 21m. in length from the door at one end to the raised *suggestus* at the other, and is covered, except for reserved areas 2m. long at either end, by a marble intaglio pavement. On either side of it, running back to the lateral walls of the building, are three stepped platforms, each approx. 19m. long, the two lower each 1.80m. wide, the upper on the right of the entrance 2.05m. wide, that on the left 2.58m. wide.[1]

In addition, there are two rear doors, one either side of the *suggestus*. In its present state the latter is of only modest elevation, rising approximately to the level of the middle stepped platform at the side. There is no reason to doubt the general belief that Diocletian reproduced in the surviving structure the size and orientation of the Curia Julia. With regard to interior arrangements, however, there can be less certainty overall.

In the first place it is at least clear that the consuls (or other magistrates) did preside over the meeting from a raised platform or tribunal. Thus in 66 Barea Soranus and his daughter are brought to be tried "before the consuls' tribunal,"[2] while in 203 the *Quindecimviri Sacris Faciundis* stand "before the platform of the most exalted consuls."[3] Epictetus can contemptuously enumerate "sitting three or four times on the tribunal"[4] as a privilege of holding the consulship. Dio[5] speaks of the consuls coming down from their seats to talk to Claudius in the body of the House. Similarly Pliny speaks of Trajan as president "stepping down to the floor"[6] to embrace candidates at the elections in 100, while Tiberius reminded the consuls that it was consistent with neither their dignity nor rank to sit in an ordinary place (that is, among the members), as they did on the death

[1] *TAPA* 100. 1969. p. 541. See further Figures 5 and 7 above.
[2] Tac. *Ann.* 16.30.
[3] G. B. Pighi, *De Ludis Saecularibus*, p. 140 I line 5.
[4] 4.10.21.
[5] 60.6.1.
[6] *Paneg.* 71.1.

of Drusus in 23, and previously on that of Augustus in 14.[7] On their tribunal the consuls sat on seats (*sellae curules*) with a third chair for the emperor (whenever he was not consul) in between them.[8] The structure itself must at least have been high enough for them to see over members who might be standing close by.[9]

In 40 a decree was passed that the emperor should sit on so lofty a platform in the House that no one should be able to approach him.[10] This arrangement presumably did not continue after Gaius' death. It would seem that Claudius sat either on the consuls' tribunal or on the tribunes' bench in the body of the House.[11] At trials in the senate and on other great occasions, according to Dio, "he would pronounce the charge seated between the consuls on a *sella curulis* or on a bench; then he would go to his accustomed place [in the body of the House], and *sellae* would be placed for the consuls."[12] At such hearings Claudius presumably intended to indicate by this move that his part would be no more than that of any other member.[13] By the late second century the emperor's seat had possibly become a grand affair: at any rate Herodian can speak of it as a "royal throne."[14] The emperor might invite others to join him, as Elagabalus certainly did when he placed his mother and grandmother on either side of him at the adoption of Alexianus in 221,[15] and as Pertinax presumably did when he asked Claudius Pompeianus and Acilius Glabrio to sit beside him. We may imagine that the bench upon which they sat, according to Dio,[16] was one set on the platform in place of the emperor's chair.

It seems plain enough that in the Republic members had sat on wooden benches, rather than on individual chairs,[17] and we may assume that this

---

[7] Tac. *Ann.* 4.8; Dio 56.31.3.

[8] Dio 54.10.5; cf. Suet. *Galba* 18; Plin. *Paneg.* 61.1. Martial (11.98.17-18) portrays the magistrate sitting in his curule chair on a lofty tribunal laying down the law for the nations— possibly within the senate house, therefore, rather than in a court.

[9] Cf. Plin. *Ep.* 2.11.22.

[10] Dio 59.26.3.

[11] Suet. *Claud.* 23, reading with Mommsen "medius inter consulum sellas tribunicio⟨ve⟩ subsellio sedebat." Cf. Dio 60.6.1. B. M. Levick (*AJP* 99. 1978. p. 89) prefers to retain Suetonius' text unamended: thus in her view Claudius stayed on the tribunal, but had the tribunes' bench specially placed for himself between the consuls, thereby symbolizing his preference for tribunician power. This opinion of his intention is entirely reasonable. Yet it would not be conveyed clearly when (so far as we know) one bench looked much like another. Claudius would surely have made his point much better by sitting with the other tribunes in the body of the House, as Dio indicates.

[12] 60.16.3-4.

[13] See further chap. 16 sect. 1 note 126.

[14] 2.3.3-4. At the meeting in Apuleius, *Metam.* 6.23, Jupiter presides from a "sedes sublimis."

[15] Dio 79.17.2; cf. HA, *Elagab.* 4.2.

[16] 74.3.3.

[17] Note Asconius, p. 33 Clark; Appian, *Bell. Civ.* 2.21.

continued to be the usual practice during the Principate.[18] However their seating was constructed, it no doubt came to feel uncomfortable as sessions wore on, and we may only hope that it was at least fitted with backrests. To some extent members may have occupied regular places. It was definitely the case that certain benches were reserved for at least two colleges of magistrates. Thus we hear of the praetors' bench[19] and the tribunes' bench.[20] The former was presumably close to the tribunal, because on one occasion it was helpful for an elderly senator of unknown rank to be moved to it so that he could hear the proceedings better.[21] More generally, in his description of the first meeting after Augustus' death in 14, Dio can say that "most of the members sat in their accustomed places,"[22] which does suggest that there was a certain regularity about seating arrangements. And, as cited above, Claudius is mentioned as customarily occupying the same place when he sat in the body of the House. Unfortunately, however, there is no further sound evidence about the arrangements. Thus for the imperial period, at any rate, Taylor and Scott[23] assume too readily that *consulares* and *praetorii* did each sit together as groups, occupying the front rows on either side of the central aisle. Even if there had been established conventions previously, we can claim with confidence that they are likely to have undergone change during the first century or more of the Principate, as *consulares* and *praetorii* gradually increased in number and junior senators correspondingly declined.[24] But in fact information that would clarify how the different ranks sat is lacking.[25] For all we know, if (say) *consulares* sat as a group at all, they might have filled a whole block, rather than spreading out along a particular row. Regular groupings of some kind or other could certainly have helped the president when calling for *sententiae* in order, but we find no mention of them, and on many

---

[18] "Sedes" at Plin. *Paneg.* 73.6 could be interpreted as individual chairs, but other evidence would not support this view, and the context is not suitable for strictly literal interpretation. Earlier in the chapter (sect. 2) Pliny uses the vaguer term "vestigium." Contrast Seneca, *De Ira* 2.25.3, "tracti subsellii stridor."

[19] Dio 56.31.3; 60.12.3.

[20] Dio 56.31.3; 60.6.1. Note also an allusive passage in Horace (*Sat.* 1.6.40-41), where the poet imagines one magistrate (cf. lines 38-39, only a magistrate could order executions) saying of another: " 'At Novius collega gradu post me sedet uno:
            namque est ille, pater quod erat meus.' "
The reference has commonly been taken to mean seating in the theater; but it could just as well be to the senate, indicating that one magistrate might sit behind another.

[21] Dio 60.12.3. However, the suggestion of Taylor and Scott (*TAPA* 100. 1969. p. 535), that such benches for magistrates were placed directly in front of the president's tribunal, is not an attractive one, above all because the central aisle would then be blocked.

[22] 56.31.3.

[23] For example, at *TAPA* 100. 1969. p. 545.

[24] Cf. *TAPA* 100. 1969. pp. 550-551 and see further chap. 4 sect. 2.

[25] See further Extended Note B, and note 35 below.

occasions they would anyway have been disrupted by the widespread movement of members about the chamber, which (as we shall see) was so common during debate.

In Diocletian's reconstruction of the Curia there are three stepped platforms running along almost the entire length of the building, on which seating could be placed so that senators faced each other across the wide central aisle. We do not know if such platforms were ever a feature of the Curia Julia, or if the benches were instead arranged so that members sat facing the tribunal, rather than each other. There seems to be no literary reference which would help determine this question,[26] but the Diocletianic arrangement whereby members faced each other is strongly suggested by the assumption in our sources that non-members could gain a reasonable grasp of proceedings from standing at the door of the House.[27] That is likely to have been awkward enough at the best of times, but to do so if all members sat facing the tribunal (and so all spoke with their backs to spectators) would have been well-nigh impossible.

However the benches were arranged, the Curia Julia, like Diocletian's reconstruction, must have incorporated a wide central aisle. If the *Historia Augusta*[28] is to be believed, Caracalla stationed a double line of troops here in between the benches, before addressing members to justify the murder of Geta. In complaining of bad behavior at elections in the senate around the beginning of the second century, Pliny mentions how "everyone rushed forward with his candidate and crowds mingled with small groups of people in the center [of the floor] in disgraceful confusion."[29] A considerable amount of open space was required for any vote to be taken, with supporters and opponents of a motion being instructed to form separate groups within the chamber.[30] The movement required is reflected in the traditional idiomatic expression "pedibus in sententiam ire."[31] Open space in the center is also suggested by frequent movement among senators at earlier stages in the proceedings. We hear of them dashing to and fro between two speakers in their eagerness to catch every word.[32] Before a vote was taken they commonly began to form up in groups for or against

[26] Though the meeting at Apuleius, *Metam.* 6.23, recalls the senate, it cannot be taken as an accurate reflection of Roman practice: it is interesting that the setting is a theater.

[27] See chap. 6 sect. 3.

[28] *Caracalla* 2.9.

[29] *Ep.* 3.20.4.

[30] Plin. *Ep.* 8.14.19-20 and chap. 7 sect. 25.

[31] Literally, "to vote for a proposal with the feet." For use by authors of our period see, for example, Seneca, *Apocol.* 11.6; Tac. *Ann.* 14.49. For figurative use of the idiom, note Apuleius, *Metam.* 2.7; 6.32.

[32] Plin. *Ep.* 6.5.5. Arguably, these restless members were spurred on more by the excitement which had developed over an acrimonious issue than by any serious defect in the acoustic qualities of the chamber, treated below.

a motion, and might change from one to the other if they felt persuaded by arguments raised as the debate proceeded.[33] As Tiberius' letter to the senate on 18 October 31 was being read out, some of those sitting near Sejanus stood up and moved.[34] On another occasion, after Pliny had spoken first by special permission, a consular remonstrated with him before it was his turn to speak again in order.[35] In much the same way Hercules, in Seneca's parody,[36] runs here and there during the debate seeking to raise individuals' support for a motion which he fears will be lost. When Claudius was present at a session where it seemed likely that there would be approval for a motion to punish those who had broken an ancient ban on any remuneration for legal services, inculpated members crowded round the emperor, urging forgiveness of the past.[37] Though members commonly stood up in their places to address the House, they might instead speak from the central aisle.[38] So far as we can tell, however, there was never any separate tribune or desk from which they might do this, having left their own places.

The arrangements made to accommodate non-members who had to attend sessions are largely hidden from us. It is not known where the shorthand writers sat in our period, nor where advocates, plaintiffs, and witnesses were placed at trials. Referring to the trial of Arvandus in 469, Sidonius Apollinaris[39] speaks of plaintiff and defendant, with their accompanying groups, ranged opposite one another in the House. This would be the natural arrangement, but we cannot say whether it reflected earlier practice. As defendants, Barea Soranus and his daughter were certainly required to stand "before the consuls' tribunal," and were kept far enough apart for lictors to stop them embracing.[40] When the *Quindecimviri Sacris Faciundis* approached the House as a college in 203, they stood "before the platform of the most exalted consuls," as mentioned above, and presumably all envoys would do the same. In other words, defendants, envoys, and other non-members too no doubt, must have faced the president with their backs to the entrance. It is hardly to be imagined that they stood facing the body of the House, with their backs to the president. Thus it would have been especially difficult for non-members on the threshold to catch their words.

[33] Plin. *Ep.* 2.11.22.

[34] Dio 58.10.4. The fact that this happened at a session on the Palatine does not affect the general demonstration of movement at meetings.

[35] *Ep.* 9.13.10-12. I assume that the consular had to move in order to deliver his warning. Of course, if he did not, then we might have evidence for two members of different rank sitting close to one another from the start of a meeting.

[36] *Apocol.* 9.6.

[37] Tac. *Ann.* 11.6. He does not state where Claudius was sitting at this session.

[38] See, for example, Dio 60.16.5; 76.8.6; Josephus, *AJ* 19.261.

[39] *Ep.* 1.7.9.

[40] Tac. *Ann.* 16.30 and 32.

Of course we have no idea of the acoustic qualities of the Curia Julia, although it is worth noting that, whether by accident or design, the dimensions of the existing building do conform approximately to those recommended by Vitruvius[41] as calculated to render speakers most easily audible: namely, that where a senate house is oblong, the interior height should be half its combined length and breadth. As we have seen, Diocletian's Curia is approximately 26 meters long and 18 meters wide, while its height to the ceiling is 23 meters. We cannot say whether the original facings of the interior also incorporated a cornice half way up all around, as Vitruvius further recommended.

As a lofty structure the Curia Julia is likely to have remained tolerably cool in summer, but could no doubt prove freezing cold in winter. Under the latter circumstances any opportunity to move about the chamber, rather than stay seated, must have been welcome. Thus trial sessions—which occurred commonly enough in winter, were lengthy almost by definition, and provided members with very limited opportunity for movement—would have proved especially arduous. There is no evidence that the House was heated, nor would there have been much gain from any heating system when the doors had to remain open during sessions and birds might even fly in and out.[42] At least, however, there is no incident known for our period similar to that on 12 February 54 B.C., when in response to members' protests about the cold the consul agreed to dismiss the meeting he had summoned![43] Equally, if Diocletian's Curia reproduces the windows of the Curia Julia, then the latter was reasonably well lit, with three above the main doors, and one high up in the center of each of the other three sides. We may imagine that confinement of the windows to this elevation was intended in part to reduce distraction from the ceaseless hubbub of the city which must always have enveloped the Curia, especially during the mornings when work was done. Windows here also offered the chance of drawing light even from the long side to the left of the tribunal, where the Argiletum formed only a narrow passageway between the Curia and the Basilica Aemilia. Unlike today, the interior walls would also have been faced and, as we shall see, there would have been decoration to add brightness. On the other hand a portico beyond the main doors (if there was one, as seems likely) would not have helped to make the chamber lighter, nor would the presence of spectators crowded on the threshold.

[41] *De Arch.* 5.2.

[42] Dio 78.37.5.

[43] Cic. *Ad Q. Fr.* 2.11.1 = SB 15; A. W. Lintott, "Popular justice in a letter of Cicero to Quintus," *Rhein. Mus.* 110. 1967. pp. 65-69 fails to convince fully when he argues that the "cold" here is only metaphorical. For the generally unhealthy winter climate in Rome, note Suet. *Aug.* 72.

We hear of Augustus posting up proposals on boards in the senate house for members to read, and also of lampoons against him being scattered around there.[44] A proposal that the decree of 22 conferring *tribunicia potestas* on Drusus be set up in the House in letters of gold was treated by members with derision, and marked out for censure by Tiberius.[45] Yet the Curia Julia was decorated by a number of monuments and dedications, presumably placed away from the central aisle. A golden shield in honor of Augustus' "clementia, iustitia, pietas" was set up in 27 B.C., and was joined by golden shields and spears of Gaius and Lucius.[46] Shields set up in honor of Domitian were torn down on his assassination in 96.[47] Augustus himself placed at least two pictures in the House, which we know of from the Elder Pliny's descriptions.[48] Augustus' name was also inscribed in the Curia Julia, and a statue of him had been placed there by 14.[49] So it is tempting to think that Hadrian is referring to decoration of the senate house itself in the oration quoted by Charisius: "I ask you, Conscript Fathers, and I am particularly keen to gain your consent that very close to the statue of Augustus you should preferably place a silver shield likewise in honor of Augustus."[50]

Statues of others were set up, too, though how long they were allowed to remain of course is not always clear.[51] After Agrippina's murder in 59 it was proposed that golden statues of Minerva and Nero be set up in the chamber.[52] Commodus is said by Herodian[53] to have deliberately tried to frighten members by erecting in front of the House a statue of himself as an archer with a bow stretched ready to shoot; this statue was removed after his death and replaced with one of Liberty. Elagabalus had an enormous picture of himself hung over the statue of *Victoria* inside,[54] while Maximinus had similarly huge pictures of his German battles set up in front of the House; these were later torn down by the senate.[55]

In prominence and fame this statue of *Victoria* outdid all other monu-

---

[44] Dio 55.4.1; Suet. *Aug.* 55.

[45] Tac. *Ann.* 3.57 and 59.

[46] *RG* 34.2; Dio 55.12.1; for what may have been intended as a copy of the shield in honor of Augustus, found at Arles, see F. Benoit, "Le sanctuaire d' Auguste et les cryptoportiques d' Arles," *Rev. Arch.* 39. 1952. pp. 31-67 and figure 11.

[47] Suet. *Dom.* 23.

[48] *NH* 35.27-28 and 131.

[49] *RG* 35.1; Tac. *Ann.* 1.11.

[50] *Art. Gramm.* II p. 287 Barwick.

[51] Drusilla, Dio 59.11.2; Domitian, Suet. *Dom.* 23; M. Aurelius, Dio 71.34.1; Septimius Severus, Dio 78.37.5.

[52] Tac. *Ann.* 14.12.

[53] 1.14.9-15.1.

[54] Herodian 5.5.7.

[55] Herodian 7.2.8; HA, *Maximin.* 12.10.

ments in the House.[56] It was brought to Rome from Tarentum at some stage, dedicated in the Curia Julia by Octavian on 28 August 29 B.C.,[57] and was still there in Dio's time and long beyond.[58] The description of it by Prudentius[59] tallies with that of statues which appear on Augustan coins.[60] Its size is not known, though it cannot have been too cumbersome if it was to head Augustus' funeral procession.[61] What appear to be remains of its pedestal have been found at the rear of the tribunal,[62] and there seems no sound reason to doubt that this was where it stood. Herodian[63] must be inaccurate when he suggests that it stood in the very middle of the chamber. With the statue was associated an altar. In the passage just cited Herodian explains how it was at the former that members made their offerings and libation on entering the chamber.[64] So it would seem most natural for the altar to be below the statue, a notion perhaps supported from the action of Barea Soranus' daughter, who, called "before the consuls' tribunal" and interrogated, first clasped "altaria et aram" before replying.[65]

We may conclude that in the Curia Julia, its one purpose-built meeting place, the senate was provided with a structure at once impressive, centrally situated, and altogether likely to add dignity to its proceedings. The chamber, too, seems to have been well enough designed and equipped by contemporary standards. Finally, as we shall see, there is reason to believe that the seating available and the customary level of attendance were suitably matched, at least into the early second century.

3. Senate House Staff

Almost nothing is known of the staff who maintained the House and were in attendance at sessions. From the delay which senators had to face after the deaths of Titus and Commodus while waiting for the building to be unlocked during the night, we gather that there was a custodian (*aedituus*)

---

[56] For a summary of the work on it, see H. A. Pohlsander, "Victory: the story of a statue," *Historia* 18. 1969. pp. 588-597.

[57] *EJ*, Calendars p. 51.

[58] Cf. Dio 51.22.1-2.

[59] *Contra Orat. Sym.* 2.27-38.

[60] References in Platner-Ashby, p. 144.

[61] Suet. *Aug.* 100.

[62] See A. Bartoli, *Curia Senatus*, p. 57.

[63] 5.5.7.

[64] On this ceremonial see chap. 7 sect. 2.

[65] Tac. *Ann.* 16.31. Whether he means this expression to be taken as literally more than one structure is not clear. For discussion of Herodian's unacceptable testimony on the location of the altar, see Extended Note C.

who kept the key and lived off the premises.[1] The House was likewise found locked before a meeting during Augustus' last illness, and by Didius Julianus after the death of Pertinax.[2] There must also presumably have been attendants to look after the water-clocks for use at trials, to bring in lamps, to distribute *tabellae* when these were used for voting at elections during Trajan's reign,[3] and to place furniture in position.[4] These attendants were perhaps the *servi publici* who, according to the *Historia Augusta*,[5] were normally present at sessions together with *scribae* and *censuales*. The function of the latter, who are never mentioned elsewhere for our period, is unknown. The former presumably had clerical duties, which perhaps included helping with the important job of keeping a tally of the members present.[6] Their aid might be enlisted, too, whenever an accurate count was made of members voting for and against a particular *sententia*.[7] In addition to *scribae*, one or more shorthand writers (*notarii*) must have been present from fairly early on in our period, though they are mentioned only in Seneca's parody of a meeting.[8] Two undatable bronze collars for runaway slaves mention as owners an *exceptor senatus* ("copyist"),[9] and, if an uncertain supplement is accepted, a *scriniarius senatus* ("keeper of *scrinia*," or boxes where scrolls would be stored).[10]

Defendants brought from prison to the senate for trial[11] must have been escorted by lictors, and the latter apparently remained during the hearing to keep their prisoners in custody. Thus when the *eques* Vibulenus Agrippa swallowed poison and collapsed in the House itself after a case against him had been completed, he was rushed to prison by lictors.[12] During the trial of Barea Soranus and his daughter in 66, the father tried to move across to embrace his daughter at one point, but lictors kept them apart.[13] In 24 the senator Vibius Serenus, brought back from exile, had to stand trial in chains, so he must have had an escort of some description.[14]

Lictors do not seem to have been present during debates, as they were at trials, and the presiding magistrate evidently had no one at his disposal

---

[1] Cf. Suet. *Tit.* 11; Eutrop. *Brev.* 7.22; HA, *Pert.* 4.9.
[2] Dio 56.29.3; HA, *Did. Jul.* 2.4.
[3] See Plin. *Ep.* 2.11.14; 4.9.14; 3.20; 4.25 respectively.
[4] Note the omen of Galba's chair, Suet. *Galba* 18.
[5] *Gord.* 12.3. It should be noted that the general reliability of this passage is doubtful.
[6] Cf. Dio 55.3.4.
[7] See chap. 7 sect. 25.
[8] *Apocol.* 9.2. See further chap. 9 sect. 3 note 50.
[9] *ILS* 8726; cf. 1958.
[10] *ILS* 8728, "serv. sum Leonti scrin. s."
[11] We are specifically informed that Asilius Sabinus, for example, was so brought (Seneca, *Controv.* 9.4.20).
[12] Tac. *Ann.* 6.40.
[13] Tac. *Ann.* 16.32.
[14] Tac. *Ann.* 4.28.

whom he could call upon to help maintain order. This lack of a Serjeant-at-Arms or any equivalent officer can be seen as one manifestation among many of the president's weak position.[15] Senators who feared that their safety was threatened in some way during a meeting might appeal direct to the tribunes for aid. Thus Vitellius made such an appeal in 69 when he felt insulted by Helvidius Priscus.[16] After Domitian's death Fabricius Veiento likewise appealed to the aid of tribunes (with scant success) when opposing Pliny's attack on Publicius Certus.[17] When order ("disciplina curiae")[18] had to be maintained, magistrates acted themselves—though how much on their own initiative, and how much at the president's instigation, we cannot say. Praetors and tribunes certainly acted to ensure that Sejanus did not leave while Tiberius' letter was being read out on 18 October 31.[19] And tribunes actually arrested Helvidius when he would not stop reviling the emperor Vespasian to his face. Helvidius was then handed over to their assistants.[20] If the House looked in danger of becoming uncontrollable, as a last resort the president could always dismiss the session, as he did when Fabricius Veiento persisted in trying to reply to Pliny's attack on Publicius Certus.[21]

Magistrates in person might also convey senatorial decisions requiring action. It was tribunes themselves who brought Claudius the message that he was required to attend the senate after Gaius' murder.[22] In particular, praetors and quaestors are heard of conveying death warrants and supervising the executions. It was very natural that this task should fall to a *quaestor consulis*, as the *aide-de-camp* of the presiding magistrate in the senate.[23]

[15] See further chap. 7 sect. 23.
[16] Tac. *Hist*. 2.91; Dio 65.7.2.
[17] Plin. *Ep*. 9.13.19.
[18] Seneca, *Apocol*. 9.1.
[19] Dio 58.10.5.
[20] Dio 66.12.1. For a tribune's right to compel silence, cf. Plin. *Ep*. 1.23.2; 9.13.19. For tribunes' assistants, cf. Dio 54.36.1, where they are said to have been inefficient in helping the tribunes and aediles to preserve decrees; see also 60.12.2.
[21] Plin. *Ep*. 9.13.20.
[22] Suet. *Claud*. 10.
[23] Tac. *Ann*. 2.34; Dio 58.3.3 (praetor); 58.4.6 (quaestor); Tac. *Ann*. 16.34 (quaestor consulis). For the presence of soldiers and of members' personal attendants during sessions, see chap. 4 sect. 4.

4

ATTENDANCE

This chapter examines the important matter of attendance at meetings of the senate. Naturally the attendance of senators themselves forms the core of the discussion, not least because the widespread assumption that they were generally slack in this respect merits considerable modification. Linked with this major section are two shorter ones on the total number of senators, and on their retirement age. The chapter concludes with a treatment of the circumstances in which non-members might gain admittance to the chamber during sessions. Special attention is paid to the presence of soldiers and women. Attendance by the emperor is covered separately in the following chapter.

1. The Total Number of Senators

Information on this key point is predictably thin, though it is quite clear that Augustus did take steps to reduce the number of senators to well below the total which it had reached under Caesar's dictatorship and during the subsequent civil war. Dio[1] says that when Augustus began his work of reduction in 29 B.C., the total was 1,000; Suetonius[2] puts it over that figure. The senate had swollen to this size, partly because of large-scale adlections by Caesar himself, which took the numbers up to 900,[3] and partly because after his death others succeeded in having themselves adlected "through influence and bribery."[4] In addition, by increasing the number of quaestorships from 20 to 40,[5] Caesar doubled the number of members elected each year, since the magistracy effectively carried with it a seat in the senate for life.

In 29 B.C. Augustus removed 190 members by one means or another.[6] Dio claims that in 18 B.C. he planned to cut the senate to as few as 300

[1] 52.42.1.
[2] *Aug.* 35.
[3] Cf. Dio 43.47.2.
[4] Suet. *Aug.* 35.
[5] Dio 43.47.2.
[6] Dio 52.42.2.

members, its size in "olden days,"[7] but in the end he bowed to pressure against so drastic a reduction, and enrolled 600 or so members—removing about 200, in other words. The plan may be viewed variously as antiquarian folly or as a subtle step towards more sweeping changes never made. Certainly the military and administrative posts reserved for senators could only have continued to be filled with the greatest strain on a total of 300 members,[8] and the number left to attend meetings would have slumped. Dio[9] mentions two further revisions of the roll by Augustus, in 13 B.C. and again just two years later in 11. He may, however, have misunderstood his sources in recording the former; alternatively it is possible that these two revisions are really one and the same, begun in 13 but not finished until 11.[10] Augustus himself in *Res Gestae*[11] claims to have revised the roll only three times. Dio[12] mentions a final revision in the reign, entrusted to a commission of senators in A.D. 4, though he specifically notes that there was no severe reduction on this occasion. It would appear therefore that during the reign the total membership was reduced to about 600—in other words, to approximately the size of the Sullan senate. Almost certainly this figure was just a notional optimum, not a fixed maximum or fixed total.

Unfortunately, after Augustus' reign no source offers any figure for the total number of senators, while the only known later reviews of the roll are those carried out by Claudius and Vespasian as censors. It is clear that the normal means of entry remained through the twenty annual vacancies in the quaestorship, usually gained by men around the age of 25. Since this fixed number of entrants came to be recruited over an increasingly wide area, it is a fair assumption that in general there did continue to be sufficient enthusiasm on the part of those qualified for all twenty vacancies to be filled each year. That said, we do have two reasons to reckon that a slight shortfall might sometimes occur. First, when there were no more vacancies for the Vigintivirate (which had to be held beforehand) than for the quaestorship, a slight natural shortfall among holders of the latter office was only to be expected from time to time, caused by the occasional man dying prematurely in the interval after he had held the Vigintivirate and before he was to stand for the quaestorship. The length of that interval was variable, but it could be as many as six years or so.[13] Second, according

---

[7] 54.14.1.

[8] For the number of such posts, see sect. 2 below.

[9] 54.26.8 and 35.1.

[10] For these arguments see respectively A.H.M. Jones, *Studies in Roman Government and Law*, Oxford, 1960, pp. 22-23; A. E. Astin, "Augustus and 'Censoria Potestas,' " *Latomus* 22. 1963. pp. 226-235, in sect. IA.

[11] 8.2.

[12] 55.13.3.

[13] See J. Morris, *List. Fil.* 87. 1964. p. 321.

to Dio,[14] there were some years in which insufficient quaestors were available to fill the posts occupied by these magistrates, so that quaestors from the previous year had to serve a second term. He gives no details, but we can point to a number of individuals spread over our period who do appear to have served two terms, or even three, no doubt for this reason among others.[15] It is notable that from the mid first century the need to call upon them thus would indicate a shortfall of at least four quaestors in each year concerned, since after that date there were never more than seventeen posts to be occupied regularly by the twenty magistrates.[16] Yet from the same period any such occasional shortfall in the corporate body's numbers would come to be compensated for elsewhere by adlected members, while in any event we have no strong cause to think that there was ever a serious or persistent lack of quaestors. This minor difficulty aside, therefore, to maintain total membership at 600 it would be necessary for twenty entrants annually aged around 25 to have an average life expectancy of 30 years. Demographically speaking, that is apparently a plausible expectation. We lack Roman figures of course, but the notion is consistent with evidence for European ruling families and British ducal families in the sixteenth and seventeenth centuries.[17]

The conjecture that total membership of the senate remained at around 600 will at least not conflict with related evidence available to us. As we shall see, surviving figures for attendance at individual meetings guarantee that there were over 500 active senators in the mid first century at the most cautious estimate. Equally, having counted the number of senators known in each reign during the first two centuries, Hammond[18] reached totals in 1959 ranging from a maximum of 483 under Augustus to a minimum of 243 under Commodus. Then, as we have already noted, the number of recruits brought into the senate by adlection (above the twenty quaestors

---

[14] 57.16.1; cf. 53.28.4; and more generally 58.20.4.

[15] To the eight listed by A. R. Birley, *The Fasti of Roman Britain*, p. 282, add *ILS* 8842; *ILS* 1002 with E. Groag, *PW* 8 A s.v. Tullius no. 56, cols. 1325-1326. The second quaestorship attributed to M. Vettius Valens in *CIL* XI. 383 is likely to represent a stonecutter's error (cf. R. Hanslik, *PW* 8 A s.v. Vettius no. 52, col. 1869). Recruitment difficulties aside, second quaestorships may equally have been made necessary by, say, premature deaths of colleagues or some temporary crisis: thus, very remarkably, at one session of the House in 217 not a single quaestor could be present (Dio 78.16.4). For what appears to be a triple quaestorship, perhaps late in Hadrian's reign, see *PIR*[2] I 391 = H. Halfmann, *Die Senatoren*, no. 83.

[16] See chap. 1 sect. 2. My figure of seventeen assumes only two *quaestores Caesaris*. The question of whether Sicily continued to merit two quaestors, as in the late Republic, rather than the normal one, must remain open for lack of evidence: but Birley (*The Fasti of Roman Britain*, p. 12 n. 6) may be right to doubt the continuance of two there.

[17] See K. Hopkins, *Death and Renewal*, chap. 2 (forthcoming).

[18] M. Hammond, *The Antonine Monarchy*, p. 254; see further, idem, "Composition of the senate A.D. 68-235," *JRS* 47. 1957. pp. 74-81.

each year) was always small. For the first century we know of only three adlections by Claudius,[19] upwards of twenty by Vespasian,[20] and two by Domitian. For the whole of the second century—between 96 and 192— we know of only thirty-five adlections.[21] Naturally these figures are likely to be raised by new discoveries: but it would take an unprecedented wave of finds to alter the impression that adlection made only a slight impact upon the total membership.

Barbieri[22] collected evidence for known senators in the reigns of Septimius Severus and Caracalla, and on the basis of identifying up to 604 members for certain together with 333 possible ones, he argued for a marked rise in membership during these reigns. But his claim will not hold. Starting with, say, a possible 600 members in 193, and adding twenty quaestors each year until 217, we should expect there to be at least 1,080 names, even without allowing for adlections and the possibility of a rapid turnover in membership during such unstable times. So there is no compelling reason to believe that the total did rise above 600. After 217 the evidence is too thin to produce any helpful figures on membership.[23] But altogether, allowing for the many uncertainties which surround the question, we shall probably not err too seriously if we imagine that the number of senators remained around 600 after the revisions of Augustus.

2. Members' Attendance

By tradition a conscientious senator considered it his duty to attend sessions. "In the first place I assert that a good senator should always attend the House," claimed Cicero.[1] Making the same point elsewhere, he adds:

---

[19] CIL X. 6520; AE 1925. 85; ILS 968. On the last, see further G. Alföldy, "Ein Senator aus Vicetia," ZPE 39. 1980. pp. 255-266. A fourth possibility is conjectured by A. Chastagnol in Studien zur antiken Sozialgeschichte: Festschrift F. Vittinghoff, p. 270 n. 2.

[20] See G. W. Houston, "Vespasian's adlection of men in senatum," AJP 98. 1977. pp. 35-63; J. Devreker, "L'adlectio in senatum de Vespasien," Latomus 39. 1980. pp. 70-87. R. Syme (HSCP 73. 1969. p. 228 = Roman Papers II pp. 766-767) may seem a little rash in asserting that Tacitus' description of P. Licinius Caecina (PIR² L 178) as "novus adhuc et in senatum nuper adscitus" (Hist. 2.53) must mean that he was adlected to membership by Galba.

[21] See A. Chastagnol, BHAC 1975/6. pp. 116-118; for equites adlected as either aedilicii or tribunicii note further H.-G. Pflaum, "La carrière de C. Iulius Avitus Alexianus, grand'père de deux empereurs," Rev. Et. Lat. 57. 1979. pp. 298-314 at pp. 302-305.

[22] G. Barbieri, L'albo senatorio da Settimio Severo a Carino (193-285), Rome, 1952, pp. 415-419. See also G. Alföldy, "Septimius Severus und der Senat," Bonn. Jahrb. 168. 1968. pp. 112-160.

[23] See further K. Dietz, Senatus contra principem: Untersuchungen zur senatorischen Opposition gegen Kaiser Maximinus Thrax, Vestigia 29, Munich, 1980.

[1] De Domo 8.

"for a full attendance adds dignity to the senate's deliberation."[2] Of course senators had always come out of mutual obligation, and continued to do so. Friends and relatives helped each other, and "one good turn deserves another," as Hercules reminded fellow members when he needed support for the *sententia* he favored in Seneca's parody.[3] For the same reason Pliny[4] specially apologizes for having to miss the meeting on 1 September 107 when his friend C. Valerius Paulinus will be taking up the suffect consulship.

But there likewise persisted a sense of duty which ran far deeper. A Roman of suitable standing and inclination considered that it was his destiny to serve the state in public life, and for a senator attendance in the House was regarded as an integral part of that service. Such a sense of duty emerges most strongly from the dialogue between Vespasian and Helvidius Priscus written by Epictetus: "When Vespasian sent him word not to attend a meeting of the senate, he answered 'It is in your power not to allow me to be a member of the senate, but so long as I am one I must attend its meetings.' "[5] In 66 one of the principal complaints lodged against Thrasea Paetus by Cossutianus Capito was that "he has not entered the senate house for three years."[6] Nero took up this particular point in the *oratio* which he sent to the senate: "Without mentioning any names he rebuked members for neglecting their public duties and setting the *equites* a slovenly example. What wonder (he wrote) if senators from distant provinces stayed away, when many consulars and priests showed greater devotion to the embellishment of their gardens?"[7]

Thrasea's accusers seized the weapon which this *oratio* gave them, and pressed the charge of non-attendance.[8] The reference to absenteeism by senators from "distant provinces" which Tacitus puts into Nero's mouth is perhaps more appropriate to the historian's own time in the early second century than to the 60's, when the number of members from distant areas had still to grow beyond a mere handful.[9] Yet Nero's rebuke highlights

[2] *De Legibus* 3.40.

[3] *Apocol.* 9.6.

[4] *Ep.* 9.37.1 with Sherwin-White ad loc.; cf. 4.17.6.

[5] 1.2.19.

[6] Tac. *Ann.* 16.22.

[7] Tac. *Ann.* 16.27. Compare how in Tacitus' version of the speech where he asks for Nero's leave to retire, Seneca refers deprecatingly to the gardens and villas with which he is so preoccupied (*Ann.* 14.53 and 54). For meetings of the *equites* as a corporate body, see briefly A. E. Gordon, *Quintus Veranius Consul 49 A.D.*, California, 1952, p. 259 n. 88.

[8] Tac. *Ann.* 16.28; cf. Dio 62.26.3.

[9] Clearly Nero's outburst is an emotional attack made to urge Thrasea's downfall. The emperor's point is not to be pressed, nor can "distant" ("longinquus") be defined. But there is no question that the number of provincials from areas more distant than Gaul and Spain was tiny at this stage: see further chap. 1 sect. 4. For similar exaggeration on the provenance of senators, note Tac. *Hist.* 1.84; 4.74.

how fear of offending the emperor acted as a fresh spur to senators' attendance during our period. Under an evil ruler, this new, negative reason could on occasion prove more powerful than traditional, positive ones. Thus Dio explains why he and others were prompted to attend the first meeting called after Didius Julianus had seized power in 193:

As for us senators, when the news was brought to each of us individually and we realized the situation, we were gripped by fear of Julianus and the soldiers, especially all of us who had done any favors for Pertinax or anything to displease Julianus. I was one of these, for I had received various honors from Pertinax, including the praetorship, and when acting as advocate for others at trials I had frequently proved Julianus to be guilty of many offenses. All the same we made our appearance, not least because it struck us as unsafe to remain at home, in case such action might in itself arouse suspicion.[10]

Senators' absenteeism during the Principate was no new problem.[11] But in contrast to the Republic there was now an emperor who could exert pressure to combat it. Though few of them genuinely sought Tiberius' ideal of a well-attended senate which would play a full, independent part in government, it remained important to the standing of all sane emperors that attendance be kept up. The senate represented continuity and tradition, and it alone legitimized the position and measures of the emperor.[12] Most rulers of our period, no less than the members of the Second Triumvirate earlier,[13] were eager for such approval to be bestowed in due form. Thus in extreme circumstances for a senator to attend the House casually or not at all might amount to contempt for the emperor himself. In the various descriptions of Thrasea's accusers, such conduct was "secession," "party warfare," "war," "treachery," "hostility."[14] Significantly, it was to the emperor, rather than to the consuls, that members' apologies or excuses for absence were regularly made.

If we move now to efforts by individual emperors in turn, Augustus' difficulties in securing a good attendance were considerable. While many of his measures served to enhance the dignity of the senate in the long term, inevitably his *lectiones senatus* sapped members' confidence and morale in the short term. For older members it was awkward to adjust to a new regime, while the preparatory work of the senatorial *consilium* was

---

[10] 74.12.2-3. For fear and hatred of Julianus, cf. Dio 74.12.5.

[11] For poor attendance in the Republic, see A. O'Brien Moore, *PW* Suppl. 6 s.v. senatus, col. 705.

[12] Cf. Otho's speech in Tac. *Hist*. 1.84.

[13] See F. Millar, "Triumvirate and Principate," *JRS* 63. 1973. pp. 50-67.

[14] Tac. *Ann*. 16. 22 and 28.

no doubt felt to infringe seriously upon the discussion of issues laid before
the House. Its lapse in Tiberius' reign must have been welcome.

Dio[15] tells us that when Augustus revised the senatorial roll in 11 B.C.
he abandoned the rule in force at the time that no decree could be passed
with fewer than 400 senators present. With total membership now standing
at no more than 600 or so, and meetings apparently sometimes poorly
attended, it is understandable that a quorum as high as 400 may have been
proving an obstacle to the passage of decrees. Two years later, in 9 B.C.,
Augustus regulated members' attendance among many other matters in a
Lex Julia de senatu habendo.[16] At the same time as he introduced the
innovation that meetings should be held on fixed days free from other
official business,[17] he laid down different quorums for different kinds of
business; stipulated heavier fines for members who were absent from sessions without excuse; and arranged for the names of all senators to be
posted on a board.[18]

Quorums were no novelty, though under Augustus' arrangements they
perhaps came to be stipulated for a wider variety of business than hitherto.[19]
As a result, the number of senators present for practically every kind of
business was now to be counted accurately (except when the emperor
attended in person), and this practice remained in force throughout our
period.[20] The number was recorded at the end of *senatus consulta*.[21] We
have no detailed knowledge of the types or sizes of quorums introduced
by Augustus, except that the senatorial decree of which he sent a copy to
Cyrene in 4 B.C. stipulated a quorum of no fewer than 200 when a committee to hear cases of extortion was being chosen.[22] As we shall see,

---

[15] 54.35.1. This quorum perhaps dated from Caesar's dictatorship, as Mommsen, *St. R.*
III. 2. p. 990 n. 3 suggested.

[16] See chap. 7 sect. 1.

[17] See further chap. 6 sect. 4.

[18] See further chap. 1 sect. 2.

[19] In the late Republic, "frequens senatus" probably came to acquire the technical meaning
of a meeting at which there would be business on the agenda requiring the presence of a
quorum (see J.P.V.D. Balsdon, *JRS* 47. 1957. pp. 18-20). After 9 B.C., when the *Lex Julia*
stipulated quorums for such a wide range of business, that technicality perhaps lost its point,
and "frequens / infrequens senatus" arguably came to signify no more than a well-/ill-
attended session. Note how in a bombastic despatch after his German expedition Gaius ordered
the courier to deliver the letter to the consuls "frequente senatu" (Suet. *Calig.* 44).

[20] For examples with specific figures, see below. For a general reference, Plin. *Paneg.*
76.2. Note also Calpurnius Siculus, *Buc.* 1.71 Verdière, "numerabit," with note 50 below
for dating.

[21] See further chap. 9 sect. 1. Presumably it was the number here which was most likely
to have indicated to Tiberius on Capri that a decree of which he disapproved had been passed
at a poorly attended session in 32 (Tac. *Ann.* 6.12).

[22] *FIRA*[2] I no. 68 V lines 106-107. For a quorum of the same size introduced in 67 B.C.,
Asconius, *In Cornelian.* p. 59 C.

there should have been no difficulty in ensuring such an attendance at that period and for long afterwards.[23] If the *Historia Augusta*[24] can be believed, a quorum of only seventy was sufficient to pass a *senatus consultum* by the reign of Severus Alexander.

In the surviving evidence for our period there is no occasion where the matter of a quorum is raised by any member. Festus' entry under the heading "Numera senatum"[25] explains that it was possible for business to be obstructed by a call to have the House "counted out," and instances of this demand are known from the late Republic.[26] It may well have remained possible for any member to invoke a count in our period, especially when quorums were such a feature of Augustus' arrangements. At the same time it is hardly surprising that we never hear of an instance.

Presiding magistrates had long possessed the right, first to require in advance the attendance of a senator at a specified meeting, and second to fine an absentee afterwards.[27] There is scant indication, however, that these rights were being exercised in the normal course of procedure by late Republican times. Even in polemic, Cicero[28] is no doubt correct in representing as quite unusual and unwarranted Antony's demand that he attend the meeting on the day before the *First Philippic* was delivered in 44 B.C. According to Gellius, the matters which M. Varro discussed in the handbook prepared by him for Pompey's entry to the senate in 70 B.C. did include "the imposition of a fine upon a senator who was not present when it was his duty to attend a meeting."[29] Since Varro's book was intended for practical use, we might conclude that fines were still being exacted during the late Republic. But further evidence is lacking, and it may be rather that the passage merely reflects Varro's antiquarian bent.

Thus, as so often, Augustus was reviving a lapsed ancient practice, rather than introducing a complete novelty, when in 17 B.C., according to Dio, he sought to improve poor attendance on the part of members by increasing the fines "for those who missed meetings without some good excuse."[30] By 9 B.C., when the *Lex Julia de senatu habendo* was passed, these fines were evidently not being enforced, partly because the number

---

[23] It is true that the *Tabula Hebana* of 19/20 (*EJ* 94a lines 33-34) makes provision for the contingency that no senator or *eques*, or fewer than five (?), might be present to represent a tribe in the *destinatio* procedure. But this clause is just part of an attempt to cover every eventuality; it cannot be used to suggest that generally speaking only a limited number of senators might be available.

[24] *Sev. Alex.* 16.1.

[25] P. 174 L.

[26] See Cic. *Ad Att.* 5.4.2 = SB 97; *Ad Fam.* 8.11.2 = SB 91.

[27] Cf. Livy 3.38.

[28] *Phil.* 1.11-12.

[29] 14.7.10.

[30] 54.18.3; see further chap. 7 sect. 24 note 14.

of members liable to punishment was so high. Augustus now increased further the fines for those who were absent without some good excuse. But he expected that the number of absentees would remain high, and that the law would consequently prove awkward to enforce. So an arrangement was made that if many were guilty they should draw lots, and one out of every five should be fined.[31] We have no evidence on enforcement of this regulation thereafter by Augustus or his successors. We may only note the tremendous stir caused by the officious praetor of 105, Licinius Nepos, when he sought to fine a senator for failure to appear on a jury.[32] (The unfortunate absentee had to plead his case before the senate, where his plea for pardon was granted.) Though a *quaestio* is not the senate, the shock produced by Nepos' action could suggest that fines for non-attendance at the latter were by now unheard of. Altogether, the reintroduction of fines by Augustus is perhaps best dismissed as a clumsy, antiquarian revival which predictably failed.

It evidently remained the right of a presiding magistrate in our period to require in advance the attendance of a senator at a specified meeting— yet examples of its use are rare. However, Dio[33] says that Augustus *forced* Lepidus to attend meetings, while in the confusion after Gaius' murder in 41, tribunes brought Claudius the message that he was *required* to attend the senate (in vain).[34] When the senate sat as a court, senators, like any other persons, could naturally always be summoned to appear.[35]

Although *legationes liberae* (that is, travel warrants entitling the bearer to treatment reserved for government officials) had commonly been granted to senators in the late Republic, a reaction set in against their abuse, and only one such grant can be cited for our period, allowed by the senate contrary to Tiberius' wishes.[36] Members were restricted not only in this way: Augustus also reaffirmed the rule that any senator who wished to leave Italy should gain permission. Such applications had always been handled by the senate, but as early as 29 B.C., according to Dio,[37] Augustus

[31] Dio 55.3.3.

[32] Plin. *Ep.* 4.29; see further chap. 16 sect. 1 note 24.

[33] 54.15.5.

[34] Suet. *Claud.* 10. Note how in the fictitious meeting at Apuleius, *Metam.* 6.23, Jupiter requires the gods to attend a heavenly council on pain of a fine of 10,000 *nummi*.

[35] Cf., for example, Plin. *Ep.* 2.11.9 and 12.2.

[36] Suet. *Tib.* 31. For general references, cf. *Dig.* 50.1.22.6; 50.7.15. For *commeatus* as equivalent to *legatio libera*, Cic. Schol. Bob. p. 107 Stangl. Regulations concerning the provision of transport for official use by Sagalassus in Pisidia early in Tiberius' reign may be admitting the possibility of a *legatio libera* when they stipulate an entitlement for "senator populi Romani," though it does then seem odd that such a man should be placed within the general category of "militantes" (*JRS* 66. 1976. pp. 107-108 = *SEG* 26. 1976/7. no. 1392 lines 17-19 and 41-43).

[37] 52.42.6-7. Egypt was virtually debarred to senators of course: cf. Dio 51.17.1; Tac. *Ann.* 2.59.

ruled that they must now be referred to him. At the same time he declared
Sicily an area for which permission was no longer needed. He considered
the law to be still very much in force in A.D. 6, because in the severe
famine of that year he temporarily relaxed both it and the normal quorums
for decrees.[38] Tacitus[39] reports under 32 that one Rubrius Fabatus fled from
Italy and headed for Parthia; he was apprehended, brought back, and placed
under guard. His crime was apparently that he could not offer an adequate
explanation for his distant travels, and this could suggest that he was a
senator against whom the regulations about absence were being invoked,
since no such restriction on movement is known to have been placed upon
other classes.[40] We later hear of a *praetorius* applying unsuccessfully to
Gaius for extensions of leave,[41] and Claudius finally required that all
requests should come before the emperor. He also ruled that senators could
visit their estates in Narbonese Gaul, as well as in Sicily, without seeking
permission.[42]

   The regulations as laid down by him still applied unchanged in the early
third century, according to Dio,[43] though we are not able to judge how
strictly they were adhered to by that time. Gavius Clarus, for example,
surely took all proper steps before making the private visit to Syria in the
160's about which Fronto writes to L. Verus.[44] But in framing his recommendation he never mentions to the co-emperor whether or not Gavius
had sought permission to leave Italy. Since all emperors were no doubt
pleased to be kept informed of the movements and plans of senators, and
since there were sound political reasons for keeping them out of certain
provinces, we might reasonably guess that some observance of the regulations did persist. Yet at the same time it would only be natural to think
that increasing recruitment of non-Italian senators, the absence of emperors
from Italy at the time of their accession in several cases, and their tendency
to be out of Italy more and more during their reigns, were all developments
which came to make enforcement more awkward in practice. In the winter
of 69/70, for example, not only a deputation sent by the House, but also
many individual members on their own initiative went to join Vespasian
in Alexandria, of all places![45] During more normal times it was understandable that members from distant provinces might seek, or take, longer

[38] Dio 55.26.1-2.
[39] *Ann.* 6.14.
[40] Claudius' attempts as censor to enforce the regulations against *equites* were a complete
surprise (Suet. *Claud.* 16).
[41] Suet. *Calig.* 29.
[42] See Dio 60.25.6-7; Tac. *Ann.* 12.23; Suet. *Claud.* 23.
[43] 52.42.6; see further Extended Note D.
[44] *Ver. Imp.* 2.7 = p. 127 H; H. Halfmann, *Die Senatoren*, no. 106.
[45] Tac. *Hist.* 4.6-8 and 51; cf. Plin. *NH* 19.3.

leave to return home than the one month in spring or two to two-and-a-half months in autumn, which was the maximum that the routine of the House would otherwise allow them.[46]

Among Tiberius' efforts to secure good attendance, Suetonius[47] tells us that he expected magistrates designate to remain in Rome, and that he went so far as to degrade a senator who moved from the city to his *horti* before the end of June in the interests of economy. In a letter of 32 read out in the senate and reported by Tacitus,[48] Tiberius made a number of criticisms of a priest's action in raising a particular matter, not least among them being that he had brought the issue before a poorly attended senate. According to Dio,[49] Claudius was so severe in requiring the attendance of members whenever they were summoned, that some who failed to respond actually committed suicide. The poet Calpurnius Siculus goes further, and depicts a senate house almost denuded of members by the end of the reign, as a result of Claudius' arrests and executions.[50] In more sober vein a sentence preserved by Suidas perhaps offers a garbled memory of emergency steps taken by him to detain members for consultation during a crisis: "Claudius, the king of the Romans, promulgated a law to the effect that no senator might travel more than seven 'markers' from the city without the king's orders."[51]

The lawyers of our period understood senators to have their domicile in Rome. As Paulus says: "Senators are always considered to have their residence at Rome; still, they are understood to have a residence in the place where they were born, for the reason that the rank of senator is considered rather to give an additional domicile than to change the old one."[52] So when Claudius would not brook any refusal from those whom he wished to introduce to the senate during his censorship, Surdinius Gallus (unwilling to serve, but anticipating an approach nonetheless) sought escape from his embarrassing predicament by leaving Rome for Carthage. The ruse was in vain: the emperor held him back.[53]

---

[46] See chap. 6 sect. 4 and note Pliny's plea (*Ep*. 10.8.6) that he would need at least one month for a worthwhile visit to estates something over 150 miles from Rome.

[47] *Tib*. 31 and 35.

[48] *Ann*. 6.12, "apud infrequentem senatum." For poor attendance under Tiberius, see further Dio 58.21.2, discussed in chap. 7 sect. 24 note 16. Valerius Maximus (2.2.6) draws an exaggerated contrast between the spontaneity with which senators attended meetings in the "good old days," and the need for members of his own day (in Tiberius' reign) to be summoned by edict.

[49] 60.11.8.

[50] *Buc*. 1. 69-71 Verdière. On dating, see G. B. Townend and R. Mayer, *JRS* 70. 1980. pp. 166-174 and 175-176, against E. J. Champlin (*JRS* 68. 1978. pp. 95-110), who argues for the beginning of Severus Alexander's reign.

[51] Dio 60.29.7[a]. For similar measures during the Republic, note Livy 36.3.3; 43.11.4-5.

[52] *Dig*. 1.9.11; cf. 50.1.22.6.

[53] Dio 60.29.2; see further chap. 1 sect. 1 note 42.

It was from the Flavian period, perhaps, that the growing number of non-Italian senators first came to have a notable effect upon attendance. Inevitably, if many of their concerns were abroad, they might be tempted to stay away. Trajan's requirement that all candidates for office should invest one third of their capital in Italian real estate may be relevant in this connection.[54] It was perhaps introduced principally for the immediate purpose of reducing electoral corruption, yet it could also have been intended to remedy a situation where senators were not present in Italy as often as was desirable. In his account of the measure Pliny goes on to comment that some candidates for office treated Rome and Italy "not as their native country but as a mere inn or lodging-house for them on their visits."[55] Trajan's requirement may have fallen into abeyance before being revived on a more modest scale by M. Aurelius, who demanded that senators of non-Italian origin should invest one quarter of their capital in Italy.[56] Again we do not know how long this stipulation remained in force. It might be rash, however, to conjecture too readily that non-Italian senators were guilty of widespread absenteeism when, as the second century progressed, it was increasingly they, rather than Italians, who showed ambition and enthusiasm to become senators.

Really from the early second century onwards it is impossible for us to trace how the attitudes of emperors and members developed towards attendance. As we shall see,[57] curtailment of the *interrogatio*, where each member was asked his opinion in order, was a notable development in procedure during the century, and it may be that this change played a part in encouraging absenteeism. The names of members who attended a session, or took part in a vote, were evidently never recorded: thus it was only when names were called during an *interrogatio* that absence became really conspicuous. Once consultation of no more than a few members was established as common practice, others could hope that they would hardly be missed in the throng.

It is tempting to conjecture from the very fragmentary letter *Ad Antoninum Pium* 1[58] that Fronto is passing some comment about how full the senate was when he delivered his consular *gratiarum actio* to the emperor on 13 August 143—unusually full perhaps. And it is interesting to note the detail that the young member, L. Fabius Severus, does not seem to have been present in person when fulsome thanks were expressed to him by his native town of Tergeste in Antoninus' reign. Since he was either

[54] See chap. 2 sect. 3 note 14.
[55] *Ep*. 6.19.4.
[56] HA, *Marcus* 11.8.
[57] Chap. 8 below.
[58] P. 156 H.

serving as *quaestor urbanus*, or had done so recently, he would probably not have been abroad then: rather we may guess that he was in Rome.[59] But in general it is only fair to imagine that there was some decline in attendance as the second century progressed. Conceivably Severus and Caracalla had this matter in mind early in the third century when they ruled that senators could not be required to take on the duties of *tutor* more than 200 miles from Rome; in fact, Marcianus, referring to the same restriction in more general terms, puts the limit at only 100 miles.[60] In our period a final complaint about slack attendance is made by Caracalla from Antioch in 215.[61]

Apart from general references to the absence of senators from meetings, we know of a number of individual absences (beyond, of course, those senators away on official business). The difficulty with certain of these cases, however, is that we can rarely be sure of the age of the members concerned, or of whether they had sought the emperor's prior permission. The senators M. Pompeius Macrinus Neos Theophanes in the mid second century,[62] and Astyrius in the reign of Gallienus,[63] may both have reached retirement age before returning to live in Mytilene and Syria respectively; but we cannot be certain in either instance. Ill health was naturally an acceptable excuse for absence in most circumstances,[64] offered by emperors[65] and members[66] alike, not always in good faith.[67] Presumably the famous jurist M. Antistius Labeo gained leave from Augustus and Tiberius for the routine whereby he spent half of each year in Rome and the other half in seclusion so as to be able to press on with his writing.[68] T. Aurelius Quietus, consul in 82, likewise withdrew every year to his estate at Ravenna:[69] but

---

[59] Mommsen (*CIL* V. 532 = *ILS* 6680) thought that symbols at the head of the inscription dated the meeting in question to the Kalends of November, which would of course have been the very day of a stated session of the House in Rome. Yet in his revised edition of the text (*Inscr. Ital.* X. 4. no. 31) Degrassi has shown how attachment of any such significance to the symbols is invalid. See further chap. 2 sect. 6 note 61.

[60] *Frag. Vat.* 147; *Dig.* 27.1.21.3.

[61] Dio 77.20.1.

[62] H. Halfmann, *Die Senatoren*, no. 44; R. Hodot, *ZPE* 34. 1979. p. 224, a new document which makes a withdrawal seem likely.

[63] Eusebius, *Hist. Eccl.* 7. 16 and 17; *PIR*[2] A 1269 and B 67; *PLRE* 1. p. 120.

[64] Cf. *FIRA*[2] I no. 68 V line 114.

[65] Cf., for example, Tac. *Ann.* 3.31.

[66] See, for example, Fronto, *Ad Ver.* 2.1.5 and 7.6 = pp. 115, 128 H.

[67] For example, Claudius Pompeianus and Acilius Glabrio at Dio 74.3.1-3. Technically the former is likely to have reached retirement age by 193. Publicius Certus claimed to have been absent through ill health when Pliny attacked him (*Ep.* 9.13.22). For another example of feigned illness, by Oclatinius Adventus in 217, see Dio 78.14.2. According to some, Libo Drusus' illness on 13 September 16 was assumed—though he attended all the same (Tac. *Ann.* 2.29).

[68] *Dig.* 1.2.2.47.

[69] *PIR*[2] A 1592; Ulpian, *Dig.* 17.1.16.

quite possibly he made this excursion during one of the senate's recesses. No doubt Vespasian and Helvidius Priscus the Younger just withdrew without a word, the one afraid of Agrippina, the other of Domitian.[70] But we just do not know whether C. Sulpicius Galba had made excuses to Tiberius before retiring from Rome; if not, it might be strange that he still expected to be eligible for a proconsulship after his withdrawal.[71] Equally we do not know whether Mucianus[72] and Bruttius Praesens[73] had made their excuses to Claudius and Trajan respectively, nor even whether they had been expected to do so. If either had failed to excuse himself, their later advancement at least shows that lasting offense had not been taken. In the late second century the sophist and consular Tiberius Claudius Aristocles could evidently reside in Pergamum,[74] while throughout the same century it is notable that senators are consistently found visiting the Asclepieium there as a religious, cultural, and medical center.[75] In the latter instance, naturally, if excuses were made, reasons of age or health could conveniently be put forward. Earlier in the second century the consulars Iulius Quadratus[76] and Arrian the historian[77] seem likewise to have spent much of their time in Pergamum and Athens respectively. Yet whether they actually had imperial permission, and whether they did also visit Rome quite regularly, are both unanswerable questions. At any rate, it is plain enough that no general conclusion can be reached on how conscientiously emperors demanded excuses, or members offered them, beyond the obvious point that much would depend on the individuals involved.[78]

Quite apart from other reasons, the level of members' attendance would vary according to the time of year. As we shall see,[79] all members except a quorum chosen by lot were excused without further ado in the months of September and October. It is conceivable that similar arrangements were made for the period of the customary spring holiday (much of April and early May), if meetings were held at all at that season. But we have no information on the point. In describing the trial of Marius Priscus in January 100, Pliny[80] remarks that this was a month in the year when Rome was

---

[70] Suet. *Vesp.* 4; Plin. *Ep.* 9.13.3.
[71] Suet. *Galba* 3; Tac. *Ann.* 6.40.
[72] Tac. *Hist.* 1.10; *PIR²* L 216.
[73] See chap. 1 sect. 2 note 54.
[74] *PIR²* C 789; H. Halfmann, *Die Senatoren*, no. 121.
[75] See especially Aelius Aristides, *Sacred Tales* IV; and C. Habicht, *Altertümer von Pergamon*, VIII. 3: *Die Inschriften des Asklepieions* (Deutsches Archäologisches Institut, Berlin, 1969), pp. 14-18.
[76] H. Halfmann, *Die Senatoren*, no. 17.
[77] See chap. 2 sect. 6 note 91.
[78] For what you say to an emperor who has excused you, cf. Epictetus 1.2.23.
[79] Chap. 6 sect. 4.
[80] *Ep.* 2.11.10.

full of people, particularly senators. Their good attendance is understandable, partly because elections took place at this time (preceded of course by entertainments and the distribution of candidates' gifts),[81] and partly because the oath "in acta Caesarum" was taken at the New Year.[82] By contrast, when writing of a session in December 57 B.C., Cicero[83] had been pleasantly surprised by an attendance of about 200, a total which he thought would be hardly possible because of all the festival days in that month.

At any one time a substantial number of senators would be out of Italy on official duties. By the late first century over eighty were absent thus. With an increased number of "special missions" for senators, this figure would have continued to grow gradually as the second century progressed, although the trend should not be overrated.[84] For long stretches, too, both a new appointee and the retiring holder of a post would be out of Rome at the same time, thus reducing still further the number of senators available to attend meetings. In normal circumstances all governors of senatorial provinces would change annually, and the ten or so new appointees would depart with their legates[85] and quaestors around the same date—before mid April, if a ruling of Claudius was adhered to.[86] Such an arrangement allowed a proconsul to leave Rome soon after the opening of the sailing season and to reach his province by midsummer at the latest. Only then could the retiring governor depart,[87] in the expectation of conveniently arriving back in Rome by early autumn, when the senate was in recess anyway.[88] Augustus in fact required governors to leave their provinces as soon as their successors arrived, and to spend no more than three months on the return journey,[89] while Claudius ordered retiring governors to remain in Rome for a year after their return.[90] The latter rule came to be ignored

---

[81] Plin. *Ep.* 6.19.1-2.

[82] Note Tac. *Ann.* 16.22.

[83] *Ad Q.F.* 2.1.1 = SB 5.

[84] See W. Eck, *ANRW* II.i. 1974. pp. 227-228. As G. P. Burton shows (*Chiron* 9. 1979. pp. 465-487), the number of senators known to have been appointed as *curator reipublicae* in the provinces is modest—for example, only seven in Asia up to c. 260 (and some of these may have been legates to the proconsul at the same time), and only nine in Africa from the first attested appointment of a *curator* here in 196 up to 282.

[85] These would mostly be of praetorian rank: see W. Eck, "Zu den prokonsularen Legationen in der Kaiserzeit," *Epig. Stud.* 9. 1972. pp. 24-36; cf. idem, *Senatoren von Vespasian bis Hadrian*, chap. 3.

[86] Dio 60.17.3.

[87] *Dig.* 1.16.10 pr. It was exceptional for governors in mid term to be temporarily away from their provinces, as happened in 44 when they were invited to attend Claudius' British triumph (Suet. *Claud.* 17).

[88] See Appendix 3.

[89] Dio 53.15.6; cf. Ulpian, *Dig.* 4.6.38.1.

[90] Dio 60.25.5; *Sent. Paul. Frag. Leidense* 5; cf. Plin. *Paneg.* 92.2.

when able men were needed urgently; the *Historia Augusta*[91] can claim that Pertinax (who was adlected into the senate) never set foot in the House till Commodus' reign, when he had already governed four consular provinces.

Imperial appointees were not changed simultaneously in the same fashion as senatorial ones, so far as we know, nor with the same frequency. Much depended on each emperor's policy, his appraisal of individuals, and his view of the situation in different sectors. Tiberius, for example, was notorious for leaving his appointees at their posts for long stretches. By contrast, Galba was alleged to have planned a two-year limit on all senatorial and equestrian posts.[92] However, despite exceptions and uncertainties, we may at least plausibly suggest that two to three years was the normal tenure for a legionary legateship,[93] and we may claim with more confidence that praetorian and consular *legati Augusti pro praetore* would normally govern their provinces for two-and-a-half to three years.[94]

A regular appearance was no doubt expected of the Praefectus Urbi in view of his responsibilities for law and order, but other senators with official duties in Rome and Italy might not always be able to spare the time for attendance at every session. *Curatores aquarum*, for example, sometimes had to be away on official tours of inspection,[95] as would *curatores viarum* also.[96] The same applied to the few members who supervised *alimenta*,[97] and to the greater number who were appointed to act as *curator reipublicae* from the latter part of the second century.[98] We know from Pliny[99] that *praefecti aerarii Saturni* were kept fully occupied. And it hardly needs demonstrating that among other senatorial officials in Rome *praefecti frumenti dandi* and curators of the banks and bed of the Tiber in particular had duties too vital to be neglected for long—for all their routine nature.[100]

It follows that the pattern of the senatorial career and the availability of

[91] *Pert.* 3.2.

[92] Suet. *Galba* 15.

[93] See B. Campbell, *JRS* 65. 1975. p. 19.

[94] See B. Campbell, ibid. p. 26; also A. Birley, "The duration of military commands under Antoninus Pius," in *Corolla memoriae Erich Swoboda dedicata, Römische Forschungen in Niederösterreich* 5. 1966. pp. 43-53.

[95] See Frontinus, *Aqued.* 2.100-101; for his own conscientiousness cf. also 2.117.

[96] During the second century up to about ten senators at a time would be serving as *curatores viarum*: see W. Eck, *Die staatliche Organisation Italiens in der hohen Kaiserzeit, Vestigia* 28, Munich, 1979, pp. 80-86.

[97] See W. Eck, ibid. pp. 184-186.

[98] 92 senators are known to have served as *curator* in Italy between 160 and 235: see W. Eck, ibid. pp. 193 and 243-246.

[99] See *Ep.* 3.4 (where the *praefecti* were present at a session); 5.14.9; 10. 3A and 8. Cf. 1.10.9; 10.9; *Paneg.* 91.1.

[100] On the former, note *FIRA*² I no. 68 V line 114.

official posts would significantly affect the composition of the House at any typical meeting. First, the number of senators of junior rank (that is, members to be called after the *praetorii*) shrank significantly during our period. As we have seen, there were always twenty quaestorships each year, normally held around the age of 25. The praetorship could be held five years later: here about fifteen vacancies were available annually throughout most of the first century, rising to eighteen thereafter.[101] So about five junior senators, later reduced to two, would be disappointed each year. (Strictly these figures should be a fraction higher, since from the mid first century there would be extra competition from the small number of senators adlected below praetorian rank.) Assuming for the sake of argument that a senator's life expectancy aged 30 might be 25 years,[102] we can reckon that at any one time during the first century there were up to 125 members disappointed of the praetorship, reducing to 50 thereafter. Otherwise there were in theory up to 80 senators who had held the quaestorship but were not yet eligible for the praetorship. Even allowing for individual exceptions, this total was significantly reduced in practice. Up to twelve members would still be serving in the provinces during the first seven months or so in which they ranked as *quaestorii*. A few might later serve abroad as legate to a governor (after the first century there were no other official posts which would normally keep a junior senator out of Rome).[103] At any time six would be serving as aediles and ten as tribunes (and then not called upon to speak), while up to eighteen would presumably be called as *praetores designati* during the year before they took up the magistracy itself. So it was a modest number of members who were eligible to be called upon to speak but could not yet stand for election to the praetorship—between, say, thirty-five and fifty according to season and date. To achieve grand totals, the number of senators eligible for the praetorship, but disappointed of it, must be added in from above. None of these figures should be regarded as better than an approximation, especially those based on the conjecture about life expectancy. Yet, provided any reasonable expectancy is conjectured, it seems fair to conclude that the maximum number of senators eligible to be called after the *praetorii* did shrink considerably during our period—say, from never more than about 175 during the first century, to no more than about 110 during the second century. It is self-evident that by the latter stage the overwhelming majority of the senate's total membership belonged to the two senior grades.

Most official posts in Italy and the provinces were assigned to senators

---

[101] See chap. 1 sect. 2.

[102] Cf. sect. 1 above.

[103] Exceptionally, some junior senators were appointed to legionary legateships in the first century: see chap. 1 sect. 2 note 15.

of praetorian rank. There were upwards of sixty such positions by the beginning of the second century, and at the same time about eighteen for consulars. Both these figures would rise gradually during the century as the number of "special missions" entrusted to *praetorii* and *consulares* increased. Some occupants of posts in Italy might be able to attend the House of course; yet in the case of distant posts both new appointees and retiring holders would be simultaneously absent from Rome for a stretch. Although again they should be treated strictly as approximations, the figures can still give some impression of how the ranks of *praetorii* and *consulares* might be depleted at a session.

In contrast to certain other groups, patricians of all ages, together with others of noble background, were likely to be well represented at sessions. Normally, though not invariably, they would serve their quaestorships in Rome rather than abroad, hold the praetorship next, and then proceed swiftly to the consulship with no official post in between. As consulars, too, they would hold few posts outside Italy, being always expected to attend upon the emperor.[104]

It is more awkward, on the other hand, to imagine the likely level of attendance by the considerable number of members who came to see little or no prospect of advancement beyond the praetorship. No doubt morale was kept up so long as they were appointed to posts and a chance of the consulship remained. But once hope faded with the passing years, would they still continue so assiduous? For a lucky few, of course, reward might come at last: Q. Junius Arulenus Rusticus, for example, praetor in 69, was finally awarded the consulship in 92, while Cornutus Tertullus, *adlectus inter praetorios* in 73/74 became consul in 100.[105] But Bruttius Praesens cannot have been alone in losing heart and abandoning Rome.[106]

All the same, it seems fair to conclude that in general three types of members were likely to make up the majority at an average session—the high-born, the elderly, and the less successful. Though they might dominate numerically, this is not to suggest that they would also be the most active participants in proceedings. The individuals whose absence was most striking, and who were most sorely missed perhaps, were the more successful *praetorii*—men aged between 30 and 40 whose energy and ripening experience had to be devoted to command of the army and to administration of the empire, not to the deliberations of the senate.

[104] On the careers of patricians, see H.-H. Pistor, "Prinzeps und Patriziat in der Zeit von Augustus bis Commodus," pp. 79-124; for A.D. 138-180, G. Alföldy, *Konsulat und Senatorenstand*, pp. 37-40 and 327-328; R. Syme, "An eccentric patrician," *Chiron* 10. 1980. pp. 427-448.

[105] *PIR²* I 730; H. Halfmann, *Die Senatoren*, no. 22.

[106] See chap. 1 sect. 2 note 54.

The few figures which we possess for attendance at meetings in our period must be assessed in the light of the relevant features mentioned above; and some brief comparison with what we know of attendance in the late Republic may be enlightening. The attendance of 405 or just over recorded on a small fragment of a decree passed in 23 B.C.—when total membership was perhaps 800 and the *Lex Julia* still very much in the future—is highly respectable.[107] Equally respectable for the season is the attendance of between 250 and 299 members at the passage of the *SC de nundinis saltus Beguensis* on 15 October 138.[108] This was one of the meetings for which Augustus' regulations required the attendance of no more than a quorum. By contrast, it need be no surprise that only 100 members are said to have assembled when the consuls summoned a meeting during the night after Gaius' murder, even though it was January.[109] As always in times of violent crisis, some senators preferred to remain in hiding in the city, while others had fled to their estates. Thus late on the day of Vitellius' murder it proved impossible to call any meeting at all, because there had been a wholesale disappearance of magistrates and senators. In panic, according to Tacitus,[110] they had slipped out of the city, or were taking cover in the houses of their various dependents. They behaved similarly on the murder of Pertinax in 193.[111]

Most impressive of all are two figures for attendance in the first century. From a speech delivered over one hundred years later, we learn that in 26, when eleven cities of the province of Asia vied for the privilege of erecting the temple to Tiberius, Livia, and the senate permitted two years earlier, 400 senators voted in favor of Smyrna, while the other ten cities received a combined total of only seven votes.[112] It is true that the emperor was present throughout the discussions and that the matter was very much one which touched his own prestige, but otherwise the subject would hardly seem calculated to attract the attention of as many as 407 members over several days. If that is a surprise, however, the attendance of 383 members at the passage of the *SC de aedificiis non diruendis* on 22 September 44[113] may in turn be considered quite astonishing for an occasion when no more

---

[107] *CIL* VI. 32272. For epigraphic commentary on this and other attendance figures recorded in inscriptions, see M. Hammond, *The Antonine Monarchy*, p. 279 n. 67.

[108] *FIRA*² I no. 47 line 9.

[109] Josephus, *AJ* 19. 249.

[110] *Hist.* 3.86.

[111] Herodian 2.6.3.

[112] Ael. Aristid. *Or.* 19.13 Keil. Cf. Tac. *Ann.* 4.15 and 55-56. For discussion of the possibility that the round figure 400 is no more than an estimate, see chap. 7 sect. 25. For another instance where only seven senators dissented from the general view, cf. Plin. *Ep.* 6.13.5.

[113] *FIRA*² I no. 45 I line 20; for date, P. A. Gallivan, *CQ* 28. 1978. p. 420.

than a quorum would be required.[114] Certainly if the seating capacity of the Curia Julia was between 450 and 500, as Taylor and Scott reasonably suggest,[115] then at such meetings the available accommodation would have been well filled. Indeed the trial of Marius Priscus in January 100 may even have been an occasion at which a number of members had to stand because the House was so crowded for this celebrated case. At least, it is difficult to suggest any other convincing reason why an informal group should have been standing by the president's tribunal during the *interrogatio* on the third day—a feature unique in surviving evidence for our period, although Pliny[116] sees no cause to account for it.

In fact, assuming total membership of the senate in the first century to be something over 600, attendances higher than those found in the two latter instances for which we have figures could hardly be expected on any routine occasion. Four hundred and seven or 383 members are accounted for here at once. In addition, 90, say, must have been absent on official duties, or were traveling to or from official posts. Others must have been absent through illness or on some other more or less valid excuse, especially in September. A proportion had reached the age limit and thus was no longer required to attend, though some would always choose to do so. Only a guess may be hazarded at the total of "retired" senators, especially when the retirement age itself cannot be established with certainty. But on the basis used earlier (average life expectancy of 30 years or just over for entrants aged 25),[117] we might reckon between 80 and 90 senators to be aged over 60 at any time. Finally, all 38 or more magistrates should have been excluded from the voting figures of 400 to 7, since technically (as always in the Republic) they were not members for their term of office, and were neither asked for *sententiae* nor eligible to vote.[118] We do not

---

[114] See further chap. 6 sect. 2 note 35. We do not know the size of the quorum, but the total of 250/299 members known for October 138 is plainly much closer to it than 383.

[115] *TAPA* 100. 1969. p. 548.

[116] *Ep.* 2.11.22. Conceivably these were members who wished to make it entirely plain that they remained open minded about the appropriate verdict and sentence, yet were ready to move from this neutral position towards whichever speaker swayed them. On the other hand, in normal circumstances a member could just as well indicate such reservation of judgment by staying seated in his place. If the benches were full, it would be natural—and considerate—to stand by the tribunal so that spectators on the threshold did not have their view blocked. In general, compare how on Domitian's death senators "vied to fill the House" ("repleta certatim curia"), according to Suet. *Dom.* 23. For what may be a reference to further meetings where members had to stand during Claudius' reign, note Dio 60.12.3. For spectators standing in the Centumviral court, note Plin. *Ep.* 4.16.2; 6.33.3.

[117] See sect. 1 above.

[118] For the position of magistrates, see chap. 7 sect. 11. The figure of 38 is the total of 2 consuls, 12 praetors (at least), 6 aediles, 10 tribunes; 8 quaestors with duties in Rome would regularly have attended as magistrates, too, but only gained a senator's right to vote *after* their term of office.

know whether or not they were excluded from attendance, as opposed to voting, figures.

It is true that the holders of some magistracies might anyway be out of Rome for all or part of their term of office. This was regularly the case with the twelve or so quaestors serving in the senatorial provinces. From an early stage, too, the emperor and members of his family might hold the consulship in absence—notably Augustus himself.[119] But from the evidence collected by Syme[120] there is no sign that in normal circumstances the highest magistracy was occupied in absence by others before the second century.[121] It is hard to substantiate Dio's claim[122] that in Augustus' day many praetors and consuls governed provinces while still in office. As Pliny[123] indicates, even in 100 it was thought proper that a consul should hold office in Rome. Just over a century later Dio[124] argues likewise that all magistrates should remain there.

Altogether there can be no doubt that our information about the first-century meetings discussed above allows us to account for well over 500 senators.[125] It should be stressed that the attendances compare very favorably with three figures we have for meetings in the late Republic (total attendances all approximately between 400 and 450),[126] and are better than the 200 or so for a meeting in December 57 B.C.,[127] and the 340 for the taking of an oath in October 39 B.C.[128] So against the dissatisfaction expressed by emperors from time to time, there does need to be set the evidence of our two random figures for first-century meetings, which prove high attendances even on routine occasions at this period. Moreover, a total of between 250 and 299 present during the recess in 138 could point

---

[119] Cf. Suet. *Aug.* 26.

[120] R. Syme, "Consulates in absence," *JRS* 48. 1958. pp. 1-9 = *Roman Papers* I. pp. 378-392.

[121] For a list of consulships held in absence between 138 and 180 (the majority prompted by the military crises of M. Aurelius' reign), see G. Alföldy, *Konsulat und Senatorenstand*, p. 104.

[122] 53.14.1. We have only the statement of Suetonius (*Aug.* 43) that Augustus on twenty-three occasions celebrated games for magistrates who were either out of Rome or lacking in means. Cf. *RG* 22.2.

[123] *Paneg.* 60.1.

[124] 52.20.4.

[125] Suetonius (*Nero* 12) may hardly be reliable in claiming that Nero mustered 400 senators fit enough to fight in the arena at his *Ludi Maximi*. But at least the figure is generally consistent with our other evidence for the number who might be available in Rome during the first century. Note also how Domitian had 500 *tesserae* thrown into the section of seats reserved for the senatorial order at a show (Suet. *Dom.* 4).

[126] Cic. *Ad Att.* 1.14.5 = SB 14 in 61 B.C.; *Red. Sen.* 26 in 57 B.C.; Appian, *Bell. Civ.* 2.30 in 50 B.C. (magistrates should be added to voting figures).

[127] Cic. *Ad Q.F.* 2.1.1 = SB 5.

[128] J. Reynolds, *Aphrodisias and Rome*, no. 8 lines 94-95 and no. 9 line 7 with discussion, p. 91.

to substantially larger totals still being achieved at that date, whenever more than just a quorum was expected.

On further reflection, these figures should impress, but perhaps not surprise us. For two main reasons we should in any event expect to find the great majority of senators in Rome. First, as we have seen, most were committed to a participation in public life which involved far more than attendance at sessions. Such attendance should not be viewed in isolation, but rather linked with the whole range of duties and obligations, formal and informal, which have already been discussed. Second, we should expect to find most senators at the seat of the empire's government. Columella,[129] in his agricultural treatise of the mid first century, appreciated very well how men of substance were drawn from the countryside to the city by "civilis ambitio," and once drawn were detained there. To fulfill his obligations, further his career, and satisfy his ambitions, a senator had to be present where the supreme power lay. That meant remaining close to the emperor, and for most of our period he was normally resident in Rome or near it. It need be no surprise that senatorial writers—Tacitus in particular—have been censured for undue preoccupation with affairs at Rome, matched by allegedly scandalous disregard of events elsewhere.[130] Even in the early third century we find members expelled from the senate wishing to continue living in Rome, and according to Modestinus,[131] Septimius Severus and Caracalla permitted them to do so. But from the second century onwards emperors were increasingly absent from Italy, accompanied by selected senior senators. That trend was critical for the senate as a corporate body, because it could not move from Rome with the ruler, and was thus left more and more isolated.

3. Retirement Age

During the Republic it would seem that senators were summoned to meetings as long as they lived. Under the Empire, however, a "retirement age" was introduced, beyond which they were not required to attend. This was possibly an innovation of Augustus' *Lex Julia de senatu habendo* of 9 B.C., if we may interpret a remark in Dio as an allusion to it, when he says that Augustus "appointed two regular meetings each month, so that senators were required to attend—*at least those of them whom the law summoned.*"[1]

---

[129] *De re rust.* 1.1.19.
[130] For assessment of the criticism, see, for example, R. Syme, *Tacitus*, Appendix 70.
[131] *Dig.* 1.9.3.
[1] 55.3.1, with my italics. See also Plin. *Ep.* 4.23.3 for confirmation that the retirement age was laid down by law.

There survive two specific figures for the retirement age: Seneca the Elder,[2] quoting Publius Asprenas, puts it at 65, while his son[3] puts it at 60. Whether the discrepancy is due to inaccuracy on the part of one author or the other, or whether there was actually a reduction in the age during the first century, we do not know. The suggestion that Claudius deliberately lowered it as part of his general concern for senators' welfare and efficiency must remain speculation.[4] There are further general references to a retirement age in pseudo-Quintilian[5] and in the letter which Pliny[6] wrote to the elderly Pomponius Bassus.

The law relieved a senator of the requirement to attend meetings, but it did not exclude him if he wished to come. That point is specifically made in Seneca the Elder's quotation of Publius Asprenas,[7] and can be borne out by a number of individual instances. T. Manlius Valens held an ordinary consulship in 96 aged 90,[8] for example, while Vestricius Spurinna was consul for the second time in 98, and aged over 77 when Pliny described his retirement in a letter possibly written about 101.[9] The family of L. Volusius Saturninus plainly took immense pride in the fact that he was still in harness as *praefectus urbi* when he died at the age of 93.[10] Fronto continued to attend past retirement age, but it is understandable that he should find a lengthy session in November or December wearisome.[11] Quite apart from the duration of meetings, it may well not have been just the infirm who were deterred by low winter temperatures in the chamber.

Far from merely tolerating elderly members, the House in fact showed respect for age. Most notably, whenever it was free to choose an emperor, its candidates were all men over retirement age—Galba, Nerva, Pertinax, Balbinus, and Pupienus. So it is altogether hardly surprising that the senate was widely thought of as a body of elderly men.[12] Only one ban on such members' participation in the work of the House is known. It occurs in the decree of which Augustus sent a copy to Cyrene in 4 B.C.: according to this, when a committee to hear cases of extortion was being chosen,

[2] *Controv.* 1.8.4.

[3] *De Brev. Vit.* 20.4.

[4] See D. McAlindon, "The senator's retiring age: 65 or 60?" *CR* 7. 1957. p. 108.

[5] *Declam.* 306 = p. 203, 1 Ritter.

[6] *Ep.* 4.23.

[7] Cf. Epictetus 3.24.36, "You are a senator for life."

[8] Dio 67.14.5.

[9] *Ep.* 3.1.10. A third consulship for 100, once generally assumed, is now discounted by new epigraphic material, however: see R. Syme, *Tacitus*, Appendix 6; idem, *Roman Papers* I. p. 256.

[10] *AE* 1972. 174.

[11] *Ant. Imp.* 1.5.1 = p. 95 H with E. J. Champlin, *Fronto and Antonine Rome*, p. 82 and Appendix B; see further chap. 6 sect. 2 note 38 below.

[12] See Dio 68.5.1, discussed in chap. 6 sect. 5 below; and in the fourth century, Ammianus 14.6.6.

no senator aged 70 or over was to be picked.[13] That limit was not derived from the new retirement age, however. Rather it was taken from earlier Republican arrangements to hear these cases.[14] In contrast, it is notable that Verginius Rufus had to excuse himself from membership of the commission set up by the senate to reduce public expenditure, when he was a ripe 83![15]

It should be recognized that while a senator no longer had to attend meetings, his retirement might still not free him from other obligations. As we have seen,[16] in Pliny's view Silius Italicus gained a special concession when he was excused the journey from Campania to greet Trajan on his first entry to Rome as emperor in 99; yet Pliny knew Silius to be over 70 at the time. Dio[17] tells us of Lusianus Proculus, an elderly senator who felt that he should emerge from retirement to assist Domitian in the crisis presented by Antonius Saturninus' rebellion in 89. In disturbed times even a member who had retired completely to the country could still be in danger: it is Dio[18] again who relates how the aged Quintillus, for example, became the victim of informers at the beginning of the third century.

4. Arms, Soldiers, and Other Non-Members

As we shall be seeing,[1] sessions of the senate were neither exactly secret, nor exactly open. Anyone might stand at the open door of the chamber and learn what he could of the proceedings. But technically, non-members were forbidden to advance over the threshold into the chamber itself during meetings. Thus in 21, C. Cestius, complaining of scandalous harassment by a woman whom he had caused to be convicted of fraud, can cite the ultimate insult of being slandered by her "on the threshold of the House":[2] in other words, she pursued him absolutely as far as she could go. In looking forward to the day when the young sons of an *eques* might become senators, Statius expresses the hope that they will be able to "tread the threshold of the senate."[3] And in Seneca's parody[4] it eventually occurs to

---

[13] *FIRA*[2] I no. 68 V lines 111-112.

[14] Cf. *FIRA*[2] I no. 7 line 17 (*Lex Acilia*).

[15] Plin. *Ep.* 2.1.4 and 9.

[16] Plin. *Ep.* 3.7 with chap. 2 sect. 4 note 38 above.

[17] 67.11.5; *PIR*[2] L 372.

[18] 76.7.4; perhaps M. Peduc[a]eus Plautius Quintillus (R. Hanslik, *PW* 21. cols. 43-44, s.v. Plautius, no. 54), to whom may have been addressed the essay *On long-lived men* attributed to Lucian. Cf. O. Hirschfeld, "Die Abfassungszeit der MAKPOBIOI" in *Kleine Schriften*, Berlin, 1913, pp. 881-884.

[1] Chap. 6 sect. 3.

[2] Tac. *Ann.* 3.36.

[3] *Silv.* 4.8.60-61.

[4] *Apocol.* 9.1; cf. 8.1; *Ep. Mor.* 44.2, "non omnes curia admittit."

the president, Jupiter, that while private persons are lingering in the House it is not lawful for senators to give their opinions or to debate. The strictness with which this rule was observed evidently declined somewhat during our period, but it is interesting that it could be invoked as late as 218 by Elagabalus on his accession, when he denounced his predecessor Macrinus in the following terms. The charge may read strangely, coming from one who was likewise not a senator before he became emperor,[5] but that is not the point here.

This man to whom it was not permitted even to enter the senate house after the proclamation debarring all others than senators, dared treacherously to murder the emperor whom he had been trusted to guard, dared to appropriate his office and to become emperor before he had been senator.[6]

Pliny's account[7] of the procedure for election to magistracies in the senate implies that candidates for the quaestorship, even though non-members, would be invited to attend and speak for themselves. This is entirely the arrangement we might expect. Likewise, envoys from near and far had regularly been allowed to address the senate in person, and this practice naturally continued during our period. Claudius even allowed Agrippa of Palestine and his brother Herod to enter and express their thanks to him in Greek.[8] Earlier, as is well known, Agrippa had been invited to give advice to the senate in person in the crisis after Gaius' murder.[9] It was presumably at Claudius' invitation, too, that Meherdates was present when the senate received the Parthian delegation which had come to ask for him as king in 49.[10] Not surprisingly, after his adoption by Galba on 10 January 69, Piso (the son of a senator, but never a member himself) was invited to enter the House and speak.[11]

Equally there was nothing strange about attendants of senators being permitted to enter the chamber for specific purposes. For example, the sick were commonly conveyed to the door of the chamber, or even inside it, by litter.[12] But the bearers would then leave. Under normal circumstances senators can hardly have been permitted to keep an attendant with

[5] Cf. Dio 79.8.3.
[6] Dio 79.1.2; cf. 78.41.4.
[7] *Ep*. 3.20.5.
[8] Dio 60.8.3.
[9] Josephus, *BJ* 2.206; *AJ* 19.239. By contrast, the tale that Philo was invited to read to the senate sounds fanciful (Eusebius, *Hist. Eccl.* 2.18.8).
[10] Tac. *Ann.* 12.11; cf. Dio 53.33.1.
[11] Tac. *Hist.* 1.19; *ILS* 240; *PIR*[2] C 300.
[12] Dio (57.17.6) mentions the practice in general, and records that Archelaus of Cappadocia (ibid.) and Libo Drusus both had to be conveyed to their trials thus (57.15.4; cf. Tac. *Ann.* 2.29; Seneca, *Ep. Mor.* 70.10). See also Suet. *Tib.* 30; Dio 58.27.4. For safety Piso was carried home by litter during his trial in 20 (Tac. *Ann.* 3.14).

them in the chamber during sessions. Admittedly we do hear of individuals appearing at the imperial *salutatio* with secretaries,[13] but this was a very different type of occasion. If every member were allowed an escort inside the senate house, and if the majority did bring one, then a well-attended session would become impossibly overcrowded, and the customary movement of members during debates and votes would be obstructed. It is true that we learn from Pliny[14] how one of his freedmen stood behind him as he delivered a prosecution speech against Marius Priscus. If it was customarily allowed that a senator or advocate be attended thus, it is curious that we know of no other example of the practice. But it is more likely that Pliny was allowed an attendant as a special concession, because of the strain he was putting on his health. Otherwise only emperors seem to have been accompanied by freedmen attendants. We hear of Polybius reading out Augustus' will for Tiberius—"because it was not proper for a senator to pronounce anything of the sort," claims Dio[15]—and of documents being read out for Gaius by freedmen.[16]

As early as Augustus' reign younger members of the imperial family were invited to attend meetings before they became senators: we hear of the privilege being bestowed upon Augustus' grandsons Gaius and Lucius, and upon Tiberius' son Drusus.[17] An invitation was extended to Claudius, but revoked by Tiberius.[18] In addition, Nero was permitted to address the senate, apparently before he became a member.[19] It is not certain whether M. Aurelius or L. Verus attended before holding magistracies, though the *Historia Augusta*[20] implies that Marcus was granted the privilege, whereas Lucius was not. It is clear, however, that at the time of Drusus' death in 23, Germanicus' sons Nero (aged 18) and Drusus (aged 15) did not attend, since after seeking permission Tiberius had them conducted in by the consuls and then commended them to the senate's care.[21]

It is notable that class distinctions were strictly observed at two formal occasions early in our period. The first occurred in A.D. 5, when daughters of *equites* and freedmen were allowed to draw lots for selection as Vestal Virgins. Fathers who were *equites* were permitted to accompany their daughters into the chamber, but fathers who were freedmen had to remain

---

[13] Suet. *Claud.* 35.

[14] *Ep.* 2.11.15.

[15] 56.32.1; Suet. *Tib.* 23.

[16] Dio 59.16.3. Protogenes was perhaps one such freedman of Gaius: see Dio 59.26.1-2 and R. Hanslik, *PW* 23 s.v. Protogenes no. 1, col. 980.

[17] Dio 55.9.4 and 9-10; 56.17.3; *RG* 14.1.

[18] Suet. *Claud.* 5-6.

[19] Dio 60.33.9; Suet. *Nero* 7.

[20] *Verus* 3.5.

[21] Tac. *Ann.* 4.8. The suggestion that Herodes Atticus' infant son was granted the privilege of attendance is probably unsound (see *PIR²* C 785 and references there).

outside.[22] Likewise in 14, when Augustus' will was proved, only signatories of the senatorial class were admitted to the House; the others acknowledged their signatures outside.[23]

Considerable numbers of non-members had to attend those sessions where the senate sat as a court, as it did from very early in our period. It does not need demonstrating that men of all classes (except slaves) appeared as prosecutors, defendants, and witnesses. Women of all classes, too, commonly appeared as defendants and witnesses.[24] Women were not allowed to prosecute except in special circumstances,[25] although we hear that Rhescuporis of Thrace was accused before the senate by the widow of his son Cotys.[26] While such a detail is not to be pressed perhaps, Tacitus[27] does imply that in 66 Ostorius Sabinus, the *eques* who accused Barea Soranus, was only permitted to enter the chamber when it was time for him to speak. By contrast, we hear from Pliny[28] of how another advocate in 105, also not a senator, could appear there while other business was being handled prior to his own case. Claudius evidently invited his prefects and freedmen to be present at trials in the senate, and indeed one of the latter, Narcissus, was even able to interrogate a freedman defendant.[29] On the other hand, the accounts of Tacitus[30] and Pliny[31] would seem to indicate that Pallas was not present at the sessions where honors were voted to him in 52. *Equites* are said to have been present at Gaius' first meeting as emperor, and at the discussions immediately after his death.[32]

The senate was a civil gathering[33] to which members and others were expected to come unarmed, free from all threat of military intervention. It was only ceremonial, of course, when Dacian envoys brought their arms into the House in 102; after they had laid them down, the peace which they sought was granted, and the arms handed back.[34] More seriously, however, there was a marked decline from traditional standards during our period. Augustus was allegedly so nervous of assassination that he frequently wore a breastplate under his clothing at meetings of the senate and

[22] Dio 55.22.5; for the ceremony, Gell. 1.12.12.
[23] Suet. *Tib.* 23.
[24] For the former, note Mauricianus in Ulpian, *Reg.* 13.2; for the latter, cf. Suet. *Claud.* 40, where the emperor described one such witness as the "liberta et ornatrix" of his mother.
[25] Cf. Plin. *Ep.* 7.6.8 and 9.13.15 with Sherwin-White ad locc.
[26] Tac. *Ann.* 2.67. At Tac. *Hist.* 4.42 Sulpicia Praetextata is presumably acting behind the scenes, rather than coming before the senate itself.
[27] *Ann.* 16.30.
[28] *Ep.* 5.13 with Sherwin-White ad loc.
[29] Dio 60.16.3-5.
[30] *Ann.* 12.53.
[31] *Ep.* 7.29; 8.6.
[32] Dio 59.6.1; Josephus, *AJ* 19.185.
[33] On its representation in art as a civil institution see chap. 6 sect. 5.
[34] Dio 68.10.1.

elsewhere, even though (Dio[35] adds) he did not think it would really protect him in a crisis. Suetonius[36] certainly mentions that Augustus wore a sword and steel corselet beneath his tunic when presiding at a *lectio senatus*; and on the same occasion he took the further precaution of having senators searched before they approached him one by one. The only other emperor specifically said to have entered the senate in armor (with a corselet under his clothing) is Caracalla on the day after Geta's murder, according to the *Historia Augusta*.[37]

The point that members were not to come armed is underlined by Augustus' search already mentioned, and further by the resolution passed in 33 that senators should be searched for hidden weapons as a matter of course.[38] In 24 the charge brought against Calpurnius Piso, that he had entered the House wearing a sword, had been passed over as too atrocious to be true.[39] Similarly, there had been a scandal in 30 when the wife of a condemned senator, herself accused of some offense, smuggled a dagger into the chamber and committed suicide on the spot.[40] Not surprisingly, Tiberius politely declined the offer made by members in 32 that whenever he entered the chamber, he should be guarded by twenty of their number armed with daggers. His reason was partly, says Dio, that the offer was without precedent, partly that "he was not so simple as to give swords to the very men he hated and by whom he was hated."[41]

Whether members were still being searched properly for weapons by the end of Gaius' reign, we cannot say. But Josephus[42] mentions that everyone in the vicinity of a meeting of the senate shortly before the emperor's assassination carried arms—members included. We have no further information until the end of our period, when members again came armed. According to the *Historia Augusta*,[43] when Septimius Severus arrived to have his claim to the Principate ratified in 193, he entered with soldiers and friends, both armed. More reliably, Herodian explains how certain senators attended a meeting in 238 with daggers concealed under the folds of their clothing, and he comments: "Because of the rioting and unrest, everyone was carrying daggers, some openly and others secretly,

[35] 54.12.3.
[36] *Aug.* 35.
[37] *Caracalla* 2.9.
[38] Dio 58.18.6.
[39] Tac. *Ann.* 4.21.
[40] Dio 58.4.6.
[41] 58.18.1. Cf. Tac. *Ann.* 6.2, where Tiberius aptly stresses the horrifying vision of senators girding themselves with swords "in limine curiae."
[42] *AJ* 19.62.
[43] *Sev.* 7.4.

alleging that this was a protection against the sudden, treacherous attacks of their enemies."[44]

Soldiers of course, like other non-members, were not to enter the chamber during sessions,[45] but again we find them coming to be stationed there, particularly during the latter part of our period. In fact, after Sejanus' downfall senators were prepared to allow the emperor to attend escorted by a guard. Up till that time soldiers seem to have remained scrupulously outside the chamber.[46] Thus on 18 October 31 the Praetorian Prefect, Macro, did enter the chamber to deliver Tiberius' letter, but then left at once to go to the Guards' camp.[47] During the session Laco, the Praefectus Vigilum, seems to have remained outside until the consul called Sejanus forward: only at that point did Laco come in to stand beside Sejanus, and later escort him to prison.[48] In 33, however, the senate allowed Tiberius' request that he be permitted to enter the chamber with an escort of the Praetorian Prefect, Macro, and a few military tribunes and centurions.[49] Of course Tiberius never came, nor is it certain whether Gaius ever used the "military guard" likewise voted to him in 40.[50] On Tiberius' death Macro had again acted as envoy to the senate, when he was sent by Gaius to read out the old emperor's will. But there is no sign in Dio's account[51] that he took any further part in the proceedings. Claudius does seem to have been in the habit of bringing an escort of the Praetorian Prefect and military tribunes. According to Suetonius,[52] he made a point of always requesting the senate's prior permission.

Cornelius Sabinus, *tribunus militum* and one of the leading assassins, intervened passionately in a debate after Gaius' murder,[53] while at the same time a soldier interjected a plea that civil war be avoided and Claudius accepted as emperor; he then rushed through the midst of the senate, followed by his comrades.[54] It is not clear whether he was on guard in the chamber itself, or stationed near enough outside to hear the discussion.

---

[44] 7.11.4.

[45] A decree passed at Claudius' instigation even forbade soldiers to attend the *salutatio* in senators' homes (Suet. *Claud.* 25).

[46] On the Praetorian Prefect, see below. Tacitus' remark about Tiberius in 14, "miles in curiam comitabatur" (*Ann.* 1.7), is perhaps not to be taken literally, especially as the latter seems to have been behaving with such studied propriety in all other respects. Note his immediate dismissal of *comites* when he was brought to the senate by litter (Suet. *Tib.* 30).

[47] Dio 58.9.6.

[48] Dio 58.10.6-8.

[49] Tac. *Ann.* 6.15; Dio 58.18.5; cf. Suet. *Tib.* 65.

[50] Dio 59.26.3.

[51] 59.1.2-3.

[52] *Claud.* 12.

[53] Josephus, *AJ* 19.261; *PIR*² C 1431.

[54] Josephus, *BJ* 2.211-212; cf. *AJ* 19.249.

According to Dio,[55] soldiers carried into the senate heads of people killed on 15 January 69. But thereafter soldiers are not heard of again in the House until the end of the second century.[56] In 193 there were large numbers of soldiers—and freedmen—present at a meeting in Pertinax's reign; Didius Julianus brought in a large number, too, to his first meeting as emperor; and Septimius Severus likewise came with soldiers and friends, both armed.[57] In addition, according to the *Historia Augusta*,[58] Caracalla stationed a military guard in a double line in the midst of the benches when he entered the senate on the day after Geta's murder. Soldiers were evidently not present at the meeting where members opposed Didius Julianus' proposal that a delegation should go out to treat with Septimius Severus' force, because Didius thought of ordering in soldiers "either to force the senators to obedience, or to slaughter them."[59]

From the inception of their office by Augustus, Praetorian Prefects naturally developed a close relationship with the emperor. A few of the Prefects were senators on appointment,[60] and a few became senators during their tenure of the office.[61] The majority, however, were chosen deliberately from the equestrian class, and therefore by definition were excluded from the senate.[62] Though it might be imagined otherwise, there is no evidence for a general attempt on the part of emperors to have membership of the senate extended to such Praetorian Prefects during their term of office. Instead Prefects commonly gained senatorial rank (though not membership) through the award of *ornamenta praetoria* or *consularia*, and in many cases from the second century became senators *after* laying down their office.[63] Claudius was therefore unusual in asking that his Praetorian Prefect, Rufrius Pollio, be granted a seat in the senate. Evidently the latter was to occupy it only when he was escorting the emperor; whether the privilege actually allowed him to take a part in proceedings, as opposed to merely witnessing them, is not clear. Claudius claimed that the same privilege had been allowed to a Ligurian, Valerius, when Augustus requested it, but nothing further is known of the precedent.[64] When the

---

[55] 64.6.5ᵃ.

[56] For soldiers being stationed outside the House, however, see chap. 6 sect. 3.

[57] Dio 74.8.4 and 12.5; HA, *Sev.* 7.4.

[58] *Caracalla* 2.9; cf. Herodian 4.5.1.

[59] HA, *Did. Jul.* 6.7.

[60] For example, Arrecinus Clemens (Tac. *Hist.* 4.68), and Titus.

[61] For example, Sejanus and Plautianus.

[62] Note M. Aurelius' public expression of regret about Pertinax, "that he was a senator and therefore could not be made Praetorian Prefect," according to HA, *Pert.* 2.9.

[63] See W. Ensslin, *PW* 22 s.v. Praefectus Praetorio, cols. 2398-2400; A. Chastagnol, *BHAC* 1975/6. pp. 123-127; and chap. 11 sect. 6 below.

[64] Dio 60.23.2-3. On Valerius, see M. Lambertz, *PW* 7 A s.v. Valerius no. 220, col. 52. If the speech of the consul Falco at HA, *Pert.* 5.2 is to be taken literally, the Praetorian

senate permitted the Praetorian Prefect, Nymphidius Sabinus, to "initiate and confirm all its decrees"[65] in mid 68, it remains obscure whether or not this honor would consequently have allowed him to attend sessions.

It appears that women might be present at sessions of the imperial *consilium*,[66] and, as we have seen, they certainly attended trials in the senate as defendants and witnesses; at least one exceptional case of a female prosecutor is also known. Just conceivably, too, an exceptional lady might appear as envoy.[67] Women might further be invited to the House for a particular purpose, as was Domitian's wife after his assassination, according to legend.[68] But otherwise they were strictly excluded. It was quite natural therefore that Alliatoria Celsilla's male relatives should apply to the senate on her behalf for exemption from a *senatus consultum* which forbade the demolition of buildings.[69] Though Livia was often criticized in strong terms for meddling in affairs of state, it was at least acknowledged in her favor that she never ventured to enter the senate chamber, camps, or public assemblies.[70] The same could not be said of Agrippina by her son. In the letter he wrote to the senate after her death, Nero claimed, among other examples of her intolerable behavior, that she could hardly be restrained from bursting into the House.[71] It is true that Pliny the Elder[72] makes a barbed remark about Agrippina, "the wife of Claudius Caesar," ordering the senate to vote *ornamenta praetoria* to ex-slaves—an allusion which has frequently been linked with the award to Pallas in 52.[73] But Nero's charge against his mother is supported neither by this remark, nor by Tacitus' narrative. He recounts how at the beginning of the reign the senate was required to meet in the palace, where an extra door had been

Prefect Laetus would seem to have been present at Pertinax's first meeting as emperor: but it would be best to put no weight on this reference. The way in which Elagabalus taunted Macrinus with his usurpation of a senator's rights has already been noted.

[65] Plut. *Galba* 8.

[66] Note H. A. Musurillo, *The Acts of the Pagan Martyrs*, no. 4 col. ii lines 7-8; cf. Dio 60.33.7. For Plotina allegedly interfering with the business of Trajan's *consilium*, see Musurillo, ibid. no. 8 lines 26-32.

[67] For one who did serve as envoy from Ephesus to M. Aurelius and Commodus, perhaps accompanying her father, see H. Engelmann and D. Knibbe, "Aus ephesichen Skizzenbüchern," *JÖAI* 1978-80 Hauptblatt 52. pp. 19-61, no. 22 with *PIR²* I 177 and 686.

[68] Procopius, *Historia Arcana* 8.15-18.

[69] *FIRA²* I no. 45 II.

[70] *Consolatio ad Liviam* 49-50; Dio 57.12.3; but cf. 56.47.1. On meddling by Livia, note the rumor that Tiberius' letter to the senate denouncing Agrippina and Nero Caesar in 29 had arrived so soon after Livia's death that it might actually have arrived earlier and been suppressed by her (Tac. *Ann.* 5.3). It was to her, too, at the beginning of the reign that Sallustius Crispus expressed his disapproval of Tiberius' intention to refer all matters to the senate (ibid. 1.6).

[71] Tac. *Ann.* 14.11.

[72] *NH* 35.201.

[73] Cf. Tac. *Ann.* 12.53; Plin. *Ep.* 7.29; 8.6.

opened into the chamber, veiled by a curtain. Behind this curtain Agrippina listened to the proceedings in the same way that any other man or woman was entitled to do. Yet even she did not dare to proceed further.[74]

Only for Elagabalus' reign is there any evidence of women actually attending the senate.[75] Dio[76] states that Maesa and Soaemias were present at Elagabalus' formal adoption of Alexianus in 221, though it may well be, of course, that this was a strictly ceremonial occasion with no other business conducted.[77] All further evidence comes from the *Historia Augusta* and cannot be relied upon. But for what it is worth, both Elagabalus' mother and grandmother are said to have been invited to the senate by him, and to have attended as participants, not just spectators;[78] after the emperor's death, the senate allegedly forbade any further attendance by women in the strongest possible terms.[79] This is at least consistent with the fact that while Severus Alexander's mother and grandmother are criticized for exerting undue influence, in our extant sources they are never alleged to have attended the senate during his reign.[80]

In short, then, even though there were infringements at moments of crisis and at the whim of certain provocative emperors, the traditional exclusion of all but members from the chamber during sessions does seem to have been generally upheld in the Principate. This is in itself a notable conclusion for the character of the senate as a working assembly over the period. At the same time, however, it is appropriate to recall that there still remained a variety of means by which non-members could, and did, learn of senatorial business, as we shall be seeing in later chapters.

[74] Tac. *Ann*. 13.5. Only John of Antioch at Dio 61.3.2 goes so far as to claim that Agrippina did attend the senate.

[75] If the speech of the consul Falco at HA, *Pert*. 5.2 is taken literally, Commodus' concubine Marcia might have been present at Pertinax's first meeting as emperor: but, as mentioned above, it is best to put no weight on this reference.

[76] 79.17.2.

[77] Cf. Dio 55.22.5, where girls were admitted to cast lots for becoming Vestal Virgins.

[78] HA, *Elagab*. 4.1-2; 15.6.

[79] Ibid. 18.3. The testimony of the *Historia Augusta* (*Elagab*. 4.3) about a "women's senate" ("senaculum"; for this term, cf. chap. 3 sect. 1) founded by Elagabalus sounds highly dubious: but see further J. Straub, "Senaculum, id est mulierum senatus," *BHAC* 1964/5. pp. 221-240. In a figure of ridicule Pliny the Elder (*NH* 37.85) remarks that the question of which gemstone is supreme has been determined by a "mulierum senatus consultum."

[80] There is no suggestion that the title "mother of the senate," by which Julia Domna, Julia Maesa, and Julia Mamaea were hailed in the early third century, allowed them to take any part in proceedings. They were, of course, hailed as "mother" of much else besides (see *PIR*[2] I 663, 678, 649 respectively).

5

THE EMPEROR IN THE SENATE

In considering attendance at meetings of the senate it is naturally most important to examine the emperor's practice and its development; as already mentioned, this topic has been reserved to form the principal theme of a separate chapter. First, however, in this connection the emperor's formal position in the House must be understood.

1. The Emperor's Position

In any discussion of the emperor's position it should always be borne in mind that his contact with senators was by no means confined to sessions in the House. For although it is an outstanding feature of our period that he grew increasingly detached from the sessions of the corporate body and also came to absorb its functions (as this book will amply demonstrate), at the same time there was significantly little shift in the pattern whereby his social contacts remained almost exclusively confined to the senatorial class and certain closely related *equites*.[1] Not only were the advisers in his *consilium* always drawn from this narrow group, but much of his business was done with senators,[2] and it was above all senators with whom he mixed socially. The affable emperor visited them when they were sick,[3] invited them to dinner, and accepted invitations in return.[4] Predictably, senators responded well to such imperial civility. It was an emperor's

---

[1] On the closeness of leading *equites* in Rome to the senatorial class, cf. Josephus, *AJ* 19.3.

[2] Whatever the town council of Tergeste may claim in honoring their fellow citizen L. Fabius Severus in the mid second century, to them the practical value of his senatorial status was plainly the figure he could cut in the imperial court and his advocacy there. See chap. 2 sect. 6 note 61.

[3] Suet. *Aug.* 53; cf. Tac. *Agr.* 43; Dio 60.12.1; 69.7.4; 71.35.4 (M. Aurelius as Caesar); HA, *Hadr.* 9.7; *Sev. Alex.* 20.1.

[4] Suet. *Aug.* 53 and 74; *Vesp.* 2; Tac. *Ann.* 2.28; Plut. *Galba* 8 (Nymphidius Sabinus playing emperor); *Otho* 3; Dio 65.2.2-3; 66.10.6 and 16.3; 67.9; Plin. *Paneg.* 49; HA, *Hadr.* 22.4; *Sev.* 1.7; Dio 74.14.2; 78.8.4. By contrast, M. Aurelius learned from Antoninus to allow his close friends leisure by *not* always inviting them to dinner (*To Himself* 1.16.2). For senators at the imperial *salutatio*, see chap. 2 sect. 4.

tyrannical behavior that aroused hostility. For example, on a personal level the extravagant demands for obeisance made by Gaius and Domitian were unacceptable.[5] The tragic consequences of a clash between a tactless emperor and the majority of senators are well known. In the end no ruler could seriously alienate the senatorial class and survive.[6] But he might wreak untold harm before he was removed. In particular, Gaius,[7] Nero,[8] and Commodus[9] openly displayed their hatred of the class and threatened to wipe it out. In the same way, Elagabalus did not disguise his contempt.[10]

Almost to the end of our period emperors had all been members of the senatorial class themselves before their accession. During their reigns their formal status was that of patrician senator. Thus when Dio[11] speaks of senatorial decrees stipulating that the emperor should not put to death anyone of the same rank as himself, he means senators. Similarly, Martial's description of Nerva as "iustissimus omnium senator"[12] is intended as a compliment. Emperors continued to hold ordinary consulships,[13] while members of their families occupied senatorial magistracies in the regular order, even if ahead of time. When he revised the senatorial roll in his first *lectio senatus* of 28 B.C., Octavian took the Republican title *princeps senatus*, accorded to the senator who headed the list of members.[14] It seems reasonable to believe that all his successors continued to head the list during their reigns, but the only later one who can be proved to have followed Augustus in taking the Republican title is Pertinax. As Dio explains: "He took all the customary titles belonging to the office, and also a further one to indicate his wish to be democratic; for he was called *princeps senatus* in accordance with the ancient practice."[15] Inscriptions and a papyrus accord Pertinax the title, but it does not seem to have appeared on his coins.[16] Dio's unique claim[17] that Tiberius was called *princeps senatus*, and even used the title himself during the reign, is altogether unsubstantiated. Equally, according to the *Historia Augusta*,[18]

[5] Seneca, *De Benef.* 2.12.1-2; Plin. *Paneg.* 24.2; Epictetus 4.1.17.

[6] It is not difficult to see how there grew up a legend that Domitian had been murdered by the senate (preserved in Malalas pp. 266-267 Dindorf).

[7] Suet. *Calig.* 48-49; Dio 59.25.5.

[8] Suet. *Nero* 37, 43, cf. 39; Dio 63.15.1 and 27.2; cf. Tac. *Hist.* 4.42.

[9] Dio 72.21.2; Herodian 1.8.7 and 14.9; HA, *Commod.* 3.9.

[10] HA, *Elagab.* 20.1.

[11] 67.2.4; cf. 53.17.10.

[12] 10.72.9.

[13] See Appian, *Bell. Civ.* 1.103; Dio 53.17.4; 79.8.2-3.

[14] *RG* 7.2; Dio 53.1.3, πρόκριτος τῆς γερουσίας. J. Suolahti, "Princeps Senatus," *Arctos* 7. 1972. pp. 207-218, is unreliable.

[15] 74.5.1.

[16] *ILS* 408, 409, 5842, 5845; *Arval Acta*, para. 85a line 10; *BGU* II. 646 = U. Wilcken, *Chrestomathie*, no. 490 line 15.

[17] 57.8.2.

[18] *Gord.* 9.7. *PIR²* L 258.

the future emperor Valerian was *princeps senatus* in 238; but the description is presumably informal, and not to be taken in the technical sense. The title *pater senatus*, which Claudius refused in 48,[19] had no significance beyond its novelty. Coins show that Commodus, Balbinus, and Pupienus later took it.[20]

From 23 B.C., even when he was not occupying the consulship, Augustus possessed *imperium* and *tribunicia potestas*, and from 19 B.C. he had the right to sit on a curule chair in between the two presiding consuls.[21] His successors were likewise privileged, and, as we have seen,[22] certain of them were also permitted to bring an escort into the House. Both powers gave the emperor authority to summon the senate. He usually seems to have done so by virtue of his *imperium*.[23] In 22 B.C., if Dio[24] is accurate, Augustus received the right to summon the senate as often as he pleased, while the *Lex de Imperio Vespasiani* confirmed that meetings summoned specially by the emperor had full legal standing: "And that, when a session of the senate is held in accordance with his pleasure or authority or order or mandate or in his presence, the authority of all proceedings therein shall be maintained and shall be observed, just as if that session of the senate had been announced and was held in accordance with a statute."[25]

To expedite the handling of the emperor's business, Augustus in 23 B.C. had been granted "the privilege of bringing before the senate at each meeting any one matter at whatever time he liked, even if he were not consul at the time."[26] By convention modern studies refer to this privilege as the *ius primae relationis*, though there is no ancient testimony for that name. Rather than stipulating blatantly that the emperor shall have priority, it is notable how in Dio's description the grant is more discreetly and more widely drawn. Such a privilege is not known to have been granted again until the second century. The earliest evidence which may be relevant is perhaps the *senatus consultum* whereby Cyzicus' right to have an association of *neoi* ("young men") is confirmed: "Sententia dicta ab Appio Gallo cos. desig. relatione IIII concedente imp. Caes[are Tito A]elio Hadriano Anto[nino Aug. Pio . . .] IIII relatione sua [. . . Kyzicen]os ex Asia, [. . . quos neos a]ppellant [. . . . .]"[27]

Presumably we may gather from the phrasing that the emperor Antoninus

---

[19] Tac. *Ann.* 11.25.

[20] See *BMC* IV, pp. 730, 811-812; VI, Balbinus and Pupienus, nos. 81, 92-94, 102.

[21] See chap. 3 sect. 2.

[22] Chap. 4 sect. 4.

[23] See chap. 6 sect. 1.

[24] 54.3.3.

[25] *FIRA*[2] I no. 15 lines 7-9.

[26] Dio 53.32.5.

[27] *FIRA*[2] I no. 48 lines 11-17.

had the right to make at least four *relationes* at a meeting. It was certainly privileges of this type which, according to the *Historia Augusta*, were granted to M. Aurelius as Caesar in 147,[28] and later to Pertinax[29] and Severus Alexander.[30] There is no obvious explanation of why such grants should have been made only to some emperors, or of why the number of *relationes* should have varied.

When he wished to be present and preside, the emperor exercised the normal presidential prerogative: in particular, during the *interrogatio* he called members in the order of his choice, and he spoke himself wherever he liked. It was notable that Tiberius even called upon magistrates during the *interrogatio*, though Trajan does not seem to have done likewise at the trial of Marius Priscus in 100.[31]

When the emperor attended as *privatus*, he might occupy a technically curious position. Like a normal *privatus*, he might be called upon to speak, and he might vote.[32] On the other hand, more like a magistrate than a *privatus*, he might keep silent, or he might exercise the right to speak at any stage of the proceedings.[33] Of the emperors who attended the senate as *privati*, it is Tiberius' practice that we can appreciate best. He understood the unique, and difficult, position of the emperor. As he wrote in a letter of 21,[34] he considered that when a *relatio* was made by a magistrate, the emperor should be present to give his opinion in the course of the *interrogatio*: yet when the latter did speak, a statement even greater and more lofty than that made by a magistrate was expected. By giving notice during the trial of Granius Marcellus in 15 that he would definitely offer his *sententia* in this instance, Tiberius immediately provoked from Cn. Piso the question of whether he would speak first or last.[35] In the former case members might feel deprived of their freedom of opinion; in the latter, those with whom the emperor turned out to disagree might feel apprehensive. In 25, according to Dio,[36] the presiding consul prevented what was otherwise expected to be inescapable condemnation for a defendant on a charge of *maiestas*, by calling upon Tiberius to give his opinion first: for fear of appearing to favor himself, he then supported acquittal.

If the emperor was absent from a meeting, he might communicate by

---

[28] *Ius quintae relationis (Marcus* 6.6).
[29] *Ius quartae relationis (Pert.* 5.6).
[30] *Ius quintae relationis (Sev. Alex.* 1.3).
[31] See chap. 7 sect. 11.
[32] See, for example, Suet. *Tib.* 31.
[33] See chap. 7 sect. 19.
[34] Tac. *Ann.* 3.53.
[35] Tac. *Ann.* 1.74.
[36] 57.24.7.

letter, and he had the unique right to put forward a *relatio* by this means.[37] Germanicus sometimes read for Augustus, and Vespasian's letters were read by his sons.[38] Wills and other documents might be read by imperial freedmen. Nero stipulated that the consuls themselves should read his communications.[39] Otherwise it was normal practice for a *quaestor Caesaris* to act for the emperor.[40] Exceptionally, a praetor read once at a session in 217 when no quaestor happened to be present.[41]

Whether they were to be present or absent, all emperors expected to be kept informed of senatorial business. From some time between 27 and 18 B.C. onwards Augustus was able to achieve this end through his senatorial *consilium*, which considered items in advance. From A.D. 13 its composition was changed and its power increased. But Tiberius abandoned it. Thereafter there was no such *consilium* until the reign of Severus Alexander at the very end of our period, when this body was revived in a significantly modified form.[42]

Augustus did not wish to convey the impression too openly that he influenced discussion in the senate. He seldom put forward measures in his own name. It was more discreet, and more convenient, for them to be proposed by his supporters. In 13, when alternatives to the five percent inheritance tax were under discussion, he specifically forbade Germanicus and Drusus to make any suggestion, for fear that it would be regarded as his, and adopted without more ado.[43] Similarly, in the following year Tiberius required a member to assure the House that he had not been prompted in advance to make a particular proposal. And when presiding at a trial in 20 the emperor deliberately omitted to call first upon Drusus (as consul designate), so that others should not feel obliged to agree with his opinion.[44]

---

[37] Cf. *FIRA*[2] I no. 15 line 3, where in my view the distinction drawn is between making ("facere") a *relatio* in person and communicating ("remittere") one by letter, not between making a *relatio* and referring one back for reconsideration (the interpretation of, for example, *Ox. Lat. Dict.* p. 1612 s.v. remitto, no. 4 b). Though instances can be cited of the latter practice (see below), to speak of it as an emperor's right would make no sense when by definition everything had to depend upon a decision by the House to refer in the first place.

[38] Dio 56.26.2; 66.10.6; Suet. *Tit.* 6. Compare Lucius Caesar reading out the dispatches of his brother Gaius (Dio 55.10a.9). Drusus read for Tiberius when the latter broke down during the meeting after Augustus' death (Suet. *Tib.* 23; cf. Dio 56.33.1).

[39] Suet. *Tib.* 23; Dio 56.32.1; 59.16.3; Suet. *Nero* 15.

[40] Note in general Ulpian, *Dig.* 1.13.1.4; also Tac. *Ann.* 16.27; Suet. *Aug.* 65; Dio 54.25.5 (when Augustus was present, but hoarse); 60.2.2; HA, *Hadr.* 3.1. On known holders of the office, see M. Cébeillac, *Les 'Quaestores Principis et Candidati' aux Ier et IIème Siècles de l'Empire*, Milan, 1972.

[41] Dio 78.16.4.

[42] On Augustus' senatorial *consilium*, see Suet. *Aug.* 35; Dio 53.21.4-5; 56.28.2-3; and the treatment of the whole topic in J. A. Crook, *Consilium Principis*, chap. 2.

[43] Dio 56.28.5.

[44] Tac. *Ann.* 1.8; 3.22.

Once the senatorial *consilium* had been abandoned, emperors who were especially anxious for the smooth passage of a particular item of business had to make their own preparations, in the same way that Octavian had forewarned his close associates in the senate before offering to lay down his powers in January 27 B.C.[45] Tiberius laid elaborate plans before making his denunciation of Sejanus on 18 October 31.[46] In 37 Gaius arranged in advance that the senate should declare Tiberius' will invalid, while Claudius persuaded members to propose his marriage to Agrippina, and Nero planned to do likewise when he wished to marry Acte.[47] In 48 Agrippina herself induced the consul designate to frame a *sententia* in which the senate begged Claudius to betroth Domitius (Nero) and Octavia.[48] Similarly, Hadrian sent a *libellus* to the consuls a few days in advance of a stated meeting in 129, requesting them to put forward certain legislative proposals.[49]

When potentially contentious items were to be put forward by others, emperors were pleased to be informed in advance. In a letter Tiberius expressed regret that the aediles of 22 had not consulted him first, before making a *relatio* about curbing extravagance, and he was critical of a tribune and a *Quindecimvir Sacris Faciundis* who in 32 had successfully pressed for a book of Sibylline oracles to be included in the official canon without first consulting the *magistri* of the college, of whom the emperor was almost certainly one.[50] When cases were laid before the emperor (charges of *maiestas* in particular), he might decide to quash them without further ado, or hear them himself, or refer them to the senate, or elsewhere.[51] By the end of our period, if Dio can be believed, the senate's handling of issues was governed by the emperor. Unfortunately, the fragmentary nature of the passage leaves the context unclear, but he does say: "It was not lawful that an investigation of any matter should take place in the senate except on the instructions of the emperor."[52]

When the emperor was present at a meeting, he could express disagreement with unacceptable proposals on the spot. If he were actually presiding, presidential prerogative itself allowed him to modify or reject proposals, as Tiberius did after the trials of Piso and Plancina in 20.[53] Equally, when present but not presiding, he could simply voice disagree-

---

[45] Dio 53.2.7.
[46] Dio 58.9.3 and 13.1.
[47] Dio 59.1.2; Suet. *Claud.* 26; *Nero* 28.
[48] Tac. *Ann.* 12.9; cf. Dio 60.32.2.
[49] *Dig.* 5.3.20.6.
[50] Tac. *Ann.* 3.53; 6.12.
[51] See chap. 16 sect. 2.
[52] 78.19.5.
[53] Tac. *Ann.* 3.17-18.

ment, as Tiberius frequently did. Thus he rejected almost all the honors proposed for Livia in 14, as well as a proposal to consult the Sibylline books the following year.[54] He asked for the separation of charges of adultery and *maiestas* against Appuleia Varilla in 17, opposed the abolition of rewards for informers in 24, and modified the proposed punishment of Catus Firmius shortly afterwards.[55] He also spoke against a proposal made "off the question" by Cornelius Dolabella in the *interrogatio* after the trial of C. Silanus in 22.[56] Among later emperors we hear of Pertinax and Septimius Severus rejecting proposals, and of Didius Julianus asking for one to be modified.[57] It is not clear whether Nero was present or absent when he begged mercy for M. Asinius Marcellus, defendant in a forgery case in 61.[58]

When the emperor was absent, a *relatio* which he had not previously considered might be referred to him without any discussion—as happened to the aediles' *relatio* about curbing extravagance in 22, already mentioned. In 56 the consuls did allow some members to speak first, out of order, about the offenses of freedmen, and to make *sententiae*, but they did not dare begin a formal *relatio* on the issue without first enquiring about the emperor's attitude. So they merely wrote to Nero explaining the views taken.[59] Similarly, in 29, when the consuls were uncertain about what reaction Tiberius expected in response to a very harsh letter he had sent, they preferred to make no *relatio* at all.[60]

Even when certain issues had been raised in the House, the senate often preferred to leave a decision to the emperor. This was understandable when the matters were those which he normally handled, such as finance, or diplomatic relations with foreign kings, for example.[61] It was arguably good sense, too, to raise with the Pontifex Maximus the request of the Flamen Dialis to be considered for a governorship.[62] But there was perhaps less sound reason to leave to the emperor the choice of a governor of Africa, or a decision on whether to curb extravagance, or the verdict in certain trials—unless to postpone an inevitable death sentence.[63] Yet after the condemnation of Clutorius Priscus for slight offenses, and his immediate execution without any consultation of the emperor, Tiberius consid-

---

[54] Tac. *Ann*. 1.14 and 76.
[55] Tac. *Ann*. 2.50; 4.31-32.
[56] Tac. *Ann*. 3.69.
[57] Dio 74.8.5; 76.6.1; 74.14.2ª.
[58] Tac. *Ann*. 14.40.
[59] Tac. *Ann*. 13.26-27.
[60] Tac. *Ann*. 5.3-4.
[61] Tac. *Hist*. 4.9; Dio 53.33.2; 69.15.2.
[62] Tac. *Ann*. 3.59.
[63] Tac. *Ann*. 3.32, 35, 52; 4.66; 16.9.

ered it necessary to establish a ten-day interval between the passage of decrees and their registration in the *aerarium Saturni*, so that he could always review them.[64] Fear of the emperor was shown in 62 when the consuls felt bound to report to Nero the unexpectedly lenient verdict successfully urged by Thrasea Paetus at the trial of Antistius Sosianus.[65]

From Pliny's *Letters* we hear of the senate appealing for action by Trajan to curb abuses of the written ballot, newly introduced for elections.[66] A tribune in the course of a session calls for him to stop sharp practices by advocates, while on another occasion a member asks that he be called upon to limit scandalously high expenditure by candidates seeking office.[67] In the arguments over whether Varenus Rufus (to be tried on a charge of *repetundae*) should be allowed to summon witnesses from his province, both sides evidently entertain hopes of enlisting the emperor's support.[68] Even if a matter were not specifically referred to the emperor, he would learn of it through *acta senatus*, and might take action in consequence. Thus Nero learned of Thrasea's motion "off the question" at the trial of Claudius Timarchus in 62, and later made a *relatio* about it himself.[69] According to the story in the *Historia Augusta*,[70] it was his fury on reading of the honors paid to a relative of Clodius Albinus by the senate that prompted Septimius Severus to deify Commodus. By contrast, Nerva evidently did not react (as he might have done) to the motion which Pliny made against Publicius Certus.[71]

The emperor was not only in a position to influence the business and decisions of the senate by informal means; by virtue of his tribunician power he also had the right of veto, and was prepared to exercise it.[72] When notice of prosecutions was given, he might forbid their hearing—as Tiberius did in the case of L. Ennius, an *eques* charged with *maiestas* for having melted down a silver statue of the emperor in 22. Nero acted likewise to protect the son of P. Suillius Rufus, condemned in 58.[73] When present at meetings the emperor might veto a *relatio*: no such instance can be cited for our period, but a member does mention the possibility to Tiberius in 14.[74] Equally he might veto *sententiae*. There was rarely the

[64] See no. 26 in list, chap. 15 sect. 5.
[65] Tac. *Ann*. 14.49.
[66] 4.25.2.
[67] *Ep*. 5.13.7; 6.19.3.
[68] *Ep*. 6.5.5.
[69] Tac. *Ann*. 15.22.
[70] *Sev*. 11.3; see further chap. 9 sect. 3 note 86.
[71] Plin. *Ep*. 9.13.22.
[72] Cf. Tac. *Ann*. 14.48.
[73] Tac. *Ann*. 3.70; 13.43. For other cases which Nero may have vetoed in advance, see ibid. 13.10.
[74] Tac. *Ann*. 1.13.

need for such a step, since, as we have seen, an expression of disagreement from him was normally sufficient in itself. But Tiberius did actually veto proposals that Vibius Serenus be executed *more maiorum* in 24, while Nero (as president) vetoed the ominous proposal of the consul designate after the Pisonian conspiracy in 65 that a temple be erected to the Divine Nero.[75] If Suetonius[76] is to be believed, Domitian had certain defendants on a charge of *maiestas* condemned to death *more maiorum*, but then vetoed the sentence and asked that they be allowed to choose the manner of their deaths.

The emperor might veto decrees or verdicts passed at meetings which he had not attended. This happened frequently in the Julio-Claudian period.[77] Where honors were offered, a veto was unnecessary. They could simply not be accepted, or not acted upon. Thus when an arch was voted to Livia on her death in 29, Tiberius hesitated to annul the decree; instead he promised to do the work himself, yet never attended to it.[78] In an extreme case the emperor might veto consideration of proposals in advance: in an effort to prevent flattery of Sejanus, Tiberius forbade consideration of any measure which proposed honors for himself.[79] According to the *Historia Augusta*,[80] M. Aurelius forbade the senate to impose heavy sentences on those who had supported the revolt of Avidius Cassius. Dio does not clarify whether it was before, or after, proposals had been made that Tiberius forbade the deification of Livia, and Claudius the grant of honors to his grandson.[81] The stage at which Antoninus forbade prosecution of conspirators against him in the senate is also unclear.[82]

Fronto[83] speaks about the duty of a Princeps to "urge necessary steps in the senate." Persuasion rather than command was the tactful approach commonly adopted by considerate emperors.[84] But it was hardly essential, when from the beginning of the Principate there could rarely be any question of rejecting imperial proposals. At the New Year, for example, all senators took an oath to observe the past measures of emperors whose memory was

---

[75] Tac. *Ann.* 4.30; 15.74. Nero was probably present when he likewise exercised his veto in 54/55, but this is not entirely clear from Tac. *Ann.* 13.10-11.

[76] *Dom.* 11.

[77] For example, Tac. *Ann.* 1.73; 5.2; 14.45 and 48; 16.11; Suet. *Tib.* 17, 26, 33; *Claud.* 6.

[78] Dio 58.2.6. For rejection of honors, see further, for example, Dio 51.20.4; 53.26.5; 54.35.5; 74.7.1; Plin. *Ep.* 8.6.8-12; HA, *Antonin.* 5.2; 10.1; *Pert.* 6.9.

[79] Dio 58.8.4; cf. 58.12.8; possibly Suet. *Aug.* 56 for another instance.

[80] *Marcus* 25.5.

[81] 58.2.1; 60.30.6ª.

[82] HA, *Antonin.* 7.3; *Epit. de Caes.* 15.6.

[83] *De Eloq.* 2.7 = p. 136 H.

[84] Note Papinian (*Frag. Vat.* 294.2) writing of Severus and Caracalla: "maximi principes nostri suaserunt et ita senatus censuit."

not condemned, as well as the future ones of the current ruler.[85] An *eques* on trial in 32 for friendship with Sejanus reflected upon such lack of independence in his address to the absent Tiberius, according to Tacitus: "It is not for us to comment on the man whom you elevate above others and on your reasons. The gods have granted you supreme control of affairs: to us is left the glory of obeying."[86] More formally, in its decree of 53, acknowledging Pallas' refusal of the offer of fifteen million sesterces, the senate: ". . . declares that though it had freely and justly taken steps to grant this sum to Pallas amongst the other distinctions offered him on account of his loyalty and devotion to duty, yet since it holds that in nothing is it lawful to oppose the emperor, in this matter also it must bow to his wishes."[87] In a similar vein Tacitus has Maternus reflect on how state issues are now decided by "a single man of highest wisdom,"[88] while Pliny, regretting the rarity of the same issues in the senate early in the second century, admits: "Everything today, it is true, depends on the will of one man who has taken upon himself for the general good all our cares and responsibilities."[89]

We do hear of senatorial disagreement with Augustus and Tiberius,[90] though the only two specific instances known for the former were perhaps cases where he expected opposition to be voiced anyway—a request to have not one colleague, but two, whenever he held the consulship, and an offer after his illness in 23 B.C. to read out his will.[91] Thereafter disagreement with the emperor still occurs, but it is extremely rare.[92] In 37 Gaius' demand for the deification of Tiberius met with so hesitant a response from the senate that he abandoned it,[93] while in 58, after the serious doubts expressed, Nero likewise withdrew his suggestion that *vectigalia* be abolished. However, this matter was probably aired in the emperor's *consilium* rather than in the full senate:[94] even at a time when

---

[85] Dio 57.8.4. On the oath see P. Herrmann, *Der römische Kaisereid, Hypomnemata* 20, Göttingen, 1968, pp. 107-110, and further chap. 6 sect. 4 below.

[86] *Ann*. 6.8.

[87] Plin. *Ep*. 8.6.10.

[88] *Dial*. 41, "sapientissimus et unus."

[89] *Ep*. 3.20.12.

[90] Suet. *Aug*. 54; *Tib*. 31.

[91] Suet. *Aug*. 37; Dio 53.31.1.

[92] It seems best to set aside Tertullian's story (*Apol*. 5.1-2), variously reproduced in other sources, that the senate rejected Tiberius' proposal to recognize Christ as a god. For discussion see T. D. Barnes, "Legislation against the Christians," *JRS* 58. 1968. pp. 32-50 at pp. 32-33.

[93] Dio 59.3.7.

[94] Tac. *Ann*. 13.50. For support of the former notion, see J. A. Crook, *Consilium Principis*, p. 46; P. A. Brunt, *JRS* 56. 1966. p. 86 n. 72; for the latter, R. Syme, *Tacitus*, p. 416. I would incline to private discussion, in the same way that objections to the application of Gallic notables for "ius adipiscendorum in urbe honorum" seem to have been made privately

relations between Nero and the House were still cordial, it strains credibility
to imagine that an imperial proposal would be rejected there. Yet we do
still hear of some remarkable verdicts by the senate in cases where it knew
the emperor's wishes, but did not act upon them. Thus at the very end of
his life Tiberius, for example, was furious that certain defendants about
whom he had written to the senate (albeit briefly) were discharged without
a hearing. Nero, too, did not disguise his displeasure over the unexpectedly
lenient sentence passed at the trial of Antistius Sosianus in 62.[95]

Later the leniency of both Nerva and Antoninus towards conspirators
evidently met with senatorial criticism; so, too, did Macrinus' handling of
the bid for the Principate made by Elagabalus.[96] But the most celebrated
occasion when the senate opposed imperial wishes in the second century
was its refusal to deify Hadrian in 138: only when Antoninus actually
threatened to abandon the Principate did it relent.[97] Later, senate and people
were said to have dissuaded Commodus from embarking upon a third
northern expedition.[98] In 193, as Didius Julianus' rule was crumbling, the
senate took the initiative in ignoring or rejecting his proposals, and in the
end deprived him of power.[99] Finally, according to the *Historia Augusta*,[100]
it showed little sympathy for Caracalla's account of why he had executed
his brother Geta, and received in complete silence Elagabalus' instruction
that Severus Alexander be deprived of the name Caesar.[101] But essentially
such behavior was an aberration, usually prompted by quite extraordinary
circumstances. Otherwise the senate carried out the emperor's wishes. It
is true that under a sympathetic ruler like M. Aurelius dissent on points
of detail might be hazarded. But even then, as we shall see,[102] the wise
member put forward any counterproposal with extreme deference and elaborate justification.

Altogether it is obvious that the senate and its proceedings were pro-
foundly affected by the nature of the emperor's position there. He could
exercise full control, even if it was seldom his wish to adopt such an
autocratic stance. At least it was common for others' proposals to be

---

to Claudius, before he explained his support in the full senate—a speech which led to the
passage of a *senatus consultum* without further debate, if Tacitus (*Ann.* 11.23-25) be taken
literally.

[95] See further chap. 16 sect. 1.

[96] *Epit. de Caes.* 12.6; 15.6; Dio 78.38.2.

[97] Dio 69.23.3; 70.1.2; HA, *Hadr.* 27.2; *Antonin.* 2.5; Aur. Vict. 14.13-14; Eutrop. *Brev.*
8.7.

[98] HA, *Commod.* 12.8.

[99] Herodian 2.12; HA, *Did. Jul.* 6 and 8.

[100] *Caracalla* 2.11; *Elagab.* 13.2.

[101] Dio (78.19.4) speaks of senators delivering "ambiguous" *sententiae* in 217, but the
fragmentary nature of the passage leaves the context unclear.

[102] Chap. 8.

discussed with him both before and after they were voiced publicly, while *acta senatus* furnished him with reports of all business transacted. Measures of which he did not approve could be vetoed. For putting forward his own business he was able to summon the House at any time, and might exercise the unique privilege of making proposals even when absent. Most important of all, he could be confident that his proposals would gain assent. Naturally these sweeping imperial prerogatives drastically curtailed the freedom which the senate had enjoyed during the Republic.

2. Attendance and Participation by the Emperor

Attendance by the emperor is a further topic on which we are not nearly so well informed as we might wish. It might be misleading, too, to discuss it without at the same time paying some attention to the degree of participation by him. Any generalization on either of these matters is to be attempted with caution when, despite the influence of custom and tradition, each emperor's practice was in the end determined individually. But there is still value in reviewing such knowledge as we do possess, and in seeing what trends develop. Each of the Julio-Claudian emperors will be taken separately, and then later emperors will be examined together.

As an extreme, the argument might be put forward that the emperor hardly needed to attend the senate in person. We have just noted how his formal powers gave him absolute control, so that from the narrowly practical viewpoint of having business conducted to his satisfaction, his presence was seldom required. Yet most emperors did naturally wish to make suitable appearances in the public gathering, and saw that there was much to be gained from them. In particular, on their accession all wished to gain the senate's formal recognition, and during their reigns sought its support in crises. To be sure, Gaius' aim never to write to the senate (thus by implication always attending in person) was only a short-lived piece of "Republican" enthusiasm on his accession,[1] and perhaps a reaction against Tiberius' behavior during the last eleven years of his reign. But even in the latter half of the second century, as we have seen, Fronto can place first in his list of an emperor's duties "to urge necessary steps in the senate."[2] Moreover, almost to the end of our period all emperors before their accession had been senators themselves, or members of the senatorial class, and thus appreciated the traditional feeling that it was a vital part of any senator's role to attend the meetings of the corporate body.

Octavian only returned to Rome from the East in 29 B.C. He left again

---

[1] Dio 59.3.1.
[2] *De Eloq.* 2.7 = p. 136 H.

during 27, to return in 24. In all this time he was consul, and he continued to hold the office until his resignation on 1 July 23. Although dated references to his presence at meetings during this period are few,[3] there is every reason to believe that whenever he was in Rome he did carry out the consul's duty of presiding in the senate. After 23 Augustus took up the consulship again only briefly for the entry of his grandsons Gaius and Lucius to public life in 5 and 2 B.C. respectively. He was out of Italy from 22 to 19, from 15 to 13, and again in 10 B.C. Otherwise all the evidence suggests that he regularly attended debates in the senate, both as president and as *privatus*, as well as an occasional trial.[4] However, old age forced him to reduce the activities he undertook in public—attendance at the senate among them—from A.D. 8, and again even more rigorously in 13, so that thereafter he would attend the senate only on very rare occasions.[5] The one meeting which he seems to have missed deliberately was the occasion in 2 B.C. when the discovery of Julia's scandalous behavior had to be made public: in his shame he could not face the House in person, but sent a letter instead. By contrast, he had made complaints in person at the time of Tiberius' retirement to Rhodes in 6 B.C.[6]

In the course of his reign Tiberius never left Italy. Except for about a year which he spent in Campania (21-22),[7] his absences from Rome were brief until he retired to Capri in 26.[8] Thereafter, although he did visit the mainland, he never set foot in the city itself nor in the senate. Between 14 and 26, however, the evidence (both specific and general) for his assiduous attendance in the senate is so copious that detailed citation becomes superfluous.[9] Tiberius was present at debates and trials, as president and *privatus*, and even on election day.[10] Indeed he provoked comment by his insistence on being present even during times of acute personal

[3] Cf. Dio 52.43.1 (29 B.C.); 53.2.7 and 20.2 (27 B.C.); 53.31.1 (23 B.C.).

[4] Dated references after 1 July 23 B.C.: Dio 53.33.1 (23 B.C.); 54.16.3-5; Livy, *Epit.* 59 (18 B.C.); Dio 54.15.5 (pre-13 B.C.); 54.25.5; 27.2 and 4 (13 B.C.); 55.4.1 (9 B.C.); *FIRA*[2] I no. 68 lines 75-76 (4 B.C.); Suet. *Aug.* 58 (2 B.C.); Dio 55.24.9 (A.D. 5); Vell. 2.111.1 (A.D. 6); Dio 56.26.2 (A.D. 12). In general: Suet. *Aug.* 35; 37; 53-58; 84; 89; *Claud.* 1; Dio 54.12.3 and 15.6. This final reference, among others, shows clearly how Augustus attended sometimes as president, sometimes as *privatus*; cf. Dio 56.41.3.

[5] Dio 55.34.1; 56.28.2. For Augustus writing a letter to the senate (most probably in old age), see Seneca, *De Brev. Vitae* 4.2-4.

[6] Suet. *Aug.* 65; *Tib.* 10.

[7] Cf. Tac. *Ann.* 3.31 and 64. Note his apology during this year for giving an opinion about a *relatio* of the aediles by letter, instead of appearing in person as *privatus* (ibid. 3.53).

[8] His intention to be absent during *res prolatae* in 16 is unexceptional, since it is likely to have been normal for all meetings of the senate to be suspended during this season. See Tac. *Ann.* 2.35 and chap. 6 sect. 4.

[9] Note especially Tac. *Ann.* 4.6; Suet. *Tib.* 30-33; Dio 57.7.2.

[10] Note Tac. *Ann.* 11.21.

stress, such as Drusus' final illness in 23;[11] and according to Tacitus,[12] it took the ordeal of attendance at a trial in 25—where he was abusively insulted—to prompt a reassessment of his practice. The only meetings which we know him to have regularly avoided (out of courtesy to the incoming consuls) were the formal sessions on 1 January.[13]

While Augustus and Tiberius both attended the senate conscientiously, the latter probably participated more, as Crook[14] suggests. Inevitably, such a conclusion may reflect our fuller and more hostile sources for Tiberius. But he would still appear to have suffered more than Augustus in embarrassing and undignified exchanges, and was perhaps by nature a less skillful debater. Unlike his successor, Augustus did not introduce such a wide range of business to the senate, and was wise generally to avoid such trial hearings as took place in the House in his day. During his reign, too, prior preparation in the senatorial committee must often have smoothed discussion of measures.

Gaius went to Sicily for a short spell in summer 38, and campaigned in the north from autumn 39 to August 40. While he is known to have attended debates and trials in the senate, it would be rash to claim that he was assiduous in so doing, and there is no clear evidence that he ever came as *privatus* rather than president.[15] But his comparatively short time in Rome as emperor, his unbalanced behavior, and the dearth of sources make any coherent assessment of his practice impossible. We should also remember that for him, not yet aged 25 on accession, any attendance in the senate in his new role was certain to be a daunting ordeal.

Apart from a six months' absence on campaign in 43-44, Claudius did not leave Italy during his Principate. Out of caution he waited a month after his accession before entering the House itself, and suffered from the same fears as Gaius about attendance there, though for different reasons.[16] From the many references in the sources, however, it is clear that while not so assiduous as Tiberius perhaps, he did regularly attend meetings and trials, both as president and as *privatus*, and was an eager participant.[17]

[11] Tac. *Ann.* 4.8; note also 4.55.

[12] *Ann.* 4.42.

[13] Dio 57.8.5-6.

[14] J. A. Crook, "The Participation of Augustus and Tiberius in Senatorial Debates," in *Consilium Principis*, Appendix I.

[15] He is shown as present by Dio 59.6.1 and 7; 18.1; 19.3 and 7 (the latter three are trials); Aurel. Vict. 3.8. At Dio 59.16.1 and 8 he was presumably not president, but merely entered to make his own speech and then left. We may reckon that he was absent on the two occasions mentioned by Suet. *Calig.* 23 and 28.

[16] Suet. *Claud.* 12; 35-36; Dio 60.3.2.

[17] See many references in Tac. *Ann.* Books 11, 12; Dio, Book 60; Seneca, *Cons. Polyb.* 13.2; Suet. *Claud.* 23, 25, 36, 37, 42, 46; *FIRA*² I no. 43. Note Dio 60.16.3 for his singular practice of opening trials as president, and then sitting in the body of the House. Plin. *Ep.* 3.16.9 could relate to such an occasion.

He is also found present on election day.[18] Dió implies that his attendance was altogether a little less regular towards the end of the reign.[19]

Except for a visit to Greece in 66/68, Nero stayed in Italy during his Principate. No general statement about his attendance in the senate is made by Tacitus or Suetonius, but such references as are given by the sources suggest that he came only as president and even then seldom—in marked contrast to Augustus and Tiberius. Of course, youthfulness, personality, and circumstance influenced his departure from respectable precedent. Except on his accession in 54, the only meeting he is definitely cited as attending is that called after the suppression of the Pisonian conspiracy in 65.[20] In addition, Suetonius' *Life of Lucan* preserves an anecdote of the emperor calling an immediate session to show disapproval of a reading by the poet. If the story can be credited, Nero presumably attended that meeting in person. Otherwise Tacitus and Suetonius strongly imply that he was present later in 54 and in 55, but do not explicitly claim it.[21] Nero did preside at the trial of Suillius Rufus in 58, but Tacitus' account[22] omits to make clear where these proceedings took place. Equally he remains ambiguous on whether the emperor was present or absent on four further occasions: twice in 58, when he favored acquittal of two proconsuls of Africa charged with *repetundae*; in 61 when he begged mercy for M. Asinius Marcellus, defendant in a forgery case; and later when a *sententia* of Thrasea Paetus in 62 was afterwards put forward and passed ''auctore principe.''[23]

On certain significant occasions we know Nero definitely to have been absent, out of fear or nonchalance. He announced the death of Agrippina in 59 by letter.[24] For the trials of Thrasea and others in 66 he took the initiative in summoning the senate himself, but never attended.[25] In this instance he presumably saw no incongruity in his approval of the accusation that Thrasea had not entered the House for three years,[26] when his own record remained little better, so far as we can see. Rather, he had long

[18] Suet. *Claud.* 40.

[19] 60.2.2. Since Claudius was at Baiae on the Ides of March 46 (cf. *FIRA*[2] I no. 71 lines 1-2), he was presumably not present if a stated meeting of the senate duly took place the day before. On the attribution to him of two anonymous speeches to the senate preserved on papyrus, see Appendix 4.

[20] Tac. *Ann.* 13.4; 15.73-74.

[21] It is likely all the same that ''crebrae orationes'' (Tac. *Ann.* 13.11) were delivered in person; cf. Suet. *Nero* 10.

[22] *Ann.* 13.43.

[23] Tac. *Ann.* 13.52; 14.40; 15.22. Note also *AE* 1972. 174.

[24] Quintilian, *Inst. Or.* 8.5.18; Tac. *Ann.* 14.10; Dio 61.14.3. Nero was still concerned by senatorial reaction even after the complimentary proposals passed at the meeting (Tac. *Ann.* 14.13).

[25] Tac. *Ann.* 16.24 and 27.

[26] Tac. *Ann.* 16.22 and 27.

considered himself detached from the corporate body and its sessions. In 68 he merely wrote to the senate from Campania on hearing of Vindex's revolt, and even on returning to Rome did not summon a formal meeting.[27] In other instances, too, it was by letter, rather than appearance in person, that Nero preferred to give a reply or take an initiative.[28] The detailed evidence would certainly uphold Tacitus' generalization that in the case of senatorial trials for *maiestas*, Nero (unlike Domitian) "withdrew his eyes and did not witness the crimes which he had authorized."[29] In Tacitus' version, Cossutianus Capito appreciates Nero's normal practice when in his plea for permission to prosecute Thrasea, he leaves to the end the special request: "Finally write nothing about Thrasea yourself. Leave the senate to decide between us."[30]

After the Julio-Claudian period evidence for emperors' attendance in the senate becomes thinner, and only in a few cases is it possible to form a coherent picture of an individual ruler's practice. Of course we must allow for wide variations in the availability of evidence, on the one hand, and in the character and circumstances of different emperors, on the other. Some emperors never even came to Rome during their reigns (Macrinus, Maximinus, Gordian I and II); others were present, but reigned only for brief periods (Galba, Otho,[31] Vitellius, Titus,[32] Nerva, Pertinax, Didius Julianus);[33] while yet others spent a substantial proportion of their reigns outside Italy (Trajan, Hadrian, M. Aurelius, Septimius Severus, Caracalla). Frequently, therefore, the emperor was able to make contact with the senate only by letter, yet this method commonly came to be preferred, too, even when it was not strictly necessary. As to attendance, there is no question that all emperors who were able to do so did come to the senate in person on their accession, and thereafter on occasions of great importance. Thus, for example, Galba[34] and Nerva[35] attended the sessions which confirmed the adoption of Piso and Trajan respectively, while Caracalla appeared after the murder of Geta.[36] The evidence does suggest that there is now

[27] Suet. *Nero* 41 and 46; Dio 63.26.1 and 4.

[28] Cf. Tac. *Ann.* 13.26; 14.49 and 59; 16.7.

[29] *Agr.* 45.

[30] *Ann.* 16.22.

[31] For Otho's appearances in the senate (apart from his accession), see Tac. *Hist.* 1.85 and 90; Suet. *Otho* 8.

[32] For Titus as emperor in the senate, note Suet. *Tit.* 11.

[33] For Didius Julianus' appearances in the senate (apart from his accession), see Dio 74.14.1 and 2ª; 17.2; HA, *Did. Jul.* 4.5; 5.3; 6.5. Herodian (2.12.3) mentions an occasion when Didius summoned the senate but did not attend himself.

[34] Tac. *Hist.* 1.19; cf. Suet. *Galba* 18.

[35] Dio 68.3.4. For other appearances by Nerva, note Dio 68.2.3, and (presumably) Fronto, *Ver. Imp.* 2.1.7 = p. 117 H; possibly also Plin. *Ep.* 2.7.1 (see Sherwin-White ad loc.). Absent: Plin. *Ep.* 9.13.

[36] He merely made his own speech and then left: Dio 77.3.3; Herodian 4.5.1; HA, *Caracalla* 2.9.

almost no impromptu participation by emperors: when they come to the House, they merely make formal speeches, so far as we can tell. What is harder to establish, however, is the extent to which they attended meetings at all with any regularity after the Julio-Claudian period. A considerable number of legal texts cite orations in the senate made by emperors from Hadrian onwards,[37] and it may seem puzzling that these are not referred to below. Yet valuable though this material may be for giving some notion of the relative frequency with which different emperors cared to bring business to the senate, it does not enable us to determine whether they attended in person on particular occasions, instead of merely communicating by letter.

We may take first those emperors of whose attendance some impression can be formed. Vitellius' frequent appearances in 69, even when there was no matter of special significance on the agenda, reflect a traditional view of how an emperor should properly behave—though our hostile witness Tacitus omits to interpret the short-lived usurper's conduct in so favorable a light.[38] Vitellius' ideal was shared by his successor Vespasian. In early 70 Domitian opens his remarks on his first appearance in the senate with an apology for the absence of his father and brother.[39] Later Dio comments that Vespasian: ". . . regularly attended the meetings of the senate, whose members he consulted on all matters, and he frequently heard cases in the forum. Whatever items he was prevented by old age from reading and whatever communications he sent to the senate when unable to be present, he usually caused to be read by his sons [that is, rather than merely by the *quaestor Caesaris*], thus showing honor to the House even in this detail."[40]

According to Dio and the *Historia Augusta*, Hadrian attempted to attend the senate regularly when he was in Rome,[41] and Antoninus, too, would seem to have been reasonably conscientious.[42] M. Aurelius was evidently

[37] For a list see chap. 15 sect. 4.

[38] Tac. *Hist.* 2.91; cf. 3.37 and 80; Suet. *Vitell.* 16; Dio 65.7.2.

[39] Tac. *Hist.* 4.40.

[40] 66.10.5-6. For Vespasian in the senate, cf. 66.12.1; Suet. *Vesp.* 25; *ILS* 986 lines 29-35. For deference to the senate in what may be a speech by him delivered at Alexandria, see F. Preisigke, *Sammelbuch griechischer Urkunden aus Ägypten*, no. 9528. A. Henrichs (*ZPE* 3. 1968. p. 54 n. 11) plausibly argued that the speech was delivered later than Vespasian's arrival in Alexandria, as its first editor had suggested (H. Gerstinger, "Neue Texte aus der Sammlung Papyrus Erzherzog Rainer in Wien," *Anzeiger der phil.-hist. Kl. d. öst. Akad. d. Wiss.* 1958. no. 15. pp. 195-202). But if the handwriting is correctly dated, there seems no reason to doubt the identification of Vespasian as the speaker (cf. C. P. Jones, *Historia* 22. 1973. p. 309).

[41] Dio 69.7.1; HA, *Hadr.* 8.6. For appearances by Hadrian, cf. ibid. 7.4; 26.8-9; Gell. 16.13.4; possibly Dio 69.15.2.

[42] For appearances by Antoninus (apart from his accession) cf. HA, *Antonin.* 6 and 12.3; possibly Dio 69.15.2. It is uncertain whether he was actually present to hear Fronto's *gratiarum actio* on 13 August 143. He may well not have been: cf. E. J. Champlin, *JRS* 64. 1974. pp. 140 and 149, and chap. 7 sect. 5 note 26 below.

scrupulous, both in attending whenever he was in Rome, and in keeping the senate informed by letter when he was on campaign;[43] such deference was no doubt in part the product of his teacher Fronto's influence.[44] The emperor's reply (jointly with Commodus) to Miletus in 177 shows how he consulted the senate on many issues, even some of no special significance like the Milesian request about the celebration of games.[45] In the surviving *sententia prima* about reducing the expense of gladiatorial shows, he and his co-emperor (almost certainly Commodus) are addressed as if present, as Oliver and Palmer say.[46] But this in itself does not guarantee their attendance in person, while the reference to the "reading" of the imperial *oratio* is similarly ambiguous.[47] The question must remain open. In an *altercatio* recorded by Pliny,[48] for example, Trajan was appealed to as if present, although he was probably away at the time. Finally, among emperors of whose practice some impression can be formed, Pertinax in his short reign is said always to have attended meetings of the senate.[49]

From the evidence about these rulers' attendance it is awkward to discern whether they ever went to meetings as *privati* rather than to preside or to put forward their own items of business only. In his *Panegyricus* Pliny reflects what was no doubt widespread feeling about the emperor's position by 100, when he says to Trajan: "It is not enough for you to enter the House if you do not bid us to assemble; you should not be present at our meetings without presiding, nor listen to the delivery of *sententiae* unless you call on the speakers."[50] Equally, many emperors came to see themselves as loftier than senators. What Pliny says of Domitian in particular was to be true of others: "Earlier despots, in all their pride, were convinced that if ever they acted as senators they would cease to be emperors in their own eyes."[51] In contrast, the *Historia Augusta* says that Antoninus "in his dealings with the senate rendered it, as emperor, the same respect that he desired another emperor to render him when he was a private citizen."[52] But of course the claim here refers merely to Antoninus' tact: there is no

---

[43] For attendance see Fronto, *Ant. Imp.* 1.2.5-12 = pp. 90-93 H; Dio 71.33.2; many references in HA, *Marcus; Verus* 7.7; *Pertinax* 2.9.

[44] See E. J. Champlin, *Fronto and Antonine Rome*, pp. 91-93.

[45] No. 125 in list, chap. 15 sect. 5.

[46] *Hesperia* 24. 1955. p. 324. For Commodus as co-emperor, see *Aes Italicense* line 6. Provided that his name is read in this line, the dating of the speech within the period 177-180 is not disturbed. Whether the emperors were themselves present in the senate, or not, is irrelevant to the problem of dating.

[47] *Aes Italicense* line 13.

[48] *Ep.* 6.5.5; cf. 6.13.2.

[49] HA, *Pertinax* 9.9; cf. 13.2.

[50] *Paneg.* 60.1.

[51] *Paneg.* 63.6.

[52] *Antonin.* 6.5.

sign that he attended as *privatus*. M. Aurelius' presence as *privatus* on occasion, however, is strongly implied by the claim of the *Historia Augusta*[53] that he would attend even if he had no *relatio* to make. Equally, neither Vitellius nor Vespasian seems to have been presiding over or addressing the respective sessions in which each became upset by the outspokenness of Helvidius Priscus.[54] Pertinax, too, was evidently not president when the consul Falco was about to be condemned, nor perhaps was Septimius Severus when Euodus was praised.[55]

Lack of evidence makes it impossible to tell how regularly other emperors attended meetings. It is frustrating that we cannot begin to form an impression of Domitian's practice.[56] The attitude of his successor Trajan is unusually awkward to assess. We know that he attended as *consul ordinarius* on 1 January 100, and presided at an election day and at the trial of Marius Priscus later the same month.[57] A decade or so later he writes to Pliny about his policy in bestowing the *ius trium liberorum*: "You are certainly well aware, my dear Pliny, that I grant these favors sparingly, seeing that it is my custom to state even in the senate that I have not exceeded the number which I originally said would satisfy me."[58] Despite the temptation, it might be rash to infer Trajan's later practice from his attendance during the first January he spent in Rome as emperor. Similarly, the custom referred to in his letter cannot prove attendance in person: his wishes may well have been relayed in an *oratio* read by a *quaestor Caesaris*.[59] Millar[60] hazards the guess that Trajan *may* have appeared in the senate to hear those Bithynian envoys who wanted to pursue the prosecution of Varenus Rufus, arguing against others who had brought fresh instructions to abandon the case. Pliny's account[61] does not indicate where this proceeding took place, and is brief anyway. All the same, it seems unlikely, if the emperor were presiding in the senate in this instance, that he would curtly announce a decision (however uncontentious) without any *interro-*

---

[53] *Marcus* 10.7. In his discussion of how the House should be addressed, Fronto's use of *sententia*, rather than *relatio*, could even imply that Marcus took part in debates: but we should probably not expect such very precise use of terms (*De Eloq.* 2.7 = p. 136 H).

[54] Tac. *Hist.* 2.91; Dio 66.12.1.

[55] Dio 74.8.5; 76.6.1.

[56] For his appearance in the senate, note Suet. *Dom.* 13 and 18; Dio 67.4.6. It is tempting to speculate that Statius' description of "lectus concilio divum ordo" (1. 198), summoned and addressed by Jupiter in the *Thebaid*, owes something to a glimpse caught by the poet of Domitian presiding over the Roman senate. Note how Jupiter enters after the assembled gods, and how they await his signal before presuming to sit down (1. 201-205).

[57] Plin. *Paneg.* 66, 69, 76; *Ep.* 2.11.

[58] *Ep.* 10.95.

[59] In Trajan's case, note HA, *Hadr.* 3.1.

[60] *Emperor*, pp. 348-349.

[61] *Ep.* 7.6.14 and 7.10.

gatio. Though the point is a small one and certainty impossible, I should prefer to guess that he heard the dispute alone.

Millar[62] also follows Sherwin-White[63] in being struck by Trajan's absence from the sessions of the senate described by Pliny. But we should bear in mind that some of these were trials for *repetundae*,[64] which the emperor would almost never attend anyway, while others were election days, to which the same point applies.[65] Conceivably it may just have been an accident that he attended even the trial of Marius Priscus for *repetundae*. The hearing must have been fixed to take place late in 99, and it was only postponed to the next suitable date in the New Year because of the defendant's failure to appear when the House was convened.[66] Our further knowledge that Trajan was at Antium during the first half of November 99[67] prompts the conjecture that he had never intended to be present at this hearing at the time originally arranged. In January 100, however, he was *consul ordinarius* and as such felt an obligation to attend. Later, in 105, he left Rome on 4 June, and so would have been absent from the proceedings which followed the death of Afranius Dexter, found dead on 25 June.[68] The meeting described in *Ep*. 4.12 did take place in 105, but hardly before 4 June.[69] The letters concerning the prosecution of Varenus Rufus[70] can be dated with reasonable certainty to early 107, and it was probably not until then that Trajan himself returned to Rome:[71] notably, in the third letter of this group he is said to be absent, but he must have been in Rome or its vicinity by the time of the last.[72] *Epistulae* 6.19 is difficult to date, but again if the elections mentioned are those of 107, Trajan may still have been out of Rome at the time of the meeting described. Otherwise, of two meetings which he evidently did not attend, one was during the summer period when only a quorum was required, and the other may have taken place at the same time.[73] For the rest we are left with only three meetings which he might have been expected to attend, but apparently did not—all of them early in 105.[74] This is too slender a foundation on

[62] *Emperor*, p. 348 n. 47.
[63] *Pliny*, p. 369.
[64] *Ep*. 2.12; 3.9; 4.9.
[65] *Ep*. 3.20; 4.25.
[66] Plin. *Ep*. 2.11.9-10.
[67] A. Plassart, *Fouilles de Delphes* III. 4. no. 288.
[68] *Ep*. 8.14; *Fast. Ost*.
[69] See Sherwin-White ad loc.
[70] *Ep*. 5.20; 6.5 and 13; 7.6 and 10.
[71] *Fasti Ostienses* give the earliest attestation of his presence in Rome in 107 on "VII K. I[un? or ul?]."
[72] *Ep*. 7.10.2.
[73] *Ep*. 3.18; 3.4.
[74] *Ep*. 4.29; 5.4 and 13.

which to base conjectures about the regularity of his attendance over the whole reign. The matter must remain open.

No statement may be made about Commodus' attendance.[75] Nor, unfortunately, can we discern Septimius Severus' practice after he consolidated his position; we only know that he did appear in the senate after the fall of Plautianus in late January 205.[76] Some appearances by Elagabalus are mentioned,[77] but his practice is unknown, as is that of Severus Alexander.[78] In general, however, the notion that by the third century emperors attended seldom may be borne out by the frequency with which the Severan rulers are said to have issued rescripts on the Kalends and the Ides, the days of stated meetings.[79] This frequency remains striking even when allowance is made both for the possibility that the emperor would have time to deal with his own business as well as attend the House on the same day, and for his absences from Rome.

Our knowledge of the presence of emperors at trial hearings after the Julio-Claudian period is slight. As we might expect, normally the only ones which they might consider attending were those for *maiestas*. It would seem to have been definitely unusual for Trajan to preside at the trial of Marius Priscus for *repetundae* (*saevitia*) in January 100.[80] But, as we have noted already, his presence may really have been an accident, and he could well never have attended another such trial: from Pliny's account it is notable that he makes no initiative during the proceedings.[81] However, according to Dio,[82] Trajan was prepared to bring defendants charged with *maiestas* before the senate. Domitian had gained a bad reputation for his constant practice in this regard.[83] Later Dio suggests that M. Aurelius would not attend in person the *maiestas* trials he had instigated. He tells us, too, that Severus did not attend the trial of Apronianus.[84] Yet Severus had evidently secured the condemnation of Didius Julianus' friends in person.[85]

---

[75] For one appearance, HA, *Commodus* 8.9; for letters to the senate, Dio 72.15.5.

[76] Dio 76.5 and 6.

[77] Note Herodian 5.7.4; Dio 79.17.2 and perhaps 18.4.

[78] But in the notoriously unreliable *Historia Augusta* biography, note *Sev. Alex.* 48.2.

[79] See Justinian, *Codex*, pp. 489-492 Krüger. The reliability of the dates given is questioned by C. E. van Sickle, "Headings of rescripts of the Severi," *Class. Phil.* 23. 1928. pp. 270-277, but defended by A. M. Honoré, " 'Imperial' rescripts A.D. 193-305; authorship and authenticity," *JRS* 69. 1979. pp. 51-64 at p. 51 n. 8.

[80] Plin. *Ep.* 2.11; cf. *Paneg.* 76.

[81] No other emperor except Tiberius is known to have attended a trial for *repetundae*, unless Claudius was present at the trial of Statilius Taurus in 53, as Tacitus implies (*Ann.* 12.59).

[82] 68.16.2.

[83] Tac. *Agr.* 45; Suet. *Dom.* 11; Dio 67.4.5.

[84] 71.28.2; 76.8.3.

[85] HA, *Sev.* 8.3.

Although emperors commended candidates beforehand, they seem rarely to have attended the senate on election days. But Trajan did preside at elections in 100, and the *Historia Augusta* says of Antoninus: "When he sought offices for himself or for his sons all was done as by a private individual"[86]—which might suggest attendance in person on an election day. Again, the *Historia Augusta*[87] claims that Marcus Aurelius frequently attended on election days, and stayed for the whole session.

From the very beginning of the Principate, formal prerogative and informal *auctoritas* set the emperor apart from his fellow senators. The notion of a Princeps attending sessions as a *privatus*, and allowing himself to be exposed along with others to the cut and thrust of debate, was an unworkable ideal which barely outlasted Claudius' time. In practice senators could not be the *domini* of the emperor, as Tiberius once termed them.[88] A claim can fairly be made that certain emperors continued to come as *privati* on occasion right up to Pertinax at the end of the second century. But such attendance perhaps gained value only if the emperor also participated in debate. Of that, not surprisingly, there is no sign. Some "good" emperors did try to attend sessions conscientiously. The practice of the rest—"good" and "bad"—is unfathomable. With few exceptions, certain cases of *maiestas* were the only trials which any of them attended. Of course this is not to say that they were necessarily unconcerned about the verdicts reached—merely that they stayed away from most hearings. By the same token they would seldom come to senatorial elections. At the least, however, to the end of our period all emperors who were able to do so did attend in person on their accession and on occasions of great importance thereafter. But that is all.

[86] HA, *Antonin.* 11.6.

[87] *Marcus* 10.9.

[88] Suet. *Tib.* 29. Ironically, it was the same emperor who dismissed senators as "homines ad servitutem paratos" (Tac. *Ann.* 3.65).

6

ROUTINE

Now that meeting places of the senate and attendance have both been reviewed, this chapter aims to examine further general arrangements for sessions. In particular, it considers the handling of recurrent business throughout the year, while its discussion of the frequency and duration of sessions prompts a reappraisal of the current misconception that the senate met seldom and speedily dispatched its business.[1]

1. Summons

Senators could always convene informally and pass as a result of their deliberations an *auctoritas*, a considered opinion.[2] Othonian members seem to have met thus at Mutina shortly after that emperor's death in 69.[3] In Rome too, on 1 January 40, when no qualified magistrate would preside, members met nonetheless, though they conducted no business.[4] Similarly, on Titus' death in 81 they anticipated any summons, hurried to the House, and began their praises of the dead emperor while waiting for the doors to be opened.[5] But if a valid decree was to be passed, the senate had to be summoned by a magistrate or tribune.[6] The following had this authority according to the handbook compiled by Varro for Pompey's entry to the senate in 70 B.C.: "dictator, consuls, praetors, tribunes of the plebs, interrex and prefect of the city."[7] In effect, only consuls, praetors, and

---

[1] See, for example, Sherwin-White, *Pliny*, pp. 230-231; F. Millar, *Emperor*, pp. 211, 341.

[2] Cf. Dio 55.3.4-5.

[3] Tac. *Hist.* 2.52-53.

[4] Dio 59.24.5.

[5] Suet. *Tit.* 11.

[6] In origin tribunes were not magistrates of course, though by our period they were regarded as such for all practical purposes: note Appian, *Bell. Civ.* 1.100 and J. A. Crook, *Consilium Principis*, p. 8 n. 3. However, for what might be interpreted as a "purist" reference to tribunes as promagistrates with the right of summons in a senatorial decree of 39 B.C., see J. Reynolds, *Aphrodisias and Rome*, no. 8 line 80 with discussion, pp. 88-89.

[7] Gell. 14.7.4; cf. 14.8.1-2, and general reference to such magistrates in *FIRA*[2] I no. 68 V lines 100-101.

tribunes remained during our period. As the most senior, the consuls usually summoned the senate,[8] no doubt with the help of their *viatores* as they had done in the Republic.[9] Gellius[10] implies that consular summons was normal practice, and it is further borne out by the difficulty on 1 January 40 when the emperor Gaius was consul, but away from Rome. He had no colleague, since the other consul designate had died just before taking up office and had not been replaced. According to Dio,[11] no praetor nor tribune dared to convene the senate that day, and it was not till 3 January that the praetors plucked up courage to issue a joint summons. It was the *praetor urbanus* who summoned the senate on the day of Galba's death and Otho's accession, and again on 1 January 70.[12] On the former occasion both consuls had been killed earlier in the day (Galba and T. Vinius); on the latter both were absent (Vespasian and Titus). Subsequent meetings early in 70 were likewise called by Domitian as praetor.[13] On 1 January 222 it was the *praetor urbanus* who carried out most of Elagabalus' duties as consul.[14]

On the very rare occasions when there was need for a meeting during the absence of both consuls and praetors, the tribunes would act. Dio[15] records an instance of their so doing in 218, though, as he adds, not surprisingly, the practice of tribunician summons had largely fallen into disuse. In a crisis tribunes might summon the senate without waiting for other magistrates to act, as they did in 14 when a popular actor's strike for more pay led to rioting.[16] In a less urgent situation in 42, when one of their number had died, the tribunes again did not wait for the consuls to act (even though the latter were in Rome), but convened the senate on their own initiative to have a successor elected.[17] Under 32 and 33 Tacitus[18] may provide one further example each of a tribune and a praetor convening the senate even when the consuls were available. In both cases, however, it is equally possible that these magistrates were allowed to make *relationes*

---

[8] Note how by the end of the second century, when writing of their initiative in issuing a summons to the meeting at which Didius Julianus was stripped of power, Herodian thinks it appropriate to explain "the consuls, who normally manage the affairs of state when there is a crisis over the succession" (2.12.4; cf. Suet. *Calig.* 60).

[9] On *viatores*, who happen never to be mentioned fulfilling this function during our period, see C. Habicht, *PW* 8A cols. 1928-1940.

[10] 3.18.7.

[11] 59.24; cf. Suet. *Calig.* 17.

[12] Tac. *Hist.* 1.47; 4.39.

[13] Tac. *Hist.* 4.40, 44, 47.

[14] HA, *Elagab.* 15.7.

[15] 78.37.5.

[16] Dio 56.47.2.

[17] Dio 60.16.8.

[18] *Ann.* 6.12 and 16; cf. Mommsen, *St. R.* III. p. 317 n. 4.

by consular presidents. Tribunes had the right to do this, while praetors were granted it as a privilege.[19]

By virtue of their *imperium* all emperors had the right to summon the senate, and exercised it frequently. Meetings called thus were confirmed by the *Lex de Imperio Vespasiani* as having full legal standing.[20] *Tribunicia potestas*, bestowed upon emperors and a few others, conferred the same right of summons, but would seem to have been invoked seldom. It was a mark of Tiberius' caution that he chose to convene the senate by this means on Augustus' death in 14.[21]

According to Gellius' account of contemporary practice in the mid second century, a summons (*edictum*)[22] was addressed to "senators and those with the right to deliver an opinion in the senate."[23] In the Republic a summons to each meeting had been essential, because neither time nor place was normally fixed. In our period not only were sessions at fixed times introduced from 9 B.C.; we have also seen how increasingly (though not invariably) the Curia Julia came to be the normal meeting place. But even for stated meetings some confirmation of place would still generally be required, and in any event it is reasonable to assume that tradition for long demanded the continued issue of a summons to such sessions, however slight the need may have become in time. There is a little evidence to support the notion that the practice did continue at least in the Julio-Claudian period. The summons sent out by Tiberius as consul to the meeting on 1 January 7 B.C. was important, because the place chosen seems to have been highly unusual.[24] Late in Augustus' reign Ovid refers to "senators summoned in traditional fashion"[25] on 1 January. By contrast, Dio[26] seems to say that the stated meeting on 1 January 40 did not take place, specifically because no praetor nor tribune (to whom it fell to act) would issue a summons. Any such call to this type of session was so routine a matter that infrequent mention of it in our sources is hardly a surprise.

[19] See further chap. 7 sect. 7.
[20] *FIRA*[2] I no. 15 lines 4-10.
[21] Tac. *Ann.* 1.7; Suet. *Tib.* 23.
[22] For the term, cf. *Lex de Imperio Vespasiani* (*FIRA*[2] I no. 15) line 9.
[23] Gell. 3.18.7-8, "senatores quibusque in senatu sententiam dicere licet." The clause is ancient Republican terminology, probably retained under the Principate (cf. *FIRA*[2] I no. 68 V line 110; *EJ* 94a lines 9-10 etc.; Festus p. 454 L) for the sake of tradition, rather than because any effective category of non-member with the right to speak still existed. It was now only quaestors in office who might strictly be described thus. They were not yet members, but as magistrates they were permitted to speak, although they would not be called in order (see chap. 7 sect. 11). The formula is discussed by M. Hammond, *The Antonine Monarchy*, p. 263 n. 3.
[24] Dio 55.8.1.
[25] *Ex Ponto* 4.4.35, "patres e more vocati"; cf. 4.5.21.
[26] 59.24.2.

But Tacitus[27] does relate how in convening the stated meeting for the Ides of September 16 the consuls indicated that a matter of particular importance would be raised (the trial of Libo Drusus in fact). Naturally in this instance a good attendance had to be secured for a session where business would normally be light and only the minimum number of members to form a quorum was required to come.[28]

Subject to the fulfillment of any quorum which might be necessary, it had always been legal for a meeting to begin almost as soon as it was called, and this evidently remained the case with special sessions during the Principate. It was by no means unusual that when the mob rioted over an actor's strike for more pay in 14, the tribunes should summon the senate to meet on the same day.[29] Such lack of notice would suggest that a summons was not broadcast more than a short distance from the House itself. Of course throughout much of the year members without a valid excuse were expected to be close at hand, and we know that at least some actually lived close by.[30] The houses of others were scattered all over the city.[31] When a meeting was expected to begin almost as soon as it was summoned, we hear of senators running to arrive in time.[32] The *senatus consultum* of which Augustus sent a copy to Cyrene in 4 B.C. regards those within a twenty-mile radius of Rome as eligible for panels chosen at short notice to hear charges of extortion by provincial governors.[33]

Scrappy evidence suggests that, as in the Republic,[34] the form of a summons might vary. Gaius apparently went so far as to give all senators in advance a written outline of business which he wished to have discussed at a particular meeting.[35] Narrating events in his own day, Dio[36] implies that members were told individually of Pertinax's death, and summoned to attend the senate the same evening. However, it was perhaps more

[27] *Ann.* 2.28 and, for the date, 32.

[28] On arrangements for the stated meetings in September and October, see further below, sect. 4.

[29] Dio 56.47.2.

[30] Cf. Seneca, *Controv.* 9.4.18 with *PIR*[2] D 127; Asconius p. 27 C; Tac. *Ann.* 3.9; 15.69; *Hist.* 3.70; Suet. *Nero* 37; cf. Dio 62.27.1. The *senaculum*, a place where senators might gather in anticipation of a meeting being called, apparently still existed in Valerius Maximus' day, but he implies that it had become more common for members to await the *edictum* and proceed straight to the House (2.2.6; on *senaculum* see also chap. 3 sect. 1 note 20).

[31] Predictably the volumes so far published of *Fontes ad topographiam veteris urbis Romae pertinentes* (ed. G. Lugli), Rome, 1952-, show that many senators lived in the more fashionable parts; but there is no sign that their dwellings were all concentrated within, say, one particular quarter.

[32] Tac. *Hist.* 1.47; Aur. Vict. 14.11.

[33] *FIRA*[2] I no. 68 V lines 107ff.

[34] Cf. W. K. Lacey, *JRS* 64. 1974. p. 176 n. 4.

[35] Dio 59.24.8. If HA, *Gord.* 11.3 could be considered reliable, it would provide another example of a written summons.

[36] 74.12.2-3.

common for them to be assembled simply by proclamation, which they or their servants would be expected to hear.[37] This is what happened during the night in the confusion following Gaius' death, according to Josephus.[38] Similarly, Suetonius[39] tells an anecdote of Claudius panicking at attempts on his life and sending out heralds (*praecones*) to assemble the senate swiftly. To be sure, in any crisis there would be no time to produce a written summons for each senator.

The proclamation could include more or less indication of the business for which the magistrate was convening the senate. In the edict which he issued to summon it after Augustus' death, Tiberius is said to have taken particular care over specifying the matters to be raised, while in 16 we are told how the consuls summoned the House to try Libo Drusus with merely "the additional indication that the matter to be discussed was grave and terrible."[40] What was said when the senate was summoned "in specially solemn terms"[41] to try C. Silius in 24 must remain uncertain. Not surprisingly, on Gaius' assassination in 41 the consul Q. Pomponius offended troops loyal to the imperial house by issuing a summons "in the cause of liberty."[42] Altogether, we should probably be right to conclude that the proclamation before most meetings gave members at best a sketchy indication of the matters to be raised. That said, the senators in Rome were of course a small, tightly knit group. If one of them did specially wish to gain further details of the proposed agenda for a session, it cannot normally have been difficult for him to direct his enquiries to the right quarter.

2. Time and Duration of Sessions

There should be no need to illustrate more than briefly the points that it was normal for an industrious Roman to start work at home before dawn, and for public business to begin as early as dawn itself. Among emperors Vespasian was by no means unique in working so early,[1] while Dio[2] relates that L. Norbanus even found time for a little private trumpet practice at dawn before proceeding to take up his office as consul on 1 January 19.

---

[37] Cf. HA, *Did. Jul.* 2.4.
[38] *AJ* 19.248.
[39] *Claud.* 36.
[40] Tac. *Ann.* 1.7; 2.28, "addito consultandum super re magna et atroci."
[41] Tac. *Ann.* 4.19, "multa adseveratione."
[42] Josephus, *AJ* 19.263; cf. Suet. *Claud.* 10.
[1] See Plin. *Ep.* 3.5.9 with Sherwin-White ad loc.; cf. Dio's account (76.17.1) of Septimius Severus' routine.
[2] 57.18.3.

At dawn, or even before it, formal calls were paid;[3] the corpse of Tiberius was laid out; Tiridates was ceremoniously received by Nero; the triumphal procession of Vespasian and Titus began.[4]

By law no decree of the senate might be made before dawn.[5] Technically, therefore, the House was not debarred from just assembling during the night, and such an occurrence is reported on one or two special occasions in our period. Josephus[6] says that it was summoned during the night in the confusion following Gaius' assassination, and discussion was still continuing inconclusively at dawn. On Titus' death there was such universal grief, according to Eutropius,[7] that members burst into the House and began to praise him, even though it was still night. Likewise it was night-time when Pertinax announced to the assembled senate his elevation to the Principate at the end of 192.[8]

In normal circumstances, however, it was not considered proper to conduct public business at night,[9] and dawn was the earliest time at which meetings might be expected to begin. It is clear from a number of passages that they could indeed start as early as this. Even if Pliny's reference[10] to Trajan's enthusiastic entry to the consulship on 1 January 100 be dismissed as rhetorical exaggeration, there is further confirmation of a start around dawn in Dio's story mentioned above (of L. Norbanus playing the trumpet) and in his account of Sejanus' downfall on 18 October 31.[11] An early start is also implied in Seneca's anecdote[12] of Cossus, *Praefectus Urbi* under Tiberius, attending a session after a party the previous night, and falling into a slumber from which he could not be roused. Cossus needed Fronto's advice to M. Aurelius,[13] that he take a good night's sleep before meetings of the senate: then he would be able to enter with a good color in the morning, and read with a strong voice.

Naturally the exact time at which a meeting might begin would vary according to the arrival of the presiding magistrate or other prominent figures, together with the members escorting them. When consuls were

---

[3] Plin. *Ep.* 3.12.2; Martial 4.8.1; Dio 57.21.4; 77.17.3; Herodian 7.6.8.

[4] Dio 59.3.7; 63.4.3; Josephus, *BJ* 7.124. Note Titus' entry to Alexandria at the second hour on 25 April 71 (*Ox. Pap.* 2725 lines 18-19).

[5] Gell. 14.7.8.

[6] *AJ* 19.248 and 254.

[7] *Brev.* 7.22; cf. Suet. *Tit.* 11.

[8] Dio's eye-witness account at 74.1.4 is to be preferred to that of Aurelius Victor, *Lib. de Caes.* 17.10, who delays the meeting until the customary hour of dawn.

[9] Note the offense which Gaius seems to have given by summoning leading senators (Dio 59.5.5) and ordering the execution of others, both by night (Seneca, *De Ira* 3.18.4 and 19.2).

[10] *Paneg.* 66.2.

[11] 58.9.3 and 11.1.

[12] *Ep. Mor.* 83.15. For another early start by Caracalla, cf. Petr. Patr. in Dio, Loeb 9, p. 284 n. 4.

[13] *Ad M. Caes.* 5.1 = p. 71 H; cf. Plin. *Ep.* 7.3.2.

entering office, the start would regularly be delayed until the completion of certain ceremonies on the Capitol.[14] However, since all sessions were limited to daylight hours, as we shall see shortly, a late start was both inconvenient and undesirable, especially during winter. Julius Caesar's indecision had caused such a delay on the fateful Ides of March 44 B.C.,[15] while it was characteristic of Elagabalus' volatile temper that not until the sixth hour (that is, about noon) would he consent to enter the senate on 1 January 222 as consul with his cousin Alexianus.[16] But otherwise it is only at moments of crisis that meetings seem to be convened late in the day. For example, it was necessary to call a second session on 18 October 31 to condemn Sejanus to death.[17] Four further instances occur after the death of an emperor, in order to confirm a successor in power as soon as possible. Thus only after presenting himself to the Guard between the sixth and seventh hours on the day of his accession (13 October 54) did Nero proceed to the senate house; it was evening when he left.[18] Only after a long day of bloodshed did the senate meet to confer power on Otho on 15 January 69.[19] Likewise it was evening (at the end of March 193) when it met to confirm Didius Julianus' position after the death of Pertinax and the auction in the Praetorian camp.[20] On 18 September 96, too, it cannot have been early when a meeting was summoned after Domitian's murder, and in fact we know that the session continued on the following day in this instance.[21] Any hope of calling a late meeting on the day of Vitellius' death in December 69 was dashed by a wholesale "disappearance" of magistrates and senators: in any case dusk was coming on.[22]

According to Varro,[23] no decree made after sunset was valid, while Seneca,[24] arguing against overwork, mentions an ancient provision that no new *relatio* should be made after the tenth hour. Pliny[25] indicates that it was equally unusual for senatorial trial hearings to be continued beyond

---

[14] See sect. 4 below.

[15] See Appian, *Bell. Civ.* 2.115-116; Dio 44.16-18 with discussion by N. Horsfall, "The Ides of March: some new problems," *Greece and Rome* 21. 1974. pp. 191-199, sect. (iv).

[16] HA, *Elagab.* 15.5-6.

[17] Dio 58.11.4.

[18] Suet. *Nero* 8.

[19] Tac. *Hist.* 1.47; Suet. *Otho* 7.

[20] Dio 74.12.1 and 3.

[21] *Fast. Ost.* For the time of Domitian's murder, cf. Suet. *Dom.* 16.

[22] Tac. *Hist.* 3.86. For discussion of the possibility that Caracalla addressed the senate during the latter part of the day after Geta's murder, see C. R. Whittaker on Herodian 4.5.1 (Loeb 1, p. 396 n. 1).

[23] Gell. 14.7.8.

[24] *De Tranq. Anim.* 17.7. If a *relatio* made so late were followed by an *interrogatio*, it would presumably have been impossible to complete the latter on the same day in normal circumstances (see chap. 7 sect. 25 below).

[25] *Ep.* 2.11.16 and 18.

nightfall. Thus on the first day of the trial of Julius Bassus his speech for the defense was cut short at that time, and he was obliged to reserve the final 1½ hours of it to the following morning. Not surprisingly, he reports that when the Bithynian prosecutor Theophanes likewise had up to 1½ hours outstanding that evening, he added to the generally bad impression he had made, by requesting to continue in order to finish on the same day. Lamps were brought in after dark.[26]

Dio[27] implies that the meeting called immediately after Gaius' assassination continued to sit for the rest of the day and all through the night with no decision being reached: yet this was an exceptional crisis. So although sessions would seldom continue beyond nightfall, but would be adjourned by evening, it evidently was common enough for them to last right up until that time, especially on days of trial hearings. Seneca confirms the general point: "Toil summons the best men. The senate is often kept in session the whole day long."[28] Until 42, when Claudius stopped the practice, it seems that members had regularly been detained until evening on 1 January every year to endure the recitation of certain speeches of Augustus and Tiberius—for up to nine hours in other words, if they actually sat from sunrise to sunset.[29] Epictetus' short sketch[30] of the reception accorded to a man who had just been elected to the tribunate portrays him as arriving home in the early evening, as the lamps were being lit. Similarly, according to the *Historia Augusta*,[31] M. Aurelius was noted for remaining in the House on election days until night fell and the consul dismissed the meeting.

Senatorial sessions were kept long not least by cumbersome procedure—the *interrogatio* especially, where (as will appear in the next chapter) each member in turn was asked his view on a matter, and was free to speak either on this or on any other issue for as long as he chose. In addition, because of the modest number of stated meetings during the year, items conceivably piled up at busy times to make such a long agenda that the House sometimes had to reconvene soon afterwards in order to complete its business. Generally speaking, the practice noted below of restricting the session on 1 January every year to formal matters could have caused some strain later that month. More specifically, it may have turned out that items scheduled for 1 March 56 could not all be handled on that day,

---

[26] Plin. *Ep.* 4.9.14 and Appendix 5.

[27] 60.1.2. By contrast, Josephus (locc. citt. in note 6 above) seems to envisage two sessions—one on the day of the murder, and then a second called during the night.

[28] *De Provid.* 5.4.

[29] Dio 60.10.2; cf. 59.24.5. For hours of daylight, see Appendix 6.

[30] 1.19.24. Admittedly the man could have been returning from the *comitia* rather than the senate.

[31] *Marcus* 10.8.

and had to be cleared in a special session the following morning. So it was on 2 March, rather than on the 1st, as they had originally been told to expect perhaps, that the relatives of Alliatoria Celsilla were able to make a plea for her exemption from the *SC de aedificiis non diruendis*.[32] We cannot say what business took up an unexpected amount of time on 1 March, though it is tempting to conjecture that this was the day when members raised first the offenses of freedmen, a grievance on which many no doubt enjoyed waxing passionate and eloquent.[33] But this is speculation. In their letter to Miletus of late 177, however, M. Aurelius and Commodus do particularly mention the long agenda in the senate on the day when the city's request was granted, and this is consistent with what we know from elsewhere of Marcus' meticulousness in referring matters there.[34] By contrast, the need for a special session to pass the *SC de aedificiis non diruendis* on 22 September 44 is a puzzle.[35] It is hard to believe that the agenda for the Ides of that holiday month had been so full as to demand another meeting before the beginning of October, unless controversy over the demolition of buildings or some other matter had already consumed an inordinate amount of time, and pressure had now been brought to resolve the issue with all speed. We may only guess that many of the 383 members who broke their summer recess to come were estate owners concerned by the possibility of restrictions being introduced that would be damaging to their interests.

On some days the session may indeed have been dismissed early,[36] but equally it could be argued that regular attendance would prove hard work, especially since by convention members were expected to arrive in time for the beginning of a meeting and stay until the end.[37] In the course of a day's session there were no doubt short, natural breaks at appropriate stages, but no sign of any long interval. So when Fronto[38] in his old age cites a laborious day in the senate as a reason for not writing earlier to M. Aurelius, his excuse must be genuine enough. For though, as we have seen, an upper-class Roman might start work very early in the day, he would perhaps not normally reckon to continue much beyond lunch around noon, followed by a siesta (in summer at least). For example, when he was *praefectus classis* in Misenum in 79, Pliny the Elder's work, bath, lunch, and siesta were all over by the seventh hour, while Septimius Severus

---

[32] *FIRA²* I no. 45 II.
[33] Tac. *Ann.* 13.26; see further chap. 7 sect. 7.
[34] No. 125 in list, chap. 15 sect. 5.
[35] See *FIRA²* I no. 45 I and chap. 4 sect. 2 note 113.
[36] Note the unexpected adjournments of hearings at Plin. *Ep.* 2.11.9-10 and 5.4.2.
[37] See chap. 7 sect. 24.
[38] *Ant. Imp.* 1.5.1 = p. 95 H. For dating to November/December 161 (when a full day's session would occupy 9 to 10 hours), see E. J. Champlin, *JRS* 64. 1974. pp. 145-146.

did little or no work beyond noon (the sixth hour).[39] The tenth hour, after which Seneca thought that no new *relatio* ought to be made, was the time when dinner was normally being served in an upper-class household.[40]

No source specifies the hour at which trial hearings in the senate usually began, though Pliny's descriptions do seem to assume the customary start at dawn. It is true that Martial[41] writes of courts sitting at the third hour, while *vadimonia* found at Herculaneum dating from Vespasian's reign cite agreement to appear before the urban praetor at the second hour.[42] Yet there is no sound reason to think that hearings in the senate would have started at a different time from its other meetings.

For the House to be kept sitting "the whole day long," as Seneca puts it, could mean a stretch varying from approximately nine to fifteen hours, according to season. But it is really only from two trial hearings in which Pliny took part that we can form some more specific impression of the length of individual sessions, and his descriptions are therefore of special interest in this respect. The first trial, that of Marius Priscus, began during autumn 99 and then took up three further days late in the following January: nothing is known about the length of the sitting on the third of these, but on each of the first two days it lasted 9 to 9½ hours. The second trial, that of Julius Bassus, was a more severe test. It occurred in late January or the first three weeks of February 103, and demanded sittings of approximately 10 to 10½, 11½, and 9 hours on three successive days, with one, or possibly two, further days to hear witnesses and reach a verdict.[43]

A succession of uninterrupted all-day sessions of this duration perhaps never featured frequently in the senate's routine; but neither can this have been an exceptional rarity, especially when trial hearings were common enough. By any standard such lengthy sessions must have imposed a tremendous strain upon members' patience and stamina, and especially so in Roman society where, as we have seen, serious work was commonly abandoned after mid-day. Not surprisingly, there were those who harped on the need for brevity in all court proceedings.[44] In the senate Pliny[45] was

[39] Plin. *Ep*. 6.16.4-5; Dio 76.17.2. See in general J.P.V.D. Balsdon, *Life and Leisure in Ancient Rome*, London, 1969, pp. 17-26; and F. Millar, *Emperor*, pp. 209-210, 270.

[40] Balsdon, op. cit. p. 33. This was the hour when the young Octavian could respectably arrive at banquets (Nicol. Dam. *Vit. Caes*. 3 and 13 = *FGrH* II A. pp. 393, 396 Jacoby). For the tenth hour as late in the day, cf. Fronto, *Ad M. Caes*. 1.3.12 = p. 5 H.

[41] 4.8.2.

[42] See G. P. Carratelli, "Tabulae Herculanenses," *La Parola del Passato* 3. 1948. pp. 165-184 at pp. 168-169. For a provincial governor in the third century hearing cases from the first hour, see *Corp. Gloss. Lat*. III. 640 para. 9, cited by F. Millar, *Emperor*, p. 327 n. 85.

[43] See further Appendix 5.

[44] Plin. *Ep*. 1.20; cf. 6.2.5.

[45] *Ep*. 3.9.9, 19 and 24.

quite right to consider the possibility of both advocates and judges becoming confused and exhausted by long hearings in the complicated case against Caecilius Classicus and others. At other times the different manifestations of extreme behavior which will be considered in the next chapter could well be attributed in part to the strains which interminable proceedings imposed upon even the coolest temperament. It is conceivable, moreover, that the sheer length of meetings—not to mention their frequency—positively discouraged regular attendance on the part of certain members who found that they had no appetite for such endurance tests. When all this has been said, however, we should bear in mind equally the value which the educated, leisured classes of our period set upon oratory. For many senators it would have been a pleasure, not a penance, to listen to a Pliny or a Fronto speaking for hours on end.[46] Nor were such lengthy orations exclusively a feature of the senate. Pliny,[47] for example, in a letter to a fellow senator, tells of how he once spoke for seven hours at a stretch in the Centumviral court, while we may hope that the Cinna whom Martial[48] takes to task for a court speech of ten hours was only a figure of the poet's imagination!

3. Confidentiality of Sessions

There is value in asking how far senatorial proceedings were confidential, but it proves awkward to offer any clear-cut answer. On the one hand, the senate was an open council (''publicum consilium''),[1] not the secret conclave where many of the emperor's decisions were taken. Yet we have seen how sessions were never fully open to the public, although in certain circumstances—at trial hearings especially—non-members might be present in the chamber itself, and there was apparently no ban on a decree being made public as soon as it was approved. A reasonably complete record of business was kept in *acta senatus*, but Augustus banned its publication. Items were still published in *populi diurna acta*, however, though we do not know how they were selected or presented.[2]

While meetings, then, were never open, in normal circumstances they were not exactly secret either. The Curia Julia especially, where most

---

[46] See, for example, E. J. Champlin, *Fronto and Antonine Rome*, chap. IV passim. Compare M. Aurelius' willingness to spend as much as eleven or twelve days over single cases in his own court, and the relaxed approach of Septimius Severus (Dio 71.6.1 and 76.17.1).

[47] *Ep*. 4.16.2.

[48] 8.7.

[1] Tac. *Ann*. 6.15; Plin. *Ep*. 2.12.5; cf. *RG* 14.1; *Dig*. 48.11.6.2; for the Republic, Mommsen, *St. R*. III. p. 1028 n. 1.

[2] On all these aspects see further in general chap. 9.

meetings were held, was in the heart of Rome.[3] Thus in 49, after L. Vitellius had asked that Claudius be permitted to marry his niece Agrippina, some senators rushed out of the House, saying that they would force the emperor to marry her, and the "mixed throng"[4] who had gathered in the vicinity soon took up their cry. But whatever chamber was being used, it was customary for the doors to remain open throughout, and people could, and did, gather on the threshold to learn what was being said. When, in advance of his arrival in person, Elagabalus sent to Rome an enormous picture of himself in Eastern priestly garb, so that senate and people could become accustomed to his appearance, he chose well to have it displayed above the statue of Victory in the Curia Julia.[5] Spectators looking in through the main doors would see their new emperor looming down upon them straight ahead. Augustus had revived the ancient custom that sons of senators in particular should stand at the threshold during meetings in order to learn how state business was conducted.[6] So in 16 M. Hortalus had his four sons strategically placed at the door of the chamber on the Palatine when he made his plea for financial aid to Tiberius.[7] Later Pliny[8] says that by tradition candidates for office had learned from the same position.

Since senatorial business regularly attracted great public interest, on many occasions a crowd gathered outside the House during meetings. In 27 B.C. we hear how when the tribune M. Ampudius tried to "dedicate" himself to Augustus in the senate, and was obstructed by the latter, he rushed over to the crowd outside, and compelled them to "dedicate" themselves.[9] So great was the rejoicing at Gaius' accession that the crowd actually burst into the House as the senate was conferring power upon him.[10] Later, a voice which seemed to come from the crowd as Cassius Chaerea entered the senate inspired him to persevere with his scheme to murder Gaius.[11]

---

[3] As Suet. *DJ* 80 implies, it was an absurdity that anybody who claimed to be Roman should not know the whereabouts of the senate house.

[4] Tac. *Ann.* 12.7, "promisca multitudo."

[5] Herodian 5.5.7.

[6] Cf. Val. Max. 2.1.9; Suet. *Aug.* 38.

[7] Tac. *Ann.* 2.37.

[8] *Ep.* 8.14.5. It is unclear from the letter whether or not the practice was defunct in his own day. He could be taken to imply in sect. 5 that it was; but there is also something to be said for Mommsen's view (*St. R.* III. 2. p. 932 n. 2) that in sect. 8 Pliny is referring to the sight glimpsed by himself and his young contemporaries when they stood on the threshold of the House. For the conjecture that Dio Cassius, as the son of a senator, attended thus from early in Commodus' reign, based on his testimony at 72.4.2, see F. Millar, *A Study of Cassius Dio*, p. 14.

[9] Dio 53.20.2-3; *PIR*[2] A 569.

[10] Suet. *Calig.* 14; Dio 59.6.1.

[11] Josephus, *AJ* 19.60.

Even though it was excluded from the House, a hostile crowd outside could make its wishes all too clear. As an extreme, in 22 B.C., according to Dio, when the people wished to elect Augustus dictator, "they shut the senate up in the House and forced them to vote this measure, threatening to burn them alive otherwise."[12] Yet during the trial of Piso in A.D. 20 the crowd threatened to lynch the defendant if he were allowed to escape with his life.[13] Four years later it was Vibius Serenus, prosecuting his father, who incurred popular hostility.[14] In 29 a crowd demonstrated outside the House against any possible denunciations of his relatives by Tiberius, while in 61, after the murder of the Praefectus Urbi by one of his slaves, there were riotous demonstrations when the execution of the whole *familia* was debated.[15] In 193, on the morning of Didius Julianus' first full day as emperor, the people voiced their hatred as he entered the House: their shouts on this occasion are said to have sounded all the more terrifying as they rebounded with the echo from nearby buildings.[16] And in 238, after the senate's closed session on the Capitol to elect Balbinus and Pupienus emperors, the crowd outside reacted so violently against the decision when it was announced, that finally Gordian (III) had to be elected Caesar in order to placate it.[17] In contrast, according to Pliny,[18] the acquittal of Julius Bassus on charges of extortion in 103 had been celebrated by a joyful, noisy crowd.

It is never clear to what extent members' speeches or voting may have been affected by the attitude of crowds outside. But certainly when they feared trouble either from members inside or from a mob outside, some emperors were prepared to keep the public away altogether by posting an armed guard around the House. Soldiers must have been on hand at least for the latter stages of the trial of Piso in 20, because we hear that in order to give protection from the menacing crowd, the defendant was carried home in a litter, under escort of a Praetorian tribune.[19] A guard was posted likewise on the day of Sejanus' downfall in 31, and also evidently during 32.[20] We are told that Nero took the same precaution for the trial of Thrasea Paetus in 66, and in a rhetorical passage Tacitus implies that Domitian did likewise for more than one such session.[21] At the meeting when he sought

[12] 54.1.3.
[13] Tac. *Ann.* 3.14; cf. Suet. *Calig.* 2.
[14] Tac. *Ann.* 4.29.
[15] Tac. *Ann.* 5.4; 14.42 and 45.
[16] Dio 74.13.3-4.
[17] Herodian 7.10.5-9.
[18] *Ep.* 4.9.22.
[19] Tac. *Ann.* 3.14.
[20] Dio 58.9.6 and 17.4.
[21] *Ann.* 16.27; *Agr.* 45.

confirmation for his seizure of power in 193, Didius Julianus evidently
stationed soldiers not only outside the House, but inside as well.[22]

How well spectators awkwardly placed on the threshold could in fact
follow the proceedings would of course depend on a variety of factors,
such as the position of each speaker, the strength of his voice and the
direction which he faced, the attentiveness of members inside, and equally
the size of the crowd outside and the amount of noise in the vicinity. As
we have already noted, Augustus and Pliny evidently did think that a
worthwhile grasp of the conduct of business could be gained from standing
on the threshold, and it must have been partly in order not to block
spectators' vision altogether that members stood by the president's platform
on the third day of the trial of Marius Priscus in 100, rather than, say, in
the central aisle.[23] By contrast, Herodian's description[24] of a meeting in
238 might suggest that little could be gleaned, except by those bold spirits
who crept over the threshold and into the chamber itself (as two or three
did on this occasion). However, we are told that a whole mass of people
had gathered outside the House on this particular day, and there are further
difficulties about the account, which have been discussed earlier.

To listen from the threshold might in itself not always prove very in-
formative. But unquestionably a non-member who was prepared in addition
to study relevant written material and to discuss items with members could
learn much. Pliny, like Cicero before him, willingly furnished full accounts
of senatorial business to members and non-members alike.[25] The *sententia
prima* following an imperial *oratio* about reducing the expense of gladiatorial games around 177 provides what seems to be an unusual instance
where consideration of the emperor's wishes was evidently deferred, and
the proposals were leaked in the meantime. Later, the senator who delivered
the *sententia prima* was able to refer to the joy of the Gallic priests at the
"rumor" they had heard.[26] In the late Republic (when the senate did not
sit as a court, so that non-members would have far fewer chances of
admission than they did for trials under the Principate) Varro had written
a handbook for Pompey's entry to the senate in 70 B.C., which sooner or
later became generally available, and another senator, Ateius Capito, wrote
De Officio Senatorio in Augustus' day.[27] As already indicated, from 59
B.C. a record of proceedings was of course published in *acta senatus*. This
practice was stopped by Augustus. But Pliny[28] can still appeal to his lawyer

[22] Dio 74.12.4-5.

[23] Plin. *Ep.* 2.11.22.

[24] 7.11.1-3; see further Extended Note C.

[25] See further chap. 2 sect. 5 note 6.

[26] *Aes Ital.* lines 13-19, *Hesperia* 24. 1955. p. 331; see further chap. 8.

[27] See further chap. 7 sect. 1 on both.

[28] *Ep.* 8.14; Sherwin-White, *Pliny*, p. 136; W. Kunkel, *Herkunft und soziale Stellung der
römischen Juristen*, pp. 143-144 and 318-319.

friend, Titius Aristo, as a great expert on senatorial procedure, although the latter was almost certainly not a member. The Nicostratus who is said to have written a work *De Senatu Habendo* is not likely to have been a senator either, if (as seems plausible) he is to be identified with the sophist of the mid second century, T. Aurelianus Nicostratus.[29] Yet apart from his literary reputation, he had senatorial friends and pupils, and was honored by the emperor. With their historical interests the authors Asconius in the first century,[30] and Appian in the second,[31] were two further non-members who moved in senatorial circles and manifestly took trouble to become acquainted with the workings of the House. In his commentary on speeches of Cicero the former is to be found carefully explaining details of procedure for his young sons.[32]

Closed, or secret, sessions were held in the Republic, mainly perhaps to discuss matters of war and peace.[33] In our period there was seldom such need for secrecy. Yet effectively, if not formally, Tiberius, Nero, Domitian, and Didius Julianus did make certain meetings secret by placing guards around the House, as we have already seen. In the third century, too, Septimius Severus called a specifically closed session after the downfall of Plautianus.[34] In 238, when news was received of the deaths of the Gordians, there was another closed session, this time in the inner sanctuary of the temple of Jupiter on the Capitol.[35] According to the *Historia Augusta*,[36] the senate's decree declaring Maximinus a public enemy and making the Gordians Augusti had likewise been a secret one ("senatus consultum tacitum"). The discussion claims that there were precedents for such a decree, but none are known, and the testimony of the *Historia Augusta* here is perhaps best ignored.

Altogether, while the publication of *populi diurna acta* usually represented the only official step taken to acquaint non-members with senatorial proceedings, those who wished to learn more of current business were nearly always free to do so. It would really be necessary for them to come to Rome, however. Once here they might gain the acquaintance of mem-

---

[29] Festus, p. 470 L with *PIR*[2] A 1427 (note especially *Dig.* 39.5.27); see further chap. 7 sect. 1.

[30] *PIR*[2] A 1206 and R. Syme, *Tacitus*, p. 88 n. 7.

[31] *PIR*[2] A 943; for contemporary references and opinions in *Bellum Civile*, see E. Gabba, *Appiano e la storia delle guerre civili*, Florence, 1956, pp. 219-220, and further chap. 7 sect. 11 note 27 below.

[32] Note especially p. 43 C, "quid sit 'dividere sententiam' ut enarrandum sit vestra aetas, filii, facit."

[33] See W.V. Harris, *War and Imperialism in Republican Rome, 327-70 B.C.*, Oxford, 1979, Additional Note I p. 255.

[34] Dio 76.5.2.

[35] Herodian 7.10.2-3.

[36] *Gord.* 12.1-4.

bers, and stand at the doors of the House to follow sessions as best they could.

4. The Annual Calendar of Business

In the *Lex Julia de senatu habendo* of 9 B.C. the innovation was introduced that meetings of the senate should be held regularly on fixed days, as Dio explains:

Augustus ordered that the sessions of the senate should be held on fixed days. Previously, it seems, there had been no precise regulation about these, and thus members often missed them. He accordingly appointed (two)[1] regular meetings for each month, so that they were under compulsion to attend—at least those of them whom the law summoned—and in order that they might have no other excuse for being absent, he commanded that no court nor anything else which demanded their attendance should occur at that time.[2]

Suetonius gives the following account:

Augustus encouraged those chosen and approved as senators to a more devout and less inconvenient discharge of their duties, by ruling that each member should offer incense and wine at the altar of whatever temple had been selected for a session; that a stated meeting (*legitimus senatus*) should not be held more than twice a month, on the Kalends and the Ides; and that in September and October no member need attend apart from those whose names were drawn by lot to provide a quorum for the passing of decrees.[3]

For reasons which will quickly become apparent, neither of these accounts gives a full and accurate description of the senate's annual round. As it happens, the continuation of a stated meeting on 1 October is confirmed by a fragment of a calendar from Viterbo, which most probably dates to the third century.[4] But otherwise we have only much later sketches, relating to the fourth and fifth centuries, when significant changes from earlier practice had occurred.[5] It is the purpose of this section, therefore, to piece together the annual calendar of recurrent business in our period.

The year regularly opened with a meeting on 1 January at which the new *consules ordinarii* entered office together with all the praetors and

---

[1] "Two" is missing from the manuscripts, and is supplied from Suetonius' account below.
[2] 55.3.1-2.
[3] *Aug.* 35.
[4] G. Colonna, "Viterbo—Calendari romani dai Bagni Communali e da Riello," *NSc* 29. 1975. pp. 37-42 = *AE* 1977. 252.
[5] See *Inscr. Ital.* XIII.2. p. 363. H. Stern (*Rev. Et. Lat.* 51. 1973. pp. 44-45) argues persuasively that *senatus legitimi* listed by the fourth-century calendar of Philocalus for 15 October and 3 December are confirmed in the contemporary painted calendar cited in note 65 below.

aediles:[6] they would be greeted with "prayers, rejoicing, congratulations."[7] The consuls were escorted from home at dawn, and back again at the end of the day, by a large crowd of senators and others. The meeting then took place after the completion of certain ceremonies on the Capitol. These also seem to have occurred when suffect consuls took up office: at least this is the procedure imagined by Ovid when he sent congratulations to Pomponius Graecinus, suffect in 16.[8]

On 1 January the business of the meeting regularly included an oath "in acta Caesarum." We hear of such an oath being sworn to Octavian as early as 29 B.C.,[9] and the practice was still being followed in the early third century, according to Dio.[10] Considerable variation might occur in the form of the oath and the manner in which it was taken, according to the wishes of the emperor. Tiberius specifically required of senators an oath to uphold Augustus' acts, but would not allow one to uphold his own.[11] Claudius followed this practice too, and when consul in 55 Nero was thought to do his colleague, L. Antistius, great honor by not requiring him to swear "in acta sua."[12] At one stage members had evidently sworn individually, though by 32, according to Dio,[13] the practice was for one to recite the oath while the others merely expressed assent. So it was a novelty when they reverted to former custom on the single occasion of 1 January 32 and later during Gaius' reign.[14] Under Claudius one member of each college of magistrates recited the oath for his colleagues.[15] After their deaths Tiberius and Gaius were omitted from the oath.[16] In all reigns it was no doubt considered important for members to be present for the taking of the solemn oath, and it need be no surprise that Thrasea Paetus' absence from New Year meetings was made a charge against him in 66.[17]

Apart from the swearing of the oath, the meeting on 1 January was traditionally regarded as a festal occasion in keeping with the happy atmosphere of this day.[18] Members would expect business to be formal and

---

[6] See in general M. Meslin, *La Fête des kalendes de janvier dans l'empire romain,* Collection Latomus 115, Brussels, 1970, pp. 23-36.

[7] Plin. *Ep.* 9.37.5, "votis, gaudio, gratulatione."

[8] *Ex Ponto* 4.9.15-38. Lines 59-60 suggest that Ovid knew Graecinus to be a suffect; for time of writing, cf. ibid. 4.10.1-2.

[9] Dio 51.20.1; cf. 53.28.1.

[10] 57.8.4.

[11] Tac. *Ann.* 1.72; 4.42.

[12] Dio 60.10.1; Tac. *Ann.* 13.11.

[13] 58.17.2.

[14] Dio 59.13.1.

[15] Dio 60.25.1-2.

[16] Dio 59.9.1; 60.4.6; cf. Suet. *Claud.* 11.

[17] Tac. *Ann.* 16.22.

[18] Cf. Dio 57.8.6; Herodian 1.16.3; Aur. Vict. 17.10. In general, Ovid, *Fasti* 1.71-74; Suet. *Tib.* 34; *Inscr. Ital.* XIII.2. pp. 388-389.

uncontentious—a consul's speech of thanks to the emperor, for example.[19] In fact, by 42 the whole day was taken up with readings from speeches by Augustus, Tiberius, and possibly Gaius; Claudius was good enough to stop the practice at his first opportunity.[20] It was regarded as characteristic of Tiberius' harshness that he wrecked the happy atmosphere of the day by bringing accusations before the meeting, and ordering executions.[21] Only in a crisis would substantial items be raised, as for example on Pertinax's accession in 193. Even on 1 January 70 business remained largely formal according to Tacitus' account,[22] and the trial of Publius Celer, fixed at the end of 69 for "proximus dies" (that is, the next day on which the senate was to meet), was deferred. During 99/100 there must have been a similar postponement in the trial of Marius Priscus.[23]

Possibly on 3 January the senate took vows for the well-being of the emperor and his family, though an actual meeting may not have been convened for this purpose.[24]

It is clear enough that from A.D. 14 onwards magistrates were elected in the senate.[25] But the timetable for holding such elections is hard to establish, and we must pause to consider this problem next. Such information as there is about the time of elections in the first century relates mainly to consuls in the Julio-Claudian period, and no consistent pattern emerges. Indeed, at least under emperors noted for their erratic habits over the election or appointment of magistrates,[26] it would clearly be wrong to expect one. It can be shown that sometimes not only *consules ordinarii* were elected in the year before that in which they held office (as we would expect), but *consules suffecti* too. So in some years both *ordinarii* and *suffecti* may well have been elected on a single occasion, rather than at separate sessions, as we know to have happened later. Both *ordinarii* and *suffecti* for 40, for example, must have been elected in 39. One *ordinarius* died before he could take up office, and the other, the emperor Gaius, resigned on 12 January, and the two were immediately replaced by *suffecti* originally elected to hold office from July. We are specifically told by Dio[27] that no business had been transacted at any meeting of the senate

---

[19] See chap. 7 sect. 5. In the Republic it had been equally unusual for Cicero as consul to proceed beyond formal matters and deliver his speech *De Lege Agraria* I on 1 January 63 B.C. On these atypical years see the full discussion of G. B. Townend, "The consuls of A.D. 69/70," *AJP* 83. 1962. pp. 113-129.

[20] Dio 60.10.2; cf. 59.6.7.

[21] Suet. *Tib.* 61; Tac. *Ann.* 4.70; cf. 4.17.

[22] *Hist.* 4.10, 39, 40.

[23] See Sherwin-White, *Pliny*, pp. 57 and 166.

[24] For the date, cf. Gaius, *Dig.* 50.16.233.1; Dio 59.24.3; HA, *Pertinax* 6.4. For the vows, Plin. *Paneg.* 67-68, with Sherwin-White, *Pliny*, pp. 611-612.

[25] In general see further chapter 10 below.

[26] Cf. Dio 58.20 on Tiberius.

[27] 59.24.

between 1 and 12 January. *Suffecti* for 69 had evidently been elected before Nero's death in June 68.[28]

In the Arval records C. Vipstanus Apronianus, *consul ordinarius* in 59, is mentioned without further comment at the meeting of the Brethren on 13 October 58, but he is described as *consul designatus* when he attends the next meeting on 6 November.[29] So it might be suggested that the *ordinarii* for 59 were designated on, say, 1 November 58. Yet for 57 that date seems less plausible. On 6 November that year M. Valerius Messalla Corvinus, *consul ordinarius* in 58, likewise appears as *consul designatus*. But he also bears the title on his attendance at the previous meeting of the Brethren, the date of which is not known because the stone is broken.[30] Except in the unlikely event of the previous meeting being squeezed in between, say, 1st and 5th, it would look as if the *ordinarii* were designated earlier in this year than they were to be in 58. In 59 *comitia consularia* were evidently held for Nero on 4 March.[31]

Yet also from 59 we have an example of a *consul suffectus* designated early in the same year that he took up office. As an Arval Brother, T. Sextius Africanus was present to sacrifice "ob comitia consularia Neronis" on 4 March, and on the following day too. But only at the next meeting of the Brethren after these occasions, on 28 March, is he described as *consul designatus*.[32] Unfortunately, from this isolated piece of evidence it is impossible to say whether other suffects for 59 were designated thus, or whether the time of Africanus' election is exceptional—as it might be if he were replacing someone who had died suddenly, for example.

Two instances remain ambiguous. It is possible to infer from Dio[33] that the suffects who entered office on 1 September 37 had been elected before Tiberius' death in March of the same year; but we cannot tell whether the election took place in late 36 or early 37. Similarly, Barea Soranus, who as *consul designatus* proposed honors for Pallas on 23 January 52, could have been elected either during 51, or earlier in January 52.[34]

Further miscellaneous references leave an equally bewildering impression. They certainly do not suggest any fixed dates, nor any special "election days," in the Julio-Claudian period. Thus if the *ludi* which interrupted the trial of Aemilia Lepida in 20 were the well-known *Ludi Romani* cel-

---

[28] Cf. Tac. *Hist.* 1.6, 14, 77.

[29] *Arval Acta*, para. 25 lines 13 and 18.

[30] *Arval Acta*, para. 23 lines 2-3 and 11.

[31] *Arval Acta*, para. 25 line 65.

[32] *Arval Acta*, para. 25 line 68; para. 26 lines 3 and 7.

[33] 59.7.9; cf. *Fast. Ost.*; *PIR*² C 103 and 393.

[34] For the day, see Plin. *Ep.* 8.6.13; for the incident, ibid. 7.29; Tac. *Ann.* 12.53. Cf. C. Anicius Cerealis, cos. suff. from July or August 65 (P. A. Gallivan, *CQ* 24. 1974. p. 310), described as designate the previous April (Tac. *Ann.* 15.74).

ebrated from 4 to 19 September, then at least one *ordinarius* for 21 had already been elected by that time, because Drusus appears at the trial as *consul designatus*.[35] By contrast, when Claudius died on 13 October 54, consuls even for the following month had apparently still not been elected.[36] Likewise in 69 (in no sense a normal year), when Vitellius heard of the disastrous defeat of his troops at Cremona at the end of October, he is said to have hurried on the elections for 70, together with the *destinatio* of consuls for many years ahead.[37]

There was, then, it seems, no regular timetable for consular elections during the Julio-Claudian period. Where lower magistrates are concerned, our knowledge remains almost a blank beyond the point that the future emperor Nerva can be described as *praetor designatus* at the time of the suppression of the Pisonian conspiracy in April 65.[38] Later, 100 is the one year for which we have some insight into election arrangements, gained from Pliny's *Panegyricus*. It is a fair guess (but no more than a guess) that the program revealed there was developed under the Flavians, and that it set a pattern which remained standard. Only the designation of emperors and others to ordinary consulships evidently continued to conform to no set pattern.[39]

According to Pliny,[40] Trajan and Julius Frontinus took up office as *ordinarii* on 1 January 100, having naturally been elected in 99. We do not know the time of their election in that year, although it may be noted that later, when delivering his *Panegyricus* on entry to office in September 100, Pliny can urge Trajan to take a fourth (ordinary) consulship for 101, so that in this year he had not already been elected to one by that time.[41] From one of Pliny's letters[42] we gather that *ordinarii* must at least have been elected later in the year than quaestors, who were perhaps elected in January to take office the following December, as we shall see. In this letter Pliny writes to his friend Minicius Fundanus (who, he believes, will

---

[35] Tac. *Ann.* 3.22. It should be recognized that Drusus' designation here may well tell us nothing about the wider pattern of elections in 20, since this could be just another instance where members of the imperial family were elected to magistracies long in advance (see, for example, Mommsen, *St. R.* I. pp. 586-587 and references there).

[36] Suet. *Claud.* 46.

[37] Tac. *Hist.* 3.55.

[38] Tac. *Ann.* 15.72. On the timing of the conspiracy see further below in this section. For speeches by Pomponius Flaccus as consul designate and, just possibly, by Cotta Messalinus as praetor designate in mid September 16, see chap. 7 sect. 11.

[39] On the former see M. Hammond, *The Antonine Monarchy*, pp. 82-85. Note how it may have been at the stated meeting on 1 July 221 that the future emperor Severus Alexander, as Caesar, was designated ordinary consul for 222 (*Feriale Duranum* in R. Cavenaile, *Corp. Pap. Lat.* no. 324 col. 2 line 18 with restoration).

[40] Cf. *Paneg.* 63 and 66.2.

[41] *Paneg.* 78-79. Trajan did hold such a consulship.

[42] 4.15.

be elected *consul ordinarius* for the following year), and urges him to choose as his quaestor, Asinius Bassus, who has already been elected to that magistracy. Sherwin-White[43] goes on to argue cautiously from this entreaty that *ordinarii* must therefore have been elected before 5 December, when quaestors took up office. This is likely, since only one *legitimus senatus* remained thereafter until the New Year, in a session when attendance might not be at its best.[44] But it should be acknowledged that the argument is not quite watertight. *Ordinarii* did not take up office till 1 January and might not choose their quaestors formally until that date, nor could the quaestors become their aides till then.

At any rate, having been elected at some time in 99, Trajan and Frontinus took up office as *ordinarii* on 1 January 100, and at a meeting very soon thereafter presided over the election of other magistrates. These others unquestionably included the *suffecti* for 100 itself, since Pliny[45] explicitly states the point. In addition, one candidate that day was a *quaestorius*,[46] so it is reasonable to guess that praetors and aediles to take up office on 1 January 101 were also elected then, along with tribunes for 10 December 100. Quaestors are not specifically mentioned. Mommsen[47] suggested on the basis of fifth-century practice—one election day on 9 January in the calendar of Silvius, followed by another for quaestors on 23 January—that their election was left to a later session. Sherwin-White disagreed.[48] But neither of his arguments is strong. He cites first Pliny's description of how each candidate for a magistracy "produced as witnesses and supporters either the person under whom he had served in the army, or the one whose quaestor he had been, or both if he could."[49] As Sherwin-White justly comments, the first alternative here would be one appropriate to those seeking the quaestorship. But it was not exclusive to them, nor would anywhere near all candidates for the quaestorship have done military service. The former point likewise weakens his second argument—that Trajan's favor towards members of noble families was also appropriate to candidates for the quaestorship.[50] Yet nobles might expect favor at all stages of their career, not just at the beginning.

A strong argument in favor of two election days in 100 must be the

---

[43] *Pliny*, p. 26.

[44] See chap. 4 sect. 2 note 83.

[45] *Paneg.* 92.3.

[46] *Paneg.* 70.1.

[47] *St. R.* I. p. 590.

[48] *Pliny*, p. 27.

[49] *Ep.* 3.20.5. It should be remembered that, strictly, Pliny is here describing behavior in some past "golden age." But he is presumably to be taken as meaning that the old procedure was still being followed in his own day, though in a far more disorderly fashion (cf. sect. 4).

[50] Plin. *Paneg.* 69.4-6.

sheer practical difficulty of completing in one day for all magistrates the procedure which Pliny describes. As he explains it,[51] each candidate spoke for himself, and was then supported by others whom he called upon. Even suffect consuls were recommended to the House,[52] though they faced no competition, and merely had their appointment confirmed. Assuming for the sake of argument that there was no competition for any magistracy, at the least two or three speeches would still be needed for each of, say, 4 suffect consuls, 18 praetors, 10 tribunes, 6 aediles, and 20 quaestors. In fact, at all levels below the consulship we know that there was modest competition, so each of the relevant figures should be increased. Altogether there would be well over, say, 120 speeches, as well as the actual business of election. Even if limits were placed upon the length of speeches,[53] and upon the number made in each candidate's favor, Sherwin-White's view requires an impossible quantity of work to be crammed within the 9 to 9½ hours of daylight during this month. One hundred twenty speeches rigidly restricted to, say, as little as four minutes each would still occupy a bare minimum of 8 hours, and in practice significantly longer amidst the prevailing excitement and confusion. Indeed even with two days available the schedule would remain tight, so it is natural enough that the *Historia Augusta*[54] should portray an election-day session continuing until evening in the latter part of the second century. In *Panegyricus* Pliny's failure to mention a second day, on which quaestors were elected, need be no puzzle. His concern in the work is with the occasions when he and the emperor were involved.

Pliny does not tell us the date of the election day in 100 described by him. All we can be sure of is that it fell before the trial of Marius Priscus, which was held late enough in January for Cornutus Tertullus to speak at it in his new capacity as consul designate.[55] Certainly, if the practice of 100 dated back to Domitian's reign, an election day between the Kalends and the Ides might have enabled a *suffectus* to take up conveniently the ordinary consulship which that emperor was in the habit of resigning on the Ides.[56] So altogether there is good reason to conjecture that a tiny fragment of a calendar from Lanuvium, now lost, which mentions "sen[– – –]" against 12 January, is recording a *senatus legitimus*.[57] Elec-

---

[51] *Ep.* 3.20.5.

[52] Cf. *Paneg.* 92.3.

[53] See chap. 7 sect. 15.

[54] *Marcus* 10.8.

[55] Plin. *Ep.* 2.11.19; Acutius Nerva also spoke thus at the next session, 2.12.2.

[56] Suet. *Dom.* 13; cf. Plin. *Paneg.* 65.3.

[57] See *NSc* 1907. pp. 125-126; *Ephem. Epig.* 9. pp. 388-389; *Inscr. Ital.* XIII.2. p. 236; and discussion by G. Colonna, *NSc* 29. 1975. p. 39. It would be satisfying, but perhaps unduly speculative, to conjecture "Sen[atūs]" against 12th, followed by "Leg[itimi]," rather than "Leg[– – –]" or "Lex[– – –]," against 13th.

tions seem its most likely purpose. It may be objected at once that if a suffect consul so elected by the senate on that day had been required to fill a place vacated by Domitian on the Ides (the following day, in other words), there could hardly have been time for the incoming magistrate's appointment to be ratified by the *comitia* before he took up office. This is true. But of course whether regular elections on 12 January really dated back so far, and even if they did, whether such a technical difficulty bothered Domitian, are both open questions. Had he wished to preserve the people's prerogative, in such circumstances it would have been easy enough to have one *suffectus* elected during the previous year with the two *ordinarii*. At any rate, 12 January appears the most plausible guess for the date of the election day described by Pliny.

In summary, therefore, the following timetable may be suggested for the election of magistrates around 100. The two ordinary consuls who entered office on 1 January were elected at some date in 99, though there was not necessarily a special meeting just for this purpose. But then during January there were two "election days." On the first, possibly 12 January, were elected all the suffect consuls to hold office later in 100; the praetors and aediles to enter office on 1 January 101; and the tribunes to enter office on 10 December 100. On the second day were elected the quaestors to enter office on 5 December 100. Though proof is lacking, it could be that these arrangements generally became standard from the Flavian period onwards. Under them, election of Baebius Macer as consul designate in January 103 would certainly tally with Pliny's report of the trial of Julius Bassus later that spring.[58] Significantly, under this scheme members had a regular obligation to attend for two days in succession, with elections on 12 January and a stated meeting on the 13th.

Assignment by lot of the proconsular provinces was another item in the senate's annual round, handled in March during the late Republic.[59] Evidence for the time in our period is lacking, but it is at least likely to have been around the turn of the year, because by a ruling of Claudius in 43 proconsuls had to set out from Rome no later than 15 April.[60] This was six weeks in advance of the date previously fixed by Tiberius, 1 June,[61] and time still had to be allowed for making preparations. We possess

---

[58] See Appendix 5. The only other time of year at which there would be 10 to 10½ hours of daylight is late October and early November. If the trial had taken place at that season in 102, we are faced with the unlikely prospect of Baebius being elected suffect consul for 103 no later than the first stated session of the House after the summer recess of 102. Such a radical departure from the arrangements outlined by Pliny for only two years earlier is hardly to be expected.

[59] Cf. Cic. *Ad Att.* 6.1.24 = SB 115 for 50 B.C.

[60] Dio 60.17.3.

[61] Dio 57.14.5.

Fronto's account[62] of the steps he took to assemble staff, while according to Papinian,[63] before departure a proconsul might wish to move furniture, clothes, medicines, and other items from his town house to his *horti* for safekeeping. Though it would seem natural enough to incorporate the actual drawing of lots into the business of a meeting, at the same time there can have been no absolute need for the corporate body to be present: for all we know, the draw was conducted separately from any session.

An anecdote in Suetonius[64] suggests that in the imperial period quaestors continued to draw lots together on a particular day for the posts they were to occupy during their year of office. In this connection a fragmentary fourth-century calendar which has come to light under the church of S. Maria Maggiore in Rome preserves the entry under 2 December: "II [II non] quaest(orum) sor[titio]."[65] If the supplements printed here be accepted, then we have our first evidence of a date for this draw, three days before the quaestors entered office on 5 December. Naturally it is still impossible to be sure whether the draw was held on 2 December during the Principate. Yet since the quaestorship was at best only a faded relic of its former self by the fourth century, the date recorded then seems all the more likely to be the traditional one. December 2 was never the day of a stated meeting; but it is understandable that this draw among quaestors designate—who strictly still lacked any right to attend the House—should not have taken place at such a time. The day might also seem too close to the moment when quaestors would have to take up their offices. Yet many would be going to provinces, and would not need to depart for three months or so; the duties of the others were all performed in Rome. So it would certainly have been possible for the draw to be held on 2 December during the Principate.

Nominations to major priesthoods came to be made in the senate from early in our period. By the end of the first century Pliny[66] can speak of a regular day each year on which they were made. But we do not know which day it was, nor when it came to be fixed.

In the late Republic the senate had regularly given priority to the reception of embassies in February each year, and might sit for days on end to hear them.[67] For envoys who had to travel any distance, especially by sea, a less convenient month than February could hardly have been fixed.

[62] *Ant. Imp.* 8 = p. 161 H.

[63] *Dig.* 33.7.12.40-41.

[64] *Tib.* 35.

[65] F. Magi, "Il calendario dipinto sotto Santa Maria Maggiore," *Pontificia Accademia Romana di Archeologia: Memorie* 11. 1972. pp. 26-27. Alternatively, H. Stern (*Rev. Et. Lat.* 51. 1973. p. 46) would read under 2 December "QUAEST(ores) SORT(iunt)."

[66] *Ep.* 2.1.8; 4.8.3. See further chap. 10 sect. 2.

[67] See Pseudasconius, p. 244 Stangl, and Mommsen, *St. R.* III. 2. pp. 1155-1156 with references there.

But conceivably this was an arrangement unaltered since early times, when the communities making approaches would almost all have been situated close by in Italy itself. As it was, the month of February no doubt continued to suit the senate, insofar as the reports or pleas of embassies might affect the allocation of provincial commands handled in March. For long into our period embassies continued to approach the House, and might be heard with equal patience.[68] To what extent they now aimed to arrive in February, and what priority they would be given in this month, we do not know.[69] Delegations of Italians and provincials were still waiting to be heard in 16 at the time of the debate on *res prolatae* discussed below, which would hardly have been later than 1 April. But presumably once the allocation of proconsular provinces was shifted to a date earlier than March, the pressing need for embassies to time their arrival for February disappeared. In any event, governors for only a limited proportion of provinces were now chosen in the senate.

Our fourth-century calendar lists a stated meeting on the day before the Ides of March, rather than on the Ides itself. Avoidance of the latter day presumably dates from shortly after Caesar's murder, when the senate voted that it should never meet on that day again.[70] We know of two, or just possibly three, stated meetings duly held on 14 March.[71]

In the Republic there was a recess of senate and law courts, variously called *discessus senatus* or *res prolatae*, for much of April (when many days were taken up by celebration of games anyway) and early May.[72] Thus in Cicero's time no meeting of the senate is known to have occurred between 5 April and 15 May,[73] except in the years of crisis, 44 and 43 B.C.[74] There is every reason to believe that observance of this recess

---

[68] See chap. 14 sect. 2.

[69] Since in all likelihood the problem of abuse of asylum rights in Greek cities was only referred to the House by the emperor (see chap. 14 sect. 2 note 80), it must be pure accident that the relevant hearing occurred in the spring of 22. No precise dating is possible, but we do know that before the senate reached its final decision on the matter, Livia had dedicated a statue to Augustus near the theater of Marcellus on 23 April (Tac. *Ann.* 3.60-64; *EJ* Calendars, p. 48).

[70] Suet. *DJ* 88; cf. Dio 47.19.1.

[71] Tac. *Hist.* 1.90 for 69; *Dig.* 5.3.20.6 for 129. The initial request for senatorial sponsorship of the Secular Games was made in 203, "Prid. [6]ias" (if not "ias," then "tas"). Into the six-letter gap would fit "id. mart," "kal. iun," "non. iun," "kal. iul," "non. iul," "k. augus." "Id. mart" is attractive in that 14 March is the only one of these days on which a stated meeting would fall. Of course the senate might have met in special session for this purpose, and the interval before the next action by the college (in November) is long. But at the very least (restoring "k. augus") the interval is still a puzzling three months or so (G. B. Pighi, *De Ludis Saecularibus*, p. 140 I line 5 and p. 144 I line 49).

[72] See P. Stein, "Die Senatssitzungen der Ciceronischen Zeit (68-43)," diss. Münster, 1930, pp. 110-111.

[73] For that precise interval in 56 B.C. (when the Conference of Luca took place), see Cic. *Ad Fam.* 1.9.4 = SB 20.

[74] For a list of all meetings of the senate which can be securely dated up to and including 49 B.C., see A. K. Michels, *The Calendar of the Roman Republic*, Princeton, 1967, pp. 55-58; for meetings 68-43 B.C. in tabular form, P. Stein, op. cit. p. 119.

continued into the imperial period. A variety of evidence shows how, just as during the late Republic, this long continued to be the smartest season of the year in the Campanian resorts, and all the fashionable set would plan to be there then[75]—even in 44 B.C.[76] Among the reasons which delayed Nero's reaction to the revolt of Vindex, for example, could well have been that he first heard the news of it around 20 March, just before the start of the holiday season.[77] News of Galba's revolt in Tarraconensis, raised on 2 April, presumably came during the recess too.[78]

Only a single specific reference to *res prolatae* in our period survives, made by Tacitus[79] under 16. It may be significant that not only is the matter treated as routine: Tacitus omits to add any explanation as he does, for example, in mentioning Tiberius' habit of calling even upon magistrates when he presided in the senate,[80] a practice which would apparently be unfamiliar to second-century readers. He also narrates the incident out of sequence.[81] The emperor had given notice that he would be absent. Asinius Gallus argued provocatively that the senate should continue to conduct its business nonetheless, whereas Calpurnius Piso proposed that its reception of various delegations be postponed until the emperor could be present. The debate might suggest that at this time a decision was taken year by year whether or not to suspend *senatus legitimi* (those of the Ides of April and Kalends of May?) for the period of the recess. Though the claim is of slight value perhaps when our evidence is thin, it is the case that in the imperial period, as in the late Republic, only emergency meetings during *res prolatae* are known. One was called after the discovery of the Pisonian conspiracy in 65,[82] another to confer power on Vitellius in 69.[83] The conspiracy had in fact been planned not so much to coincide with *res*

[75] See J. H. d'Arms, *Romans on the Bay of Naples*, Harvard, 1970; F. Millar, *Emperor*, pp. 24-28. For the possibility that a decline in popularity set in after the Julio-Claudian period, see J. H. d'Arms, *Commerce and Social Standing in Ancient Rome*, chap. 4 sect. 4.

[76] Cic. *Ad Att.* 14.9.2 = SB 363; cf. 12.40.3 = SB 281.

[77] Suet. *Nero* 40; cf. Tac. *Ann.* 14.4.

[78] Cf. Dio 64.6.5².

[79] *Ann.* 2.35.

[80] *Ann.* 3.17.

[81] For 16 he opens with foreign affairs (*Ann.* 2.1-26), next deals with the trial of Libo Drusus on 13 September (2.27-32), then with business on "proximo senatus die" and soon afterwards (2.33-34); and only after all these with the debate on *res prolatae*, which can hardly have occurred later than 1 April (2.35). I would not follow Sherwin-White (*Pliny*, p. 361) in believing Tacitus to refer in this passage to the autumn recess—which would still start before 13 September.

[82] For the timing of the conspiracy, see Tac. *Ann.* 15.53. Milichus seems to have informed Nero on the very day when the plot was to have been carried out (ibid. 55). One or two more days (cf. 57) were spent on investigations, and the senate was then summoned (72).

[83] Tac. *Hist.* 2.55. Vitellius' *dies imperii* was 19 April according to *Arval Acta*, para. 34. I. line 85.

prolatae as to catch Nero at the *Ludi Ceriales* (12-19 April), one of his rare appearances in public. Meetings on the Ides of April and Kalends of May are listed without comment in the fourth- and fifth-century calendars. The only other references to *res prolatae* in our period relate to the vacation of the law courts, which was in November and December.[84]

There is no evidence that Augustus made for *res prolatae* the arrangement which he introduced for the *senatus legitimi* (presumably four of them) in September and October. Since this was the season of the grape harvest, and September anyway was taken up by a great many public holidays,[85] all members were excused, except a sufficient number to provide a quorum for the passage of decrees. The senators who thus remained were to be chosen by lot. Some at least may have been willing enough to stay if they had also been drafted to serve as jurors on *quaestiones*, who evidently sat through these months and then, as we have just noted, took their vacation in November and December.[86] Conceivably it was on purpose that Tiberius therefore delayed his denunciation of Sejanus until a meeting of the senate in October when attendance would be lower than usual. It is quite clear that September and October were the months in which Pliny, for example, habitually visited his estates.[87]

If a matter of national importance arose, or a death occurred in the imperial family, then excused senators might have to return. Two months is a long stretch, and not surprisingly the recess was interrupted thus in a number of years. Meetings of the House would not have been essential in every instance perhaps, but members' presence at public ceremonials would certainly have been expected. As an extreme, during the decade beginning in 14 there are likely to have been interruptions of the recess in as many as five years of the ten—in 14 for the accession of Tiberius; in 16 for the trial of Libo Drusus; in 19 for rites in honor of Germanicus;[88] in 20 for the trial of Aemilia Lepida; and in 23 on the death of Drusus. In other years there occurred during the recess the accessions of Nero, Domitian, and Nerva; the deaths of Lucius Caesar[89] and Trajan's sister, Marciana;[90] the trial of Cornelius Priscianus in 145;[91] and most probably the arrival of

---

[84] *FIRA²* I no. 44 col. 2 line 4; Seneca, *De Brev. Vitae* 7.8; *Laus Pisonis* 86 Verdière. For the season, Suet. *Aug.* 23; *Galba* 14.

[85] Cf. Plin. *Ep.* 10.8.3 with Sherwin-White ad loc.

[86] For senators as jurors see chap. 16 sect. 1 note 23.

[87] Cf. *Ep.* 1.7.4; 7.30; 8.1 and 2; 9.37. *Ep.* 4.13 and 5.14 may also belong to the same season: both are addressed to fellow senators with movements comparable to his own (for the virtual certainty that L. Pontius Allifanus was a senator, see *AE* 1956. 187 with W. Eck, *PW* Suppl. 14 s.v. Pontius no. 24 b, col. 445).

[88] *EJ* p. 53; cf. p. 41.

[89] *Fasti Gabini*, 19 September A.D. 2.

[90] Strictly, she died at Rome on 29 August 112; a public funeral followed on 3 September (*Fast. Ost.*).

[91] *Fast. Ost.*; *PIR²* C 1418.

Galba in Rome as emperor.[92] In addition, Tiberius[93] and Commodus[94] both celebrated triumphs in October. The surprisingly high attendance of 383 at a special meeting on 22 September 44 remains unexplained.[95] There may also have been a session on 25 September in an unknown year.[96] Lastly, although we have no information on the point, it seems fair to imagine that news of Trajan's death in Cilicia around 9 August 117[97] reached Rome during the summer recess.

Apart from 15 March perhaps, there is no clear evidence of other days in the year on which the senate *could not* meet during our period. A fragmentary inscription from Samos relating to 23[98] might be interpreted to indicate that in this year the stated session scheduled for the Ides of September was brought forward to the previous day by choice, perhaps as a consequence of the Ides itself having been declared "dies festus" after Libo Drusus' suicide in 16.[99] Unfortunately, no other meeting can be dated securely to either of these days, so that we have no inkling of whether the arrangement conjectured for September 23 became standard practice, and if so, for how long. In the fourth century, at any rate, the stated meeting was on the Ides itself. More generally, the view that there could be no meeting during a *iustitium* has been proved false.[100] Yet even though there was no legal obstacle, certain days were always likely to be avoided except in a crisis. We may guess that the stated meeting for the Ides of July was shifted so as not to coincide with the *transvectio equitum* on that day,[101] and we have already gathered from Dio how Augustus arranged stated sessions in such a way that members should be deprived of all possible excuses for absence.[102] We can be fairly sure that it was the *Ludi Romani* (4-19 September) which were allowed to interrupt the trial of Aemilia

---

[92] See Tac. *Hist.* 1.6-7 with Chilver ad loc.

[93] *Fasti Praenestini*, 23 October. For discussion of the year (A.D. 12?) see *Inscr. Ital.* XIII. 2. pp. 524-525.

[94] HA, *Commodus* 12.7.

[95] See above, sect. 2 note 35.

[96] Lines 3 and 4 of *Fast. Ost.* XXXVIII would need to refer to the same item for this conjecture to be proved.

[97] For the date see M. Hammond, *MAAR* 24. 1956. p. 90.

[98] The stone is so badly damaged that its identity as a *senatus consultum*, or part of one, is uncertain. More to the point here, there is also no knowing whether the day of the month in line 5 (which at least is clear) relates to the day when the consuls delivered their decision, or to the day when the senate issued its decree. Naturally, both events could have occurred on the same day. See P. Herrmann, "Die Inschriften römischer Zeit aus dem Heraion von Samos," *Ath. Mitt.* 75. 1960. no. 5 pp. 90-93; R. K. Sherk, *Roman Documents*, no. 32; S. M. Sherwin-White, *Ancient Cos, Hypomnemata* 51, Göttingen, 1978, p. 149.

[99] Tac. *Ann.* 2.32.

[100] See K. Wellesley, *JRS* 57. 1967. p. 24.

[101] Perhaps for that reason our fourth-century calendar lists a meeting on 17 July, rather than 15th.

[102] Dio 55.3.2.

Lepida in the senate in 20.[103] In all likelihood, sessions due to coincide with days when the emperor was to dedicate major building projects on completion would at the very least have been curtailed: for example, Augustus is known to have dedicated the temple of Mars Ultor on 1 August 2 B.C., Claudius two new aqueducts on the same day in 52,[104] and Trajan his forum and the Basilica Ulpia on 1 January 112. Similarly, the stated meeting scheduled for 1 March in the latter year must have been moved or canceled, since on that day Trajan gave a circus and banqueted senate and *equites*.[105] But otherwise we cannot establish in detail how far sessions—whether stated or summoned specially—were arranged to avoid days of games, circuses, and festivals.[106]

Altogether the number of fixed sessions in a year during our period was modest—a maximum of twenty-four, of which in practice most senators were automatically excused four or more. However, there would always be one meeting or more for elections, and special meetings in addition. These were called for a variety of reasons, entirely at the discretion of those with authority to summon the senate and sometimes at very short notice. It was perhaps standard practice at least to call an immediate session not only on emperors' accessions, but also whenever dispatches were received from them on campaign. Thus we find the House meeting for the latter reason on 20 or 21 February and again on 6 May 116 (during *res prolatae*),[107] when Trajan was in the East. As to other business, we have already noted how remarkable it is to find a special meeting called to discuss legislation during the summer recess on 22 September 44. It may be set beside another special meeting with a similar purpose on 25 August 56.[108] Conceivably this represented part of an effort to clear outstanding items just before the recess formally began. But its timing must have proved a severe test of many members' patience, since twelve days had already elapsed from the last stated meeting in August, and they were straining to escape the unbearable city heat. In any event, special sessions seem all the more astonishing during summer when days were at their longest. Stated meetings might have been expected to suffice for dispatching even very substantial agendas at this season. In mid August there were up to

[103] Tac. *Ann.* 3.23.

[104] Dio 60.5.3; Frontinus, *Aqued.* 1.13.

[105] *Fast. Ost.* A.D. 112.

[106] For sacrifices (on the Capitol) by Arval Brethren on the days of stated sessions in the first century, see J. Scheid and H. Broise, *MEFR* 92. 1980. pp. 236-240. In our fourth-century calendar some stated sessions do seem to avoid festivals and the like, but others do not: see *Inscr. Ital.* XIII. 2. p. 363.

[107] *Fast. Ost.*; cf. Suet. *Calig.* 44. For two sessions probably called specially for the same purpose in 217 and 218, see Dio 78.16.5 and 37.5.

[108] *Dig.* 36.1.1.1.

14 hours of daylight, and in mid September 12½—if flesh and blood could stand uninterrupted sittings of this length. In the second century Hadrian's adoption of Antoninus Pius was confirmed at a special meeting on 25 February 138,[109] but we no longer hear of extra sessions to discuss legislation.[110]

Irritatingly for members, the business at special meetings might not always turn out to be critically urgent: in 42, for example, tribunes summoned the House merely to elect a successor to one of their number who had died.[111] If the session on 23 January 52 was a special one,[112] we may hope for the sake of offended senators that honors for the imperial freedman Pallas were not the only item on the agenda![113] The business at special meetings called by certain emperors might prove minimal; Nero is said to have issued an immediate summons simply for the purpose disrupting a reading by Lucan.[114]

We have noted earlier[115] how on certain occasions failure to reach the end of an agenda because of unforeseen difficulties or delay (whether at a stated meeting or otherwise) might require the House not just to postpone items for a period, but instead to continue sitting on the following day and even beyond. More commonly, the reception of embassies could extend over several days. But trials were the most time-consuming extra sessions of all. Though they might begin at *senatus legitimi*,[116] they would regularly take more than a single day, and extra sessions therefore had to be arranged as necessary. We know that when charges of provincial misgovernment were brought, the normal allowance of time was six hours (measured by water clocks) to prosecuting counsel, and nine to the defense. Examination of witnesses would follow, and then the *interrogatio* to fix the verdict and any sentence. It is hard to believe that less time would customarily be allowed for other cases, so that altogether any trial could be expected to take two days at the very least, and usually three. As we shall be seeing,[117] adjournments of hearings were frequent too. By contrast, questions to be

---

[109] HA, *Antonin.* 4.6.

[110] Note two stated meetings on 14 March 129 and 13 June 195 (*Dig.* 5.3.20.6; 27.9.1.1).

[111] Dio 60.16.8.

[112] Plin. *Ep.* 8.6.13. We happen to hear of another meeting (its agenda unknown) on this day in 138: see HA, *Hadr.* 26.8; cf. 1.3. But the earliest evidence for a stated meeting then (to elect quaestors) remains the fourth- and fifth-century calendars.

[113] Unless all the items mentioned in *Ann.* 12.52 were handled before 23 January (which is unlikely), Tacitus has presumably not treated senatorial business of this year (or 16) in strict chronological sequence. The matter of honors for Pallas has been held back for fuller coverage.

[114] Suet. *Vita Lucani.*

[115] See sect. 2 above.

[116] For example, the trials of Libo Drusus; possibly also P. Celer (Tac. *Hist.* 4.10 and 40); Marius Priscus (Plin. *Ep.* 2.11.10 and 24).

[117] Chap. 16 sect. 2.

decided at once might arise unexpectedly, thus requiring a special session straightaway. In early 107, for example, the Bithynians' objection to the unprecedented request of the defense for the right to summon witnesses from the province led to an immediate hearing of this controversy, continuing into the following day.[118] In general, Pliny seems to think a continuous three-day hearing entirely normal.[119] For the trial of Piso in 20 we find time being allotted according to the standard proportions, with two days for the prosecution, and then, after an interval of six days, three for the defense. Even Plancina's "sham" trial, which followed, took two days.[120] For charges of provincial misgovernment the trial of Julius Bassus in 103 cannot have been unusual in taking four, or possibly five, days within a short span (they may even have been consecutive).[121] In certain terrible years—32, for example, after Sejanus' fall—trials in the senate must have been extremely time-consuming. Yet Tacitus[122] can comment upon the pressure of accusations even in 25, a year which brought notably heavy diplomatic business, too, it would seem.[123]

Although most active senators could enjoy generous recesses of three months or more each year (unless they were unlucky in the lot), it is fair to conclude that they would usually be called to a substantial number of sessions throughout the rest of the year. Such regular continuation of meetings, with no lengthy break except possibly for just one month in the spring, stands in marked contrast, say, to the practice of Parliament at Westminster which as late as the reforms of 1928/9 aimed to sit only from February to July each year.[124] Of course Parliament by no means always achieved this leisurely ideal, and in a whole variety of ways it has always been a very different type of institution from the Roman senate: but the comparison does at least serve to underline the latter's demanding routine. It would be mistaken to deduce from the modest total of fixed meetings during the Principate that the senate now met much less often than it had done in the late Republic or that members would be significantly less

---

[118] Plin. *Ep.* 5.20.

[119] Cf. *Ep.* 2.11.18; *Paneg.* 76.1.

[120] Tac. *Ann.* 3.13 and 17.

[121] See Plin. *Ep.* 4.9.1 and 15 (it is not clear whether the debate on a verdict occurred on the fourth day, after the examination of witnesses, or was held over until a fifth day). On the length of trials, cf. also Plin. *Ep.* 2.11.14.

[122] *Ann.* 4.36.

[123] See chap. 14 sect. 2 note 10.

[124] See E. Taylor, *The House of Commons at Work* (ed. 9), London, 1979, pp. 48-50.

Supplementary note: M. R. Salzman, "New evidence for the dating of the calendar at Santa Maria Maggiore in Rome," *TAPA* 111. 1981. pp. 215-227, reached me only after this section had gone to press. A convincing case is made for re-dating the calendar (see above, note 65) to the late second or third centuries, rather than the fourth. Its significance for our period, to which it is now seen to belong, is thus increased.

occupied with senatorial business. The character of business did indeed change, but there was still much to be done. Well into the second century at least, in almost all years *senatus legitimi* are likely to have represented only a small proportion of sessions, especially now that the senate met as a court, which it had never done in the Republic.

5. Senatorial Dress

Roman costume is a large topic, but a short section on senatorial dress does merit a place in a chapter on the routine of the corporate body.[1] Not only was that dress distinctive; it was also considered important that members should be correctly attired when appearing in public. First, members of the class were privileged to wear the broad purple stripe (*latus clavus*) upon their tunics.[2] This was presumably the "distinctive dress" which those removed from the senate by Augustus were allowed to retain.[3] Traditionally the white toga had always been the special garb of all Roman citizens on formal occasions, and those in exile continued to be forbidden its use.[4] It symbolized formal civilian dress. But by the beginning of our period it would seem that the majority of folk no longer bothered with such an impractical garment. Efforts by Augustus to bring it back into general use made little lasting impact.[5] *Equites* perhaps continued to wear it for some time, but in practice the toga gradually came to be the special clothing of senators alone, and remained so throughout our period. In their case its heavy, ample folds did perhaps serve a practical purpose in offering some protection against freezing temperatures in an unheated chamber during winter sessions.[6]

In time, therefore, it was the toga which marked out senators more than the *latus clavus*. Indeed Pliny the Elder[7] grumbles about this badge being adopted even by public criers, and there is evidence from wall paintings to show how stripes of varying widths and colors were commonly worn throughout Italian society.[8] At a banquet given by Gaius togas were evidently suitable gifts to be presented to senators and *equites*.[9] But it was

---

[1] See in general L. M. Wilson, *The Clothing of the Ancient Romans*, Baltimore, 1938; on the toga, F. W. Goethert, *PW* 6 A. s.v. toga, cols. 1651-1660.

[2] Cf. Plin. *NH* 9.127; Epictet. 1.20-22; Juvenal, *Sat.* 1.106.

[3] Suet. *Aug.* 35, "insigne vestis"; cf. in general Tac. *Ann.* 11.23.

[4] Cf. Seneca, *Apocol.* 3.3 for citizens described as "togati"; Plin. *Ep.* 4.11.3; Marcianus, *Dig.* 49.14.32.

[5] Suet. *Aug.* 40 and 44; cf. Juvenal, *Sat.* 3.171-172; Plin. *Ep.* 5.6.45; 7.3.2.

[6] On lack of heating, see chap. 3 sect. 2.

[7] *NH* 33.29.

[8] See Wilson, op. cit. p. 61.

[9] Suet. *Calig.* 17.

presumably his toga which Umbonius Silo ostentatiously sold at auction after his expulsion from the senate had been engineered in 44; he would no longer need it in private life.[10] Nero allegedly gave offense not only by appearing in public wearing an ungirt tunic, but also by receiving senators in a flowered tunic and muslin neck-cloth.[11] According to the *Historia Augusta*,[12] Hadrian stipulated that senators and *equites* must wear the toga in public except when returning from a banquet. If an anecdote in the same source[13] is to be trusted, a toga was the required dress for guests at an imperial banquet in M. Aurelius' time—as the young Septimius Severus discovered when, strangely, he arrived wearing a *pallium*. Gellius[14] was witness to an incident in the city when Castricius—a noted teacher of rhetoric, well thought of by Hadrian—met some of his pupils, who were senators, wearing tunics and light cloaks (*lacernae*) on a holiday. Even so strict and old-fashioned a teacher acknowledged that well-established custom had made such attire acceptable, and that togas might have been unduly formal wear in the circumstances. But he tells the senators reprovingly that he would have preferred to see them in girt tunics and heavy cloaks (*paenulae*).

In the mid second century, Appian[15] commented that slave and free citizen were dressed alike; only the senatorial order stood out as different. Dio[16] confirms that early in the third century members still wore togas on public occasions, and it was no doubt the antique formality of this dress which gave an added barb to Elagabalus' insulting dismissal of senators as "slaves in togas."[17] Herodian[18] reflects Julia Maesa's concern that the willful young emperor might enter the House in unconventional dress.

According to Dio, the traditional representation of "the senate" was said to be "an elderly man in a tunic and purple bordered clothing, and with a crown upon his head."[19] No pictures have survived, but the personifications of the senate on Roman coins and monuments certainly conform to this description, as does the unique statue from Merida, plausibly identified as a "genius senatus."[20] By contrast, the personifications of

[10] Dio 60.24.6, τὴν βουλευτικὴν ἐσθῆτα.
[11] Dio 63.13.3. Quintilian (*Inst. Or.* 11.3.138-139) advises as to how a speaker of the senatorial class should gird his tunic—a detail, he claims, which must be attended to carefully, if criticism is to be avoided.
[12] *Hadr.* 22.2.
[13] HA, *Sev.* 1.7.
[14] 13.22.1.
[15] *Bell. Civ.* 2.120.
[16] Frag. 39.7.
[17] HA, *Elagab.* 20.1, "mancipia togata." Cf. Epictetus' description (4.1.57) of a consul as "a slave in a *toga praetexta.*"
[18] 5.5.5.
[19] 68.5.1.
[20] See, for example, *BMC* I. p. 359; III. p. 21; IV. p. 31; further chap. 2 sect. 6 note 122 and Figure 1 above.

ἱερὰ σύγκλητος which appear on coins of Greek cities throughout our period adhere to a wholly different tradition. The most common Greek image is the head of a beardless young man with long, flowing hair, sometimes crowned with laurel or a diadem, but quite frequently, too, the head of a young woman. The head of a bearded older man—closer to the Roman conception—is very much a rarity among these Greek coins.[21]

Consuls, praetors, and aediles in office wore the *toga praetexta*, the purple-bordered toga,[22] and on very special occasions others might do so too: for example, we hear of the senators who had shared Octavian's victory being allowed to wear it at his triumph in 29 B.C.[23]

Private citizens in mourning were accustomed to wear dark clothing. Senators, too, might do so both when the death of a public figure occurred, and at the time of some public or private crisis. To take one example from the late Republic, Dio explains how in the chaotic situation over elections in late 53 B.C. the consuls "laid aside their senatorial dress and convened the senate in the costume of *equites*, as on the occasion of some great calamity."[24] By the costume of *equites* he presumably means the *sagum*, a heavy cloak of dark color.[25] Further references suggest that it was normal for senators to wear dark equestrian costume at all public functions, including sessions of the House, after the death of an emperor or of a member of his family.[26] It was a mark of respect in similar fashion that the magistrates removed their insignia before coming out to meet Agrippina with the body of Germanicus in 20.[27] In 192, when Commodus ordered senators to enter the arena "in equestrian costume and woolen cloaks," it was taken as an omen of his impending death. For, as Dio explains: "We never do this when going to the arena except when an emperor has died."[28]

Individual senators facing a crisis are found changing their dress to

----

[21] See G. Forni, "ΙΕΡΑ e ΘΕΟΣ ΣΥΝΚΛΗΤΟΣ," pp. 60-61, with chap. 2 sect. 6 note 105 and Figure 8 (a) and (b) above. For the Greek tradition, B. Ashmole, "A lost statue once in Thasos," in D. J. Gordon (ed.), *Fritz Saxl 1890-1948: A Volume of Memorial Essays*, London, 1957, pp. 195-198.

[22] Cf. Dio 56.31.2 and 46.5; 57.21.2; 76.8.5-6; Plut. *Quaest. Rom.* 81 = *Mor.* 283 B-D; Fronto, *Ad M. Caes.* 5.37 = p. 77H; perhaps also Epictet. 1.2.18. For the question of whether plebeian, as well as curule, aediles were thus honored, see in brief L. R. Taylor and R. T. Scott, *TAPA* 100. 1969. p. 551 n. 51.

[23] Dio 51.20.2. It is not clear whether Tacitus (*Ann.* 14.13) is thinking of this costume when he speaks of "festo cultu senatus" on the occasion of Nero's return to Rome after the murder of Agrippina.

[24] 40.46.1; cf. 41.3.1.

[25] Cf. Wilson, op. cit. in note 1, p. 105.

[26] *Consolatio ad Liviam* 186; Dio 54.35.5; 55.8.5; 56.31.2; 75.4.4; Herodian 4.2.3; cf. Suet. *Calig.* 13; *EJ* 94a lines 55-56.

[27] Tac. *Ann.* 3.4.

[28] 72.21.3; cf. HA, *Commod.* 16.6. By contrast, according to Dio (60.7.4), Claudius had not required senators to sit in their specially reserved seats at shows, and even permitted them to wear ordinary dress.

highlight their distress. Libo Drusus did so when seeking help in answering the charges brought against him in 16, as did L. Vitellius before begging Gaius for his life.[29] After the defeat of his troops at Cremona in 69, the emperor Vitellius, whose concern to conform to what he saw as correct imperial behavior we have noted earlier with reference to attendance in the senate,[30] was in a complete quandary about fitting dress for himself—wearing a purple military cloak with a sword at some times, at others dark clothing.[31] Juvenal[32] maliciously claims that all leading citizens would put on mourning when the town house of one of their number is burned down.

It was a longstanding tradition that a senator in formal costume was marked out not just by his clothing, but also by his shoes.[33] This is another topic which it would not be appropriate to discuss in detail here.[34] But it should be emphasized that in our period the senatorial *solea* remained a distinctive badge of the class. Although Plutarch[35] and Statius do speak of "patrician shoes," there is no good evidence that a difference in the design between "patrician" and "plebeian" wear (which may once have existed) still continued during the Principate. Rather, just one type was worn. It was a special sandal, red or black in color,[36] decorated with a crescent,[37] and tied some way up the leg with black straps.[38] In the incident mentioned above, where Castricius met some senators dressed informally, it seems to be their unsuitable footwear which upset him almost more than their costume.[39] And in recounting the charge of having murdered his wife Regilla, brought against Herodes Atticus by her brother, Appius Annius Atilius Bradua, Philostratus has the sophist ridicule his accuser's haughtiness with a jibe which refers to his special shoes: "Bradua was a very illustrious man of consular rank, and the outward sign of his high birth, a crescent-shaped ivory buckle, was attached to his sandal. And when he appeared before the Roman tribunal he brought no convincing proof of the charge that he was making, but delivered a long panegyric on himself

[29] Tac. *Ann.* 2.29; Dio 59.27.5.

[30] See chap. 5 sect. 2 note 38.

[31] Dio 65.16.4.

[32] *Sat.* 3.213.

[33] See Plin. *Ep.* 7.3.2; Apuleius, *Florida* 8.

[34] For modern discussions, Mommsen, *St. R.* III. 2. pp. 888-892; A. Mau, *PW* 3 s.v. calceus, cols. 1340-1345. For illustration see, for example, F. Magi, *I rilievi Flavi del Palazzo della Cancellaria*, Rome, 1945, p. 22 and fig. 21.

[35] *De Tranq. Anim.* 10 = *Mor.* 470 C.

[36] Martial 2.29.7-8; Juvenal, *Sat.* 7. 191-192.

[37] Stat. *Silv.* 5.2.27-28; Martial 1.49.31. See further G. Dossin, "La 'lunule' des sénateurs romains" in *Hommages à Marcel Renard, Collection Latomus* 102, Brussels, 1969, vol. 2 pp. 240-243.

[38] Hor. *Sat.* 1.6.27-28; Seneca, *De Tranq. Anim.* 11.9.

[39] Cf. Seneca, *De Ira* 3.18.4.

dealing with his own family. So Herodes made fun of him and said: 'You have your pedigree on your toe-joints.' "[40]

It is ironic therefore that the poet who composed verses of consolation on Regilla's funeral monument outside Rome should have singled out her son's special shoes as symbolic of his elevation to patrician status.[41] It was this footwear, together with the *latus clavus* on the tunic, and above all the formal white toga, which distinguished the senator from all other classes in public.

[40] *Vit. Soph.* 555.
[41] *IG* XIV. 1389 I lines 23ff; cf. H. Halfmann, *Die Senatoren*, nos. 68, 128.

7

PROCEDURE

We now come to the major topic of procedure at senatorial sessions.[1] Plainly, it did not remain static during the two centuries and a half of our period. Yet such development as did occur was only gradual and informal, not the result of clearly defined, precisely datable change. So on the one hand we can rarely, if ever, tell when a novelty was first introduced; nor, on the other, can we claim with confidence that an older practice was definitely superseded after a particular date. That said, we do know enough to fix the second century as the period of most striking development, although sadly it is for this formative time that our evidence is thinnest, and the actual evolution of change must therefore remain largely untraced.

Surprising though the judgment may seem at first glance, there is no reason to think that procedure in our period up to the early second century had changed radically from late Republican practice.[2] A senator of Cicero's day might have been puzzled by the scope and nature of business in Trajan's senate, and he would have needed to adjust to the pervasive influence of the emperor. But procedure itself he would not have found so strange. Pliny's own letters about sessions in the time of Nerva and Trajan show how he exaggerated in claiming that traditional practice had become irretrievably forgotten during Domitian's reign.[3] Unfortunately, none of the letters included in his collection seems to have been written before Nerva's time. Some do still treat earlier events—for example, the case of Licinianus and the Vestal Virgin Cornelia[4]—but there is no description of a session under Domitian.

Among modern scholars it has been fashionable to stress how trivial the business of the senate soon became under the Principate, and how meetings,

---

[1] While both M. A. de Dominicis, ''Il 'ius sententiae' nel senato romano,'' *Annali*, Facoltà di giurisprudenza, Perugia, 44. 1932. pp. 243-300, and A. Ormanni, *Saggi sul ''regolamento interno'' del senato romano*, Milan, 1971, have some relevance to the subject of this chapter, their focus is principally confined to the Republic.

[2] For an excellent summary of that practice, see C. Nicolet, *Rome et la conquête du monde Méditerranéen 264-27 avant J.-C., 1. Les structures de l'Italie romaine* (ed. 2), Paris, 1979, chap. 10 with bibliography on pp. 62-64.

[3] *Ep.* 8.14.2.

[4] *Ep.* 4.11.

or correct procedure at them, no longer held members' interest. Of course there is truth in these views. Yet an examination of the evidence shows that many members did nonetheless continue to take seriously their work in the House, so that a full study of procedure is entirely justified. Senators may often have been frightened and tongue-tied at sessions, but for all its changed circumstances they were too proud of their ancient high assembly and of their own station to let meetings slide into mocking farce. Contemptuous behavior such as the spoiling of ballot papers with jokes or obscenities (recorded by Pliny)[5] is conspicuous by its rarity; what is more, we are told that even in this instance it was widely disapproved of. Perhaps the spoiling was not childishness at all in fact but rather a deliberate, and apparently effective, ploy to achieve the return of open voting at elections.

Whatever view is taken of the quality of procedure, there is no doubt that after the second century, while some traditional elements remained, change clearly did set in. In this chapter procedure will therefore be examined with special reference to practice up to that time. Separate consideration of major changes thereafter follows in Chapter 8.

1. *Lex Julia*

Procedure was one of the matters regulated in a comprehensive *Lex Julia de senatu habendo* put forward by Augustus in 9 B.C., and never formally superseded, so far as we know. Such a law was an innovation, since previously, with certain exceptions,[6] it had been custom which mainly governed the workings of the House. Yet the apparent lack of change in the workings of senatorial procedure between the late Republic and the first century A.D. could suggest that the law for the most part served to codify existing practice rather than to introduce sweeping changes. Dio[7] mentions the new law in connection with the fixing of stated meetings, the establishment of quorums, and the levying of fines for non-attendance. But it is certain that further matters were covered too. Gellius,[8] who states that the law was still operative in the latter part of the second century, mentions it as laying down the order in which *sententiae* were to be asked for. In one letter Pliny quotes a sentence of its clause on how a vote should

---

[5] *Ep.* 3.20; 4.25; see further sect. 25 note 41 below.

[6] For example, quorums for particular types of business were laid down by law in the later Republic. See chap. 4 sect. 2 note 19.

[7] 55.3.1-4; cf. Suet. *Aug.* 35, both quoted in chap. 6 sect. 4 above. The latter's references to senatorial procedure are assembled by P. Ramondetti, "La terminologia relativa alla procedura del *senatum habere* in Svetonio," *Atti Accad. Sc. di Torino*, Classe Sc. Mor., Stor. e Filol. 111. 1977. pp. 135-168.

[8] 4.10.1.

be taken, while in another he relates how a clause (evidently seldom invoked) whereby one member could require another to swear that his *sententia* was in the interests of the state, was among several cited by a member and a tribune in the course of a session.[9]

Sadly, we have no further information on this vital law. In particular we do not know whether it was ever revised to take account of new procedures, such as elections within the House, which were established after 9 B.C. Conceivably these just continued to be run in accordance with the practice which developed. To compensate for loss of the law there is no alternative ancient guide to which we may turn instead. The Roman senate of our period had no commonly cited authority like Erskine May, or *Manual of Procedure in the Public Business*, to which we might refer. Before 70 B.C. a written manual of guidance for members was perhaps unknown, since Varro felt the need to produce his own to assist Pompey. He also repeated much of the material later for Oppianus in a letter, according to Gellius.[10] We have no further knowledge of Oppianus, nor can we tell whether the letter was even part of genuine correspondence.[11] With the changes introduced in 9 B.C. much of this work was presumably superseded, and in the late second century Gellius[12] can even cite Varro's own testimony that it had been lost, though copious extracts survived. C. Ateius Capito, the consular and legal expert of the Augustan period, wrote a volume *De Officio Senatorio*, known only from Gellius' citations.[13] But there is no telling whether this work was more a handbook of contemporary practice than an antiquarian treatise. The same problem recurs with the work by Nicostratus, entitled *De Senatu Habendo*, known only from a single citation in Festus.[14] In this case, however, the title drawn from the *Lex Julia* might well suggest a handbook, no doubt aimed in part to meet the needs of the many new entrants to the senate in the first half of the second century.

Instead of turning to these works (such as they were), members who sought to make a claim about procedure, or to raise a query in connection with it, seem to have cited the *Lex Julia* itself, or to have relied, in traditional fashion, on guidance handed down by word of mouth. When Pliny has a query, he consults his lawyer friend Titius Aristo, citing no written document on procedure other than the law itself. He alleges that new senators of his own generation, under the "tyranny" of Domitian,

---

[9] *Ep.* 8.14.19; 5.13.5-7.
[10] 14.7.
[11] See H. Dahlmann, *PW* Suppl. 6 s.v. (M.) Terentius (Varro) no. 84, cols. 1225-1226.
[12] 14.7.3.
[13] *PIR*[2] A 1279; Gell. 4.10.7-8; cf. 14.7.13 and 8.2.
[14] P. 470 L; see chap. 6 sect. 3 above.

did not have their elders' opportunity to be taught ". . . by example (the surest method of instruction) the powers of putting forward a *relatio*, the rights of making a *sententia*, the authority of magistrates, and the privileges of other members; *they* were taught when to give way and when to stand firm, when to keep silent and how long to speak, how to distinguish between conflicting *sententiae* and how to make additions to earlier *sententiae*, in short the whole of senatorial procedure."[15]

Such prejudice is to be discounted, however, and we may fairly assume that in practice new members always continued to receive guidance from their relatives and their elders, just as Pliny himself certainly did from two consulars, Verginius Rufus, his guardian,[16] and Corellius Rufus.[17] Relationships of mutual help and obligation developed: thus Fronto makes a general reference to the services he had been rendered by his junior, Gavius Clarus.[18] In such circumstances a lack of handbooks on procedure mattered little. In any event, as we shall see, it would only be after attendance for five years or more, on becoming *praetorii*, that most members would ever be called upon to take much individual part in proceedings. Thus even if they had to spend a year abroad as quaestors, new entrants were still left ample time to learn by the example of their seniors.

2. Religious Ceremonial

Not least because it could only be held in a place appointed by an augur and called a "temple,"[1] any regular session had to be preceded by religious ceremonial. According to Varro's handbook of 70 B.C.,[2] a magistrate should sacrifice a victim and take the auspices before holding a meeting of the senate. In 12 B.C. Augustus ordered that the senators should burn incense in the House whenever they met—in order to increase their respect for the gods, according to Dio.[3] Then as a further effort to promote a more devout attitude towards their duties, he prescribed that before taking their places all members should offer incense and wine at the altar of the god in whose temple the meeting had been convened.[4] As usual during Roman sacrifices, a flute player would perform. So it was notable that on the first entry which Tiberius and Drusus made to the senate after Augustus' death,

---

[15] *Ep.* 8.14.6.

[16] *Ep.* 2.1.8.

[17] *Ep.* 4.17.6; 9.13.6; cf. 1.12; 5.1.5.

[18] *Ver. Imp.* 2.7 = pp. 127-128 H; cf. Plin. *Ep.* 10.26.1 and further in general R. P. Saller, *Personal Patronage Under the Early Empire*, pp. 142-143.

[1] See further chap. 3 sect. 1.

[2] Gell. 14.7.9.

[3] 54.30.1.

[4] Suet. *Aug.* 35.

they offered the customary wine and incense, but dispensed with the flute player.[5]

This religious ceremonial before meetings evidently continued to the end of our period. In the mid second century, Appian[6] refers in the present tense to the taking of the auspices by magistrates as they entered a meeting. More specifically, Dio[7] later describes how in the presence of senators Didius Julianus offered to Janus the sacrifices of Entrance in front of the House in 193, while Herodian[8] seems to record it as a matter of course that Caracalla made a sacrifice before entering the senate in 212. He also explains, as we have seen in another context, that when a picture of Elagabalus was sent to Rome prior to his arrival there, orders were given that "it should hang in the middle of the senate house, very high up over the head of the statue of Victory. This is where all members, on arriving for meetings in the House, burn an offering of incense and make a libation of wine."[9]

3. The Opening of Sessions

Once the required religious ceremonial had been completed, the magistrate who had summoned the session proceeded to open it.[1] In effect only an emperor might call a session which he did not preside over himself. It was thus very much an "imperial" privilege which Tiberius exercised in 14 after Augustus' death, when he summoned a meeting by virtue of his tribunician power, and attended it, but left the presidency to the consuls.[2] Generally by definition there was a close link between summons and consultation. Consuls (who normally presided) continued to follow the traditional Republican practice of acting jointly in their presidential capacity,[3] although they would of course determine by mutual agreement which of them should take the lead as chairman on a particular occasion.[4] Whenever a session continued for hours on end one consul would be able to relieve the other in the chair. If special difficulties arose, they would

[5] Suet. *Tib.* 70; Dio 56.31.3.
[6] *Bell. Civ.* 2.116; for a similar use of the present tense by him, see sect. 11 note 27 below.
[7] 74.13.3 and 14.4.
[8] 4.5.1.
[9] 5.5.7. On the location of the statue of Victory, see chap. 3 sect. 2.
[1] On summons see chap. 6 sect. 1.
[2] Tac. *Ann.* 1.7-8.
[3] For the background, A. O'Brien Moore, *PW* Suppl. 6 col. 701. Joint consular sponsorship of *senatus consulta* remains normal in our period.
[4] Note the reference in the *senatus consultum* of which Augustus sent a copy to Cyrene in 4 B.C. to τῶν ὑπάτων τόν τε προηγορούντα (*FIRA*[2] I no. 68 V lines 138-139). Predictably, it is only one consul whom Pliny addresses at *Ep.* 9.13.9.

consult together and assume joint responsibility.[5] There can be little doubt that the need for both to approve any strong action contributed to the weakness persistently shown by presidents, a feature discussed further below. It is easy to appreciate the damage which might be done by disputes between consuls, such as occurred in late 31.[6] In the last resort each did retain the right to consult the House separately, and to veto his colleague's measures; but no such extremes are heard of in our period.

The actual opening of a session was possibly marked by a traditional proclamation excluding all but members from the chamber. It is referred to only by Dio,[7] quoting a speech by Elagabalus, and its wording is not known. Neither do we know whether it was dispensed with before trial hearings at which non-members would have to be present.

A modern observer might wish to divide the meetings of our period into three types: consultations by the president or others; trials; and elections. While each of the three has its special features (to be treated elsewhere),[8] it should be recognized with reference to the first two that procedure at trials evolved out of that for consultations. In particular, at a trial, after prosecution and defense had made their cases and witnesses had been heard, the president consulted members about a verdict and sentence just as he might about any other matter. Not surprisingly, therefore, contemporaries hardly drew a clear-cut distinction between sessions where the senate was consulted about non-judicial matters, and sessions where it sat as a court. Just as it was possible for trial proceedings to be conducted even at a stated meeting,[9] so, too, a meeting which opened with non-judicial business could proceed to hear a case.[10] Those aspects of procedure common to both consultation and trials will therefore be covered here.

4. The Language of Proceedings

Senatorial proceedings were generally conducted in Latin. We hear that Tiberius went to great lengths to ensure that no foreign words were used

---

[5] Thus, for example, Tacitus (*Ann.* 13.26) can explain "sed consules relationem incipere non ausi ignaro principe. . . ."

[6] Tac. *Ann.* 5.11; 6.4; Dio 58.9.3.

[7] 79.1.2.

[8] See chapters 10 and 16 below.

[9] See chap. 6 sect. 4.

[10] Cf., for example, Tac. *Hist.* 4.40. It may be noted, incidentally, that the senate resembled the *consilium principis* in this absence of any sharp division between its administrative and judicial roles. The different view taken of the latter body by W. Kunkel seems to me misplaced: see briefly his *Kleine Schriften*, Weimar, 1974, p. 178 and references there.

at sessions or in *senatus consulta*.[1] According to Tacitus,[2] however, it was in Greek that he habitually exclaimed to himself as he left sessions. Claudius, too, is said to have thrown out hints in Greek,[3] and it may be no accident that in his parody of a meeting in the *Apocolocyntosis*,[4] with that emperor present, Seneca works Greek quotations into the speeches of no fewer than three divine members. Fiction aside, the only exception to the general rule was that trials or investigations involving envoys or witnesses from Greek-speaking provinces might be conducted either in Latin, or, if necessary, in Greek. According to Valerius Maximus,[5] the practice of allowing Greek to be used thus without an interpreter dated from the late Republic. We have a number of references to such proceedings in Greek under Tiberius, Claudius, and Nero.[6] Claudius in particular enjoyed replying to Greek-speaking envoys in their own language. But he was horrified when a chance question in Latin to a Lycian envoy with Roman citizenship revealed that the man could not understand Latin, while on another occasion when the proceedings were otherwise in Greek, Tiberius insisted that a Roman centurion give his testimony in Latin.[7]

5. Speeches of Thanks

In the Republic consuls had thanked the people for their election.[1] But during our period these thanks soon came to be rendered instead to the emperor in the House as incoming holders took up their office.[2] The speech which Pliny delivered (presumably on 1 September 100) was later expanded by him and published. It alone survives today, usually referred to as *Panegyricus*.[3] Pliny[4] seems to suggest that such a speech was required of

---

[1] Suet. *Tib.* 71; cf. Dio 57.15.2 and 17.1-3.

[2] *Ann.* 3.65.

[3] Dio 60.16.8.

[4] 8-11.

[5] 2.2.2-3.

[6] Dio 57.15.3; Suet. *Claud.* 25, 42; *Nero* 7 (cf. Tac. *Ann.* 12.58); Quintil. *Inst. Or.* 6.1.14. By contrast, there is no indication from Pliny that any of the proceedings against Julius Bassus or Varenus Rufus were conducted in Greek.

[7] Dio 60.17.4; Suet. *Tib.* 71.

[1] Note, for example, Cic. *De Leg. Agr.* II, *ad populum*, 1-4.

[2] *Laus Pisonis* 68-71 Verdière. The speech would not necessarily be made at the first possible session; all the same, Fronto, who was suffect consul for July and August 143, was perhaps unusual in delaying until 13 August—the last possible stated meeting, in other words (*Ad M. Caes.* 2.1.1 = p. 24 H).

[3] M. L. Paladini, "La 'gratiarum actio' dei consoli in Roma attraverso la testimonianza di Plinio il Giovane," *Historia* 10. 1961. pp. 356-374, says little. More useful are B. Radice, "Pliny and the *Panegyricus*," *Greece and Rome* 15. 1968. pp. 166-172; S. MacCormack, "Latin Prose Panegyrics" in T. A. Dorey (ed.), *Empire and Aftermath: Silver Latin II*, London, 1975, pp. 143-205, esp. sect. 3.

[4] *Paneg.* 4.1.

an incoming consul by *senatus consultum*. There is no further evidence for the decree, but the practice of delivering such a speech certainly dated back to Augustus' reign, because Ovid[5] writes of it as normal for the entry of S. Pompeius to the ordinary consulship on 1 January 14. Pliny[6] mentions Verginius Rufus rehearsing such a speech, and admits that in general members found them extremely boring, which is hardly surprising in view of their frequency. In his day there were at least six or eight consuls every year, and the number was to increase during the second century.[7] It is true that at least in the published version Pliny speaks not only on his own behalf, but also for his colleague, Cornutus Tertullus. If other pairs of consuls were willing and able to offer thanks jointly in this way, the tedium of the ritual would certainly have been reduced; but we have no further information on whether this was done. Our only hope must be that the length of Pliny's speech was atypical. With the speed of delivery and the extent to which the original was later expanded both uncertain, no figure can be set: but it does seem to be acknowledged that the text in its present form would demand at the very least three hours to deliver, and more probably well over that.[8] Of course Pliny is likely to have been speaking at the first meeting of the summer recess, for which the amount of pressing business was conceivably reduced. And the pleasing opportunity to discourse at unusual length perhaps partially compensated for the disappointment that his entire two-month term of office was to fall within the recess, when so many members would be away throughout.[9] In the mid second century Fronto[10] tells us something of how he tackled the composition of his own speech, which evidently included praise, indeed overpraise, of the young M. Aurelius,[11] and in general must have adopted the type of encomiastic tone to be found throughout Pliny's *Panegyricus*.

In addition to incoming consuls, it was evidently the custom for governors appointed by the emperor to express their thanks to him in the senate, until they were forbidden to do so by Claudius in 42.[12] However,

---

[5] *Ex Ponto* 4.4.35-39.

[6] *Ep*. 2.1.5; 3.18.6.

[7] In addition, consuls designate were obliged to deliver thanks in the senate (see sect. 9 below), and consuls also had to do so by edict (*Ad M. Caes*. 2.1.1 = p. 24 H).

[8] See Sherwin-White, *Pliny*, p. 251.

[9] See Sherwin-White, *Pliny*, p. 78 with R. Syme, *Roman Papers* I. p. 256; and note Pliny's own apology (*Ep*. 9.37) to the friend who took up the consulship in September 107.

[10] *Ad M. Caes*. 2.1.1 = pp. 24-25 H; for discussion, see E. J. Champlin, *Fronto and Antonine Rome*, pp. 83-86.

[11] *Ad M. Caes*. 2.3.3 = p. 27 H; *Ant. Imp*. 4.2.3-4 = p. 110 H.

[12] Dio 60.11.6-7. Yet those who had been *un*successful in gaining a magistracy or post, or had excused themselves, might still express thanks to the emperor privately. Note Tac. *Agr*. 42; *Hist*. 2.71; cf. Seneca, *De Ira* 2.33.2.

Nero still addressed thanks to Claudius there on his introduction to public life,[13] and speeches of thanks by L. Ceionius Commodus and Antoninus Pius on their adoption by Hadrian were likewise allowed.[14] M. Aurelius expressed thanks for the deification of L. Verus.[15]

Elsewhere we hear of a variety of benefits for which thanks were expressed, though the stage in the proceedings at which such speeches came is not always clear. Tiberius was thanked by leading members for his relief efforts after a fire in Rome in 27, for example, and Claudius for adopting Nero.[16] On 1 January 70, when there would be none of the customary speeches from the incoming consuls (they were Vespasian and Titus, and both were absent anyway), the meeting opened instead with a general vote of gratitude to legates, armies, and client kings.[17] We may guess that it was common for expressions of the same type to be made by previously condemned senators to whom rights were later restored,[18] and by those to whom the emperor granted financial support.[19] The whole custom became ridiculous late in Tiberius' reign when the emperor could be thanked for not having had Agrippina strangled,[20] and even more so in Gaius' reign, when the future emperor Vespasian thanked Gaius in the senate for an invitation to dinner, and others expressed gratitude that the emperor had kissed them.[21] Possibly it was in the senate ("in conspectu principum") that Pompeius Pennus thanked Gaius for sparing his life, and was forced to kiss the emperor's left foot.[22]

The speeches of thanks by Germanicus' son Nero and by the future emperor Nero[23] were presumably delivered when delegations from the cities concerned were received by the senate. Such was the occasion too, no doubt, of Fronto's "gratiarum actio in senatu pro Carthaginiensibus."[24] We hear that he likewise praised Antoninus on the completion of a British war.[25] It is easy to imagine how a formal speech of thanks by an acknowl-

---

[13] Suet. *Nero* 7.

[14] See HA, *Hadr.* 23.15; *Aelius* 4.7; *Antonin.* 4.6.

[15] HA, *Marcus* 20.2.

[16] Tac. *Ann.* 4.64; 12.26.

[17] Tac. *Hist.* 4.39.

[18] Cf. Tac. *Ann.* 3.24; Suet. *Otho* 2. Cicero had made a speech of thanks in the senate on his recall from exile in 57 B.C. (*Ad Att.* 4.1.5 = SB 73).

[19] Cf. Tac. *Ann.* 2.38, where out of fear or pride M. Hortalus himself said nothing, but others tactfully covered for him.

[20] Tac. *Ann.* 6.25; Suet. *Tib.* 53.

[21] Suet. *Vesp.* 2; Dio 59.27.1.

[22] Seneca, *De Benef.* 2.12.1-2.

[23] Tac. *Ann.* 4.15; 12.58.

[24] Pages 241-242 H with B. Bischoff, "Der Fronto-Palimpsest der Mauriner," *Sitzungsberichte der Bayerischen Akademie der Wissenschaften*, phil.-hist. Klasse, Heft 2, Munich, 1958, pp. 27-28.

[25] *Pan. Lat.* 8(5).14.2; for discussion, Champlin, op. cit. p. 85.

edged master might well have attracted members' attention. Yet behind Antoninus' praise of Fronto after one such oration there is perhaps a hint of the boredom generally felt on these occasions, when he compliments him on finding "in such a hackneyed and threadbare subject . . . anything to say that is new and worthy of your abilities."[26]

6. Communications

In the late Republic it had been common enough for communications to be addressed to the senate, and when there were such, they were normally heard first.[1] This practice continued throughout our period, when above all there were letters from the Princeps to be heard—increasingly so as the emperor came to stay away from sessions or to be out of Rome in any case.[2] Such letters did not of course always require action. They might simply relay information or justify measures already taken[3]—as when Caracalla at Antioch in 215 ". . . slaughtered so many persons that he did not even venture to say anything about their number, but wrote to the senate that it was of no interest how many of them or who had died, since all had deserved to suffer this fate."[4] Frequently the emperor kept the senate informed by letter of the progress of campaigns.[5] Where imperial letters did require action (as was very common),[6] the necessary steps could be taken later in the session.

Letters might be read, too, from other members of the imperial family,[7]

---

[26] *Ant. Imp.* 2.1 = p. 156 H. It has often been assumed that Fronto's speech on 13 August 143 is referred to here, but, as Champlin says (*JRS* 64. 1974. p. 149), such confidence is unwarranted. At the same time, he is wrong to rule out the identification altogether, despite the emperor's failure to address Fronto as consul. It should be remembered that the latter gave thanks for his consulship only just over a fortnight before its end. Antoninus was perhaps absent from the meeting (possibly at Baiae: Champlin, pp. 140-141), so that Fronto could well have laid down his office before the emperor had received the relevant *acta senatus*, appreciated the speech, and composed his congratulations.

[1] See A. O'Brien Moore, *PW* Suppl. 6. col. 708.

[2] For the standard opening of an imperial letter to the senate, note Dio 69.14.3; cf. 72.15.5; 77.18.2.

[3] See, for example, Seneca, *De Brev. Vit.* 4.3; Tac. *Ann.* 6.29; Dio 69.1; 78.8; 79.4; Herodian 5.6.2; HA, *Sev.* 11.4.

[4] Dio 77.22.3.

[5] For example, Dio 54.9.1 (Augustus); Tac. *Ann.* 3.47 (Tiberius); Suet. *Calig.* 44 (Gaius); *Fast. Ost.* A.D. 116; Dio 68.29.1-2 (Trajan); 69.14.3 (Hadrian); Fronto, *Ver. Imp.* 2.1 = pp. 114ff. H (L. Verus); HA, *Marcus* 14.6 (M. Aurelius and L. Verus); Dio 71.10.5, 17.1, 27.1 (M. Aurelius); HA, *Sev.* 9.1 and 3 (Severus); Dio 77.18.2; HA, *Caracalla* 6.5 (Caracalla).

[6] For example, Tac. *Ann.* 3.47; 4.70; 5.3 and 4; 6.3, 9, 15; 14.10 and 59; *Hist.* 4.3; Dio 58.10; cf. Suet. *Tib.* 65; Dio 78.27.

[7] For example, Tac. *Ann.* 3.59; Dio 55.10a.9.

or from commanders,[8] or from foreign notables.[9] We might also expect to hear of letters from governors of senatorial provinces, yet mention of these is curiously lacking.[10] Also, it was at this early stage of a meeting that documents such as emperors' wills,[11] or the account kept of Drusus' behavior in captivity,[12] are most likely to have been read, as well as certain speeches of Augustus, Tiberius, and Nero, for so long as this custom continued.[13]

7. Permission to Speak First

It had always been possible for any member to raise a matter outside those referred to the House by the president: he would mention it when called upon for his *sententia* in order, and would ask for a suitable *relatio* to be made. In 58 Thrasea's critics cite this procedure as normal.[1] The right was a valuable one, because it represented the only secure method by which members (other than consuls, praetors, and tribunes in office) could draw attention to anything not raised by the president.[2] It was not suitable, however, in an instance where a member urgently sought action, because once other business was in progress, the president might be unable to bring forward a fresh item, even if he were willing. To avoid this awkwardness, therefore, a different practice was employed whereby as soon as a session opened, a member asked the president's leave to speak; if so permitted, he might gain the sympathy of the House and prompt the president to bring forward the fresh item for discussion and decision at the same meeting.[3] Of the two clearest instances of the practice in our period the first occurs in 49, when the ex-censor L. Vitellius sought to gain the senate's support for overcoming Claudius' hesitation in marrying Agrippina, a match technically illegal because she was his niece.[4] Vitellius' request was then acted

[8] For example, Tac. *Hist.* 2.55 (from Valens); 4.4 (from Mucianus). As Syme suggests, part of the reason that Tacitus treats the proconsuls' campaign against Tacfarinas so fully may be that he found detailed reports in *acta senatus*—the kind of record which an imperial legate was much less likely to send to the corporate body (P. R. Coleman-Norton [ed.], *Studies in Roman Economic and Social History in Honor of A. C. Johnson*, Princeton, 1951, p. 120 = *Roman Papers* I. p. 223); cf. Dio 54.11.6 and 24.7.

[9] For example, Tac. *Ann.* 2.88 (from Adgandestrius).

[10] But note Suet. *Tib.* 32, and see further chap. 13 below.

[11] Augustus: Tac. *Ann.* 1.8 and 11; Suet. *Aug.* 101; *Tib.* 23 (according to this passage Tiberius had already tried to make a speech *before* the will was read); Dio 56.33. Tiberius: Dio 59.1.2-3.

[12] Tac. *Ann.* 6.24; Dio 58.25.4.

[13] Dio 60.10.2; 61.3.1.

[1] Tac. *Ann.* 13.49.

[2] See further below, sect. 16.

[3] For Republican examples, cf. Mommsen, *St. R.* III. 2. pp. 948-949.

[4] Tac. *Ann.* 12.5-6.

upon immediately. The second dates to 97, when Pliny, as *praetorius*, sought permission to bring a charge against an unnamed member. In his account he first speaks of the practice as a senator's right, though in a remark made soon afterwards he implies it to be a privilege, albeit one which the presiding consul concerned had never denied to anyone else who sought it.[5] Strictly, it would indeed seem more accurate to regard the practice as a privilege exercised at the president's discretion rather than as a right. When he had heard enough, the consul withdrew the privilege by instructing Pliny to stop speaking; and in the earlier instance Vitellius is perhaps not just being polite when Tacitus[6] portrays him as *asking permission* to speak first because the matter was of the highest national importance.

In 97, once the consul had stopped Pliny speaking, the meeting proceeded, no doubt as planned, with other business. Pliny does not clarify the point well, but later the consul must actually have returned to his charge and put it forward for discussion, because we next hear of members giving their *sententiae* on it.[7] Finally, after Pliny had spoken again in his due place, a vote was taken, presumably on his *sententia*, however it was framed exactly; and presumably the vote was passed.

This view of procedure at the session is essentially the one formed by Mommsen[8] and must be preferred to that of Sherwin-White.[9] The latter argues that the members who pronounce an opinion on Pliny's charge are all being called to give their *sententiae* on another matter, but are consistently speaking ''off the question.'' It would indeed have been possible for them to exercise this right. But only if a *relatio* had been made on the matter by the president could a vote on it later be taken: a vote on any matter not formally placed before the House was impossible.[10] The fact that in this case a *senatus consultum* on the matter was passed must show that a *relatio* had duly been made by the president.

Other instances have been suggested as examples of the practice where members asked to speak first out of turn. First, Tacitus[11] describes an occasion in 47 when the consul designate C. Silius, applauded by other members, attacked unscrupulous advocates like P. Suillius Rufus by demanding enforcement of the ancient *Lex Cincia*, which forbade acceptance of money or gifts for legal services. Evidently this matter was not one

---

[5] *Ep.* 9.13.7 and 9; cf. 2.11.9 discussed below.

[6] *Ann.* 12.5, ''summamque rem publicam agi obtestans veniam dicendi ante alios exposcit.''

[7] *Ep.* 9.13.13ff.

[8] *St. R.* III. 2. p. 950 n. 1.

[9] *Pliny*, p. 495.

[10] See further below, sect. 16.

[11] *Ann.* 11.5-6; cf. 13.42.

already referred to the House by the consul, because Tacitus goes on to explain: "Others expressed agreement with what the consul designate said, and a resolution was prepared inculpating offenders under the extortion law."[12] We may reasonably assume that it was the consul who proceeded to take some action here, though in precisely what form is not certain. Possibly he was intending to respond to the strong feeling already expressed by formally putting forward the matter for discussion. But in that case the alarm of those members who felt inculpated would still seem puzzling, since they would gain due opportunity to make their pleas and their defenses when called upon for *sententiae* in the normal course of discussion. Instead the key to a more accurate explanation may lie in the strength of the feeling expressed by Silius' supporters. In the face of this, the president perhaps gauged the atmosphere to be so overwhelmingly in favor of Silius' proposal that he decided to dispense with further discussion on the matter, and was preparing to take a vote at once—in other words, in effect, by *discessio*— on a resolution formulated by himself.[13] Suillius and the other members who felt inculpated were then extremely alarmed, because they would never have the chance to put forward their views, and thus they appealed for Claudius' intervention.

Second, in late 99, when charges of *saevitia* against the former proconsul of Africa, Marius Priscus, were to be investigated, and one key witness appeared, but not Priscus himself, the consular Tuccius Cerealis clearly gained permission to speak before the proceedings opened, and asked that Priscus be informed.[14] As a result, the hearing was adjourned.

It can be argued that a third example of members asking to speak first out of turn is to be seen on the occasion in 56 when, according to Tacitus,[15] the offenses of freedmen were discussed, and a demand was made by a number of senators that patrons be granted the right to re-enslave the undeserving. Tacitus' account of this occasion only makes sense if the matter is one raised first by special permission, rather than put regularly to the House in a *relatio*, because he goes on to explain how even when faced by members' pressing demands, the consuls still did not dare to begin a formal *relatio* on the matter without first consulting the emperor.

Sherwin-White[16] suggests that a further example of members asking to speak first out of turn is to be seen in Pliny's account[17] of the dispute

---

[12] *Ann.* 11.6, "Talia dicente consule designato, consentientibus aliis, parabatur sententia qua lege repetundarum tenerentur."

[13] For *sententia* as "resolution" or "decision," as opposed to "opinion," cf. Tac. *Ann.* 12.59; 13.44; and chap. 9 sect. 3 note 1 below. On *discessio* see further sect. 25 below.

[14] In Pliny's words, "iure senatorio postulavit, ut Priscus certior fieret" (*Ep.* 2.11.9).

[15] *Ann.* 13.26.

[16] *Pliny*, p. 166.

[17] *Ep.* 5.4.2.

between a senator and a delegation from Vicetia heard by the House in 105. For the hearing proper the Vicetians appeared without their counsel and claimed that they had been cheated. The praetor Nepos exercised the magistrate's right to intervene[18] and demanded that the counsel who had agreed to act be required to attend: the case was then adjourned. Whether or not this incident should rightly be categorized as an example of the practice under consideration may be seen as a quibble, though it is perhaps more naturally taken as an unavoidable part of the proceedings, given the unfortunate circumstances in which the Vicetians unexpectedly found themselves at the opening of the hearing proper.

8. *Relatio*

Once any communications had been heard, and members' requests to speak first out of turn had been met, the president began the *relatio*, in other words the items formally constituting the main part of the meeting, during which he raised one or more matters and might go on to seek members' individual opinions. Strictly, it remained his exclusive right to choose which matters to put forward at the session he had himself summoned, and to place them in order—subject to two restrictions. First, in accordance with traditional practice, sacred matters should take precedence over human, as Varro[1] said in his handbook of 70 B.C. There is no reason to doubt that this precedence was usually observed,[2] though inexplicably, at a meeting in December 69, the restoration of the Capitol does seem to have been considered after secular business.[3] The second restriction was a new development of our period—namely, that from an early date the emperor, whether present or absent, gained the right to put forward business at any stage of a session. Normally any matters raised by the emperor would be taken first. His authority and involvement were naturally such that presidential prerogative came to be seriously curtailed.[4]

As we have noted already,[5] it would appear that the majority of members would rarely be given much advance notice by a president of the matters to be considered. However, if it is right to assume that those who attended were expected to stay for the full course of the session from the very beginning,[6] then this absence of an agenda or order paper would be less

---

[18] See sect. 19 below.

[1] Gell. 14.7.9.

[2] Note how at the meeting after Augustus' death, absolution of Tiberius for having touched the corpse is the first item, according to Dio 56.31.3.

[3] Tac. *Hist.* 4.4.

[4] On the emperor's position see above, chap. 5 sect. 1.

[5] See chap. 6 sect. 1.

[6] See below, sect. 24.

serious than in a modern parliament. To a significant degree, too, the course of any session was unpredictable. Not only did it depend upon members' reaction to successive items; plans made by the president might also be upset by special requests raised on the spot.

Magistrates other than the president who had the right to make a *relatio* might wish to do so, although they were required to wait until presidential business was completed. In our period, when almost all sessions were summoned by consuls, only a tribune had the right to raise an item on the same occasion. In practice it would of course have been extremely rare for a tribune to act thus, but Tacitus[7] does record what may have been an instance in 32. Although praetors, unlike tribunes, did not have the right to make a *relatio* at a meeting called by a consul, for a time they were granted this prerogative as a privilege by Augustus.[8] Their agitation for the honor perhaps indicates their vanity more than any urgent desire or serious need to transact business with the House. All the same, the financial problems which the praetor Gracchus raised in 33 were pressing ones.[9]

In theory a tribune might veto the *relatio* of a magistrate: not surprisingly, this right seems rarely to have been exercised in our period. But Mamercus Scaurus does mention the possibility of Tiberius using it in 14, while Vulcacius Tertullinus vetoed a *relatio* about the management of the *aerarium Saturni* in 69.[10]

In his handbook of 70 B.C. Varro said that a *relatio* should be made "either in general terms, concerning the state, or in specific terms, on particular matters."[11] In the Republic a general *relatio* "de republica" was commonly made in times of crisis,[12] but there is no explicit evidence that the practice continued under the Principate.[13] Indeed the remark was hurled at Augustus: "To speak *de republica* ought to be the right of senators."[14] We cannot be sure whether a general *relatio* is meant here, or just a vague reference to matters of state. But no doubt both Augustus and most of his successors would have been unhappy to see the House offered opportunities to discourse upon the state of the nation too often, even if the more prudent senators were to prove fairly guarded in their remarks on such occasions. In the circumstances it would be understandable enough if a general *relatio* was now made seldom.

---

[7] *Ann.* 6.12. Equally, this meeting could have been one which the tribune himself summoned, rather than the consul: see chap. 6 sect. 1 note 18.

[8] Dio 55.3.6, under 9 B.C.

[9] Tac. *Ann.* 6.16.

[10] Tac. *Ann.* 1.13; *Hist.* 4.9.

[11] Gell. 14.7.9, "referri oportere aut infinite de republica aut de singulis rebus finite."

[12] Cf. Mommsen, *St. R.* III. 2. p. 956 n. 3.

[13] Ovid's portrayal of a contemporary consul "publica quaerentem quid petat utilitas" (*Ex Ponto* 4.9.48) could refer to either type of *relatio*.

[14] Suet. *Aug.* 54.

It is impossible to determine whether Syme[15] is right in claiming that at the meeting on 17 September 14 (following Augustus' death) the *relatio* laid before the House was a general one "de republica," or whether the consuls were more specific. As Goodyear says,[16] Tacitus' silence here is one of his most lamentable omissions. His account of late 69 may provide a more secure example, however. Members' reaction to Mucianus' despatch of letters to the senate was evidently that "he could have given the same report verbally in a few days' time when called upon to deliver his *sententia* in order."[17] If Mucianus had given his report thus, would he have spoken very much "off the question," or might a general *relatio* "de republica" have been framed to afford him a suitable opportunity?

Each *relatio* was perhaps preceded by a standard invocation: "Quod bonum faustum felix fortunatumque sit populo Romano Quiritium."[18] The emperor Gaius is alleged to have altered it thus: "Quod bonum felixque sit C. Caesari sororibusque eius."[19] The *relatio* then opened with the words, "Refero / referimus ad vos, patres conscripti . . . ," and closed with the words, ". . . de ea re quid fieri placeat."

In the late Republic it would seem that a number of minor matters might be raised in a single *relatio*, though major issues had to receive separate consideration.[20] While the point cannot be checked, practice during the Principate was no doubt similar. There was also the new, related development that matters raised by the emperor in particular evidently came to be dealt with in a single *relatio*. But there is no reason to think that this development occurred before the second century.[21]

9. Explanation ("Verba Facere")

In the *relatio* proper the president traditionally confined himself to putting forward an issue on which he sought guidance—as the clause "quid fieri placeat" implies. Yet it was normal for the *relatio* to be accompanied by an explanation or discussion, and here some solution or course of action might be proposed. In Latin this part of the proceedings can be expressed

[15] R. Syme, "Historiographia Antiqua," *Symb. Fac. Litt. Philos. Leuven* Ser. A Vol. 6 (1977) p. 236.

[16] *The Annals of Tacitus* 1, p. 174. B. Levick's suggestion (*Tiberius the Politician*, London, 1976, pp. 78-79) that the wording of the *relatio* is reflected in Velleius' clause "ut stationi paternae succederet" (2.124.2) has been trenchantly criticized by P. A. Brunt, *JRS* 67. 1977. p. 97 n. 15.

[17] *Hist.* 4.4, "potuisse eadem paucos post dies loco sententiae dici."

[18] Cf. Suet. *Aug.* 58; A. O'Brien Moore, *PW* Suppl. 6 col. 711 and references there.

[19] Suet. *Calig.* 15; cf. *Arval Acta*, para. 9b lines 1-2.

[20] Cf. Mommsen, *St. R.* III. 2. p. 955 n. 3.

[21] See further chap. 8.

verbally ("verba facere"), but apparently not by any noun. Where appropriate, the president would deliver the explanation himself—as C. Silanus did, for example, in connection with two items concerning the Secular Games of 17 B.C.,[1] or as Ovid[2] could imagine Pomponius Graecinus doing in A.D. 16. Augustus actually furnishes us with a unique quotation of such a consular explanatory speech in his fifth Cyrene edict of 4 B.C.[3]

If the matter were religious, the explanation would be supplied by a priest of the appropriate college, as happened in 203, when the *magister* of the *Quindecimviri Sacris Faciundis* asked the senate to sponsor the Secular Games.[4] On other occasions magistrates or officials, as appropriate, might be invited to make the explanation. Five such instances can be identified with more or less certainty. Thus in 15 the consuls presumably allowed the Tiber commissioners, Arruntius and Ateius, to explain the possible diversion of streams feeding the river, and to introduce the different delegations.[5] In 22 Bibulus and other aediles were certainly permitted to raise the issue of whether steps might be taken to restrain excessive expenditure on food and banquets,[6] while during the following year it was only after "numerous and generally unsuccessful complaints" from the praetors that Tiberius eventually consulted the House about the bad behavior of *histriones*.[7] In late 69 we find the *praetores aerarii* explaining the state's financial difficulties.[8] Finally, in 105 it was the emperor who gave leave for a quaestor to bring up the question of what was to be done with the salary of his *scriba*, the man having died the day before payment was due.[9]

A private member, too, would commonly be allowed to make an explanation by prior arrangement. For such cases commentators have some-

---

[1] G. B. Pighi, *De Ludis Saecularibus*, p. 111 line 52; p. 112 line 59.

[2] *Ex Ponto* 4.9.47.

[3] *FIRA*[2] I no. 68 V lines 85-90; cf. J. Reynolds, *Aphrodisias and Rome*, no. 8 lines 26ff. with discussion, pp. 74-75.

[4] Cf. Mommsen, *St. R.* III. 2. p. 959; G. B. Pighi, *De Ludis Saecularibus*, pp. 140-142 lines 7-25. In other circumstances, too, it is evident that priests played a prominent part, as we should expect, when matters of religion arose. Note their role alongside the consuls at the meeting when prayers were said for Claudius on his deathbed (Tac. *Ann.* 12.68). In a different context, it is the very experienced augur, Cn. Cornelius Lentulus (*PIR*[2] C 1379), who is the foremost opponent of the request by the Flamen Dialis to be considered for the governorship of Asia in 22 (Tac. *Ann.* 3.58-59).

[5] Tac. *Ann.* 1.79.

[6] Tac. *Ann.* 3.52-53. As Furneaux appreciates (Vol. I. p. 453), the aediles would not be able to make an actual *relatio*, since they lacked the *ius relationis*. However, Nipperdey's explanation (ad loc. p. 280), followed by him, that the matter was therefore raised "off the question" in the first instance, will not do, because magistrates were not normally called upon to speak in the *interrogatio*.

[7] Tac. *Ann.* 4.14.

[8] Tac. *Hist.* 4.9.

[9] Plin. *Ep.* 4.12.

times suggested that the members spoke "off the question."[10] But for no instance cited below is that method specified, and in any event it might be a clumsy expedient. Instead, members (like magistrates) might always approach the president before a meeting, and seek his leave to bring forward an item. Only if the latter refused permission would the member have to resort to speaking "off the question." In either case, as he made his points to the House, the president would be able to judge the general reaction and decide whether to pursue the matter with an *interrogatio*. Unlike asking to speak first before the *relatio*, or speaking "off the question" during the *interrogatio*, this third method alone required a member to run the risk of explaining his business to the president beforehand, and thus possibly meeting an adverse reaction before the matter could ever reach the House at all. We need hardly be surprised, therefore, that this was *not* the method chosen by Pliny, for example, for his controversial attack on Publicius Certus. Rather he confided his purpose to nobody beforehand, not even to Corellius Rufus.[11]

Whether or not the impression be accurate, it would seem at least that the items most commonly raised with prior presidential permission were complaints and pleas, some of them more private than public in nature. In the debate about Pliny's attack on Certus one member even speaks of a "ius querendi" (by women of the senatorial class),[12] but perhaps that phrase should not be interpreted too literally. Despite the preponderance of complaints, a wide variety of private members' items can be cited. We hear of Asinius Pollio complaining "bitterly and angrily"[13] in the senate during Augustus' reign of how his grandson had broken a leg in the "Troy game." In 15 a member sought the senate's aid after his house had been damaged by the construction of a road and an aqueduct. At the same time a *praetorius* begged leave of the House to resign on the grounds of poverty. Tiberius made him a grant of money, but when others began to apply, he required them to put their cases before a meeting.[14] It might seem a private affair for the *praetorius* Domitius Corbulo to complain in 21 that a noble youth had refused to give up his seat to him at a gladiatorial show,[15] and likewise for a member in 70 to complain of ill-treatment in Sena.[16] Yet of course both these incidents reflected upon the dignity of the House as a

[10] See, for example, Furneaux (Vol. II. p. 29) and Koestermann (Vol. III. p. 70) on the proposal of P. Dolabella mentioned below.

[11] *Ep.* 9.13.16.

[12] Plin. *Ep.* 9.13.15; cf. Tac. *Ann.* 2.71, "erit vobis locus querendi apud senatum, invocandi leges" (Germanicus' dying speech to his friends).

[13] Suet. *Aug.* 43, "graviter invidioseque." *PIR*² A 1241.

[14] Tac. *Ann.* 1.75.

[15] Tac. *Ann.* 3.31; for the situation, cf. Suet. *Aug.* 44.

[16] Tac. *Hist.* 4.45.

body, especially in the latter case where insults had been hurled at the entire senate. Corbulo's further complaints about unsatisfactory upkeep of Italian roads were perhaps made more for the public good—though the same did not apply to the subsequent prosecutions, adds Tacitus.[17] In this instance, and in that of 70, the complaints did lead to action being taken.

In 21 C. Cestius raised the matter of abuse of effigies of the emperor to escape punishment for bad behavior: this was an issue on which a number of members spoke, and on which Drusus, as presiding consul, took action.[18] Eligibility to wear gold rings of the equestrian order was at last established in 23 after C. Sulpicius Galba, having enacted penalties for keeping eating-houses as consul the previous year, went on to complain in the senate that "peddling tradesmen, when charged with that offense, commonly protected themselves by means of their rings."[19] In 22 M. Aemilius Lepidus had asked the senate's permission to strengthen and beautify the Basilica Pauli, the family monument of the Aemilii, just across the Argiletum from the Curia.[20] At some date before 25 Caecina Severus complained about improper female dress,[21] though it was evidently not his proposal, but that of Cn. Cornelius Lentulus[22] put forward then or on another occasion, which the House chose to pass. Later, in summer 31, Cossus Cornelius Lentulus had a motion passed forbidding accusation of an imperial legate.[23] Finally, in 47 P. Dolabella successfully proposed that quaestors should mount an annual gladiatorial display,[24] while in Nero's reign we hear of Otho seeking the restoration of a member condemned for extortion.[25]

An item of a special type, which members neither wholly private nor yet magistrates must regularly have sought to bring forward, was the proposal "in honorem principis" expected of *consules designati*, according to Pliny and Fronto.[26] Nothing further is known of the formal side of this procedure, but it would be a fair guess that an opportunity to make such proposals was granted by the president at a meeting soon after the elections (that is, early each year from the Flavian period at least).

When ambassadors or others were introduced by the president, he would naturally allow them, or their *patronus*, to put their case.

---

[17] *Ann.* 3.31; Dio 59.15.3.

[18] Tac. *Ann.* 3.36.

[19] Plin. *NH* 33.32; nos. 27-28 in list, chap. 15 sect. 5.

[20] Tac. *Ann.* 3.72.

[21] Tertullian, *De Pallio* 4.9. *PIR²* C 106. For another antifeminist complaint by Caecina, see sect. 11 below.

[22] Cos. 14 B.C., augur; he died in 25 (*PIR²* C 1379).

[23] *Dig.* 48.2.12 pr.; no. 31 in list, chap. 15 sect. 5.

[24] Tac. *Ann.* 11.22; cf. 13.5 and Suet. *Claud.* 24; *PIR²* C 1349.

[25] Suet. *Otho* 2.

[26] Plin. *Ep.* 6.27; Fronto, *Ant. Imp.* 4.2.3 = p. 110 H.

10. *Interrogatio*

Once a *relatio* had been made and an explanation delivered, the mood of the House might seem overwhelmingly in favor of the solution or course of action advocated. In such a case the president would commonly take a vote without more ado.[1] Alternatively, once the explanation had been made, members' reaction or his own inclination might lead the president to conclude that there was no value in pursuing the matter further, and it would thus be dropped. Members who disputed this view might shout "consule":[2] in other words, they asked for individual opinions to be sought in turn. There is no explicit example of this practice from our period, but we may guess that Thrasea Paetus successfully resorted to it in 58 over the minor question of authorizing Syracuse to exceed the numbers permitted at gladiatorial displays.[3] This was exactly the type of measure which in normal circumstances would have been passed without comment. When an issue was contentious, the president would usually wish to consult the House anyway, in accordance with recognized practice throughout Roman public and private life.[4] This part of the proceedings was termed the *interrogatio*.

11. The Order in Which Members Were Called

Gellius relates what Varro said in 70 B.C. about the order in which members should be called: ". . . the senators ought to be asked their opinions in order, beginning with those of consular rank. And in that rank in former times the one to be called upon first was always the one who had been enrolled in the senate as its *princeps*; but at the time when he was writing he said that a new custom had become current, through partiality and a desire to curry favor, of asking first for the opinion of the one whom the president wished to call upon, provided however that he was of consular rank."[1] Elsewhere Gellius (writing in the late second century) does imply that the *Lex Julia* of 9 B.C. itself came to stipulate the order in which members should be called, when he explains: "before the passage of the law which is now observed in the proceedings of the senate, the order in

---

[1] See below, sect. 25.

[2] Festus p. 174 L; cf. Cic. *Ad Att.* 5.4.2 = SB 97.

[3] Tac. *Ann.* 13.49. From his account, the alternative possibilities—that the president did consult the House anyway, or that Thrasea spoke "off the question" on another matter—seem less likely.

[4] In general, see J. Crook, *Consilium Principis*, chap. 1. Note also Plin. *Ep.* 1.22.8 with Sherwin-White ad loc.; and the striking caricature at Juvenal, *Sat.* 6. 497-501.

[1] 14.7.9.

calling for opinions varied.''[2] But with the *Lex Julia* now lost we are thrown back upon other evidence in order to form an impression of normal practice.

Such general statements as survive about the practice of presidents are mostly of slight help for this purpose. In a passage included in his account of 18 B.C. (thus before the *Lex Julia*) Dio[3] explains how Augustus, copied by the consuls, continued a practice akin to that of the late Republic, whereby all consulars were called upon at random, and other members in order of seniority. So Lepidus was always shamed by being called last of the consulars. This humiliation was later likewise inflicted upon Claudius by the emperor Gaius, though he was in fact near the bottom of the list anyway, having only held office in 37.[4] It seems that Tiberius as consul in 13 B.C. exercised the same kind of prerogative when rather curiously he chose to call upon L. Cornelius Balbus first, in recognition of his completion of a theater.[5] Suetonius[6] goes further than Dio with his claim that in order to gain more alert discussion of major issues Augustus as president would abandon ''custom and order'' altogether, in favor of simply calling upon members as he pleased. Even after the passage of the *Lex Julia*, there was clearly still some scope for presidents to vary the order in which they called members. Thus we are told how at the trial of Aemilia Lepida in 20, Tiberius sought to save Drusus embarrassment by not calling upon him first as consul designate, as would have been normal.[7] At the beginning of Gaius' reign it would seem that all consuls were in the habit of calling M. Junius Silanus[8] first, no doubt because of his preeminence. He cannot have been the senior consular, however,[9] for we are told that Gaius, in an attack on his position, arranged that henceforth consulars, like other members, should be called upon in order of seniority.[10]

In general, certainly, it would seem to have been seniority which most presidents followed in our period. Strictly, the emperor outranked all other members, heading the *album senatorium*; but as he came to attend less and less except to preside, there was rarely any question of calling upon

---

[2] 4.10.1.

[3] 54.15.5-6.

[4] Suet. *Claud.* 9; cf. 6.

[5] Dio 54.25.2; *PIR²* C 1331. For a vague reference to an instance where a senator was called upon first, presumably out of order, ''post acceptam hereditatem'' (''after he had accepted a legacy,'' an odd reason), see Quintilian, *Inst. Or.* 6.3.97.

[6] *Aug.* 35.

[7] Tac. *Ann.* 3.22; cf. Dio 57.7.4 in general.

[8] *PIR²* I 832 (cos. 15).

[9] This must be self-evident from the action Gaius proceeded to take. L. Volusius Saturninus (cos. A.D. 3), for one, was certainly by far Silanus' senior, and long outlived him (see Extended Note G).

[10] Dio 59.8.6; on Silanus' position, cf. Philo, *Leg. ad Gaium* 75.

him.[11] By tradition magistrates were not called upon either, although they, like the emperor, could speak whenever they wished.[12] However, according to Tacitus,[13] Tiberius did call upon magistrates when he presided, evidently at the head of their grades. By contrast, we know that Trajan did not do this when he presided at the trial of Marius Priscus in 100.[14]

In normal circumstances, whenever designated magistrates were available (that is, members who had been elected to an office, but had not yet taken it up) they were probably taken to outrank all others in their grade, and were called at the head of it. Among consulars this was without doubt the case, so that, when he could, the president would call first one or more consuls designate. Thus Seneca[15] reflects standard procedure in his parody, by having two consuls designate deliver their opinions first. The strength of established custom in this respect is underlined by the incident in 14 when Tiberius refrained altogether from requesting for Drusus the *imperium proconsulare* which he sought for Germanicus, "because Drusus was consul designate and was present in person."[16]

It remains uncertain whether Townend[17] is correct in his claim that the consuls designate immediately in line to take up office were given precedence over others. The point is not proved by the passages of Tacitus which he cites, since none gives a sufficiently full account of who else spoke on these occasions, or in what order. So Townend may not be right to infer that the appearance of L. Calpurnius Piso as consul designate must date the session reported by Tacitus, *Annals* 13.28, to the last two months of 56. In his view, if the session were earlier, L. Duvius Avitus (suffect consul during these months) would have been called upon in this capacity; the same function would only fall to Piso after Avitus had taken office in November. Yet in Trajan's time it seems not to have been the case that *designati* immediately in line to hold office were called upon first as a matter of course, nor need it have been in Nero's day for all we know. Thus in January 100 we find Cornutus Tertullus apparently called upon first, even though a number of *designati* present were due to become consul before his own entry to office in September.[18] Just conceivably he was

---

[11] But note Dio 57.24.7; possibly also 60.12.3.

[12] See sect. 19 below.

[13] *Ann.* 3.17.

[14] Plin. *Ep.* 2.11.19-20.

[15] *Apocol.* 9.2 and 4.

[16] Tac. *Ann.* 1.14. Tiberius arguably had a double motive: first, such power was unsuitable for one who would shortly be consul (as Furneaux, ad loc., appreciated); second, since the president would feel obliged to adhere to established practice in seeking opinions, it would be embarrassing for Drusus to be called upon first (as Mommsen, *St. R.* II. 2. p. 1152. n. 1, understood).

[17] *AJP* 83. 1962. p. 126 n. 20.

[18] Plin. *Ep.* 2.11.19 and 12.2. Admittedly, the likelihood is that the emperor presided on

singled out in this way because of his age.[19] In the case discussed by Townend, if Piso had been elected considerably earlier in 56—and this is where our knowledge of Julio-Claudian practice fails us altogether[20]—then the session in question reported by Tacitus could have been earlier than November too.

The precedence of praetors designate in their grade is well enough attested for the late Republic, but not for the Principate. All the same, it is fair to assume that it continued. Support for the notion might come from Tiberius' reaction to the suggestion of Asinius Gallus that praetors be designated five years in advance—"the number of *magistrates* would be increased fivefold"[21]—reflecting the special position of *designati* midway between magistrates and *privati*. Whether aediles designate or tribunes designate had a corresponding precedence (as might seem likely) is unknown for both Republic and Principate. Quaestors designate of course did not sit in the senate.[22]

If it be accepted that from the Flavian period onwards elections for senatorial magistracies were carried out according to the timetable suggested above,[23] we may reckon that magistrates designate should then have been available at most sessions. Only for about two weeks at the beginning of January would there have been no praetors or aediles designate (those elected in the middle of the previous January having taken up office on 1 January, and the next elections having not yet taken place). In the case of tribunes the corresponding hiatus was a little longer, beginning on 10

---

the first of these occasions, and he might have varied the conventional order; but there is no sign that he was president on the second occasion. See further the discussion of Sherwin-White, *Pliny*, pp. 78 and 172. As he says, it is still possible that Pliny has twice distorted the actual order of speakers for stylistic reasons. In addition, we can now be certain that Q. Acutius Nerva's term of office preceded that of Cornutus Tertullus (R. Syme, *Roman Papers* I. p. 256). But it is more natural to reckon that Pliny did retain the actual order of speakers in these up-to-the-minute accounts.

[19] He must have been in his late fifties at least (H. Halfmann, *Die Senatoren*, no. 22)—unusually elderly for tenure of a first consulship. With one exception all the other *suffecti* of 100 were likewise only holding the office for the first time, so far as we know (R. Syme, *Roman Papers* I. p. 256). L. Julius Ursus, however, as cos. suff. III, is very likely to have been older than Cornutus, but he might not have wished to take an active part, or might even have already succeeded Julius Frontinus, *consul ordinarius*, by the time of either or both the sessions in question.

[20] See chap. 6 sect. 4.

[21] Tac. *Ann.* 2.36, "quinquiplicari prorsus magistratus" (my italics). Were any such scheme to have been implemented, the inevitable inflation in the number of *designati* might well have called for some modification of the customary order in which members were called. There must indeed have been a real problem of this type during the Triumviral period, though we lack insight into how it was tackled: see discussion by J. Reynolds, *Aphrodisias and Rome*, p. 70.

[22] Note Vell. 2.111.3; HA, *Verus* 3.5; cf. Mommsen, *St. R.* III. 2. p. 973 n. 2. See further Extended Note E.

[23] Chap. 6 sect. 4.

December. Yet naturally it was the hiatus in the case of the consulship which mattered most. Here there would again regularly be a gap during the first two weeks or so of January, as for other magistracies. Whether there would have been one earlier, too, depended entirely on the time at which the ordinary consuls were elected to take up office on the following 1 January, and so far as we can tell a date for this particular piece of business was never fixed. It is certainly possible that when the final pair of suffect consuls for a year took up office on, say, 1 October, ordinary consuls for the following year had not yet been elected, and that an earlier hiatus of the type we have been considering did therefore ensue for a time. Whenever a man was elected to open the year with the emperor, he might expect to face an unusually onerous duty as *designatus*, since in practice either from the day on which the last pair of *suffecti* entered office, or from the day of his own election (if it came later), he was likely to be put in the position of having to speak first in every *interrogatio* up to 31 December. He could hardly expect his imperial colleague to share the burden with him. When all this is said, however, it is only right to recall that many ordinary consuls were experienced men who had seen long service, holding the office for a second, or even third, time.

Mommsen,[24] followed by O'Brien Moore,[25] correctly noted that the precedence of consuls designate in the *interrogatio* eventually lapsed. But it is puzzling that both scholars dated the lapse to the time of Hadrian or Antoninus Pius. Mommsen gave no reason for this view, while O'Brien Moore suggested that it might be linked with an increase in the number of consulships at that time—the latter itself a doubtful presumption. To be sure, when detailed evidence about the conduct of meetings after Trajan's reign is so thin, it is difficult to affirm whether or not consuls designate did still take precedence. But there is nothing to suggest that well-established tradition was broken as early as the second century. We certainly continue to hear of a part played in meetings by consuls designate as such,[26] and it is interesting that Appian, in his treatment of the debate on the Catilinarian conspiracy, can write as follows: "Silanus, the consul elect, spoke first, as it is the Romans' custom for the man who is about to assume that office to deliver his opinion first, because, I think, he will have most to do with future business and thus will consider each matter

---

[24] *St. R.* III. 2. p. 976.

[25] *PW* Suppl. 6 col. 768.

[26] Cf. *FIRA²* I no. 48; Fronto, *Ant. Imp.* 4.2.3 = p. 110 H; HA, *Did. Jul.* 7.2. By contrast, the speaker in the *Aes Italicense* (*Hesperia* 24. 1955. p. 330) does confirm that he is making the *prima sententia* (line 21), but of course his identity and status remain unknown. This is also the case with Calpurnius Maximus, who spoke about the *Ludi Saeculares* in 203 (G. B. Pighi, *De Ludis Saecularibus*, p. 142 line 25; cf. Mommsen, *Ges. Schriften* VIII p. 625).

with greater care and good sense.''[27] It might be rash to place too much weight on the use of a present, rather than a past tense in this explanation supplied by a Greek about 160. But despite certain shortcomings, Appian did possess some historical sense; he also came to know Fronto, and as *eques* and procurator was generally well acquainted with contemporary Roman society.[28] On other grounds too, as we have seen, it is indeed credible that consuls designate were still being called first in M. Aurelius' reign.

So far as we are aware, a member's seniority within his grade was determined exclusively by the year in which he had held the magistracy concerned.[29] As will emerge, it was plainly on this basis that a consular's eligibility to draw lots for the governorships of Africa and Asia was determined. It can be shown with varying degrees of certainty that in the Republic any member might gain a higher place through patrician status (till Sulla's time),[30] tenure of major priesthood, distinguished military service, or a successful prosecution.[31] In our period it is true that the senators who successfully prosecuted Libo Drusus in 16 were awarded praetorships *extra ordinem*,[32] and it was still recognized that a junior member might seek to make himself a reputation by attacking a prominent figure.[33] In 28 four *praetorii* are even said to have brought a prosecution in order to please Sejanus and thus gain the consulship.[34] At that time such services might well have improved a man's prospects of advancement, as military distinction always would. But we still cannot point to any instance of a senator in the Principate being granted a higher place as a direct reward either for a successful prosecution, or for any of the other reasons mentioned above. Equally, while fathers might seek magistracies earlier than childless men,[35] there is no evidence for the size of a member's family also serving to improve his seniority within a grade.

As we have seen, members and non-members alike came to be adlected to a grade. Yet their placing within it remains uncertain. All we may say is that, if the report of the *Historia Augusta* about Pertinax's action in 193 can be believed, it had evidently not been customary just to leave all *adlecti* at the bottom of their grade: "Since Commodus had mixed up the ex-

---

[27] *Bell. Civ.* 2.5.
[28] See *Prooem.* 15; *PIR*[2] A 943; G. W. Bowersock, *Greek Sophists in the Roman Empire*, pp. 112-113; and further chap. 6 sect. 3 note 31 and sect. 2 above.
[29] Note, however, Pupienus' special pleading in Herodian 8.4.4.
[30] Mommsen, *St. R.* III. 2. pp. 967-968.
[31] Mommsen, *St. R.* III. 2. p. 971; L. R. Taylor and R. T. Scott, *TAPA* 100. 1969. pp. 553-556.
[32] Tac. *Ann.* 2.32.
[33] Tac. *Hist.* 1.2; 2.53; 4.42; cf. *Ann.* 12.42; Plin. *Ep.* 9.13.2.
[34] Tac. *Ann.* 4.68.
[35] See chap. 1 sect. 2.

praetors by countless adlections, Pertinax framed a senatorial decree and ordered that those who had not held praetorships, but had gained the rank by adlection, should be junior to those who had actually been praetors: but thereby he also stirred up abundant hatred against himself on the part of many.''[36] While no check is possible, it would thus be natural to reckon that before Pertinax's change, adlected members had entered at the bottom of the relevant grade alongside elected ones and had automatically risen with them, rather than being left permanently at the bottom.[37] As it is, if the *Historia Augusta* is to be taken literally, even Pertinax's change was to apply only to *praetorii*, not to any other grade. After his death there was no doubt a complete reversion to previous practice.

Since Tacitus devotes such attention to senatorial proceedings, we might expect to learn much from him of the order in which members were called. In fact, from his accounts of sessions it is impossible ever to be certain of the order because, understandably, in many cases he has abbreviated and molded fuller sources to suit his own purpose. Thus the order of speakers after the hearing of the case against Libo Drusus in 16[38] is perhaps better taken as deliberately designed to illustrate "a climax of shameful enormity,''[39] on which Tacitus lays stress, than as an exact record of the precise order in which members were called on this occasion. Any attempt to see it as the latter quickly runs into difficulty. Cotta Messalinus is mentioned first. It seems most natural to assume cautiously that he is M. Aurelius Cotta, consul in 20, and the suggestion has been advanced that he spoke here as *praetor designatus*, even though that does make the interval between his tenure of the two magistracies a short one. But in Tacitus' order he is followed by a senior consular, Cn. Cornelius Lentulus (cos. 14 B.C.), and only then by Pomponius Flaccus, *consul designatus* for 17.[40] There follow, according to Tacitus, one speaker whose name is lost beyond L.P. . . . (L. Piso, cos. 1 B.C.? or L. Piso, cos. 15 B.C.? or L. Plancus, cos. A.D. 13? or L. Voluseius Proculus, cos. suff. 17?), Gallus Asinius (cos. 8 B.C.), Papius Mutilus (cos. A.D. 9), and L. Apronius (cos. A.D. 8). It would be awkward to maintain that this order preserves faithfully that of the actual occasion: a *praetor designatus* would hardly be called

---

[36] *Pert*. 6.10-11. For further discussion see A. Chastagnol, *BHAC* 1975/6. pp. 121-122.

[37] Similar arrangements can be conjectured in the rare instances where senators were granted the *ornamenta* of a higher grade: see chap. 11 sect. 6. Once they actually gained election to this rank, it is a nice question whether they would retain the position in it which they had already attained, or whether they would then be required to revert to the bottom along with their fellow magistrates!

[38] *Ann*. 2.32.

[39] R. Syme, *JRS* 46. 1956. p. 19.

[40] Cf. *Ann*. 2.41.

upon first, to be followed by a *consul designatus* in third place.[41] As we shall see, a *praetor designatus* might never even have made a full speech in the senate before, except to recommend himself at election time.[42]

Later in 16, in his report of a debate about "nationwide extravagance," Tacitus[43] explains first the points made by the two foremost advocates for imposing restraint—the consular Q. Haterius[44] and the *praetorius* Octavius Fronto[45]—before noting the outburst of the consular L. Calpurnius Piso,[46] who spoke "off the question." In all probability Piso really preceded Fronto in the debate, but Tacitus' order is clearer for readers, and also allows him to move smoothly on to reporting another "display of outspoken indignation" by Piso, namely summoning Livia's friend Urgulania to court.

Likewise, in his account of a discussion in 21 about suitable governors for Africa and Asia, Tacitus[47] must again have altered the order of points to help the reader's understanding of a rambling debate. He mentions first the attack by Sextus Pompeius[48] on the suitability of Manius Lepidus as a candidate, and only then does he pass to the *sententia* made by Caecina Severus,[49] "off the question," and the comment it occasioned. However, since Caecina was a considerably more senior consular than Pompeius, it is likely that his *sententia* was actually made *before* the latter ever spoke. Caecina's main opponent, Valerius Messalinus[50] (cos. 3 B.C.), outranked him in turn, and therefore would have needed special permission to speak a second time out of order.[51] It must have been above all to achieve clarity that Tacitus shifted the actual order in which these members had spoken. In his account of the trial of C. Junius Silanus in 22 this will again be his purpose in leaving to the end, out of order, treatment of another proposal

[41] As Varro explained (Gell. 14.7.9, quoted above), the member whom a president chose to call first had to be of at least consular rank.

[42] On the whole debate, cf. R. Syme, "Some Pisones in Tacitus," *JRS* 46. 1956. pp. 17-21 = *Ten Studies in Tacitus*, pp. 50-57; Goodyear ad loc. With reference to both, however, it should be understood that the epigraphic basis for Syme's identification of the speaker Cotta Messalinus here as the praetor of 17 is by no means firm, and that even were it proved correct, his occupation of first place in Tacitus' account would still be remarkable, since he is plainly below the rank of consul. Normally even a *praetor designatus* should not have been called until after all the *consulares*.

[43] *Ann.* 2. 33-34.

[44] *PIR*² H 24, cos. 5 B.C.

[45] Otherwise known only as one of those present in 19 at the "writing" of the decree no. 22 in list, chap. 15 sect. 5: clearly a man of strong moral views!

[46] *PIR*² C 290, cos. 1 B.C.

[47] *Ann.* 3.32-34.

[48] R. Hanslik, *PW* 21 s.v. Pompeius no. 62, cols. 2265-2267, cos. A.D. 14.

[49] *PIR*² C 106, cos. 1 B.C.

[50] R. Hanslik, *PW* 7 A s.v. Valerius no. 265, col. 162.

[51] See below, sect. 19.

made "off the question." It was put forward by P. Cornelius Dolabella,[52] who in actual debate (though not in Tacitus) probably spoke later than Cn. Cornelius Lentulus.[53] In this instance, however, it must be admitted that a conjecture about the order of speeches when the emperor was presiding is hazardous, since he may well have varied the order more freely than a consul.

In the fullest account which Pliny[54] gives us of an *interrogatio*, he understandably enough lists speakers according to the view they took, rather than strictly in order of speaking. But it is reasonable to assume that there was fairly close adherence to seniority on this occasion in 97. He gives the following as favoring one view, in this order: Domitius Apollinaris, consul designate, Fabricius Veiento,[55] Fabius Postuminus (cos. suff. 96), Bittius Proculus (*praetorius*, later cos. 98), Ammius Flaccus (otherwise unknown; presumably *praetorius*). The opposing view was taken by Avidius Quietus (cos. suff. 93) and Cornutus Tertullus (*praetorius*, later cos. suff. 100). Later than all these in the order Pliny himself spoke as a *praetorius*.[56] Finally, in his account of the debate in 105 on treatment of the freedmen of the dead consul, Afranius Dexter, Pliny[57] altogether omits proposers' names other than his own. But here, too, he is more likely to be listing the three motions made—release (his own), exile, execution—in a logical sequence of increasing severity rather than in the actual order in which they were put forward. If the latter were the case, we would be left wondering what had been proposed by the consuls designate, and by all the consulars before Pliny, who was still comparatively junior in the rank. In this instance they can hardly have done other than choose one of the three sentences mentioned, or something close to them.[58] Really it looks as if they all took a harsher view than Pliny; at least one of the other two sentences had been put forward before he was called. Thus if he is fair in claiming that by the end of the debate more members favored release than either of the other two sentences,[59] then on this occasion he either drew notable support from those junior to himself, or at least succeeded in persuading a number of consulars to change their minds.

[52] Tac. *Ann.* 3.69; *PIR*² C 1348, cos. 10.

[53] *PIR*² C 1379, cos. 14 B.C.

[54] *Ep.* 9.13.13-15.

[55] Cos. suff. III in 82 or 83 perhaps: see discussion by P. Gallivan, *CQ* 31. 1981. pp. 209-210.

[56] *Ep.* 9.13.18.

[57] *Ep.* 8.14.12.

[58] This is the key problem not resolved by Sherwin-White (*Pliny*, p. 464), when he takes the opposite view.

[59] *Ep.* 8.14.24.

12. The Participation of Junior Members

By any reckoning it would be a time-consuming business to call upon all members individually in order, even if the meeting were only moderately well attended, and the opinions delivered were of the briefest. Inevitably there arises the question of whether the president really did call upon everybody, or whether he was permitted to curtail the *interrogatio* at his discretion. The scanty evidence for Republican practice would suggest that then no such discretion was normally open to him, and that he did genuinely call upon every member—until he reached the end of the list, or night fell.[1] Otherwise, at all periods, curtailment was customary only when opinion seemed so unanimous that the president could proceed to a vote *per discessionem*[2] without more ado. As Tacitus[3] relates it, the trial of Clutorius Priscus in 21 may have been an occasion of this type, with the president not troubling to continue the *interrogatio* beyond the *consulares*, because only two[4] had dissented from the *sententia* of the consul designate. In such circumstances it is understandable that afterwards Tiberius criticized the precipitate haste of the hearing and the execution of sentence.

During the Principate was there some modification of Republican practice? Tacitus' account of the period up to 70 gives no sign of one.[5] It is true that then, as ever, the influential opinions were those delivered by the senior members, the *consulares* and *praetorii*. In any event they formed together a much larger group than their juniors.[6] But in writing under the year 22 about the growth of senatorial sycophancy during Tiberius' reign, Tacitus[7] can state quite explicitly that many junior senators (*pedarii senatores*, those who had not yet reached the praetorship) did deliver *sententiae*. Presumably they were called in the order *aedilicii, tribunicii, quaestorii*.[8] Tacitus' own narrative would seem to supply some specific examples of such participation, although he never again uses the term *pedarius*.[9] Instead the simple description *senator* often, though not invariably,[10] seems

---

[1] Cf. Mommsen, *St. R.* III. 2. pp. 982-983.

[2] This term was used of such occasions, though strictly it denoted a vote without any discussion at all: see further sect. 25 below.

[3] *Ann.* 3.49-51.

[4] M. Aemilius Lepidus, cos. 6; C. Rubellius Blandus, cos. 18.

[5] Plainly it was an exceptional crisis when on 18 October 31 the consul asked only one senator if Sejanus should not be imprisoned after Tiberius' letter had been read (Dio 58.10.8).

[6] For the lead which might be given by the more senior members, cf. Tac. *Hist.* 4.8 and 41.

[7] *Ann.* 3.65.

[8] *Aedilicii* had preceded *tribunicii* in the Republic (Mommsen, *St. R.* III. 2. p. 967), and must surely have continued to do so later too, though the point cannot be checked.

[9] On it see further Extended Note F.

[10] At *Ann.* 4.31, for example, Firmius Catus is simply called *senator*, although he had

to denote a junior member. In all cases certainty is impossible, when by definition most of the members concerned are obscure, and many are never heard of again. But there must be a strong suspicion that M. Hortalus, whom Tacitus describes as "juvenis," was a junior senator in 16, when he sought financial help; it is notable that he makes his plea "loco sententiae."[11] Others who may be junior members and who take an active part in debate once each are Aurelius Pius (*senator*),[12] C. Cestius (*senator*),[13] Junius Rusticus,[14] Togonius Gallus "ignobilis,"[15] Caecilianus or Caesilianus (*senator*),[16] Cingonius Varro,[17] Junius Mauricus,[18] and Manlius Patruinus (*senator*).[19] In addition, Cossutianus Capito may not yet have reached the praetorship when Tacitus portrays him as wishing to speak in 47.[20]

In the same way Livius Geminus may still have been a junior senator when he testified to having seen Drusilla ascend to heaven in 38.[21] It is just conceivable that the poet Lucan as *quaestorius* was prepared to speak; at least we are told that he went out of his way to advertise openly his violent hatred of Nero.[22] The future emperor Otho certainly seems to have spoken as *quaestorius*.[23] We even have a miscellaneous reference to a "maiden speech" by Passienus Crispus, but unfortunately there is no evidence to determine his senatorial rank when he made it.[24] More gen-

---

been advanced to the praetorship *extra ordinem* for his part in the trial of Libo Drusus eight years earlier (*Ann.* 2.27 and 32). In the same chapter (4.31), the description *senator* is also used of Cominius, not least to distinguish him from his brother, an *eques*, mentioned here, as Furneaux suggests (*The Annals of Tacitus* I, pp. 278-279). Iuncus Vergilianus is no doubt termed *senator* at *Ann.* 11.35 to make the same distinction, though he may in fact have been a *praetorius*, if the reference thus in Seneca, *Apocol.* 13, is to him (cf. *PIR²* I 712). Goodyear (*The Annals of Tacitus* 2, p. 167) is too restrictive when he suggests that Tacitus sometimes uses *senator* to denote no more than a *quaestorius*.

[11] *Ann.* 2.37. For his ancestry see J. Geiger, "M. Hortensius M. f. Q. n. Hortalus," *CR* 20. 1970. pp. 132-134.

[12] *Ann.* 1.75.

[13] *Ann.* 3.36; *PIR²* C 690.

[14] *Ann.* 5.4.

[15] *Ann.* 6.2.

[16] *Ann.* 6.7.

[17] *Ann.* 14.45; *PIR²* C 736. We know him to have been consul designate in 68, so it is at least possible that he had not yet reached the praetorship in 62.

[18] *Hist.* 4.40; *PIR²* I 771.

[19] *Hist.* 4.45.

[20] *Ann.* 11.6-7; *PIR²* C 1543. We know only that he had returned from governing the praetorian province of Cilicia by 57.

[21] Dio 59.11.4. If it is he to whom Seneca refers in *Apocol.* 1, he was still only *praetorius* (as *Viae Appiae curator*) in 54.

[22] Cf. Suet. *Vita Lucani*; Tac. *Ann.* 15.49; *PIR²* A 611.

[23] Cf. Tac. *Hist.* 1.85; A. Nagl, *PW* 2A s.v. Salvius no. 21, cols. 2035-2055.

[24] Scholia on Juvenal, *Sat.* 4.81, p. 60 Wessner. We know only that Tiberius was emperor (and presumably present) at the time of the speech, and that Crispus was cos. II in 44. See R. Hanslik, *PW* 18 s.v. Passienus no. 2, cols. 2097-2098. The only other "maiden speech"

erally, throughout almost the entire Julio-Claudian period junior members were of course frequently involved in trials in the senate as advocates, defendants, and witnesses. After playing an active role on these occasions it would be extraordinary if they had all remained silent, or allowed themselves to be passed over, at every *interrogatio*: the evidence plainly shows any such notions to be false. Might we even speculate that the senate's new role as a court, and junior members' participation in trials, now gave them more confidence to speak in an *interrogatio* than they had possessed under the Republic?[25]

If we now move beyond the Julio-Claudian period, the confrontation between Vespasian and Helvidius Priscus depicted by Epictetus[26] hinges, among other points, on the fact that the former as president must ask for the opinion of the latter as senator when he attends a meeting. Helvidius would have been a *praetorius* at the time. Later, in an oblique reference in the *Panegyricus* to proceedings at the end of the trial of Marius Priscus (whose prosecutor he was), Pliny can claim that on this occasion in 100 Trajan as president asked every member for his *sententia*: "Each senator when called upon for his opinion spoke as he thought fit; he was free to disagree, to vote in opposition, and to give the state the benefit of his views. We were all consulted and even counted. . . ."[27]

As it happens, Pliny's descriptions in the *Letters* of his own experiences in the senate give no strong indication that it remained normal practice in his day for the president to call upon every member in this way. Yet equally it is true that, apart from one exceptional instance considered below, there is nothing in any of his accounts to show that junior senators were passed over. All the same, he never mentions the participation of any member below the rank of praetor, except for a tribune in office on one occasion.[28] At best, therefore, the contribution made by junior members to debates recorded by him is likely to have been slight. This is indeed entirely what we might expect from the knowledge that by his day the number of such members present at sessions, and eligible to be called upon, was notably smaller than it had been during the Julio-Claudian period described by Tacitus.[29] Yet the important point that junior members were still called upon even after Pliny's time may find confirmation in Fronto's

---

known is that delivered by Augustus "sententiae suae loco dicendae," in Seneca's parody, *Apocol.* 10.

[25] For consideration of claims by two consulars relevant to the question of junior members' participation, see Extended Note G.

[26] 1.2.19-21.

[27] 76.2, "interrogatus censuit quisque quod placuit; ⟨licuit⟩ dissentire discedere, et copiam iudicii sui rei publicae facere; consulti omnes atque etiam dinumerati sumus. . . ."

[28] *Ep.* 5.13.6. Cf. Sherwin-White, *Pliny*, pp. 168, 359.

[29] For approximate figures, see chap. 4 sect. 2.

description of M. Aurelius as a man whose *sententia* is asked for in the senate, when the latter was still only *quaestorius* (that is, before 140).[30]

An exceptional incident recorded by Pliny remains to be discussed. It occurred at the meeting in 97 when he himself attacked Publicius Certus,[31] and may provide an unusual instance where the consul called only the *consulares* and *praetorii*, and then at once took the vote, even though the opinions expressed thus far had not been unanimous. However, the reason for the curtailment here lies paradoxically in the extreme contentiousness of the issue, raised by Pliny (as we have seen) at the beginning of the meeting with the consul's special permission, and later put forward formally by the consul. By the time Pliny had spoken a second time (in order, among the *praetorii*), passions were rising, and his opponents were seeking the tribunes' aid, although the majority of the House was showing itself to be firmly on his side. Despite the support of the tribune Murena, Pliny's opponent Veiento was refused permission to speak a second time. We are then told that the consul "called out names,"[32] took a vote, and dismissed the meeting. Sherwin-White[33] envisages that *all* the other members were called. But even if their replies remained brief, this would still have been a lengthy business. Any delay which gave Pliny's opponents time to recover their composure represented a risk. In this volatile situation did the consul perhaps confine himself rather just to some, or all, the *praetorii* junior to Pliny? Since he was himself one of no more than four years' standing,[34] they formed a group of manageable size.[35]

13. The Need to Reply

Just as it evidently remained the duty of the president to call upon every member for an opinion when making the *interrogatio*, so, too, it remained the duty of every member thus called to make some reply.[1] After Poppaea Sabina had been driven to suicide by Messalina in 47, two of her minor associates were tried in the senate. When the president consulted members about the verdict, even her husband, P. Cornelius Lentulus Scipio, was asked for an opinion, and Tacitus speaks of the "*senatoria necessitas*"[2] which compelled him to give one. Helvidius Priscus, in the confrontation

---

[30] *Ad M. Caes.* 4.3.6 = p. 59 H. For dating, E. J. Champlin, *JRS* 64. 1974. pp. 143-144. It may be, of course, that Marcus would have been called out of order as Caesar.

[31] *Ep.* 9.13.6-20.

[32] *Ep.* 9.13.20, "citatis nominibus"; for the phrase, cf. *Ep.* 3.20.5.

[33] *Pliny*, p. 497.

[34] See Sherwin-White, *Pliny*, Appendix IV.

[35] For discussion of another incident recorded by Pliny, see Appendix 7 below.

[1] For Republican practice, note especially Livy 28.45.

[2] *Ann.* 11.4.

with Vespasian depicted by Epictetus,[3] affirmed that when called upon to speak he must say what he considered right, rather than just keep quiet. And there is no question that Thrasea Paetus came to cause offense by his habit of passing over flattering proposals in silence.[4] Silence was always open to interpretation as rebellion—as in the delicate situation when Vitellius' challenge to Otho was growing in strength.[5] So it was notable that Agrippa once refused to give an opinion when he was asked;[6] while near the end of our period, in 221, the emperor Elagabalus was naturally thunderstruck to have his instruction that the senate deprive Severus Alexander of the name Caesar met there by "a colossal silence," according to the *Historia Augusta.*[7] Only in special circumstances would it be appropriate to pass over a proposal in silence, as when members ignored the tactless motion of Helvidius Priscus in late 69 that the Capitol be restored at public expense with the assistance of Vespasian.[8] In the early second century, when the consul designate Acilius Rufus omitted all mention of Varenus' request for the right to summon witnesses from Bithynia for his trial, Pliny[9] naturally interpreted his attitude as a rejection.

14. Delivery of *Sententiae*

It was the duty of the first member called upon either to make a positive proposal about the issue put to the House in the *relatio*, or to argue that no action be taken. All later speakers could then either indicate agreement with an opinion already expressed, or make a new proposal. Indeed even *consules designati* might disagree at the very beginning of an *interrogatio.*[1] An opinion did not have to be supported by argument, but some support was normal unless a member were just agreeing with what appeared to be the majority view. A speaker in Tacitus, *Dialogus*, however, does claim that discussion in the senate had slipped in this respect under the Principate, and recalls with approval the good old days ". . . when it was not enough to move a brief resolution in the senate, unless one made good one's opinion in an able speech."[2]

With all the relevant evidence lost we cannot say how many members

[3] 1.2.20-21.
[4] Tac. *Ann.* 14.12; cf. 16.28.
[5] Tac. *Hist.* 1.85.
[6] Dio 54.11.6 (the correct reading of this passage is uncertain).
[7] *Elagab.* 13.2, "ingens silentium."
[8] Tac. *Hist.* 4.9.
[9] *Ep.* 5.20.6.
[1] See, for example, Plin. *Ep.* 2.12.2.
[2] *Dial.* 36, "cum parum esset in senatu breviter censere, nisi qui ingenio et eloquentia sententiam suam tueretur." The speaker may be Vipstanus Messalla.

on a typical occasion would go beyond a very brief indication of agreement with an opinion already expressed, and actually make a speech. Naturally there must have been wide variations, but it does seem fair to reckon that the number of speeches would in many instances have been small, especially in an atmosphere of fear under certain emperors, or when the mood of the House rapidly made itself clear. In any event, the judicious member appreciated that his influence was only likely to be weakened by over-frequent speeches, and especially by over-frequent opposition to popular proposals.[3] When this is said, however, the fact remains that an *interrogatio* was set to prove a long drawn out affair. My own attendance at Graduation ceremonies indicates how today it can take approximately 45 minutes just to read out about 350 names with due solemnity, pausing for a few seconds between each name. To estimate the full duration of an *interrogatio* in the Roman senate where that number of members was present to be consulted, time for speeches must then be added: say, for the sake of argument, 145 minutes, which would allow 5 speeches of 10 minutes each (50 mins.), 12 or 13 speeches of about 4 minutes each (50 mins.), and sundry other contributions (45 mins.). We might reckon 20 minutes for voting thereafter. If 30 minutes are allowed first for the *relatio* and the accompanying "explanation," then altogether, from the opening of the *relatio* to the conclusion of voting in a single instance might span as much as four hours. This seems a very considerable time, though not so much to Roman senators perhaps as to us today, especially when it is viewed in the context of the even longer periods for which the House was accustomed to sit, as seen in the previous chapter. Moreover, discussion of any controversial issue which gave rise to "variae sententiae," as contemporaries put it,[4] was always likely to exceed the span estimated above. The latter naturally remains guesswork, but it may at least be matched against the one surviving figure for the number of speeches delivered in the course of an *interrogatio*—a total of 44 *orationes*, probably on the punishment of Livilla, in late 31. Reckoning on no more than the modest average of just four minutes per speech, that number of *orationes* would still occupy about three hours. If Tacitus[5] offered any reason for this citation of a precise total of speeches (unique in all the accounts of senatorial sessions in his extant work), unfortunately the fragmentary nature of the passage has deprived us of it.

A proposal might be very simple, as in this example, which is presumably the first proposal of the *interrogatio*, made by the consul designate: "I move that Didius Julianus be named emperor."[6] The divine Augustus, in Seneca's parody, provides a clear example of a member making a new

---

[3] For the sentiment, cf. C. Cassius Longinus at Tac. *Ann.* 14.43.

[4] Seneca, *Apocol.* 9.6; Plin. *Ep.* 4.9.2; cf. Tac. *Ann.* 3.59, "varie dissererent."

[5] *Ann.* 5.6.

[6] HA, *Did. Jul.* 7.2, "Didium Julianum imperatorem appellandum esse censeo."

proposal, justified with a speech: "For my opinion I move as follows
. . . ."[7]

It was entirely in order to move that no action be taken. So in 15, when
the possibility of diverting streams which fed the Tiber was discussed, it
was such a proposal by Piso which carried the day.[8] Equally, where an
issue was complex or awkward, it was in order to propose that it first be
referred ("reicere," "deferre") to another authority before reaching any
decision. In our period, as might be expected, it was normally the emperor
who was consulted thus. For example, in 21 the House referred to Tiberius
(as consul) the choice of a proconsul for Africa, not least because discussion
of the issue had stirred up acrimony, and in his reply by letter the emperor
indirectly criticized members "because they referred all their problems to
the emperor."[9] Nonetheless, in the following year an issue raised by the
aediles was likewise referred to him.[10]

As might be expected, senators normally stood up to speak:[11] any trained
orator naturally wished to do so, in order to make the greatest possible
impact.[12] However, a member who was weak or unwell might remain
seated.[13] Otherwise not to rise was considered a sign of bad manners,[14]
unless nothing more than simple agreement with a previous speaker was
being expressed.[15] This could be indicated briefly by a single word like
"adsentior" ("I agree"), or apparently just by facial expression or gesture.[16] Thus in his speech preserved on papyrus[17] the mid first century
senator (Claudius?) may not only be criticizing his fellow members' un-
thinking agreement at sessions, but also pouring scorn on their self-sat-
isfaction at having voiced it with the one word "adsentior," rather than
merely indicating it by gesture.

In certain circumstances, especially where the interests or prestige of a
sensitive, cruel emperor like Nero were concerned, such curt assent could
seem inadequate and cause offense, as it did in the case of Thrasea Paetus.[18]

---

[7] *Apocol.* 11.4, "Ego pro sententia mea hoc censeo. . . ."

[8] Tac. *Ann.* 1.79, "nil mutandum censuerat." Cf. elsewhere, for example, 4.16, "placitum
instituto flaminum nihil demutari"; 14.42, "pluribus nihil mutandum censentibus."

[9] Tac. *Ann.* 3.32 and 35 (quoting from the latter), "quod cuncta curarum ad principem
reicerent."

[10] Tac. *Ann.* 3.52. For the senate referring matters to the emperor, see further chap. 5
sect. 1.

[11] Plin. *Ep.* 4.9.18; 9.13.9.

[12] Plin. *Ep.* 2.19.3.

[13] Plin. *Ep.* 4.9.18; cf. Dio 60.2.2 and 12.3.

[14] Cf. Plin. *Paneg.* 71.2.

[15] Pliny speaks bitterly of "sedentaria adsentiendi necessitas" under Domitian (*Paneg.*
76.3). Note Asconius, p. 44 C. For similar Republican practice, cf. Livy 27.34.7; Cic. *Ad
Fam.* 5.2.9 = SB 2.

[16] Cf. Tac. *Hist.* 4.4.

[17] *FIRA*[2] I no. 44 col. III lines 21-22.

[18] Tac. *Ann.* 14.12.

Pliny[19] refers to the need for any *sententia* to be accompanied by praise of the emperor in Domitian's time. In the same way, the extensively preserved *sententia prima* about curbing the cost of gladiatorial shows (A.D. 177) shows the speaker opening with a rhetorical passage where the benefits of the emperors' proposed measure are praised at some length;[20] only then does he turn to deal with the details in more matter-of-fact style.

A member who strongly supported a previous speaker's view might underline his agreement with, for example, "Hoc amplius censeo."[21] In his speech he might then add to the proposal already made. Pliny[22] lists this practice as a recognized part of senatorial procedure, and preserves an excellent example in the action of Valerius Paulinus at the trial of Julius Bassus: "Valerius Paulinus agreed with Caepio, but made the further proposal that Theophanes should be the subject of a *relatio* once he had made his report on his mission."[23]

15. Scope of *Sententiae*

Traditionally, once a senator had been called upon to speak, he could first discourse upon any subject he wished, at whatever length he chose, as Ateius Capito said: "For it was a senator's right when asked his opinion to speak beforehand on any other subject he wished, and as long as he wished."[1] Capito was writing in the Augustan period about a filibuster by the younger Cato in the late Republic.[2] Because he uses a past tense ("erat"), it has been thought[3] that the old rights no longer applied in his own day, possibly having been curtailed by Augustus. But in the passage as Gellius quotes it there is no sign that the use of the imperfect tense is intended to have this significance, and any better evidence for some curtailment by Augustus is lacking. It does seem highly dubious whether he would have risked giving the serious offense which any such attempted infringement on traditional rights would have provoked, especially when in public, at any rate, he paraded a desire to encourage senatorial freedom of debate. Outspokenness could be controlled in other ways, while coaxing

---

[19] *Paneg.* 54.3.

[20] *Aes Italicense* to line 26 (*Hesperia* 24. 1955. pp. 330-334).

[21] Cf. Seneca, *De Vita Beata* 3.2.

[22] *Ep.* 8.14.6.

[23] *Ep.* 4.9.20, "Valerius Paulinus adsensus Caepioni hoc amplius censuit, referendum de Theophane cum legationem renuntiasset." For other examples, cf. Cn. Lentulus and C. Cassius Longinus in Tac. *Ann.* 3.68 and 13.41; Ulpian, *Reg.* 11.23; in general, Seneca, *De Vita Beata* 3.2.

[1] Quoted by Gellius, 4.10.8, "erat enim ius senatori, ut sententiam rogatus diceret ante quicquid vellet aliae rei et quoad vellet."

[2] See, in general, P. Groebe, "Die Obstruktion im römischen Senat," *Klio* 5. 1905. pp. 229-235.

[3] For example by Mommsen, *St. R.* III. 2. p. 940.

any words at all out of some members was to become a greater problem than halting a full flow of eloquence. It could be that some curtailment of speeches was one of Augustus' schemes, like the levying of fines for non-attendance, which was introduced only to fall rapidly into disuse. But in any such attempt he could not claim to be reviving ancient practice, as he could with fines.[4]

Not surprisingly, filibusters are unheard of in our period. Indeed in Tacitus, *Dialogus*, Maternus, regretfully comparing conditions under the Principate with those of the good old days, even poses the question: "What is the use of long *sententiae* in the senate, when the best people quickly agree?"[5] In any event, as Pliny indicates,[6] the considerate member disciplined himself to keep his speeches to a reasonable length. Yet it is still true that we have no instance in our period of a president cutting short members delivering *sententiae*,[7] even when they rambled.[8] The phrase "tempus loquendi" used once by Pliny[9] could be taken as a unique reference to a "time limit" for speeches. But here he is talking only of recommendations made by candidates themselves, or by others in their favor, on election days. It is entirely understandable that limits may have been introduced on such occasions to allow each candidate's merits an equal airing, and to prevent undue delay in the completion of a lengthy process. In the same way there were time limits for the speeches of prosecution and defense at trials. These were based on Republican practice and were laid down by law, though evidently the president might vary or extend them.[10] For the delivery of *sententiae* in the course of a normal *interrogatio*, however, there is no sign that any restriction had come to be imposed upon either length or scope.

16. The Right to Speak "Off the Question"

Members certainly did still speak on any matter they wished, and this is claimed by opponents of Thrasea Paetus as a senator's right: "Whenever

---

[4] Even though the point of the reference is not clear to us, note that Dio does have Tiberius say at the funeral of Augustus: "In connection with the senate's decrees he did not do away with senators' privilege of voting, but even added safeguards for their freedom of speech" (56.40.3).

[5] *Dial.* 41.

[6] Cf. *Ep.* 8.14.6, "dicendi modus"; Asconius, p. 44 C; for a similar attitude in the late Republic, see Cic. *De Legibus* 3.40.

[7] In *Ep.* 9.13.9 Pliny is cut short by the president, but in this case he is only speaking with the latter's special permission. Later on the same occasion (sect. 19) Fabricius Veiento tries to speak and is shouted down by other members: however, he is out of turn, and has not gained the president's leave.

[8] Note Tacitus' remark (*Hist.* 4.44) that Mucianus spoke "prolixe" early in 70.

[9] *Ep.* 3.20.3.

[10] On both limits see further chap. 6 sect. 4.

a senator exercises his right to speak, he may draw attention to any matter
of his choice and demand a *relatio* on it."[1] In 16, when replying to Marcus
Hortalus' request for aid, Tiberius represented the practice as ancient custom, though he expressed disapproval of its use to raise private matters:
"When our ancestors permitted senators occasionally to digress from the
relatio and raise matters of public importance while delivering a *sententia*,
this was not to enable us to promote our private interests and personal
affairs."[2]

M. Hortalus is by no means unique in raising an extraneous matter *loco
sententiae* during our period. Indeed earlier in his account of the same
year, 16, Tacitus can claim that the practice was then common: "It was
still usual practice for senators, when delivering their *sententiae*, to put
forward any matter that they believed to be in the public interest."[3] He
implies that it had fallen out of use by his own day. This may be largely
true, although, as we shall see, at least one instance from the early second
century is known. Scholars have been puzzled by the fact that his remark
is made in a context where, strictly, no extraneous matter was raised, but
rather a member, Octavius Fronto, supported and amplified the proposal
of an earlier speaker, Q. Haterius—a common practice mentioned above.
All the same, it is easy to see how the point occurred to Tacitus here.
Since other asides not strictly apposite may be found in his work,[4] there
seems no call either to brand the sentence as interpolation, or to try and
claim that Octavius Fronto did introduce entirely new issues.[5]

The member, however, who really did speak "off the question" in this
discussion about nationwide luxury was L. Calpurnius Piso.[6] Having denounced "official sharp practice, corruption in the courts and bullying by
advocates, with their continual threats of prosecution,"[7] he then declared
that he would retire far from Rome, and dramatically walked out of the
senate house. In 21, when the choice of suitable proconsuls for Africa and
Asia was under discussion, Sextus Pompeius strayed far from the question
by making the occasion an opportunity to launch a bitter personal attack

---

[1] Tac. *Ann.* 13.49, "licere patribus, quoties ius dicendae accepissent, quae vellent ex-
promere relationemque in ea postulare."

[2] Tac. *Ann.* 2.38, "nec sane ideo a maioribus concessum est egredi aliquanto relationem
et quod in commune conducat loco sententiae proferre, ut privata negotia et res familiares
nostras hic augeamus."

[3] *Ann.* 2.33, "erat quippe adhuc frequens senatoribus, si quid e republica crederent, loco
sententiae promere."

[4] Much of the comment in *Ann.* 12.60, for example, is irrelevant to the issue of granting
jurisdiction to imperial equestrian procurators.

[5] See Koestermann ad loc. (Vol. I p. 310) for rejection of the first alternative, and support
of the second.

[6] *PIR*[2] C 290.

[7] Tac. *Ann.* 2.34.

on the consular Manius Lepidus as most *un*suitable for selection. But it was probably earlier in the same debate[8] that an even more senior consular, Caecina Severus, departed completely from the question by proposing that "no-one appointed to a governorship should be allowed to take his wife." Not surprisingly, there were protests at the irrelevance of this *sententia*, and opposition to it was expressed. In 28 many proposals were again made "off the question" according to Tacitus,[9] as senators out of fear sought to flatter Tiberius and Sejanus. In 69, when the state of the *aerarium* was under discussion, Helvidius Priscus not only made a *sententia* on this, but also strayed "off the question" to propose restoration of the Capitol.[10]

We hear from Tacitus of three occasions in the Julio-Claudian period when members consulted about the verdict in a trial sought to go further and make a proposal "off the question" concerning some general issue raised by the case. Thus in 22 Cornelius Dolabella proposed "that anyone of scandalous life and evil reputation should be excluded from the drawing of lots for a governorship—the emperor to be judge."[11] As it happened, Tiberius was present himself at this session to express his disagreement on the spot. In 62, however, there was considerable support for the motion of Thrasea Paetus, when asked for a verdict on Claudius Timarchus, that provincials be forbidden to pass votes of thanks to governors. This was indeed an occasion which, as Tacitus says, Thrasea turned "ad bonum publicum,"[12] but no measure could be passed, "since the consuls ruled that this was not the question on which the *relatio* had been made."[13] The proposed ban was only introduced later, at the instigation of the emperor. Though Tacitus[14] does not say so, the same technical difficulty presumably had to be overcome in the case of the proposal of Cotta Messalinus[15] at the trial of C. Silius in 24, that officials should be punished for their wives' wrongdoing in the provinces as though it were their own.

In recording meetings he had attended, Pliny furnishes one striking example of an issue raised "off the question." In early 107 Varenus Rufus, indicted by the Bithynians on a charge of misgovernment, had asked Pliny as his leading defense counsel to make the unusual request to the senate that he be permitted to summon witnesses from the province. After a hearing, the request was granted.[16] But among a number of members who

---

[8] Tac. *Ann.* 3.32-34; see further above, sect. 11 note 47.
[9] *Ann.* 4.74.
[10] Tac. *Hist.* 4.9.
[11] *Ann.* 3.69.
[12] Cf. Tiberius at *Ann.* 2.38, quoted above; and for the general sentiment, Plin. *Ep.* 9.13.21.
[13] *Ann.* 15.22, "abnuentibus consulibus ea de re relatum."
[14] *Ann.* 4.20; cf. Ulpian, *Dig.* 1.16.4.2.
[15] *PIR*² A 1488.
[16] *Ep.* 5.20.

still considered the concession inadmissible was the *praetorius* Licinius Nepos. At the next meeting of the House, when other business was under discussion, he reopened the question and made proposals to have a general reexamination of the whole issue initiated. Predictably, this behavior provoked a hostile reaction,[17] followed by speeches in opposition. Nepos was even accused of seeking to set himself up as "emendator senatus." In view of this reaction the president—unlike on the occasion of Pliny's request at *Ep*. 9.13[18]—presumably never made a *relatio* in accordance with Nepos' wishes, so that there could be no fresh vote. The dissatisfied Bithynians therefore had to seek further ways of having the matter formally reopened.[19]

Two further instances where Pliny has been seen to record speeches "off the question" may not be correctly interpreted thus. First, Sherwin-White[20] considered that Homullus spoke in this way at the meeting described in *Ep*. 6.19. But we cannot be altogether certain, when Pliny omits to explain what issue was under discussion at the time. Second, in *Ep*. 9.13, after he has himself with permission raised a matter before the beginning of the regular business, the consul finally stops him with the words: "Secundus, you shall say whatever you wish when you offer your *sententia* in order."[21] In Sherwin-White's view[22] the president was thus offering Pliny the chance to pursue his matter further by speaking "off the question" later. But the remark was perhaps rather intended as a signal that the matter would be put forward formally later, as indeed must have happened. Certainly Pliny himself seems well satisfied at this stage, and those friends who hurriedly take him to one side for a private word must also think that the issue will be pursued further. In contrast, the mere opportunity to speak "off the question" later would have been of little service.

17. Withdrawal of *Sententiae*

Though we seldom hear of the practice, it evidently was possible for a member to withdraw his *sententia*. Tacitus[1] implies that Thrasea might have done so, but chose not to, after his popular proposal of less severe

---

[17] Plin. *Ep*. 6.5.3, "fuerunt quibus haec eius oratio ut sera et intempestiva et praepostera displiceret, quae omisso contra dicendi tempore castigaret peractum, cui potuisset occurrere."
[18] See sect. 7 above.
[19] Cf. Plin. *Ep*. 6.13.
[20] *Pliny*, p. 360.
[21] *Ep*. 9.13.9, "Secunde, loco sententiae dices, si quid volueris."
[22] *Pliny*, p. 494.
[1] *Ann*. 14.49.

punishment for Antistius Sosianus on a charge of *maiestas* had infuriated Nero in 62. Yet in order to compromise, the proposer of the death penalty did withdraw his motion when the fate of the freedmen of the murdered consul, Afranius Dexter, was being discussed in 105.[2] In 32 Tiberius effectively required Togonius Gallus to withdraw an extravagant *sententia*.[3] Though a formal *sententia* was perhaps not involved, as soon as he had consented to prosecute Caecilius Classicus for the Baeticans, Pliny[4] took a similar step voluntarily in begging leave to withdraw the excuses offered earlier.

18. Delivery of *Sententiae* on Oath

If he wished, a senator could deliver his *sententia* under solemn oath;[1] he might also add that his proposal was "in the interests of the state."[2] Thus in 14 Tiberius swore that, despite the senate's encouragement, he would not increase the number of praetors above the total stipulated by Augustus. Two years later, when Libo Drusus committed suicide before his trial was completed, the emperor stated on oath that he would have interceded for his life if he had been found guilty.[3] In 38 Livius Geminus swore that he had seen Gaius' sister, Drusilla, ascending to heaven on her death,[4] while at the opening of his reign Nero frequently pledged himself to clemency.[5] In early 70 all magistrates, followed by other members as they were asked for their *sententiae*, swore on oath "that they had done nothing to harm anyone, and had gained neither reward nor preferment from the downfall of citizens."[6] Members' verdicts after trial hearings might equally be given under oath: Tiberius undertook to do this at the trial of Granius Marcellus in 15, and definitely acted thus in proposing exile for P. Suillius Rufus in 24.[7] We are told that the whole senate had actually delivered its verdict on oath at the trial of Cassius Severus.[8]

In addition, the *Lex Julia* evidently allowed a member to require of another a sworn statement that his *sententia* had been in the interests of

[2] Plin. *Ep.* 8.14.24.
[3] Tac. *Ann.* 6.2.
[4] *Ep.* 3.4.4.
[1] This was Republican practice: for examples, see Mommsen, *St. R.* III. 2. p. 979 n. 5.
[2] "E re publica." For the expression, see, in addition to references below, Tac. *Ann.* 2.33; 3.53; Gell. 4.10.8; Suet. *Claud.* 26, "rei publicae maxime interesset."
[3] Tac. *Ann.* 1.14; 2.31.
[4] Dio 59.11.4; Seneca, *Apocol.* 1.3. Cf., on Augustus' death, Suet. *Aug.* 100; Dio 56.46.2.
[5] Tac. *Ann.* 13.11.
[6] Tac. *Hist.* 4.41.
[7] Tac. *Ann.* 1.74; 4.31, ". . . amovendum in insulam censuit, tanta contentione animi, ut iure iurando obstringeret e re publica id esse."
[8] Tac. *Ann.* 4.21; *PIR*² C 522.

the state. We may guess that Augustus had intended this provision to serve as one means of curbing irresponsible or ill-conceived proposals.[9] But only one instance of its use is known—where an oath was required from a consul designate early in 105.[10] Syme[11] suggests that it was Fabius or Flavius Aper, as a consular of recent standing, who had the temerity to press this unusual demand. The idea is attractive, but strictly Pliny's account of the session can give no indication of his status, so that the arguments for it must really rest on the other evidence which Syme adduces.

Under the procedure in the *senatus consultum* of which Augustus sent a copy to Cyrene in 4 B.C.,[12] it was only on oath taken before the House that defendants could challenge senators chosen by lot to hear the cases, while again it was only on oath, supported by the sworn testimony of fellow members, that such senators could excuse themselves in advance, or withdraw during the proceedings.[13]

19. Character of Debate

For the president merely to call upon each member in order for his opinion might seem to make for an inflexible, dull occasion, lacking the cut and thrust of, say, many modern parliamentary debates, where members seek to contribute only if they wish to, and the order of speakers is determined afresh each time by the chairman. Without doubt, for a variety of reasons, many sessions of the Roman senate were dull. Members were reluctant to speak out of fear, for example.[1] Or, very frequently, the business comprised only routine, uncontentious matters, such as authorizing an increase in the number of gladiators, or licensing a *collegium*, both of which Pliny cites.[2] Thrasea Paetus' attempt to oppose a proposal like an increase in the number of gladiators at Syracuse in 58 was plainly unusual,[3] and his enthusiasm

[9] Cf. his distaste for a suggestion by Antistius Labeo (Suet. *Aug.* 54).

[10] Plin. *Ep.* 5.13.5.

[11] R. Syme, *JRS* 58. 1968. pp. 139-140 = *Roman Papers* II pp. 701-702.

[12] *FIRA*[2] I no. 68 V lines 115-130.

[13] For emperors swearing an oath not to execute senators, see chap. 16 sect. 1.

[1] Cf. Plin. *Paneg.* 76.3-4; Epictet. 1.2.24; 4.1.139-140; cf. *FIRA*[2] I no. 44 col. III lines 10-22, where the reason for senators' reticence is not made explicit.

[2] *Paneg.* 54.4. Cf. the reference to generally trivial business at Tac. *Hist.* 2.91. Note also Plin. *Ep.* 4.12.3; 5.4.1; 8.14.8; 10.2 and 95, with Sherwin-White ad loc. (*ius trium liberorum*); Dio 54.23.8 (assigning names to cities); HA, *Max. Balb.* 1. 3-4. Dio (72.4.2-3) comments on how Commodus driveled in his first speech to the senate after the death of M. Aurelius.

[3] Tac. *Ann.* 13.49. Tacitus speaks of the *senatus consultum* as "vulgarissimum"; Thrasea's critics consider such matters "tam levia," and he in reply terms them "levissima."

for taking sides even on such "trivial" issues was later made a charge against him by Cossutianus Capito in 66.[4]

Yet in practice the *interrogatio* was not so stereotyped as it might appear from the description so far. There are a number of reasons for this, which need to be examined in turn. First, as we have seen, it was possible for the president to vary at his own discretion the order in which members were called, although admittedly there is little sign of this right being exercised, except by emperors. At the same time the president shared with all magistrates and with the emperor the right to intervene and speak whenever he wished. As mentioned above, magistrates were not normally called upon for their *sententiae* in the course of the *interrogatio*, although Tacitus[5] records that exceptionally the emperor Tiberius did call them thus when presiding. Yet the right of intervention was exercised frequently— not only by presidents[6] and by the emperor (whether or not presiding),[7] but also by praetors[8] and tribunes,[9] among other magistrates.[10] We hear of certain emperors even bursting in with remarks as others were speaking.[11]

The right to intervene at any time naturally offered the opportunity to ask questions, and there is little doubt that both magistrates and the emperor commonly did this.[12] Equally, when non-members were introduced for one purpose or another, it seems that the whole House could be offered the chance to question them.[13] At other sessions, too, it was evidently

---

[4] Tac. *Ann.* 16.22, ". . . qui vulgaribus quoque patrum consultis semet fautorem aut adversarium ostenderet."

[5] *Ann.* 3.17.

[6] For example, Tac. *Ann.* 3.31 and 34; cf. Josephus, *AJ* 19.251.

[7] For example, Tiberius: Tac. *Ann.* 1.74; 3.68-69; 4.30 and 42; perhaps also 4.6 ("cohibebat ipse"); Suet. *Tib.* 29. Claudius: Tac. *Ann.* 12.7; Dio 60.16.8. Nero: Tac. *Ann.* 13.43. Vitellius: Tac. *Hist.* 2.91. Domitian: Suet. *Dom.* 11. Septimius Severus: Dio 76.6.1. Cf. Plin. *Ep.* 2.11.15 (Trajan) and Tac. *Ann.* 1.46 (popular vision of Tiberius, faced by mutinies in 14, "sedere in senatu, verba patrum cavillantem").

[8] Suet. *Vesp.* 2; Tac. *Hist.* 4.43; Dio 66.12.1; Plin. *Ep.* 6.5.4. Syme's inference (*Symb. Fac. Litt. Philos. Leuven* Ser. A Vol. 6. 1977. p. 236 n. 15) that Mamercus Scaurus was in office as praetor in 14 because Tacitus (*Ann.* 1.13) reports him as "intervening among consulars," seems rash. From elsewhere we know only that he did not reach the consulship till 21, and the account here will not help us further. Since Scaurus' remarks are the last in this debate to be reported, we cannot fix his rank with more precision. It is not clear whether he was delivering his *sententia* at the time, or making an intervention. If the former, we could at least be sure that he was not a magistrate in office; if the latter, the question would remain open, because although magistrates alone intervened of right, others were commonly permitted to do so.

[9] Tac. *Ann.* 13.28, where a tribune attacked a quaestor; Plin. *Ep.* 5.13.6; Dio 53.20.2-3.

[10] For references to magistrates in general speaking, cf. Tac. *Hist.* 1.47; 4.41.

[11] Claudius: Suet. *Claud.* 40. Pertinax: Dio 74.8.5. Didius Julianus: HA, *Did. Jul.* 7.1.

[12] For example, Tac. *Ann.* 1.8; 2.50.

[13] Note especially Seneca, *Apocol.* 9.1; cf. Dio 60.17.4. For interrogation of witnesses at trial hearings, see chap. 16 sect. 2.

permitted for private members to ask questions in the course of the proceedings, even if they had no strict right to do so. Such queries might be put to the president,[14] the emperor,[15] or any other member.[16] A reply was normally allowed too.

In the same way, though members had no right to interrupt or speak out of turn, in practice they were commonly permitted to do so. Most notably, when the *interrogatio* came to develop in an unexpected fashion as it proceeded, or when points were made which merited rebuttal, a more senior member (who had already delivered his *sententia* earlier) might seek to speak again.[17] Thus in the debate about *res prolatae* in 16 Asinius Gallus (cos. 8 B.C.) probably spoke before Cn. Piso (cos. 7 B.C.) in the normal order, and then broke in again. He acted likewise later in the same year to oppose the *sententiae* of the consular Q. Haterius and the *praetorius* Octavius Fronto.[18] In 21, when the House was asked to appoint a governor to Africa, we have already seen how the *interrogatio* took a strange turn with the consular Caecina Severus proposing "off the question" that nobody appointed to a governorship be allowed to take his wife. Valerius Messalinus, who outranked Caecina and would therefore already have delivered his *sententia* in the normal order, gained leave to speak against the irrelevant proposal.[19] Tacitus' comment that M. Lepidus (cos. A.D. 6) "often palliated the brutalities caused by other people's sycophancy"[20] perhaps implies that he frequently spoke out of turn to good effect. Later Vitellius could boast that he had been in the habit of speaking in opposition to Thrasea Paetus[21]—again out of turn presumably, since as a consular eight years senior to Thrasea, he would have been called upon first in the normal order. Pliny's account[22] of the *interrogatio* about the treatment of the freedmen of the murdered consul of 105, Afranius Dexter, is not altogether lucid, but presumably he must have spoken at least twice himself—

[14] For example, Tac. *Hist.* 4.40; Dio 58.10.6.

[15] For example, Tac. *Ann.* 1.12-13 and 74; 3.53; Dio 54.16.5; 57.2.5-6. The question of "Domitius orator" cited by Jerome (*Ep.* 52.7.3), "ego te habeam ut principem, cum tu me non habeas ut senatorem?" was perhaps addressed by Cn. Domitius Afer to Claudius in the senate. See *PIR*[2] D 123 and 126; for questions of similar type in the late Republic, cf. Cic. *De Orat.* 3.4; Quintil. *Inst. Or.* 8.3.89; 11.1.37.

[16] For example, Tac. *Ann.* 3.18; 13.49 (when Thrasea responded to requests that he justify the attitude taken by him earlier in the session); *Hist.* 4.41.

[17] This was recognized Republican practice. Cf. Scholia on Cicero, p. 170 Stangl.

[18] Tac. *Ann.* 2.35 and 33.

[19] Tac. *Ann.* 3.33-34. See further above, sect. 11 note 47.

[20] *Ann.* 4.20, "pleraque ab saevis adulationibus aliorum in melius flexit"; cf. 3.50-51; 6.27; R. Syme, "Marcus Lepidus, *Capax Imperii*," *JRS* 45. 1955. pp. 22-33 = *Ten Studies in Tacitus*, pp. 30-49.

[21] Tac. *Hist.* 2.91; cf. *Ann.* 14.49.

[22] *Ep.* 8.14.

once to make his *sententia* (sect. 12), and again later to ask that each of the three *sententiae* made be voted upon separately (sect. 14).

Speeches made out of order in this way extended to the senatorial *interrogatio* something of the vigor of a modern parliamentary debate. Such vigor was even more in evidence when one speech made out of order was allowed to lead to further exchanges, so that an *altercatio* developed.[23] The most celebrated such disputes in the senate during our period were perhaps those between Eprius Marcellus and Helvidius Priscus in 69 and 70,[24] but we do hear of a number of others too.[25] Significantly, Tacitus[26] does not fail to record in contrast how Nero's toady, the future emperor Vitellius, when answered back by those members he insulted, did not have sufficient fiber to make any rejoinder.

20. Expression of Feeling

The *interrogatio* on any contentious issue was enlivened by members' readiness to express their feelings volubly. In a body so large, as in the House of Commons today, time and circumstance made it impossible for all members to speak individually as and when they would wish. So a member might convey a point simply by a brief "aside." As Tiberius hesitated to accept the Principate, many must have shared the frustration of the unidentified senator who blurted out "Let him take it or leave it!"[1] Cassius Severus' remark about a member who flattered Tiberius was also remembered: "Such frankness will be the death of this man."[2] And according to Seneca, it was after exclaiming "Now the theater is ruined indeed!"[3] (when a statue of Sejanus was being voted, to be placed in the rebuilt theater of Pompey) that Cremutius Cordus began to starve himself to death. Mommsen[4] was surely wrong when he saw the brief paragraph in Claudius' speech on the admission of Gallic notables to the senate as an interruption by confused members, rather than as merely the emperor addressing himself: "It is now time, Tiberius Caesar Germanicus, for you

---

[23] For the term see, for example, Cic. *Ad Att.* 1.16.9-10 = SB 16; 4.13.1 = SB 87; Suet. *Aug.* 54.

[24] See Tac. *Hist.* 4.7-8 (note that on this occasion Eprius, as consular, must already have had an opportunity to speak before Helvidius, as *praetor designatus*); 4.43. From the *Histories* there is little sign that Helvidius was a novice in this kind of contest compared to Eprius, as Aper claims at *Dial.* 5.

[25] For example, Tac. *Ann.* 2.51; 3.31; 5.11; 6.4; 13.28; Plin. *Ep.* 2.11.4-7; 6.5.

[26] *Ann.* 14.49.

[1] Suet. *Tib.* 24, "aut agat, aut desistat!"

[2] Plut. *How to Tell a Flatterer* 18 = *Mor.* 60 D; *PIR²* C 522.

[3] *De Cons. ad Marciam* 22.4, "exclamavit Cordus tunc vere theatrum perire."

[4] *Ges. Schriften* VIII. p. 506. For acceptance of his view, however, note J. H. Oliver and R.E.A. Palmer, *Hesperia* 24. 1955. p. 323.

to disclose the direction of your speech to the conscript fathers; for you have already reached the furthest boundaries of Narbonese Gaul.''⁵ But at least an interruption of the type envisaged was entirely characteristic of senatorial debate.

On certain occasions the expression of feeling might be more widespread, and thus safely anonymous. So in 61 no individual dared oppose the *sententia* of C. Cassius Longinus that all the slaves of the murdered *Praefectus Urbi* be executed, but members generally were prepared to raise a clamor of protest in their pity for "the numbers affected, and the women, and the young, and the undoubted innocence of the majority."⁶ Elsewhere Tacitus describes vividly the senators' dilemma in Otho's reign and the solutions adopted:

But when the senate was assembled in its chamber there was the continual hazard of steering a middle course. Here silence might seem rebellious and free speech suspect. Otho had recently been an ordinary senator and had used the same language as his peers. So he knew all about flattery. In delivering their *sententiae*, therefore, the senators tacked and veered this way and that. They denounced Vitellius as "parricide." But those with a keen eye to the future confined themselves to perfunctory abuse. Certain others did hurl genuine insults, yet timed their denunciations for moments of uproar when many were shouting, or blurted out their words in an incoherent torrent which nobody could quite catch.⁷

Although it was considered proper for all to keep silent while a member was delivering his speech⁸ (and a genuine effort to observe such courtesy was no doubt made for "maiden speeches"),⁹ more or less coherent general interruptions were plainly common in the course of an *interrogatio*¹⁰ and even perhaps of a *relatio*.¹¹ In the final stages of the session in 97 when Pliny had attacked Publicius Certus, the uproar reached such a pitch that Veiento, who had already spoken in order, was prevented from making any reply at all to the points in Pliny's *sententia*, despite having gained a tribune's support.¹²

Interruptions were only one of the ways in which a member who spoke could expect to find the House a lively audience (unless it were frozen by

⁵ *FIRA*² I no. 43 col. 2 lines 20-22.

⁶ Tac. *Ann.* 14.45.

⁷ *Hist.* 1.85.

⁸ Cf. *Laus Pisonis* 69 Verdière; Plin. *Ep.* 3.20.3, "tacendi modestia"; 8.14.6, "silentii tempus."

⁹ See above, sect. 12 note 24.

¹⁰ For example, Tac. *Ann.* 3.34; 4.42; 6.24; Plin. *Ep.* 2.11.7; 5.13.6; 9.13.7 (strictly, before the *relatio*); Suet. *Aug.* 37. At a trial, Plin. *Ep.* 3.9.25-26.

¹¹ For a possible example (assuming that the phrasing is chosen with such precision), note Suet. *Aug.* 54 ("in senatu verba facienti," that is, following the *relatio*). Note also Dio 53.11.4.

¹² Plin. *Ep.* 9.13.19.

fear). In another context Pliny[13] describes how a person who reads poetry in public will gauge the reaction of his audience from their "facial expressions, glances, nods, gestures, murmurs and silence." We should remember, too, that the spectators in a Roman court were notoriously noisy.[14] So likewise in the senate members made their reactions plain.[15] They applauded proposals which they supported[16]—normally when the speaker sat down, but once even, in anticipation, as he rose to speak.[17] We hear of mixed reactions on some occasions: when Octavian laid down his powers in January 27 B.C., for example;[18] in the discussions at the time of Tiberius' accession;[19] when Tiberius rejected M. Hortalus' request for aid in 16;[20] or when the same emperor's letter was read on 18 October 31.[21] The extremes of laughter—when ludicrously extravagant proposals were made to flatter Tiberius, for example[22]—and tears—as on the death of Drusus in 23[23]—were known. Equally, members could range between lavishing obsequious flattery on an emperor they feared,[24] and hurling insults at Lepidus in his disgrace.[25] Piso suffered a reception of the latter sort when he stood trial in 20. By contrast, it was to avoid a similar occurrence that Thrasea's friends advised him against attending the senate and attempting to defend himself in 66.[26] On the most tense occasions interruptions and altercations led to plain uproar—for example, early in 70, when the House turned on members who had been notorious *delatores* under Nero, shaking fists at them, and hauling them out of the chamber.[27]

Pliny[28] implies that it was proper behavior for all to remain seated (as well as silent) during a member's speech. But it is clear enough that this convention, too, was infringed with impunity. So in addition to heckling and hubbub, a speaker would often have to persevere against background

---

[13] *Ep.* 5.3.9.

[14] Cf. Plin. *Ep.* 2.14; Suet. *De Rhet.* 6.

[15] Cf. in general Pliny's comment at *Ep.* 9.13.18.

[16] For example, Tac. *Ann.* 12.6 and 7; 15.22; *Hist.* 4.4; Plin. *Ep.* 2.11.11 and 14; 3.4.4; 5.13.3; 9.13.7 and 21; 9.23.2.

[17] Plin. *Ep.* 4.9.18.

[18] Dio 53.11.1 and 4.

[19] Tac. *Ann.* 1.11, "questus, lacrimas, vota."

[20] Tac. *Ann.* 2.38.

[21] Dio 58.10.3ff.

[22] Laughter (often sneering): cf. for example Tac. *Ann.* 3.29 and 57; 6.2; *Hist.* 2.91; Plin. *Ep.* 6.13.5; Dio 57.17.5; HA, *Hadr.* 3.1; perhaps Herodian 5.7.4.

[23] Tears: cf. for example Tac. *Ann.* 1.11; 4.8-9; Plin. *Paneg.* 73.4-6; *Ep.* 2.11.3 (at a trial); *Epit. de Caes.* 16.13 (on the death of M. Aurelius).

[24] For example, Tac. *Hist.* 3.37; cf. in general Epictet. 1.2.24.

[25] Dio 54.15.5.

[26] Tac. *Ann.* 3.15; 16.26.

[27] Tac. *Hist.* 4.41; cf. also, for example, *Ann.* 1.13; *Hist.* 1.85; Plin. *Ep.* 2.11.4-7; 3.20.4; 4.25.2; Dio 54.16.3; 57.24.8.

[28] *Ep.* 3.20.3.

disturbance. As we noted in an earlier chapter,[29] there might also be considerable movement in the chamber during a session, especially by members coming together to confer privately or proceeding to stand near one whose *sententia* they supported. Such conditions called above all for firmness and resolution on the part of speakers.

21. Style of Speaking

Formally a speech in the senate was addressed to the whole House, not just to the president. More important, it was to be made with due attention to rhetorical rules and other proprieties. This would have been the agreed opinion of emperors, who prepared their speeches carefully, with or without help, as well as of members like Pliny and Fronto, and of a teacher like Quintilian. It is no surprise, therefore, to hear of the octogenarian Verginius Rufus rehearsing a formal *gratiarum actio*.[1] Accent and style were important.[2] What Pliny said with reference to trials applied broadly to all sessions: "much can be gained or lost by the speaker's memory, voice and gestures, the occasion, and lastly the good or bad impression made by the defendant."[3] We are told that when Hadrian first had to speak for the emperor during his quaestorship, his provincial accent provoked laughter, while Septimius Severus was alleged to have retained an "African" accent even to old age.[4] In the same vein Pliny commented adversely on the breathless, monotonous style of many Greek advocates; by contrast he complimented "pure accent."[5]

So a good Roman education, with its stress on the ability to speak both after preparation and impromptu, would always have been invaluable to the member who aimed to make an impression upon the House. Tacitus, himself a speaker of note, pitied the senior consular, C. Silanus,[6] on trial in 22 after his governorship of Asia. Accused by a battery of able senators and the best rhetoricians from the province, Silanus had to reply "alone, an inexperienced speaker, in mortal fear—which incapacitates even practiced orators."[7] In his sole reference to the senate in the *Meditations*, it is significant that Fronto's pupil M. Aurelius wrote: "Speak both in the senate and to any person whatsoever with propriety, without affectation.

---

[29] Chap. 3 sect. 2.

[1] Plin. *Ep.* 2.1.5. For the help allegedly sought by L. Ceionius Commodus, cf. HA, *Aelius* 4.7.

[2] For senatorial interest in *facundia*, note Fronto, *Ad amicos* 1.4.2 = p. 167 H.

[3] *Ep.* 5.20.3; cf. Ovid, *Ars Amat.* 1. 461-462.

[4] HA, *Hadr.* 3.1; *Sev.* 19.9.

[5] *Ep.* 5.20.4; 6.11.2, "os Latinum."

[6] *PIR*² I 825.

[7] *Ann.* 3.67.

Use words that ring true."[8] Fronto himself stresses to M. Aurelius that
"you are mistaken if you think that an opinion blurted out in the language
of Thersites would carry equal weight in the senate with a speech of
Menelaus or Ulysses, whose looks in the act of speaking and their expression and stance and melodious voices and the differences of cadence in
their oratory Homer did not disdain to describe . . .";[9] and he explains in
the same passage how it falls to a Caesar to carry by persuasion necessary
measures in the senate. Imperial letters to the senate, he urges,[10] should
be eloquent, dignified, restrained; in speeches there, as elsewhere, far-
fetched words, as well as unintelligible or unusual figures, should be
avoided.[11] Quintilian[12] serves to sum up this whole attitude when he em-
phasizes that advocates' speeches before the senate demand a certain loft-
iness and gravity.

For the converse, Pliny[13] maintains that wit (*urbanitas*) is not becoming
in the senate. For this reason his contemporary Quintilian disapproves of
the opening, "Conscript fathers—for so I must open my address to you,
that you may remember the duties of fathers,"[14] and we may guess that
the jokes of Asilius Sabinus,[15] preserved by Seneca the Elder,[16] went down
badly.[17] However, Dio[18] does record a proposal to give Tiberius a guard
in 14 which he regards as facetious, and Pliny[19] tells how jokes and
obscenities were scribbled on ballot papers when this method of voting
was tried at elections—though here there may also have been a more serious
motive. All the same, members clearly shared Pliny's disgust at such
behavior, and, while sessions were not uniformly solemn, most senators
manifestly did take their functions seriously. The apprehension of Pliny
and Tacitus at having to address the House on a tense occasion like the
trial of Marius Priscus, with the emperor presiding, can readily be appreciated.[20]

[8] 8.30.

[9] *De Eloq.* 2.7 = p. 136 H.

[10] *Ver. Imp.* 2.1 = pp. 114ff. H, esp. p. 120 H.

[11] *Ad M. Caes.* 3.1 = p. 36 H; cf. *Ant. Imp.* 1.2.5 = p. 90 H.

[12] *Inst. Or.* 8.3.14; 11.1.45 and 47; 11.3.150 and 153. The sentiments of Quintilian and
Fronto are predictably close to those of Cicero: see, for example, *De Oratore* 1.31; 2.333;
3.210-211, and the analysis by D. Mack, *Senatsreden und Volksreden bei Cicero*, Würzburg,
1937.

[13] *Ep.* 4.25.3; 8.6.3.

[14] *Inst. Or.* 8.5.20, "patres conscripti, sic enim incipiendum est mihi, ut memineritis
patrum."

[15] *PIR*[2] A 1213.

[16] *Controv.* 9.4.20-21.

[17] But one flash of wit by Antistius Labeo was evidently appreciated: cf. Dio 54.15.8.

[18] 57.2.3.

[19] *Ep.* 4.25.1.

[20] Plin. *Ep.* 2.11.11; cf. Tac. *Dial.* 11.

Ancient styles of public speaking were more vigorous than many modern ones, so that for all the formal strictures outlined above, the senate was often the scene of emotional or flamboyant behavior on the part of speakers, especially defendants, and sometimes of members in general.[21] Thus in 2 B.C., for example, Augustus replied in tears to salutation as Pater Patriae, while on another occasion Claudius, likewise in tears, protested vociferously about the risk of assassination which he faced as emperor.[22] Antoninus wept and groaned as he begged the House to deify Hadrian.[23] In seeking to encourage Tiberius' acceptance of the Principate, members threw themselves at his feet, according to Suetonius.[24] Earlier, in indignation at Augustus' proposals for senatorial membership in 18 B.C., Licinius Regulus "tore his clothes in the chamber itself, laid bare his body, enumerated his campaigns, and showed them his scars."[25] Defendants, however, behaved most dramatically of all. Servilia, the daughter of Barea Soranus, for example, on trial in 66 ". . . at first collapsed on the ground, weeping incessantly and not answering. But then she grasped the altar and its steps, and cried. . . ."[26] Instances of defendants on the charge of *maiestas* actually drinking poison in the House are reported for Tiberius' reign.[27]

22. Personal Abuse

Although speeches to the senate were to be framed with care, this ideal still left the way open for rudeness and personal abuse, just as much as it did for emotion. The senate tolerated slanderous allegations, damaging to character and standing,[1] of a far more vicious kind than anything permissible in, say, the Houses of Parliament today. So far as can be seen, it made little difference whether those attacked were living or dead, members or non-members. It is true that many speakers did seek to maintain decent standards. Though it would appear that apologies were not demanded, strong objection was often taken to insults:[2] indeed, in Suetonius' view,[3]

---

[21] On one aspect of this theme, note R. Macmullen, "Romans in tears," *Class. Phil.* 75. 1980. pp. 254-255.

[22] Suet. *Aug.* 58; *Claud.* 36.

[23] Dio 70.1.2.

[24] *Tib.* 24; for a Republican parallel, cf. Cic. *Ad Att.* 4.2.4 = SB 74.

[25] Dio 54.14.3.

[26] Tac. *Ann.* 16.31. For dramatic pleas by other defendants, cf. Tac. *Ann.* 6.49; Plin. *Ep.* 5.13.3; Dio 59.19.4-5; 76.9.3. Outburst after sentence: Tac. *Ann.* 4.70.

[27] Suet. *Tib.* 61; Dio 58.21.4; cf. 58.27.4.

[1] Cf. Seneca, *De Const. Sap.* 17.1, "maledicta mores et vitam convulnerantia."

[2] See, for example, Tac. *Ann.* 3.32; 5.11.

[3] *Tib.* 29.

Tiberius was really being over-polite when he begged Q. Haterius' forgiveness for speaking against him more freely than he should as a senator.
It is notable that in 69 the majority of members did resist an extraordinary
attempt by Vibius Crispus to have the *eques* Annius Faustus sentenced to
death without defense or hearing,[4] while Dio[5] can comment upon the
marked restraint with which M. Aurelius spoke and wrote about the rebel
Avidius Cassius a century later. In his essay *On Anger* Seneca argues that
a man should not be too "sensitive." Otherwise, he asks, ". . . will he
be able to bear with equanimity the strife of public life and the abuse
rained down on him at a *contio* or in the senate house?"[6]

Such behavior may be found throughout the Principate. First, in the
Julio-Claudian period, remarks of Augustus in a speech made some time
during the last ten years of his life were interpreted by Tacitus[7] as deliberately critical of Tiberius' deportment, dress, and behavior. Tiberius himself was later to be even more outspoken about members of his family in
letters sent to the senate,[8] and insisted that all Drusus' statements in captivity be read out after his death.[9] We have already seen how in 21 Sextus
Pompeius could attack his fellow consular Manius Lepidus as a "lazy
pauper of no credit to his ancestors,"[10] while Seneca describes how Corbulo[11]
drove Fidus Cornelius[12] to tears by calling him "a plucked ostrich."[13]
Gaius was rude about Livia in a letter to the senate, and indeed abused
the corporate body in general.[14] The future emperor Vitellius gained a bad
reputation for publicly insulting his fellow members at sessions during
Nero's reign.[15] Seneca's brother Gallio was denounced as "public enemy
and parricide"[16] after the Pisonian conspiracy in 65; the same terms were
used against Vitellius as he was claiming the Principate early in 69.[17] The

---

[4] Tac. *Hist.* 2.10.

[5] 71.27.1.

[6] *De Ira* 2.25.4, "feret iste aequo animo civile convicium et ingesta in contione curiave
maledicta?"

[7] *Ann.* 1.10; cf. Suet. *Tib.* 68. By contrast, Augustus perhaps said no more in public about
Julia and Agrippa Postumus than was absolutely necessary (Tac. *Ann.* 1.6; Suet. *Aug.* 65).

[8] For example, Tac. *Ann.* 5.3.

[9] Tac. *Ann.* 6.24; Dio 58.25.4. Cf. Tiberius' insult to an *eques* on trial (Suet. *Tib.* 57).

[10] Tac. *Ann.* 3.32.

[11] For discussion of the identity of this "Corbulo," see M. Griffin, *Seneca: A Philosopher
in Politics*, p. 44 n. 4.

[12] *PIR*[2] C 1360.

[13] *De Const. Sap.* 17.1, "struthocamelum depilatum."

[14] Suet. *Calig.* 23 and 30; cf. Seneca, *De Const. Sap.* 18.1.

[15] Tac. *Ann.* 14.49.

[16] Tac. *Ann.* 15.73, "hostis et parricida"; for similar terms used in our period of great
figures of the Republic, ibid. 4.34.

[17] Tac. *Hist.* 1.85. Similarly, the whole senate had been cursed as "parricide" by the
people when a rumor was spread that Claudius had been killed on a journey to Ostia (Suet.
Claud. 12).

"taunts and insults" hurled at Otho before his accession were a source of acute embarrassment later.[18] In contrast, by autumn 69 members had learned to be more cautious; they took care to voice no criticism against the Flavian leaders, and avoided even mentioning Vespasian's name.[19] Yet in the course of the informal meeting of Othonian senators held at Mutina after that emperor's death in April 69, the junior senator, P. Licinius Caecina, is found launching a violent attack on Eprius Marcellus, and the quarrel had to be ended by those with greater level-headedness. In the same vein, soon afterwards, during Vitellius' Principate, Caecilius Simplex was accused of having bought the consulship by means of bribery and the murder of Marius Celsus.[20]

Later, quite apart from wrangles with Eprius Marcellus and his associates, Helvidius Priscus allegedly would not cease slandering Vespasian, and even drove him to tears on the sensitive issue of the succession to the Principate.[21] According to Pliny, at the trial of Arulenus Rusticus in 93 the prosecuting counsel M. Aquillius Regulus could abuse the defendant as "a Stoic ape, branded with a Vitellian scar."[22] Elsewhere Pliny's reference[23] to an incident at a senatorial hearing is kept sufficiently vague for its interpretation to remain uncertain, but it seems that Publicius Certus attacked a defendant so brutally that he ended by striking him. Thrasea's friends, too, we may note, had been apprehensive that he might actually be assaulted if he tried to attend the senate and defend himself in 66.[24] Early in the second century Pliny[25] found the language and behavior of two members in an *altercatio* too distasteful and offensive to repeat any of their words in a letter. According to the *Historia Augusta*,[26] senators interpreted certain remarks made by M. Aurelius on the death of L. Verus as critical of his fellow emperor. Finally, insults were hurled at fallen emperors in the early third century,[27] as previously.[28]

In sum, while the rudeness of senators to each other on certain occasions may readily be illustrated, this aspect of their behavior must nonetheless be viewed in perspective. Against it should be set the voluntary restraint

[18] Tac. *Hist.* 1.47.
[19] Tac. *Hist.* 3.37.
[20] Tac. *Hist.* 2.53 and 60.
[21] Dio 66.12.1-3.
[22] *Ep.* 1.5.2, "Stoicorum simiam, Vitelliana cicatrice stigmosum."
[23] *Ep.* 9.13.2.
[24] Tac. *Ann.* 16.26. In a high-flown passage elsewhere (*Agr.* 45), Tacitus suggests that senators in a body laid hold of Helvidius Priscus the Younger after his trial in 93 and escorted him to prison; but it is difficult to know whether this statement should be taken literally.
[25] *Ep.* 6.5.5-7.
[26] *Marcus* 20.3-4.
[27] Dio 79.2.5-6 and 3.2.
[28] Suet. *Dom.* 23.

on the part of many, treated above; the favor which the House could show towards its own members on trial for certain offenses;[29] and the underlying feeling, shared by all to a greater or lesser degree, that as a body they represented a proud and dignified élite.[30]

23. The Role of the President

Altogether it is not difficult to appreciate how the *interrogatio* on a contentious issue could be a lively, even turbulent, occasion. The modern observer, however, might justly be puzzled at the apparent lack of control exercised by the president. In theory his prerogative was enormous: he alone could decide matters on which to make a *relatio* (no member could force any *relatio*), and, as will appear, he alone chose which *sententiae* to put to the vote. In Seneca's parody the divine president, Jupiter, did rebuke members for turning the interrogation of Claudius into "a real shambles," and desired them to maintain "the rules of the House."[1] But we hear of no such stern initiatives from human presidents in our period.[2] Rather Roman convention would seem to have been for them to do little towards influencing or directing proceedings. Not least at trial hearings such a passive stance was traditional; the praetor in a Republican *quaestio* (from which, as we shall see, the senate derived its trial procedure) had exercised only a supervisory role.

Instead, while in session the House was governed mostly by the mood of its members, especially the more senior ones. These always remained a loose group, but it is worth remembering that among them *consulares* in particular grew significantly more numerous than they had ever been in the Republic, once regular suffect consulships were introduced from 5 B.C. In 97 Fabricius Veiento's attempt to speak a second time, for example, was perhaps stopped more effectively by the protests of members than it would have been by presidential intervention.[3] In extreme circumstances, if a member felt threatened, he would appeal to a tribune—as Veiento did.[4] It was almost unheard of for a president to take decisive action spontaneously. Senatorial initiative after the violent deaths of Caligula and Domitian, as well as in the disturbed years 68, 193, and 238, might be considered honorable exceptions. But even in these instances it is seldom

---

[29] See chap. 16 sect. 1.

[30] See chap. 2 sect. 6.

[1] *Apocol.* 9.1, "vera mapalia"; "disciplina curiae."

[2] Pliny (*Paneg.* 73.2) does refer obliquely to the possibility of Trajan as president restraining members' enthusiasm on election day in 100, but only to dismiss it.

[3] Plin. *Ep.* 9.13.19.

[4] See further chap. 3 sect. 3.

clear from our sources how far action was inspired specifically by the president,[5] and it was arguably only in 238 that the initial decisiveness was sustained. Much more typical was the occasion in 29 when the consuls were completely at a loss to know what action should be taken in regard to an accusing letter from Tiberius about his own family. They were equally nonplussed at other times when they were uncertain of imperial reaction.[6] Predictably, in all these instances they chose to consult the emperor before proceeding further. It might be added that on certain occasions, even when his reaction was never in doubt, he could still be consulted for the strategic purpose of delaying an inevitable condemnation.[7]

Lack of initiative by presidents in our period should not really be cause for surprise. None attained the consulship without the emperor's approval, and all were keenly aware that their actions in office were reported to him, whether or not he attended meetings. Not only was a consul's prerogative in selecting items for discussion, and presenting them as he wished, significantly diminished when so much business came to be put forward by the emperor; for any controversial motion, or any action out of the ordinary, he would also need to ensure in advance the approval of his colleague in office.[8] In the normal course of debate, too, he was debarred from curbing irrelevance, or pulling up an unduly prolix speaker. These were formidable obstacles to the exercise of independence. Moreover, as tenure grew progressively shorter, a consul presided over fewer meetings, and thus had less opportunity to gain experience and confidence. So, once short terms of office became the rule, it would have been unrealistic to expect much skilled presidential guidance of sessions. Yet there is no question that the senate, in its parliamentary capacity, came to suffer in consequence. As with any body of its size, it could only benefit from some restrained, tactful chairmanship; with such help the acrimony of the disgraceful sessions in late 69 and early 70 might have been avoided. Members and non-members alike must have had their confidence in the corporate body severely shaken at that time. And—even more damaging for the future, as it turned out— these sessions afforded the young Domitian a devastating introduction, which must have colored his estimate of the senate ever afterwards. It is hardly remarkable that our sources seldom supply evidence, or make comments, which would help towards assessing the skill of an individual president (other than emperors). Tacitus' attention[9] to Drusus' handling of

---

[5] Yet Josephus does indicate the leading role played in January 41 by the consuls Q. Pompeius Secundus (esp. *AJ* 19.263) and Cn. Sentius Saturninus (esp. *AJ* 19.166-186). Cf. *BJ* 2.205; Suet. *Claud.* 10; Dio 59.30.3.

[6] Tac. *Ann.* 5.3-4; 13.26; 14.49; cf. *Hist.* 4.9.

[7] Cf. Tac. *Ann.* 4.66; 16.8.

[8] See above, sect. 3.

[9] *Ann.* 3.31-37; *Hist.* 4.40-47.

awkward items during his second consulship in 21, and to Domitian's presidency early in 70, are very much the exception.

24. Members' Attention

When they sat as the jury during a trial in the House, members who intended to vote upon the verdict had a natural obligation to remain in the chamber for the full duration of the hearing. There is reason to think that they were expected to stay likewise for other sessions which they attended, and it is easy to see how such a convention might impose strain. In theory they were indeed free to come and go as they pleased, but in practice it would seem that they did usually stay in the chamber throughout, rather than adopt the kind of behavior for which members of the modern House of Commons are often criticized—that is, attending the debate on an issue desultorily, if at all, and only appearing when the bells ring for a division. At Westminster such behavior is encouraged in a number of ways. To put it crudely, under a "party" system a loyal member need never form his own view of an issue. He must simply vote with his leader, and if one party outweighs all others, then the result of votes is largely a foregone conclusion. Even when he does wish to contribute to a debate, he still faces the uncertain business of "catching the Speaker's eye," and may not be successful, especially when the "guillotine" can impose a severe limit on time allowed for discussion.

By contrast, many features of the procedure and practice of the Roman senate did press a member to remain throughout. First, he would seldom receive in advance a full agenda from which to determine whether or not the business specially roused his concern. Then not only was the course of any meeting unpredictable, but, as we shall see, it was also common for a matter to be raised, and a decision taken, at the same session. If a senator was absent on the day when a matter was first raised, there would not necessarily be the equivalent of a second or third reading at which he could speak instead. Since no member attended as a representative, it was strictly inappropriate for him to consider, say, whether business was likely to touch constituents' interests. Rather, by definition all items were of concern to him simply as a senator. In practice, however, senators as *patroni* of communities did come to represent the interests of local areas to a degree, and it was perhaps in order to prevent undue application of local pressure, among other purposes, that a clause in Caesar's law of 59 B.C. regulating provincial government had made it an offense to accept a bribe for delivering a *sententia* in the senate.[1] Yet as diplomatic business

[1] Venuleius Saturninus, *Dig*. 48.11.6.2.

came to be handled more and more by the emperor, in many instances a patron would perhaps render greater service to his community by, say, making informal contact with imperial advisers than by taking an active role in the House itself. It would be most instructive, for example, to know whether it was before the latter or before the emperor that the senator of the Severan period, M. Nonius Fabius Arrius Paulinus Aper, had displayed the "industria" as *patronus* which earned him the thanks of the *collegium dendrophorum* at Brixia for having its *immunitas* confirmed.[2] Certainly Lucian[3] represents influence in the palace as the great benefit which the bogus seer Alexander gained from the favor shown to him by the consular, P. Mummius Sisenna Rutilianus; while it was M. Aurelius, not the senate, whom Alexander petitioned to have Abonoteichos renamed Ionopolis.

The convention whereby members should escort the emperor or president from home immediately before a meeting, and then back again afterwards, naturally acted to demand their attendance for its duration. Hadrian perhaps appreciated how tiresome the return journey in particular was for members, and thus spared them trouble by leaving in a litter.[4] Then during the session itself every senator knew that he would be asked in order his opinion in each *interrogatio*, and that he could speak freely for as long as he liked. It was when names were called that absence became conspicuous. Moreover, where a matter was controversial, the outcome of a debate could hardly be foreseen. A fresh *sententia* could be made by each speaker, but at the end, as we shall see, the president put to the vote only the *sententiae* of his choice. By contrast, the outcome was never likely to be uncertain in the same way when an item was raised by the emperor. Yet of course it would be particularly disrespectful, and thus perilous, for members to leave while business raised by him, or concerning him, was before the House.

It is fair to guess that at all times informal groupings or "parties" of senators existed, though our knowledge of any is slight. We may claim with more assurance that none made a lasting impact upon sessions of the House. Thus there were no "party lines" for members to follow regularly on particular issues, beyond the obvious one that the emperor's wishes could hardly be refused. No doubt in practice, where a senior member keenly advocated a proposal, he did expect the support of junior colleagues indebted to him for help in gaining election to a magistracy, for instance, or appointment to a post. So it may be that the strikingly lavish contributions proferred by the unsavory consulars Paullus Fabius Persicus[5] and C. Ca-

[2] *ILS* 1150 with P. Lambrechts, *PW* 17. s.v. Nonius no. 12, cols. 864-865. Note also discussion of *Inscr. Ital.* X. 4. no. 31, chap. 2 sect. 6 note 61.

[3] *Alexander* 48 and 58.

[4] Dio 69.7.2. See further chap. 6 sect. 4.

[5] *PIR*[2] F 51.

ninius Rebilus[6] for the games given by Agricola's father, L. Julius Graecinus[7] as praetor, actually represented a crude bid to buy the support of a *novus homo* from Narbonensis.[8] It was quite exceptional, however, for Thrasea Paetus to be accused of establishing a "party" in the senate, though the charge lost point when it had to be acknowledged that his associates did not imitate his rebellious *sententiae*.[9] In desperation after the death of Britannicus, Agrippina, too, had allegedly sought to form a "party" to work in her interest,[10] but at best it can only have been short-lived. Later Pliny[11] hints that in Domitian's time a split between senators emerged— in support of the emperor and his close associates, and against them. Though in this instance he claims the return of unanimous support soon afterwards under Trajan, it is plain enough that in all reigns individual members would vary widely in their attitude towards the Princeps, and even to the Principate itself. Yet both the groups to which Pliny refers must always have been loose, and the latter of the two ineffective.

Members did join together, as we find at the trial of Marius Priscus,[12] for example, or as Hercules trots round the chamber soliciting support for his view in Seneca's parody.[13] But mostly such groupings shifted with each individual occasion or issue. There was all the more need, therefore, for members to give their full attention to business throughout a meeting, while the complex tangle of mutual obligation demanded that they stay to listen to their friends' speeches and vote with them.

It is perhaps only to be expected that late arrival at meetings on the part of individuals is almost unheard of. Although strictly the Greek of our informant Dio[14] is ambiguous, the main aim of Augustus' fines must surely have been to punish members who missed meetings altogether rather than those whose attendance was lethargic. Equally, his instruction in 12 B.C. that members should not call upon him beforehand[15] was to prevent a delayed start to a whole session, not just the late arrival of a few individuals. Tiberius, too, "made a special point that senators should always meet as often as was appropriate, and that they should neither assemble later than

---

[6] *PIR*² C 393.

[7] *PIR*² I 344.

[8] Seneca, *De Benef*. 2.21.5 with comment by J. Morris, "Senate and Emperor," in *Geras, Studies Presented to George Thomson on the Occasion of His 60th Birthday*, Prague, 1963, pp. 149-161 at p. 154.

[9] Tac. *Ann.* 16.22.

[10] Tac. *Ann.* 13.18.

[11] *Paneg.* 62.

[12] Plin. *Ep.* 2.11.20-22.

[13] *Apocol.* 9.6.

[14] 54.18.3; 55.3.2. ὑστερίζειν may mean "come late" or "come too late" (and thus miss).

[15] 54.30.1.

the prescribed time, nor disperse earlier.''[16] Arguably the emperor's concern here was really with the slackness of individual senators, not of the whole body, which hardly met according to prescribed hours. Yet the aim of this instruction is by no means clear, and it remains open to interpretation.

These instances aside, it is striking that we do not hear of late arrival or early departure from meetings under normal conditions. Instead, such behavior appears exceptional. Among emperors, Augustus is said to have twice left meetings early in 13 B.C., first to avoid acceptance of further honors after he had been appointed *pontifex maximus*,[17] and second to avoid expressing his fury at an allegation made by Cornelius Sisenna. As Dio describes the latter incident, "He did not do or say anything violent, but rushed out of the senate house, and then returned a little later, choosing to act thus even though it was not proper behavior, as he said to his friends afterwards, rather than to remain where he was and be forced into taking some harsh step.''[18] Similarly, according to Suetonius,[19] Augustus several times hastened away when altercations became excessive. Later, in 39, Gaius dashed from the House after defending the memory of Tiberius and restoring the charge of *maiestas* in a devastating tirade.[20] In 49 senators received L.Vitellius' plea that Claudius be permitted to marry his niece Agrippina with such enthusiasm that they rushed out of the House to press his acceptance; he then entered the meeting and asked for the necessary legislation to be passed.[21] It was presumably before the end of a meeting that Vespasian walked out in tears, upset by what had been said about the succession.[22] After the murder of Geta in 212, Caracalla merely entered the senate to make his own speech, and then left.[23]

We do hear of a number of exits by other members, all of them dramatic. In 16, having denounced corruption in public life, L. Calpurnius Piso walked out, saying that he would leave Rome altogether. Then in 25 Cremutius Cordus walked out and starved himself to death after making a defense against trumped-up charges.[24] C. Fufius Geminus in 30 likewise did not wait to hear the verdict in his case, while in 22, when a praetor was accused of having insulted the emperor, he went out, took off his robe of office, and returned demanding as a *privatus* to be prosecuted at once.[25]

---

[16] Dio 58.21.2 (under A.D. 33).
[17] Dio 54.27.2.
[18] 54.27.4.
[19] *Aug.* 54.
[20] Dio 59.16.8.
[21] Tac. *Ann.* 12.7.
[22] Dio 66.12.1.
[23] Dio 77.3.3.
[24] Tac. *Ann.* 2.34; 4.35.
[25] Dio 58.4.6; 57.21.2.

Beyond any question Thrasea Paetus made a deep impression by walking out as honors were being proposed to the emperor after Agrippina's death in 59.[26] Members who had been notorious *delatores* under Nero were actually hounded out of the chamber early in 70, while later in the same session Eprius Marcellus and Vibius Crispus moved to withdraw of their own accord when the former was attacked by Helvidius Priscus.[27]

In contrast to all these instances, if it really was also a common habit among members to walk casually in and out of sessions, then we may only say that evidence for such behavior is striking by its absence. Such movement may have been too mundane to show up anywhere in the surviving record, it is true.[28] Yet on the other side there is much to suggest that members did usually stay present in the chamber throughout and, as has been argued, there was good reason for them to do so.

25. The Taking of Votes[1]

Where appropriate, matters brought before the House by the president were sooner or later put to the vote. The stage at which this was done would depend on whether or not the matter was contentious. Thus Varro, quoted by Gellius, explained in his handbook of 70 B.C.: "a decree of the senate is made in two ways: either by *discessio*, if there is general agreement, or, if the matter is disputed, by calling for the opinions of individual senators."[2]

In our period the practice of voting on uncontentious matters without any prior discussion must have continued, though it is difficult to cite examples[3] when on the one hand we know that sources use *discessio* in the broad sense of any vote, but on the other we cannot identify usage in Varro's more limited, technical sense with the same confidence. The problem is that separate nouns which would specifically distinguish the background to senatorial votes were not in use.[4] Tacitus, for example, can speak of the consul allowing a *discessio* after the trial of Antistius Sosianus

[26] Tac. *Ann.* 14.12; 16.21; Dio 61.15.2.

[27] Tac. *Hist.* 4.41 and 43.

[28] The instance of the advocate who slipped away before his case was called might be cited. He was not a member, however, and he behaved thus not out of slackness, but because his nerve had failed (Plin. *Ep.* 5.13).

[1] For its length M. L. Paladini, "Le votazioni del senato Romano nell' età di Traiano," *Athenaeum* 37. 1959. pp. 3-133 is unrewarding.

[2] 14.7.9, "senatus consultum fieri duobus modis: aut per discessionem, si consentiretur, aut, si res dubia esset, per singulorum sententias exquisitas."

[3] For one atypical possibility, where there had been discussion but no *interrogatio*, see my view of Tac. *Ann.* 11.5-6, sect. 7 note 11 above.

[4] The consequent difficulty of making distinctions is reflected in Gellius' confusion at 14.7.12-13.

in 62; yet on this occasion the consul designate and Thrasea Paetus had made conflicting *sententiae*, each of which was voted upon.[5] Pliny likewise uses *discessio* even after there had been an *interrogatio* and conflicting proposals.[6] Elsewhere Tacitus[7] specifies that the contents of a letter from Tiberius in 29 were not discussed after it had been read out. But it is not so clear whether the senate then proceeded just to loyal protestations or to the passage of a formal *senatus consultum*. By contrast, it is entirely credible that there had not been discussion in the case of the *SC de nundinis saltus Beguensis* (an uncontentious request to hold fairs on an estate), which is described as "s. c. per discessionem factum."[8]

When a matter was contentious, the vote would follow the *interrogatio*. The debate and vote upon many issues would presumably be completed on the same day. But there was no need for them to be, and we know that in the late Republic major questions or disputes were not always dispatched so conveniently.[9] In our period there was still the same opportunity to continue consideration of an issue at a later date. It must regularly have taken more than one session to settle the requests of embassies and to finalize much of the complex civil legislation which continued to be handled even into the Severan period. There is reason to think that the issue settled by the *SC de aedificiis non diruendis*, for example, might already have been discussed on one or more occasions before its passage on 22 September 44,[10] while we know that proposals to reduce the expense of gladiatorial shows late in M. Aurelius' reign were on the agenda of more than one meeting.[11] In general, too, few trial hearings would ever be completed within a single day. Two further occasions may be mentioned in this context, although we should recognize that neither is a straightforward case of prolonged discussion upon a contentious or complex issue. First, it may well have taken more than one session to secure Tiberius' formal acceptance of the Principate in 14, in whatever terms exactly that proposition was put to him. Here, of course, the delay was caused not by general argument among members, but by Tiberius' own hesitations.[12]

---

[5] *Ann.* 14.48-49. For further references to *sententiae* made in the course of an *interrogatio* being passed by *discessio*, cf. *Ann.* 3.69; 6.12.

[6] Cf. *Ep.* 2.11.22; 8.14.19; 9.13.20. He can also use *sententiae* to mean "votes," not "proposals," at *Ep.* 2.12.5; cf. Gell. 3.18.2.

[7] *Ann.* 5.5.

[8] *FIRA*[2] I no. 47 line 9. *Discessio* is also found in Seneca, *De Vita Beata* 2.1, *FIRA*[2] I no. 15 line 4, and Suet. *Tib.* 31, though whether used in the broad or the technical sense, it is impossible to say.

[9] See W. K. Lacey, *JRS* 64. 1974. p. 177 n. 9; in general, Gell. 1.23.5.

[10] *FIRA*[2] I no. 45. See further chap. 6 sect. 2 note 35.

[11] See chap. 8.

[12] On the whole chronology of Tiberius' accession, see B. Levick, *Tiberius the Politician*, chap. 5.

Second, it is true that the unknown speaker (Claudius?) on a mid first century papyrus does offer a pause for pondering his suggestions, followed by their reconsideration at a later date.[13] Yet here, too, the difficulty was hardly one of prolonged argument over the issues; rather it was the complete absence of any response.

When a number of conflicting proposals[14] had been made, the president had sole discretion over the selection of those to be put to the vote and in what order, except of course that he had to pass over *sententiae* vetoed by tribunes or the emperor.[15] In normal circumstances he was hardly likely to ignore any proposal which had seemed to attract some support, but strikingly Pliny[16] tells us how at the trial of Julius Bassus a proposal made by Valerius Paulinus was in fact treated thus, even though it had gained great favor. No explanation for the omission is offered: we may only speculate that the consuls were in some way concerned at the vindictiveness of the proposal, or at its entry to the discussion at a comparatively late stage, since Valerius can have been no more than a *praetorius*. It was perhaps usual to put forward *sententiae* in the order they had been made.[17] Each was voted upon individually, and the first to gain the support of the majority was carried.[18] So on the occasion in 26 when Smyrna is said to have received 400 votes and the ten other cities competing with her a combined total of only seven, the natural conclusion must be that the *sententia* in favor of Smyrna was put first, thereby resolving the matter without further ado.[19]

Pliny writes a rambling, wordy letter in which he seeks to justify an attempt to undermine the normal voting procedure.[20] In the *interrogatio* concerning treatment of the freedmen of the dead consul Afranius Dexter in 105, three proposals were made about their treatment—release, exile, or execution. As explained above, the regular practice was for each proposal to be put to the vote separately until one gained an outright majority. Thus each senator here would vote up to three times. As proposer for release, Pliny is incensed that the supporters of exile and execution will combine against him (as he expects they will), even though these latter

---

[13] *FIRA*[2] I no. 44 col III lines 14-16.

[14] Cf. Plin. *Ep.* 8.14.6, "pugnantes sententiae."

[15] Cf., for example, Tac. *Ann.* 1.77; 6.47 (tribune). For the emperor's veto, see chap. 5 sect. 1 note 72.

[16] *Ep.* 4.9.20-21 with Sherwin-White ad loc.

[17] Cf. Plin. *Paneg.* 76.3, where it is noted as a sign of liberty that "vicit sententia non prima, sed melior." The *sententia prima* was naturally the one most likely to reflect the emperor's wishes, especially under Domitian.

[18] Pliny (*Ep.* 2.11.6) speaks of a *sententia* which gained a good deal of support when put to the vote as "frequens."

[19] See above, chap. 4 sect. 2 note 112.

[20] *Ep.* 8.14, esp. sect. 22.

proposals are very disparate. He therefore seeks a method of voting whereby each sentence may be put to the House, but every member will have only *one* vote; under this arrangement he reckons that release will gain the greatest support of the three. As it turned out, the effect of his protest was to prompt the proposer of execution to withdraw his *sententia*, thus leaving members a straight choice between release and exile. There is every reason to share Pliny's doubts about whether his alternative method of voting was legal. Though it is not certain that such was the intention, his efforts at least did have the strategic effect of eliminating one rival proposal before any vote was taken. But irritatingly he never makes clear whether release did then carry the day against exile.

A senator who felt that a single *sententia* which was being put to the vote in fact covered more than one point could ask for it to be "divided" and for each point to be voted upon separately. So Seneca can write in a letter: "I think that the custom in the senate should be followed in philosophy too: when someone has made a proposal, part of which I support, I tell him to divide his *sententia* and I vote for the part which I approve."[21] Seneca's contemporary, Asconius,[22] likewise refers to the practice as current, but no example can be cited from the reports of sessions in our period.

In putting a *sententia* to the vote the president used the formula: "Those who agree with this proposal go to this side; those who agree with all other proposals go to the side you support,"[23] and indicated the respective sides by a movement of the hand. Having moved to the side chosen, each member then sat down.[24] Every member (though not magistrates) had a vote, even at trials of more senior fellow members.[25] All votes were of equal value, and a straight majority prevailed.[26] Senators were not bound to vote for the proposal they had supported in their *sententia*, and certainly did not always do so, as Pompeius Collega bitterly complained when those who had agreed to act with him at the trial of Marius Priscus did not lend their support in the end.[27] Notoriously, opinions might shift in the course of the *interrogatio*, as they did at an earlier stage of the same hearing.[28] So while it is true, as we might expect, that the result of a vote was normally in

[21] *Ep. Mor.* 21.9, "quod fieri in senatu solet, faciendum ego in philosophia quoque existimo: cum censuit aliquis, quod ex parte mihi placeat, iubeo illum dividere sententiam et sequor, quod probo."

[22] Page 43 C.

[23] Plin. *Ep.* 8.14.19, "qui haec censetis, in hanc partem, qui alia omnia, in illam partem ite qua sentitis."

[24] Plin. *Ep.* 8.14.13.

[25] Cf. Plin. *Ep.* 2.12.4. Dio (52.32.2-3) advocated that in such cases a member should have a vote only if the defendant was of an equal grade or lower.

[26] Plin. *Ep.* 2.12.5; cf. Seneca, *Ep. Mor.* 66.41.

[27] Plin. *Ep.* 2.11.22.

[28] Cf. Plin. *Ep.* 2.11.6; Tac. *Ann.* 4.30; *Hist.* 2.10.

accordance with the views already expressed,[29] this was not invariably the case. The president declared the result of a vote with the words: "This side seems to be in a majority."[30]

It is natural to ask how long the formal procedure outlined above continued in use for the passage of imperial proposals, all of which were likely to be approved unanimously as a matter of course.[31] In consequence was there perhaps no actual voting on such occasions? Or were members still regularly required to go through the charade of grouping themselves all together on one side of the chamber to register approval? We cannot say for certain. As will appear,[32] it is at least plain enough that by the latter half of the second century separate decrees may no longer have been formulated for individual items put forward by the emperor. Instead a single, brief decree would give general assent. But we just do not know how it was passed at this date, or earlier. It is true that in addressing members M. Aurelius and Commodus can speak of "voting" ("suffragari"),[33] while Dio consistently writes as if decrees were passed thus in his day. Yet the actual procedure which any of them envisaged for such "voting" is still obscure. Herodian[34] and the *Historia Augusta*[35] do suggest instances of formal votes—the accessions of Pertinax and Didius Julianus, for example, and Elagabalus' appointment of Severus Alexander as Caesar. These were especially momentous occasions, however, and it could well be argued that even if members did all move to one side of the chamber in these instances, that is no guarantee of their having done so regularly at other sessions. Thus it remains an open question whether normal voting procedure at some date came to be suspended or modified in the case of certain imperial proposals, or even all of them.

More generally, we do not know whether presidents always relied just upon impressions in taking a vote, or if sometimes an actual count of each side was made once it was seated. By law, at least, it was only the numbers present in the House which had to be recorded in each *senatus consultum*, not the numbers voting on each side, nor individual voters' names. To take a count for the vote on every *sententia* without exception would have

[29] Cf. Plin. *Ep.* 3.4.4.

[30] Seneca, *De Vita Beata* 2.1, "haec pars maior esse videtur." Cf. Tacitus' phrasing in *Ann.* 14.45: "praevaluit tamen pars quae supplicium decernebat."

[31] Naturally many matters—not only those put forward by the emperor—must have been uncontentious, and passed unanimously. In this connection it is interesting that in his *De Notis Iuris* (late first century?) Probus listed an abbreviation for "quid de ea re fieri placeret, de ea re *universi* ita censuerunt" (*FIRA*² II p. 455, with my italics). In fact no extant version of a *senatus consultum* includes this adjective in the formula.

[32] See chap. 8.

[33] No. 125 in list, chap. 15 sect. 5 line 28.

[34] 5.7.4.

[35] *Pertinax* 5.2-6; *Did. Jul.* 3.3; cf. Eutropius, *Brev.* 8.16.

been time-consuming, pointless, and altogether impracticable. That said, the effort was no doubt made when appropriate, as perhaps on the occasion in 17 when Tacitus speaks of an issue being decided "by a few votes."[36] Paradoxically, the only session for which we are offered explicit testimony of a count is the trial of Marius Priscus in 100,[37] when in fact precision should hardly have been necessary, since it is certain that overwhelming support emerged for the motion of the consul designate.[38] So this occasion should warn us both against seeking to draw conclusions from the conspicuous absence of voting figures in surviving sources generally (for which there could just as well be many other reasons) and against conjecturing that our one extant set (400 to 7 in A.D. 26) is merely an estimate. While 400 may look a suspiciously round figure, we have seen elsewhere[39] how the total attendance of which it forms a part is at least entirely plausible, and it could represent an accurate count. Thus the question of whether a count was taken on this occasion, let alone upon others when counting would likewise appear to have been strictly unnecessary, is best left open. Whether there is significance in the point that the emperor was present in person both in 26 and for the trial of Marius Priscus, is equally obscure. Sessions which the emperor attended were, of course, the only ones for which the law did not require a record of attendance to be kept.

So far as is known, voting in the senate was always open in the manner described. Thus we find open voting prescribed in the judicial procedure laid down by the *senatus consultum* of which Augustus sent a copy to Cyrene in 4 B.C.[40] Exceptionally, under Trajan, there was what perhaps turned out to be a short-lived experiment whereby secret ballot was tried at elections as a precaution against excessive personal influence. This method was soon abused by certain members, however, who spoilt their *tabellae* in an offensive fashion—perhaps deliberately.[41] Mommsen[42] thought that Tiberius' outburst during the trial of Granius Marcellus in 15 implied the possibility of secret voting: "se quoque in ea causa laturum sententiam *palam* et iuratum."[43] Here, however, Tiberius is merely referring emphatically to delivery of his *sententia* after the trial; the vote which then

---

[36] *Ann.* 2.51, "paucis suffragiis."

[37] Plin. *Paneg.* 76.2, "consulti omnes atque etiam dinumerati sumus," where in my view "dinumerati" is most naturally taken in the literal sense "counted" (cf. *Ox. Lat. Dict.* s.v. 1a p. 546), not as "reckoned with" (B. Radice in Loeb edition). "Numerantur" in Plin. *Ep.* 2.12.5 remains vague, but can at least admit the possibility of a count being taken.

[38] Plin. *Ep.* 2.11.22. His "etiam" in *Paneg.* 76.2 perhaps hints at this lack of any real need for a count.

[39] Chap. 4 sect. 2 note 112.

[40] *FIRA*² I no. 68 V lines 142-144.

[41] Plin. *Ep.* 3.20; 4.25; see further the introduction to this chapter, note 5.

[42] *St. R.* III. 2. p. 993 n. 3.

[43] Tac. *Ann.* 1.74 with my italics.

followed was a completely separate process.[44] As emperor, Tiberius of course had the right to speak at any point in the *interrogatio*. Cn. Piso, who proceeds to enquire at what point he will deliver his *sententia*, correctly appreciates that Tiberius' view will influence those members left to speak after him. The notion of introducing secret voting to the senate is at least raised explicitly, though not developed, in one of the letters to Caesar attributed to Sallust, and thus ostensibly of late Republican date. But there are strong arguments for regarding it as just a rhetorical exercise, perhaps of the early Principate.[45]

Once a *senatus consultum* was passed, its wording had to be fixed after the meeting, and the text deposited in the *aerarium Saturni*. This task would normally occupy up to perhaps half a dozen members in every case, and constituted an important responsibility.[46] Equally, once passed, a *senatus consultum* could be vetoed by the emperor or by a tribune. The latter's right remained,[47] but, as we might expect, was hardly ever exercised during the Principate. Thrasea Paetus was only sensible to reject Arulenus Rusticus' offer to use it in 66.[48] Strictly, a *senatus consultum* passed irregularly in some respect, or later vetoed, was termed an *auctoritas*.[49]

A session was closed by the president announcing: "We detain you no longer, *patres conscripti*."[50]

26. Delegation of Business

It is clear that much of the senate's work was of a routine, uncontentious nature. Sessions might be long and dull, so that members understandably suffered boredom and frustration. Naturally we might ask whether the House ever chose to delegate the handling of any items to smaller groups which would nonetheless remain responsible to the corporate body. The

[44] Cf. Tac. *Ann.* 14.48-49; Plin. *Ep.* 2.11.19-22. For emphatic use of "palam" elsewhere, cf. Tac. *Ann.* 4.30 and 36.

[45] See *Ep. ad Caes. senem* 2.11.5-7 with discussion, for example, by R. Syme, *Sallust*, California, 1964, Appendix 2, esp. pp. 342-348.

[46] See further chap. 9 sect. 1 note 2. The group of twenty or more which wrote up a decree of October 39 B.C. is quite exceptional, and must reflect the importance attached to the matter concerned: see J. Reynolds, *Aphrodisias and Rome*, no. 8 lines 4-13 with discussion, p. 67.

[47] Cf. Dio 55.3.5.

[48] Tac. *Ann.* 16.26. Dio 57.15.9 may provide an instance of a tribune vetoing a *senatus consultum*, though the passage is not entirely clear.

[49] See Dio 55.3.4-5. At *Ann.* 2.32 it is not clear whether Tacitus means "auctoritas" to be taken in the technical sense (with *Ox. Lat. Dict.* s.v. 4a p. 206), or just informally as, say, "proposal" (with Goodyear ad loc.).

[50] HA, *Marcus* 10.9, "nihil vos moramur, patres conscripti." For Republican practice, cf. Cic. *Ad Q.F.* 2.1.1 = SB 5. Sources commonly use the expression "senatum mittere" or "dimittere" (e.g. Plin. *Ep.* 4.9.22; 9.13.20; Gell. 6.21.2).

answer would seem to be that not only was this seldom done, but that all the known instances except perhaps one concern special problems rather than routine. In fact, such a refusal to delegate responsibility seems characteristic of Roman administrative practice; there is much evidence to show that emperors and governors, for example, dealt personally with the whole range of matters referred to them.[1]

It is true that Augustus' senatorial *consilium* must have considered in advance some, or all, of the items to be raised at full sessions, as we know specifically that it discussed the measure of 4 B.C. which made new arrangements for hearing cases of *repetundae*.[2] It may be that such prior discussion of business could sharpen the quality of debate in the House and reduce its length. Yet it more probably served to stifle the expression of views, as members felt there was little they could do to influence opinions already formed. At least, however, the senatorial *consilium* still had to refer all matters to the House. Only in A.D. 13 did it gain authority to bypass the larger body and enact binding decisions independently. But, as it turned out, there was small opportunity for this major development to be exploited, since the *consilium* was abandoned altogether by Tiberius only a year or so later.[3]

At all times the consuls, as joint presidents of the senate, must have looked over the agenda for meetings beforehand, and no doubt often consulted the emperor, too, in this connection. They would receive applications from members who wished to raise a matter, and from others who sought to appear before the House. In theory, as presidents they had almost complete discretion to choose the agenda as they pleased, though again— very much as we have just seen with the *consilium*—the binding decisions they could take without reference to the House were extremely limited. In all likelihood few presidents wished to act independently anyway. We noted earlier how they were more than ready to be swayed by the House.

We do know of instances where the detailed investigation of complex issues was delegated to the consuls. In 19, as directed by the House, they drew up a *commentarium* concerning the problem of those members of the upper classes who by their degrading activities were thought to be undermining the majesty of the senate. Three years later they were asked to examine the mass of documents on which many Eastern cities rested claims to grant asylum, while in 59 an enquiry into the outbreak of fighting at a gladiatorial show was put in their hands.[4] In all three cases they reported back to the House to enable it to decide what action should be taken.

[1] Cf. F. Millar, *Emperor*, p. 6; G. P. Burton, "Proconsuls, assizes and the administration of justice under the empire," *JRS* 65. 1975. pp. 92-106.

[2] *FIRA*[2] I no. 68 V line 87.

[3] For full discussion of the institution, see J. Crook, *Consilium Principis*, chap. 2.

[4] No. 22 in list, chap. 15 sect. 5 lines 4-6; Tac. *Ann.* 3.63; 14.17. For comparable Republican instances, note for example, R. K. Sherk, *Roman Documents*, nos. 12 and 23.

Though we hear about the appointment of several committees composed of senators, it would seem that in each case a special task was to be fulfilled. Not one was a standing committee which relieved the House of regular, routine business. Thus altogether during the first century five boards of senators were established at different times to deal with pressing difficulties of public finance.[5] For a review in A.D. 4 Augustus nominated ten senators, three of whom were then drawn by lot to examine the qualifications of their fellow members.[6] During Tiberius' reign two committees relieved unusual difficulties—one commissioned in 20 to resolve confusion and fear produced by the *Lex Papia Poppaea*, and the other to distribute papyrus during a shortage.[7] A further board was elected in 16 to recover lost public records and to copy others made illegible by time. Another committee did similar work after the civil war of 69.[8] Finally, at the end of the first century, it was senators who were commissioned to buy and distribute the land granted by Nerva to impoverished Romans.[9]

We might imagine that annual arbitration of market prices by the senate—as advocated by Tiberius—would have been delegated to a committee, which could regularly have relieved the House of a routine obligation. But so far as we know, this proposal failed.[10] There remains the procedure under the *senatus consultum* of 4 B.C. mentioned above, whereby a panel of five senators would be chosen to hear provincial claims for money extorted by governors.[11] Since up to this date there appears to have been no change in the Republican arrangement whereby such cases went to the *quaestio de repetundis*, the work of the senate was in fact not affected. But, as we shall be seeing in more detail later,[12] the procedure was modified not many years after its introduction, so that all charges of provincial misgovernment against senators were heard by the full senate, and only the assessment of compensation due to injured provincials after a conviction continued to be referred to a panel. In this limited respect, therefore, the senate did then delegate business to a committee. Yet prosecutions for *repetundae* can hardly be considered regular, recurrent items, while in all likelihood a fresh panel was constituted in each instance. There was no standing committee for the purpose. Thus in general the senate maintained its characteristically Roman reluctance to delegate, and as a result members had to endure the transaction of much time-consuming, routine business

[5] See chap. 12 sect. 2.
[6] Dio 55.13.3.
[7] Tac. *Ann*. 3.28; Plin. *NH* 13.89.
[8] Dio 57.16.2; Tac. *Hist*. 4.40.
[9] Dio 68.2.1.
[10] Suet. *Tib*. 34.
[11] *FIRA*[2] I no. 68 V lines 104ff.
[12] Chap. 16 sect. 1.

by the whole House. At least, however, they could ensure thereby that the risk of encroachment upon its prerogative, such as had occurred in Augustus' reign, was for ever afterwards securely eliminated.

27. Conclusion

It is frustrating that there remains not even an outline record of just one complete session to aid an evaluation of senatorial procedure. To reach any conclusions from such other evidence as does survive may therefore be rash, but some attempt should be made, and attention can be drawn to certain features at least. First, even though senatorial procedure may have been seen as a norm by the wide range of other bodies in the Roman world which copied it closely,[1] to modern readers its whole character is likely to seem alien. Our recommendation might be to offer the president stronger authority (if only for curbing prolixity and irrelevance on the part of speakers); to abandon the tedious canvassing of members' opinions in rank order in favor of allowing the president to invite speeches at will from those who sought to make them; to grant private members some guarantee of having their business considered; and to modify the cumbrous system of taking a separate vote upon each *sententia* judged worthy of consideration by the president; in short, to bring the workings of the Roman senate much closer to those of a modern parliamentary institution. It is true that during our period innovation in certain areas—the order in which members were called, for example, or the manner in which votes were taken—was suggested, and there was even some experimentation. But the remarkable fact is that no such novelty was retained, and that despite all the other changes and pressures faced by the senate as the Principate developed, the traditional character of procedure was proudly upheld. Today it may indeed seem baffling that so large an assembly could function effectively, not only in view of its time-consuming procedures, but also in an age before the invention of printing, where drafts of measures could not be circulated to individuals in advance, and even the most complex matters might need to be carried in the head.[2] Yet this is partly, as has been noted, the result of the loss of the right type of evidence, and partly a reflection of modern failure or inability to acknowledge just how very great the differences are between the Roman senate and modern parliamentary institutions. That said, however, the senate can have been no

---

[1] In particular, Western city councils (see R. K. Sherk, *The Municipal Decrees of the Roman West*, Buffalo, 1970, esp. chap. 3) and *collegia* (see, for example, *ILS* 7216-7218, 7220-7221; *FIRA*[2] III no. 40); for church councils, see Extended Note B.

[2] It is thus no surprise to find members taking writing material with them into the chamber: see chap. 9 sect. 3 note 67.

exception to the rule that all large bodies must pass a substantial number of items "on the nod" if they are to make headway with their business. It should certainly have been rare for the authorization of gladiators beyond the permitted number to be queried, for example, or for an application for a market license to be contested. So even though much is often made of how certain imperial proposals were hardly discussed, this must in fact have been equally true of a much wider range of business. By no means all items would demand an *interrogatio*.

Finally, since Pliny's descriptions give the impression that in its idiosyncratic way senatorial procedure was functioning reasonably enough at the beginning of the second century, there is the puzzle of why it was that later in the same century the significant changes discussed in the next chapter were gradually introduced. As will be seen, these were alterations that really could just as well have been made at any stage during the previous fifty years or so. In view of the consistent respect for the senate's dignity shown by Nerva and all his successors to M. Aurelius, pressure for change can hardly have come from these emperors. Rather, the corporate body must itself have been responsible for the shift. It would thus be especially instructive to learn contemporaries' views of the developments, insofar as they were aware of them; as it is, however, we may only note that no comment is passed in what survives of the correspondence of our one witness, Fronto.

8

PROCEDURAL CHANGE IN THE
SECOND CENTURY

The difficulties of discussing procedural change in the senate during the second century have already been mentioned at the beginning of the previous chapter. In particular, from the reign of Hadrian to 193 our evidence is rarely more than scrappy, so that it is impossible to trace the evolution of changes which unquestionably developed in this period. The best we may do is to concentrate upon two new features.

The more striking of these is the way in which an imperial *oratio* to the House, rather than any *senatus consultum*, now frequently comes to be cited by jurists as a statement of law. At the same time, too, the *interrogatio* was evidently curtailed on many occasions when the emperor put forward business. The imperial oration would be heard; one senator would be called upon, and he would propose briefly the adoption of all the measures sought. In such an instance this is all that remained of the *interrogatio* proper. The measures would then be approved by some means, though we cannot say whether a formal vote continued to be taken when its outcome was a foregone conclusion.

It is fair to guess that the whole procedure developed from the long-standing impossibility of considering imperial proposals freely. From early in the Principate it would regularly have been embarrassing to attempt intelligent discussion of such business in the knowledge that approval must follow in any event. The problem had been tackled by Augustus,[1] and it may have been this issue which likewise concerned the mid first century speaker whose words are preserved on papyrus: "For, Conscript Fathers, it is most unbecoming to the high dignity of this order here that one member only, the consul designate, should deliver a *sententia*, and that drawn word for word from the *relatio* of the consuls, while others utter the one word *adsentior*, and then when they depart say 'Well, we spoke.' "[2] Although

---

[1] Suet. *Aug.* 35.

[2] *FIRA*[2] I no. 44 col. III lines 17-22, "Mini[me] enim dec[o]r[um] est, p(atres) c(onscripti), ma[iestati] huius or[di]nis hic un[um ta]ntummodo consule[m] designatum [de]scriptam ex relatio[n]e consulum a[d ver]bum dicere senten[tia]m, ceteros unu[m] verbum dic[ere]: 'adse[nti]or,' deinde c[um e]xierint 'di[ximus].' "

Domitian's reign had been notorious for sessions of the same meaningless character, if Pliny³ is to be believed, the testimony of his *Letters* confirms that in meetings under Nerva and Trajan open debate continued. Yet Trajan's successor Hadrian is the earliest emperor whose addresses to the senate (*orationes*)⁴ are cited by legal writers as statements of law.⁵ Such citations from the *orationes* of M. Aurelius are particularly abundant.

The next available non-legal evidence likewise relates to the latter part of M. Aurelius' reign, unless note be taken of the parody in Apuleius, *Metamorphoses*.⁶ Here the meeting at which Jupiter arranges for Psyche to enter heaven and marry Cupid is surely meant to recall the Roman senate,⁷ and it may not be entirely frivolous to reflect that the session evidently consisted of a speech from Jupiter and nothing else! Fiction aside, from the reply which M. Aurelius and Commodus sent jointly in 177 to a request of Miletus in connection with celebrating games, it is clear that formal ratification of imperial proposals had developed by that date:

Having received your message about the festival, we thought it fitting to consult the sacred assembly of the senate, to gain its agreement to your request. There were many other matters to speak to it about too. Since, therefore, it did not ratify individually each item which we raised, but its decree was instead a joint, collective one about the matters on which we had spoken that day, we have attached to this answer for your information the section of the speech delivered by us relevant to your request.⁸

The prevalence of the same practice is implied in the contemporary oration of the first senator to speak after an imperial request that steps be taken to reduce the expense of gladiatorial shows in various ways:

Moreover, although many think that everything which our mighty emperors have referred to us should be proposed in only one succinct motion, nevertheless, with your permission, senators, I shall deal with each point individually, taking over

---

³ *Paneg.* 76.3-4.

⁴ This is the standard Latin term. For Greek equivalents note ὁρατίων (Modestinus, *Dig.* 27.1.1.4); ὁ ῥηθεὶς λόγος (M. Aurelius and Commodus, *AE* 1977. 801 line 18).

⁵ For a list of the *orationes* by Hadrian and other emperors of our period cited thus, see chap. 15 sect. 4.

⁶ 6. 22-23.

⁷ Note the references to *Lex Julia*; fine; "sedes sublimis"; "dei conscripti Musarum albo."

⁸ P. Herrmann, "Eine Kaiserurkunde der Zeit Marc Aurels aus Milet," *Istanb. Mitt.* 25. 1975. pp. 149-166 = *AE* 1977. 801, Ἐντυχόντες οἷς ἐπεστείλατε περὶ τοῦ ἀγῶνος προσήκειν ἡγησάμεθα διαλεχθῆναι πρὸς τὴν ἱερὰν σύγκλητον βουλήν, ὅπως συγχωρήσειεν ὑμῖν ὅπερ ἠξιοῦτε. Ἐδέησεν δὲ καὶ περὶ ἑτέρων πλειόνων ποιήσασθαι πρὸς αὐτὴν τοὺς λόγους. Ἐπεὶ τοίνυν οὐκ ἰδίᾳ καθ' ἕκαστον ὧν εἴπομεν ἐπεκύρωσεν, ἀλλὰ κοινῇ καὶ συλλήβδην περὶ τῶν λεχθέντων ὑφ' ἡμῶν ἐκείνης τῆς ἡμέρας τὸ δόγμα ἐγένετο, αὐτοῦ τοῦ ῥηθέντος λόγου τὸ συντεῖνον μέρος πρὸς τὴν ὑμετέραν ἀξίωσιν ὅπως εἰδείητε ὑποτέτακται τῇ ἀποκρίσει ταύτῃ. See further chap. 14 sect. 2 note 87.

from the most sacred oration the very same words to clarify the motion, so that there be no room anywhere for misinterpretation.[9]

Two features of this *sententia prima* are notable. First, the senator does indeed take the trouble to discuss each point individually at some length, even if in fact he adds little of his own. Piganiol[10] argued that amendments to the imperial oration are suggested in three places. Since the publication of his article, however, the texts of these documents have been significantly improved, and it is perhaps only the second of his suggestions which still seems really convincing, namely, that the senator does offer his own advice about the fixing of prices for gladiators in smaller, or less wealthy, cities.[11] As the editors note in the most up-to-date study of the inscription,[12] the senator may also be putting forward his own views in lines 59-61 and 62-63 (where the stone breaks off), but in all instances the divergence from the imperial oration remains modest. It is still an open question, of course, whether any of his suggestions were adopted in the *senatus consultum* as eventually passed. We also do not know what further opinions, if any, were delivered later on this occasion. A second striking feature of the *sententia prima* is its separation from the imperial *oratio* by an interval sufficient for a rumor of the proposals to reach Gaul and for a favorable reaction to be reported back.[13] Such a delay in the consideration of imperial proposals is unexpected, and it is impossible to do more than speculate about whether it occurred on imperial or senatorial initiative.[14]

In the terrifying atmosphere under Septimius Severus and Caracalla it is entirely credible that discussion of imperial proposals might sometimes be muted, and quite apart from the legal writers' continued citation of imperial *orationes*, the absence of debate is borne out by Caracalla's complaint in a letter of 215 from Antioch: "He found fault with the senate, declaring that in addition to being lazy in other respects members did not assemble with any eagerness and did not give their opinions individually."[15] There was evidently no more than one speech in response to the request of the *Quindecimviri Sacris Faciundis* in 203 for senatorial spon-

---

[9] J. H. Oliver and R.E.A. Palmer, "Minutes of an Act of the Roman Senate," *Hesperia* 24. 1955. pp. 329-349, *Aes Ital.* lines 26-29, "quamquam autem non nulli arbitrentur de omnibus quae ad nos maximi principes rettulerunt una et succincta sententia censendum, tamen, si vos probatis, singula specialiter persequar, verbis ipsis ex oratione sanctissima ad lucem sententiae translatis, ne qua ex parte pravis interpretationibus sit loc⟨u⟩s."

[10] A. Piganiol, "Les *trinci* Gaulois, gladiateurs consacrés," *Rev. Et. Anc.* 22. 1920. pp. 283-290.

[11] *Aes Ital.* lines 46-55.

[12] *Hesperia* 24. 1955. p. 339.

[13] Lines 13-19.Compare how adjournment of the hearing of Marius Priscus' case was said to produce "rumors and expectations" (Plin. *Ep.* 2.11.10).

[14] Cf. *FIRA²* I no. 44 col. III lines 11-15.

[15] Dio 77.20.1.

sorship of the Secular Games.[16] Yet of course this particular occasion was a solemn one steeped in tradition, where full discussion of the request would hardly have been expected. As it is, the single speech is painstaking, not merely "succinct."

Despite the major change which curtailment of the *interrogatio* represented, it is important to recognize at the same time that discussion in the traditional style was never wholly superseded. On appropriate occasions it did continue, especially when the fear of an autocrat was removed. Various explanations of a delay in the consideration of imperial proposals for reducing the cost of gladiatorial shows can be conjectured. But the most likely one is a deliberate effort to allow members time for thinking over the matter. From our point of view the provision of this opportunity is surely a more significant feature than the first speaker's general agreement with the co-emperors. In this instance the senate was neither expected nor required simply to offer immediate, uncritical ratification of imperial proposals. The painstaking character of the discussion when the general reaction of the House was certain to be favorable can even be seen as rather impressive; after all, nobody in the latter part of the second century would have wished to reject the offer of a reduction in the expenses to be borne by office-holders throughout the empire! The fact that in this particular instance there was sure to be widespread support for the emperor's intentions should strike a note of caution for those who would wish to draw sweeping conclusions from this set of documents about the general character of contemporary senatorial proceedings. We still have no clue as to how the House would have handled any more controversial proposals made by M. Aurelius. It does seem to have offered immediate ratification on the day when the co-emperors put forward the uncontentious request of Miletus for a small concession of a type already granted to other cities. In the imperial reply to the city the explanation of the senate's action may just reflect Marcus' characteristic desire for meticulous clarification of every point. Yet equally it could suggest that such ratification was not the invariable, well-known practice of the House, so that it would merit explanation.[17]

At other times items raised by magistrates rather than by the emperor could presumably call for discussion. In this connection we may note the

---

[16] G. B. Pighi, *De Ludis Saecularibus*, pp. 142-144. I. lines 25-48.

[17] The argument might be strengthened if the phrase ἐκείνης τῆς ἡμέρας in note 8 above were taken with the words following it ("its decree that day was instead a joint, collective one. . . . "—but would not necessarily always be such). This is the interpretation of Herrmann himself (translation, p. 152) and of the editors of *AE* 1977. 801. All the same, it is probably better to follow W. Williams (*JRS* 66. 1976. p. 80) in taking the phrase in the natural way, with the words preceding it, as translated above.

claim of the *Historia Augusta*[18] that M. Aurelius would attend regularly even if he had no *relatio* to make; he must have come not least to hear what others had to say. There was debate, as there had to be, at the meeting to consider the collapse of Didius Julianus' rule in 193,[19] and again at the sessions following the death of the Gordians in 238.[20] Elsewhere we hear of Septimius Severus arranging for a member to frame a decree;[21] and certainly, if the story can be in any way credited, it was not that emperor who prompted a resolution in 196/7 praising Clodius Celsinus, a relative of his rival Albinus.[22] Though fragmentary, a passage in Dio[23] relating to 217, when Macrinus was emperor and absent from Rome, specifies that senators were asked individually about a matter. Finally, if the whole episode is not just more fiction, the *Historia Augusta*[24] represents Elagabalus introducing his grandmother to the senate, where she duly delivered her *sententia*.

In considering how far debate continued it should be stressed that the jurists give no support to the commonly accepted notion of a smooth transition from decision-taking by means of *relatio, interrogatio,* and *senatus consultum*, to curt adoption of the imperial *oratio* as a statement of law in itself.[25] Rather the picture which emerges from the surviving extracts of their writings is notably more complex. It confirms the impression that while discussion of uncontroversial business may often have been abandoned, it could nonetheless continue for greater or more contentious issues. As already mentioned, the jurists do indeed cite imperial *orationes* from Hadrian's time onwards as statements of law without more ado. Yet into the third century they continue to cite *senatus consulta* alongside them without mention of any imperial *oratio*.[26] Most striking of all, however, is the considerable number of measures for which they refer both to the imperial *oratio* and to the subsequent *senatus consultum*. Datable instances of this practice are found from 129 in the reign of Hadrian right up to nearly the last known occasion when a legislative matter was put before the House—by Caracalla in 206.[27] As one quotation from Macer shows,[28]

---

[18] *Marcus* 10.7.
[19] Cf. Dio 74.17.4; Herodian 2.12.5; HA, *Did. Jul.* 7.2; note also 6.6.
[20] Herodian 7.10.2-3 and 11.3.
[21] Dio 75.2.2.
[22] HA, *Sev.* 11.3. For strong arguments against acceptance, however, see T. D. Barnes, "A senator from Hadrumetum, and three others," *BHAC* 1968/9. pp. 47-58 at pp. 51-52.
[23] 78.19.4-5.
[24] *Elagab.* 12.3.
[25] See, for example, H. F. Jolowicz and B. Nicholas, *Historical Introduction to the Study of Roman Law* (ed. 3), Cambridge, 1972, p. 365.
[26] Note *SC Gaetulicianum*, no. 165 in list, chap. 15 sect. 5.
[27] See nos. 81, 100, 108, 111-113, 128-130, 134-135 in list.
[28] *Dig.* 48.21.2.1 and no. 111 in list.

such *senatus consulta* could clearly be full resolutions, not just brief, general acceptances of the emperor's views. Lack of parallel texts makes it impossible to determine whether the senate's provisions were identical to those of the imperial *oratio* in every case. Adoption of the emperor's wishes can mostly be expected. Indeed it is sometimes specifically confirmed,[29] and altogether it might be assumed from the instances in some jurists' discussions where citations seem to alternate between *oratio* and *senatus consultum* quite indiscriminately.[30] Yet for all we know, the *senatus consulta* may have incorporated modest additions or changes such as those advocated by the speaker of the *sententia prima* of 177 discussed above. It is conceivably significant that when choosing titles for commentaries Gaius and Paulus both decided upon *Ad senatus consultum Orphitianum*, although M. Aurelius' *oratio* on the measure was also available and was even cited by the former.[31] By contrast, in two other instances Paulus chose to head commentaries *Ad orationem* of the emperors concerned, though the relevant *senatus consulta* were again available and were cited by him.[32]

In the absence of parallel texts it is difficult to estimate the degree to which these choices by the jurists have significance. It is equally difficult to draw conclusions from the manner in which emperors refer to those measures for which we know that an *oratio* and a *senatus consultum* were both available. The scatter of such measures and of references to them is highly random; it may be that little weight should be placed on what are arguably no more than stylistic quirks of individual emperors.[33] Yet with all this understood, it is at least interesting that in the overwhelming majority of such instances, with not a single exception before Gordian,[34] *senatus consulta* are cited rather than *orationes*.[35] In fact on one occasion Caracalla even refers to the corresponding *senatus consultum* instead of to the *oratio* which his own father made.[36]

In claiming that by the late second century emperors expected their proposals to be ratified without discussion, and thus framed their *orationes* accordingly, scholars have often drawn attention to the opening of a quo-

[29] Note especially with reference to no. 129 in list, Paulus, *Dig.* 23.2.16 pr.: "Oratione divi Marci cavetur, ut, si senatoris filia libertino nupsisset, nec nuptiae essent: quam et senatus consultum secutum est"; Papinian, *Frag. Vat.* 294.2.

[30] For example, discussion of no. 130 in list by Paulus and Tryphoninus (23.2.16 pr. and 67.1-4); Ulpian (*Dig.* 23.1.16; 24.1.3.1) on no. 129.

[31] *Dig.* 38.17.9.

[32] See list of commentaries, chap. 15 sect. 2.

[33] Note how Diocletian and Maximian evidently refer to no. 134 in list as *senatus consultum* and *oratio* respectively on successive days! (*CJ* 5.71.8-9).

[34] I leave out of account the letter of M. Aurelius and Commodus to Miletus, where we know that the senate's decree was brief and general.

[35] See Extended Note H.

[36] *CJ* 5.71.1, citing no. 134 in list.

tation from Septimius Severus in 195: "Moreover, Conscript Fathers, I shall forbid *tutores* and *curatores*. . . ."[37] The uncompromising use of a future indicative here has been compared to Hadrian's conciliatory appeal in 129: "Conscript Fathers, consider whether it is not more equitable that . . . ."[38] The difference in tone between these two quotations is indeed unmistakable. But it can hardly serve to support the notion that by the late second century emperors had ceased to have regard for senatorial views. Other passages suggest a more reasonable approach and need to be taken into account equally. Elsewhere in the same speech of 195, for example, Severus adopts a persuasive tone: "This difficulty will be met, Conscript Fathers, if you approve, by . . . [the following action]."[39] With the same tone Papinian writes of proposals by Severus and Caracalla in 206: "Our mighty emperors advocated these proposals, and the senate thus gave its approval."[40] The style in which Ulpian describes the introduction of the same measure is also strikingly traditional: "By the speech he made in the senate before the death of his father, the divine Severus, our emperor Antoninus Augustus was the instigator of the senate's resolution in the consulship of Fulvius Aemilianus and Nummius Albinus that there should be some relaxation in the rigor of the law."[41]

In none of these passages is there an assumption of blunt disregard for the opinions of the House on the part of the emperor. Naturally it is awkward to draw conclusions when our knowledge of the relevant speeches is so slight; but modern claims about the tone which imperial *orationes* had adopted by the late second century have perhaps been too sweeping. In any event, it is obvious that much would always depend upon the approach of individual emperors and the nature of the business in hand. Even M. Aurelius, noted for his painstaking tact towards the House, could use a future indicative in a certain context,[42] while arguably among the least conciliatory of any surviving speeches to the senate in our period are two attributed to Claudius as far back as the mid first century.[43] The

[37] Ulpian, *Dig*. 27.9.1.2, discussing no. 134 in list: "praeterea, patres conscripti, interdicam tutoribus et curatoribus. . . ."

[38] Paulus, *Dig*. 5.3.22, discussing no. 81 in list: "Dispicite, patres conscripti, numquid sit aequius. . . ." For another tactful appeal to the House by Hadrian, note Charisius, *Art. Gramm*. p. 287 Barwick, no. 102 in list.

[39] *Frag. Vat*. 158, "Cui rei obviam ibitur, patres conscripti, si censueritis, ut. . . ."

[40] *Frag. Vat*. 294.2, ". . . maximi principes nostri suaserunt et ita senatus censuit." Cf. Fronto, *De Eloq*. 2.7 = p. 136 H, "nam Caesarum est in senatu quae e re sunt suadere. . . ."

[41] *Dig*. 24.1.32 pr. ". . . imperator noster Antoninus Augustus ante excessum divi Severi patris sui oratione in senatu habita auctor fuit senatui censendi Fulvio Aemiliano et Nummio Albino consulibus, ut aliquid laxaret ex iuris rigore."

[42] Cf. Ulpian, *Dig*. 49.4.1.7, discussing no. 124 in list.

[43] *FIRA*[2] I no. 44; attribution discussed in Appendix 4.

frequency with which the speaker resorts to the imperative here is unparalleled, while the hectoring tone in which comment is called for sounds anything but inviting.

Because Hadrian is the earliest emperor whose *orationes* are cited by the jurists, there is a temptation to conjecture some notable shift in the character of the senate's proceedings during his time. Yet further signs of such a change are absent, and altogether there is no sound basis for the notion, especially when it may be sheer accident that his *orationes* are the first to be cited. Since it was as much the case before his time, as after it, that the House would broadly accept imperial proposals, the surprise is rather that not a single juristic reference to any *orationes* by earlier emperors remains extant. Some of their speeches were certainly in circulation,[44] and we even find a legal point in Augustus' *oratio de statu municipiorum* referred to by Frontinus[45] in a work on land-surveying composed at the end of the first century. Moreover, it is clear that the jurists considered any statement by an emperor to carry authority. Thus in one instance Paulus,[46] for example, cites as a precedent merely what Augustus said ("dixit"), while Ulpian[47] can refer to what he wrote "libro decimo de vita sua." Equally, Macer[48] takes over from Tarrutenus Paternus a quotation of Augustus' rules of military discipline. It is likely to be pure chance that citations of imperial *orationes* before Hadrian's time are missing from the jurists. The same may perhaps be said for the even more puzzling absence of references to statements made in the House by Antoninus Pius. Dozens of his rescripts and other decisions are cited.[49] We know that he addressed the senate: a single *oratio* by him is even cited by Diocletian and Maximian.[50] But all such references are absent from the jurists.[51]

To pass to the second development, scholars have commonly maintained that in the course of the second century, along with curtailment of the *interrogatio*, the traditional form of voting in the senate came to be superseded simply by acclamation.[52] It is true that more is heard of acclamations in the senate from this time, so that we do need to enquire into both their

---

[44] See chap. 9 sect. 3 note 55.

[45] *De Controversiis*, p. 7 Thulin; no. 18 in list.

[46] *Dig.* 40.12.23.2.

[47] *Dig.* 48.24.1.

[48] *Dig.* 49.16.12.1.

[49] See G. Gualandi, *Legislazione imperiale e giurisprudenza* I, Milan, 1963, pp. 58-102.

[50] *CJ* 10.53.4.

[51] An ingenious solution to the puzzle might be to speculate that some of the numerous undated *orationes* attributed to M. Aurelius were actually delivered on Antoninus' behalf during the latter's reign. But no matter who delivered them, they are still likely to have been recorded as *orationes* of the reigning emperor, not of any deputy.

[52] See, for example, M. Hammond, *The Antonine Monarchy*, p. 259.

nature and the extent to which they superseded voting in the passage of decrees.

If "acclamation" is to be defined not just as a loud outburst of applause, but as, say, the "measured, rhythmical cadences" with which the people of Rome cheered Nero's musicianship,[53] then its introduction to the senate and development there are hard to trace. On the one hand, there is no question that groups of Romans—especially soldiers, for example, or spectators at games or shows—had long been accustomed to shouting words in unison, and to "acclaiming" the emperor when he was seen in public.[54] On the other hand, it is also clear that at sessions senators had always expressed their feelings volubly. In particular, it was from these reactions that the president had traditionally determined whether issues mentioned should be pursued or not.[55] And since "acclamation" and similar terms have as vague a meaning in Latin as they do in English,[56] a problem results in determining how early it was that "acclamation" in the senate became the "rhythmical, measured cadences" which the *Historia Augusta* reports from there on the death of Commodus, for example: "Let the parricide be dragged down. We beg, Augustus, that the parricide be dragged down. This we beg, that the parricide be dragged down. Listen, Caesar: to the lions with informers. Listen, Caesar: to the lions with Speratus. Good fortune to the victory of the Roman people. Good fortune to the loyalty of the troops. Good fortune to the loyalty of the Praetorians. Good fortune to the Praetorian cohorts."[57]

Suetonius[58] implies that the senate might have chosen to hail Augustus *pater patriae* "by acclamation" in 2 B.C., though it is impossible to tell how formal a salute that might have involved. Similarly we cannot determine exactly how members expressed their demand on Augustus' death, as recorded by Tacitus ("conclamant patres corpus ad rogum umeris sena-

---

[53] Tac. *Ann.* 16.4, "certis modis plausuque composito"; cf. Dio 74.2.3.

[54] Cf., for example, Tac. *Hist.* 1.32 and 78; Suet. *Dom.* 13. In general A. Cameron, *Circus Factions: Blues and Greens at Rome and Byzantium*, Oxford, 1976, chap. 7 and pp. 231-232.

[55] For the expression of strong feelings in the Republic, cf. for example, Livy 29.16.3; 30.21.10; 42.3; Sallust, *Catil.* 48.5; Cic. *Ad Fam.* 10.16.1 = SB 404.

[56] Equally, *acclamatio* would appear to have no particular equivalent in contemporary Greek sources (no entry in H. J. Mason, *Greek Terms for Roman Institutions*).

[57] *Commod.* 18-19, quoting 18.9-11. As argued below, it is possible that there were formal acclamations on an occasion such as this (cf. *Pert.* 5.1), though it should hardly be thought that the *Historia Augusta* preserves their form accurately. For other acclamations in HA, cf. *Avid. Cass.* 12; *Macrinus* 2.4; *Sev. Alex.* 6, 12, 56.9; *Maximin.* 16, 26; *Gord.* 11; *Max. Balb.* 2 (all unreliable records). *Epit. de Caes.* 18.6 records favorable acclamations on the death of Pertinax. In general see O. Hirschfeld, "Die römische Staatszeitung und die Akklamationen im Senat" in *Kleine Schriften*, pp. 682-702; B. Baldwin, "Acclamations in the *Historia Augusta*," *Athenaeum* 59. 1981. pp. 138-149.

[58] *Aug.* 58.

torum ferendum''),[59] just as we cannot tell the form of its reaction to a proposal by Thrasea Paetus in 62 ("magno adsensu celebrata sententia''),[60] or to a speech by Montanus early in 70 ("tanto cum adsensu senatus auditus est Montanus ut spem caperet Helvidius . . .'').[61] The nature of the *adsensio* (after a plea by envoys) which Pliny mentions as common in the early second century presents the same problem: "secuta est senatus clarissima adsensio, quae solet decreta praecurrere.''[62] Most difficult of all to assess, perhaps, is Fronto's report of a speech he made in 143: "What ears men have nowadays! What taste in judging of speeches! You can learn from our Aufidius what shouts of applause were roused in my speech, and with what a chorus of approval were greeted the words 'in those days every bust was decorated with patrician insignia'; but when, comparing a noble with a plebeian race, I said 'as if one were to think the flame kindled on a pyre and on an altar to be the same because both alike give light,' at this a few murmurs were heard.''[63]

In none of these cases cited above is there specific indication that the applause was more than informal. In two instances, however, Suetonius (who was not himself a senator) mentions what would appear to have been orchestrated acclamations, uttered in unison. He reports that after a letter from Nero against Vindex had been read out in the senate, "conclamatum est ab universis: 'Tu facies, Auguste!' ''[64] He also describes how Domitian on his death was lacerated by the senate: "contumeliosissimo atque acerbissimo adclamationum genere.''[65]

Pliny's *Panegyricus*, delivered in September 100, refers more fully to "acclamations" than any other source in our period. He makes it clear that the senate had expressed itself in this way before Trajan's time, though he claims[66] that previously acclamations had never been preserved in official records. Pliny uses a variety of terms which are not carefully distinguished, and are perhaps not meant to be—"acclamationes," "adsensus,"[67] "clamores,"[68] "consensus,"[69] "exclamationes."[70] Some of the

---

[59] *Ann.* 1.8. Since the use of language is the point at issue here, this passage, along with certain others below, is quoted only in the original.

[60] Tac. *Ann.* 15.22.

[61] Tac. *Hist.* 4.43.

[62] *Ep.* 3.4.4; cf. 4.9.18 below.

[63] *Ad M. Caes.* 1.9.1 = p. 17 H. For discussion of this obscure fragment, probably delivered in the senate, see E. J. Champlin, *Fronto and Antonine Rome*, pp. 88-90.

[64] *Nero* 46.

[65] *Dom.* 23.

[66] 75.2.

[67] E.g. 71.6.

[68] E.g. 73.1.

[69] E.g. 95.2.

[70] E.g. 72.5.

acclamations were conceivably orchestrated. He can describe how it was the whole senate which cried to Trajan "Haec faciat, haec audiat,"[71] and which hailed him on election day in 100 as "Tanto maior, tanto augustior!"[72] and as "O te felicem!"[73]

That said, however, it is perhaps misconceived to make the easy general assumption that an acclamation claimed to have been uttered by "all" was most likely to have been formally orchestrated; there are instances where the shouts of "all" were more probably spontaneous.[74] In the *Panegyricus* Pliny does not explain whether the whole senate likewise joined in other acclamations quoted—"Crede nobis, crede tibi" and "O nos felices."[75] Perhaps in these cases the expressions were in fact uttered by individuals at random. Pliny does not report them with such precision, though he does mention in passing "those acclamations which have no time for artifice."[76] He is more exact elsewhere when describing his attack on Publicius Certus (as yet unnamed) and the reaction to it: "There was a general outcry against me, 'Let us know whose case it is that you are raising out of order.' 'Who is being put on trial before a *relatio*?' 'Let us survivors remain unharmed!' "[77]

It is difficult to believe that certain other acclamations mentioned in the *Panegyricus* were necessarily orchestrated. Would the expressions of joy have been so formal when the names of sponsors for candidates at elections were read out, or when the designation of a suffect consul like Pliny himself was announced?[78] In such instances the expressions were surely as informal as those which greeted a popular *sententia* were likely to have been—as on this occasion mentioned by Pliny in the *Letters*: "Caepio's proposal was carried; in fact on rising to speak he was greeted with the acclamation which is usually given when a speaker resumes his seat."[79] The acclamation of Tuscilius Nominatus by a few members must likewise have been quite informal.[80]

The adulatory tone and rhetorical style of the *Panegyricus* make it an untrustworthy guide to the character of normal senatorial procedure at the beginning of the second century. Moreover, the principal context in which

[71] 2.8.
[72] 71.4.
[73] 74.1; cf. 2.8.
[74] Cf. Suet. *Aug*. 37; Dio 58.10.7.
[75] 74.2 and 4.
[76] 3.1.
[77] *Ep*. 9.13.7, ". . . undique mihi reclamari. Alius: 'Sciamus, quis sit de quo extra ordinem referas,' alius: 'Quis est ante relationem reus?' alius: 'Salvi simus, qui supersumus.' "
[78] 71.6; 95.2.
[79] *Ep*. 4.9.18, "praevaluit sententia Caepionis, quin immo consurgenti ei ad censendum acclamatum est, quod solet residentibus"; cf. 3.4.4 above.
[80] Plin. *Ep*. 5.13.3.

Pliny mentions acclamations in this work is an election day where the emperor was present. In fact it was the first such session attended by Trajan as emperor, and with the memory of Domitian still green, the atmosphere was no doubt tense; members were more eager than ever to please. By contrast, the sessions described in the *Letters* cover a wider range of business and are more matter-of-fact; in addition, the emperor seems to be present only once—at a trial.[81] In all these accounts there is no reference to formal, orchestrated acclamations, nor any sign that decrees were passed by such means rather than by formal vote.[82] The most that Pliny can be said to show perhaps, is that in his day formal, orchestrated acclamations in the senate were reserved for the honor of the emperor, on certain of the infrequent occasions when he was present.

Even for the late second and early third centuries, the end of our period, sound evidence of formal acclamations in the senate remains thin. The clearest example comes from the contemporary member, Dio, and relates to praise of Septimius Severus, presumably at a meeting: "The senate, while chanting his praises, once went so far as to shout out these words: 'All do all things well, since you rule well.' "[83] Later, in writing of the death of Caracalla in 217, Dio relates the following incident: "Some thought that Antoninus had foretold his own end, since in the last letter which he sent to the senate he said 'Cease praying that I may be emperor for one hundred years'; for from the beginning of his reign this cry was always raised to him, and this was the first and only time that he had found fault with it. So while he intended merely to rebuke them for praying for the impossible, in fact he was foretelling that he would not rule any longer at all."[84] These passages may be evidence for formal acclamations, but nonetheless they are still only praises or prayers. Decrees are not passed by this means.

We cannot tell whether it is a formal acclamation to which Herodian refers when describing Pertinax's entry to the senate at the beginning of 193: "as soon as he appeared all with one accord greeted him as Augustus and hailed him emperor."[85] Dio, who was present on this occasion, is

---

[81] *Ep.* 2.11.10.

[82] Sherwin-White (*Pliny*, p. 376) sees the request of Homullus at *Ep.* 6.19.3 as "an early stage in the development of passing a *SC.* by *acclamatio*, without a formal debate and vote. . . . The informally expressed opinions . . . lead to a regular proposal." For such opinions he refers to "voces" in sect. 1. In fact "voces" merely seems a loose way of referring to the electoral regulation passed by the senate on an earlier occasion, while in any case Homullus was hardly pressing for the passage of a *senatus consultum*; he was just requesting the consuls to act, which they did. For "voces" used likewise loosely to mean "speeches," "proposals," cf. Tac. *Ann.* 4.42.

[83] 76.6.2.

[84] 78.8.3.

[85] 2.3.3.

likewise vague. He says that after a short announcement by Pertinax, "we gave heartfelt praise and chose him in truth [sc. as emperor]."[86] According to the accepted interpretation, the rhetorical question framed in the *sententia prima* about reducing the expense of gladiatorial shows (c. 177) raises the same uncertainty as to whether formal, or informal, expression is meant: "Therefore when your advice is so good and its objects so salutary, what other first opinion can there be for me to give than that which each (*singuli*) feels, and all (*universi*) cry from the bottom of their hearts?"[87] But a more basic difficulty with this passage hinges on the identity of the subject of *singuli* and *universi*. It has commonly been taken as the senators in the House.[88] Yet it is perhaps better understood as the Gallic priests, since their joy at the proposals and their renewed enthusiasm for service have just been described. So this passage possibly does not concern senatorial acclamation at all.

Our contemporary witness Dio can show the senate shouting in unison on various public occasions—after the death of Commodus, for example, or at the funeral of Pertinax.[89] It need be no surprise, therefore, if formal acclamations did come to be uttered at certain sessions as early as the late first century perhaps. But as the investigation above has shown, they were merely brief greetings and praises reserved for the emperor. Common sense rejects the notion that anything longer or more elaborate could have been chanted effectively in unison without rehearsals; and these there can hardly have been. In some sense, therefore, the result of our extended enquiry is negative and disappointing. Yet at least one important conclusion does emerge, namely, that in the present unsatisfactory state of the evidence there is no sign of acclamations having a part to play in the conduct of business. In particular, not one example survives from our period of a *senatus consultum* said to have been passed "per acclamationem."

Altogether therefore, while procedural changes in the second century were striking, they were perhaps not so radical as has often been assumed, and they did not entirely supersede established practice. In fact, during this period the senate was affected far more seriously by developments in the character and scope of its business than ever it was by procedural change. But these are matters to be treated in later chapters.

[86] 74.1.5.

[87] *Aes Ital.* lines 21-22, "quae igitur tantis tam salutarium rerum consilis vestris alia prima esse sententia potest quam ut quod singuli sentiunt, quod universi de pectore intimo clamant {e} ego censeam?"

[88] See, for example, M. Hammond, *The Antonine Monarchy*, pp. 259-260.

[89] Dio 74.2.1; 75.5.1. Cf., for the first century, idem 60.32.2 (Claudius); 63.20.4 (Nero); *Epit. de Caes.* 1.28 (Augustus). For acclamations by Arval Brethren, see especially *Arval Acta*, para. 86 lines 16ff. (A.D. 213).

9

RECORDS AND THEIR USE

This chapter examines first the manner in which resolutions and proceedings of the senate were recorded and published, and then their use by
ancient writers.

1. Form of *Senatus Consulta*[1]

As in the Republic, the *relator* of each decree fixed its wording with a
small group of senators. We have evidence of such drafting from one
decree of 19 and two others of the mid second century by seven members
in each case, as it happens, including the two *quaestores urbani*.[2] If the
Historia Augusta[3] can be believed, the practice still continued in the early
third century. *Senatus consulta* only attained validity when they had been
deposited in the *aerarium Saturni*. From 21 onwards there was an obligatory interval of at least ten days between the passage of a decree and its
deposit. Tacitus' account implies that this delay applied to all decrees, but
our other sources limit it to death sentences.[4] Even in those instances the
legal requirement might still be ignored.[5]

After deposit, the originals of decrees, inscribed on wooden tablets,[6]
never left the care of the *quaestores urbani* in the *aerarium*.[7] Since all
have perished, our knowledge rests entirely on copies rendered less than

---

[1] For discussion, especially of Republican practice, see R. K. Sherk, *Roman Documents*,
pp. 7-13, and idem, *The Municipal Decrees of the Roman West*, pp. 59-63. Certain unusual
features are considered by D. Daube, *Forms of Roman Legislation*, Oxford, 1956, pp. 78-
91.

[2] No. 22 in list, chap. 15 sect. 5; *FIRA*[2] I nos. 47, 48.

[3] *Elagab.* 4.2 and 12.3.

[4] See no. 26 in list, chap. 15 sect. 5; and Appendix 10.

[5] Note, for example, Tac. *Ann.* 4.70; 6.18; Dio 76.9.2.

[6] For the use of such a *tabula* in 69, see *FIRA*[2] I no. 59 line 3.

[7] For full discussion of the care of documents here during the imperial period, see
M. Corbier, *L'Aerarium Saturni et l'Aerarium Militare: administration et prosopographie
sénatoriale*, Rome, 1974, pp. 674-682. Note also Malalas' story of Antoninus Pius burning
a *senatus consultum* of Julius Caesar's time stored in the *aerarium*—all fiction! (p. 281, 11
Dindorf with A. Schenk Graf von Stauffenberg, *Die römische Geschichte bei Malalas*,
Stuttgart, 1931, p. 318).

perfect in various ways: by inaccurate transcription, for example; by imperfect transmission of a text or damage to an inscription; and by incomplete
rendering where an interested party preserved only those clauses which
concerned him. In such circumstances it might be unwise to expect the
form or style of *senatus consulta* to adhere to a strict pattern, and indeed
there is little sign that they did so. This is not to deny that there may have
been certain recognized norms, as is implied by Ulpian's comment upon
the "singularis sermo"[8] in which one *senatus consultum* of the mid first
century was written. But so far as we can detect from extant verbatim
quotations, the basic format of decrees seems to have altered little throughout our period, and (more importantly) there is only slight practical significance to be attached to the many trivial variations which do occur.
Detailed study may proceed from those decrees for which verbatim quotation survives, as listed below.[9] In confining the treatment here to an
outline, however, it is at least fair to claim that decrees would commonly
open with the names of the consuls in office together with the day and the
month, the meeting place, and the names of those members who fixed the
wording. Next would follow an account at greater or lesser length of the
"explanation" made to justify the proposal, framed as a causal clause:
"Quod . . . verba fecit/fecerunt."[10] The sentence would then be completed
by a transition to the decision of the House, phrased "quid de ea re fieri
placeret, de ea re ita censuerunt."[11] There followed the motives for the
decision in one or more clauses introduced by "cum" and the decision
itself phrased as "placere" or "placere senatui." At the end the passage
of the decree was signified by "censuere/censuerunt,"[12] while the *Lex
Julia* required the number of senators present to be recorded ("in senatu
fuerunt . . .")[13] except when the emperor attended the session.[14]

Modern legislative assemblies, like the British Houses of Parliament or
the U.S. Congress, have adopted systems of numbering which allow each
of their resolutions to be readily identified. By contrast, for the decrees of
the Roman senate there is little, if any, sign of a system. Exceptionally,
by the second century decrees in favor of individual groups or cities may
have been identified by a brief reference to the type of business and the

---

[8] *Dig.* 38.4.1.1.

[9] See chap. 15 sect. 5.

[10] The latter words might be abbreviated "v.f."; see, for example, *FIRA*[2] I no. 40 I, II.
Normally, but not invariably, this explanation was made by the *relator* himself. See chap.
7 sect. 9.

[11] Abbreviated as "q. d. e. r. f. p. d. e. r. i. c.": see, for example, *ILS* 6043 (misprinted
in *FIRA*[2] I no. 45 II).

[12] See, for example, *Dig.* 5.3.20.6d.

[13] Abbreviated as "i. s. f.": see *CIL* VI. 32272 and Probus, *De Notis Iuris* 3 (*FIRA*[2] II
p. 455).

[14] On this provision see further chap. 4 sect. 2 note 20.

names of those raising it.[15] These instances apart, there might still be confusion over identifying decrees, as much for contemporaries as for us today. Thus, during his governorship of Bithynia-Pontus, Pliny[16] consults Trajan about a decree which he identifies merely by subject-matter; the emperor replies with a request for a copy of the document.

A decree was most securely identified by the names of both consuls at the time of its passage, together with the day and month. Yet in surviving texts such precision is rare.[17] Admittedly most of our references derive from the jurists, and there is little doubt that these would be fuller if we possessed complete works rather than merely extracts from their discussions. As it is, they most commonly refer to the provisions of decrees without giving any date, or with only a vague indication of one—"Hadriani temporibus," for example, or "auctore divo Marco." It is true that certain decrees—generally those most discussed—are "named" informally on the pattern *SC Tertullianum, SC Trebellianum*.[18] The name is usually derived from the *nomen*[19] or *cognomen*[20] of a presiding consul or from that of the emperor, although the *SC Macedonianum* was named after the man whose crimes led to its introduction.[21] Where the text shows both consuls sponsoring a decree (as was customary), it is not always named after the first of the pair,[22] and we do not know whether it was at random, or with the help of further information now lost, that the choice was made. Such names could still be confusing. In extant texts three different measures are cited as *SC Claudianum*, for example, while the frequency with which men of the same name gained the consulship must have made dating *senatus consulta* from such titles as awkward in ancient times as the list below shows it to be today. Yet when these names do go some way towards facilitating identification, it is the curiously sparing use of them which becomes puzzling. The proportion of decrees referred to in such a fashion by the jurists (in extant texts at least) is very limited, and even some much-discussed measures are never identified thus. An outstanding example is the decree passed on 14 March 129, which only modern scholars term *SC Iuventianum*. The same point could be made about many other decrees.

---

[15] Note "s.c. factum de postulatione [Pergamenorum?]" (no. 76 in list); "SC de nundinis saltus Beguensis in t(erritorio) Casensi" (no. 104); "[SC de p]ostulatione Kyzicenor(um) ex Asia" (no. 105).

[16] *Ep*. 10.72-73.

[17] But note, for example, Plin. *NH* 22.13.

[18] See list, chap. 15 sect. 3.

[19] For example, *SC Ninnianum*.

[20] For example, *SC Gaetulicianum*.

[21] See its text quoted by Ulpian, *Dig*. 14.6.1 pr.

[22] Note *Dig*. 16.1.2.1 (no. 53 in list, chap. 15 sect. 5); cf. *Dig*. 36.1.1.1 (no. 56 ibid.).

2. Publication of *Senatus Consulta*[1]

So far as is known, there was no regular procedure for the publication of *senatus consulta* either in Rome itself or beyond. We do happen to be aware that certain speeches of Augustus and Tiberius were inscribed at Claudius' instigation, while the House itself voted that the text of Nero's accession address be set up in silver; Trajan's speech on 1 January 100, together with members' enthusiastic response, was likewise to be engraved on bronze.[2] As may readily be imagined, it was thus all the more flattering that the decrees honoring Pallas should be posted on bronze "ad statuam loricatam divi Iulii."[3] Certain ancient *senatus consulta* were among the documents on bronze destroyed by fire on the Capitol in late 69; but we cannot say whether decrees of our period were placed there thus.[4] Equally, while the so-called *Lex de Imperio Vespasiani* survives on bronze, we do not know where it was displayed.[5] At least we may distrust the claim of the *Historia Augusta*[6] that by the late third century decrees relating to emperors had for long been specially preserved in books of ivory! Among emperors Gaius is known to have ordered that certain of his requests to the senate be written up in public.[7] Magistrates might be sent personally to communicate urgent decrees and see their provisions carried out—death sentences above all.[8] In June 68 the consuls likewise made arrangements for "public servants" to convey the relevant decrees of the senate to Galba in Tarraconensis after he had been made emperor.[9] In addition, we shall see later how it is reasonable to think that some record of senatorial business might be circulated in *populi diurna acta*. That said, however, we remain altogether ignorant about the choice of items for this record, the degree of detail, and the readership.

In certain circumstances—when a treaty was made, for example[10]—a decree might stipulate that steps be taken to inform those concerned by its provisions. In the so-called fifth Cyrene edict Augustus himself commu-

---

[1] T. Mommsen, "Sui modi usati da' Romani nel conservare e pubblicare le leggi ed i senatusconsulti," *Ges. Schriften* III. pp. 290-313, is mainly, but not exclusively, devoted to the Republican period.

[2] Dio 60.10.2; 61.3.1; Plin. *Paneg.* 75.1-3.

[3] Plin. *Ep.* 8.6.13; cf. Tac. *Ann.* 12.53. Note ibid. 3.57 for a proposal of 22 to display the texts of certain *senatus consulta* in the House itself.

[4] Suet. *Vesp.* 8; note, however, that Appian (*Syr.* 39) in the mid second century mentions the display of treaties there on bronze as contemporary practice.

[5] *FIRA*[2] I no. 15.

[6] *Tacitus* 8.2.

[7] Dio 59.4.4 and 16.8.

[8] See chap. 3 sect. 3.

[9] Plut. *Galba* 8.

[10] See Sherk, *Roman Documents*, no. 26 col. c lines 22-26.

nicated a *senatus consultum* of special interest to provincials,[11] while in 177, after an imperial request for measures to reduce the expense of gladiatorial shows in various ways, the *sententia prima* recommends that provincial governors be informed about a particular point.[12] We know that in permitting certain temples to continue granting asylum rights in 22, the House required its provisions to be displayed on bronze in each shrine.[13] Though testimony is lacking, we may hope that it likewise arranged to make known its offer of a re-trial for anyone sentenced by Julius Bassus, after his acts as governor of Bithynia-Pontus had been annulled.[14]

Of course interested parties—in particular those who had approached the House on a matter—could always ask for a copy of any decree.[15] We may guess that Italica (in Baetica) and Sardis (in Asia) did this after measures had been taken to reduce the expense of gladiatorial shows in 177. Certainly it is astonishing and puzzling that both went to such trouble in having the relevant documents set up publicly, not least because the measures seem to have made their greatest impact in Gaul (unless this just happens to be the area where the speaker of the *sententia prima* had his contacts). In a less formal way, at least the upper classes throughout the empire would regularly be able to tap private sources of information on issues of concern to them. As we have noted elsewhere, senators must have communicated current business in the House to friends and associates, and in general great public interest was shown too.[16] Thus according to the *sententia prima* mentioned above, rumors of the imperial proposal had already met with a favorable reaction in Gaul. Earlier Pliny[17] suggests that after the trial of Julius Bassus senators and non-senators alike argued over the merits of the two principal *sententiae* regarding his sentence, while no doubt the representatives of the *koinon* who had successfully prosecuted him helped to spread the word that all his sentences as governor could now be reviewed. Yet by contrast it is interesting that the unidentified individual who asked Severus and Caracalla in 204 whether senators could be required to receive guests, evidently did not know of the relevant decree granting exemption—as the emperors indicate to him.[18]

The imperial recommendation here that *periti* (that is, jurists?)[19] be

---

[11] *FIRA*[2] I no. 68 V.

[12] *Aes Ital.* lines 53-55, *Hesperia* 24. 1955. p. 333.

[13] Tac. *Ann.* 3.63.

[14] Plin. *Ep.* 10.56.4.

[15] On Roman willingness to make official communications available on request, note in general the comments by J. Reynolds, *Aphrodisias and Rome*, p. 97.

[16] See chap. 6 sect. 3.

[17] *Ep.* 4.9.19.

[18] See no. 164 in list, chap. 15 sect. 5. Note that no details are offered to help the enquirer in any search for the text of the decree!

[19] Cf. Plin. *Ep.* 10.6.1.

consulted leads to the further puzzle of how such professional experts were kept informed. Since they were naturally interested in more than just an occasional decree from time to time, were they still reduced to the chore of painstakingly requesting each one, or was some smoother arrangement devised? We cannot say. Equally it is unclear whether provincial archives contained only those decrees which governors happened to bring with them or to obtain from Rome by special request, or whether the senate itself took the initiative in furnishing some, or all, its resolutions to high officials.

3. *Acta Senatus*

We know that in the Republic resolutions of the senate deposited in the *aerarium* would be stored in order of registration, each month's decrees being further copied and bound in some kind of volume.[1] Otherwise before 59 B.C. there was apparently no official record of business whatever. Although there was nothing to stop a senator from compiling his own account, any such document was not only private and unofficial, but would also normally remain in private hands.[2]

Suetonius alone tells us that in 59 B.C. Julius Caesar "having entered office (as consul), was the very first person to arrange that daily records of senate and people should be compiled and published."[3] Both these journals apparently continued in existence right through our period. A close examination of the second, *populi diurna acta*,[4] lies outside the scope of this study,[5] but the record deserves mention here because it is clear that it might include some news of senatorial business. The evidence is adequate, even if not abundant. Caelius, for example, is likely to have been drawing upon it when he sent a compilation of news from Rome to Cicero in Cilicia during April 50 B.C., with the following comment: "The *sententia*

---

[1] See R. K. Sherk, opp. citt. in sect. 1 note 1; J. Reynolds, *Aphrodisias and Rome*, no. 8 lines 1-3 with discussion, pp. 65-66. The *liber sententiarum in senatu dictarum* mentioned in a copy of a *senatus consultum* of 138 (*FIRA*[2] I no. 47 lines 2-3) suggests that Republican practice was kept up. *Sententiae* here cannot mean "opinions delivered by members," but must have the force of "decisions" or "resolutions" as, for example, in the title of Paulus' *libri imperialium sententiarum in cognitionibus prolatarum* (*Dig.* 35.1.113). See further *Ox. Lat. Dict.* p. 1736 s.v. 5, and chap. 7 sect. 7 note 13.

[2] Cf. Cic. *Pro Sulla* 42. For the consequent difficulties faced by writers seeking to discover views expressed at sessions, see especially W. V. Harris, *War and Imperialism in Republican Rome 327-70 B.C.*, pp. 6-7.

[3] *DJ* 20, "inito honore primus omnium instituit, ut tam senatus quam populi diurna acta confierent et publicarentur."

[4] A whole range of titles is known, all of which seem to refer to the one journal. At least, this is the assumption made here throughout, in preference to the suggestion that the titles cover two or more journals (for the latter view, see, for example, R. Syme, *Tacitus*, p. 120 n. 2).

[5] For a full treatment, see B. Baldwin, "The *acta diurna*," *Chiron* 9. 1979. pp. 189-203.

which each expressed you will find in the *commentarium* of affairs in the city; select from it what is worth noting. There is much to pass over, especially who was hissed at the games, the number of funerals and other trivia. But it contains more of value."[6]

Naturally it need not follow from these remarks made in 50 B.C. that *populi diurna acta* adhered to the same pattern during our period. Yet Pliny, in his *Panegyricus*, having described at length Trajan's conduct at the elections in the senate in 100, concludes:

> But why trouble to assemble all these details? I could hardly hope to keep in mind or cover in a speech all that you, Conscript Fathers, decided to save from oblivion by publishing in the official records (*publica acta*) and inscribing on bronze. Hitherto, only the speeches of the emperors were made safe for all time by records of this kind, while our acclamations went no further than the walls of the senate house; and indeed these were such that neither senate nor princeps could take pride in them. Today these have been sent out into the world and passed on to posterity both in the general interest and to do honor to us all. . . .[7]

The style and tone of the *Panegyricus* are such that we may not wish to trust literally the claim that *acclamationes* of senators had *never* before been recorded in *populi diurna acta*. But it does seem clear that, if the House so decided, the latter could commonly include some form of record of emperors' speeches to the senate. In a letter written later than 100,[8] Pliny offers Tacitus his version of an incident which had occurred in 93 as potential material for the latter's *Histories*. Though the exchange actually took place before the consuls sitting in their administrative capacity, rather than presiding over the House, it was still of significance to the senate and its members, and thus it is striking that Pliny can say of it apologetically to the historian: "I am sending you this account although the incident can hardly have escaped your watchful eye, since it appears in the official records [*publica acta*]."[9]

The first journal, *acta senatus*,[10] contained some account of proceedings

---

[6] *Ad Fam.* 8.11.4 = SB 91, "Quam quisque sententiam dixerit in commentario est rerum urbanarum; ex quo tu quae digna sunt selige, multa transi, in primis ludorum explosiones et funerum ⟨numerum⟩ et ineptiarum ceterarum. Plura habet utilia."

[7] *Paneg.* 75.1-3.

[8] For dating see Sherwin-White, *Pliny*, pp. 38 and 41.

[9] *Ep.* 7.33.3. In making accusations against Thrasea Paetus, Cossutianus Capito declares to Nero: "Diurna populi Romani per provincias, per exercitus curatius leguntur, ut noscatur quid Thrasea non fecerit" (Tac. *Ann.* 16.22). Since one of Capito's main charges is that Thrasea "triennio non introisse curiam," the remark just quoted—for all its color and exaggeration—does not diminish the likelihood that *diurna populi Romani* did include some news of senatorial business. Further, unreliable testimony is supplied by HA, *Sev. Alex.* 6.2.

[10] For the Greek equivalents ἄκτα and ὑπομνήματα, see H. J. Mason, *Greek Terms for Roman Institutions*, s. vv. Single references are also made by Tacitus to *commentarii senatus* (*Ann.* 15.74) and to *acta patrum* (*Ann.* 5.4), both of which may fairly be taken as synonymous with *acta senatus*. At any rate they will be considered so in this chapter, and the one latter term will be used throughout.

in the senate. Next to nothing is known of these *acta* before the beginning
of the Principate. But it is at least plain that two changes did occur in
relation to them thereafter. First, Suetonius[11] is again our own only authority for the significant prohibition made by Augustus, "ne acta senatus
publicarentur." He mentions this item briefly at the head of a list of
innovations introduced by the emperor; he offers neither date nor explanation for it. There is no sign that the prohibition was ever rescinded. In
Suetonius' references[12] the force of "publicarentur" remains unclear. We
know that *populi diurna acta* were "published" in the sense that copies
were made and sent throughout the empire. We never hear of such "publication" for *acta senatus*. The only readers of them outside Rome ever
mentioned are the emperors Tiberius and Septimius Severus.[13] For *acta
senatus* therefore, "publicarentur" in these instances may really mean "to
put into circulation." Again, we do not know how access was gained after
Augustus' ban on "publication." We may guess that no objection was
normally made to consultation by a senator like Tacitus, although he would
have faced considerable labor in sifting through records made up to a
century before his own time, and he remains unique in his claim to have
explored them. If Suetonius makes his single citation firsthand (quoted
below), it is conceivable that he gained access as a member of the imperial
service. It could well be that copies were kept in the imperial archives
(wherever these were housed), and that he read them while he worked in
the imperial secretariat.[14]

A second change is that we hear of an *ab actis senatus* for the first time
under the Principate. The date when this post was created is a puzzle which
has perhaps been overlooked. Because the first known holder, Junius Rusticus, is mentioned by Tacitus[15] under 29, it has generally been accepted
that the office was instituted by Augustus or Tiberius. There is no reason
to doubt Tacitus' specific testimony, but it may be an unsound deduction
that the office was regularly occupied from 29 onwards, if not from some
even earlier date. For it is striking that while we can suggest at least a
very approximate date for the tenure of all known holders except one,[16]
only Rusticus falls before c. 90. Thereafter a reasonable number are known
right up to the end of the Severan period, the last of them probably serving

[11] *Aug.* 36.
[12] Cf. *DJ* 20, quoted above, note 3.
[13] See further below, notes 85 and 86.
[14] On the vexed question of when Suetonius wrote his imperial biographies, see G. W.
Bowersock, "Suetonius and Trajan," in J. Bibauw (ed.), *Hommages à Marcel Renard,
Collection Latomus* 101, Brussels, 1969, vol. 1 pp. 119-125. On imperial records, see
F. Millar, *Emperor*, chap. V. 6.
[15] *Ann.* 5.4.
[16] No. 27 in list, sect. 5 below.

under Severus Alexander.[17] If there was likewise regular occupation during most of the first century by senators who changed at not too distant intervals, it seems remarkable that we lack any example. It could be that the office was held but never mentioned by contemporaries; yet that is inherently unlikely, and it is hard to imagine why it alone and not, say, the Vigintivirate should have been so despised. It would not be strange if the office were occasionally omitted from the record of a man's career, as it was from that of Hadrian set up at Athens in 112.[18] But regular omission in many such records over a long span would be puzzling. Not only does there survive a satisfactory spread of individual senators' careers from the first century; lists drawn up of other senatorial office-holders with duties in or around Rome reveal no such yawning gaps.[19] It is true that tenure of these offices might commonly extend over more than the single year which, as we shall see, was perhaps normal for an *ab actis senatus* in the second century. On the other hand, the functions in question were often performed by more than one senator at a time. Among the office-holders regularly appointed, *praefecti aerarii militaris* happen to be the most poorly documented group perhaps, but even here the gaps are never such as to arouse suspicion that the office fell into abeyance—hardly a likely prospect anyway in this case.

Caution is still called for, especially when the argument from silence brings special risks. The conjecture that the office of *praefectus frumenti dandi* fell into abeyance between the reigns of Claudius and Nerva must serve as a warning: it has not long ago been demolished by reappraisal of the career of L. Caesennius Sospes.[20] New evidence may likewise emerge which will no longer allow us to think that *curatores tabularum publicarum* only existed as a separate board at the most from late in Augustus' reign to 56.[21] Yet while it must remain speculation liable to be overturned by fresh discoveries, a suspicion arises that Domitian first instituted a regular

---

[17] No. 26 in list.

[18] *ILS* 308 with no. 4 in list.

[19] See in general H.-G. Pflaum, *ANRW* II. i. pp. 129-130. For *curatores operum publicorum*, A. E. Gordon, *Quintus Veranius, Consul A.D. 49*, pp. 283-285, with G. Molisani, "Un nuovo curator operum publicorum in un' iscrizione inedita dei Musei Capitolini," *ZPE* 13. 1974. pp. 7-17. For *curatores alvei Tiberis*, M. J. le Gall, *Le Tibre, fleuve de Rome dans l'antiquité*, Paris, 1953, pp. 137-140. For *praefecti aerarii Saturni* and *militaris*, M. Corbier, op. cit. in sect. 1 note 7 above, pp. 476-478 and 570-571.

[20] R. Syme, "The enigmatic Sospes," *JRS* 67. 1977. pp. 38-49, especially pp. 48-49. See further G. E. Rickman, *The Corn Supply of Ancient Rome*, Oxford, 1980, pp. 213-215.

[21] At present five holders would seem to be known from three inscriptions. The whole topic is discussed most fully by M. Hammond, "Curatores Tabularum Publicarum," in L. W. Jones (ed.), *Studies in Honor of E. K. Rand*, New York, 1938, pp. 123-131 (note especially concluding paragraph); see further F. Millar, "The aerarium and its officials under the Empire," *JRS* 54. 1964. pp. 33-40 at p. 35; and M. Corbier, op. cit. in sect. 1 note 7 above, p. 75. Neither Millar nor Corbier cites Hammond's discussion.

ab actis senatus. Earlier Tiberius had indeed wished to be kept closely informed of senatorial business during his absence in Capri. Logically or not, he perhaps felt that a special nominee could supply a record in some way better or more reliable than the *acta* themselves. But Junius Rusticus' task was an invidious one. It understandably lapsed in the revulsion after Tiberius' death, and never needed to be revived so long as the emperor either attended conscientiously (like Claudius and Vespasian), or by contrast showed little interest (like Gaius and Nero). In any case we may presume that *acta senatus* continued to be kept whether or not they had a special senatorial custodian, and their record was always available.

Domitian, however, learned from Tiberius.[22] He was the first emperor since 37 to spend significant periods out of Rome. And he had a passion for administrative efficiency. It would be understandable for him to institute a *quaestorius* who could maintain *acta senatus* in order, and keep the emperor informed, especially during any prolonged absences from Italy. The office was the only one open to a junior member. Though the importance of its supervisory duties should not be overrated, on Domitian's death it presumably came to be seen as another of his measures which was worth retaining.[23] During the absences of Trajan and Hadrian it must again have proved its value.

While the argument cannot be pressed, the varying titulature of the first known holders might support the notion that the office was still a novelty at the end of the first century. Nothing may be deduced from Tacitus' phrasing, since he eschews official terminology in any event. The next holders in sequence are cited on inscriptions as *curator actorum senatus, ab actis imperatoris, ad acta senatus.* If the office had been regularly occupied far back into the first century, citation in a standard form might have been expected, but only in Hadrian's time does *ab actis senatus* occur. It is used in all the Latin inscriptions thereafter, with just two or three exceptions.[24]

In the second century it evidently became normal for an ex-*quaestor urbanus* to take the post. In his magistracy he had had duties which would help prepare him for keeping the *acta*, not only remaining in Rome to attend meetings, but also assisting at the writing up of *senatus consulta.*[25] Though the choice was not invariable, it remains perhaps a small, yet significant, sign that the keeping of *acta senatus* continued to be taken

[22] Cf. Suet. *Dom.* 20.

[23] See in general K. H. Waters, "Traianus Domitiani Continuator," *AJP* 90. 1969. pp. 385-405.

[24] Nos. 24 and 25 in list for certain; no. 12 remains very fragmentary. No. 27 may be left aside.

[25] See sect. 1 note 2 above.

seriously during the second century. Under the Severi two senators adlected *inter quaestorios* are even found occupying the office.[26] Normal length of tenure is unknown, but we may reckon that it was seldom above one year. Except in the case of patricians, the customary promotion from quaestorship to praetorship through tribunate or aedileship within a six-year span would hinder longer tenures. Leaving aside two doubtful cases,[27] only one early holder of the office is known to have been a patrician.[28] Yet during the second century few of his successors are likely to have been, because these aristocrats were most commonly *quaestor Caesaris* rather than *quaestor urbanus*. Following service as *ab actis senatus* a number of holders were curule aedile, and Dio[29] implies that progression to this particular magistracy was the promotion expected after the office even in the early third century.

Though evidence is lacking, we may guess that *acta senatus* were stored in the *aerarium Saturni*. Their introduction, however, did not mean the end of the former arrangement whereby *senatus consulta* continued to be kept in the same building. Similarly, in the House of Commons the institution of *Hansard* as a daily, verbatim record of all proceedings has not meant the end of the annual *Journal*, which remains the official record of the proceedings of the House.

It is natural to enquire about the nature and fullness of *acta senatus*. But even these basic features are hard to establish when this record is only cited once each by two authors of our period (discounting the *Historia Augusta* as unreliable). At the very end of his treatment of the Pisonian conspiracy and its aftermath in 65, Tacitus says: "I find in the *commentarii* of the senate that the consul designate Anicius Cerealis proposed that a temple to the divine Nero should be erected as soon as possible at public expense. Anicius meant to indicate that the emperor had transcended humanity and earned its worship. But Nero vetoed it."[30] This unique citation in Tacitus would at least seem to demonstrate that rejected *sententiae* were recorded there.

Suetonius mentions *acta senatus* in describing the birthplace of Augustus, where (he says) there is now a shrine set up some time after the emperor's death. He continues: "For it is recorded in *acta senatus* that when C. Laetorius, a young man of patrician family, was pleading for a milder punishment for adultery because of his youth and birth, he further

---

[26] Nos. 19 and 25 in list.

[27] Nos. 17 and 28 in list.

[28] No. 2 in list.

[29] 78.22.2.

[30] *Ann.* 15.74. I leave out of account Mommsen's attempt to produce a second reference by emendation of *Ann.* 2.88: see Goodyear ad loc.

urged upon the House that he was the possessor and as it were the warden
of the spot which the deified Augustus first touched at his birth, and begged
that he be pardoned for the sake of what might be called his own special
god. Whereupon it was decreed that that part of his house should be
consecrated."[31] C. Laetorius is otherwise unknown, and no further evidence exists to fix the date of his trial.

Neither these citations nor indeed any ancient author's mention of *acta
senatus* seems to resolve for us the nature and fullness of the record. For
example, after Fronto had been elected consul in 143, he justified to
M. Aurelius his dilatoriness in delivering the *gratiarum actio* by explaining
his desire to honor the emperor Antoninus with a most carefully prepared
oration: "Him I must so praise, that my praise should not lie hidden away
in *acta senatus*, but come into the hands and under the eyes of men;
otherwise I am ungrateful to you."[32] Though it might imply a fairly full
report, this remark still does not clarify further the exact form in which a
gratiarum actio would appear in *acta senatus*. Likewise the form cannot
be securely adduced from two instances where Pliny might have been
expected to consult this record but did not do so.

In the first, according to his own account, having decided to write up
for publication a speech he had made in the senate in 97, "Afterwards I
set down what I could remember of my speech, and made numerous
additions."[33] And he also wrote up the speeches of those who had opposed
him on this occasion: "What else they said I need not tell you, as you
have it all in the published speeches—I gave it all in full, in the words of
the speakers."[34] Pliny's composition from memory and his apparent failure
to consult *acta senatus* could suggest that the latter would not provide a
verbatim record of what was said. But equally the omission might be
explained by a typically Roman desire to provide a polished, literary
account of the affair, beside which a verbatim record would hold little
attraction. Thus Quintilian[35] disowns those verbatim versions of speeches
delivered by him as an advocate, pieces taken down by *notarii* and sold
for profit.[36] Elsewhere Pliny shows no special concern for the text of the
Panegyricus as he delivered it, and afterwards he set about "giving the
same subject a fuller and more elaborate treatment in a written version."[37]
As another example of this practice, Tacitus is all but certain to have

[31] *Aug.* 5.
[32] *Ad M. Caes.* 2.1.1 = p. 24 H.
[33] *Ep.* 9.13.23.
[34] *Ep.* 9.13.14.
[35] *Inst. Or.* 7.2.24.
[36] For similar disdain shown by Greek orators in the Late Empire for copies taken down
thus, see A. F. Norman, *JHS* 80. 1960. p. 123.
[37] *Ep.* 3.18.1; cf. 3.13.5, "adnota, quae putaveris corrigenda."

consulted Claudius' speech on the admission of Gallic senators, yet still would never have wished to reproduce even extracts verbatim in his *Annals*.[38]

Secondly, when Pliny's anger had been so roused by reading the inscription on a monument to Pallas that he decided to look up the senate's decree,[39] it is notable that he seems to have sought out only the relevant *senatus consulta* (which would have been deposited in the *aerarium Saturni*) and not *acta senatus*, which might have been expected to give an account fuller in some degree than the decrees alone. But his action cannot sway any debate about the fullness or otherwise of *acta senatus*. It was almost certainly more convenient for him to look up the *senatus consulta* first; once he had found them, he had quite sufficient material with which to vent his spleen against Pallas. Any deeper investigation would serve only to bring into prominence features of the affair which he preferred to forget. In particular, his strictures against the senators who voted honors for Pallas are harsh, but they remain strikingly vague. Though he must have learned who moved the resolution, he never mentions that it was the consul designate Barea Soranus, whose memory he would surely have revered.[40]

The fact that after meetings each *relator* apparently continued to gather together a small group of members in order to fix the wording of the *senatus consultum* proposed by him could be used to suggest that the record of proceedings was not a verbatim one. If it had been, why did senators still need to finalize the wording afterwards? The answer is not far to seek. First, such a procedure was hallowed by tradition, and was therefore not to be given up lightly. Second, any body wishes to have its proceedings and decisions checked after each meeting: for that reason today minutes are circulated and later signed by chairmen as a "correct record" with the consent of members. Shorthand writers are fallible, and in Rome some might prove corrupt,[41] while to entrust the final wording of *senatus consulta* to mere penpushers would have struck members as outrageous. Seneca saw the invention of shorthand as the achievement of "the lowest type of slaves."[42]

Some scholars have readily concluded that *acta senatus* were a full, verbatim record of all proceedings in the House.[43] Neither of the citations

---

[38] *Ann.* 11. 24; *FIRA²* I no. 43.

[39] *Ep.* 7.29; 8.6.

[40] For Barea's part, see Tac. *Ann.* 12.53. Sherwin-White (*Pliny*, p. 453) seems to confuse *acta senatus* with the archive of *senatus consulta* in the *aerarium Saturni*.

[41] For corrupt *scribae* in the *aerarium Saturni*, see Plut. *Cat. Min.* 17; cf. Suet. *Dom.* 9.

[42] *Ep. Mor.* 90.25, "vilissima mancipia."

[43] See, for example, A. Stein, "Die Protokolle des römischen Senates und ihre Bedeutung als Geschichtsquelle für Tacitus," *Jahresberichte der I. deutschen Staatsrealschule in Prag*

by Tacitus and Suetonius quoted above proves this view, and it is hard to find other evidence which might do so. Attention must therefore be given equally to an alternative possibility, namely, that they were an edited record of proceedings, either in direct or indirect speech.[44]

It has been doubted whether Latin shorthand writers would ever have been competent to make a verbatim record of a meeting.[45] This is certainly too sweeping a claim, but the earliest date at which they were sufficiently adept remains unclear. In 63 B.C., in the absence of any official record, Cicero as consul specially asked for a written record to be made of "all statements, questions put to them, and replies"[46] when he examined informers about the Catilinarian conspiracy. His description of the four senators chosen as all being men "who could, as I knew, most easily take down what was being said, because of their memory, their knowledge, their practice and speed at writing"[47] need not imply that they wrote in any form of shorthand. Indeed according to Plutarch it was only a few days later that shorthand writers were first employed in the senate. He explains how Cicero took special steps to ensure that a verbatim record was made of Cato's speech urging the death penalty for the Catilinarian conspirators, and he then comments:

This is the only speech of Cato which has been preserved, we are told, and its preservation was due to Cicero the consul, who had previously given to those clerks who excelled in rapid writing instructions in the use of signs, which, in small and short figures, comprised the force of many letters; these clerks he had then distributed in various parts of the senate house. For up to that time the Romans did not employ or even possess what are called shorthand writers, but then for the first time, we are told, the first steps towards the practice were taken.[48]

There is no certainty that shorthand writers were regularly present at sessions from the introduction of *acta senatus* in 59 B.C. In the context of judicial proceedings there has been only partial support for interpreting a passage of Asconius to understand that shorthand writers took down and

---

43. 1904. pp. 5-33, esp. 10-15; and (in less detail) idem, "Die Stenographie im römischen Senat," *Archiv für Stenographie* 56. 1905. pp. 177-186; also W. Kubitschek in *PW* 1. s.v. acta, col. 290.

[44] For the general point, cf. R. A. Coles, *Reports of Proceedings in Papyri* (*Papyrologica Bruxellensia* 4), Brussels, 1966, pp. 9-13.

[45] For example, by F. B. Marsh, *The Reign of Tiberius*, Oxford, 1931, p. 263. On the development of shorthand at Rome, see further T. N. Winter, "The publication of Apuleius' Apology," *TAPA* 100. 1969. pp. 607-612; H. Boge, *Griechische Tachygraphie und Tironische Noten*, Berlin, 1973.

[46] *Pro Sulla* 41.

[47] *Pro Sulla* 42.

[48] *Cat. Min.* 23.

preserved a verbatim version of Cicero's *Pro Milone* (delivered in 52 B.C.) different from the version later published by the orator himself.[49]

However, Tacitus' *Annals* do treat senatorial business in remarkable detail from A.D. 14 onwards—reports arguably drawn from accounts taken down in the first instance by shorthand writers. More specifically, by early in Nero's reign when Seneca wrote his parody of a meeting of the senate, he can explain of the *sententia prima* delivered by Father Janus: "As he lives in the forum he delivered a long and eloquent speech which the *notarius* could not keep abreast of; and so I do not report it since I don't wish to put what he said into different words."[50] It must be sheer accident that, except in this piece of fiction, we have no evidence for the presence of one or more *notarii* at sessions of the senate during our period. Further testimony to the standard which Roman shorthand writers had attained by the second half of the first century is supplied by Seneca again, who mentions among recent innovations of his time "the signs for words, which make it possible for a speech to be taken down however rapidly it is uttered, matching speed of tongue to speed of hand."[51] Suetonius, too, remarks on the ability of the emperor Titus: "I have gathered from many sources that he used also to take very rapid shorthand, and enjoyed friendly competition with his secretaries."[52]

The attempt by a *notarius* to take down the *sententia prima* verbatim is significant, but does not of itself prove that such a full version would appear in *acta senatus*. Nor can proof be derived from the survival of verbatim orations by emperors, of a lengthy extract from a *sententia prima* delivered c. 177,[53] and of a *relatio* and a *sententia* made about the Secular Games in 203.[54] As shown above, senatorial proceedings could be reported in *populi diurna acta*. In 203 the *Quindecimviri Sacris Faciundis* naturally wished to preserve for their own *commentarium* a complete record of speeches which were written out beforehand anyway. Or the speakers themselves could publish versions. Emperors' speeches certainly seem to have been available for study. Among others, Fronto[55] and Tacitus[56] both make comments on the rhetorical abilities of successive *principes*, and we

---

[49] Asconius p. 42 C. Coles (op. cit. in note 44) would incline towards acceptance of this interpretation. But against it see A. Mentz, "Die Entstehungsgeschichte der römischen Stenographie," *Hermes* 66. 1931. pp. 369-386 and J. N. Settle, "The trial of Milo and the other *Pro Milone*," *TAPA* 94. 1963. pp. 268-280, especially pp. 274-277.

[50] *Apocol.* 9.2. For *notarius* as specifically a shorthand writer, note Paulus, *Dig.* 29.1.40 pr.

[51] *Ep. Mor.* 90.25; cf. Manilius 4.197-199.

[52] *Tit.* 3.

[53] *Hesperia* 24. 1955. pp. 320-349.

[54] G. B. Pighi, *De Ludis Saecularibus*, pp. 140-144 I lines 7-48.

[55] *Ver. Imp.* 2.1.8-10 = pp. 117-118 H.

[56] *Ann.* 13.3.

know that a book of twelve speeches by Hadrian was in circulation.[57] Tacitus specifically tells us that a particular speech by Tiberius had survived,[58] and as already mentioned, he is all but certain to have consulted the verbatim text of Claudius' speech on the admission of Gallic senators before composing his own version.

The senate itself must have preserved emperors' speeches with care in cases where it was laid down that these should be read out on future occasions. According to Dio,[59] it was decreed that the speech delivered by Gaius on taking up the consulship in 37 should be read every year. There was likewise a decree of the senate stipulating that certain speeches by Augustus and Tiberius be read on 1 January every year. The pieces must have been substantial, since Dio remarks that the readings went on until evening. In 42, at his first opportunity, Claudius therefore ended this practice, declaring that it was sufficient for the speeches to be engraved on tablets.[60] But in 54 the senate voted that the speech which Nero made on his accession should be inscribed on a silver tablet and read every time the new consuls took up office.[61]

Verbatim texts would naturally be available when emperors, or other members of the imperial family, or occasionally other senators had sent communications to be read out in their absence.[62] Fronto[63] could compare the despatches sent to the senate by both Trajan and L. Verus, having been too unwell to attend when those from the latter were read out. Even when emperors were present, it was common for them to read out a prepared statement.[64] Others, too, sometimes read their speeches, or spoke from notes. In 203, when the *magister* of the *Quindecimviri Sacris Faciundis* sought senatorial sponsorship of the Secular Games, he read from a *libellus*, and a *sententia* was then formulated by a senator reading from a *manuarius*, a term otherwise unattested.[65] In Seneca's parody[66] Augustus seems to deliver his speech ex tempore, and then reads *ex tabella* the wording of his actual *sententia* formulated beforehand. It was evidently accepted prac-

---

[57] See Charisius, *Art. Gramm.* II. p. 287 Barwick. Gellius (16.13.4) seems to have had access to Hadrian's speech in the senate *De Italicensibus* (though he does not actually quote from it, he can explain its contents at length).

[58] *Ann.* 2.63; cf. 1.81.

[59] 59.6.7.

[60] Dio 60.10.2.

[61] Dio 61.3.1.

[62] See chap. 7 sect. 6.

[63] *Ad Ver. Imp.* 2.1.5 = p. 115 H; *Princ. Hist.* 20 = p. 200 H.

[64] Note the following references in Dio: for Augustus, 53.2.7, 11.1 and 4; Gaius, 59.19.3; Claudius, 60.2.2 and 12.3; Nero, 61.3.1; Vespasian, 66.10.6; Septimius Severus, 75.8.1; also perhaps Hadrian or Antoninus, 69.15.2. For Claudius, Plin. *Ep.* 8.6.13.

[65] G. B. Pighi, *De Ludis Saecularibus*, p. 140 I line 6 and p. 142 I line 25. For further examples, see Plin. *Ep.* 5.13.6; 6.5.6; and compare Suet. *Tit.* 6 (speech to troops).

[66] *Apocol.* 11.

tice for senators to keep their own writing materials to hand during sessions. At least we hear of them stabbing with their pens on a number of occasions.[67] Senators must have needed a writing instrument when voting with *tabellae* was instituted for elections during Trajan's reign.[68]

It was not only respect or piety towards an emperor which might demand that a verbatim record of his words in the senate be preserved. When the emperor was the *relator* of a ratified *sententia*, he might hardly be expected to come in person to the "writing" of the decree afterwards, and in fact only one example of such attendance is known.[69] Thus an accurate verbatim record of his words would be invaluable. Such a record became essential once the stage was reached in the second century where the senate might do little more than ratify the emperor's speech.

We do know of instances in the ancient world where verbatim accounts of meetings were kept,[70] and one in particular is discussed below. But it seems to have been more common for any account to be an edited record—at greater or lesser length, in direct or indirect speech—which sought to bring out significant points. In some cases such records are likely to have been based on a verbatim version, or on vivid recollection.[71] As examples in this category we may cite *P. Ryl.* 77 (the election of a cosmete at Hermopolis Magna, 192) or the so-called Dmeir inscription (the case of the Goharieni against Avidius Hadrianus, heard by Caracalla at Antioch on 27 May 216).[72] Though these documents are carefully set out in direct speech, the remarks of each participant remain so brief that neither record as it stands could have taken more than a few minutes to transact. The main purpose was to represent the essence of the proceedings in a vivid form.[73]

The obvious technical difficulties of providing a full verbatim account may seem to rule out this particular possibility altogether. To be sure, in the case of any body which holds lengthy meetings, such a record is bulky,

---

[67] Suet. *DJ* 82; *Gaius* 28; *Claud.* 15 and 35; Seneca, *De Clem.* 1.15.1. *Grammateia*, mentioned by Dio 44.16.1, could be documents or writing materials.

[68] Plin. *Ep.* 3.20; 4.25.

[69] Augustus in *FIRA*[2] I no. 68 V lines 75-76.

[70] Coles, op. cit. in note 44, p. 22, rightly refers to *Ox. Pap.* 2407 as a striking example.

[71] On the general point, see Coles, op. cit., pp. 14-27. As he stresses (p. 16), the whole question is complicated by the fact that surviving papyrus records are almost invariably not the official ones, but private copies, which may well have incorporated only those matters of interest to the individual requiring the copy.

[72] *SEG* 17. 1960. 759 with J. H. Oliver in *Mélanges Helléniques offerts à Georges Daux*, Paris, 1974, pp. 289-294.

[73] See Coles, op. cit., p. 16. Despite their vividness, and even the irrelevance which they contain (e.g. *P. Ryl.* 77, lines 39-40), these records are too brief in themselves to be considered verbatim versions on the scale of, say, *Ox. Pap.* 2407. J. H. Oliver and R.E.A. Palmer are not alone in somewhat rashly regarding the Dmeir inscription and others as verbatim records comparable to the *Aes Italicense* and *Aes Sardianum* (see *Hesperia* 24. 1955. p. 323).

and its production a most demanding task, especially if speed is imperative. Yet in the *Acts* of the conference of Donatists and Catholics held at Carthage in 411 we do have striking proof that such an achievement was feasible in antiquity.[74] At this crucial disputation the significance of every word was of course measured with special care, so that four shorthand writers were furnished by the official secretariat to take down the proceedings verbatim, together with eight supplied by either side. Each group evidently split into two teams, working alternate shifts of about six hours' duration, so that at any one time six writers were present.[75] While no exact lengths for the sessions can be given, the texts themselves show how the first one on 1 June was long,[76] and the second one on the following day short. At the close of the latter full transcripts of both sessions were promised for 8 June, but in fact by working round the clock it proved possible to deliver several copies on the morning of 6 June.[77]

Naturally the arrangements for recording the conference of Carthage in 411 can shed no light directly upon the practice of the Roman senate a century and a half or more earlier. But in general, as we have seen above, a satisfactory system of shorthand was in use by the mid first century at the latest, while more specifically these *Acts* do prove the feasibility of recording a long meeting verbatim and issuing a full transcript of it within a short time. In the case of the senate, leaving aside trials and special sessions, the fortnightly interval between stated meetings would require a record to be produced well within that span if it was going to be read and pondered (among others) by an emperor who was in Rome or nearby, but had been absent from the meeting. It is notable that in 21 Tiberius evidently considered a ten-day interval between the passage of a decree and its lodgement in the *aerarium* adequate for him to receive the text, weigh up the issue, and take further action when necessary. This interval remained unchanged even after his removal to Capri, and would clearly have de-

---

[74] This is not to overlook the point that extensive records were made of most, if not all, church councils, some of them still surviving—Ephesus in 431 and Chalcedon in 451, for example (see E. Schwartz, *Acta Conciliorum Oecumenicorum* I and II, Berlin and Leipzig). I confine myself to Carthage alone here simply because the relevant evidence is so clear in this instance.

[75] See S. Lancel, *Actes de la conférence de Carthage en 411*, vol. 1 (*Sources Chrétiennes* no. 194, Paris, 1972), esp. pp. 342-353 and 390-391, with E. Tengström, *Die Protokollierung der Collatio Carthaginiensis*, Göteborg, 1962. Until Lancel's edition is complete, consult J.-P. Migne, *Patrologia Latina* XI. cols. 1223-1420.

[76] The starting time is unknown; it finished after eleven hours of daylight (on the Roman "12 hour" system? *Gesta* I. 219, "exemptae sunt horae undecim diei"). By modern reckoning sunrise to sunset at Carthage on this day is a span of approximately 14 hours 24 minutes.

[77] Summaries survive to show that the third and final session on 8 June was also a long one. Since pressure had been eased, the full text was not delivered until 26 June, and much of it is now lost.

manded that the document reach him at most five to six days after the decree had been passed.[78] If the full record of proceedings were to have been sent, as well as the decrees themselves, speedy transcription of verbatim notes would have been required: but, as we have seen, it could have been achieved.

So altogether there seems no argument for claiming that it would have been a physical impossibility to make a verbatim record of the senate's proceedings. While the task would certainly have been very arduous,[79] it should always be remembered that the House would not usually meet in continuous daily sessions except for trials and the reception of embassies. Equally not many copies of its proceedings would be required, though this was hardly a consideration to affect the speed of production, since a shorthand writer could just as well dictate his notes to, say, ten copyists as to three.

Even when all this is said, however, we still cannot determine whether *acta senatus* were in fact a verbatim account of proceedings, or an edited record, or a mixture of the two. As soon as technical shorthand difficulties were overcome, a full verbatim account might really have been easiest to produce, since this would have entailed no editorial decisions. Alternatively, in the case of a mixed record, the speeches of more senior members might have been reproduced in full, and only those of more junior ones in briefer form; thereby the bulk of the record would be reduced somewhat, and the editorial function limited. In favor of a mixed record may be the point that only in the rarest of instances does any source preserve verbatim quotations from senators' speeches in our period, excluding those of emperors or *sententiae primae*.[80] Tacitus' description of Junius Rusticus, the first *ab actis senatus* known to us, as "chosen by the emperor to write up the senate's proceedings and thus believed to have insight into the recesses of his mind,"[81] also could suggest that some editorial function was involved (especially in the choice of material and phrasing) beyond the formal task

[78] See above, sect. 1.

[79] To employ just the single *notarius* indicated by Seneca, *Apocol.* 9.2 can only have added to difficulties; but there is no need to think that the parody reproduces this detail with the same accuracy that it does certain others.

[80] The comic opening of Passienus Crispus' "maiden speech" preserved in the fragment of Suetonius' *Vita* is one such rarity (for "maiden speeches," see chap. 7 sect. 12 note 24). However, it should be remembered that the whole ethos of ancient literature was to shun verbatim quotation: see further sect. 41 below. If F. Millar (*Emperor*, p. 350 n. 59) is right to doubt the attribution of *FIRA*[2] I no. 44 to Claudius, or indeed any emperor, then this papyrus might be a rare verbatim record of a senator's contributions, thereby raising the possibility that such a record was sometimes kept of speeches other than those of emperors or *sententiae primae*. But, as Millar appreciates, a definite attribution is impossible; see further Appendix 4.

[81] *Ann.* 5.4, "componendis patrum actis delectus a Caesare eoque meditationes eius introspicere creditus."

of overseeing a purely verbatim record. Yet against these points it must be admitted that the lack of verbatim quotations from members' speeches may be either coincidence, or explicable on other grounds, while the character of Junius Rusticus' commission could well be unique. Once permanently established at a later date (as argued above), the junior office of *ab actis senatus* may have played a more mechanical role.

If *acta senatus*, whatever their precise form, did give fairly ample coverage of proceedings, we may at first be puzzled by the small use apparently made of them by the writers of our period, let alone the statesmen. But on closer inspection we should perhaps not be puzzled. *Acta senatus* were instituted in the freedom of the Republic by a politician who had reached a critical point in his career, a time at which he was bitterly opposed by significant numbers of influential senators. It was of value to him to introduce the innovations of having the senate's proceedings recorded and made public. But under the Principate an utterly different situation rapidly developed. The senate lost much of its old power. Augustus saw no value in continuing to allow open circulation of a record which preserved proceedings in unflattering detail. Any items which he did wish to make more widely known—in particular his own speeches—could conveniently be published in *populi diurna acta*. For the same reasons as the emperor, contemporary senators can themselves have sustained little interest in *acta senatus*. Augustus took steps to ensure that members without reasonable excuse for absence should attend all meetings in person anyway. In the longer term *acta senatus* were too unwieldy, too full of trivia, for all but the most painstaking historian to consult—and only then if he could gain access to this unpublished material. Its bulk, alluded to above, should be emphasized again here. The size of the extant *Acts* of the Conference of Carthage in printed form today, representing less than three full days of discussion in 411, can give some inkling of how large, say, one year's *acta senatus* might have looked during the first century especially, when the House was at its busiest. In any event, the type of historical research which involved combing such records was never the fashion.[82] Equally, members who came to prepare their speeches for circulation among the literary public had little interest in checking back to the precise words of the original, where these were preserved.

In effect *acta senatus* retained their importance only insofar as they could supply the emperor himself with an accurate record of those meetings from which he was absent. It need not surprise us that the first known *ab actis senatus* at least, if not his successors, was chosen by the emperor

[82] See especially A. D. Momigliano, "Historiography on written tradition and historiography on oral tradition," in *Studies in Historiography*, London, 1966, pp. 211-220.

rather than by the senate, and that he was thought to have gained special insight into the mind of Tiberius. That description characterizes *acta senatus* as above all a record for the emperor's attention. Thus of two titles by which later holders of the office are described, *ab actis imperatoris* seems significantly more apt than *ab actis senatus consulum*—the first used of two holders under Trajan and Hadrian respectively,[83] the second uniquely of S. Asinius Rufinus Fabianus, whose tenure possibly dates to the third century.[84] Again it need not surprise us that the only references to *acta senatus* being read outside Rome concern two emperors taking exception to measures passed in the House. Near the end of his life Tiberius was furious with the senate's handling of certain cases,[85] while Septimius Severus bitterly objected to praise of Clodius Celsinus, a relative of his rival Albinus.[86]

4. Ancient Writers' Use of *Acta Senatus*

I. SUETONIUS, DIO, AND OTHERS

The fact that words said to have been uttered in the senate are quoted verbatim is plainly no guarantee that they were actually spoken there thus. We have already noted how ancient literary convention positively encouraged a man to improve his own speeches before publication, while in historical works neither authors nor readers demanded verbatim accuracy in speeches, and certainly not verbatim quotation.[1] Among authors who have left us speeches alleged to have been made in the senate during our period, the point applies not only to Tacitus, but also to Dio and Josephus.[2]

Similarly, the fact that an author quotes words said to have been spoken in the senate is no guarantee that he consulted *acta senatus*, or that the latter were a verbatim record. Access to a wide range of other sources was easier—for example, *populi diurna acta*, where many emperors' speeches were published; texts of speeches by prominent men (emperors among them), published by themselves or by others; family records of one kind or another; personal reminiscence, and so forth. It should not be overlooked either that educated men in the ancient world could have an amazing memory for the spoken word. Seneca the Elder is an outstanding example,

---

[83] See nos. 3 and 8 in list, sect. 5 below.
[84] See no. 24 in list.
[85] Suet. *Tib.* 73.
[86] HA, *Sev.* 11.3 (where I take *acta* to refer to *acta senatus*, not to *populi diurna acta*). The whole story may be fiction: see T. D. Barnes, *BHAC* 1968/9. pp. 51-52.
[1] The *Historia Augusta* is an exception; but it was written long after our period, and its extensive verbatim quotations are probably all fabricated.
[2] For the latter, cf. *AJ* 19. 166-184.

even if the claims he makes for his own retentive powers should not altogether be trusted.[3] Authors' quotations of brief remarks said to have been made in the senate may conceivably have been drawn from *acta senatus*, but in most cases they are more likely to have come from the wide range of more accessible sources just cited. Leaving aside Tacitus for the present, Suetonius is the only extant author of our period who gives the impression of having consulted *acta senatus*, and as we have seen he does cite them once.[4] Unlike Tacitus in particular, he was not aiming to write that elevated type of literature which shunned verbatim quotation. He twice specifically claims to give the exact words of speakers in the senate: first, those of Valerius Messalla in saluting Augustus as *pater patriae*, and of the latter's reply; second, those of Tiberius in the ''accession'' debate of 14.[5] Elsewhere he gives what seem to be verbatim remarks made in the senate by Augustus,[6] Tiberius,[7] Claudius,[8] Nero,[9] Vespasian,[10] and Domitian.[11]

Some of these quotations are notable in that the words spoken clearly did not form part of formal, prepared speeches by the emperors concerned—for example, a jibe by Tiberius or Claudius' interjections.[12] But even so we can perhaps do no more than admit the possibility that Suetonius gained these quotations from a firsthand exploration of *acta senatus*, instead of deriving them from more accessible sources of one kind or another. The same caution must apply to his mention of honors refused by emperors;[13] such refusals might regularly be publicized. Likewise the two occasions for which he specifically claims to give the exact words of speakers in the senate were both very well-known ones—the bestowal of the title *pater patriae* upon Augustus in 2 B.C. and the ''accession'' debate of 14. It must remain equally unclear whether the quotation of members' acclamatory response to Nero's threats against Vindex may be attributed to firsthand exploration of *acta senatus*.[14]

Only in the case of Tiberius may the suggestion be made with any

---

[3] See *Controv.* 1 pref. 1-5 with discussion by L. A. Sussman, *The Elder Seneca*, Leiden, 1978, pp. 75-78.

[4] *Aug.* 5.

[5] *Aug.* 58; *Tib.* 24; cf. 67.

[6] *Aug.* 56 and perhaps 66.

[7] *Tib.* 27-29 (note ''extat et sermo eius in senatu percivilis'' in 28), 57, 71, and perhaps 25; letter to senate, 67.

[8] *Claud.* 40, 42; *Otho* 2.

[9] *Nero* 10.

[10] *Vesp.* 25.

[11] *Dom.* 11, 13, 18.

[12] *Tib.* 57; *Claud.* 40, 42.

[13] Cf. *Aug.* 100; *Tib.* 17, 26; *Claud.* 11.

[14] *Nero* 46.

confidence that Suetonius might have explored *acta senatus* at firsthand in order to determine emperors' conduct in the senate. In Suetonius' biography we have not only a remarkably large number of quotations of Tiberius' words; he can even cite specific words to which the emperor objected in two different *senatus consulta*.[15] Moreover, in the same context he explains Tiberius' caution over using the word *monopolium* in the senate.

What survives of Dio's account of our period includes a considerable number of verbatim remarks made in the senate. Those datable within the span of his own career as a senator are presumably reproduced from memory.[16] Thus he quotes verbatim remarks addressed to the senate by the emperors Pertinax,[17] Didius Julianus,[18] Septimius Severus,[19] Caracalla,[20] and Elagabalus.[21] He also quotes verbatim a remark to senators possibly made by the Praetorian Prefect, Plautianus; cites remarks made at the trial of Apronianus; and gives the words of an acclamation addressed to Caracalla.[22] He also quotes the terms in which Caracalla would send messages to the senate.[23]

For his account of the period prior to his own time Dio does quote statements by emperors and others in the senate, but there is no clear sign that his researches extended to a perusal of *acta senatus*. Two famous sessions are recounted in some detail—the "accession" debate in 14 and the fall of Sejanus in 31.[24] In addition, among emperors Dio quotes remarks made in the senate by Tiberius,[25] Gaius,[26] Vitellius,[27] Domitian,[28] Antoninus,[29] and M. Aurelius.[30] Of others there survive quotations only of Antistius Labeo and of the freedmen Galaesus and Narcissus at the former's trial before the senate.[31] Antistius' remark in particular is very much a *bon mot*.

---

[15] "Liviae filius" in 50, ἔμβλημα in 71; cf. also 27.
[16] Cf. his personal statement at 72.18.4, and note his comment at 74.12.5.
[17] 74.1.4 and 8.3-5.
[18] 74.14.2ᵃ.
[19] 75.8.1; 76.6.1-2.
[20] 77.3.3; cf. 78.8.3.
[21] 79.18.4.
[22] 75.15.2ᵇ; 76.8; 78.8.3.
[23] 72.15.5.
[24] 57.2; 58.10.
[25] 57.18.2 and 24.8.
[26] 59.16.1-7. J.-C. Faur seems to have no good grounds for believing that Dio's sources in this section were especially reliable; see his "Un discours de l'empereur Caligula au Sénat (Dion, Hist. rom. LIX, 16)," *Klio* 60. 1978. pp. 439-447.
[27] 65.7.2.
[28] 67.4.6.
[29] 70.1.2-3.
[30] 71.33.2. In addition, the remarks of Claudius at 60.5.5 and 11.7 probably fit this category. John of Antioch purports to give the exact words of a letter from M. Aurelius to the senate (cf. Loeb Dio 71.30.2).
[31] 54.15.8; 60.16.4.

Among other authors it is impossible to believe that *acta senatus* were consulted by Plutarch, for example, who quotes verbatim remarks made by members to Tiberius in the senate.[32] On the other hand, there is room for the possibility that Seneca might have found in *acta senatus* the letter of Augustus to the senate, from which he quotes.[33] Yet we know that some letters of Augustus were in circulation.[34] Quintilian's quotations of remarks made in the senate seem to be no more than *bon mots*.[35] Finally, the words of Vespasian in proposing *triumphalia ornamenta* for Tiberius Plautius Silvanus Aelianus might have been taken from *populi diurna acta*, or more probably had been cherished in the memory of his family.[36]

In contrast to authors with greater or lesser literary pretensions, grammarians and legal writers by definition both maintained a special concern for verbatim quotation. Though such quotations of words spoken in the senate during our period do survive, there is no sign that any were drawn from *acta senatus*. To illustrate use of "valdissime" the grammarian Charisius cites a sentence of Hadrian, yet gives as his source Hadrian's *orationum XII liber*.[37] Likewise legal writers show knowledge of *orationes* delivered to the senate by most emperors from Hadrian to Caracalla: the verbatim texts were of vital importance as such *orationes* could acquire the force of law without further discussion or alteration. But again there is no sign that *acta senatus* were the source of the legal writers' quotations.[38]

II. TACITUS

Scholars might generally agree that some material in Tacitus' *Histories* and *Annals* is drawn ultimately from *acta senatus*. But there has been controversy both over the extent to which he used this record, and over whether he consulted it at firsthand.[1] To deny that he ever consulted *acta senatus* at all would perhaps be extreme when, as we have seen, he cites them once to mention a *sententia* put forward after the Pisonian conspiracy

[32] *Mor.* 60 C-D.
[33] *De Brev. Vitae* 4.2-3.
[34] Gell. 15.7.3.
[35] Cf. *Inst. Or.* 6.1.14, remark in Greek made by the accuser of Cossutianus Capito; 8.5.18, Nero's letter after the death of Agrippina; and perhaps 6.3.97.
[36] *ILS* 986 lines 32-35.
[37] *Art. Gramm.* II. p. 287 Barwick. For his citation of Augustus' will (which we know to have been read in the senate), no source is given (ibid. p. 132).
[38] See list, chap. 15 sect. 4.
[1] For a summary of views, see, for example, R. Syme, *Tacitus*, pp. 282-283; cf. more generally pp. 185-188, chap. XXII passim, Appendix 40; further, idem, "The senator as historian," Fondation Hardt, *Entretiens*, Geneva, 1956, pp. 187-201 = *Ten Studies in Tacitus*, pp. 1-10; and "How Tacitus wrote *Annals* I-III" in *Historiographia Antiqua, Symb. Fac. Lit. Phil. Lovaniensis* Ser. A Vol. 6, 1977, pp. 231-263, esp. pp. 248-249. For an older view, T. Mommsen, "Das Verhältniss des Tacitus zu den Acten des Senats," *Ges. Schr.* VII. pp. 253-263.

of 65. Yet scholars who argue that he did not explore them thoroughly for himself have pressed the point that this is the only citation of the record in the whole of his extant work. It remains doubtful whether this uniqueness is significant in a historian who mostly seeks to hide his sources, rather than display them. Syme[2] goes so far as to speculate that Tacitus might have erased even his single reference if he had produced a finished version of the later books of the *Annals*.

Some scholars have attached weight to certain passages in the *Annals* which could indicate a failure to consult *acta senatus*. The most significant of these passages and the arguments about them, as discussed by Marsh[3] for example, may be summarized as follows:

(1) When writing about the degree of Tiberius' involvement with the consular elections in his reign, Tacitus states: "About the elections to consulships, from the first year of Tiberius until his death, I hardly venture to make any definite statement. The evidence in historical accounts, and indeed in his own speeches, is conflicting."[4]

Nipperdey[5] argued that Tacitus might have settled this doubt by consulting *acta senatus*.

(2) Under 19 he mentions: "I find from the writings of contemporary senators that a letter was read in the senate from a chieftain of the Chatti named Adgandestrius, offering to kill Arminius if poison were sent him. The answer was given that Romans take vengeance on their enemies, not by underhand tricks, but by open force of arms. By this elevated statement Tiberius invited comparison with generals of old who had forbidden, and disclosed, the plan to kill King Pyrrhus."[6]

Nipperdey[7] argued that Tacitus would have cited the letter and the response from secondary sources only if he had not drawn upon *acta senatus*.

(3) Having mentioned an exchange of correspondence between Maroboduus and Tiberius, Tacitus[8] summarizes the latter's speech in the senate about the threat posed by the king, and vouches for the truth of his account by explaining "the speech survives." Fabia[9] argued that in this instance Tacitus had consulted the emperor's speech (in some collection perhaps), but not *acta senatus*.

(4) Under 32 he records of trials in the senate: "But on condemnation

---

[2] *Tacitus*, p. 742.

[3] F. B. Marsh, *The Reign of Tiberius*, pp. 259-264.

[4] *Ann.* 1.81.

[5] K. L. Nipperdey, *Tacitus*, Annals I-VI (ed. 11, revised G. Andresen), Berlin, 1915, p. 28.

[6] *Ann.* 2.88.

[7] Op. cit. p. 28.

[8] *Ann.* 2.63.

[9] P. Fabia, *Les sources de Tacite dans les Histoires et les Annales*, Paris, 1893, p. 327.

Minucius and Servaeus turned informer. Julius Africanus from the community of the Santones in Gaul was forced to the same plight, along with Seius Quadratus, whose background I have not discovered."[10]

Fabia[11] argued that Quadratus' *origo* must have been recorded in *acta senatus* and that Tacitus' inability to discover it shows that he omitted to consult this source.

None of these arguments can be considered wholly convincing. In the case of (1) it would have been a formidable task to collate from *acta senatus* all the relevant information about consular elections during Tiberius' long reign, and even then the bare record of proceedings might not serve to reveal the emperor's attitudes or behavior accurately. In the case of (2) no particular significance should perhaps be attached to Tacitus' citation of secondary sources rather than a primary one. He may just as well have read *acta senatus* but decided to cite contemporary writers for this matter, because it was only by comparing their selective accounts against the great mass of varied material in *acta senatus* that he could discern more clearly which affairs had been of particular concern at the time. It is hard to see how any reasonable conclusion can be drawn from (3) about whether he did, or did not, consult *acta senatus* in this instance. Likewise, with regard to (4), there can be no certainty that the record would have revealed Quadratus' origin.

In itself each of these disputes about whether Tacitus did, or did not, consult *acta senatus* for a particular passage is of small significance. However, some scholars have made one or more passages the basis for a general claim that throughout the *Annals* he consulted *acta senatus* at firsthand no more than casually. Fabia, for example, justified such a claim by explaining: "Il n'y a pas lieu de s'étonner que Tacite n'ait point pris les documents officiels pour source principale dans les parties des *Annales* qui sont relatives aux séances du sénat. Ces matériaux avaient été exploités par ses devanciers. Les recherches étaient faites, il eût été superflu de les refaire, selon la doctrine des anciens."[12] To make the general claim on the basis of the particular passages seems unsound in this instance; and in the light of research pursued since Fabia's day, the claim cannot now be considered to gain support from a highly questionable assumption about "la doctrine des anciens" with regard to the use of primary source material.

---

[10] *Ann.* 6.7.

[11] Op. cit. pp. 313-314.

[12] Op. cit. p. 319. Cf. A. D. Momigliano in *Studies in Historiography*, p. 131: "The surviving books of Tacitus' *Annals* are the most conspicuous example of a great work of history written with a minimum amount of independent research." F.R.D. Goodyear in E. J. Kenney (ed.), *The Cambridge History of Latin Literature* 2, Cambridge, 1982, p. 648, is scarcely less extreme in stressing how little Tacitus used *acta senatus*. But his view seems to be modified in *The Annals of Tacitus* 2, pp. 136 and 397.

We may more profitably investigate what material Tacitus might have drawn from *acta senatus*, and then consider whether there is any argument to determine whether or not he took it at firsthand. On the first point it is hard to escape the conclusion that the wealth of detail about the senate in the *Histories* and *Annals* must have been derived ultimately from *acta senatus*. In this connection it should be remembered first that the length at which the affairs of the senate are reported is astonishing, with the record of meetings in 20 to 23 particularly full.[13] Later, in a fragmentary passage presumably about a meeting of 31, Tacitus[14] can state with precision that 44 speeches were delivered on one matter. In the latter part of the *Annals* coverage continues to be full, with a notable amount of space devoted to the fall of Thrasea Paetus and Barea Soranus together with their relations and alleged accomplices.[15] In the *Histories* likewise there is detailed coverage of sessions of the senate in early 70.[16] This length of treatment is matched by a remarkable total of persons named as speakers in the senate, or as prosecutors, defendants, or witnesses there. In the *Annals* the best part of two hundred persons in these categories are named, on a rough calculation;[17] in the *Histories* a count on the same basis produces about thirty names. Many of the persons thus mentioned in the *Annals* in particular are otherwise unknown.

Use of *acta senatus* is suggested further by exceptionally detailed reporting throughout the works of a variety of matters of lesser importance. Some of these might certainly have been recorded by contemporary senatorial historians, but it is difficult to believe that such well-informed reports of the whole range were to be found outside *acta senatus*. As examples there might be cited the pleas put forward by Florence, Interamna, and Reate at a discussion about Tiber floods, or the submissions made by Greek cities about asylum rights, by Sparta and Messene about the ownership of the temple of Diana Limnatis, and by cities in Asia competing for the honor of erecting a temple to Tiberius.[18] In the same vein Tacitus can list precisely those cities in Asia to which the senate sent an "inspector" after an earthquake in 17.[19] Elsewhere he reproduces the argument of a recondite discussion about the choice of a Flamen Dialis.[20] He can likewise relate the complaint of Domitius Corbulo against L. Sulla, and the resulting

[13] *Ann.* 3.2-4.16.
[14] *Ann.* 5.6.
[15] 16.21-35.
[16] Cf. 4.3ff.; 4.40-44.
[17] Note how as many as seven proposers of *sententiae* are named in the single chapter, *Ann.* 2.32.
[18] *Ann.* 1.79; 3.61-63; 4.43 and 55-56.
[19] *Ann.* 2.47.
[20] *Ann.* 4.16.

exchange, together with the names of Sulla's supporters. This incident is followed immediately by another of Corbulo's complaints, and then a detailed account of a meeting, where names of persons, irrelevant points, and the to-and-fro of debate are unfolded with what seems to be vivid accuracy.[21] The order of dull business, together with suggestion and countersuggestion, seems to be well reproduced, too, for a debate in 52.[22]

Along with matters of lesser importance the number of abortive proposals recorded is striking, and here also we would hardly expect the whole range to be found outside *acta senatus*. For example, while those proposals rejected by Nero in 54-55 might have been advertised to underline imperial modesty, the three rejected by Tiberius at the trial of Vibius Serenus in 24 are unlikely to have been publicized outside the House.[23] Likewise references to what did *not* happen, so to speak, might all go back to contemporary accounts, but the frequency with which such details occur could equally suggest derivation from *acta senatus*. For example, Tacitus says that Tiberius made no statement to the senate about the death of Agrippa Postumus, and no reply to a remark by Scaurus.[24] He did not speak in the discussion on actors' behavior in 15; similarly, he kept silent when *res prolatae* was debated.[25] In 21 he did not criticize Haterius Agrippa for advocating that Clutorius Priscus be sentenced to death; at the trial, we are told, Rubellius Blandus was the only consular to support M. Aemilius Lepidus' plea for a lesser penalty.[26] In the same way Tacitus can describe how in 16 Tiberius replied unpromisingly to Hortalus' plea for aid; next sensed from the virtual silence that he had not pleased members; and so then offered money for Hortalus' sons. The father made no reply.[27] The steps by which Tiberius had eventually decided to make his gift in this grudging manner would hardly have been publicized—they must have been drawn either from a senatorial eye-witness, or from *acta senatus*.[28] Later Tacitus can state that in his speech to a Parthian embassy before the senate in 49, Claudius recalled how Augustus had been asked for a Parthian king, but did not mention the similar request made to Tiberius.[29]

Use of *acta senatus* is suggested, too, by Tacitus' habit of reporting developments exactly as they arose at successive meetings of the House, without any attempt to draw them together in a single passage. Thus in

---

[21] *Ann.* 3.31-34.
[22] *Ann.* 12.53.
[23] *Ann.* 13.10-11; 4.30.
[24] *Ann.* 1.6; 1.13.
[25] *Ann.* 1.77; 2.35.
[26] *Ann.* 3.51.
[27] *Ann.* 2.38.
[28] Cf. Tiberius' delayed revelation at the trial of Lepida in 20 (*Ann.* 3.23).
[29] *Ann.* 12.11.

Annals, Book 3, the question of choosing a proconsul of Africa is raised at one meeting (chapter 32), and then taken further at a later one (35). The opening of the case against Caesius Cordus is mentioned in chapter 38, and the verdict given in chapter 70. In the same way the request of the Flamen Dialis to be considered for the proconsulship of Asia is made in chapter 58, but Tiberius' decision does not follow till chapter 71.[30]

While we may fairly claim that Tacitus had access to a range of material which at one stage or another was derived from *acta senatus*, it is less easy to go further and show that he necessarily consulted this source at firsthand. In seeking to explore the latter point, however, we may first note the historian's own belief that he had a comprehensive range of source material at his disposal in writing of senatorial affairs in the *Annals*. He declares first: "The only *sententiae* which I have seen fit to mention are particularly praiseworthy or particularly scandalous ones."[31] Elsewhere he says: "I realize that many writers omit numerous trials and condemnations, bored by repetition or afraid that catalogues which they themselves have found overlong and dismal may equally depress their readers. But numerous unrecorded incidents, which have come to my attention, ought to be known."[32] Thirdly he asks: "How long must I go on recording the thank-offerings in temples on such occasions? Every reader about that epoch, in my own work or others, can assume that the gods were thanked every time the emperor ordered a banishment or murder: and, conversely, that happenings once regarded joyfully were now treated as national disasters. Nevertheless, when any senatorial decree reaches new depths of sycophancy or abasement, I will not leave it unrecorded."[33]

In this connection the claim that Tacitus may not always have fulfilled his promises does not matter; he still *felt* able to select material from a wide range of sources. From his own citations it is clear that this range included both reminiscences[34] and literary accounts of the period.[35] These must at least have been drawn upon for reports of sessions in the senate where details are included which can never have appeared in *acta senatus*.[36]

---

[30] It should not be thought, however, that the practice illustrated here is one which Tacitus invariably adopts. By contrast, having explained how the consuls were asked by the senate to investigate rights of asylum granted by Greek cities, he then proceeds to report their findings at once (*Ann.* 3.63).

[31] *Ann.* 3.65.

[32] *Ann.* 6.7.

[33] *Ann.* 14.64.

[34] See R. Syme, *Tacitus*, pp. 176-177; 299-303.

[35] See R. Syme, *Tacitus*, pp. 177-185; 274-278; 287-298.

[36] At least it is a fair assumption that they were not recorded. Admittedly when Drusus was in prison Tiberius could require the recording of "vultum, gemitus, occultum etiam murmur," according to Tacitus (*Ann.* 6.24), but no inference should be drawn from this exceptional demand.

For example, in a number of passages Tacitus describes the bearing or expression of individuals in the senate. Tiberius' reception of Libo Drusus before his trial is vividly portrayed: "He was carried in a litter to the door of the senate-house. Leaning on his brother's arm he stretched out his hand to Tiberius and cried for mercy. The emperor, without altering his expression, read out the accusation and its signatures in a toneless voice calculated neither to aggravate nor to extenuate the charges."[37] Later he can explain how Piso became terrified because "he saw Tiberius pitiless, passionless, adamantly closed to any human feeling."[38] After Piso's suicide we are told how Tiberius appeared in the senate "with an expression turned to sorrow."[39] Elsewhere Tacitus comments on his expression in the "accession" debate and at the trials of C. Silanus in 22 and Cremutius Cordus in 25, even though no statement by the emperor is recorded on this latter occasion.[40] In the case of senators we are told of laughter or derision,[41] weeping,[42] warm applause,[43] silence,[44] and horrified interruptions,[45] as well as the confused chorus of flattery which met Tiberius' shocked interjections at the trial of Votienus Montanus in 25.[46] In some of these instances it may be that Tacitus is just writing imaginatively, rather than making a careful comparison of sources; that is certainly a fair supposition about the powerful image of Tiberius, after executions in 35, "almost gazing at the homes deluged in blood, and the executioners at work."[47] But on the other hand, the caution with which he opens his account of the trial of Lepida in 20 does suggest a serious attempt to weigh up Tiberius' attitude from source material which did not explain it adequately: "The emperor's attitude during the trial is not easy to reconstruct. Alternately, or simultaneously, both anger and indulgence were perceptible."[48]

While it is clear that Tacitus' reports of senatorial meetings drew upon both reminiscences and literary accounts, these alone cannot invariably have been sufficient for his purpose. Otherwise, especially for his full account of senatorial business from 20 to 23, we must envisage him first finding a most detailed historical account, and then drawing upon it so heavily that he might almost seem a plagiarizer or hack copyist. It makes

[37] *Ann.* 2.29.
[38] *Ann.* 3.15.
[39] *Ann.* 3.16.
[40] *Ann.* 1.12; 3.67; 4.34.
[41] *Ann.* 3.29 and 57; 6.2.
[42] *Ann.* 4.9.
[43] *Ann.* 12.6.
[44] *Ann.* 5.3.
[45] *Ann.* 6.24.
[46] *Ann.* 4.42.
[47] *Ann.* 6.39.
[48] *Ann.* 3.22.

better sense to believe that he explored *acta senatus* of these years for himself, and thereby gained the comprehensive grasp of *sententiae, senatus consulta*, and trials which he claims. He was so fascinated by the death of Germanicus and the trial of Piso that he took the trouble not only to check *populi diurna acta* for a detail about the former's funeral,[49] but also to adduce the reminiscences of *seniores* about the latter's behavior as defendant. He would surely have wished to peruse the relevant *acta senatus* as well. The latter were records of a high assembly in which he took intense pride. It would be fantastic if he consulted them only in the single instance which he documents. On the contrary, while proof is lacking, there is much in his work to confirm the belief that he frequently used them elsewhere, too, in conjunction with other material.

If the claim that Tacitus drew substantially upon *acta senatus* be accepted, further conclusions may be hazarded. We have already noted how research of this type was unusual among ancient historical writers. Tacitus' use of *acta senatus* may thus be one of the most significant innovations in his writings, developed fully in the last work, *Annals*. Indeed altogether it may be a unique, and very successful, experiment in method. We may be sure that such historians as wrote later in the second century were disinclined to follow his example in this respect.[50] The extent to which his lost predecessors in the first century had shown him the way is of course a much larger question, impossible to answer definitely.[51] Yet we may note with more or less assurance that three of the writers known to have treated his period were non-members,[52] and therefore not likely to have drawn heavily upon *acta senatus*; only two were senators.[53] How far the latter pair drew upon this material, and Tacitus upon them, is equally unfathomable in each instance. Yet there are at least strong negative arguments for suggesting that he both consulted *acta senatus* more systematically, and incorporated more material from this record in his work, than any predecessor. Were it not so in either case, he would become (as has been said) a dull plagiarizer of other men's researches, and his claims that he could select material should stand as utterly false. In reality any such impression of Tacitus must be dismissed. Rather the conjecture may be ventured that the use of *acta senatus* was not only a notable influence upon the character of *Annals*, but also represented a significant development in contemporary historical method. It is a tribute to Tacitus' literary artistry

---

[49] *Ann.* 3.3.

[50] For a brief survey, see E. J. Champlin, *Fronto and Antonine Rome*, pp. 55-56.

[51] For the authors cited below, and their works, see R. Syme, *Tacitus*, chaps. XXII and XXIII; idem, "The historian Servilius Nonianus," *Hermes* 92. 1964. pp. 408-414 = *Ten Studies in Tacitus*, pp. 90-109.

[52] Aufidius Bassus, Fabius Rusticus, Pliny the Elder.

[53] Servilius Nonianus, Cluvius Rufus.

that such heavy reliance upon documentary research is so unobtrusively incorporated into the narrative as a whole.

There remains the question of how and why he was led to undertake historical research of this type. The character and fullness of the record offered an unparalleled opportunity, it is true. In addition, as Syme remarks,[54] Asconius' investigations into the period of the late Republic might have pointed the way towards exploiting it, though the latter was more antiquarian than historian. Equally it could be that the regular appointment of a senatorial *ab actis senatus* was a contemporary development which served to draw fresh attention to the record—if that innovation really dated from Domitian's reign, as conjectured above. Then Tacitus' own talent and inclination must have played a role. Perhaps above all, however, it was his deep sense of pride in the achievements and sufferings of the corporate body that prompted a marked departure from long-established traditions and the creation of nothing less than a new type of history.

5. Known Holders of the Office *ab Actis Senatus*

Information on holders of this office was gathered long ago by de Ruggiero[1] and Stein,[2] for example, but the only more recent lists seem to be an unpublished one by Morris[3] for 69-193, and a fuller review by Pflaum.[4]

1. Iunius Rusticus (*PIR*[2] I 813), otherwise unknown, reported by Tacitus (*Ann.* 5.4) under 29 as "componendis patrum actis delectus a Caesare."

2. L. Neratius Marcellus (A. R. Birley, *The* Fasti *of Roman Britain*, pp. 87-91), patrician, quaestor Augusti, curator actorum senatus, praetor.

3. C. Iulius Proculus (Cébeillac no. 48, cos. 109), quaestor Augusti, ab actis imperatoris, tribunus plebis.

4. P. Aelius Hadrianus (Cébeillac no. 49, *PIR*[2] A 184), quaestor Caesaris (101), "acta senatus curavit" (HA, *Hadr.* 3.2), tribunus plebis (105).

5. Unknown = *ILS* 1039 (A. Larcius Macedo? *PIR*[2] L 98, cos. ?123), quaestor, ad acta senatus, tribunus plebis.

6. Unknown = *ILS* 1062 (Claudius Maximus? Alföldy, *Konsulat*, p. 334, cos.

---

[54] *Tacitus*, p. 186.

[1] *Diz. Epig.* I (1895) s.v. *acta senatus*, pp. 45-48.

[2] See the works cited in sect. 3 note 43 above: "Die Protokolle," pp. 15-18 and "Die Stenographie," p. 184 n. 25.

[3] J. Morris, "The Roman Senate 69-193 A.D.," unpublished Ph.D. thesis (London, 1953), vol. 2, pages not numbered.

[4] H.-G. Pflaum, *Les fastes de la province de Narbonnaise* (*Gallia*, Supplement 30, Paris, 1978), pp. 27-28.

?142; not T. Statilius Maximus, *PIR*[1] S 602), quaestor urbanus, ab actis senatus, tribunus plebis.

7. M. Pontius Laelianus Larcius Sabinus (Alföldy, *Konsulat*, p. 334, cos. 144), quaestor Galliae Narbonensis, ab actis senatus, tribunus plebis.

8. . . . Plautius Aelius Lamia Silvanus [Aelianus?]: in compiling his list Stein considered Bormann's restoration of *CIL* XI. 5171 too uncertain (a[b actis? imp. Caes. Hadr]iani), but Groag retained it in *PIR*[2] A 206.

9. M. Servilius Fabianus Maximus (Alföldy, *Konsulat*, p. 336, cos. 158), quaestor urbanus, ab actis senatus, aedilis curulis.

10. M. Claudius Fronto (Halfmann, *Die Senatoren*, no. 99, cos. 165), quaestor urbanus, ab actis senatus, aedilis curulis.

11. C. Arrius Antoninus (Alföldy, *Konsulat*, p. 338, cos. c. 173), quaestor urbanus, ab actis senatus, aedilis curulis.

12. Unknown = *IRT* 552, tribunus militum decorated by M. Aurelius and L. Verus, quaestor, p[raepositus?] act[is senatus?] (very fragmentary).

13. P. Ennius Saturninus Karus (A. Beschaouch, *CRAI* 1979. pp. 400-403), quaestor urbanus, ab actis senatus, aedilis curulis designatus. Mid second century?

14. L. Cestius Gallus Cerrinius Iustus Lu[t]atius Natalis (Alföldy, *Konsulat*, p. 341; A. R. Birley, *The* Fasti *of Roman Britain*, pp. 258-259), quaestor urbanus, ab actis senatus, aedilis curulis. Second half of second century.

15. Unknown = *CIL* VI. 3850 = 31809, quaestor, ab actis senatus, aedilis curulis, praetor, honored (?) by the senate on the motion of M. Aurelius.

16. Ti. Claudius Frontinus Niceratus (Halfmann, *Die Senatoren*, no. 126), quaestor Achaiae, ab actis senatus / ἐπὶ τῶν ὑπομνημάτων τῆς συγκλήτου, aedilis curulis, praetor c. 174/5.

17. M. Cassius Paullinus (*PIR*[2] C 513; H.-G. Pflaum, *Archivo Español de Arqueologia* 39. 1966. pp. 21-22, reprinted in *Scripta Varia* II), quaestor Macedoniae, ab actis senatus, perhaps died prematurely. For discussion of the possibility that he was a patrician, see *AE* 1977. 811. Second century date?

18. T. Marcius Cle[mens] (A. R. Birley, *The* Fasti *of Roman Britain*, p. 263), quaestor Achaiae, ab actis senatus, aedilis curulis. Second half of second century?

19. C. Porcius Priscus Longinus (C. Wolff, *PW* 22 s.v. Porcius no. 40, col. 228), adlected inter quaestorios, ab actis senatus, aedilis curulis, magister fratrum Arvalium (224-31).

20. Domitius Florus (*PIR*[2] D 147), reported by Dio (78.22.2) as τὰ τῆς βουλῆς ὑπομνήματα διὰ χειρὸς ἔχων when Plautianus was influential (c. 200).

21. M. Iunius Hermogenes (*PIR*[2] I 758; C. Habicht, *Altertümer von Pergamon*, Band VIII. 3, *Die Inschriften des Asklepieions*, no. 24), quaestor Asiae (under Septimius Severus), [ἐπὶ] ἄκτων τῶν τῆς ἱερᾶς συ[νκλ]ήτου.

22. Q. Comius Armiger Crescens (*PIR*² C 1274), quaestor (between 193 and 211?), ab actis senatus, aedilis curulis.

23. M. Annaeus Saturninus Clodianus Aelianus (*PIR*² A 615), quaestor urbanus (between 193 and 211?), ab actis senatus, tribunus plebis. For Severan date see further G. Camodeca, *Atti dell' Accademia di scienze morali e politiche, Napoli,* 85. 1974. pp. 260-261.

24. Sex. Asinius Rufinus Fabianus (*PIR*² A 1247), quaestor urbanus, ab actis senatus co(n)s(ulum), aedilis Cerealis. Severan date, if he is the son of the consul c. 184 commemorated in *AE* 1954. 58.

25. L. Iulius Apronius Maenius Pius Salamallianus (*PIR*² I 161), adlected inter quaestorios (by Severus/Caracalla?), praepositus actis senatus, aedilis curulis.

26. M. Antonius Me[mmius Hiero], quaestor Lyciae Pamphyliae, aedilis curulis. For the post mentioned between these two, Cagnat (*IGRR* 3.238) and Groag (*PIR*² A 850) followed Ramsay's original restoration (*BCH* 7. 1883. p. 26 no. 17): πράξεις συν]κλήτου εἰλη[φότα. More attractive, however, are two further suggestions: ὑπομνήματα συγ]κλήτου εἰλη[φότα (Stein); ἄκτα συν]κλήτου εἰλη[φότα (Habicht, op. cit. in no. 21 above). If he is identical with Antonius Memmius Hiero (*PIR*² A 851) recorded as legate of Cappadocia under Philippus (244-249), as seems likely, then he was *ab actis senatus* under Severus Alexander perhaps.

27. J. M. Reynolds, *PBSR* 34. 1966. p. 60 = *AE* 1968. no. 166 (S. Etruria). Very fragmentary inscription, by its lettering of second or third century date, commemorating an unidentifiable senator who was quaestor urbanus and aedilis curulis. The gap in between these offices may be filled by ab actis senatus.

UNCERTAIN CASES

28. Unknown = *CIL* XI. 572 (Forum Popili), restored [trib.] mil. leg. . . . [quaest] August . . . [ab actis] senatu[s p]raetor. In compiling his list Stein was understandably cautious about these restorations. It would indeed be unusual, though not unprecedented, for a quaestor Caesaris (and one who would seem to be a patrician) to become ab actis senatus. Ignored by Cébeillac.

29. . . . CANIUS M. . . . = *CIL* IX. 1593 (Beneventum): only the following letters survive: CANIUS. M
                                    TRIB. PL. A
                                    BI. A. L. P
"Trib. pl. a[b actis sen." or "trib. pl. a[dl. inter" have been suggested, both equally uncertain.

30. Unknown = *CIL* XIV. 182. A. R. Birley, *The* Fasti *of Roman Britain,* pp. 282-283, sees the possibility of restoring curator actorum senatus in this record of a career. But the stone is too fragmentary for this to be more than speculation.

31. A. R. Birley, *The* Fasti *of Roman Britain,* pp. 250-251, argues that a stone

recording the career of A. Claudius Charax may have mistakenly conflated his adlection inter aedilicios and tenure of the post of ab actis senatus. For further comment, and a simpler explanation of the curious phrasing in question, see chap. 1 sect. 2 note 35 and Extended Note E.

32. Sex. Oppius Priscus: the only evidence for his career, alleged to include ab actis senatus, is a forged inscription (*CIL* XIV *386 = *Inscr. Ital.* IV. 1. 35*).

Part Three

FUNCTIONS

10

ELECTIONS AND THE LOT

In moving to consider the functions of the senate, we may take first the significant matter of elections and the assignment of appointments by lot.

1. Magistracies

Elections to senatorial magistracies under the Principate have received much attention in recent years,[1] although the most widely discussed aspect—the role of the emperor—is not one which it would be appropriate to treat in detail here. Rather this section will be confined to explaining succinctly the role of the senate as a corporate body.

In the Republic magistrates had been elected by the popular assemblies. The latter evidently continued to function in the traditional manner during the period of the Second Triumvirate, although at the same time many magistrates were simply appointed by the Triumvirs.[2] Not till 27 B.C. were elections in the old style fully restored by Augustus. In A.D. 5 the procedure for the election of praetors and consuls was modified by a *Lex Valeria Cornelia*, known to us through the so-called *Tabula Hebana*.[3] The law gave an important preliminary role to senators and all *equites* enrolled in the *decuriae iudicum*. This group voted in ten centuries—increased to fifteen in A.D. 19 and twenty in 23—to reach a corporate decision. The candidates whom they chose were termed *destinati* and probably matched the number of places to be filled. There followed a vote by the full assembly, at which these *destinati* were likely to gain election, although it was never guaranteed to them. In effect the ten or more centuries acted like the old *centuria praerogativa* in legislative assemblies. Yet despite

---

[1] For discussion and bibliography see, for example, R. Frei-Stolba, *Untersuchungen zu den Wahlen in der römischen Kaiserzeit*, Zurich, 1967; B. M. Levick, "Imperial control of the elections under the early Principate: commendatio, suffragatio and 'nominatio,' " *Historia* 16. 1967. pp. 207-230; A. E. Astin, " 'Nominare' in accounts of elections in the early Principate," *Latomus* 28. 1969. pp. 863-874; F. Millar, *Emperor*, chap. VI. 4; A. J. Holladay, "The election of magistrates in the early Principate," *Latomus* 37. 1978. pp. 874-893.

[2] See F. Millar, "Triumvirate and Principate," *JRS* 63. 1973. pp. 50-67, esp. pp. 52-54.

[3] See P. A. Brunt, "The Lex Valeria Cornelia," *JRS* 51. 1961. pp. 71-83.

their weight it seems false to infer that they were introduced as a means whereby the emperor could influence the outcome of elections. Rather they served mainly to enhance the electoral status of their members. If it had been further intended that they should serve to reduce disturbingly lively contests in the full assembly, riots in 7 soon dashed such hopes.

Any aim that there may have been to restrain the assembly only achieved final success in 14, when during the early weeks of Tiberius' reign elections were transferred entirely to the senate.[4] All the same, as late as the early third century the assemblies still continued to meet for the purpose of ratifying the choice of candidates.[5] It is true that for a short time Gaius did restore to the assemblies their ancient prerogative.[6] Yet senators soon forced him to abandon the scheme by regularly bargaining among themselves beforehand to ensure that no more candidates stood for office than there were vacancies, thus depriving voters of any choice.[7]

Whatever the precise intention behind the transfer of elections to the senate and its timing, there was certainly never any relaxation of the existing constraints upon candidates and voters. For the former, as we have already seen in considering senators' advancement,[8] eligibility for office was governed by various legal provisions. In practice it was also necessary for any candidature to gain the general approval of the emperor. Altogether the degree of influence exercised by him was substantial. Above all, it was apparently he alone who determined the key issue of how many vacancies there should be in the two senior magistracies, the consulship and praetorship.[9] He would also declare positive support for certain candidates, whom members could then hardly reject.[10] Most notably, in the case of the consulship he would always declare support for as many candidates as there were vacancies, with the result that elections to this magistracy were a formality. For all other offices, however, candidates supported by him would usually occupy no more than a proportion of the vacancies, thus allowing genuine competition for the remaining places. In many instances it may be that the number of candidates did not greatly exceed the vacancies available. But into the second century our sources indicate that competition stayed keen: canvassing was taken seriously, and the prospect of rejection

---

[4] Tac. *Ann.* 1.15, "tum primum e campo comitia ad patres translata sunt."

[5] Dio 58.20.4; cf. *ILS* 6044; Suet. *Vesp.* 5; *Dom.* 10; Plin. *Paneg.* 63.2; 92.3.

[6] Suet. *Calig.* 16; Dio 59.9.6-7.

[7] Dio 59.20.3-4.

[8] Chap. 1 sect. 2.

[9] Note, for example, how the number of consulships varied considerably from year to year under Nero, according to P. A. Gallivan, "Some comments on the *Fasti* for the reign of Nero," *CQ* 24. 1974. pp. 290-311.

[10] The *Lex de Imperio Vespasiani* required the election of such candidates (*FIRA*[2] I no. 15. lines 10-13).

was real. As late as Trajan's time efforts were made to reduce the amounts spent on canvassing,[11] and to eliminate the exercise of excessive personal influence by the introduction of secret ballot in place of open voting.

As we have concluded earlier,[12] such evidence as there is argues against any notion that there was a regular time during the Julio-Claudian period at which elections for the consulship were held; of the others we really know nothing. Only by the beginning of the second century does a clear pattern seem to emerge whereby most elections were accomplished on two days in January set aside for this purpose: the first for the election of suffect consuls (to hold office later the same year), praetors and aediles (to hold office the following year), and tribunes (to hold office from 10 December the same year); the second for the election of quaestors to hold office from 5 December the same year. Ordinary consuls were evidently elected at some later session.

While we lack a precise account of the procedure at elections, it is fair to assume that a letter by Pliny[13] preserves the outline: each candidate was called upon in turn; he urged his own merits and might also criticize his opponents; he then called upon some of his principal supporters to speak in his favor. Because of sharp competition, however, this procedure was no longer adhered to in the traditional, orderly fashion by the early second century. The voting which followed was certainly open in the customary senatorial style, but beyond that the arrangements are obscure. It seems reasonable to guess that there was a vote only after all the candidates for a magistracy had been heard, rather than after each individual had recommended himself, and that each candidate was taken in turn—the president, as usual, instructing those in favor to move to one side of the chamber, those against to the other.[14] We cannot say whether the numbers on each side were then counted. It is conceivable that the House followed the same practice in elections as it did when voting upon *sententiae*, namely, a majority in favor was itself sufficient to secure a candidate's election, and names were put to the vote only so long as there remained vacancies to fill. Thus in, say, an election for the tribunate, if the first ten candidates who were voted upon all gained narrow majorities, they would secure election even though the eleventh candidate was widely expected to gain a much larger majority. The order in which candidates were voted upon could then assume considerable importance. We know that the pres-

---

[11] See chap. 2 sect. 3 note 14.

[12] Chap. 6 sect. 4.

[13] *Ep*. 3.20.1-8. There seems to be nothing in Pliny's remarks at *Paneg*. 69ff. inconsistent with the outline in this letter. It should be remembered that in *Panegyricus* he is striving neither for completeness nor for accuracy, and that it was unusual for an emperor to preside, as Trajan did in 100.

[14] See in general chap. 7 sect. 25.

ident put *sententiae* to the vote in the order of his choice. But a similar prerogative at elections might appear to leave him undue discretion, and it would not be surprising to find that recourse was had to the lot. All the same, whatever method was chosen, it must have been arranged that candidates supported by the emperor were placed first; and conceivably in their case the formality of a vote might even have been dispensed with.

According to Pliny,[15] in Trajan's time members called for the introduction of secret ballot at elections, not to eliminate any element of potential unfairness in the system of open voting, but rather to reduce the exercise of excessive personal influence. After a ballot an accurate count of the votes cast for each candidate was presumably made, and those with the highest poll were elected; so here the number of votes cast could be especially important. The administrative arrangements made for the ballot—distribution of *tabellae*, tellers, counts, and so forth—are hidden from us not least because the whole experiment seems to have been so short-lived. There was perhaps a return to open voting after certain members had brought the new method into disrepute by spoiling their *tabellae* in an offensive fashion.[16] It is impossible to say whether they were merely childish, or rather perhaps calculatingly irresponsible.

There can be little doubt that the degree of influence exercised over elections by the emperor increased with time. In addition, imperial adlection of members to a higher grade came to provide an alternative to advancement through magistracies, and thus lessened the urgency of securing election to them.[17] We cannot say how long open competition survived for vacancies below the consulship, though it did perhaps continue at least to the end of M. Aurelius' reign. The *Historia Augusta*[18] mentions one Vetrasinus who appears to have been thoroughly disapproved of by Marcus, yet competed for an unspecified office all the same. Equally, in recording Septimius Severus' election to the praetorship in the same reign, the *Historia Augusta* seems to draw a contrast between candidates of the emperor and those, like Severus himself, who were elected "in the crowd of competitors."[19] On a very strict interpretation, of course, this passage may simply indicate that some candidates received the emperor's support, while others did not, rather than that there were more candidates than vacancies. In the same way the reference in the *Historia Augusta*[20] to the continuation of proceedings until nighttime on election days during Marcus' time might

---

[15] *Ep.* 3.20.7.
[16] Plin. *Ep.* 4.25.
[17] See chap. 1 sect. 2.
[18] *Marcus* 12.3.
[19] *Sev.* 3.3, "in competitorum grege."
[20] *Marcus* 10.8.

not indicate competition, when even in Pliny's day speeches were made in support of consuls whose election was assured. All the same, competition is again the natural inference here.

From a reference in Dio[21] relating to 217, we know that one or more "election days" survived into the early third century. If the contemporary jurist Modestinus is to be believed, the occasion was now only a formality. In commenting on the *Lex Julia Ambitus*, he opens by explaining: "Today this law no longer applies in the City, since the appointment of magistrates is a matter for the consideration of the emperor, not the favor of the people."[22] Likewise Ulpian[23] writes quite plainly of praetors and consuls being granted their magistracies by the emperor—without reference to the senate. We lack further evidence to check whether or not such claims for the role of the emperor are too sweeping, and in any event the question is of limited significance. Not only had election to the highest office, the consulship, regularly been determined by him, but the importance of all magistracies had also long declined. Throughout our period the senate had never played more than a subordinate part in elections to them.

2. Priesthoods

There is no question that the senate made the emperor a member of all the priestly colleges on his accession[1] (subject to formal ratification by a popular assembly perhaps),[2] and voted likewise that priesthoods be conferred upon members of his family.[3] There are also many references throughout our period to conferment of priesthoods on others by the emperor alone,[4] and it is plain that he came to acquire authority to act thus.[5] Though the formal power may not have been conveyed as early as 20,

---

[21] 78.14.2.

[22] *Dig.* 48.14.1 pr., "haec lex in urbe hodie cessat, quia ad curam principis magistratuum creatio pertinet, non ad populi favorem."

[23] *Dig.* 42.1.57.

[1] See chap. 11 sect. 1. Note the co-option of Elagabalus and Maximinus as *Sodales Antoniniani* (?) *ex s.c.* on their accession (*CIL* VI. 2001) and the conjecture that the former was likewise co-opted as Arval Brother at the same time (*Arval Acta*, para. 88b. lines 25-26).

[2] *RG* 10; *EJ* Calendars p. 47, 6 March (Augustus); ibid. 10 March (Tiberius); *Arval Acta* para. 34 I. lines 70, 73-74 (Otho).

[3] Cf. Suet. *Claud.* 6; HA, *Marcus* 6.3; *ILS* 5025 (Nero, Titus, and Caracalla "adlectus ad numerum ex s.c." or "super numerum cooptatus ex s.c." into the *Sodales Augustales* in 51, 71, and 197 respectively); *BMC* I. p. 176 nos. 84-88 and p. 397 (Nero SACERD COOPT IN OMN CONL SUPRA NUM EX S C); *CIL* VI. 2001 (the future emperor Severus Alexander co-opted *Sodalis Antoninianus* (?) *ex s.c.* as Caesar in 221).

[4] See list in M.W.H. Lewis, *The Official Priests of Rome under the Julio-Claudians*, p. 16 n. 47.

[5] Cf. Dio 51.20.3; 53.17.8; F. Millar, *Emperor*, chap. VI. 8.

Tiberius was arguably just displaying tact in this year when he took to the House the proposition that three of the prosecutors be granted priesthoods after the trial of Piso.[6]

So far as we can tell, the senate normally played no part in elevating priests to the lesser colleges; these co-opted their members, commonly on imperial recommendation.[7] Yet the procedure for elevation to the four major colleges—pontiffs, augurs, *quindecimviri sacris faciundis, septemviri epulonum*—is less certain. Normally no man outside the imperial family would hold more than one of these priesthoods. The arrangement of the late Republic whereby candidates were elected in a special assembly of 17 of the 35 tribes chosen by lot must have been ended early in our period—perhaps in 14 when, as we have seen, elections for magistracies were transferred to the senate. We lack information about the new procedure until the mid first century when the tombstone of Q. Veranius mentions that as consul in 49 he was created augur on the nomination of a person whose name has been lost.[8] At the end of the century Pliny writes of a day "on which the priests customarily nominate those they judge most worthy of a priesthood"; he claims that his guardian, Verginius Rufus, always used to nominate him.[9] Later he says[10] that Julius Frontinus regularly did the same, perhaps with the intention of co-opting him as a successor. Though such nominations were presumably made in the House, they are otherwise unheard of[11] and their purpose remains unclear. Were they merely a means of indicating to the emperor members approved by the House whom he might later call upon to fill vacancies at his pleasure? Or were the nominations followed, either at once, or later, by an election in the House? We cannot say, although any such vote must have been a formality for members, since everything would seem to have depended upon the emperor's wishes, and his choice of candidates can never have been confined to senatorial nominees. Not surprisingly, it was Trajan from whom Pliny first sought an augurate or septemvirate, and the emperor likewise to whom he felt grateful after his elevation.[12] We never hear of aspiring priests attempting to canvass members, in the way that candidates certainly did when seeking magistracies where the House was left a choice. In sum, it was indeed a new development for the senate to become involved in the choice of holders of major priesthoods during the Principate, but there is nothing to suggest that its role was ever more than slight.

[6] Tac. *Ann.* 3.19.

[7] See M. Hammond, *The Antonine Monarchy*, p. 70.

[8] See A. E. Gordon, *Q. Veranius Consul A.D. 49*, pp. 254-256.

[9] *Ep.* 2.1.8, "sic illo die quo sacerdotes solent nominare quos dignissimos sacerdotio iudicant, me semper nominabat."

[10] *Ep.* 4.8.3.

[11] But note that Seneca (*De Benef.* 7.28.2) can speak of a candidate for priesthoods.

[12] *Ep.* 10.13; 4.8.

3. The Lot

In our period, as in the late Republic, the House preferred to use the lot in selecting members for most special tasks. Predictably enough, in late 69 Helvidius Priscus' novel suggestion that envoys to Vespasian be chosen individually by magistrates under oath provoked a bitter reaction from Eprius Marcellus. The latter's hostility was personal; but he also urged adherence to tradition. As he said, according to Tacitus: "It was the consul designate who had put forward the [original] proposal in accordance with long-standing precedents which fixed lot as the method employed to choose deputations, in order to give no scope for self-seeking or personal animosities. Nothing had happened to render an established principle obsolete. . . ."[1]

After debate the lot was used in this instance, as no doubt on other such occasions. We can cite two specific examples—deputations sent to Gaius, and to Trajan on his adoption by Nerva.[2] Yet it was by no means only envoys who were chosen thus. Though the scheme was never carried through, membership of the senate as revised by Augustus in 18 B.C. was to depend on the lot to a significant degree.[3] The fifteen private members who sat on his advisory *consilium* for six-month periods were chosen by this method, as were those to form a quorum at sessions of the House in September and October, and those to pay a fine when there had been many absentees from a session.[4] *Praefecti frumenti dandi, curatores alvei Tiberis*, and *praetores aerarii* were picked thus.[5] The lot was used to divide the celebration of festivals between praetors,[6] and the *cura urbis* between praetors, aediles, and tribunes: Dio[7] notes that the latter arrangement continued in his own day. When there were insufficient men to serve as quaestor in 24 B.C., or as aedile or tribune on a number of occasions, former junior magistrates were required to cast lots to fill the vacancies.[8] The twenty members whom Togonius Gallus proposed should guard Tiberius at sessions were to be selected by lot.[9] More seriously, the composition of committees set up for special tasks might be determined thus—in A.D. 6, for example, the board of three consulars to regulate expenditure; in 20 the five consulars, five *praetorii*, and five other senators commis-

[1] *Hist.* 4.8.
[2] Dio 59.23.2; Martial 10.6.1-4; see further chap. 14 sect. 1.
[3] Dio 54.13.2-4.
[4] Suet. *Aug.* 35; Dio 53.21.4; 55.3.3; *FIRA*[2] I no. 68 V line 87.
[5] Tac. *Ann.* 13.29; Dio 54.17.1; 57.14.8.
[6] Dio 59.14.2; 60.31.7.
[7] 55.8.7.
[8] Dio 53.28.4; 54.26.7; 55.24.9.
[9] Tac. *Ann.* 6.2.

sioned to resolve confusion and fear produced by the *Lex Papia Poppaea*; and various boards to undertake tasks of restoration after the civil war of 68/9.[10] Similarly in 26 the extra legate attached to the proconsul of Asia for supervising erection of the temple to Tiberius, Livia, and the senate at Smyrna was chosen by lot from the *praetorii*, after the governor had declined to make an appointment himself.[11] By contrast, the five members commissioned to reduce public expenditure under Nerva were actually elected.[12]

The *senatus consultum* sent to Cyrene by Augustus in 4 B.C. laid down an elaborate scheme for selection by lot of four consulars, three *praetorii*, and two other senators to make up a panel of five for hearing provincials' claims for money extorted by governors. (Up to four of the original nine could be rejected by plaintiff and defendant.) At least 200 members were to be present, and those over seventy, incapacitated, more than twenty miles from Rome, or engaged on specified official duties, were to be ineligible.[13] As part of this procedure the provincials were to be granted the senatorial advocate they asked for, provided he were willing and able. Later, when somewhat different procedures applied, we know that the senate continued to appoint members as advocates in such cases. So in a letter from Pliny to Trajan about the prosecution of Marius Priscus at the end of the first century, it is puzzling to find the statement that these advocates were chosen by lot,[14] especially as elsewhere Pliny[15] represents himself as having acted as defense counsel at the senate's bidding.

More significant perhaps than the use of the lot on these special occasions was its regular annual use to assign posts to quaestors and praetors, and proconsulships to more senior members. The timing and the arrangements in detail are mostly hidden from us.[16] We cannot say, for example, whether members had to give notice of their intention to enter a ballot, or whether they had to be present in person for the occasion. We know only that the order in which they drew lots was determined according to whether or not they were married, and the number of their children.[17] Among quaestors, the names of those chosen as aides by the emperor or the consuls must have been set aside,[18] so that only fourteen or so out of the twenty holders

[10] Dio 55.25.6; Tac. *Ann.* 3.28; *Hist.* 4.40.
[11] Tac. *Ann.* 4.56.
[12] Plin. *Paneg.* 62.2; cf. *Ep.* 2.1.9; Dio 68.2.1.
[13] *FIRA*[2] I no. 68 V lines 104ff.
[14] *Ep.* 10.3A.2.
[15] *Ep.* 2.11.2; 3.4; 6.29.7; cf. 7.33. See further chap. 16 sect. 2 note 19.
[16] See further chap. 6 sect. 4. In mentioning the ballot for advocates Pliny (*Ep.* 10.3A.2) does speak of "nomina nostra in urnam conici," but the description might just be figurative; cf. Tac. *Hist.* 4.6.
[17] Dio 53.13.2.
[18] Note how Velleius Paterculus (2.111.4) withdrew from the lot because he had been appointed legate to Tiberius. For quaestors being chosen by consuls, see Plin. *Ep.* 4.15.

each year would draw for assignment to a province or for service as *quaestor urbanus*.[19] Augustus required *praetorii* to be of five years' standing before they were eligible for assignment to a proconsular province.[20] Presumably the ten or so most senior members in this grade who were willing and able to serve could draw for such governorships. The alternative arrangement seems less likely—namely, that any *praetorius* of five years' standing could enter automatically. If this were permitted, then some competitors might emerge with nothing. Such a result is unheard-of in surviving sources, although of course we could hardly expect it to be mentioned.[21] Certainly it was no more than the two most senior consulars free of other commitments who drew for Africa and Asia. In this instance there was normally the additional restriction that no individual should serve more than one term in one of these two exalted offices.[22] In 22, after the governor of Africa's term had been extended and the application of Servius Maluginensis to be assigned Asia had been rejected because he was *Flamen Dialis*, Tacitus[23] explains how the province was then allotted to the next consular after him. In the late 150's Fronto[24] speaks of his "right" to enter the lot for Africa or Asia. No doubt he would have preferred to serve in his native province, but, as he explains, a fellow consular was given precedence in the ballot because of his children, and he drew (or chose) Africa. The interval which would elapse before a consular became eligible for either governorship in this way naturally varied, but in practice it was usually between ten and fifteen years.[25] After the revolt of Avidius Cassius all senators were forbidden by law from governing their native provinces.[26]

[19] Cf. Dio 53.14.5. Until 44 there were posts in Italy too: see chap. 1 sect. 2 note 8.

[20] Dio 53.14.2.

[21] In the quaestors' ballot about three men must regularly have drawn "no post" from the mid first century, since there would seldom have been more than eleven or so vacancies in the provinces (and no longer any in Italy): see further above, chap. 4 sect. 1. For all we know, men not otherwise occupied may have been attached, say, to the consuls. All the same, it is striking that in many inscriptions the post held as quaestor is not specified. While there must be a variety of reasons for such an omission, one of them may well be that there was indeed no post for some men to record.

[22] Some governors had their tenure prolonged beyond one year (see Appendix 8), but the only man who governed, or was to govern, both provinces seems to have been C. Iulius Asper. Having served as proconsul of Africa in some year between 200 and 210, at the very end of Caracalla's reign he was appointed to Asia. The emperor died before considering Asper's request to decline. Macrinus at first confirmed the appointment, but then tactlessly withdrew it (Dio 78.22.3-4; *PIR*² I 182; H. Halfmann, *Die Senatoren*, no. 134).

[23] *Ann.* 3.58 and 71.

[24] *Ant. Pium* 8.1 = p. 161 H.

[25] For discussion, see B. E. Thomasson, *Die Statthalter der römischen Provinzen Nordafrikas von Augustus bis Diocletianus* I, Lund, 1960, chap. 2. Philostratus (*Vit. Soph.* 556) makes the puzzling remark that in grief at the death of his wife (c. 160) Herodes Atticus δευτέραν κλήρωσιν τῆς ὑπάτου ἀρχῆς ἐπ᾽ αὐτῇ ἀναβαλέσθαι. As Stein concludes (*PIR*² C 802, pp. 177-178), this is presumably a careless reference to drawing lots for a proconsulship of Africa or Asia, rather than actually for the magistracy itself, where such a procedure is unheard-of. We do not know why a second entry should have been necessary.

[26] Dio 71.31.1.

For many members the province to which they were allotted as quaestor or governor was not a matter of indifference. It is natural to ask therefore whether interested parties could bring influence to bear (and if so, by what means), or whether the lot was invariably left to operate at random. As usual, there are few clear-cut answers. First it should be remembered that the governorship of any proconsular province might be removed from the ballot and a governor appointed, though as far as we can tell this was only done when special circumstances arose in the area, and never for the personal reasons of securing a particular post for one individual or denying it to another. One partial exception to this claim would seem to be Gaius' action in Africa: he allegedly did nothing to stop M. Silanus from gaining the province through the lot, but was then so alarmed by the prospect of his raising a rebellion that he removed the one legion stationed there (III Augusta) from proconsular control.[27] Less rarely both emperor and senate might debar certain individuals from drawing lots in the first place. Not surprisingly, in 22 Tiberius rejected the sweeping proposal of Cornelius Dolabella that members "of scandalous life and evil reputation" be excluded from the ballot, the emperor to be judge.[28] But it was a letter from the same emperor which excluded the wastrel C. Galba, suffect consul in 22 and brother of the future emperor, from competing for Africa or Asia in 36.[29] Domitian, too, allegedly put pressure upon Agricola not to compete for these proconsulships when he became eligible.[30] As part of his policy of ensuring that governors should always remain in Rome as *privati* for one year after their service, Claudius even forbade a man who had been a legate from entering the ballot for a governorship at once.[31] In 22 Sextus Pompeius was unsuccessful in his proposal that on moral grounds the House debar Manius Lepidus from being assigned Asia, for which he was otherwise eligible.[32] But after a hearing in 100 it did sentence Hostilius Firminus, legate of the governor of Africa, Marius Priscus, to exclusion from the ballot for governorships.[33]

There is evidence to suggest that the lot did not operate altogether at random. From their respective studies of office-holders in Achaea and Baetica, for example, both Groag and Alföldy[34] considered that the number

[27] Tac. *Hist.* 4.48; Dio 59.20.7; see further below, chap. 13 note 5.
[28] Tac. *Ann.* 3.69.
[29] Tac. *Ann.* 6.40; Suet. *Galba* 3, "prohibitusque a Tiberio sortiri anno suo proconsulatum." "Anno suo" must have the sense of "when he reached the requisite seniority": cf. following note.
[30] Tac. *Agr.* 42.
[31] Dio 60.25.6.
[32] Tac. *Ann.* 3.32. Since a proconsul of Africa was to be appointed in this year, the "lot" for Asia was a formality.
[33] Plin. *Ep.* 2.12.2.
[34] E. Groag, *Die römischen Reichsbeamten von Achaia bis auf Diokletian*, Vienna and Leipzig, 1939, col. 156; G. Alföldy, *Fasti Hispanienses*, Wiesbaden, 1969, pp. 269-270.

of men with local connections serving in these provinces as quaestor and proconsul was higher than random selection was likely to produce. In general, too, among senators of Greek or eastern origin, the proportion found serving in that part of the empire, rather than in the west, is a high one[35]—although of course in any case the majority of proconsular provinces did lie to the east. Equally, it may not have been just accident which gave T. Clodius Eprius Marcellus the proconsulship of Cyprus soon after his acquittal on charges of *repetundae* as governor of Lycia in 57. Once his principal Lycian enemies had been exiled for accusing an "innocent" man, Cyprus was a remarkably convenient spot from which to renew old business contacts![36]

Some bargaining over posts by individuals is understandable; for all we know, private deals or exchanges may have been struck behind the scenes from time to time. Yet in the case of proconsulships for which *praetorii* competed, Eck[37] makes the much more sweeping claim that Cyprus and Crete with Cyrene were rated notably lower than the others—Baetica, Narbonensis, Sicily, Macedonia, Achaea, Bithynia/Pontus—and were regularly assigned to undistinguished members. As he appreciates, if this claim is well-founded, then doubt is cast on just how random the operation of the lot ever was. In fact his own comprehensive information shows that our all-important prosopographical evidence is insufficient to uphold the claim.[38] To generalize with confidence about the status of the governors of many proconsular provinces over two-and-a-half centuries or so is impossible, not least because our knowledge remains so incomplete. If we seek only the names of the governors of, say, Narbonensis in the first century A.D., let alone information about their careers before or after tenure of the post, we know fewer than ten out of a possible hundred.[39] In Sicily, too, we have the name of hardly a single proconsul from Gaius' time well into the second century,[40] and later in the same century there is another huge gap. For Cyprus likewise a similar blank begins after Hadrian's day and extends to Septimius Severus' reign. Eck recognizes that as a group proconsuls generally tended to be drawn from members pursuing less distinguished careers. So it is difficult to differentiate meaningfully between them further, especially when such a limited proportion of the relevant

[35] For discussion, see H. Halfmann, *Die Senatoren*, pp. 88-94.

[36] For his career see *PIR*[2] E 84; Tac. *Ann.* 13.33; *AE* 1956. 186, with comment by M. Griffin, *Seneca: A Philosopher in Politics*, p. 91 n. 2.

[37] W. Eck, "Über die prätorischen Prokonsulate in der Kaiserzeit. Eine quellenkritische Überlegung," *Zephyrus* 23/24. 1972/3. pp. 233-260; cf. idem, *ANRW* II.i. pp. 204-205.

[38] Note especially his table in *Zephyrus* 23/24. 1972/3. p. 256.

[39] See now H.-G. Pflaum, *Les fastes de la province de Narbonnaise*, chap. 1.

[40] But note now T. Iunius Montanus, proconsul prior to his suffect consulship in 81 (W. Eck, *PW* Suppl. 15 cols. 125-126).

evidence is at our disposal. Altogether he perhaps imposes a more schematic approach than is appropriate.

It is very likely that some provinces were considered more desirable than others on grounds of distance from Rome, size, wealth, or climate, and that therefore these were the areas most keenly sought after.[41] Certainly Dio[42] can claim that Caracalla posted officials who had lost his favor to those provinces with the most extreme climate, deliberately aiming thereby to ruin their health. In writing to Maximus on his appointment as *curator* of *civitates liberae* in Achaea Pliny[43] understandably draws a contrast between his friend's previous service as quaestor—assigned by lot to remote Bithynia with its servile inhabitants—and the prospect now before him as a specially appointed official to deal with free men in an area nearer to Rome. It is possible that Crete with Cyrene was an unpopular posting. Not only were its territories awkwardly separated by sea, but judging by a letter from Antoninus Pius to Cyrene its assize circuit also kept the proconsul notably busy.[44] The remoteness and comparatively small size of Cyprus may also have been unappealing. Yet equally a posting to Sardinia and Corsica can have held little attraction beyond the islands' proximity to Rome. The former at any rate always had a reputation for bad climate, and its inhabitants were disliked by Romans.[45]

For certain individuals, where influence could be brought to bear or special interests were at stake, the lot may well have been manipulated. But for others random operation seems most probable. Among undistinguished members like the future emperors Vespasian and Septimius Severus, it was presumably just chance that the former drew Crete with Cyrene as quaestor, while the latter drew Baetica as quaestor and Sicily as *praetorius*.[46] More generally, allegations from the Julio-Claudian period of fictitious marriages and adoptions by those entering the ballot might suggest that it was impossible for the members concerned to secure a particular post which they desired. Rather, the most they could do was to improve their position in the order for drawing lots.[47] Random selection of two *praetores aerarii* each year is certainly implied by the reason which

[41] Some provinces more than others do seem to be held by *praetorii* who proceed very soon thereafter to the consulship: for a list, see H.-G. Pflaum, *Bonn. Jahrb.* 163. 1963. p. 226. But again it should be stressed that while the number of identifiable instances is comparatively tiny, even so the spread is wide—at least one case of such promotion from every proconsular province except Crete with Cyrene and Sardinia.

[42] 77.11.6-7.

[43] *Ep.* 8.24.9.

[44] J. M. Reynolds, *JRS* 68. 1978. p. 114 lines 70-77.

[45] See H. Philipp, *PW* 1A s.v. Sardinia, col. 2495.

[46] Suet. *Vesp.* 2; HA, *Sev.* 2.3; 4.2.

[47] Tac. *Ann.* 15.19; Suet. *Tib.* 35.

Tacitus[48] gives for ending the practice in 44 and appointing quaestors instead: according to him, the lot tended to fall upon unsuitable men. Though the historical reliability of the story must remain uncertain, we may note further how during his discussion with Vespasian at Alexandria, Philostratus[49] has Apollonius ask the emperor that proconsuls should be suitable for the areas assigned to them, insofar as the lot will allow. Without naming names, he cites the difficulties which he witnessed himself between Greeks and a governor of Achaea unsympathetic to its inhabitants and unable to speak the language. Finally, Dio's remark[50] that governors of senatorial provinces came to be chosen by the emperor rather than by lot, because some men selected by the latter method had governed badly, could likewise be taken to imply random operation.

Throughout our period proconsuls are regularly referred to by contemporaries as officials "chosen by lot."[51] It is right to think that the description carried some meaning, even if eventually the ballot became no more than a formality because appointments were controlled by the emperor.[52]

---

[48] *Ann.* 13.29; cf. *ILS* 966 erected to Domitius Decidius, "qui primu[s quaes]tor per triennium citra [sorte]m praeesset aerario Saturni."

[49] *Vit. Apoll.* 5.36.

[50] 53.14.3.

[51] In addition to references in this section, note Tac. *Ann.* 2.43; Plin. *Ep.* 4.9.2; 6.22.7; Aelian, *Hist. Anim.* 13.21; Tertullian, *Ad Nat.* 1.7; Dio 55.28.2; 56.40.3; 57.14.5; 69.14.4; 78.30.4; 79.3.5; Paulus, *Dig.* 1.7.36.1; *CIL* II. 3838, VI. 1361 discussed by G. Alföldy, *Fasti Hispanienses*, pp. 166 and 172 respectively; *CIL* IX. 4119; *ILS* 1011 and 1104; *Aes Ital.*, *Hesperia* 24. 1955. p. 333, lines 53-55. For proconsuls *extra* or *citra sortem*, see chap. 13 note 34. For quaestors chosen by lot, note *CIL* VI. 1426 and chap. 6 sect. 4 note 24 above.

[52] It could be, as B. W. Jones suggests, that in time the ballot merely allocated provinces among the requisite number of *praetorii* nominated by the emperor. But such an arrangement would hardly have been introduced as early as the Flavian period (*Domitian and the Senatorial Order*, Memoirs of the American Philosophical Society 132, 1979. p. 68).

11

IMPERIAL POWERS AND OTHER HONORS

This chapter considers the senate's grant and withdrawal of imperial powers and titles, together with the bestowal of a wide range of other honors, by no means all of which are easy to classify neatly. It is inevitable, therefore, that there should be places where the treatment seems little better than an untidy patchwork. Ironically, such an impression may in fact prove a fair reflection of the character of business at many sessions, where a succession of trivial, uncontentious, and unrelated honors might be proposed.

1. Imperial Powers and Titles

In law every emperor's position rested upon investiture by the senate.[1] It must be acknowledged that this function was usually a formality. Almost without exception each emperor was designated by his predecessor, or was a usurper backed by military force: either way rejection by the senate was equally impracticable. Thus all usurpers after Vitellius dated their reigns from the day of their recognition by troops, not from the day of the senate's investiture.[2] Yet no other prerogative gave the House greater prestige. All the same, we know remarkably little of the bestowal of powers beyond the time of Augustus and Tiberius. We can trace the gradual development of the former's position over many years; and even if greater precision would be welcome, Tacitus still affords some brief insight into the transfer of power to the latter in 14. Thereafter it is clear that the accession of all emperors, no matter how they emerged, continued to be marked by bestowal of powers on the part of the senate. Unlike Tiberius, Gaius was only a *privatus* when he succeeded in 37, so that a fully comprehensive grant

[1] For full discussion, see B. Parsi, *Désignation et investiture de l'empereur romain*, Paris, 1963.
[2] See M. Hammond, "The transmission of the powers of the Roman emperor from the death of Nero in A.D. 68 to that of Alexander Severus in A.D. 235," *MAAR* 24. 1956. pp. 61-133; idem, *The Antonine Monarchy*, p. 20 n. 36.

was required at once. There seems no reason to doubt the testimony that it was duly voted at a single session.[3] This pattern of a comprehensive grant voted at a single session most probably came to be followed on all later occasions too.[4] A strong claim can be made that the so-called *Lex de Imperio* preserves part of a *senatus consultum* passed when Vespasian was formally recognized at Rome in December 69.[5] Yet even if this identification be accepted, we still lack full knowledge of any emperor's grant. In addition to receiving *imperium, tribunicia potestas*, and a whole range of lesser prerogatives, he must have been granted the name of *imperator*, as well as the office of Pontifex Maximus and membership of all the priestly colleges.[6] It is likely therefore that more than one decree would be passed initially, while we know that completion of all the formalities might be spread over weeks or even months. For example, Tiberius was not made Pontifex Maximus until 10 March 15.[7] In 69 Otho's *tribunicia potestas*, membership of all the priestly colleges, and election as Pontifex Maximus were each ratified at separate *comitia*.[8]

Names and titles appropriate to the emperor and members of his family either on accession or later were to be voted by the House, not merely usurped.[9] Galba was scrupulous enough to use none of those voted to him until in the course of his march to Rome he actually met the embassy sent by the senate at Narbo.[10] Even in the third century Dio, the consular historian, can deplore the way in which Macrinus and Elagabalus brazenly headed their letters to the senate with titles never awarded to them in due form. He explains how the appellations Caesar, Augustus, and *pater patriae* had come to be voted to emperors on accession.[11] Earlier in the period the latter title had sometimes not been offered, let alone accepted, till later in a reign.[12] Notably Gaius, though offered it on his accession, did not formally accept until eighteen months later.[13]

---

[3] Suet. *Calig.* 14; Dio 59.3.1-2.

[4] Note especially Tac. *Hist.* 1.47; 2.55; 4.3 (Otho, Vitellius, Vespasian).

[5] *FIRA*[2] I no. 15 with P. A. Brunt, "Lex de Imperio Vespasiani," *JRS* 67. 1977. pp. 95-116.

[6] See chap. 10 sect. 2.

[7] *EJ* Calendars, p. 47.

[8] *Arval Acta*, para. 34 I. lines 60, 70, 73-74.

[9] For specific mention of bestowal by the senate, see for example: Vell. 2.91.1; Plin. *Paneg.* 21.1-2; 84.6; 88.4-6; Tac. *Ann.* 12.26; Suet. *Aug.* 7, 58; *Tib.* 50; *Nero* 8; *Vesp.* 12; Dio 53.16.6; 55.10.10; 57.8.1; 70.2.1; HA, *Antonin.* 2.3; *Commod.* 8.1 and 9; *Pert.* 5.4-6; 15.2; *Did. Jul.* 4.5; *Macrinus* 11.2; Eutropius, *Brev.* 8.19; *P. Colon.* 4701. col. I lines 1-6 in *ZPE* 5. 1970. p. 226.

[10] Dio 63.29.6; Plut. *Galba* 11.

[11] 78.16.2; 79.2.2-3; 53.18.4.

[12] Note Appian, *Bell. Civ.* 2.7; and see further M. Hammond, *The Antonine Monarchy*, pp. 87-89.

[13] See the sacrifice of the Arval Brethren on 21 September 38, "Quod eo die C. Caesar

THE SENATE not only conferred powers and titles upon the emperor and members of his family. It also claimed the right to declare them public enemies, to blot out their memory, and to rescind their acts.[14] The first of these prerogatives derived from the ancient ritual of declaring war, which perhaps still continued under the Principate; at least, according to Dio,[15] Decebalus, King of Dacia, was pronounced *hostis* by the senate before each of Trajan's campaigns against him. Germanicus' elder sons Nero and Drusus were declared *hostis* by the senate at Tiberius' instigation,[16] but the first emperor to suffer this fate during his lifetime was Nero in 68.[17] It was shared by Maximinus and his son,[18] and also in effect by Didius Julianus, whose death was ordered outright.[19] Commodus was pronounced *hostis* immediately after his assassination.[20] If Dio[21] is to be believed, Macrinus hoped that Caracalla might be treated likewise, but neither emperor nor senate proved willing to take the initiative.

Rebels and usurpers might equally be pronounced *hostes*. We hear of the senate acting thus against Galba,[22] Avidius Cassius,[23] Septimius Severus,[24] and Clodius Albinus.[25] Dio describes the traditional measures taken as soon as news of Elagabalus' bid for the Principate reached Rome in 218: "The consuls uttered certain declarations against him, as is regularly done in such cases, and one of the praetors and one of the tribunes did the same. War was declared and proclaimed against not only Elagabalus and his cousin, but also against their mothers and grandmother."[26]

Other measures passed against emperors and members of their families derived from penalties for *maiestas* or treason, such as erasure of the condemned man's name from the Fasti (proposed in the case of Piso in

Augustus Germanicus cons[ensu] senatus delatum sibi patris patriae nomen recepisset in Ca[pitolio]" (J. Scheid and H. Broise, *MEFR* 92.1980. p. 225 lines 57-58, with commentary, pp. 240-242). Cf. Dio 59.3.2; *BMC* I. p. 152 no. 38; and for "consensus," ibid. p. 155 no. 55.

[14] In general see F. Vittinghoff, *Der Staatsfeind in der römischen Kaiserzeit: Untersuchungen zur "damnatio memoriae,"* Berlin, 1936; M. Hammond, *The Antonine Monarchy*, pp. 339-342.

[15] 68.10.4; cf. in general Pomponius, *Dig.* 50.16.118.

[16] Suet. *Tib.* 54; *Calig.* 7.

[17] Suet. *Nero* 49; Dio 63.27.2b.

[18] HA, *Maximin.* 15.2; Herodian 7.7.2 with Whittaker ad loc.

[19] Dio 74.17.4; Herodian 2.12.6.

[20] Dio 74.2.1.

[21] 78.17.2-4.

[22] Plut. *Galba* 5.

[23] HA, *Marcus* 24.9.

[24] Dio 74.16.1; HA, *Did. Jul.* 5.3; *Sev.* 5.5.

[25] HA, *Sev.* 9.1.

[26] 79.38.1. For loss of rights by those whom the senate pronounced *hostes*, note Paulus, *Dig.* 4.5.5.1.

20, but opposed by Tiberius),[27] or removal of his statues (required by the senate in the case of C. Silius in 24).[28] The House passed savage decrees against Livilla's statues and even her memory in 32; it was similarly harsh after the death of Messalina in 48.[29] The birthdays of Agrippina the elder and younger were declared *dies nefasti*.[30]

According to Suetonius,[31] after Gaius' assassination some senators proposed that all memory of the Caesars be wiped out. On Claudius' accession there was a further move to dishonor Gaius, including a proposal that the day of his death be celebrated. Claudius opposed these extremes, so that in the end neither Tiberius nor Gaius had any such measure passed against them. But apparently Gaius' acts were rescinded, and bronze coinage bearing his portrait was to be melted down.[32] On Domitian's death the House voted that all record of him be erased,[33] while Antoninus, on meeting with resistance to his request for the deification of Hadrian, pointedly asked if the senate intended to pronounce him *hostis* and rescind his acts—not least among the latter, of course, being the adoption of a successor.[34] Orders were given for the names of Commodus and Elagabalus to be erased.[35] Caracalla was not dishonored thus, but his acts were annulled.[36]

Our concern here must be limited to the senate's role in passing measures of this nature. But it is relevant to add that we lack evidence of any steps to enforce formally the erasure of names, say, or the removal of statues; probably there were none taken. Likewise the practical consequences of the annulment of an emperor's acts are uncertain. In the case of Julius Bassus, a former governor of Bithynia-Pontus, who was condemned on a charge of *repetundae* in 103, and his acts there annulled, we know that the senate at least permitted anyone sentenced by him to apply for a retrial within two years.[37] By contrast, we lack all details of the senatorial decrees passed against the emperor Domitian on his death. But there evidently followed such widespread uncertainty about the validity of his

[27] Tac. *Ann.* 3.18.

[28] Tac. *Ann.* 4.18-20; 11.35. On penalties see further Ulpian, *Dig.* 28.3.6.11; Paulus, *CJ* 9.8.6 pr.-2.

[29] Tac. *Ann.* 6.2; 11.38.

[30] Suet. *Tib.* 53; Tac. *Ann.* 14.12. Antony's birthday was likewise declared "vitiosus ex s.c." (*Inscr. Ital.* XIII. 2. pp. 362, 397 s.v. 14 January).

[31] *Calig.* 60.

[32] Suet. *Claud.* 11; Dio 60.4.5 and 22.3.

[33] Plin. *Paneg.* 52.4-5; Suet. *Dom.* 23; Lactantius, *De Mort. Persecut.* 3.3; Eusebius, *Hist. Eccl.* 3.20.8; Procopius, *Hist. Arcana* 8.13.

[34] Dio 70.1.3; cf. HA, *Hadr.* 27.

[35] HA, *Commod.* 17.6; 20.4-5; cf. *Pert.* 6.3; *Elagab.* 17.4; 18.1; *Sev. Alex.* 1.2.

[36] Dio 78.9.2 and 18.5.

[37] Plin. *Ep.* 10.56.4.

measures that Nerva felt compelled to issue reassurances confirming all his predecessor's acts.[38] More specifically, it is clear from elsewhere that *senatus consulta* passed during the reign, as well as other decisions taken by Domitian, did all remain valid.[39] The same applies to the decisions of Commodus and Caracalla.[40]

Emperors and members of their families were not only condemned or dishonored in various ways by decree of the senate. When the wheel of fortune turned, their memory might equally be restored by the same means. Thus once he became emperor Otho had the statues of his former wife Poppaea reinstated by *senatus consultum*, while the House also restored Galba and Piso to honor early in 70.[41] No doubt it was through the senate, too, that Septimius Severus had the memory of Commodus restored.[42] We hear of efforts by Pertinax to remove the stigma from those who had been executed by the latter.[43] The contemporary monument erected to M. Antonius Antius Lupus indicates that such measures were similarly put through the House. It records how "after being forcibly destroyed his memory was restored anew according to a decree of the senate."[44]

2. Honors

Despite its limited quantity the surviving evidence is sufficient to confirm that the bestowal of honors upon individuals occupied the House to a significant degree. Indeed we may almost be thankful that the bulk of relevant material has perished, for it would be overwhelming. Even the most assiduous of contemporaries at times found the sheer surfeit of awards unmanageable and degrading. Tacitus' outburst in this connection, following his description of the downfall of Octavia in 62, has been quoted earlier.[1] Dio found it beyond him to describe the honors bestowed by the House during Nero's visit to Greece. So many sacrifices and *supplicationes* were announced, he says, that the entire year would not hold them all. He also refuses to mention the meaningless honors conferred upon Domitian after his German campaign, or upon other emperors of similarly bad rep-

---

[38] Plin. *Ep.* 10.58.7-10.

[39] Note Plin. *Ep.* 10.66.2 and 72; *Dig.* 29.1.1 pr.; 40.16.1; 48.3.2.1 and 16.16.

[40] See, for example, the relevant entries in G. Gualandi, *Legislazione imperiale e giurisprudenza* I.

[41] Tac. *Hist.* 1.78; 4.40.

[42] Cf. Dio 75.8.1-2.

[43] Dio 74.5.2-3; HA, *Pert.* 6.8.

[44] *ILS* 1127, ". . . cuius memoriam per vim oppressi in integrum secundum amplissimi ordinis consultum restituta est"; *PIR*² A 812.

[1] *Ann.* 14.64, quoted in chap. 9 sect. 4ɪɪ; cf. *Ann.* 3.65.

utation.[2] The many extravagant honors voted to Nero after the capture of Artaxata in 58 prompted C. Cassius Longinus to move in the House "that if the gods were to be thanked worthily for their favors the whole year was too short for their thanksgiving: so a distinction should be made between religious festivals and working days on which people might perform religious duties without neglecting mundane ones."[3]

Certain emperors did take steps to moderate lavish gestures on the part of the senate. At the beginning of his reign Hadrian asked that no special honor be voted to him except at his express request.[4] At some stage Tiberius, too, evidently introduced a similar ban, which was reaffirmed once he turned against Sejanus. He likewise forbade any proposals to be made in his honor after the latter's death.[5] Though Claudius accepted honors voted on his accession, he declined all extravagant ones, according to Dio.[6] In the case of other members of the imperial family, Tiberius rejected many of the honors proposed when tribunicia potestas was conferred on Drusus in 22.[7] Later he warned the senate sternly that young Drusus and Nero Caesar were not to have their heads turned by premature honors, and he reduced awards made to Claudius.[8] He refused most of the honors voted to Livia on Augustus' death, and again on her own death in 29.[9] In 39 Gaius—out of vanity, rather than any desire for restraint—forbade the award of honors to his relatives.[10] Claudius vetoed the proposals made on the birth of Britannicus in 42, and again on the birth of a grandson in 48.[11] In the late second century Pertinax refused titles for his wife and son.[12] Septimius Severus prevented the award of honors to imperial freedmen.[13]

The House itself rarely showed moderation in proposing honors, and out of fear or flattery proved all too eager to please any emperor who craved distinction for himself or others. Thus to Dio[14] it was noteworthy

[2] 63.18.3; 67.4.1-2.

[3] Tac. Ann. 13.41.

[4] Dio 69.2.2; cf. HA, Hadr. 6.4; 8.2.

[5] Dio 58.8.4 and 12.8.

[6] 60.3.2 and 5.3-4; cf. Tac. Ann. 11.25.

[7] Tac. Ann. 3.57 and 59.

[8] Tac. Ann. 4.17; Suet. Claud. 6.

[9] Tac. Ann. 1.14 and 5.2; cf. F. K. Dörner, "Der Erlass des Statthalters von Asia Paullus Fabius Persicus," diss. Greifswald, 1935, p. 40. cols. VIII.24-IX.6 = E. M. Smallwood, Documents of Gaius etc., Cambridge, 1967, no. 380 (reading κ]αὶ in the last line cited).

[10] Dio 59.22.9 and 23.2.

[11] Dio 60.12.5 and 30.6ᵃ.

[12] Dio 74.7.1-2; HA, Pert. 6.9.

[13] Dio 76.6.1.

[14] 66.7.2. For comment, see P. Kneissl, Die Siegestitulatur der römischen Kaiser, Hypomnemata 23, Göttingen, 1969, pp. 42-43.

that Vespasian and Titus were not voted the title "Iudaicus" in 70. The *interrogatio* no doubt encouraged accumulation of lavish proposals; to make his mark each member in turn felt the need to contribute a suggestion. At the same time presidents shrank from advocating restraint. Augustus was alleged to have been passionately eager for his grandsons Gaius and Lucius to be honored,[15] and he was not disappointed in this desire. For a time Tiberius and Septimius Severus were content to see their respective favorites, Sejanus and Plautianus, exalted by the House.[16] At one stroke Gaius took the honors bestowed upon Augustus over a lifetime, and in the same way had all Livia's honors voted to his grandmother, Antonia, in a single *senatus consultum*.[17] Later he became quite uncertain about how to react to proposals from the House. Dio comments: "It irritated him to have small distinctions voted, since that implied a slight, and greater distinctions irritated him also, since thus the possibility of further honors seemed to be taken from him."[18] We have already glimpsed the appetite for honors displayed by Nero and Domitian. Though the former had shown a modest attitude at first,[19] and had also urged the senate to take a greater share in government, it was characteristic that the House paid little attention. Even in 54 the announcement of the Parthians' evacuation from Armenia was greeted by exaggerated proposals, while further lavish honors were rejected by Nero himself.[20] In the second century Commodus required the senate to vote him everything bestowed upon M. Aurelius.[21]

It remains to examine individually the honors awarded by the senate. Certain distinctions conferred upon the emperor and his family have already been treated, while further honors of a religious nature are covered in the following chapter.

3. Honorific Months[1]

To name months after a living ruler was an honor of divine character, which originated in the Hellenistic world. At Rome it was bestowed exclusively by the senate upon emperors and members of their families.

[15] Tac. *Ann.* 1.3.
[16] Tac. *Ann.* 4.74; Dio 58.2.7; 4.4; 11.1; 75.14.7; perhaps 75.15.2[b].
[17] Dio 59.3.2; Suet. *Calig.* 15.
[18] 59.23.3.
[19] Cf. Suet. *Nero* 8.
[20] Tac. *Ann.* 13.8 and 10.
[21] Dio 72.15.1.
[1] No more than the role of the senate is treated here. For full discussion of the whole topic, see K. Scott, "Greek and Roman honorific months," *Yale Class. Stud.* 2. 1931. pp. 201-278.

Quintilis was renamed Iulius in honor of the month in which Julius Caesar was born. Sextilis was renamed Augustus for reasons set out in the relevant *senatus consultum* quoted by Macrobius:

Whereas the *imperator* Caesar Augustus in the month Sextilis entered upon his first consulship and led three triumphs into the city, and the legions were brought down from the Janiculum and loyally served under his auspices; and whereas in this month also Egypt was brought under the sway of the Roman people, and in this month an end was made of civil wars; and whereas for these reasons this month is and has been fortunate for this empire, it pleases the senate that this month be called Augustus.[2]

Although Suetonius, Dio, and Censorinus associate the introduction of the new name with the restoration of the Julian calendar in 8 B.C., there are strong arguments for believing that the innovation really dated back to 27 B.C. On Augustus' death the proposal was evidently made in the House, but taken no further, that the new name be transferred to September, the month of the emperor's birth (whereas he had died in August).[3]

It seems that during Tiberius' reign more than one attempt was made to rename months in the emperor's honor. Characteristically, however, he quashed not only the suggestion that September be called Tiberius and October Livia, but also the senate's further plea that at least November, the month of his birth, be renamed Tiberius.[4] We may guess, but cannot prove, that Gaius consulted the senate about renaming September Germanicus in memory of his father.[5] Early in his reign Nero refused the senate's wish that the year start from December, the month of his birth. But in 65 he evidently raised no objection when the House renamed April, May, and June as Neroneus, Claudius, and Germanicus respectively in his honor.[6]

Domitian had September renamed Germanicus and October Domitianus.[7] The only sign that he may have referred the matter to the House is Pliny's jibe in *Panegyricus* about the trivial subjects discussed there during the reign. As he puts it, "we even dedicated the months, and not just one of them, to the name of the Caesars."[8] Like all the new names of months

---

[2] *Sat.* 1.35 = *FIRA*² I no. 42; see also Livy, *Epit.* 134; Plut. *Numa* 19; Suet. *Aug.* 31; Dio 55.6.6-7; Censorinus, *De die natali* 22.16; Servius, *In Verg. Buc.* 4.12.

[3] Suet. *Aug.* 100.

[4] Dio 57.18.2.

[5] Suet. *Calig.* 15.

[6] Tac. *Ann.* 13.10; 15.74; 16.12; Suet. *Nero* 55.

[7] Suet. *Dom.* 13; Dio 67.4.4.

[8] *Paneg.* 54.4, ". . . menses etiam nec hos singulos nomini Caesarum dicabamus."

except July and August, Domitian's pair lapsed with his death and the annulment of his acts.[9]

According to the *Historia Augusta*,[10] Antoninus rejected a senatorial decree renaming September Antoninus and October Faustinus. In contrast, at the end of his reign Commodus required the senate to rename all twelve months in his honor.[11]

4. Triumphs, Ovations, Triumphal Honors, and Salutation as *Imperator*

In our period, as in the Republic, triumphs and ovations (a lesser honor of the same type) continued to be awarded by the senate to successful commanders who fulfilled certain conditions. Among the latter was the stipulation that the commander must enjoy full *imperium*.[1] Once nearly all Roman forces were commanded by imperial legates, it was almost impossible for such a condition to be fulfilled except by the emperor or members of his family, so that the last man outside this circle to be awarded a triumph was L. Cornelius Balbus as early as 19 B.C.[2] In the same way an *ovatio* was last awarded to A. Plautius in 47 in recognition of his service as commander of Claudius' expedition to Britain.[3] Yet emperors and their close relatives still celebrated triumphs and ovations on the vote of the senate.[4] Augustus stipulated that for this purpose the House should always meet in the temple of Mars, dedicated in 2 B.C.[5]

Agrippa's refusal of triumphs afforded Augustus time to establish a new principle that this honor was to be reserved for members of the imperial family.[6] Others were to be content instead with the *insignia* or *ornamenta* of a triumph, likewise awarded by the senate. The first recipient of this fresh distinction was Tiberius in 12 B.C., followed by Drusus and L. Piso in the next year.[7] According to Suetonius,[8] Augustus had had triumphs

---

[9] Cf. Plut. *Numa* 19; HA, *Commod.* 20.5; Macrob. *Sat.* 1. 36-37; Censorinus, *De die natali* 22.17.

[10] *Antonin.* 10.1.

[11] Dio 72.15.3; Herodian 1.14.9; HA, *Commod.* 11.8.

[1] The further stipulation that all recipients of the honor must be of consular rank came to be ignored: see, for example, *ILS* 957; Dio 60.20.4 and 23.2.

[2] See *Inscr. Ital.* XIII. 1 (= *EJ* p. 36).

[3] Tac. *Ann.* 13.32; Suet. *Claud.* 24; Dio 60.30.2.

[4] See Extended Note J.

[5] See chap. 3 sect. 1 note 34.

[6] Cf. Dio 54.24.7-8; and further A. A. Boyce, "The origin of *ornamenta triumphalia*," *Class. Phil.* 37. 1942. pp. 130-141.

[7] Suet. *Tib.* 9; Tac. *Ann.* 6.10; Dio 54.33.5; 34.3 and 7.

[8] *Aug.* 38.

voted to over thirty commanders, and *ornamenta* to an even higher number. If the latter total is accurate, then many names have been lost.[9]

Naturally the initiative in the matter usually came from the emperor, and his approval was always necessary in practice.[10] But so far as we can judge from sources which often remain vague on this point, it seems that all emperors did put their proposals to the House for ratification, rather than make awards independently.[11] Contemporary complaints[12] that the distinction was conferred on men who had not achieved any success in the military sphere can be borne out in a few instances, but on present evidence these exceptions do seem to remain rare.[13]

In the Julio-Claudian period the erection of a statue seems to have accompanied the conferment of triumphal honors as a matter of course.[14] But in 69, if Tacitus[15] is to be taken literally, we first encounter the award of no more than a triumphal statue. Though triumphal *insignia* or *ornamenta* still continue to be voted thereafter, the award of a statue alone, often posthumously, becomes normal by M. Aurelius' day.[16] Even this distinction fades away in Septimius Severus' time; at least we have only a single example which can be dated as late as his reign.[17]

Two further distinctions which under the Principate soon came to be reserved for members of the imperial family should be mentioned. The first is salutation as *imperator* in recognition of victories won either by the emperor personally or under his auspices.[18] The last general outside the

[9] A valuable list of awards made during our period is furnished by A. E. Gordon, *Quintus Veranius Consul A.D. 49*, Appendix 2; see further the discussions of D. E. Eichholz, *Britannia* 3. 1972. pp. 149-163; and V. A. Maxfield, *The Military Decorations of the Roman Army*, London, 1981, chap. 5.

[10] Note that the soldiers' letter at Tac. *Ann.* 11.20 is addressed to Claudius. For imperial approval, see ibid. 4.26.

[11] For specific mention of the senate, note Vell. 2.115.3; Tac. *Agr.* 40; *Ann.* 1.72; 2.52; 3.72; 4.46; 12.28 and 38; 15.72; *Hist.* 4.4; Dio 56.17.2; *ILS* 918, 921, 986, 1022, 1023, 1056, and 8970 revised by G. W. Bowersock, *JRS* 63. 1973. p. 135 (uniquely *ex s.c.*). The restoration of *ILS* 985 offered by A. Mocsy, *Archaeologiai Értesitö* 93. 1966. pp. 203-207 (= *AE* 1966. 68) remains very uncertain: cf. G. W. Houston, *ZPE* 20. 1976. pp. 27-28.

[12] For example, Suet. *Nero* 15; Plin. *Ep.* 2.7.1; Dio 58.4.8.

[13] Note Tac. *Ann.* 4.26; 11.20-21; 15.72; Suet. *Claud.* 24; *ILS* 957.

[14] Cf. Tac. *Ann.* 4.23; Dio 55.10.3.

[15] *Hist.* 1.79.

[16] For specific mention of the senate conferring triumphal or "military" statues without *insignia* or *ornamenta*, note Plin. *Ep.* 2.7.1; *ILS* 1098, 1112; *CIL* VI. 3850 = 31809; 37087-37088.

[17] *CIL* VI. 1566, acephalous (a notable omission from Gordon's list).

[18] This use of *imperator* is to be distinguished from its meaning as "holder of supreme power" (cf. *Arval Acta*, para. 9c. line 10, "quod hoc die C. Caesar Augustus Germanicus a senatu impera[tor appellatus est]"). Even when *imperator* in the latter sense became a *praenomen* of the Princeps from Vespasian's day, the title continued to be used after the name, too, in recognition of victories.

imperial family thus honored was Q. Junius Blaesus, who fought under his own auspices as proconsul of Africa in 22.[19] Such a salutation might be offered by the senate, as it evidently was to Germanicus on Tiberius' proposal in 15.[20] More commonly soldiers in the field might hail their general. After narrating the miracle of the "thundering" legion, which had given victory over the Marcomanni, Dio explains: "He (Marcus Aurelius) was now saluted *imperator* by the soldiers for the seventh time. Although it was not his custom to accept any such honor before the senate voted it, nonetheless this time he took it as a gift from heaven, and informed the senate."[21] It remains doubtful, however, whether we may infer from this instance that all such salutations had to be ratified by the senate;[22] among emperors Marcus was unusually scrupulous in consulting the House.

The other distinction soon reserved for members of the imperial family was a title assumed from a conquered nation.[23] Under the Principate only two men outside this circle are known to have gained such titles—Cossus Cornelius Lentulus, proconsul of Africa, who became "Gaetulicus" in A.D. 6,[24] and P. Gabinius Secundus, whom Claudius permitted to become "Chaucius" or "Cauchius."[25] In addition, however, Florus[26] can claim that P. Sulpicius Quirinius might have become "Marmaricus" had he not represented his work of conquest so modestly. We do know that such titles were commonly offered to the emperor and members of his family by the senate,[27] but it is impossible to tell whether at times they also assumed them independently.

5. Statues

Military success was not the only reason for which the senate might honor a man with a statue. To vote statues in precious metals was another customary means of honoring emperors.[1] Augustus was thanked thus for his

---

[19] Tac. *Ann.* 3.74.

[20] Tac. *Ann.* 1.58.

[21] 71.10.4-5.

[22] For the contrary view, see M. Hammond, *The Antonine Monarchy*, pp. 77-78.

[23] For full treatment see P. Kneissl, *Die Siegestitulatur der römischen Kaiser*.

[24] *PIR*[2] C 1380; Vell. 2.116.2; Florus 2.31.40; Dio 55.28.4.

[25] *PIR*[2] G 9; Suet. *Claud.* 24.

[26] 2.31.41. The date of the campaign and the puzzle of Quirinius' post at the time are discussed by J. Desanges, "Un drame africain sous Auguste," in *Hommages à M. Renard, Collection Latomus* 102, Brussels, 1969, vol. 2 pp. 197-213 at pp. 208-212.

[27] Note Suet. *Tib.* 17; *Claud.* 1; Dio 60.22.1-2; 68.10.2 and 18.3[b]; 78.27.3; cf. 66.7.2; HA, *Marcus* 9.1-2; *Verus* 7.9; *Fast. Ost.* A.D. 116.

[1] Note Stat. *Silv.* 1.1.99-100; Tac. *Ann.* 13.10; Dio 72.15.3 and 6; 74.14.2[a]; possibly also Plin. *Paneg.* 52.

conduct in a court case of 12 B.C.,[2] while the House proved quick to emulate Tiberius' regard for Sejanus in the same way.[3] Later Plautianus was honored with statues too.[4] Detection of a plot against Claudius by the emperor Otho's father earned him a statue in the palace by vote of the House.[5] It was most common of all, however, for the emperor to propose statues for prominent figures after their death, often together with a public funeral;[6] altogether perhaps nine such statues preserved the memory of L. Volusius Saturninus, who died as Praefectus Urbi in 56.[7] The task of erection might be entrusted to the consuls.[8]

Gaius forbade the erection of a statue of any living man anywhere without his consent.[9] Claudius attempted to curb unregulated erection in Rome by ruling that private citizens must either have built or repaired a public work, or must have gained senatorial permission, before proceeding further.[10] If a restoration of the stone be accepted, the funerary inscription of Q. Veranius seems to provide the only trace of adherence to such a regulation: when he was *curator aedium sacrarum et operum locorumque publicorum* in the early 50's, the *equester ordo et populus Romanus* set up a statue (?) to him "consentiente senatu."[11] An approach to the senate here seems almost overscrupulous when this *curator* of all people should have built or repaired a public work. We cannot say, however, whether applications to erect statues were always put to the House thereafter. Certainly at the very least the tacit approval of the emperor would always be essential. We do indeed know of one case where he was approached in the first instance, when Titinius Capito asked Nerva for leave to erect a statue of L. Junius Silanus Torquatus in the Forum.[12] Of course as an *eques* Titinius did not sit in the House, and anyway enjoyed close contact with the emperor as *ab epistulis*,[13] so that it remains impossible to infer from his action how a contemporary senator might have made a similar request.[14]

---

[2] Dio 54.30.5.

[3] Seneca, *Cons. Marc.* 22.4; Tac. *Ann.* 3.72; 4.74; cf. 4.23; Dio 57.21.3; 58.2.7 and 4.4.

[4] Dio 75.14.7.

[5] Suet. *Otho* 1.

[6] Tac. *Ann.* 4.15; cf. 13.10; Suet. *Vitell.* 3; HA, *Marcus* 2.5 and 3.5; *ILS* 1100; 1326; 8963; possibly *CIL* VI. 1437; *AE* 1934. 177.

[7] *AE* 1972. 174, with W. Eck, "Die Familie der Volusii Saturnini in neuen Inschriften aus Lucus Feroniae," *Hermes* 100. 1972. pp. 461-484.

[8] Suet. *Claud.* 9.

[9] Suet. *Calig.* 34.

[10] Dio 60.25.3.

[11] A. E. Gordon, *Quintus Veranius Consul A.D. 49*, pp. 234, 270-271.

[12] Plin. *Ep.* 1.17.1.

[13] *ILS* 1448.

[14] The accepted interpretation of the senator Curiatius Maternus' request in Tac. *Dial.* 13 (see, for example, A. Gudeman, *P. Cornelii Taciti Dialogus de Oratoribus*, Leipzig and Berlin, 1914, pp. 281-282) could be considered to have some bearing on this problem, when

Among emperors there is no means of determining whether Trajan and Hadrian, for example, consulted the senate about all the statues they erected to their friends and marshals, according to Dio.[15] It is true that M. Aurelius did prove characteristically scrupulous in gaining senatorial approval in such instances. But it would only be sanguine to guess that certain other emperors may not have taken such pains.

6. Ornamenta[1]

During the Republic the senate had bestowed the *ornamenta* or *insignia* of a consul or other magistrate not only upon non-members but even upon members of lower rank. The practice continued in our period. This grant of "decorations" for some distinguished service allowed the recipient to wear the appropriate dress, to be classed officially with senators of the appropriate grade,[2] and to share such other privileges as were associated with the rank.[3] Yet a non-member so honored was still excluded from sessions of the House. By contrast, a member upon whom the distinction had been bestowed naturally continued to enjoy the right of attendance. It is not clear, however, whether at meetings he would stay classed in his existing rank, or would be grouped with that for which he had been awarded *ornamenta*. The latter alternative perhaps seems the more likely.[4] It was thus an extra privilege when in A.D. 9 the *quaestorius* Germanicus was voted, among other honors, *ornamenta praetoria* together with the right to give his *sententia* immediately after the *consulares*.[5] Normally we might imagine a member upon whom *ornamenta praetoria* had just been bestowed

---

he specifies how the statue on his tomb is to look, and is taken to be asking "that no one shall seek to honor my memory either by a motion in the senate or by a petition to the Emperor" (M. Winterbottom, revised Loeb edition, 1970). But in fact his words are entirely general: "et pro memoria mei nec consulat quisquam nec roget" ("in honor of my memory let nobody take advice or make any request"). Gudeman's view is passed over without comment by R. Güngerich, *Kommentar zum Dialogus des Tacitus*, Göttingen, 1980, p. 58.

[15] 68.16.2; 69.7.4; cf. A. E. Gordon, op. cit. pp. 322-323. As so often, no weight can be attached to omission of the senate. Dio (57.21.3) equally omits it when mentioning the bronze statue of Sejanus erected in the theater, about which we know from elsewhere that the House was consulted (Seneca, *Cons. Marc.* 22.4).

[1] In general see Mommsen, *St.R.* I. pp. 455-465; A. Stein, *Der römische Ritterstand*, pp. 272-275; S. Borzsák, *PW* 18. s.v. ornamenta, cols. 1110-1122; and at unnecessary length, B. Rémy, "Ornati et ornamenta quaestoria praetoria et consularia sous le haut empire romain," *Rev. Et. Anc.* 78-79. 1976/7. pp. 160-198.

[2] Note how Pliny (*Ep.* 8.6.4) refers to Pallas as "praetorius"!

[3] Cf. Ulpian, *Dig.* 50.16.100, " 'speciosas personas' accipere debemus clarissimas personas utriusque sexus, item eorum, quae ornamentis senatoriis utuntur."

[4] Rémy (op. cit. p. 161) would agree. But his deduction of normal practice from the quite exceptional case of Octavian in 43 B.C. is unsound.

[5] Dio 56.17.2; *PIR*[2] I 221.

being called among the most junior *praetorii*, not the most senior. All the same, such a privilege was still of strictly limited value for a man's advancement. Only tenure of actual magistracies could further his career, never the award of *ornamenta* alone. Thus, as Dio says,[6] Tiberius became praetor in 16 B.C. even though he had already been awarded *ornamenta praetoria*. In the same way Tettius Julianus, awarded *ornamenta consularia*, took up the praetorship in 70, while some years later another member did likewise despite the earlier bestowal of *ornamenta praetoria*.[7] By the same token anyone who had been awarded, say, *ornamenta consularia* and later gained the office itself nonetheless had to reckon this tenure of the magistracy as his first. The earlier award of *ornamenta* counted for nothing in this respect until the third century when, as Dio[8] tells us, Plautianus' arrogant greed for honors brought about a permanent change in the method of reckoning.

Awards in late 69, together with the offers made by the senate to Macro and Laco after the downfall of Sejanus, and refused, may have been proposed by members.[9] Otherwise during the Principate *ornamenta* were in effect conferred only at the instigation of the emperor. But he evidently did continue to put some, if not all, his proposals to the House in due form. At first the honor was limited to members of the imperial family— Tiberius, his brother Drusus, Germanicus, and Claudius,[10] among whom the latter was the only non-member. In the case of the others, bestowal of *ornamenta* was only one of a variety of ways to enhance the dignity of members of the imperial family at a time when no pattern had emerged in the conferment of such honors.[11]

From Tiberius' time we no longer hear of *ornamenta* being awarded to members of the imperial family. In his reign, however, *ornamenta praetoria* granted to the Praetorian Prefect, Sejanus, represent the first conferment of such an honor outside this circle during the Principate.[12] After his downfall, however, *ornamenta praetoria* and *quaestoria* offered by the House to his successor, Q. Naevius Sutorius Macro, and to the *praefectus vigilum*, P. Graecinius Laco, respectively, were declined.[13] Yet the number

---

[6] 54.19.6.
[7] Tac. *Hist*. 1.79; 4.39-40; *ILS* 1000 with reading and interpretation of A. B. Bosworth, "Firmus of Arretium," *ZPE* 39. 1980. pp. 267-277 (see further below). For discussion of such members' placing within the higher grade, see chap. 7 sect. 11 note 37.
[8] 46.46.3-4; cf. 78.13.1.
[9] Tac. *Hist*. 4.4; Dio 58.12.7.
[10] Dio 54.10.4 and 32.3; 56.17.2; Suet. *Claud*. 5.
[11] By contrast, Marcellus was adlected as *praetorius* in 24 B.C., but then elected aedile (Dio 53.28.3). In A.D. 9 the younger Drusus could speak as *praetorius* as soon as he became quaestor (Dio 56.17.3).
[12] Dio 57.19.7.
[13] Dio 58.12.7.

of instances known suggests that in fact it soon became common for Praetorian Prefects to be awarded *ornamenta consularia* either during their tenure of office or afterwards.[14] We may guess that the honor was duly conferred through the senate, though that point can be documented only up to the early second century.[15]

Under Gaius we first find *ornamenta* more widely offered—the beginning of a trend continued by Claudius as part of his notable generosity in the bestowal of honors. It was possibly Gaius who prompted an unparalleled award of *ornamenta aedilicia* which arguably was made to a *tribunus militum*, L. Julius Crassus, after service in Germany.[16] Certainly it must have been during the same reign that the House granted *ornamenta praetoria* to King Julius Agrippa.[17] At Claudius' instigation it later voted him *consularia*, and *praetoria* for his brother Herod.[18] To the disgust of Pliny the Elder[19] and his nephew,[20] *ornamenta quaestoria* and *praetoria* respectively had also to be awarded to the emperor's powerful freedmen, Narcissus and Pallas.[21] There is evidence to support Suetonius' claim that Claudius "gave *ornamenta consularia* even to *procuratores ducenarii*."[22] At least Junius Chilo, procurator in Bithynia, was awarded this distinction in 49 for conducting King Mithridates of the Crimean Bosporus to Rome, while C. Iulius Aquila, his less senior colleague who had been responsible for the king's defeat, was given *ornamenta praetoria* at the same time.[23] Having judiciously declined the senate's offer in 31, P. Graecinius Laco, *praefectus vigilum*, did accept *ornamenta consularia* from Claudius.[24]

It was presumably in Nero's reign that C. Iulius Sohaemus, king of Emesa, was granted *ornamenta consularia*.[25] In 66 the *eques* Ostorius Sabinus was rewarded by the House with *ornamenta quaestoria* for his prosecution of the consular Barea Soranus.[26] Then during the civil war of

---

[14] See W. Ensslin, *PW* 22 s.v. praefectus praetorio, col. 2399.

[15] Senatorial involvement is specified, or strongly implied, in Tac. *Ann.* 11.4 (*ornamenta praetoria*); 15.72; *Hist.* 4.4; HA, *Hadr.* 8.7.

[16] At first sight it seems natural to take the distinction as one awarded by a municipality, not by the Roman senate at all. But in that case it is curious for the award to be given such prominence in the inscription, and for it to be separated from what are unquestionably municipal honors cited later. The point was raised by Mommsen (ad *CIL* VIII. 15503), and discussed further by E. Ritterling (*Germania* 1. 1917. pp. 170-173 at p. 171). It merits consideration by *PIR*² I 279 and by Rémy (cf. op. cit. p. 178).

[17] Philo, *Flacc.* 40; *PIR*² I 131.

[18] Dio 60.8.2-3.

[19] *NH* 35.201.

[20] Plin. *Ep.* 7.29; 8.6.

[21] Tac. *Ann.* 11.38; 12.53; Suet. *Claud.* 28.

[22] *Claud.* 24.

[23] Tac. *Ann.* 12.21; *PIR*² I 166 and 744.

[24] Dio 60.23.3; *ILS* 1336.

[25] *ILS* 8958; *PIR*² I 582.

[26] Tac. *Ann.* 16.33.

69 and afterwards there was a rash of awards to members and non-members alike. Among the former, three legionary legates and Antonius Primus all received *ornamenta consularia*; one Firmus was elected quaestor Caesaris and awarded *ornamenta praetoria*;[27] while the *equites* Cornelius Fuscus and Arrius Varus likewise received *praetoria*.[28]

From the Flavian period, on the evidence available, *ornamenta* seem to be more sparingly awarded, not least perhaps because revulsion had set in against some of those thus honored in the recent past, and because more frequent recourse was now made to adlection.[29] Certainly in the case of men who were already senators the latter honor had the practical advantage of confirming them in a higher rank, whereas we have seen how the grant of, say, *ornamenta praetoria* to an *aedilicius* still did not relieve him of the necessity to stand for the praetorship itself, if he sought advancement. It is unusual, therefore, to find Ti. Claudius Atticus Herodes, father of the famous sophist, twice attested on inscriptions from Corinth as "decorated with *ornamenta praetoria* by decree of the senate."[30] He was presumably not a member at this time, though he is next known as suffect consul about 108. So the award of *ornamenta* may be a slip for adlection or (more probably) adlection soon followed it but happens never to be mentioned.

One foreign prince is known to have been granted *ornamenta praetoria*— Julius Agrippa, brother of Berenice, on the occasion of their joint visit to Rome in 75.[31] But leaving him aside with Herodes and the Praetorian Prefects, we otherwise hear of the award of *ornamenta* only to figures of some cultural distinction from the Flavian period onwards. As early as 54 Nero had asked the senate to award *insignia consularia* to his old tutor, Asconius Labeo.[32] It may be that the *eques* Cn. Octavius Titinius Capito gained *ornamenta praetoria ex s.c.* on Nerva's proposal for his work as *ab epistulis*, but no doubt his literary distinction was also taken into account.[33] Around the same time there is evidence of awards to Quintilian, allegedly on the recommendation of the emperor Domitian's cousin, Fla-

---

[27] *ILS* 1000 lines 3-5, reading with A. B. Bosworth, *ZPE* 39. 1980. p. 277, "q. Aug. orn[ament. p]raetoricis a senatu auctorib. [duob. i]mperatorib. Vesp. et Tito adiect. [in place of adlect.]." The change of one letter dispels the inexplicable peculiarity of adlection with *ornamenta praetoria*. Bosworth attractively conjectures that the man honored is C. Petillius Firmus, a younger son of the leading Flavian commander, Q. Petillius Cerialis.

[28] Tac. *Hist.* 1.79; 4.4.

[29] The sweeping claim that M. Aurelius bestowed "cuncta honorum ornamenta" upon his relatives cannot be substantiated with regard to senatorial *ornamenta* (HA, *Marcus* 16.1).

[30] A. B. West (ed.), *Corinth* VIII. 2, Harvard, 1931, no. 58; *AE* 1977. 774; H. Halfmann, *Die Senatoren*, no. 27.

[31] Dio 66.15.4; *PIR*² I 132.

[32] Tac. *Ann.* 13.10.

[33] *ILS* 1448; Sherwin-White, *Pliny*, p. 125 and references there.

vius Clemens,[34] and to Plutarch;[35] and even at the end of our period over a century later an award was made to the sophist Valerius Apsines by Maximinus.[36] But we cannot say whether the senate was consulted in any of these cases.

There seem to be only two known instances from our period where the senate granted equestrian status to persons below that rank. Both were freedmen. Antonius Musa, Augustus' doctor, was honored thus in 23 B.C. (along with other privileges),[37] and Hormus, Vespasian's freedman, on 1 January 70.[38]

7. Public Funeral[1]

In the late Republic it had become customary for the senate to vote public funerals to men of high distinction. The consuls presided, and the ceremony was paid for by the state. This practice continued under the Principate. Such funerals were naturally granted to emperors and members of their families.[2] In the case of others, while proposals were now made only by the emperor, they were still duly put to the House. Augustus and Tiberius are said to have bestowed the honor generously.[3] For the former the claim is difficult to document, though it was presumably in his reign that Sextus Appuleius, husband of the emperor's sister Octavia, was voted a public funeral. Yet strictly of course he should be considered a member of the imperial family.[4] By contrast, in Tiberius' reign we know of such funerals granted to Sulpicius Quirinius in 21, Lucilius Longus in 23, L. Piso in 32, and Aelius Lamia in 33.[5] L. Vitellius, too, was accorded one by vote of the House (in Claudius' reign?),[6] as was L. Volusius Saturninus in 56.[7] In 70 likewise it voted the same honor to Vespasian's brother, Flavius Sabinus (again, strictly a member of the imperial family).[8] More generally,

---

[34] Ausonius, *Grat. Act.* 7; *PIR*² F 59 and 240. Ausonius' "sortitus" is not to be taken literally of course.

[35] See C. P. Jones, *Plutarch and Rome*, Oxford, 1971, p. 29.

[36] See *PIR*² A 978; J. H. Oliver, *Hesperia* 10. 1941. p. 260 no. 65.

[37] Dio 53.30.3; *PIR*² A 853.

[38] Tac. *Hist.* 4.39; *PIR*² H 204.

[1] In general see A. Hug, *PW* Suppl. 3, s.v. funus publicum, cols. 530-532.

[2] For votes by the senate, note Tac. *Ann.* 1.8; Suet. *Aug.* 100 (Augustus); Dio 58.2.2 (Livia); Tac. *Ann.* 2.82-83; 4.9 (Germanicus and Drusus); Suet. *Tib.* 75; Dio 58.28.5; 59.3.7 (Tiberius); Tac. *Ann.* 12.69; 13.2; Dio 60.35.2 (Claudius).

[3] Dio 54.12.2; 57.21.3; cf. 58.19.5.

[4] *ILS* 8963; *PIR*² A 960.

[5] Tac. *Ann.* 3.48; 4.15; 6.11; 6.27; Dio 58.19.5. A vote of the senate is specified in all but the case of Aelius Lamia.

[6] Suet. *Vitell.* 3; cf. R. Hanslik, *PW* Suppl. 9, s.v. Vitellius no. 7c, cols. 1733-1739.

[7] *AE* 1972. 174.

[8] Tac. *Hist.* 4.47.

Quintilian must be speaking in terms of current practice when he says at the end of the first century: "For persons holding some public office are frequently assigned to deliver laudatory orations at funerals, and the same task is often entrusted to magistrates by decree of the senate."[9] However, the last men outside the imperial family known to have been awarded public funerals are Verginius Rufus in 97 and L. Licinius Sura under Trajan.[10] We may fairly guess that the House was consulted in each case, though in neither reference does this point happen to be mentioned.[11]

[9] *Inst. Or.* 3.7.2.

[10] Plin. *Ep.* 2.1.1; Dio 68.15.3[2].

[11] In addition to the common term "funus publicum" Tacitus sometimes uses "funus censorium." Of Claudius this was no doubt technically correct, since the emperor had occupied that magistracy (*Ann.* 13.2). In the case of others (*Ann.* 4.15; 6.27; *Hist.* 4.47), "funus censorium" is best considered merely as a variant expression; it is hardly likely to denote a different or more splendid ceremony. It is used elsewhere of members of the imperial family: see *Fast. Ost.* A.D. 112; HA, *Pert.* 15.1; *Sev.* 7.8.

12

THE SENATE'S ROLE IN
ADMINISTRATION

The nature and extent of the senate's administrative role in a variety of spheres during the Principate require careful appraisal. It is the aim of this chapter and the following one to attempt such a review under six principal headings.

1. Public Works and Services

At Augustus' instigation various administrative functions in connection with public works and services, previously handled in more or less haphazard fashion by magistrates, came to be assigned to specially designated senatorial officers. As we might expect, it was normal for the new arrangements to be established by *senatus consultum*. However, Dio[1] happens to make no reference to such procedure when he describes how two *praefecti frumenti dandi* were introduced in 22 B.C., increased to four in 18 B.C. Yet from the beginning all known holders include *ex s.c.* in their titulature. Only in the third century is it normally dropped, when the scope of the office had been significantly changed—though even then it does still appear occasionally.[2] Again Dio omits consultation of the senate in referring to the establishment of *curatores viarum* in 20 B.C.[3] Yet milestones after this date do mark construction work done by Augustus on the Viae Appia,[4] Latina,[5] and Salaria[6] *ex s.c.* From inscriptions we also know of two contemporary holders of the office who mention the senate in their

---

[1] 54.1.4 and 17.1.

[2] For known holders and their titulature, see H.-G. Pflaum, *Bonn. Jahrb.* 163. 1963. pp. 234-237, reprinted in *Scripta Varia* II.

[3] 54.8.4. The Republican office of the same title had evidently been abandoned (cf. Cic. *Ad Att.* 1.1.2 = SB 10; *ILS* 5800, 5892).

[4] *CIL* IX. 5986, 5989; X. 6914, 6917.

[5] *CIL* X. 6903.

[6] *CIL* IX. 5943, 5954; *ILS* 5815; cf. *CIL* VI. 878: repair of a bridge (?) in Rome by Augustus *ex s.c.*

titulature: C. Propertius Postumus, who was *ex s.c. viarum curator*, and P. Paquius Scaeva, *viar. cur. extra u. R. ex s.c.*[7] Yet the titulature of all later holders omits any mention of a *senatus consultum*.[8]

The survival of Frontinus' work, *De Aquis Urbis Romae* affords a full account of the establishment of *curatores aquarum* in 11 B.C. Agrippa had previously formed his own slave gang for the maintenance of the city's aqueducts; on his death in 12 B.C. Augustus inherited it.[9] It was presumably then that a working party of unknown composition was instructed by the senate to inspect public aqueducts in Rome and to make an inventory of all the public fountains. This group reported back in the following year.[10] At the same time *senatus consulta* quoted extensively by Frontinus[11] placed maintenance and administration in the hands of senatorial *curatores aquarum*. Yet known holders of the office never cite senatorial authority.[12] In Augustus' reign *ex s.c.* does appear on *cippi* erected in connection with work on aqueducts, but not thereafter.[13] Among other work done on the banks of the Tiber we hear of some carried out by the consuls of 9 and 8 B.C. *ex s.c.*[14] Yet it was not until A.D. 15 that a board of *curatores riparum et alvei Tiberis* seems to have been established.[15] Its *cippi* on the banks derived authority *ex s.c.* in Tiberius' time, but *ex auctoritate* of the emperor thereafter.[16] Once again, known holders of the office never cite senatorial authority in their titulature.[17]

We know almost nothing of two further boards, *curatores locorum publicorum iudicandorum* and *curatores tabularum publicarum*, though we do find instances of each operating *ex s.c.*[18] It may be that neither continued in existence beyond the Julio-Claudian period.[19] In addition, two *curatores aedium sacrarum et operum locorumque publicorum* were appointed from the latter part of Augustus' reign. Yet no evidence survives

---

[7] *ILS* 914, 915. For the consuls of 21 B.C. repairing a bridge *ex s.c.*, see *ILS* 5892.

[8] For lists, see W. Eck, *Die staatliche Organisation Italiens in der hohen Kaiserzeit*, pp. 80-86. He seems unjustified (p. 85) in taking T. Mussidius Pollianus as "cur. viarum . . . ex s.c." (*ILS* 913).

[9] Front. *Aqued.* 98 and 116.

[10] Front. *Aqued.* 104.

[11] *Aqued.* 100-108 and 125-127 passim.

[12] For a list, see T. Ashby, *The Aqueducts of Ancient Rome*, Oxford, 1935, pp. 17-23.

[13] *CIL* VI. 31558-31563 (cf. *ILS* 5746; and *Inscr. Ital.* IV. 1. 85-94); 37030-37035; *AE* 1953. 70; 1957. 136.

[14] *CIL* VI. 31541; 31702; *AE* 1947. 154; 1951. 182a.

[15] Dio 57.14.8; cf. Suet. *Aug.* 37; Tac. *Ann.* 1.76 and 79.

[16] See *CIL* VI. 31542-31544; 31557; XIV. 4704; with VI. p. 3109.

[17] *CIL* VI. 1552 is best set aside in this connection. For holders, see M. J. le Gall, *Le Tibre, fleuve de Rome dans l'antiquité*, pp. 137-145.

[18] For the former, *ILS* 942͵ 5939-5941; *CIL* VI. 37037; the latter, *CIL* VI. 31201.

[19] Note usurpation of the former's function by Claudius and L. Vitellius as censors (*ILS* 211). On the latter see chap. 9 sect. 3 note 21.

about the formal establishment of their office, and they are never found working *ex s.c.*[20]

In general a predictable pattern emerges. So far as we can see, these offices were established at the instigation of Augustus or Tiberius, and senatorial approval was duly gained. The holders themselves at first likewise sought such approval for their work, though they soon dropped this formality. It is true that in Tiberius' time Domitius Corbulo made complaints to the senate about negligence on the part of *curatores viarum*.[21] But from the beginning it was with the emperor and his officials that holders became involved when their duties rose above routine, not with the House at all. Most were appointed by the emperor too.[22] Even the *senatus consulta* establishing the *cura aquarum* mention a promise by Augustus to carry out certain repairs at his own expense, while imperial involvement in this sphere increased permanently once a second, much larger gang was recruited by Claudius to work alongside the "public" gang.[23] The senate could thank Augustus and Vespasian for repairing roads at their own expense.[24] In the same way it was typical that the authority cited on *cippi* of the *curatores alvei Tiberis* should change from *ex s.c.* to *ex auctoritate* of the emperor after Tiberius' time. Although by contrast *praefecti frumenti dandi* consistently retained *ex s.c.* in their titulature, it would be just as inappropriate to imagine that the House in any sense controlled their duties.[25]

In effect, wherever the first two emperors arranged that administrative tasks in Rome formerly handled by magistrates should be transferred to senatorial officials, the senate's role in supervising them soon lapsed. All this is hardly surprising of course, let alone cause for dismay. During the Republic the House had never liked to act as an administrative body in any modern sense, while neither then nor later[26] was it of a size or character

[20] But note how Paulus (*Dig.* 39.3.23 pr.) envisages the general possibility that senate or emperor might commission work which would cause water damage to the property of others.

[21] Tac. *Ann.* 3.31; Dio 59.15.3-5; 60.17.2.

[22] Notionally the *praefecti frumenti dandi* and *curatores alvei Tiberis* were chosen by lot (see chap. 10 sect. 3), while the emperor's choice of *curatores aquarum* was supposed to be ratified by the senate (Front. *Aqued.* 104). But it is natural enough for Frontinus (*Aqued.* Pref. 1) to regard himself as appointed to the latter post by Nerva alone. No doubt Pliny, too, really owed his post as *curator alvei Tiberis* to Trajan, though Sherwin-White (*Pliny*, p. 79) goes too far in claiming that his apparent reference in *Ep.* 5.14.2 indicates this. In fact "mandatum mihi officium" is entirely neutral.

[23] Front. *Aqued.* 125; 116.

[24] *ILS* 84, 245; cf. *RG* 20.

[25] See further H. Pavis d'Escurac, *La préfecture de l'annone: service administratif impérial d'Auguste à Constantin*, Rome, 1976, pp. 21-26; G. E. Rickman, *The Corn Supply of Ancient Rome*, chaps. IV. 3, VII(c) 3, and Appendix 1.

[26] For skeptical appraisal of the view that it was associated with Trajan in the foundation of alimentary schemes, see W. Eck, "Traian als Stifter der Alimenta auf einer Basis aus Terracina," *Archäologischer Anzeiger* 1980. pp. 266-270.

to undertake such functions suitably. In this connection its continuing reluctance to delegate routine business to committees has already been treated. Augustus' appointments in the sphere of public works and services were new developments for which he was personally responsible. It was natural enough therefore that the office-holders should liaise principally with him and his successors.

2. Finance[1]

During the Republic the senate controlled the finances of the Roman state. Yet in practice with the coming of the Principate this prerogative, too, was yielded to the emperor. From the beginning he contributed a large share of his own money to public expenditures, and was even in a position to publish state accounts if he wished.[2] So it is natural to ask what role remained to the senate.

Nominally the *aerarium Saturni* did continue under its control. From 29 B.C. the officials in charge there were two *praefecti* of praetorian rank chosen annually by the House. In 23 B.C., as part of an effort to eliminate excessive canvassing, they were replaced at Augustus' instigation with two praetors chosen by lot.[3] From 44, however, direct appointment by the emperor was introduced. In order to reflect traditional Republican practice Claudius placed in charge two quaestors chosen by himself for three-year terms; they were promised accelerated promotion thereafter. But it proved impossible to find men of sufficient maturity to shoulder the responsibilities of the post, so that in 56 Nero instead appointed two *praetorii*.[4] Except for an interval in 69 when praetors evidently took over again, this arrangement continued unchanged thereafter.[5]

Whatever their rank, all these officials had the right to attend the House, and they could thus participate in discussion of measures affecting them— as when one *senatus consultum* authorized the Treasury officials to redeem the *area Saturni* from private occupiers,[6] for example, or when another of Hadrian's time instructed them to examine the accounts of those whose estates had been confiscated.[7] We see the same officials coming forward

---

[1] For important recent discussions, see F. Millar, "The aerarium and its officials under the empire," *JRS* 54. 1964. pp. 33-40; P. A. Brunt, "The 'fiscus' and its development," *JRS* 56. 1966. pp. 75-91; F. Millar, *Emperor*, chap. IV. 9.

[2] Suet. *Calig.* 16; Dio 59.9.4.

[3] Tac. *Ann.* 13.29; Suet. *Aug.* 36; Dio 53.2.1 and 32.2.

[4] Tac. *Ann.* 13.28-29; Suet. *Claud.* 24; Dio 60.24.1-3; *ILS* 966.

[5] Tac. *Hist.* 4.9; Suet. *Claud.* 24, "uti nunc." See in general M. Corbier, *L'Aerarium Saturni et l'Aerarium Militare: administration et prosopographie sénatoriale.*

[6] *ILS* 5937.

[7] *Dig.* 49.14.15.3-6.

to speak when relevant issues were raised by others. Thus in 15 they resisted a request for compensation from a member who claimed that construction of a road and an aqueduct by the state had undermined his house.[8] Again, in summer 105 when the heirs of a deceased *scriba quaestorius* sought a salary payment which he had not lived to receive, the Treasury prefects countered by claiming the money for the state.[9] Naturally enough the Treasury quaestor charged by the tribune Helvidius Priscus with over-strict sale of poor men's property must have responded to the allegation (if it was made in a meeting).[10] During Pliny's absence in autumn 99, when a delegation from Baetica asked the House for his services in the prosecution of Caecilius Classicus, predictably we find Treasury colleagues seeking to have him excused on the grounds of official duties.[11]

Among emperors, Augustus and Tiberius in particular are known to have raised financial issues in the senate. In A.D. 5 the former brought forward a proposal for securing funds to pay troops, while in the following year he sought members' views on how a new *aerarium militare* might best be financed.[12] He did the same in 13 when there was pressure to find an alternative to the five percent inheritance tax.[13] Later, indirect taxes and monopolies were among the wide range of matters which Tiberius is said to have taken trouble to raise with the senate.[14]

In other ways, too, the House might feel that it retained some degree of financial involvement. Provincial governors who sought to increase taxation had to gain its permission, or that of the emperor, according to Dio.[15] By contrast, Hermogenianus[16] says that an official required imperial authority to change *vectigalia*. Yet Modestinus[17] cites a *senatus consultum* which fined anyone who imposed a new *vectigal*. To the senate were still addressed applications for remission of tribute from distressed provinces or cities in both imperial and senatorial spheres.[18] In the same way it granted relief to cities stricken by earthquake or fire.[19] It also bestowed gifts of money from the *aerarium* upon individuals—as much as 15 million

[8] Tac. *Ann.* 1.75.
[9] Plin. *Ep.* 4.12.
[10] Tac. *Ann.* 13.28.
[11] Plin. *Ep.* 3.4.2-3. Strictly Pliny had only one colleague as *praefectus aerarii Saturni*. But, as Sherwin-White suggests (ad loc.), the *praefecti aerarii militaris* may have supported the plea.
[12] Dio 55.24.9 and 25.4-6.
[13] Dio 56.28.4.
[14] Suet. *Tib.* 30.
[15] 53.15.6.
[16] *Dig.* 39.4.10 pr.
[17] *Dig.* 48.14.3.
[18] Tac. *Ann.* 1.76; 2.42; 12.62-63; cf. Suet. *Claud.* 25. Note also *ILS* 6772.
[19] Tac. *Ann.* 2.47; 4.13; 12.58; Suet. *Tib.* 8; Dio 54.23.8.

HS in one instance.[20] From the same source it could order funds to be made available for games[21] or for official purposes,[22] and in Tiberius' reign might apparently even vote that its Treasury furnish pay for the Praetorian guard.[23] The *aerarium* evidently remained responsible for paying a governor's entourage,[24] though by contrast Ulpian[25] can speak of governors paying into the *fiscus* sums of money appropriated from condemned criminals. In 70 the House itself arranged to float a state loan of 60 million HS for public subscription—an abortive project, as it turned out.[26] A century later M. Aurelius went to the trouble of asking it to vote money for his campaigns, and when his financial difficulties became severe, evidently felt that he could not turn to it again.[27] When the *Historia Augusta* says that Commodus pretended to be making a visit to Africa "in order to gain funds for the journey,"[28] the implication may be that he would apply to the senate.

On the other hand, if sums continued to be granted regularly to provincial governors from the *aerarium*, as they had been in the Republic, we lack all evidence of the practice. The unlikely notion that the emperor likewise was voted a recurrent grant from the same source is supported only by testimony from Jerome and Orosius for Nero's reign.[29] But, as we shall see, this hardly squares with more reliable information about the need for the emperor to provide subsidies. Above all, however, it should be stressed that, despite a certain involvement, the senate never exercised financial control in our period. Dio explains with reference to the occasion noted above: "Marcus asked the senate for money from the public treasury, not because such funds were not already at the emperor's disposal, but because he used to declare that all the funds, both these and others, belonged to the senate and people."[30] Marcus' second reason here might reflect highflown theory; but, as Dio acknowledges, imperial control of all state finance was the reality. From the beginning the emperor and his growing body of agents not only collected much public revenue, they also spent it on a

---

[20] Note Dio 53.30.3; Plin. *Ep.* 8.6.8.

[21] G. B. Pighi, *De Ludis Saecularibus*, p. 112 line 63 (17 B.C.); p. 143 I line 29 (A.D. 204).

[22] For example, Front. *Aqued.* 100.

[23] Dio 58.18.3.

[24] Modestinus, *Dig.* 4.6.32.

[25] *Dig.* 48.20.6.

[26] Tac. *Hist.* 4.47.

[27] Dio 71.33.2, quoted below; *Epit. de Caes.* 16.9; Eutropius, *Brev.* 8.13.

[28] HA, *Commod.* 9.1, "simulavit se et in Africam iturum, ut sumptum itinerarium exigeret."

[29] Jerome, *Chron.* p. 184 Helm; Orosius 7.7.8.

[30] 71.33.2.

large scale. They alone took censuses.[31] Equally, it was the emperor, together with his *a rationibus*, who alone attempted even the most rudimentary budgeting or forward financial planning. In brief, there developed a whole financial administration controlled by the emperor.

By contrast, the officials in charge of the *aerarium* were occupied exclusively with administering from day to day an institution which was more depository than treasury to any modern way of thought. They handled payments in and out on due authority; they lodged documents; they heard cases. Pliny describes his duties as prefect in such terms: "I sit on the bench, answer petitions, make up accounts, and write quantities of most unliterary letters."[32]

Even when financial issues were brought to the House by Augustus and Tiberius, it could have little influence on the formulation of the policies eventually adopted. Thereafter, so far as we can tell, such matters were seldom even raised.[33] In late 69 it was highly unusual for the Treasury praetors to complain of the low state of public funds, and to call for a limit on expenditure.[34] No doubt their initiative was prompted by difficulties at a time when the new emperor could not be in touch with Rome. Yet it is striking how the general reaction was one of refusal to take any steps in a sphere considered to belong to the emperor. Later the problem mentioned above—of whether relatives should receive a salary payment arguably due to a dead *scriba quaestorius* from the *aerarium*—was referred first to Trajan, and only passed by him to the House. Not surprisingly, therefore, while the senate may have authorized the five commissions set up to deal with pressing difficulties of public finance during the first century, all but one of the proposals came from the emperor.[35] Three commissions were established to limit or reduce expenditure in 6, 70, and 97 respectively.[36] One, set up in 42, was to recover money owed to the state; and another, set up in 62, was to take charge of public revenues.[37]

It is true that to the end of the Julio-Claudian period emperors did strive to support the *aerarium* when the demands made upon it were greater than its receipts. Thus Tacitus[38] implies that part of the purpose of Augustus'

---

[31] We may set aside Jerome's entry under 1 B.C., *Chron.* p. 169 Helm, "Quirinius ex consilio senatus Iudaeam missus census hominum possessionumque describit."

[32] *Ep.* 1.10.9, "sedeo pro tribunali, subnoto libellos, conficio tabulas, scribo plurimas sed inlitteratissimas litteras."

[33] In my view Nero's proposal for the abolition of *vectigalia* was put to members informally, not to the House in session: see chap. 5 sect. 1 note 94.

[34] Tac. *Hist.* 4.9.

[35] The exception is the commission of 70, which was formed quietly despite the earlier objections—at a meeting presided over by Domitian.

[36] Dio 55.25.6; Tac. *Hist.* 4.40; Plin. *Ep.* 2.1.9; *Paneg.* 62.2.

[37] Dio 60.10.4; Tac. *Ann.* 15.18.

[38] *Ann.* 3.25

marriage legislation had been to increase the revenue of the *aerarium*. According to *Res Gestae*[39] he had himself contributed 2,400,000,000 HS to the *aerarium*, the Roman plebs, and discharged soldiers. In the financial crisis of 33 Tiberius made it a loan of 100 million HS.[40] To maintain its solvency Nero paid in 40 million HS in 56, and six years later claimed that he had been providing subsidies as high as 60 million HS annually.[41]

But these attempts to maintain the *aerarium* were abandoned. The emperor and his staff worked independently, and inextricable confusion arose between revenue due to him privately, or due to the *aerarium*, or handled by him in an official capacity. As contemporaries recognized, such confusion did not matter, since the emperor was in complete charge.[42] In 100 Pliny[43] can speak quite openly of Trajan's control of the *aerarium*. At best the senate's role had only ever been subordinate to that of the emperor. Now it had disappeared altogether.

3. Coinage

It seems appropriate to consider next how far, if at all, the senate was involved in the issue of coinage under the Principate. Almost the only evidence derives from the coins themselves, and its interpretation has been the subject of controversy among numismatists in recent years. A full review which did justice to all their arguments would be out of place here. But a brief consideration of principal points is called for as part of our enquiry into the functions of the House.

During the Republic the senate enjoyed exclusive control of Roman coinage. Minting itself was supervised by *triumviri aere argento auro flando feriundo*, three junior magistrates from the Vigintivirate who held office for one year. Under the Principate these posts continued to be filled into the mid third century.[1] Until c. 4 B.C. the holders follow the traditional Republican practice of placing their names upon all issues—gold, silver, and bronze—made during their term of office. Yet when minting at Rome resumes thereafter in A.D. 10-12 the magistrates' names are omitted, and indeed never reappear. We cannot say whether the omission is a sign of some more substantial modification of the magistrates' duties, since we

---

[39] Appendix 1; cf. 17.1.
[40] Dio 58.21.5.
[41] Tac. *Ann.* 13.31; 15.18.
[42] Cf. Tac. *Ann.* 6.2; Dio 53.22.3-4.
[43] *Paneg.* 36.3.
[1] For a list, see J. R. Jones, "Mint magistrates in the early Roman empire," *BICS* 17. 1970. pp. 70-77.

lack all knowledge of the latter beyond the confident presumption that they would have been confined to routine supervision.

Some link between the senate and bronze coinage is suggested by the fact that from the start of minting at Rome c. 23 B.C. almost all issues feature prominently the legend *SC* or *EX SC*, and continue thus to the end of our period. By contrast, when gold and silver issues begin from c. 19 B.C. they make no mention of the senate except in rare cases.

It is natural to think that this regular occurrence of *SC* on bronze coins denoted senatorial supervision of the issues. Yet such a view has been challenged by Kraft,[2] who argued that the reference is rather to the type-content of the coinage: in other words, for example, *SC* on an Augustan reverse depicting an oak wreath refers to the senate's conferment of this honor upon the emperor in 27 B.C. Despite its appeal, such an interpretation is difficult to accept for a number of reasons.[3] In particular, if it were correct, we might expect *SC* to accompany the oak wreaths and other honors voted to Augustus which likewise appear on gold and silver issues; but here the legend is not found. Among bronze coins, its occurrence on *quadrantes* (the lowest denomination) cannot refer to any type, because none is displayed. In addition, it becomes awkward to sustain any notion which links *SC* to type-content in many issues made after Augustus' time. In what sense can "Spes Augusta," for example, be *EX SC*?

We may accept that *SC* on Republican issues did occasionally refer to type-content, and that this was sometimes the case under the Principate too.[4] But in the Republic *SC* most commonly referred to senatorial authority for the issue: this continues the most natural interpretation. If we ask the nature of that authority, the regular appearance of *SC* on bronze, and its omission from gold and silver issues, at once point to the notion that the former were supervised by the senate, the latter by the emperor. Yet the introduction of such a division, quite apart from its justification, remains mysterious. Moreover, there are serious difficulties if we seek to determine the nature of any such senatorial supervision and its development. As we have seen, from the beginning of the Principate financial control and initiative indisputably passed to the emperor, while despite differences in emphasis the types on coins of all metals uniformly promoted imperial virtues, powers, and honors.

[2] K. Kraft, "S(enatus) C(onsulto)," *JNG* 12. 1962. pp. 7-49.

[3] For these objections, and alternative views discussed below, see especially A. Bay, "The letters *SC* on Augustan *aes* coinage," *JRS* 62. 1972. pp. 111-122; C.H.V. Sutherland, *The Emperor and the Coinage: Julio-Claudian Studies*, London, 1976, pp. 11-22; A. M. Burnett, "The authority to coin in the late Republic and early Empire," *NC* 17. 1977. pp. 37-63. Also, for example, H. R. Baldus, "Zum Rechtsstatus syrischer Prägungen der 1. Hälfte des 3. Jahrhunderts n. Chr.," *Chiron* 3. 1973. pp. 441-450; A. Kunisz, *Recherches sur le monnayage et la circulation monétaire sous le règne d'Auguste*, Wrocław, 1976.

[4] See Bay, *JRS* 62. 1972. p. 122; Sutherland, op. cit. p. 15.

Bay suggested that *SC* was intended to vouch for new weights and metals introduced by authority of the House when the mint of Rome reopened. Yet such a guarantee or explanation by no means invariably accompanied novel issues, while it is unlikely to have been appreciated by most users. In addition, this interpretation can hardly account for the continued prominence of *SC*. If the legend was only intended to justify innovation, we might expect that it would soon lapse. Sutherland argued that *SC* on bronze coinage simply denoted senatorial permission to withdraw the required metal from the *aerarium Saturni* and use it for minting. If such permission had to be granted for each issue, the regular appearance of *SC* into the third century is indeed adequately explained. In this respect Sutherland's view may be considered more satisfying than that of Bay. Yet he in turn fails to provide any reason why it should suddenly have been considered vital to advertise with such punctiliousness that permission for minting had been given—a formality which the House had seldom bothered over previously, even with issues in precious metal. Not least for this reason Sutherland's interpretation hardly seems one which would readily occur to users of the coinage. More significantly, he leaves unexplained the striking prominence of *SC* on many issues, especially the earlier ones. Figure 8(c) above is a representative example. Can we credit that it was a control mark—included simply to indicate permission for the withdrawal of the required metal for minting—which was chosen as a major feature in designs?

It is doubtful whether we need to follow Sutherland in seeking an interpretation which will necessarily assign *SC* a meaningful place on all issues into the mid third century. For whatever reason the legend first appeared, once it had become established its indefinite continuation as a traditional feature is entirely understandable, even though it might reflect no legal or administrative reality. Thus it was surely just out of regard for propriety and tradition that *SC* was regularly inscribed on issues of the mint at Antioch throughout our period and even beyond,[5] and that it also came to feature on certain issues by Mallus,[6] Philippopolis,[7] and perhaps Damascus,[8] in the mid third century. The same applies to its appearance on pieces minted elsewhere as medallions rather than as coins for circulation.[9] L. Clodius Macer, legate of Numidia, painstakingly included the legend on each of

[5] See *BMC Galatia, Cappadocia and Syria*, pp. 166ff. For illustration of p. 180 no. 243, see Figure 8 (d) above.

[6] *BMC Lycaonia etc.*, p. 102, nos. 32-35.

[7] *BMC Arabia etc.*, pp. 42-43, nos. 2-10. For illustration of p. 43 no. 9, see Figure 8 (e) above.

[8] *BMC Galatia etc.*, p. 286, no. 25.

[9] See J.M.C. Toynbee, *Roman Medallions*, A.N.S. Numismatic Studies 5, New York, 1944, pp. 45-48.

the fourteen silver types he is known to have issued in the course of his bid for power in 68. Thereby he sought to invest these coins with the stamp of legitimacy which they otherwise lacked.[10] The pretender Uranius Antoninus had similar purposes in retaining the letters on tetradrachms he issued from Emesa in 253: partly he wished to give an impression of legitimacy, partly he was modeling his issues upon those of Antioch.[11]

Some attempts to understand the significance of the legend *SC* have paid special attention to those issues which seem to contradict the regular pattern—that is, gold and silver coins bearing the legend, and bronze ones lacking it. But there is no reason to believe that most such pieces reflect more than the whim of, say, the official who chose the design or its engraver.[12] Exceptionally, it may be that the appearance of *EX SC* on gold and silver coins minted under Nero between 54 and c. 63 is intended to advertise special deference to the senate, whereas its omission from bronze issues in 63-64 may purposely indicate that impatience with the House which the emperor allegedly felt at this time. To go further, however, and suggest that the legends are evidence for Nero "handing over" the minting of gold and silver issues to the senate in some way during the early years of the reign, and similarly "depriving" it of bronze later, is extreme.[13]

Attempts to substantiate claims of a separate senatorial mint on the basis of epigraphic evidence fail for lack of material. Likewise the decision of the House to melt down just bronze coins bearing Caligula's portrait[14] cannot necessarily prove that it was responsible for minting these issues in the first place.[15] It is conceivable that while control of all coinage rested with the emperor, separate minting of bronze still continued under senatorial supervision. But evidence is entirely lacking, while there is no sign that the senate continued to undertake any other such administrative work.

It may seem disappointing to end this section with a negative conclusion, but it is only fair to do so. If we seek to know how far, if at all, the senate was involved in the issue of coinage under the Principate, it is worth underlining again that we have little except the coins themselves to help us. The significance of *SC* or *EX SC*, which regularly appears on bronze, cannot be explained with certainty. But it is most naturally taken to mean that the senate authorized the issue, an impression which the prominence

[10] *RIC* I pp. 193-195. For illustration see Figure 8 (f) above.

[11] See *PIR*[2] I 195 and H. R. Baldus, *Uranius Antoninus: Münzprägung und Geschichte, Antiquitas* 11, Bonn, 1971, pp. 35-37 and 185-189.

[12] For discussion, especially of Gaius' "Adlocut(io) Coh(ortium)" issue without *SC* and bronze issues of 64 from Lugdunum with *SC*, see Sutherland, op. cit. in n. 3, p. 19 n. 47, pp. 31, 73-74.

[13] See Sutherland, op. cit. pp. 32-33, 117-118.

[14] Dio 60.22.3.

[15] For these points see A. M. Burnett, *NC* 17. 1977. pp. 53-56.

of the legend would encourage. Yet it must be acknowledged that we are quite unable to fathom the nature of the senate's involvement with the issue of coinage, or the nature of its relationship with the emperor in this sphere. Nor do we know how long any such involvement may have continued. It is possible that in time bronze coinage came to carry the legend *SC* or *EX SC* purely out of a sense of tradition.

4. Public Order

The need to head this section with such a general title reflects the remarkably wide range of administrative measures which the senate continued to take for the maintenance of good order in society during our period. Many of these applied to Rome and Italy, for which the House understandably felt a particular responsibility, though by no means an exclusive one. The version[1] of Nero's accession speech in Tacitus[1] is misleading when it implies that Italy and the proconsular provinces were in some sense a "senatorial sphere" for administrative purposes, in contrast to the imperial provinces. Rather, senate *and* emperor dealt with Italy and legislated for it, just as they both did for all other parts of the empire;[2] while the administrative work of *curatores viarum* throughout Italy,[3] for example, and later *iuridici*,[4] was supervised by the emperor.

That said, however, we can discern special concern for public order in Rome and Italy on the part of the senate. To this end the consuls no doubt kept in close touch with the Praefectus Urbi whenever the city seemed unsettled,[5] while in times of crisis the House itself could even direct troops. In the emergency of 19 B.C. a guard was voted for the consul, Sentius Saturninus.[6] After Gaius' murder the House attempted to calm both the populace and the troops in Rome, and apparently even contemplated liberating slaves to fight in its cause.[7] According to Dio,[8] it had been prepared to meet Tiberius' curious request for protection at the funeral of Augustus, and in 68 took the initiative in withdrawing Nero's guard.

It was to secure public order that the House passed *senatus consulta* expelling astrologers from Italy in 16,[9] and again in 52,[10] and perhaps in

---

[1] *Ann.* 13.4.
[2] See chap. 13.
[3] See above, sect. 1.
[4] See W. Eck, *Die staatliche Organisation Italiens in der hohen Kaiserzeit*, chap. VII.
[5] On the latter's responsibility for keeping order there, note Ulpian, *Dig.* 1.12.1.12-13.
[6] Dio 54.10.1.
[7] Josephus, *AJ* 19.160; 242; cf. 232; *BJ* 2.205.
[8] 57.2.2; 63.27.2[b].
[9] Tac. *Ann.* 2.32; Dio 57.15.8-9; Ulpian, *Coll.* 15.2.1, with discussion by F. H. Cramer, *Astrology in Roman Law and Politics*, American Philosophical Society, Philadelphia, 1954, pp. 237-240; and by Goodyear ad loc.
[10] Tac. *Ann.* 12.52; cf. Dio 60.33.3[b] with Cramer, op. cit. pp. 240-241.

93.[11] Expulsions of philosophers on other occasions are attributed to emperors alone; if these, too, were put to the senate, we do not hear of it. Yet it was the House which outlawed Egyptian and Jewish rites in 19 and possibly again during the 90's, while in 23, at Tiberius' instigation, it banned the performance of Oscan farces and expelled actors from Italy.[12] In all likelihood it was again consulted about a further expulsion in 56, but testimony is lacking.[13]

Burning of books was another harsh security measure. A *senatus consultum* to this effect was passed against the works of T. Labienus and Cassius Severus late in Augustus' reign,[14] and against those of Cremutius Cordus in 25.[15] Pliny[16] mentions that late in Domitian's reign the senate felt compelled to order the destruction of certain books which had belonged to Helvidius Priscus.

We hear of various other measures taken for the maintenance of public order within Italy. After deputations of council and citizens from Puteoli had brought mutual accusations before the House in 58, a special commissioner was appointed to resolve the strife. When he proved unacceptably severe, at his own request the task was handed to other members, a pair of brothers, supported by a Praetorian cohort.[17] The following year fighting between the people of Nuceria and Pompeii at a gladiatorial show held in the latter town was first brought to the attention of the emperor, and then referred by him to the House. Stern measures were passed to prevent a recurrence of the trouble.[18] Likewise those guilty of public insult to a senator at Sena in 69 were tried by the House and punished, while the people of the town were called to order by *senatus consultum*.[19] According to Suetonius,[20] an outrage by the people of Pollentia at the funeral of a *primipilus* was punished by Tiberius alone; we cannot say whether or not he consulted the senate in this instance. But we know that the senate did mete out punishments and pass severe measures to prevent any recurrence after the disastrous collapse of a jerry-built amphitheater during a show at

---

[11] The only testimony for a *SC* comes from Gell. 15.11.3-5; for date and other sources, see especially Plin. *Ep.* 3.11.2 with Sherwin-White ad loc., and Cramer, op. cit. pp. 245-246, who overlooks Gellius here.

[12] Tac. *Ann.* 2.85; 4.14; cf. Josephus *AJ* 18.83. The scope of the anti-Jewish decree of the 90's, recorded only in the Midrash Rabbah, is altogether obscure: see further Appendix 10.

[13] Tac. *Ann.* 13.25.

[14] Seneca, *Controv.* 10 pref. 8; Suet. *Calig.* 16; *PIR²* L 19; C 522.

[15] Tac. *Ann.* 4.35; *PIR²* C 1565.

[16] *Ep.* 7.19.6.

[17] Tac. *Ann.* 13.48.

[18] Tac. *Ann.* 14.17.

[19] Tac. *Hist.* 4.45.

[20] *Tib.* 37.

Fidenae in 27.[21] In Rome itself disorders in connection with the theater were discussed in 14 and again in 15; many measures were passed to curb the violence of actors' fans.[22] The question of suitable treatment of disorderly fans caused a dispute between a praetor and a tribune in 56.[23] When a corn shortage seemed set to spark off riots in 32, Tiberius criticized magistrates and senate for not using their authority to restrain the populace. A stern resolution was then duly passed, accompanied by a consular edict.[24]

More generally, the House took certain precautions to forestall disorder. A *senatus consultum* laid it down that all *collegia* except burial clubs (*collegia funeraticia, collegia tenuiorum*) had to be licensed by the senate;[25] we know how the unlicensed *collegia* which had evidently played a significant role in the fighting at Pompeii in 59 were promptly dissolved. Otherwise it is impossible to determine whether adherence to the requirement was strict or lax, though we may gather from Pliny's dismissive reference in *Panegyricus*[26] that applications for licenses were still made in the late first century, and uncontroversial, dull ones at that. We never hear of any means of checking or enforcement by the House, and it is a fair guess that none such existed.

The number of gladiators permitted at shows was likewise restricted by law. Again we may gather from the same passage of Pliny that applications to exceed the total did continue to be made in the late first century, though the only specific instance of such a request recorded in the sources is one by Syracuse in 58.[27] As we shall see,[28] this type of application later seems to have come to the emperor rather than the House.

At some unknown stage the House directed that money bequeathed to a city for shows or wild-beast hunts should be used instead to fund whatever else the community most needed.[29] It was presumably in order to forestall pressure from crowds that a ban was placed on manumission of performers in shows on the spot.[30] Gambling at any competition was forbidden, except at athletic contests mounted "for virtue."[31] Equally it must have been in connection with the maintenance of public order that the House laid down penalties for keeping eating-houses (*popinae*) in 22,[32] and discussed butch-

---

[21] Tac. *Ann.* 4.63.
[22] Tac. *Ann.* 1.77; Dio 56.47.2.
[23] Tac. *Ann.* 13.28.
[24] Tac. *Ann.* 6.13.
[25] No. 138 in list, chap. 15 sect. 5.
[26] 54.4. See further chap. 14 sect. 2 note 29.
[27] Tac. *Ann.* 13.49.
[28] Chap. 14 sect. 2 note 67.
[29] No. 169 in list, chap. 15 sect. 5.
[30] No. 109 in list.
[31] No. 195 in list.
[32] No. 27 in list.

ers and winesellers ("lanii ac vinarii") in Claudius' reign.[33] Applications
to hold markets still came before it in the second century,[34] though predictably at the end of our period Modestinus[35] mentions only the emperor
in this connection.

Finally, it is not clear what positive role, if any, the senate played in
the conflict between the Roman authorities and the Christians. The Christian claim that it passed some general resolution against their sect is extremely doubtful.[36] Even if the story of a Christian being tried before the
senate in Commodus' time is accurate, the incident remains unique in the
present state of our knowledge.[37] It is true that Justin addressed two *Apologies* to the emperor Antoninus Pius and the senate, and that in the mid
third century Origen[38] listed it among those authorities and individuals
whom he considered to have worked against Christianity. But there is no
evidence of action by the corporate body. It is more striking that in 258
Valerian did choose to send there an *oratio* concerning measures to intensify
the persecution of Christians.[39] Yet the senate was a recognized place for
an emperor away on campaign to publicize his wishes; conjecture that the
House had consciously prompted this *oratio* may thus be rash.[40]

In short, the senate can be shown to have maintained a wide concern
for public order at least up to the end of the first century. As we might
expect, for the most part its measures more often seem to represent reaction
to matters brought before it than any spontaneous initiative. But at the
same time, strikingly, it might also be prompted to take more sweeping
precautionary steps against the recurrence of trouble.

5. Religion

In Roman life a sharp distinction between secular and religious matters is
not always easily drawn, so that there is an especially wide overlap between
the subject of this section and others. Yet during the Principate the senate
clearly did continue to handle an extensive range of what might broadly

[33] Suet. *Claud*. 40.

[34] Suet. *Claud*. 12; Plin. *Ep*. 5.4 and 13; *FIRA*[2] I no. 47.

[35] *Dig*. 50.11.1.

[36] See no. 163 in list, chap. 15 sect. 5. For discussion of the legal basis for Roman
persecution of Christians, see, for example, Sherwin-White, *Pliny*, Appendix V.

[37] See Extended Note L. The *Roman Acts* of St. Ignatius, in which Trajan and the senate
jointly examine the saint, are just romantic fiction of the fifth or sixth century (J. B. Lightfoot
[ed.], *The Apostolic Fathers*, Part 2, vol. 2, London, 1889, p. 496).

[38] *Contra Celsum* 1.3; 2.79.

[39] No. 137 in list, chap. 15 sect. 5; G. W. Clarke, *Latomus* 34. 1975. p. 438.

[40] See in general T. D. Barnes, *Tertullian: A Historical and Literary Study*, Oxford, 1971,
p. 149. At the end of the second century Tertullian can claim that there were Christian
senators (*Apology* 37.4; cf. *Ad Nat*. 1.7).

be termed religious business. Indeed during certain years such items conceivably took up more time than they had done in the late Republic.

Naturally religious honors for the emperor and members of his family were a new feature. The greatest distinction was deification after death.[1] We need not trust literally Tertullian's assertion that "there was an ancient decree which forbade the consecration of any god by the emperor unless the senate approved."[2] But it is plain that senatorial approval of deification did continue to be sought regularly. Thus Dio[3] notes it as a matter of course that Caracalla was formally deified by the House under pressure from the army. Normally the emperor alone put forward names. Leaving aside the remarkable proposal of the consul designate in 65 that a temple be erected to "divus Nero" during the latter's lifetime,[4] the only proposals likely to have been made by others were those to deify Augustus in 14, Livia in 29, and just possibly Claudius in 54. Even then, however, the emperor could exercise a veto, as Tiberius did in the case of Livia.[5] Otherwise it was customary for a new ruler to request the deification of his predecessor, so long as the latter had not given irreparable offense. Though they were not his immediate predecessors, Septimius Severus' efforts to secure the deification of first Pertinax and later Commodus followed the same pattern. Such requests were normally a formality, although Gaius allegedly never pressed his demand that Tiberius receive the same honors as Augustus,[6] while it was notorious that the House only assented to Antoninus' plea for the deification of Hadrian with the greatest reluctance.[7] Deification of members of the imperial family—in some cases a considerable time after their deaths—was an innovation by Gaius, continued by a number of his successors. We can point to consultation of the senate in a number of these instances,[8] and it is fair to assume it in others.

Whether or not a member of the imperial family was deified, his or her death was certain to be marked by the vote of lesser honors. Beyond stressing how the time of the House was taken up thus, there is no cause to illustrate this practice in detail. As an example, Tacitus' account of honors bestowed upon Germanicus in 19 may suffice:

[1] For full discussion, see M. Hammond, *The Antonine Monarchy*, pp. 203-209.

[2] *Apol.* 5, "vetus erat decretum ne qui deus ab imperatore consecraretur nisi a senatu probatus." Cf. note 53 below.

[3] 78.9.2.

[4] Tac. *Ann.* 15.74.

[5] Tac. *Ann.* 1.10; 5.2; 13.2.

[6] Dio 59.3.7.

[7] See chap. 5 sect. 1 note 97.

[8] Note Drusilla in 38 (Seneca, *Apocol.* 1.3; Dio 59.11.2); Livia in 42 (Suet. *Claud.* 11); Claudia, daughter of Nero, in 63 (Tac. *Ann.* 15.23); Poppaea in 65 (ibid. 16.21); Faustina the elder in 141 (HA, *Antonin.* 6.7; *ILS* 348; *PIR²* A 715); Faustina the younger in 176 (HA, *Marcus* 26.5-7; *PIR²* A 716).

He was decreed every honor which love or ingenuity could devise. His name was to be sung in the Salian hymn; curule chairs, crowned by oak wreaths, were to be placed in his honor among the seats of the *Augustales*; his statue in ivory was to head the processions at the circus games; his posts of priest of Augustus and augur were to be filled by members of the Julian family only. There were to be arches at Rome, on the bank of the Rhine and on Mount Amanus in Syria, with inscriptions recording his deeds and his death for his country. Antioch, where he had been cremated, was to have a sepulcher; Epidaphne, where he died, a funeral monument. His statues and cult centers were almost innumerable. It was also proposed to place a huge golden medallion-portrait among the busts of the great orators. . . .''[9]

We have specific testimony for such votes by the senate after the deaths of Octavia,[10] Drusus the elder,[11] Augustus,[12] Livia,[13] Drusilla,[14] Galba,[15] Faustina the elder[16] and younger,[17] Antoninus,[18] and M. Aurelius.[19]

The birth of a child within the imperial family would prompt bestowal of honors. For example, the birth of Gaius to Agrippa and Julia in 20 B.C. was marked by the vote of an annual sacrifice, while lavish honors and celebrations greeted the birth of a daughter to Nero and Poppaea in 63.[20]

Again it would be superfluous to illustrate more than briefly the bestowal of honors of a religious nature upon emperors and other members of the imperial family at moments of success or special significance during their lifetimes. The important point is to underline the frequency of these gestures, especially under emperors who valued such tributes. It was not only in Domitian's reign that the House dedicated "colossal arches and inscriptions too long for temple architraves," as Pliny[21] so contemptuously puts it. Especially common were votes of games, festivals, holidays, priesthoods, sacrifices, altars, and other dedications.[22]

Into the second century at least a *supplicatio* continued to be voted by the House on special occasions. It represented a special opportunity for

[9] *Ann.* 2.83; cf. 4.9 (Drusus); *CIL* VI. 911, 912; *EJ* 94a, b.
[10] Dio 54.35.4-5.
[11] Suet. *Claud.* 1; Dio 55.2.3; cf. Florus 2.30.28.
[12] Tac. *Ann.* 1.8; Suet. *Aug.* 100; Dio 56.46; *Epit. de Caes.* 1.28. Consecration of part of the house where Augustus was born followed later—at some time before the early second century (Suet. *Aug.* 5).
[13] Tac. *Ann.* 5.2; Suet. *Claud.* 11; Dio 58.2.1-3.
[14] Dio 59.11.2-5.
[15] Suet. *Galba* 23.
[16] HA, *Antonin.* 6.7-8.
[17] Dio 71.31.1-2.
[18] HA, *Antonin.* 13.3-4.
[19] Dio 71.34.1; Aur. Vict. 16.15.
[20] Dio 54.8.5; Tac. *Ann.* 15.23.
[21] *Paneg.* 54.4, ''. . . ingentes arcus excessurosque templorum fastigium titulos . . . dicabamus.''
[22] See Extended Note K.

some, or all, of the gods to be approached at a time of notable success or disaster.[23] Such celebrations had been particularly associated with victories, and this link persisted. Augustus boasts: "For successful operations on land and sea, conducted either by me or my legates under my auspices, the senate decreed *supplicationes* to the immortal gods on 55 occasions. The days on which there were such *supplicationes* by decree of the senate numbered 890."[24] Two acephalous inscriptions of the time of Augustus and Trajan respectively record votes of *supplicationes*, possibly in connection with the award of *ornamenta triumphalia*.[25] We also know that they were voted in recognition of Nero's more vigorous policy on the Eastern frontier, and after Corbulo's capture of Artaxata.[26] Successes by Trajan and Hadrian were honored likewise.[27]

But there were further, diverse occasions for *supplicationes*. The deaths of Libo Drusus and Agrippina in 16 and 59 respectively were marked thus,[28] as well as the removal of Sulla and Plautus from the senate in 62.[29] Tiberius' proposed journey to Gaul in 21 was honored with a *supplicatio*; so, too, was the birth of Nero's daughter in 63.[30] It was appropriate that the gods should be approached thus during Livia's serious illness in 23, and after the fire of Rome in 64.[31] But *supplicationes* for Nero's public recitation of his poems, or for his victories on tour in Greece, represented abject flattery.[32] The voting of any *supplicationes* by the senate beyond the early second century is attested to only by the *Historia Augusta*. For example, in a speech Severus Alexander is made to remind the House of its duty to vote one in honor of his "victory" over the Parthians in 233.[33] Yet little trust can be placed in this source.

It is clear enough, however, that the senate did continue to handle a miscellaneous variety of other religious business. It supervised the selection of Vestal Virgins,[34] for instance, and praised those who filled that office piously.[35] It sanctioned celebration of the Secular Games.[36] On senatorial

[23] See in general G. Wissowa, *PW* 7A s.v. supplicationes, cols. 942-951; G. Freyburger, "La supplication d'action de grâces sous le Haut-Empire," *ANRW* 16.2. pp. 1418-1439. For *supplicatio* "ad omnia pulvinaria," note Tac. *Ann.* 14.12; for a more limited appeal, ibid. 15.44; and cf. *RG* 9.2.

[24] *RG* 4.2; cf. Dio 54.10.3; *Inscr. Ital.* XIII. 2. p. 557.

[25] *ILS* 918, 1023.

[26] Tac. *Ann.* 13.8 and 41.

[27] *Fast. Ost.* A.D. 116, "supplicationes [per omnia delub]ra"; HA, *Hadr.* 12.7.

[28] Tac. *Ann.* 2.32; 14.12; *Arval Acta*, para. 26 lines 10-13; 28c lines 15-18.

[29] Tac. *Ann.* 14.59.

[30] Tac. *Ann.* 3.47; 15.23.

[31] Tac. *Ann.* 3.64; 15.44.

[32] Suet. *Nero* 10; Dio 63.18.3.

[33] HA, *Sev. Alex.* 56.9; cf. *Maximin.* 26.6.

[34] Tac. *Ann.* 2.86; cf. 4.16; Gell. 1.12.12.

[35] See *ILS* 4928; *CIL* VI. 2133 with *PIR*² C 379; F 428.

[36] See, for example, *FIRA*² I no. 40; G. B. Pighi, *De Ludis Saecularibus*, pp. 140ff.

authority Augustus restored eighty-two temples in the city,[37] while the House likewise ordered the rebuilding of the Capitol in late 69,[38] and commissioned the college of augurs to restore the boundaries of the *pomerium* in 120/1.[39] It bestowed upon Augustus the unique distinction of having his name sung in the hymn of the Salii during his lifetime, and ordered that the temple of Janus be closed three times in the course of the reign.[40] Tiberius was absolved for having touched Augustus' corpse, while instructions were given for the bones of L. Antonius, son of Iullus Antonius, to be placed in the tomb of the Octavii on his death in 26.[41] Special sessions were called to say prayers for Augustus and Claudius shortly before their deaths.[42] The senate also joined the consul in authorizing the Arval Brethren to sacrifice for Tiberius' "safety and well-being" near the end of his life.[43] It was in accordance with a senatorial decree that the Brethren sacrificed for the "safety, victory, and return" of Domitian during his suppression of Saturninus' revolt in January 89.[44]

The senate not only received applications from provinces to erect temples to the emperor early in our period; it also continued to be consulted about the grant of neocorates over a much longer span. Both these items will be considered in connection with the diplomatic activity of the House.[45] Quintilian[46] comments at the end of the first century on how matters of religion frequently provoke discussion in the senate. While there is no reason to doubt his testimony, we can only substantiate the point for the Julio-Claudian period. In 22, for example, the request of the Flamen Dialis to hold the governorship of Asia was considered, as well as which temple should house the statue of *Fortuna equestris* vowed by the *equites* during Livia's illness.[47] In the following year, when a new Flamen Dialis had to be appointed, the opportunity was taken to review the relevant laws governing the priesthood.[48] The restrictive legal position of the priest's wife had already been eased as early as 11 B.C., while the laws governing the choice of Vestal Virgins were modified in A.D. 5.[49] In 25 the House adjudicated in a dispute between Sparta and Messene over ownership of

[37] *RG* 20.4.
[38] Tac. *Hist.* 4.4.
[39] *CIL* VI. 31539 (cf. *ILS* 311) with M. Hammond, *The Antonine Monarchy*, pp. 33-34.
[40] *RG* 10.1; 13.
[41] Dio 56.31.3; Tac. *Ann.* 4.44.
[42] Dio 56.29.3; Tac. *Ann.* 12.68.
[43] *Arval Acta*, para. 8 lines 7-11.
[44] *Arval Acta*, para. 47 lines 13, 20, 26.
[45] See chap. 14 sect. 2.
[46] *Inst. Or.* 12.2.21.
[47] Tac. *Ann.* 3.58 and 71.
[48] Tac. *Ann.* 4.16.
[49] Gaius, *Inst.* 1.136; Dio 55.22.5.

the temple of Diana Limnatis, and received a plea from Segesta for help towards rebuilding the temple of Venus on Mount Eryx.[50] Consultation of the Sibylline books was proposed in 15 and 64, while the possibility of adding a further volume to the canon was raised in 32.[51] Claudius brought up the establishment of a *collegium haruspicum*, and it was no doubt in accordance with his wishes that the *augurium salutis* was revived during the reign.[52]

Finally, according to Gaius, "That alone is considered sacred which has been consecrated under the authority of the Roman people, for example by *lex* or *senatus consultum* passed to that effect";[53] while Ulpian[54] explains how legacies could be left to gods only by permission of a *senatus consultum* or the emperor. He cites a number of instances where leave had duly been granted, but does not specify by which authority. All the same, it should not be assumed that action by the senate in such an instance is unthinkable. For while it is true that its involvement in certain other spheres does seem to have faded away completely as our period progressed, this was never so in the domain of religion. The scope and number of such items may have been reduced. But tradition plainly still ensured that some matters of a broadly religious nature did continue to be handled by the senate throughout.

[50] Tac. *Ann.* 4.43.
[51] Tac. *Ann.* 1.76; 6.12; 15.44.
[52] Tac. *Ann.* 11.15; 12.23; cf. Dio 51.20.4.
[53] *Inst.* 2.5.
[54] *Reg.* 22.6.

13

THE SENATE'S ROLE IN

ADMINISTRATION (CONTINUED)

6. Provinces[1]

It is well known that the senate was responsible for such administrative supervision of the provinces as there had been in the Republic. During the civil wars of the 40's and 30's B.C. this prerogative, along with others, was perforce yielded to the Triumvirs. Augustus' "restoration of the Republic" in 27 B.C. therefore offered the senate a welcome return of control. But it turned out to be only partial. Ovid overstated its effect when he wrote of that day: "Every province was returned to our people."[2] For at the same time Augustus was entrusted with a substantial number, including most of those in which legions were stationed. These areas he would administer through *legati pro praetore* appointed by himself and holding office at his pleasure. Meanwhile it was ostensibly the more peaceful and prosperous regions which were retained by the senate, to be governed by proconsuls chosen, in traditional fashion, by lot for one-year terms.[3] This new and radical division of provinces, made in the first instance for ten years, became permanent, and, as we shall see, the senatorial group stayed little changed throughout our period. All newly annexed areas were added to the emperor's group.[4] By Augustus' death in 14 only one legion remained under direct senatorial control, and this, too, was removed in Gaius' reign.[5] Thereafter no legions are stationed in senatorial provinces, although de-

[1] On the subject of this chapter note F. Millar, "The emperor, the senate and the provinces," *JRS* 56. 1966. pp. 156-166; and idem, *Emperor*, chap. VI. 5 and 6.

[2] *Fasti* 1.589, "redditaque est omnis populo provincia nostro."

[3] Note Florus' line "consules fiunt quotannis et novi proconsules" (poem 10 Jal). On the use of the lot, see chap. 10 sect. 3.

[4] Cf. Dio 53.12.9.

[5] Tac. *Hist.* 4.48; cf. Dio 59.20.7, with discussion by B. E. Thomasson, *Die Statthalter der römischen Provinzen Nordafrikas von Augustus bis Diocletianus* I, pp. 10-13 and 82; and E.W.B. Fentress, *Numidia and the Roman Army: Social, Military and Economic Aspects of the Frontier Zone, B.A.R.*, International Series 53, Oxford, 1979, pp. 68-69.

tachments of troops do remain there,[6] and proconsuls might have responsibility for furnishing supplies and for taking a levy.[7] Except for Africa
and Asia, which came to be reserved for senior consulars and frequently
represented the pinnacle of a man's career, all the governorships in the
senatorial group were assigned to *praetorii* and were less esteemed than
imperial posts of equivalent grade. However, any notion that it was generally more costly to support administration through proconsuls than through
imperial legates may be discounted.[8]

So far as we can discern from scanty evidence,[9] the division of 27 B.C.
was not accompanied by any statement about assignment of responsibility
for provincial affairs. Nor should we have expected it to be, when strictly
the only change made related to the method by which the governors of
certain provinces for the next ten years were to be chosen. No shift in the
nature of administration as such was intended. Yet even in Augustus' reign
some shift in fact started to occur under what became a permanent change,
so that it is important to ask how the roles of senate and emperor respectively did develop within the new scheme. For example, in broad terms
are we to picture the senate administering and legislating exclusively for
its group, while the emperor confined himself correspondingly, though
empowered to intervene anywhere in a crisis by virtue of *imperium maius*?
Support for this view might come from Nero's accession speech where he
assures the House, according to Tacitus: "The senate is to preserve its
ancient functions. By applying to the consuls, Italy and the senatorial
provinces may gain access to it. I myself will look after the armies assigned
to me."[10] Yet no other evidence supports such a rigid demarcation, and
there is much which argues against it. We shall see in the following chapter

---

[6] See E. Ritterling, "Military forces in the senatorial provinces," *JRS* 17. 1927. pp. 28-
32; R. K. Sherk, "The *inermes provinciae* of Asia Minor," *AJP* 76. 1955. pp. 400-413;
idem, "Roman imperial troops in Macedonia and Achaea," *AJP* 78. 1957. pp. 52-62;
W. Eck, "Bermerkungen zum Militärkommando in den Senatsprovinzen der Kaiserzeit,"
Chiron 2. 1972. pp. 429-436.

[7] Dio 60.24.5; Tac. *Ann.* 14.18. See further in general P. A. Brunt, "Conscription and
volunteering in the Roman imperial army," *Scripta Classica Israelica* 1. 1974. pp. 90-115.

[8] This view is taken up most recently by B. M. Levick (*Roman Colonies in Southern Asia
Minor*, p. 169; *Tiberius the Politician*, p. 129), and arises solely from Tacitus' sentence
under 15, "Achaiam ac Macedoniam onera deprecantis levari in praesens proconsulari imperio
tradique Caesari placuit" (*Ann.* 1.76). But of course there is no need to equate the support
of a governor and his staff with the unspecified "onera" here. Such support can seldom have
been a major imposition, and in any event the extent to which Roman officials could make
demands for their own needs was always limited by law. For speculation that the transfer of
the two provinces, and hence their "onera," are to be linked with disorder at Athens towards
the end of Augustus' reign, see G. W. Bowersock, *Augustus and the Greek World*, Oxford,
1965, pp. 106-108.

[9] Strabo 3.4.20; 17.3.25; Dio 53.12. The division is not mentioned by Velleius Paterculus
nor in *Res Gestae*.

[10] *Ann.* 13.4.

how far into the second century individuals and communities from all over the empire (including Italy) approached either authority according to no fixed rule. As might be expected, the choice was determined mainly by which of the two was hoped to prove more sympathetic and more effective. Naturally, therefore, most approaches were made to the emperor, and instances of, say, a direct appeal to the senate by a community in an imperial province are less common. But a few are found. By contrast, certain Italian and Asian communities continued to favor an approach to the House not least because they had influential senatorial patrons. Moreover, there were conceivably a few other Asian cities, in addition to Aphrodisias, which actually enjoyed the right to a hearing in the senate, and would seek to exercise it.[11]

We find rulings and communications addressed by the emperor to all governors, not just to his own legates. Likewise the senate's legislation applied throughout the empire,[12] and remained valid without time limit.[13] As Septimius Severus and Caracalla say in a rescript of 205 addressed to a colony in Noricum, "it is not right that privileges granted to *collegia* of *centonarii* on the instructions of the most exalted senate or by some emperor should be abolished lightly. Let what has been sanctioned by their laws (?) be safeguarded. . . ."[14] Even in Egypt the senate is mentioned as one of the sources of law which must be taken into account by the department of the Idios Logos, according to the preamble of its *Gnomon*,[15] while guardians were being officially assigned there in accordance with the relevant *senatus consultum* as late as 261.[16] During his governorship of Bithynia/Pontus Pliny cites a senatorial decree about the acknowledgment of children and granting of free-born rights to former slaves which, he says, "refers only to those provinces governed by proconsuls."[17] If the provisions of the decree were explicitly limited thus, such a restriction is unique in our knowledge. But it may rather have been the case that the decree left unclear the situation in imperial provinces, or was just intended to supplement some previous enactment by emperor or senate. Evidence of other enactments said to have been limited by the senate to imperial provinces, or by the emperor to either group, is altogether lacking.[18]

---

[11] In the present state of our knowledge the grant made to Aphrodisias in 39 B.C. is unique: see J. Reynolds, *Aphrodisias and Rome*, no. 8 lines 81-83 with discussion, p. 89.

[12] See nos. 94 and 95 in list, chap. 15 sect. 5.

[13] For a remarkable instance where a proconsul of Augustus' time (c. A.D. 4/5?) evidently respected privileges granted to Chios by a *senatus consultum* of 80 B.C., see *SEG* 22. 507 lines 10-18 with commentary in R. K. Sherk, *Roman Documents*, no. 70.

[14] *FIRA*² I no. 87, revised by G. Alföldy, *Noricum*, London, 1974, p. 269.

[15] *FIRA*² I no. 99 lines 1-7.

[16] *Ox. Pap.* 2710; cf. Cavenaile, *Corp. Pap. Lat,*, nos. 200-205, especially 200, 202.

[17] *Ep.* 10.72.

[18] Yet note that according to Gaius (*Inst.* 1.6) the aedilician edict was not published in imperial provinces.

In 27 B.C. the senatorial group of provinces comprised Achaea, Africa, Asia, Bithynia/Pontus, Crete with Cyrene, Dalmatia, Macedonia, Sardinia with Corsica, and Sicily. Thereafter changes were made under various circumstances, but it is notable that far into the second century efforts were continued to prevent undue shrinkage of the senatorial group. Direct exchanges between emperor and senate are explicitly mentioned, for example, by Dio[19] for 22 B.C. when Augustus took over Dalmatia and the senate gained Cyprus and Narbonensis. Similarly, according to Pausanias,[20] when Nero wished to acquire direct control of his beloved Achaea in 67, he compensated the senate with Sardinia. This exchange was evidently reversed early in Vespasian's reign. Although the placing of the passage has been disputed, epigraphic evidence would seem to confirm an excerpt from Dio[21] which claims an exchange around 134, with the senate ceding Bithynia/Pontus to receive Lycia with Pamphylia in return.[22] It is again epigraphic evidence which indicates further changes during M. Aurelius' reign from senatorial to imperial control in the former province, and vice versa in the latter.[23]

A province might be transferred without compensation: at least, so far as we know, the senate made Augustus no return for Baetica,[24] nor did the latter make any for Sardinia, which he took over in an unsettled condition in A.D. 6.[25] In 15 Tiberius likewise gave nothing in exchange for Achaea and Macedonia, brought under imperial control when they protested at the weight of their burdens. Claudius returned these areas to the senate in 44.[26] As we have already noted, under Vespasian Sardinia with Corsica reverted to the emperor's group of provinces. By Trajan's time, however, inscriptions show it as governed by proconsuls, who evidently give way in turn to imperial procurators under Hadrian; yet by M. Aurelius' reign proconsuls are present again, until procurators reappear under Commodus.[27]

---

[19] 54.4.1.

[20] 7.17.3.

[21] 69.14.4.

[22] See B. M. Levick and S. Jameson, JRS 54. 1964. p. 103; W. Eck, Senatoren von Vespasian bis Hadrian, pp. 18-19; H. Halfmann, Die Senatoren, no. 71.

[23] See, for example, D. Magie, Roman Rule in Asia Minor, Princeton, 1950, pp. 1532-1533; B. M. Levick, Roman Colonies in Southern Asia Minor, p. 169; G. Molisani, "Il governo della Licia-Panfilia nell' età di Marco Aurelio," Rivista di Filologia 105. 1977. pp. 166-178 (discussed further in AE 1978. 713).

[24] Although it must have been during his reign that Baetica was detached from Lusitania to form a senatorial province, the date cannot be fixed with further precision: see G. Alföldy, Fasti Hispanienses, pp. 223-224. Dio (53.12.4) errs in saying that Baetica formed part of the senatorial group from 27 B.C.

[25] Dio 55.28.1.

[26] Tac. Ann. 1.76; Suet. Claud. 25; Dio 60.24.1; cf. 58.25.4-5.

[27] For discussion of changes, see A. E. Astin, "The status of Sardinia in the second century

While these changes probably made small difference to the Sardinians, their frequency does set a puzzle in any attempt to understand the senate's involvement with its own provinces. Other senatorial provinces, too, were evidently transferred to the emperor and back again in the course of the second century, yet so far as we can tell these moves were never intended to be more than temporary. So it is certainly possible to suggest a link between them and the changes in the island's status, especially when it would be difficult to account for the latter otherwise. But if there was such a link, there arises the further problem of why the emperor should take this trouble to furnish compensation even for temporary losses. Was he so concerned to placate the House and maintain tradition? Or was there such stiff competition among *praetorii* for governorships of limited tenure and prestige that it was considered necessary to make up even the temporary removal of a province from the senate? (An imperial legate who governed a senatorial province for, say, three years would replace three proconsuls— a net "loss" of posts for two men. For the same period no quaestor would be required either.) All these questions must remain open for lack of evidence, although we might note the prefecture of the *aerarium Saturni* as a comparable post which *praetorii* evidently were very eager to compete for at one stage—so much so that from 23 B.C., reputedly in order to eliminate excessive canvassing, Augustus replaced the two praetorian *praefecti* chosen by the House with two praetors chosen by lot.[28] Unless in this case there were known to be special opportunities for private profit, such keen rivalry seems extraordinary. But it may be that there really was competition of a similar nature for proconsulships as well, not to mention comparable opportunities for private profit.[29]

Another route by which we might hope to probe the senate's involvement with its own provinces is to examine how measures were taken for their administration in special circumstances. Yet here, too, no clear pattern emerges. Whenever arrangements had to be made to cover for a proconsul unable to finish his term, we might expect the House to act—in consultation with the emperor where appropriate. But when proconsuls of Achaea and of Crete with Cyrene died in office in 6 and 15 respectively, Dio[30] is typically not concerned to specify the authority by which these provinces were temporarily divided between legate and quaestor. The description of

A.D.," *Latomus* 18. 1959. pp. 150-153; W. Eck, "Zum Rechtsstatus von Sardinien im 2 Jh. n. Chr.," *Historia* 20. 1971. pp. 510-512; B. E. Thomasson, "Zur Verwaltungsgeschichte der Provinz Sardinia," *Eranos* 70. 1972. pp. 72-81.

[28] Tac. *Ann.* 13.29.

[29] G. Clemente, "La presunta politica di scambio dei governi provinciali fra imperatore e senato nel I e II secolo," *Parola del Passato* 20. 1965. pp. 195-206, rightly warns against adopting an over-mechanical approach.

[30] 55.27.6; 57.14.4.

C. Minicius Italus as "procurator of the province of Asia, which he governed in the place of a deceased proconsul on the instructions of the emperor,"[31] hardly suggests that Domitian had consulted the House before acting in this instance. Equally it remains open whether or not the appointment of further procurators acting for proconsuls early in the third century—one each in Africa and Macedonia, two in Asia[32]—was referred to it or not. If we may accept Alföldy's conjecture[33] that Hadrian's companion C. Iulius Proculus was asked to act as temporary governor of Baetica in an emergency during that emperor's visit to Spain in 122 or 123, it may understandably have been impossible to consult the senate in advance on this occasion.

When it was seen in advance that a province needed special attention temporarily, common first-century practice was either for a governor to be picked and appointed (rather than selected at random through the lot), or for the term of an existing holder to be extended. In the earliest recorded instance of the former arrangement the senate acted on the initiative of the emperor, so that P. Paquius Scaeva could describe himself as "again proconsul outside the lot, sent by authority of Augustus Caesar and a *senatus consultum* to restore the state of Cyprus for the future."[34] In 21 Tiberius as consul duly asked the senate to appoint to Africa a proconsul with the strength and ability to subdue Tacfarinas; he was not pleased when the choice was referred back to him.[35] We may be fairly sure (though we cannot prove) that the House was likewise consulted before the future emperor Galba was sent out as governor of Africa in 44-46 or 45-47: "Chosen outside the lot, he gained Africa for two years: the province had been unsettled by internal disputes and native risings, and his task was to restore order."[36] The House was presumably consulted about the appointment of Martius Macer as proconsul of Achaea *citra sortem* very soon after the province had been handed back to the senate by Claudius.[37] We

[31] *ILS* 1374, "proc(urator) provinciae Asiae quam mandatu principis vice defuncti procos. rexit"; see further R. Syme, *Tacitus*, pp. 55-56.

[32] In Africa, Hilarianus, see B. E. Thomasson, *Die Statthalter* II. p. 104; in Macedonia, M. Aurelius Apollinarius, *IG* X.2.1 no. 140, with comment by H.-G. Pflaum, *Ecole Pratique des Hautes Etudes (IVe section): Annuaire* 1973/4. pp. 269-270; in Asia, Aelius Aglaus (*PIR*² A 133) and C. Furius Sabinius Aquila Timesitheus (*PIR*² F 581).

[33] *Fasti Hispanienses*, pp. 166-167.

[34] *ILS* 915, "procos. iterum extra sortem auctoritate Aug. Caesaris et s.c. misso [for missus] ad componendum statum in reliquum provinciae Cypri." Note also L. Aquillius Florus Turcianus Gallus, who served as *quaestor Augusti* and was then proquaestor in Cyprus "ex auctoritate Augusti": *ILS* 928; *AE* 1919. 1; *PIR*² A 993.

[35] Tac. *Ann.* 3.32 and 35.

[36] Suet. *Galba* 7, "Africam pro consule biennio optinuit extra sortem electus ad ordinandam provinciam et intestina dissensione et barbarorum tumultu inquietam." For dates, see B. E. Thomasson, *Die Statthalter* II. pp. 32-33.

[37] *ILS* 969; E. Groag, *Die Reichsbeamten*, col. 32. Some would even make Macer the first proconsul after the change.

may make the same presumption about the appointment of M. Iulius Romulus as proconsul of Macedonia *extra sortem* (in the late 50's?).[38]

Dio[39] does not explain which authority extended the terms of quaestors and proconsuls in various crises under Augustus and Tiberius. But in the latter's reign in particular the epigraphic evidence for extension of proconsular terms confirms literary testimony about their frequency under that emperor,[40] and leaves no doubt that he showed interest even in the deployment of proconsuls. Altogether we know of up to eleven such governors who served extended terms under Augustus and Tiberius. Later in the first century, leaving aside the case of Galba already mentioned, we know of extended terms served by two proconsuls in Africa (under Claudius and Nero), at least one in Asia (under Vespasian), one in Bithynia/Pontus (under Vespasian), and one, or just possibly two, in Crete with Cyrene (the more certain case under Vespasian, the less under Claudius).[41] The senate itself certainly extended the term of Q. Iunius Blaesus in Africa.[42] We might guess, though we cannot prove, that it was consulted in all the other instances. The urgent need for reconstruction in the aftermath of civil war must have been a major cause of the special arrangements in Vespasian's reign. Thereafter, however, no certain case of a proconsul serving an extended term can be found—provided we leave aside Q. Anicius Faustus, to whom so little of 217 remained once his appointment to Asia had finally been settled, that he was understandably permitted to continue in office the following year.[43] Otherwise the evidence remains uncertain in the only further possible instance, that of P. Iulius Scapula Tertullus Priscus in Africa (211-13?).[44]

Rather, in the second and early third centuries, when the need for special attention was foreseen, new measures superseded the old; provinces now seem either to have been handed over temporarily to the emperor, or to have received a *curator* or *corrector* commissioned by him. If a restoration be accepted, the senate was evidently consulted in the earliest known instance of the former arrangement, when Pliny was sent to Bithynia/

---

[38] *AE* 1925. 85; *PIR²* I 523. The conjecture that L. Tampius Flavianus was *proconsul extra sortem* in Africa late in Nero's reign (*AE* 1966. 68) is highly uncertain: cf. G. W. Houston, *ZPE* 20. 1976. pp. 27-28.

[39] 54.30.3; 55.28.2; 57.16.1; 58.23.5. Note, however, Q. Coelius "pr., aed. pl. Cer., pro pr. ex s.c., q." (*ILS* 153).

[40] Tac. *Ann.* 1.80; 6.27; Dio 58.23.5.

[41] See Appendix 8.

[42] Tac. *Ann.* 3.58.

[43] Dio 78.22.2-4.

[44] See B. E. Thomasson, *Die Statthalter* II. pp. 112-113. When Dio (78.21.5) says that Lucilius Priscillianus became governor of Achaea under Caracalla παρὰ τὸ καθῆκον, he might conceivably mean *extra sortem*. But other possibilities remain open, discussed by Groag, *Die Reichsbeamten*, col. 84.

Pontus about 110: *"legatus pro praetore* of the province of Pontus and Bithynia with consular powers when sent to that province by the emperor Trajan in accordance with a decree of the senate."[45] By contrast, an inscription in honor of Cornutus Tertullus, who is commonly taken to have been Pliny's successor in this governorship, merely terms him *"legatus pro praetore* of the divine emperor Trajan in the province of Pontus and Bithynia,"[46] with no mention of the senate nor of the *consularis potestas* which symbolized the authority of the proconsul.

The *Historia Augusta* suggests that Marcus Aurelius showed concern for the senate's interests and made an effort to maintain the size of its group of provinces, explaining how "he made provinces consular instead of proconsular, or proconsular or praetorian instead of consular, in accordance with the necessities of war."[47] Certainly we find Hispania Citerior and Baetica (imperial and senatorial provinces respectively) under a single imperial legate during the emergency of the Moorish invasions in the 170's, while the appointment of a governor of Macedonia with consular rather than praetorian rank c. 170 might equally suggest imperial intervention at a time of hostilities in that region. We may guess that it would have been in character for M. Aurelius to have consulted the senate about such changes, but predictably any such courtesy is omitted in the *cursus honorum* which form our only evidence.[48] Severus Alexander is another emperor who might likewise have consulted the House before taking the special step of appointing an equestrian governor to Asia. So it is frustrating that the relevant stone from Aphrodisias breaks off before completing its account of how this measure, too, was effected.[49] Finally in this connection Pflaum[50] has conjectured that Septimius Severus split Crete and Cyrene, leaving the former to a proconsul and assigning the latter to a procurator. Later Severus Alexander, more favorable to the senate, returned the whole to it; but the restoration probably did not last out his reign. Despite its

---

[45] *ILS* 2927, "legat. pro pr. provinciae Pon[ti et Bithyniae] consulari potesta[t.] in eam provinciam e[x s.c. missus ab] imp. Caesar. Nerva Traiano"; cf. *CIL* XI. 5272.

[46] *ILS* 1024, "legato pro praetore divi Traiani [Parthici] provinciae Ponti et Bith[yniae]."

[47] HA, *Marcus* 22.9, reading: "provincias ex proconsularibus consulares aut ex consularibus proconsulares aut praetorias pro belli necessitate fecit."

[48] Spain: G. Alföldy, *Fasti Hispanienses*, pp. 38-42, s.v. C. Aufidius Victorinus, with M. Rachet, *Rome et les berbères, Collection Latomus* 110, Brussels, 1970, pp. 203-211, and J. M. Blázquez, "Hispania desde el año 138 al 235," *Hispania* 132. 1976. pp. 5-87 at pp. 70-77. Macedonia: *ILS* 1102 with *PIR²* I 340.

[49] J. Reynolds, *Aphrodisias and Rome*, no. 47, with earlier discussion by P. Veyne, "Un gouverneur impérial en Asie," in R. Chevallier (ed.), *Mélanges d'archéologie et d'histoire offerts à A. Piganiol*, Paris, 1966, III. pp. 1395-1396.

[50] *Ecole Pratique des Hautes Etudes, IVe section: Annuaire* 1973/4. pp. 271-276. Note comment by J. Reynolds, *JRS* 68. 1978. p. 120; her remarks in *PBSR* 20. 1965. p. 52 also need to be taken into account.

accommodation of difficult epigraphic evidence, this complicated development cannot be confirmed until more material comes to light.

Epictetus[51] has the *curator* Maximus declare that he was appointed by the emperor personally. Otherwise we lack information on how these officials were formally appointed to senatorial provinces. In a number of cases we cannot even be certain whether they took over altogether from the governor, or whether their duties were confined, say, to certain cities. In Bithynia/Pontus Pliny clearly combined the functions of governor and *corrector*, as perhaps did C. Julius Severus, sent to the same province near the end of Hadrian's reign.[52] From the late second century we likewise find senators who seem to have been simultaneously proconsul of Achaea, *legatus Augusti pro praetore,* and *corrector liberarum civitatium.*[53] On the other hand, from Pliny's letter to Maximus[54] a century earlier there is no cause to believe that the latter's mission had gone beyond regulating the affairs of *civitates liberae* in Achaea. Epigraphic evidence shows the duties of L. Aemilius Iuncus there to have been similarly circumscribed during Hadrian's reign, and there is a strong temptation to believe that under Trajan the same applied to C. Avidius Nigrinus, also imperial legate in Achaea.[55]

We do hear of two legates appointed for special missions by the senate— to help the earthquake-stricken cities of Asia in 17, and to oversee the new temple to Tiberius, Livia, and the senate at Smyrna in 26.[56] Imperial legates on special missions in senatorial provinces are more commonly found, however. But again we lack knowledge of how they were formally appointed. Those who assigned land in Africa between the reigns of Vespasian and Hadrian form the largest known group, though at least some of them were stationed on the spot anyway as legates of III Augusta, rather than officials specially sent out as land commissioners.[57] The epigraphic evidence gives no hint that the senate had ever been consulted about their work. It is valuable to gain unique confirmation that there had indeed been no consultation prior to Claudius' appointment of L. Acilius Strabo as commissioner to determine ownership of lands in Cyrene left to Rome by King Apion.[58] When Acilius delivered a decision unfavorable to the oc-

---

[51] 3.7.30.

[52] Dio 69.14.4; *PIR*² I 573.

[53] See J. H. Oliver, "Imperial commissioners in Achaia," *GRBS* 14. 1973. pp. 389-405.

[54] *Ep.* 8.24.2, "missum ad ordinandum statum liberarum civitatum."

[55] See E. Groag, *Die Reichsbeamten,* cols. 54-56, 64-65; *Fouilles de Delphes* III. 4. p. 39; H. Halfmann, *Die Senatoren,* no. 55.

[56] Tac. *Ann.* 2.47; 4.56; Dio 57.17.7.

[57] For a list and discussion see H.-G. Pflaum, "Légats impériaux à l'intérieur de provinces sénatoriales," in *Hommages à Albert Grenier, Collection Latomus* 58, Brussels, 1962, pp. 1232-1242 at pp. 1234-1235; in addition *AE* 1969/70. 696.

[58] For epigraphic evidence of Acilius' activity under Claudius and Nero, note *SEG* 9. 352; *AE* 1974. 677, 682, 684.

cupiers, they initiated a prosecution in the House in 59. But Tacitus[59] explains how it was then forced to undergo the humiliation of admitting that it could not assess Acilius' decision since it did not know Claudius' instructions, and that the question must therefore be referred to the emperor. Epigraphic evidence again gives no hint that Vespasian had consulted the senate before sending Q. Paconius Agrippinus as land commissioner to Cyrene.[60]

Pflaum[61] takes the view that both these imperial officials went to Cyrene as legates of the proconsul appointed by the emperor, rather than as extra legates. This may also have been the status of C. Julius Severus, "sent as *legatus* in Asia by a letter and *codicilli* of the divine Hadrian," according to an inscription,[62] as well as later of Q. Hedius Lollianus Plautius Avitus in Asia under Septimius Severus and Caracalla,[63] and perhaps A. Egnatius Proculus in Africa.[64] We may note also a senior consular, Julius (?) Avitus, who after governing Asia was sent by Caracalla to advise the proconsul of Cyprus.[65] Whatever the precise status of such special officers, there can be no question that it was the emperor who took the initiative in having them appointed. They acted as his legates, and in all likelihood the senate was not even consulted at any stage.

It is hardly necessary to illustrate how from the beginning of the Principate the emperor issued direct instructions to individual proconsuls.[66] Even Tiberius could order as senior a figure as L. Aelius Lamia, proconsul of Africa around 16, to build a road, as the latter advertised on stone.[67] It is striking therefore to find L. Turpilius Dexter, proconsul in 64/5, delimiting land in Crete "on the authority of the emperor Nero and by decree of the senate."[68] But this apparently unusual instance of imperial consultation of the senate may be accounted for by the previous embarrassment already noted—when the House had to admit in 59 that it could not assess a decision made by Claudius' legate in the other half of the same province since it did not know his instructions. All the same, ac-

---

[59] *Ann.* 14.18.

[60] *AE* 1919. 91-93; 1974. 683; cf. Hyginus in *Gromatici Veteres* I. p. 122 Lachmann.

[61] Op. cit. in note 57, p. 1237.

[62] *ILS* 8826; for delimitation of boundaries by him in this capacity, see *MAMA* V. 60 (Dorylaeum), with discussion by Pflaum, op. cit. in note 57, p. 1236.

[63] *ILS* 1155, "leg. Augg. prov. Asiae"; *PIR*² H 36, with Pflaum, op. cit. in note 57, p. 1240.

[64] *ILS* 1167, "leg. Aug. prov. Afr. dioeces. Numid.," with Pflaum, op. cit. in note 57, pp. 1240-1241.

[65] Dio 78.30.4; for discussion of the identity of this Avitus, see *PIR*² I 190.

[66] See F. Millar, *JRS* 56. 1966. pp. 161 and 164.

[67] *IRT* 930 = *EJ* 291, "Imp. Ti. Caesaris Aug. iussu L. Aelius Lamia pro cos. ab oppido in mediterraneum direxsit m. p. XLIV". For the date of his proconsulship, see B. E. Thomasson, *Statthalter* II. p. 21.

[68] M. Guarducci, *Inscriptiones Creticae* I, Rome, 1935, XXVI. 2; cf. 3 and XXVIII. 29.

cording to the conventional estimate, Nero's tact towards the senate in this matter is not perhaps what might have been expected from him in 64. More predictably, it was just by direct order of Domitian that the proconsul C. Pomponius Gallus Didius Rufus carried out similar work in Cyrene in 88/9.[69]

In contrast to the known activities of the emperor we lack evidence for the senate taking the initiative in sending orders to any governor, whether proconsul or imperial legate.[70] It should be stressed at once, however, that this is no surprise. Even from the emperor, spontaneous communications were rare. Normally he confined himself to providing justice and responding to queries or petitions. Romans viewed these functions as the major role of government, and the senate itself acted no differently. Yet in an appropriate instance there was certainly no obstacle to action by it, and indeed the speaker of the *sententia prima* about reducing the cost of gladiatorial games c. 177 does supply an example. In the only paragraph where he is likely to be framing his own proposals independently of the imperial *oratio*,[71] he advocates steps to be taken by all governors and concludes: "Let the *viri clarissimi* who went out as proconsuls a short while ago be informed that each of them is supposed to carry out this assignment within his year; let those who govern provinces where the lot is not used likewise finish within the year."[72] If this proposal was adopted, it follows that the senate would arrange to inform governors. It certainly notified them all of its deposition of Maximinus in 238.[73]

Beyond direct orders to individual proconsuls we must consider the regular issuing of *mandata*—"instructions" given to those entering office. From the beginning, governors in the emperor's group of provinces, together with a wide range of other officials appointed by him, seem to have received these. Dio[74] goes further and states explicitly that from 27 B.C. senatorial governors likewise received *mandata* from the emperor. The

---

[69] *AE* 1954. 188. For other proconsuls assigning land or determining boundaries on the orders of the emperor (with no mention of the senate), note J. Keil and A. von Premerstein, *Bericht über eine dritte Reise in Lydien*, Vienna, 1914, no. 146 (in Asia, under Claudius); possibly also no. 137; *AE* 1933. 123 (both in Asia, under Domitian); 1963. 197 (in Narbonensis, under Vespasian).

[70] It would be possible to conjecture that a metrical fragment of the second or third century from Salamis in Cyprus mentions the senate to render thanks for building work carried out in the baths at its instigation. But no secure conclusions can be drawn from this hopelessly damaged inscription, where even the reference to the Roman senate is open to doubt. See T. B. Mitford and I. K. Nicolaou, *Salamis* vol. 6, Nicosia, 1974, no. 32.

[71] For discussion see chap. 8.

[72] *Aes Ital.* lines 53-55, *Hesperia* 24. 1955. p. 333.

[73] Herodian 7.7.5; HA, *Maximin.* 15.2-3. Note also the fragmentary decree of A.D. 7 instructing the consuls to dispatch letters (no. 12 in list, chap. 15 sect. 5), and the senate's communication to Galba in 68 (Plut. *Galba* 8).

[74] 53.15.4.

claim has been variously accepted or rejected by scholars, but until recently the persistent difficulty remained that the earliest instance of a proconsul receiving *mandata* seemed to be the future emperor Antoninus Pius as governor of Asia in 134/5[75]—in other words, a century and a half on from 27 B.C. Yet Burton[76] has now drawn attention to two earlier proconsuls of Asia citing their "instructions" in letters to cities—Cn. Domitius Corbulo writing to Cos in Claudius' reign, and Q. Fabius Postuminus to Aezani about 111/12.

The evidence for receipt of "instructions" by these proconsuls is unassailable. Yet it may not serve as an equally firm foundation for the further claims, first that they regularly received *mandata* from 27 B.C. onwards, and second that these were issued by the emperor direct. Both claims merit a pause for reflection. On the first we have no evidence, though two negative impressions might be taken into account. The first relates to the situation uncovered by Pliny in Bithynia/Pontus under Trajan. From his *Letters*, Book 10, we gain the general impression of a province whose previous governors had consistently not been directed by any authority, or at any rate had totally failed to translate instructions into action. More specifically, if these proconsuls had regularly been receiving imperial *mandata*, it seems astonishing that Trajan should have waited until Pliny's governorship before introducing a ban on *collegia*.[77] Second, a glance at the list of known *repetundae* trials up to the early second century (incomplete though this must be) suggests that imperial legates were charged less often than proconsuls. A variety of reasons may be given for the contrast, not least among them that any attack upon an imperial legate was mounted with special caution, whereas provincials might not feel that proconsuls enjoyed the same close links with the emperor.[78] Indeed it may have been partly because there was no convention of such a close working relationship that Trajan chose to depart from first-century practice in transferring Bithynia/Pontus to his group of provinces, and to appoint as governor a consular directly answerable to himself. Dio's remark[79] that governors of senatorial provinces came to be chosen by the emperor rather than by lot because some men selected by the latter method had governed badly might equally suggest the absence of any such closeness, and thus only irregular *mandata* at best.

The second claim—that *mandata* were issued to proconsuls by the em-

---

[75] *Dig.* 48.3.6.1; for date, see W. Eck, *Senatoren von Vespasian bis Hadrian*, p. 210.

[76] "The issuing of mandata to proconsuls and a new inscription from Cos," *ZPE* 21. 1976. pp. 63-68. As he says (p. 64), Tac. *Hist.* 4.48 must indicate that proconsuls of Africa, too, received *mandata* in the first century.

[77] Plin. *Ep.* 10.96.7.

[78] See P. A. Brunt, *Historia* 10. 1961. p. 211 and further below, Appendix 9.

[79] 53.14.3.

peror direct—is more delicate. None of the three references already cited specifies the issuing authority, while it is notorious that Dio had little interest in the procedural and constitutional niceties by which Augustus and certain of his contemporaries set great store. To Dio 27 B.C. marked the foundation of an out-and-out monarchy.[80] Taken literally, the claim that thereafter Augustus regularly issued his own *mandata* to proconsuls would make nonsense of the division of provinces between emperor and senate carried out at the same time, and would seem to be altogether at odds with the parity which he aimed to maintain at that date in relation to his consular colleagues.[81] With proconsuls thus instructed, from that moment the senate would effectively have been left without control of the governors in its own group of provinces, and the only difference remaining between proconsul and imperial legate would have been the method of their appointment and the length of their tenure. We may well believe that such was the case in Dio's own day, and indeed long before. But it is harder to credit that the new arrangement of 27 B.C. was intended by Augustus to be such a blatant sham from the very beginning. Equally, those of his successors who sought the senate's cooperation in government cannot have wanted to deny the House some control of its group of provinces. As we have already noted, it is true that from the beginning emperors might communicate with proconsuls from time to time on certain matters. But if they went so far as to issue *mandata* to them regularly, it seems puzzling that at the same time Augustus and Tiberius should still take trouble to gain the senate's authorization for the Eastern missions of Agrippa[82] and Germanicus,[83] for example, or that early in his reign Claudius should instruct Q. Veranius, legate of Lycia, jointly with the House.[84]

In considering the issuing authority for *mandata* there has perhaps been too ready an assumption that none were sent out by the senate, on the grounds that all relevant evidence is said to be lacking.[85] In fact there are two passages which merit consideration in this regard. First, it does seem to be *mandata* from the senate which Juvenal indicates in cautioning a prospective governor early in the second century, "Pay attention to the

---

[80] Cf. 53.11.5.

[81] The trial of M. Primus (Dio 54.3) might become an even greater puzzle too, especially if it be dated to 23 B.C.: on this vexed episode see, for example, S. Jameson, "22 or 23?" *Historia* 18. 1969. pp. 204-229.

[82] *P. Colon.* 4701 col. I lines 10-11 in *ZPE* 5. 1970. p. 226.

[83] Tac. *Ann.* 2.43; 3.12; Josephus, *AJ* 18.54. Note how Germanicus, in what was perhaps an impromptu speech at Alexandria, merely said that he had been sent by his father (*Ox. Pap.* XXV. no. 2435 recto lines 9-10).

[84] This remarkable instance of joint initiative hinges on restoration of *IGRR* IV. 902. For its punctuation see L. Robert, *Etudes anatoliennes*, Paris, 1937, p. 89 n. 2; and further A. E. Gordon, *Quintus Veranius Consul A.D. 49*, p. 240.

[85] See F. Millar, *JRS* 56. 1966. p. 159.

laws' provisions and to the instructions of the House. . . ."[86] Second, the Severan jurist Callistratus makes a specific reference to undated senatorial *mandata* in an extract from his work *De Cognitionibus* under the heading "On public works":

If anyone wishes to adorn with marble, or in any other way, a work constructed by another, and has promised to do so in accordance with the people's wishes, the senate resolved that this could be done, with his own name being inscribed upon the work, although the names of those originally responsible for it should remain. But the same *mandata* caution that where private individuals spend money of their own upon works constructed with public funds, they should mention the amount they have contributed to the work when inscribing their names upon it.[87]

By Callistratus' time oversight of the completion of new public buildings in due form had long been a notable part of any governor's duties,[88] so that it is quite natural to find the senate issuing instructions in this connection.

In the light of all the evidence cited above, consideration should be given to the possibility that the House itself did issue proconsular "instructions," most commonly perhaps on the motion of the emperor. The issuing authority would thus hardly differ in practice from the latter acting alone. But not only would the slight distinction be significant in constitutional terms; it would also avoid the offense liable to be taken above all at regular imperial instructions to the proconsuls of Africa and Asia, whose offices were so highly esteemed by members. The House would also be offered that vital degree of controlled initiative which many emperors were keen to foster. At the very least it would be reasonable to think that in the first century the senate played some part, even if only a formal one, in instructing those proconsuls who, as we have already seen, were appointed by it to areas with special needs—Paquius Scaeva to Cyprus, for example, or Galba to Africa. In addition, if a restoration be accepted, it certainly was the senate which authorized one Proculus to serve three times as legate of Narbonensis during the Julio-Claudian period.[89]

---

[86] *Sat.* 8.91, "Respice quid moneant leges, quid curia mandet." An allusion to Marius Priscus' governorship of Africa (8.120) provides one clue for dating: his trial in January 100 is well known (cf. 1.48-50). See further E. Courtney, *A Commentary on the Satires of Juvenal*, London, 1980, pp. 1-10.

[87] *Dig.* 50.10.7.1, "si quis opus ab alio factum adornare marmoribus vel alio quo modo ex voluntate populi facturum se pollicitus sit, nominis proprii titulo scribendo: manentibus priorum titulis, qui ea opera fecissent, id fieri debere senatus censuit. Quod si privati in opera, quae publica pecunia fiant, aliquam de suo adiecerint summam, ita titulo inscriptionis uti eos debere isdem mandatis cavetur, ut quantam summam contulerint in id opus, inscribant." For inconclusive discussion see R. Bonini, *I "Libri de Cognitionibus" di Callistrato*, Milan, 1964, pp. 152-153; for dating, A. M. Honoré, *SDHI* 28. 1962. pp. 215-216.

[88] Note, for example, Ulpian, *Dig.* 1.16.7.1.

[89] *CIL* XI. 5173 (Vettona) restored by G. Alföldy, *Fasti Hispanienses*, pp. 154-155 = H.-G. Pflaum, *Les fastes de la province de Narbonnaise*, p. 60.

There are difficulties enough in determining what role the senate may have taken in instructing proconsuls and communicating with them. But the uncertainties are even greater when we move on to consider how far they in turn might consult the House or the emperor. Burton has rightly stressed the unbalanced nature of the testimony for consultation of the latter. The main evidence comes from the jurists, and only dates from the early second century. For the first century there is no literary evidence, nor are there many inscriptions for either century. All the same, from meager epigraphic material it is at least clear that even in the first century proconsuls might consult the emperor.[90] Did they ever consult the senate too? Here we have no evidence. For the second century we might hardly expect any. For the first, doubt remains. If an instance were to be unearthed, it would not seem amazing. As it is, we may not draw conclusions from silence, especially when evidence for consultation of the emperor remains so slight, and when (most important of all) we just have no idea how frequently governors referred matters to Rome. Quite apart from the varying situations they encountered, much must of course have depended on their individual experience and temperament as well as upon their estimate of the emperor or the House. In addition, proconsular tenure was so short that in the more distant provinces at least there might seem little point in dispatching queries during the final months before departure each year.[91]

In any study of the corporate body and its functions the senate's involvement with its own provinces must be discussed. But an attempt to sum up the character of that involvement underlines how little can be established. At least from the early second century there is no discernible distinction between senatorial and imperial provinces beyond the method by which governors were appointed and the length of their tenure. By that date it was the emperor who issued *mandata* to proconsuls and who was consulted by them about problems. All the same, until late in the century efforts were still made to maintain the number of senatorial provinces, perhaps so that the House would be gratified and the total of posts for members kept up. Even earlier it is true that the emperor might exercise his right to give orders to proconsuls, and they in turn might consult him. Yet the point of greatest uncertainty is whether at this stage he encroached so far as to deprive the House of all involvement with its group. In my opinion he did not. Rather, as in other spheres, imperial encroachment

[90] Cf. Claudius' letter discovered at Delphi, *Fouilles de Delphes* III. 4. no. 286, with following note; possibly also Domitian's letters cited at Plin. *Ep.* 10.65.3.

[91] Naturally the reply to a proconsul's query could still be sent to his successor. See Eusebius, *Hist. Eccl.* 4.8.6 and 9.1-3; Justin, I *Apol.* 68-69. This was likewise the case with Claudius' letter to Delphi in the view of its most recent editor, A. Plassart (loc. cit. in previous note), disputed by J. H. Oliver, "The epistle of Claudius which mentions the proconsul Iunius Gallio," *Hesperia* 40. 1971. pp. 239-240.

developed gradually. In the first century the senate did take some part in such oversight as there was of its own provinces, even if it was largely a formal part. Claudius Timarchus' offensive remarks about his influence in determining whether or not retiring proconsuls received a vote of thanks seem significant in this connection.[92] The fact that these were taken as an insult to the senate shows how in 62 Crete and Cyrene was still considered to be "its" province.[93] It is true that the initiative at times of special need frequently came from the emperor; yet he can be seen continuing to consult the senate about his intentions during the first century.

Altogether, while the Principate manifestly robbed the House of initiative in provincial government as in other matters, it should be remembered that provincial affairs always occupied members and must have continued to feature prominently at sessions. Many senators of course had extensive private interests outside Italy. A growing number were of provincial origin themselves. And regardless of background, all but a handful would soon gain more or less provincial experience in the course of advancement. As we shall see, too, far into the second century matters raised by communities throughout the empire were either brought directly to the senate, or referred there by the emperor. Moreover, it continued to legislate for the whole empire, and to hear cases brought against governors for maladministration. Finally, as the following chapter will show, it is striking how emperors consistently kept the House informed about developments both in the imperial provinces and beyond the empire's frontiers.

[92] Tac. *Ann.* 15.20.

[93] Arguably it was the same feeling which made Tiberius reluctant to receive envoys from Africa (Suet. *Tib.* 31).

14

DIPLOMACY, THE ARMY, AND FOREIGN AFFAIRS

1. Embassies from the Senate

In our period, as in the Republic, embassies were still sent out by the senate, although mostly for different reasons and perhaps less often than hitherto, at least to judge by the scanty surviving evidence. The purpose for which senators might now most commonly serve as envoys seems to have been to greet a new emperor. In particular, when he was far from Rome at the time of his accession, a senatorial delegation might be sent to him in the first instance. And in all cases (except towards the end of our period, when some emperors never came to the city at all) there would sooner or later be a formal *adventus*, or arrival, in Rome. Where the latter is concerned, however, it is strictly necessary to distinguish between formal and informal practice, though the actual difference between the two may have been slight.

In the late Republic members of all classes had gone out informally to welcome distinguished citizens when they returned to Rome on certain significant occasions. Cicero was honored thus on his return from exile in 57 B.C., and Julius Caesar likewise on his return from Spain in 45 B.C.[1] When Octavian landed at Brundisium in winter 31/30 B.C., almost all senators went there to meet him, and in 30 they voted that when he should enter Rome, the Vestal Virgins, and the senate and people with their wives and children, should go out to meet him. But he specifically asked that this decree not be put into effect.[2]

In 19 B.C., however, we first hear of envoys being sent formally from the senate to meet Augustus—an unprecedented honor, as he himself claims in *Res Gestae*: "By order of the senate some of the praetors and tribunes of the plebs together with the consul Q. Lucretius and leading men of the state were sent to Campania to meet me, an honor which up to the present

---

[1] Cic. *Ad Att.* 4.1.5 = SB 73; *Phil.* 2.78; Plut. *Anton.* 11.
[2] Dio 51.4.4; 19.2; 20.4.

time has been decreed to no one except myself.''[3] Augustus implies here that the envoys had been sent merely to greet him. Yet Dio[4] may be more accurate when he explains that they were sent in the first instance to tell the emperor of the disturbed situation in Rome, where attempts to fill the consular place which he would not accept himself had provoked riots. We hear of no more such embassies to Augustus. Rather, he made it plain that he disliked the formal ceremonies of arrival (*adventus*) and departure (*profectio*) at Rome, or any other city, and did everything he could to avoid them.[5]

For the rest of our period we know only that by vote of the senate both Sejanus and Tiberius were to be formally met whenever they entered Rome,[6] and that P. Cluvius Maximus Paullinus, probably as ex-praetor, served as "envoy sent by the senate to the emperor Hadrian on his return from Africa,"[7] almost certainly in summer 128. According to the *Historia Augusta*,[8] after the death of Maximinus in 238 an embassy of twenty senators likewise went to welcome Pupienus on his return to Rome from Aquileia. It must be partly chance that we know of no further instances where the senate actually sent an embassy for the *adventus* of an emperor to Rome. In any event, the need for such a step was less pressing when every fit senator in the city appreciated an informal obligation to be present to greet him on such occasions, as we have seen in an earlier chapter.[9]

When a new emperor was far from Rome at the time of his accession, an embassy might instead be sent out to him from the senate at once. Galba (in Spain) was honored thus in 68,[10] and so was Vitellius (in Germany) the following year, as we shall see shortly. The proposal late in 69 that an embassy should go to Vespasian at Alexandria provoked a bitter altercation between Helvidius Priscus, who asked that the envoys be chosen individually by the magistrates under oath, and Eprius Marcellus, who supported the consul designate's motion that the traditional method of selection by lot be followed. In the end tradition carried the day.[11]

Similarly, at the beginning of Tiberius' reign it was arranged that an embassy led by the consul of 13, L. Munatius Plancus, should be sent from the senate to Germanicus to console him on the death of Augustus,

---

[3] *RG* 12.1. In 29 B.C. the sacrifices for Octavian's return offered by the consul on behalf of senate and people were equally unprecedented, according to Dio (51.21.2).

[4] 54.10.2.

[5] Suet. *Aug.* 53; Dio 54.10.4 and 25.4; cf. 56.41.5.

[6] Dio 58.4.4.

[7] *AE* 1940. 99, "legato misso a senatu ad imp. Hadrianum cum ex Africa reverteretur."

[8] *Max. Balb.* 12.4.

[9] Chap. 2 sect. 4.

[10] Plut. *Galba* 11; Dio 63.29.6.

[11] Tac. *Hist.* 4.6-8.

and to convey the grant of *imperium proconsulare* which Tiberius had requested for him. When this delegation reached Germanicus at Ara Ubiorum, it was caught up in the mutiny of the German legions.[12] In early January 69 the senatorial embassy originally intended to conciliate the mutinous German armies was chosen by Galba amidst "scandalous indecision,"[13] but was later recalled by Otho. A fresh deputation chosen ostensibly from the senate, according to Tacitus,[14] was later sent out to approach both armies in Germany, the Italian legion and the forces at Lugdunum. But these envoys willingly changed their allegiance and stayed with Vitellius. When Otho's death was reported at Rome in mid April, a third embassy was sent from the senate to the German armies, and met Vitellius at Ticinum. Months later, during the closing days of his reign, the latter in turn begged the senate to send envoys who might negotiate a peace with the Flavian leaders.[15]

An allusion by Martial[16] suggests that an embassy, chosen by lot and presumably including senators, was sent to convey to Trajan in Upper Germany the news of his adoption by Nerva in 97. Almost a century later in 193 a senatorial delegation was originally sent to Septimius Severus' armies to dissuade them from seeking to overthrow Didius Julianus; but these envoys deserted to Severus.[17] Julianus' later proposal that the senate, together with the Vestal Virgins and priests, should go out to meet Severus' army as suppliants was rejected by the House as futile.[18] In the end, after ordering Julianus' death, it dispatched a delegation to confer power on Severus. This was said to consist of one hundred members, and met him at Interamna.[19]

Emperors might also be approached by senatorial embassies when absent from Rome or Italy in the course of their reigns. We hear that during Augustus' absence in the West between 16 and 13 B.C. embassies of senate and people besought his return to Rome.[20] Deputations from the senate were sent to Tiberius in retirement on Capri—in 29 (when Sejanus was

---

[12] Tac. *Ann.* 1.14 and 39; Dio 57.5.4-6. The fact that Plancus had been consul only the previous year, and thus during any debate would have been one of the last to be called upon among the consulars, naturally makes it more unlikely than ever that he was the original proposer of any decree related to the handling of the mutiny, as the soldiers at Ara Ubiorum alleged. Tacitus' phrasing here (*Ann.* 1.39) furnishes a rare instance of an individual in our period, other than the emperor, being described as "auctor" of a *senatus consultum* (cf. Mommsen, *St. R.* II. 2. p. 899 n. 4).

[13] Tac. *Hist.* 1.19, "foeda inconstantia."

[14] *Hist.* 1.74; cf. Suet. *Otho* 8.

[15] Tac. *Hist.* 2.55 and 69; 3.80; Suet. *Vitell.* 16; Dio 65.18.3.

[16] 10.6.1-4.

[17] HA, *Did. Jul.* 5.5 and 6.3; *Sev.* 5.6.

[18] HA, *Did. Jul.* 6.5-6.

[19] Herodian 2.12.6; HA, *Sev.* 6.1-2.

[20] Porphyrio on Horace, *Odes* 4.5 (p. 129 Meyer).

similarly honored), and in 31 on Sejanus' death.[21] When Gaius was on campaign in Germany and Gaul during 39/40, one senatorial embassy (including Claudius, who was directly appointed, rather than chosen by lot) was dispatched to him conveying congratulations after he had sent news of Gaetulicus' execution,[22] and another, larger one was dispatched later, begging his immediate return to Rome.[23] According to Aurelius Victor,[24] it was at the senate's request—however conveyed—that Trajan set out for Rome from the East in 117. Finally in this connection P. Porcius Optatus Flamma served in 197 as "envoy sent by the most exalted senate to the same lord emperor [Septimius Severus] in Germany, and to Antoninus Caesar, destined as emperor, in Pannonia."[25]

A rare instance where we find the senate taking the initiative with an approach other than to the emperor occurred in 24, after the conclusion of the war with Tacfarinas, when one member was sent to convey to Ptolemy of Mauretania the traditional gifts of an ivory scepter and an embroidered toga, and to salute him as king, ally, and friend.[26] Much later it was of course again on senatorial initiative that selected members and well-known *equites* were dispatched to gain the support of provincial governors in 238, after Maximinus had been stripped of power and Gordian I and II proclaimed jointly instead.[27] But these instances are exceptional. It is, rather, a reflection of the emperor's dominance in all affairs of state that most embassies dispatched by the senate during the Principate, as we have seen, confined their approaches to him or to members of his family.

2. The Reception of Embassies and Other Diplomatic Business[1]

As Polybius[2] recognized in the mid second century B.C., the reception of embassies was an important, and exclusive, prerogative of the senate during

---

[21] Dio 58.2.7; 3.2; 13.2.

[22] Suet. *Claud.* 9; Dio 59.23.1-2 and 5.

[23] Suet. *Calig.* 49; Dio 59.23.6.

[24] 13.11.

[25] *ILS* 1143, "legati ab amplissimo s[enatu] ad eundem dominum [i]mp. in Germaniam et [ad] Antoninum Caes. [im]p. destinatum in Pannoni[am] missi." Cf. A. R. Birley, *Septimius Severus*, pp. 193 and 200; G. Winkler, *PW* Suppl. 14 s.v. Porcius no. 38a, col. 446. By contrast, Mommsen's view (*St. R.* II. p. 680) that the military tribune Q. Laberius Iustus Cocceius Lepidus Proculus was "l[egatus] missus ad principem" by the senate seems unlikely. There is reason to think that the occasion was the rising of Antonius Saturninus early in 89, and it is more probable that Laberius was sent from his legion to Domitian. See *PIR²* L 7; *AE* 1975. 835; M. Dondin, *Latomus* 37. 1978. pp. 156-157 (following Mommsen).

[26] Tac. *Ann.* 4.26; cf. Dion. Hal. 3.61.3, with discussion by E. Rawson, *JRS* 65. 1975. p. 155.

[27] Herodian 7.7.5 with Whittaker ad loc.

[1] On the subject of this section see also F. Millar, *Emperor*, chap. VI. 7.

[2] 6.13.7.

the Republic. In fact, late in the period the pressure of business thus generated was so great that by a *Lex Gabinia* the House might be required to sit daily throughout February each year for this purpose alone.[3] Tacitus' imagination is understandably fired by the investigation of asylum rights in Greek cities in 22: "It was a splendid sight, that day, to see the senate investigating privileges conferred by its ancestors, treaties with allies, edicts of kings who had reigned before Rome was a power, even divine cults; and it was free, as of old, to confirm or amend."[4]

Just as embassies in the late Republic had come to wait upon powerful individuals like Julius Caesar, so, with the coming of the Principate, they approached both emperor and senate. Thus the latter's role in diplomacy slowly declined as its power was eclipsed by that of the emperor. Dio[5] reminds his readers how, under the shadow of the emperor, it did continue to transact business in certain cases with embassies and heralds, from both peoples and kings, in Augustus' reign. On one interpretation the order of Augustus and Agrippa as consuls in 27 B.C. concerning possession of public places may have followed just such a provincial approach to the senate, and authorization by the latter to the consuls to carry out its ruling.[6] Yet the number of embassies to approach Augustus so increased that from A.D. 8, when he felt old and ill, he entrusted their reception to three consulars. According to Dio, the three could deliver answers, "except in matters where there was a need for the senate and Augustus to make the final decision."[7] With a striking limitation to Italy and the senatorial provinces, this prerogative was confirmed in Nero's accession speech, according to Tacitus: "The senate is to preserve its ancient functions. By applying to the consuls, Italy and the senatorial provinces may gain access to it. I myself will look after the armies entrusted to me."[8]

Though the number of embassies received by the senate plainly did decline, we have no means of discerning the speed or seriousness of the trend in detail. Some reduction in diplomatic activity after Augustus' reign might be expected anyway, with the new era of general peace; and certainly

---

[3] Cf. Cic. *Ad Q. Fr.* 2.12.3 = SB 16; see further chap. 6 sect. 4 note 67 above, and in general T. Büttner-Wobst, *De legationibus reipublicae liberae temporibus Romam missis*, Leipzig, 1876.

[4] *Ann.* 3.60.

[5] 53.21.6.

[6] See Sherk, *Roman Documents*, no. 31, and further N. Charbonnel, "A propos de l'inscription de Kymé et des pouvoirs d'Auguste dans les provinces au lendemain du règlement de 27 av. n. è.," *Rev. Int. Droits Ant.* 1979. pp. 177-225.

[7] 55.33.5; cf. 56.25.7.

[8] *Ann.* 13.4; cf. 14.11, where in reporting his mother's death and deploring her behavior Nero cites how only with great effort had he prevented her from "bursting into the senate house and issuing replies to foreign nations." Whether these two ambitions are to be considered linked, or separate, is unclear.

the exceptional need for sittings throughout February is never heard of again after the Republic. But the senate might still find itself surprisingly occupied with embassies under Augustus' Julio-Claudian successors. Thus unless it is just special pleading to spite his opponent in debate, Asinius Gallus can claim that there are plenty of deputations from Italy and the provinces awaiting a hearing at the season when the House might take its spring recess in 16.[9] Tacitus' record in the *Annals* shows a notable amount of diplomatic business in two particular years. We cannot say whether this load was really unusual, or whether in fact a comparable number of embassies in other years has gone unrecorded for one reason or another. At any rate, we may reasonably guess that in 25 the trial of the former proconsul Fonteius Capito drew some representatives from Asia, and that the Cyzicenes attempted to answer the charges brought against them. In the same year approaches were made by delegations from Baetica, Sparta and Messene, Segesta, and Massilia.[10] Likewise in 53 the trial of Statilius Taurus presumably brought representatives from Africa, while there is every likelihood that a Coan embassy would have appeared to support Claudius' proposal to exempt the island from taxation.[11] In the same year we hear of applications from Ilium and Bononia, both of which Nero supported, and also from Rhodes, Apamea, and Byzantium.[12] The impressive number of embassies coming to Rome is further reflected in general comments by Seneca[13] and Tacitus,[14] and again by Plutarch[15] early in the second century, though none of these authors is concerned to specify whether it was emperor or senate that the envoys sought.

It is our knowledge that the relevant surviving evidence is so incomplete which makes it impossible to gauge the level of diplomatic activity in the senate with any accuracy. For example, trials for misgovernment were common enough in the Julio-Claudian period, and must always have involved provincial delegations; yet it could hardly be claimed that we have a full list of all the cases brought before the House.[16] Then if it were not for Tacitus' record of the speech made by Thrasea Paetus at the trial of

[9] Tac. *Ann.* 2.35; see further chap. 6 sect. 4 note 72.

[10] Tac. *Ann.* 4.36-37, 43.

[11] Tac. *Ann.* 12.59 and 61. Cf. A. Maiuri, *Nuova silloge epigrafica di Rodi e di Cos*, Florence, 1925, no. 462 lines 13-16, in honor of L. Nonius Cornelius Aristodemus πρεσβεύσαντα πολλάκις δωρεὰν ὑπὲρ τᾶς πατρίδος ἐς Ῥώμαν ποτὶ τὸς Σεβαστὸς καὶ τὰν σύνκλητον.

[12] Tac. *Ann.* 12.58, 62-63; cf. Callistratus, *Dig.* 27.1.17.1.

[13] *Ad Helv. Matr. de Cons.* 6.2.

[14] *Ann.* 16.5.

[15] *Quaest. Rom.* 43 = *Mor.* 275 C. For the date of this work, see C. P. Jones, *JRS* 56. 1966. p. 73. On the pressure of embassies in Rome, see further F. Millar, *Emperor*, pp. 364-365.

[16] For known instances see Appendix 9.

Claudius Timarchus in 62, and of the decree passed as a result, we should never have appreciated how common a practice it evidently was by this date for provincial *concilia* to dispatch envoys to the senate with a vote of thanks for a governor.[17] To the latter such speeches would stand as valuable testimony if charges were later laid against him; by contrast, the House in general was only likely to feel bored when this occasion for rendering thanks was added to the many others.[18] One man who perhaps early in our period twice conveyed such votes from Achaea to the senate is honored at Mantinea; his pride that it was praise of proconsuls he had brought, not accusation, stands out.[19] An inscription from Gigthis in Africa in honor of Caecilius Clodianus (?) Aelianus is sufficiently preserved to show that he, too, had put much effort into serving on embassies, and that "clarissimi viri consulares" had testified to his "pietas" and "studium" on this account.[20] If the choice of virtues is significant, it is tempting to speculate that he likewise might have praised proconsuls before the senate. But unfortunately we are not told where he had gone as envoy, while it should be remembered that such praise could equally well be addressed to the emperor. We find an envoy from Stratonicea-Hadrianopolis in Asia conveying it to Hadrian in the course of making requests.[21]

Among other matters we may be quite certain that the request by Syracuse in 58 to exceed the numbers permitted at gladiatorial displays (presumably put through an embassy) was by no means the only application for a small privilege made by a city during the period. In fact, Tacitus[22] assures us that he would have passed over even this instance had it not been for the remarkable opposition of Thrasea Paetus. His lack of interest is shared by Pliny,[23] who in 100 cites applications relating to such displays as notably trivial items of senatorial business. Some further such matters normally requiring the attendance of an embassy merit notice. Thus if the restoration of two damaged inscriptions either side of a Hadrianic arch at Nicaea be accepted,[24] the senate evidently played a part with emperors in granting

---

[17] *Ann.* 15.21-22. For restrictions on the practice introduced by Augustus in A.D. 11, see Dio 56.25.6.

[18] See chap. 7 sect. 5.

[19] *SIG*³ 783 B lines 28-30, δὶς οὖν, καὶ ταῦτα [δω]ρεάν, πρεσβεύσας ὑπὲρ τὴν πόλιν προσηνὴς ἐγένετ[ο] καὶ τῇ θειοτ[άτ]ῃ συνκλήτῳ, μὴ κομίζων κατηγορίαν ἀν[θυ]πάτων ἀλλ' ἔπαινον. For dating cf. E. Groag, *Die Reichsbeamten*, col. 17; U. Kahrstedt, *Das wirtschaftliche Gesicht Griechenlands in der Kaiserzeit*, Berne, 1954, p. 133 n. 3. Achaea was governed by imperial legates from 15 to 44.

[20] *CIL* VIII.11032.

[21] *IGRR* IV. 1156 revised by L. Robert, *Hellenica* 6. 1948. p. 81. col. II lines 29-32. Cf. Plin. *Paneg.* 70.3.

[22] *Ann.* 13.49.

[23] *Paneg.* 54.4.

[24] S. Şahin, *Bithynische Studien (Inschriften griechischer Städte aus Kleinasien* 7, Bonn, 1978) no. I. 5 = *SEG* 27. 1977. 820-821.

the status of *metropolis* to that city, for instance. It emerges from what can be identified as a proconsul's letter datable no earlier than the third century,[25] that at some stage, too, the House must have granted rights of precedence to Ephesus, though we have no details beyond this general reference. In the same way a proconsul's letter to Aphrodisias in Severus Alexander's reign[26] alludes generally to immunity from visits by the governor as another privilege which might have been granted by *senatus consultum*. But again, as it happens, we can point to no example from our period. The same applies also to the possibility of privileges being granted to *collegia* by the senate, cited in general terms by Septimius Severus and Caracalla in a rescript of 205 to a colony in the imperial province of Noricum.[27] It is arguably more significant that the formation of all *collegia*, except *collegia funeraticia*, required a license from the senate, and thus presumably the attendance of deputations. Though not all associations duly complied,[28] the requirement was evidently not a dead letter since in the passage mentioned above Pliny can cite business in this connection as another equally trivial item, while as late as the mid third century documents drawn up by *collegia* do cite rights of assembly granted by *senatus consultum*.[29] Yet from all this no sign of deputations to the House survives beyond a confirmation of Cyzicus' right to have an association of *neoi* ("young men") in the reign of Antoninus Pius.[30] It is striking, however, that a *collegium funeraticium* founded at Lanuvium in 136 actually takes the trouble to quote in its regulations the relevant clause of the *senatus consultum* which proved that it did *not* need to apply for a license.[31]

Where the more vital applications of cities for aid after natural disasters are concerned, we may be sure that we have far from full knowledge; Dio[32] remarks that a complete list would be endless. Monopolies may serve as a final example of a matter on which we remain almost completely uninformed, yet which demanded both senatorial discussion and dealings with provincials. Explaining how hedgehog skin is used in dressing cloth for garments, Pliny the Elder comments in the Flavian period: "Even here fraud has discovered a great source of profit by monopoly, nothing having been the subject of more frequent *senatus consulta*, and every emperor

[25] *AE* 1966. 436.

[26] J. Reynolds, *Aphrodisias and Rome*, no. 48 lines 19-22.

[27] *FIRA*[2] I no. 87, revised by G. Alföldy, *Noricum*, p. 269.

[28] See Tac. *Ann.* 14.17, for example, and in general J.-P. Waltzing, *Etude historique sur les corporations professionnelles chez les Romains*, Louvain, 1895, vol. I pp. 132-140.

[29] See, for example, *ILS* 335, 1164, 3399, 4174, 7266; *CIL* VI. 29691 (A.D. 206); X. 1647, 3700, 5198; XIV. 168, 256, 4548, 4572, 4573 (A.D. 232).

[30] *FIRA*[2] I no. 48.

[31] *CIL* XIV. 2112. I. lines 10-13 = *FIRA*[2] I no. 46.

[32] 54.23.8.

without exception having been approached by complaints from the provinces.''[33] Fortunately, the two scraps of evidence which may be connected
with this passage are both significant for our present purpose. Suetonius[34]
mentions that monopolies were among the issues which Tiberius was scrupulous enough to discuss with the senate, and as an instance of the emperor's zeal for using only Latin words there cites his begging pardon
before using "monopolium." In the circumstances we might well expect
Tiberius, not to mention other emperors, to have introduced provincial
delegations when this issue was debated.

The senate's role in the reception of embassies declined not least because
all such business could be handled as well or better by the emperor—and
he might respond more swiftly and more decisively than would a corporate
body less confident of its prerogative than he ever was. It was precisely
when those expectations were not fulfilled that envoys to Tiberius from
the senatorial province of Africa attempted the unusual expedient of leaving
him and turning to the consuls.[35] It is interesting, too, to find a Rhodian
honored for having conveyed his city's loyalty and goodwill towards Vespasian "and his whole house and the sacred senate and the Roman people."
It remains unclear whether he thus actually appeared before the senate as
well as the emperor. But predictably the favors said to have been granted
as a result of this mission came from the latter.[36] Nonetheless, approaches
were still made to the senate in the first instance, from both senatorial and
imperial provinces, and a continuing general concern with embassies (whoever
was to be approached) is shown by an undated *senatus consultum* which
forbade envoys appointed by a city to attend to their business or their
private affairs until they had completed their mission.[37] If Nero's initial
limitation of the senate's diplomatic role to its own provinces had any
effect, we cannot discern it. But perhaps the restriction soon came to be
ignored, like so many other general instructions. We may note that it was
a later motion by Nero himself which in 62 forbade envoys from senatorial
and imperial provinces to approach the House with votes of thanks for
their governors.[38] It is true that after 54 we can cite no specific instance
of an approach about a non-judicial matter from an imperial province, but
with our evidence beyond the Julio-Claudian period so thin, it might be
wrong to attach undue significance to this accident.

Requests concerning religion are among the matters brought before the

[33] *NH* 8.135.
[34] *Tib*. 30 and 71.
[35] Suet. *Tib*. 31.
[36] *IG* XII.1.58.
[37] No. 168 in list, chap. 15 sect. 5.
[38] Tac. *Ann*. 15.22.

senate, at least in the Julio-Claudian period. For example, a Spanish application to build a temple to Augustus at Tarraco (in an imperial province) was made in 15. A similar request for a temple in honor of Tiberius, Livia, and the senate came from cities in Asia in 23, followed in 26 by senatorial adjudication over where it should be sited.[39] In 25 Baetica asked the House for leave to honor Tiberius and Livia in the same way.[40]

A number of embassies from Italy are found making a wider variety of requests. Thus in Tiberius' reign we hear of Trebiae asking to use a legacy for construction of a road rather than a theater.[41] As it turned out, the city perhaps came to regret making the request here rather than before the emperor, when his private willingness to see it granted was unexpectedly overruled by a majority of the House. Under Claudius, Bononia sought relief after a fire in 53, and five years later the council and citizens of Puteoli brought their mutual recriminations for adjudication.[42] In 105 Vicetia contested an application by a senator to hold a market on his estates.[43] Additionally, there are a number of references in inscriptions which may indicate that further disputes within Italian communities were brought before the senate for resolution.[44] It is frustrating that deeper insight into these affairs and their precise dates is at present unattainable. Also, we lack means of checking whether it is more than accident that no comparable epigraphic testimony seems to survive for any such disputes being resolved by the emperor.

Applications for relief likewise came from the provinces. After earthquakes eastern cities made appeals in the 20's B.C.,[45] in A.D. 17 and 23, followed by Phrygian Apamea in 53.[46] Earthquake relief for Cyzicus was again discussed in the senate by M. Aurelius in 161.[47] Relief from burdens was sought by Achaea and Macedonia in 15. Tacitus does not specify to whom Syria and Judaea made a similar plea in 17, though we do know that Tiberius brought the matter before the House.[48] Ilium and Byzantium were granted relief in 53; in the latter year Rhodes was restored its liberty.[49]

[39] Tac. *Ann.* 1.78; 4.15, 55-56; Ael. Aristid. *Or.* 19.13 Keil.

[40] Tac. *Ann.* 4.37-38.

[41] Suet. *Tib.* 30.

[42] Tac. *Ann.* 12.58; 13.48.

[43] Plin. *Ep.* 5.4 and 13.

[44] See W. Eck, *Die staatliche Organisation Italiens in der hohen Kaiserzeit*, p. 14 n. 24; cf. *Ephem. Epig.* 8. 120; *CIL* XI. 6167; *ILS* 2689; *Inscr. Ital.* III. 1. 51 (Buccino).

[45] Suet. *Tib.* 8. For discussion of chronology, see B. M. Levick, "The beginning of Tiberius' career," *CQ* 21. 1971. pp. 478-486.

[46] Tac. *Ann.* 2.47; 4.13; 12.58. Note that one of the appeals in 23 came from Aegium in the imperial province of Achaea.

[47] Fronto, *Ant. Imp.* 1.2.6 = p. 91 H, with E. J. Champlin, *Fronto and Antonine Rome*, p. 93.

[48] Tac. *Ann.* 1.76; 2.42-43.

[49] Tac. *Ann.* 12.58, 62-63.

Segesta sought help towards the reconstruction of the temple of Venus at Eryx in 25. Among pleas and disputes, in the same year Massilia asked permission to receive the legacy of a Roman exile, while the senate also adjudicated between Sparta and Messene (in the imperial province of Achaea) over the ownership of the temple of Diana Limnatis.[50]

In certain circumstances the senate itself might invite, or require, embassies to appear. In 15, for example, the commissioners appointed to tackle the problem of Tiber flooding presumably asked for deputations from towns involved.[51] Cyzicus, too, was no doubt invited to answer the charges laid against the city in 25,[52] and the same perhaps happened if it was the senate which judged a similar case against Rhodes in 44.[53] In 27 we may guess that a deputation from Fidenae played a part in the investigation of the catastrophe at a gladiatorial show there.[54] Certainly in 70 the authorities at Sena were summoned to account for their insulting behavior towards Manlius Patruinus and indeed the whole senate.[55]

Even though our evidence concerns mainly embassies from communities and nations, it should not be forgotten that the senate also continued to be approached by private individuals. In the late Republic the right to make such an approach in person, or through envoys, on private business had been granted to privileged *peregrini* and their descendants, with or without Roman citizenship, by the senate itself in 78 B.C. and by Octavian about 41 B.C.[56] In 4 B.C. a similar privilege was granted to provincials generally, in connection with laying charges of *repetundae*,[57] and later under modified arrangements we do indeed hear of private individuals joining to bring such a case.[58] Early in our period, too, we find the emperors Augustus and Gaius approaching the senate to be granted individual exemption from laws governing inheritance,[59] while on 2 March 56 the relatives of Alliatoria Celsilla gained for her exemption from a *senatus consultum* of 44 which prohibited demolition of buildings for profit.[60] By contrast, according to

[50] Tac. *Ann.* 4.43; for Segesta, cf. Suet. *Claud.* 25.

[51] Tac. *Ann.* 1.76 and 79.

[52] Tac. *Ann.* 4.36.

[53] Cf. Dio 60.2.4.

[54] Tac. *Ann.* 4.62-63.

[55] Tac. *Hist.* 4.45. It is no longer possible to conjecture a date early in our period for the quarrel between Pteleon and Larisa which was only settled after both sides had been bidden to appear before the senate (cf. *Diz. Epig.* IV. p. 411). A Republican date is now assured. See *IG* IX.2.520 (esp. lines 10-13), with H. Kramolisch, *Die Strategen des Thessalischen Bundes vom Jahr 196 v. Chr. bis zum Ausgang der römischen Republik*, Bonn, 1978, E7 p. 90.

[56] *FIRA*[2] I no. 35 lines 8-9; no. 55 lines 61-63 = Sherk, *Roman Documents*, nos. 22 and 58.

[57] *FIRA*[2] I no. 68 V lines 97-103; cf. 140-141.

[58] Plin. *Ep.* 3.9.4.

[59] Dio 56.32.1; 59.15.1.

[60] *FIRA*[2] I no. 45 I and II.

Severus Alexander,[61] it had been rare for senate or emperors to grant pardon to those liable for the penalty of having written themselves into another's will. Tacitus explains how in 60, at Nero's instigation, it was laid down that an appellant from a civil tribunal to the senate must pay the same deposit as was required for an appeal to the emperor. Later he mentions fathers of fictitiously adopted children putting a plea in 62, and a young man of the senatorial class, not yet a member, approaching the House in 70.[62] More generally, we hear how requests could be made to the senate for the appointment of guardians, and for the appointment of new guardians in place of ones who had become deaf or dumb or had gone insane.[63] Last in this regard, Quintilian[64] at least envisages it as theoretically possible that individuals might seek the permission of the House to commit suicide—though no instance can be cited.

We have already noted how the senate came to suffer because all types of diplomatic business referred to it by individuals or corporate bodies were equally within the emperor's competence, and did come to be handled by him. He, too, might appoint guardians,[65] issue licenses to *collegia*,[66] allow gladiators beyond the permitted number,[67] grant *ius trium libero-rum*,[68] authorize any kind of erection in a public place,[69] forbid the drawing of water from a public stream,[70] and indeed bestow all the rights and privileges cited above. In consequence it seems that the senate's role in the diplomatic sphere had all but disappeared by the mid second century. Altogether, as might be expected, the number of embassies to it mentioned in inscriptions of our period as a whole is a mere fraction of the many said to have been sent to the emperor.[71] It is true that some honorary decrees (the commonest type of document in which such missions are cited) remain vague, mentioning simply an embassy "to Rome."[72] Yet the trend is unmistakable. Only provincial prosecutions of senatorial officials for misgovernment seem to have remained immune from imperial intervention. Otherwise the emperor, like the senate, might receive ap-

---

[61] *CJ* 9.23.3.

[62] *Ann.* 14.28; 15.19; *Hist.* 4.42.

[63] Ulpian, *Reg.* 11.2; *Dig.* 26.1.6.2; Paulus, ibid. 4.5.7 pr.; 26.1.17.

[64] *Inst. Or.* 7.4.39; 11.1.56.

[65] *Dig.* 26.1.6.2.

[66] *Dig.* 3.4.1 pr.; 47.22.3.1; cf. *ILS* 4966.

[67] Note, for example, *AE* 1971. 431.

[68] Dio 55.2.5-6; Plin. *Ep.* 10.95 with Sherwin-White ad loc.

[69] *Dig.* 43.8.2 pr.

[70] Pomponius, *Dig.* 43.12.2.

[71] Though incomplete, the fullest collection of relevant material is perhaps that of G. Iacopi, *Diz. Epig.* IV. s.v. legatus, pp. 500-548.

[72] Note the striking variant where Theophilus of Iulia Gordos (Asia) is honored for having gone on embassies "to Rome and Germany and Caesar" in the mid first century (*AE* 1977. 808 line 15).

proaches from anywhere in the empire, not only from his own provinces. We have already seen how proconsuls might be praised before him rather than the senate. In the same way, as early as the 20's B.C., while Laodicea, Thyatira, and Chios appealed to the latter for aid after an earthquake, Tralles addressed a plea to the emperor direct instead.[73] In 15 B.C. it was again Augustus himself who aided Paphos in the senatorial province of Cyprus after another earthquake.[74] Then on the death of Lucius Caesar in 2 B.C. the town council at Pisa wished to perform rites in his honor exactly as the senate in Rome had laid down—but still it was to Augustus that they sent envoys seeking permission.[75] From his reign onwards, too, almost all applications in connection with the imperial cult were addressed to the emperor, and those to the senate mentioned above come to appear as the exception. Under Tiberius it was to the emperor, not the senate, that Cretans conveyed complaints about the entourage of their proconsul, Occius Flamma.[76]

Not only were individuals and communities quite free to choose which authority they might approach, but the emperor in his turn might decide to reserve for himself diplomatic business on which we could really have expected him to consult the House. Claudius in 48/49 and Hadrian in 119/120, for example, had both evidently omitted to consult thus before confirming privileges granted by previous emperors and the senate to Dionysiac artists[77] and to Aphrodisias[78] respectively. But altogether, as we shall see again with reference to legislation, it is impossible to fathom why emperors put certain matters before the senate and not others.

We may illustrate how imperial consultation did continue in certain instances up to M. Aurelius' time. As early as 23 B.C., for example, when Tiridates and envoys from Phraates approached Augustus to settle their quarrel, he brought them before the House, which then referred the decision in the matter back to the emperor.[79] From Tacitus' account of Tiberius' reign we hear how the senate adjudicated in the matter of abuse of asylum

[73] Suet. *Tib.* 8; Strabo 12.8.18. See further F. Millar, *Emperor*, pp. 422-423.

[74] Dio 54.23.7.

[75] *ILS* 139 lines 31ff.

[76] Seneca, *Controv.* 9.4.20. The episode is discussed by W. Orth, "Ein vernachlässigtes Zeugnis zur Geschichte der römischen Provinz Creta et Cyrenae," *Chiron* 3. 1973. pp. 255-263.

[77] *Milet* 1.3 no. 156 = Smallwood, *Documents of Gaius etc.*, no. 373 (b). See further M. Amelotti, "La posizione degli atleti di fronte al diritto romano," *SDHI* 21. 1955. pp. 123-156, esp. pp. 137-140.

[78] J. Reynolds, *Aphrodisias and Rome*, no. 15. In further documents confirming the privileges of Aphrodisias the senate is not mentioned at all by Septimius Severus and Caracalla (ibid. 17, 18), Gordian III (20), or Decius and Herennius (25); however, Gordian III is more meticulous on another occasion (49).

[79] Dio 53.33.1-2.

rights in cities of Asia, Crete, and Cyprus in 22.[80] Yet his phrasing suggests that the problem was one referred by the emperor, and the likelihood is increased if we are right to link with the episode an inscription from Miletus honoring a man "who had been on an embassy to the emperor over the privilege of asylum of Apollo at Didyma and the rights of the city."[81] We cannot say whom Samos and Cos first approached when they made an application in the same connection the following year.[82] It is certain, however, that the fight between Pompeians and Nucerians in 59 was first brought to the attention of Nero, and then referred by him to the senate.[83] Hadrian discussed there the requests of his home town, Italica, and others, including Utica, to be granted the status of *colonia*.[84] Although the question cannot be pursued further until full publication of the relevant inscription, it may be that he also took the initiative in putting before the senate a letter to him from Delphi.[85] We have already seen how Antoninus Pius helped Cyzicus to have its right to an association of *neoi* confirmed. In the following reign, despite the very fragmentary condition of the relevant stones, there may be some basis for the conjecture that M. Aurelius and L. Verus likewise consulted the senate in connection with a matter on which they in turn wrote to Delphi.[86] Certainly in 177, when a Milesian embassy approached the co-emperors, Marcus and Commodus, in connection with celebrating games, it was on their initiative that the question was brought before the House.[87] In the fragment of the appended imperial oration here, the remark "we have indeed excused other communities"[88] could suggest that such reference to the senate was actually common practice on Marcus' part. It was probably in 177, too, that he asked members to vote money for the restoration of Smyrna after an earthquake.[89]

Most remarkably, until a very late stage emperors evidently continued to put to the senate certain applications for a neocorate. Thus a unique coin of Laodicea ad Lycum proclaims that the city was honored in this way under Commodus "by decree of the senate,"[90] and the latter's role

---

[80] *Ann.* 3.60-63.

[81] R. Harder, *Didyma* II, no. 107 lines 9-13, [πρεσβ]εύσαντα πρὸς τὸν Σεβασ[τὸν] ὑπὲρ τῆς ἀσυλίας τοῦ Διδυμέως Ἀπόλλωνος καὶ τῶν τῆς πόλεως δικαίων. Cf. the statue of the senate erected by Hierocaesarea, possibly at this time (chap. 2 sect. 6 note 117).

[82] Tac. *Ann.* 4.14 and chap. 6 sect. 4 note 98 above.

[83] Tac. *Ann.* 14.17.

[84] Gell. 16.13.4; cf. *Dig.* 50.15.1.1 and F. Millar, *Emperor*, p. 408.

[85] For Hadrian's reply of September 125, see E. Bourguet, *De rebus Delphicis imperatoriae aetatis capita duo*, Montpellier, 1905, p. 82, and *Fouilles de Delphes* III. 4. pp. 82-83.

[86] *Fouilles de Delphes* III. 4. no. 314 lines IV and IX; note also no. 317 line III.

[87] *Istanb. Mitt.* 25. 1975. p. 150 = *AE* 1977. 801.

[88] Loc. cit. in previous note, line 32, "excusavimus sane civitatibus aliis." The first person plural seems most likely to refer to emperor(s) and senate.

[89] Ael. Aristid. *Or.* 20.10 Keil; see further F. Millar, *Emperor*, p. 423.

[90] L. Robert in J. DesGagniers and others, *Laodicée du Lycos*, Université Laval, Recherches Archéologiques, série I, Québec and Paris, 1969, pp. 284-285.

continues to be featured on further issues made there under Elagabalus and Severus Alexander.[91] Dio[92] mentions in passing that, thanks to the great influence of Commodus' *cubicularius* Saoterus, his native city Nicomedia was able to obtain from the senate the privilege of celebrating certain games and erecting a temple to the emperor. The application to Rome (otherwise hardly necessary) together with the evidence of coin legends[93] confirm that this request, too, was for a neocorate. As such it is likely to have come first before Commodus, who would then have referred it to the House. It must surely have been on him, rather than on the senate, that Saoterus brought influence to bear. From the late second century Sardis also heralds that it is "*neocoros* twice according to the decrees of the sacred senate."[94] A document from Smyrna specifically explains how the *senatus consultum* giving that city, too, its second neocorate was passed at Hadrian's behest,[95] while a number of inscriptions advertise that the award of a third one (in Caracalla's time) was conveyed likewise.[96] A letter from the latter—found at Ephesus, but possibly addressed to the *koinon* of Asia—gives no indication that he associated the senate with himself in bestowing the same honor there, unless (as Robert attractively suggested) the corporate body is indicated in the reference made to "the authorities at (?) Rome," which also gave their approval to the request.[97] That conjecture does seem to be confirmed by a contemporary inscription in which Ephesus bears the title "*neocoros* of the Augusti three times according to the decrees of the sacred senate."[98] It thus matches another, somewhat earlier inscription[99] and certain coins,[100] which in turn both associate the senate with the award of second and fourth neocorates respectively to the city, the latter grant dating to Elagabalus' reign. More generally, it is as usual not clear why only certain applications for this

[91] *BMC Phrygia*, pp. 319-322. For illustration of p. 321 no. 249, see Figure 8 (g) above.
[92] 72.12.2.
[93] B. Pick, "Die tempeltragenden Gottheiten und die Darstellung der Neokorie auf den Münzen," *JÖAI* 7. 1904. pp. 1-41 at pp. 7 and 26; L. Robert, "La titulature de Nicée et de Nicomédie: la gloire et la haine," *HSCP* 81. 1977. pp. 1-39 at p. 34.
[94] See W. H. Buckler and D. M. Robinson (eds.), *Sardis* VII.1. nos. 63-70, with L. Robert, *Rev. Phil.* 41. 1967. p. 48 n. 6.
[95] *IGRR* IV. 1431 lines 31-37.
[96] *IGRR* IV. 1419-1421, 1424-1426.
[97] *AE* 1966. 430, with L. Robert, *Rev. Phil.* 41. 1967. pp. 46 and 49-50; W. Williams, *Latomus* 38. 1979. pp. 86-87.
[98] H. Engelmann and D. Knibbe, *JÖAI* 1978-80 Hauptblatt 52. p. 25 no. 15 lines 7-10.
[99] *Forschungen in Ephesos* II. no. 40 (erected between A.D. 200 and 210); cf. ibid. III. p. 118 no. 30 lines 3-5 (fragmentary). Thus to refer to the senate under Caracalla as [τοῖς ἐπὶ Ῥώ]μης ἡγουμένοις (loc. cit. in note 97 above, lines 18-19) emerges as an interesting choice of epithet!
[100] See J. Keil, "Die dritte Neokorie von Ephesos," *Num. Zeitschr.* 48. 1915. pp. 125-130 at pp. 129-130. Evidence for the neocorates of Ephesus (to 1970) is collated by D. Knibbe and S. Karwiese, *PW* Suppl. 12 s.v. Ephesos, cols. 248-364 sects. A III.5 and C II.B.

honor should have been referred to the senate. All those known came from cities in the senatorial province of Asia, except for that from Nicomedia in Bithynia/Pontus, which was an imperial province at the time.

In illustrating emperors' consultation of the senate about diplomatic matters, the latter's dependence upon the initiative of the former emerges plainly enough. At the same time it is worth noting the outstanding value of such consultation from the emperor's viewpoint in particular. To bring forward diplomatic business in the House afforded him an unrivaled opportunity to show respect to the corporate body and to cultivate a highly esteemed sense of partnership with it. Such a sense seems to have been conveyed strongly to envoys from Mytilene early in our period. In order to make a formal alliance with Rome in 25 B.C. they dealt with both authorities (it is uncertain in which order),[101] and presumably it was in this connection that their city then voted to send an embassy which would thank Augustus in front of the senate, and vice versa.[102] Later in the reign, when an embassy from Cyrene complained to him about judicial oppression of Roman citizens there in 7/6 B.C., he issued an edict which was to be valid "until the senate has discussed this matter or I myself have found a better solution."[103] In the third Cyrene edict he again implies equal standing of emperor and senate by mentioning "those to whom by a *lex, senatus consultum,* or the *decretum* of my father [Julius Caesar] or myself, immunity of taxation has been granted together with citizenship."[104] It is the fifth Cyrene edict of 4 B.C., however, which represents an outstanding example of joint handling of diplomatic business by senate and emperor, since it consists of an edict of Augustus introducing a *senatus consultum* framed on the recommendation of the emperor and of his senatorial *consilium.*

Claudius promoted further joint action when he staged an investigation of Lycian affairs in the senate, and introduced there a Parthian delegation which had approached him.[105] He evidently enjoyed addressing a reply to it, as he did speaking in support of Cos and Byzantium and answering other Greek embassies.[106] It is likely to have been early in our period, too, that a deputation from Chersonesus on the north shore of the Black Sea

---

[101] See R. K. Sherk, *Roman Documents,* no. 26 col. b lines 36-43 and all col. c, with discussion.

[102] *OGIS* 456 b.

[103] *FIRA*[2] I no. 68 I lines 12-13. The "better solution" is perhaps put forward in the fourth edict, which is in fact Augustus' own pronouncement.

[104] *FIRA*[2] I no. 68 III lines 58-60. Not surprisingly, in practice only the emperor is ever found making a grant of citizenship during the Principate. The same applies to Latin rights (*Latii ius*), which, Gaius says (*Inst.* 1.96), "quibusdam peregrinis civitatibus datum est vel a populo vel a senatu vel a Caesare."

[105] Dio 60.17.4; Tac. *Ann.* 12.10-11.

[106] Tac. *Ann.* 12.61-63; Suet. *Claud.* 42.

approached emperor and senate on the matter of freedom for the city.[107] In the second century both Trajan and the senate acted in response to Pergamum's application for the establishment of a second set of quinquennial games.[108] We also hear of a man from Gaulos (Gozo) who appeared before Hadrian and the senate, possibly in connection with reclaiming local revenues.[109]

Early in the third century Dio still thought that it would impress envoys to be introduced before the senate for show. He has Maecenas say to Augustus:

It seems to me that you would be adopting the best arrangement if you should, in the first place, introduce before the senate the embassies which come from the enemy and from those under treaty with us, whether kings or democracies; for, among other considerations, it is both awe-inspiring and will attract attention for the impression to be given that the senate has full authority in all matters and that envoys who deal unfairly will face many opponents.[110]

During Dio's own day, however, no such role actually remained to the senate. From around the mid second century there is very little sign of embassies continuing to approach it. No doubt this is partly a reflection of a general dearth of evidence for the period, but it must also be true that the senate was at last being superseded almost entirely by the emperor in its diplomatic function. Admittedly we do know of two Ephesians about this time who are said to have been on embassies to the emperors and to the senate.[111] It was then, too, after help had been given towards repairing damage done by a fire in the city's forum, that Fronto delivered a *gratiarum actio in senatu pro Carthaginiensibus*, of which only a few broken lines survive.[112] But there is no further evidence.

Exceptionally, provincial delegations may have continued to approach the senate in connection with trial proceedings even into the early third century. At least, as late as 205 we hear of Noricum prosecuting its legate

---

[107] *IOSPE*² I 355, acephalous and badly damaged, lines 29-31, – – – – τοῦ μ]εγίστου Αὐτοκράτορος καὶ τὰς συνκλ[ή]το[υ – – – –] παρὰ τοῦ δήμου τοῦ Ῥωμαίων, καὶ ταῖς ἰδί[αις δαπάναις πορευθεὶς εἰς Ῥώμαν ἀνεκτάσατο? τὰν] πάτριον Χερσονασίταις ἐλευθερία[ν. Cf. Plin. *NH* 4.85.

[108] *IGRR* IV. 336.

[109] *ILS* 6772. The repetition of *apud* could imply a separate hearing before each authority.

[110] 52.31.1.

[111] Such missions by M. Claudius P. Vedius Antoninus Sabinus (H. Halfmann, *Die Senatoren*, no. 84a; C. Börker and R. Merkelbach, *Die Inschriften von Ephesos*, III. no. 728) and Cn. Pompeius Hermippus (ibid. VI. no. 2069; cf. III. no. 710 for family tree) could well extend into the reign of M. Aurelius. Similar visits by P. Vedius Antoninus, adoptive father of the first-named above (ibid. III. no. 728; H. Halfmann, *Die Senatoren*, no. 84b), probably belong to the early part of the second century.

[112] Pages 241-242 H and chap. 7 sect. 5 note 24.

on a charge of misgovernment.[113] But, as a later chapter will show, lack of evidence renders it impossible to form any coherent picture of hearings in the senate, or provincial involvement in them, beyond the reign of Trajan. It remains equally unclear whether or not "the excellent judgment in the senate, which, while safeguarding the provinces, also gently rebuked the defendants," referred to by Fronto in Antoninus' reign,[114] had involved representations by provincials.

Finally, although the senate's function in handling diplomatic business may not altogether have faded away until the mid second century, it is important to recognize that such respect as it may once have commanded among the empire's population as protector and benefactor of the Roman world had long been transferred to the emperor. Thus, as Millar remarks,[115] the subject of aid for the earthquake-stricken cities of Asia in 17 may have been discussed in the House, but epigraphic evidence[116] shows that it was the emperor, and only he, whom the recipients consistently regarded as their benefactor. It made no difference that Asia was a senatorial province, and one where the senate was very widely honored in cults and on coins. In similar fashion Suetonius[117] attributes exclusively to emperors three decisions on diplomatic questions which from the more precise record of Tacitus we happen to know were made by the senate. Of course, in biographies of emperors the slip is understandable, and arguably of slight importance in any case. But the attitude it reflects is significant for the eclipse of the senate's role in the diplomatic sphere. So perhaps the real surprise is that this role actually took as long to fade away as it did.

3. The Army and Foreign Affairs

From the beginning of the Principate the emperor controlled the army, thereby depriving the senate of a major prerogative. As we saw in the previous chapter, when the provinces were divided between the two authorities in 27 B.C., a few legions did remain in the senatorial group. But these were reduced to one—III Augusta in Africa—by Augustus' death in 14, and it, too, came under direct imperial control from 39. Its only campaigns during that time were those against Tacfarinas. Although tech-

---

[113] See Appendix 9, no. 36. Since an attempt by certain Gauls in the early 220's to prosecute their former governor, Claudius Paulinus, turned out abortive, we may only speculate about where such a case might have been heard. See H.-G. Pflaum, *Le Marbre de Thorigny*, Paris, 1948, p. 8 II. lines 14-26.

[114] *Ad M. Caes.* 3.21.1 = p. 52 H. Dating, E. J. Champlin, *JRS* 64. 1974. p. 143.

[115] *Emperor*, p. 423.

[116] *OGIS* 471; *CIL* III. 7096; *ILS* 156.

[117] *Tib.* 37; *Claud.* 25; *Nero* 7.

nically they were fought under senatorial auspices, Tiberius of course showed close concern.[1] Otherwise the senate directed troops only in moments of crisis when there was no emperor. Thus it gave orders after Gaius' assassination,[2] for example, while Josephus[3] comments on the sense of wonder felt when the consuls were asked for the watchword at this time.

No doubt all emperors gave the senate information of one kind or another relating to military matters, but we only have specific evidence for Augustus and Tiberius so doing. Augustus had had soldiers' terms of service laid down by *senatus consultum* in 13 B.C., and later (though it was admittedly more a fiscal question than a military one) he consulted members about sources of revenue for the *aerarium militare*.[4] He is also known to have given an opinion on whether or not the empire should be expanded in 20 B.C., and to have discussed with the House measures to be taken on the outbreak of revolt in Pannonia in A.D. 6.[5] We may possibly relate to this rising a fragmentary *senatus consultum* in some way concerning ships and troops; inscribed on bronze it was found at Pola (just within the borders of Italy), and is datable to A.D. 7.[6] In 14 one of the *libelli* which Augustus left to be read out in the senate after his death gave details of the army's strength.[7]

In explaining Tiberius' conscientiousness in consulting the senate Suetonius includes among his illustrations "the levying and disbanding of troops, and the stationing of legions and auxiliaries; finally the extension of commands and special appointments for campaigns, and the form and content of his replies to the letters of kings."[8] In a letter to mutineers in Pannonia at the beginning of the reign Tiberius did indeed undertake to submit the men's grievances for the decision of the House. Tacitus[9] has them sarcastically contrast this promise with imperial reluctance to consult about punishments or campaigns. In 19 Adgandestrius' offer to poison Arminius was presumably made to Tiberius, and then read out in a session at his instigation. He did give the House an account of the legions' strength and deployment in 23,[10] and actually invited members to a parade by the Praetorian Guard two years later. But he never even pretended to share

---

[1] Cf. Tac. *Ann.* 2.52.
[2] Josephus, *BJ* 2.205; *AJ* 19.160.
[3] *AJ* 19.186-187.
[4] Dio 54.25.5-6; 55.25.4-6.
[5] Dio 54.9.1; Vell. 2.111.1.
[6] *Inscr. Ital.* X. 1. no. 64, with A. Degrassi, *Il confine nord-orientale dell' Italia romana,* Berne, 1954, p. 59 n. 37.
[7] Tac. *Ann.* 1.11; Suet. *Aug.* 101.
[8] *Tib.* 30.
[9] *Ann.* 1.25-26; cf. 27, 39.
[10] Tac. *Ann.* 2.88; 4.4.

control of the army.[11] Despite Suetonius' claim, it is clear that during his reign, as in all others, the levying of troops always remained exclusively in the hands of the emperor.[12] According to Tacitus,[13] amidst all his other hesitations on Augustus' death, Tiberius' instructions to the armies were notably decisive. And in 32, still shaken after the fall of Sejanus, he wrote strongly criticizing a proposal by Junius Gallio to honor veterans of the Praetorian Guard with front seats at shows: "as if questioning Gallio face to face, he asked what he had to do with soldiers who were entitled to receive their orders and rewards from the emperor only."[14] We have already seen how Nero's accession speech similarly represented care of the legions as the emperor's personal charge.[15]

Augustus' instruction that matters of war should always be discussed by the senate in the temple of Mars (dedicated in 2 B.C.) envisages that such items would continue to feature on the agenda.[16] Later Seneca marks out as a worthy senator one who, among other actions, "gives his opinion about peace and war."[17] And in 58, when Thrasea Paetus objected to a Syracusan application to exceed the number of gladiators permitted at displays, his opponents asked why he did not turn his attention to a more important issue, like "war or peace, indirect taxes, or laws."[18] Formal declaration of war was indeed a ritual maintained at least up until Trajan's time.[19]

It is true, and striking, that emperors did consistently maintain the tradition of informing the senate about hostilities current or impending. At first commanders, too, were perhaps expected to make their own reports direct to the senate. Thus Agrippa stood out because he omitted to do so, and Tiberius later felt the need to reprimand governors with legions under their command for similar slackness.[20] But from an early date reports were just as likely to be relayed through the emperor. Tiberius, for example, spoke of the exploits of Germanicus and Drusus in 14, and three years later discussed the unstable situation in the East.[21] In 21 it was a matter

[11] Dio 57.24.5; cf. ibid. 59.2.1 for Gaius doing likewise at the beginning of his reign.
[12] See P. A. Brunt, "C. Fabricius Tuscus and an Augustan dilectus," *ZPE* 13. 1974. pp. 161-185.
[13] *Ann.* 1.7.
[14] Tac. *Ann.* 6.3; cf. Dio 58.18.3-4, who claims that there was a different occasion on which Tiberius had commended the senate's offer to furnish pay for the Guard from the *aerarium Saturni*. But it seems most likely that Dio has either garbled his source here, or misinterpreted Tiberius' tone.
[15] Tac. *Ann.* 13.4.
[16] See chap. 3 sect. 1 note 34.
[17] *De Tranq. Anim.* 3.3.
[18] Tac. *Ann.* 13.49.
[19] See chap. 11 sect. 1.
[20] Dio 54.24.7; Suet. *Tib.* 32.
[21] Tac. *Ann.* 1.52; 2.42-43.

of note that he wrote only a single letter about the rising of Florus and Sacrovir in Gaul—after it had been crushed.[22] The revolt of the Nasamones and its suppression were evidently reported by Domitian,[23] while M. Aurelius sought the senate's consent to send out L. Verus as commander in Parthia, and later raised the threat of an imminent Marcomannic War.[24] Given Dio's opinion of Caracalla as a most unbusinesslike ruler, contemptuous of senators, his own record of that emperor's many letters to the House about campaigns or foreign affairs seems quite remarkable.[25] We have already noted elsewhere the numerous references throughout the period to letters sent by emperors in the field,[26] while the long list of triumphal honors and other distinctions dutifully voted[27] also testifies to the reports of victories received by the House. However, Claudius' request[28] that the senate name Legions VII and IX "pia fidelis" after Scribonianus' revolt is unparalleled.

Thus the House was kept informed, and, in theory, as the quotations above from Seneca and Tacitus reflect, its members did still retain the right to raise issues of war and peace. But there is no question that in practice from the beginning of the Principate all such prerogative was ceded to the emperor. After the defeat of Tacfarinas it was indeed technically correct procedure that the Garamantes should approach the House to make peace in 24.[29] Yet in requesting Vologeses of Parthia to send envoys there in 70 Vespasian was merely displaying tact and a desire to gain public approval.[30] It was no doubt for the same reasons that a Dacian embassy arrived likewise after Decebalus' first defeat. A contemporary gold coin shows Trajan on the left presenting a kneeling Dacian to a senator on the right.[31]

Augustus' Greek contemporary Strabo could describe him as "lord of war and peace for life,"[32] while according to Dio[33] the senate formally voted Claudius authority to conclude treaties in 44. This right was confirmed in the *Lex de Imperio Vespasiani*, with not only Claudius, but also Augustus and Tiberius cited as the earlier emperors who had possessed it.[34] Equally, at the end of our period Dio[35] considers it the emperor's right

---

[22] Tac. *Ann*. 3.47.
[23] Dio 67.4.6; Ael. Aristid. *Or*. 19.9 Keil.
[24] HA, *Marcus* 8.9; 12.14.
[25] Note 77.7.2; 12.3; 13.6; 18.2; 20.1-2; 22.3; 23.2; 78.8.3.
[26] See chap. 7 sect. 6.
[27] See chap. 11 sect. 4 and Extended Note J.
[28] Dio 60.15.4.
[29] Tac. *Ann*. 4.26.
[30] Tac. *Hist*. 4.51; cf. Suet. *Nero* 57.
[31] Dio 68.9.7-10.1; *BMC* III. p. 65 no. 244.
[32] 17.3.25.
[33] 60.23.6.
[34] *FIRA*[2] I no. 15 lines 1-2.
[35] 53.17.5.

to declare war and make peace, while in a paraphrase of the *Lex Julia maiestatis* the Severan jurist Marcianus[36] explains that the death penalty was prescribed for anyone who made war without orders from the Princeps. So it was really only by the latter's courtesy that the House was ever involved in such matters.

Yet instances of such consultation, in addition to those already cited above, can be found well into the second century. Thus in A.D. 3 Augustus associated the senate with himself in granting Armenia first to Ariobarzanes and soon afterwards to his son Artabazus.[37] Tiberius gained senatorial approval for the annexation of Cappadocia in 18,[38] as did Gaius for grants of territory to Eastern kings in 38. He then ceremonially bestowed them in the Forum.[39] Claudius, too, celebrated there an alliance with Agrippa of Palestine in 41.[40] It is all the more strange, therefore, to find mention of the senate and people of Rome, but not the emperor, in the legend on a unique coin issued by Agrippa in commemoration of this treaty.[41] Tacitus[42] implies that the senate was consulted about the addition of Ituraea and Judaea to Syria in 49. Certainly Claudius did bring before it the Parthian delegation which had asked him for a king.[43] In the second century Hadrian or Antoninus introduced rival embassies from Vologeses and the Iazyges, but the House left any reply to the emperor.[44] Finally, Dio[45] claims that M. Aurelius regularly sent the senate details of treaties he had made. Only when the alarming news of Avidius Cassius' rising in Syria forced him to conclude a humiliating peace with the Iazyges did he omit to do so.

Yet with the possible exception of the curious tale that "the senate and his people" somehow dissuaded Commodus from embarking upon a third northern expedition,[46] these initiatives earlier in the second century seem to represent the final occasions when issues of war or peace are known to have been brought before the House for discussion. Thereafter emperors

[36] *Dig.* 48.4.3. Obviously a law passed in the time of Julius or Augustus would not itself have referred to the Princeps in such terms. For discussion, see J. E. Allison and J. D. Cloud, "The Lex Julia maiestatis," *Latomus* 21. 1962. pp. 711-731; R. A. Bauman, *Impietas in Principem*, pp. 96-97.

[37] Dio 55.10a.7.

[38] Strabo 12.1.4; cf. Tac. *Ann.* 2.42 and 56; Dio 57.17.7.

[39] Dio 59.12.2.

[40] Josephus, *AJ* 19.275.

[41] See J. Meyshan, "The coinage of Agrippa the First," *Israel Exploration Journal* 4. 1954. pp. 186-200 at p. 191 (i) and plate 17.14, [φιλ]ία βασ(ιλέως) Ἀγ[ρί]πα [πρὸς τὴν σύγ]κλητον [καὶ τὸν δ]ῆμ(ον) Ῥωμαίω(ν) κ(αὶ) συμ(μαχία).

[42] *Ann.* 12.23.

[43] Tac. *Ann.* 11.10; 12.10-11. It is mere politeness for him to have the Parthians say that they might approach "princeps patresque" with this request.

[44] Dio 69.15.2-3.

[45] 71.17.1.

[46] HA, *Commod.* 12.8.

certainly maintained the established practice of keeping the senate informed about campaigns or foreign affairs, as such behavior showed courtesy and a respect for tradition; they are likely to have borne in mind, too, that the senate was a convenient place of publication, and that it voted honors. But the aim was only to convey information, never to consult.

15

SENATORIAL LEGISLATION

No clear impression of the senate's functions can be gained without a complete conspectus of *senatus consulta* and *orationes* passed throughout our period. The aim of this chapter is to furnish such a review, which has not been attempted before.[1] To forestall the possibility of dissatisfaction with certain features let it be stressed that the lists below are intended to do no more than illuminate for historians the character and scope of senatorial legislation. Only explicitly attested legislative or administrative measures with broad application are covered. *Senatus consulta* of an honorary or commemorative character are excluded, while equally no notice is taken of citations on, say, aqueducts and milestones. *Senatus consulta* with exclusive application to individuals, limited groups, or communities are also omitted. Inevitably some decrees do not fall easily within a category, and I acknowledge that the decisions on whether or not to include them may not always have been consistent. In any event, reference to measures omitted will be found elsewhere.[2] Exceptionally, *all senatus consulta* and *orationes* for which any verbatim quotation survives are listed here (asterisked). Since only a conspectus is sought, descriptions are kept brief. Not even an attempt has been made at the colossal work of setting out the provisions of decrees in detail (where known), and discussing them from a legal standpoint. Rather, for guidance on these matters, and for bibliography, standard handbooks may be consulted in the first instance.[3]

Senatus consulta and *orationes* which can be assigned to a particular reign are listed first, in chronological order. Measures of uncertain date

---

[1] The list by E. Volterra makes an invaluable starting point for further investigation, but is intended to be only a selection (*Novissimo Digesto Italiano* XVI, Turin, 1969, s.v. senatusconsulta, pp. 1047-1078). Invaluable aids to research are furnished by O. Gradenwitz, *Vocabularium iurisprudentiae romanae*, Berlin, 1903- (for *senatus consulta*, see s.v. consultum, vol. I cols. 966-974); by R. Mayr, *Vocabularium codicis Iustiniani*, Prague, 1923-1925; and by A. M. Honoré and J. Menner, *Concordance to the Digest Jurists*, Oxford, 1980 (microfiche).

[2] See especially chaps. 11-14.

[3] In addition to E. Volterra, op. cit., see, for example, M. Kaser, *Das römische Zivilprozessrecht*, Munich, 1966; idem, *Das römische Privatrecht* I (ed. 2), Munich, 1971; and the excellent series of L. Caes, *Collectio bibliographica operum ad ius romanum pertinentium* (Brussels).

follow in three groups: those for which there is some indication of date; those for which the earliest citation occurs in second-century jurists;[4] those for which the earliest citation occurs in jurists and imperial constitutions of the third century or later. It should be understood that among the many *senatus consulta* within the two latter groups, some may really be of Republican date. By definition no check is possible unless further evidence emerges.[5] Throughout there is a more general difficulty in determining whether provisions on matters of a broadly similar nature derive from the same decree, or from separate ones. In doubtful cases provisions have usually been left separate for the sake of clarity; fresh evidence might well prove this approach to be too cautious.[6]

In the Republic the senate was technically never more than an advisory body of the magistrate who consulted it, so that his acceptance and action were required for the execution of its resolutions. In themselves the latter came to carry great weight, but they lacked the legal authority which could be bestowed by a popular assembly alone.[7] In our period the role of such assemblies soon faded almost to nothing. So, as the jurists explained it, *senatus consulta* gained legislative force[8] almost by default, with the House in some sense being taken to represent the people.[9] When methods of making law are listed, its decrees now duly feature.[10] Yet in typically Roman fashion, no measure was ever promulgated formally investing *senatus consulta* with legal authority. Rather a *senatus consultum* only "has the force of law," as Gaius[11] puts it briefly in the mid second century, immediately adding that this claim has been questioned.

We have no further knowledge of the controversy or of the arguments used on either side. In the civil sphere, however, modern scholars have disputed long and vigorously over when and why the House was first able to move from making *ius honorarium* (that is, law which depended for its force upon action by a magistrate) to *ius civile* (that is, law which had no

---

[4] On individual jurists, see A. M. Honoré, *Gaius*, Oxford, 1962; idem, "The Severan lawyers: a preliminary survey," *SDHI* 28. 1962. pp. 162-232; W. Kunkel, *Herkunft und soziale Stellung der römischen Juristen*.

[5] But I would assume the "ancient" senatorial ban on mining in Italy to be Republican (Plin. *NH* 3.138; 33.78; 37.202).

[6] The following pairs, for example, in the list below could conceivably each derive from the same *senatus consultum*: nos. 15 and 16; 22 and 140; 58 and 65; 159 and 194.

[7] See A. Watson, *Law Making in the Later Roman Republic*, Oxford, 1974, chap. 2.

[8] Note Pomponius on different forms of law: ". . . aut senatus consultum, quod solum senatu constituente inducitur sine lege . . ." (*Dig.* 1.2.12).

[9] Cf. Pomponius, *Dig.* 1.2.2.9; Just. *Inst.* 1.2.5.

[10] See, for example, in *Digest* Pomponius (43.12.2), Papinian (1.1.7 pr.), Ulpian (37.1.12.1). Cf. praetor's edict, quoted *Dig.* 43.8.2 pr.

[11] *Inst.* 1.4, "senatus consultum est quod senatus iubet atque constituit; idque legis vicem optinet, quamvis fuerit quaesitum." Cf. Ulpian, *Dig.* 1.3.9, "non ambigitur senatum ius facere posse."

such dependence).[12] With a profound apology I set aside this quarrel over an essentially theoretical question. It has no relevance to a study of how the senate functioned in practice. Any hypothesis which would delay the making of *ius civile* for a significant period (even as late as Hadrian's time) implies a marked shift in the character and scope of *senatus consulta*, which in my view cannot be discerned from the extant evidence. Rather, certain key practical points need to be appreciated. While technically resolutions of the senate may have lacked legal authority, in practice by the late Republic the convention had long been established that *senatus consulta* on certain matters would be considered binding in their own right, especially in the spheres of finance, foreign affairs, and public order.[13] Thus it was arguably a natural development, not a radical change, when the emperor encouraged the senate to continue its administrative work (in modified form), and to extend its interest in civil legislation. From the beginning of the Principate all *senatus consulta* enjoyed entirely adequate legislative force because the emperor himself upheld their authority. Thus while the learned may have paused to doubt their validity (as Gaius implies), men of affairs can hardly have been troubled. Perhaps, as some modern scholars suggest,[14] we should describe *senatus consulta* in their new role as *ius novum*—but the label is unimportant.

It is clear that during the Principate various *senatus consulta* did continue to be referred to the people for confirmation. The business concerned was mostly of a formal nature, in particular the bestowal of powers and honors upon the emperor.[15] But the month Sextilis was evidently renamed by both senate and people;[16] Octavian was given the new name Augustus likewise;[17] and we hear of *Ludi Martiales* mounted "s.c. et lege."[18] Later the senate passed posthumous honors for Germanicus and Drusus to the people for ratification.[19] Dedications by *senatus populusque Romanus* are common of course. It is less clear, however, whether the senate had similarly discussed and passed all those measures (none later than the end of the first century) known to us only as *leges* ratified by a popular assembly.[20]

---

[12] For bibliography and guidance on views held, see A. A. Schiller, "Senatus consulta in the Principate," *Tulane Law Review* 33. 1958/9. pp. 491-508 = *An American Experience in Roman Law*, Göttingen, 1971, pp. 161-178.

[13] See G. Crifò, "Attività normativa del senato in età repubblicana," *Boll. Ist. Dir. Rom.* 71. 1968. pp. 31-115; C. Nicolet, *Rome et la conquête du monde Méditerranéen* I. pp. 373-384.

[14] See, for example, A. A. Schiller, op. cit. pp. 505-508 = 175-178; approved by M. Kaser, *Das römische Privatrecht* I. p. 199.

[15] See chap. 11 sect. 1.

[16] Macrobius, *Sat.* 1.12.35.

[17] Vell. 2.91.1; Dio 53.16.6.

[18] *RG* 22.2.

[19] *EJ* 94 a and b.

[20] For a complete list of *leges*, see G. Rotondi, *Leges publicae populi Romani*, Milan, 1912.

Livy's *Epitome*[21] does indicate that Augustus must have raised in the senate issues related to the *Lex Julia de maritandis ordinibus* of 18 B.C. In another early instance we might guess that it had likewise been consulted: having passed six *senatus consulta* in 11 B.C. in connection with the work of the newly established *curatores aquarum*, it is likely also to have discussed the related, equally detailed *lex* of 9 B.C. Yet it is baffling that Frontinus[22] should quote all six enactments of 11 B.C. as *senatus consulta*, and only the later one of 9 B.C. as a *lex*. Generally speaking, a considerable number of innovatory *leges* on issues of wide concern were carried, especially during the reigns of Augustus and Tiberius.[23] While there was strictly no need for the senate's approval to be gained before the assembly was approached, regular reference would plainly be both tactful and in keeping with tradition. So altogether it would be valuable to know the practice favored by emperors, not least for the light to be shed on the functions of the senate.

Unfortunately, sound evidence is not available.[24] Two passages of Dio are relevant for Augustus' approach, but the lack of concern for technical terms hinders the drawing of any decisive conclusion from them. In the first, under 27 B.C., Dio gives a general description of how Augustus "did not invariably legislate on his own responsibility alone, but raised some matters in public, so that if there were any feature which caused displeasure, he might learn it in advance and make an amendment. For without distinction he encouraged everybody to give him advice, in case anyone thought of possible improvements: he was quite willing for them to speak as they wished, and even altered some provisions."[25] Since there was no discussion at popular assemblies, the reference here points to debate in the senate. A second passage under 9 B.C. is less clear for our purpose. It follows a description of the *Lex Julia de senatu habendo*: "Before taking any action in regard to these measures or any others which he enacted then, Augustus had them posted on tablets in the senate house, and allowed members to enter in pairs and read them, so that if any point did not please them, or they could suggest any improvement, they might speak."[26] It may be that Augustus considered these measures as calculated to stir unusually vigorous controversy, and thus took special care to make them known in detail among individual members before presentation to the assembled House. Equally the passage might imply that, while he sought members' private views, he never intended to bring these proposals for-

---

[21] *Epit.* 59; cf. *RG* 6.2.

[22] *Aqued.* 108, 125-127, 129.

[23] Cf. A. Watson, *Law Making in the Later Roman Republic*, pp. 13-15.

[24] It is true that a rescript of Valerian and Gallienus speaks of "decretum patrum et lex Petronia," but neither enactment can be dated (*CJ* 9.9.16.2; cf. no. 201 in list below).

[25] 53.21.3.

[26] 55.4.1.

mally to the House prior to introducing them in the assembly. In sum, it is likely that he did gain senatorial approval for at least some *leges*, but no stronger claim can be made for his practice. Later, under 23, Tacitus[27] provides an instance where Tiberius raised with the senate the question of altering the regulations governing the priesthood of Flamen Dialis by *lex rogata*. After debate such a *lex* was duly enacted in accordance with the wishes of the House, though it is notable that, according to Tacitus, a *senatus consultum* alone could have served equally well. Nothing further is known about either Tiberius' practice or that of later emperors.

1. *Senatus Consulta* to Which Titles Are Devoted in Legal Works

Claudianum	*List no.* 44
Claudianum	47
Libonianum (title with Lex Cornelia de falsis)	20
Macedonianum	70
Orphitianum	128
Pegasianum	68
Silanianum	13
Tertullianum	82
Trebellianum	56
Turpillianum	60

Note also *Dig.* 1.3, De legibus senatusque consultis et longa consuetudine.

2. Ancient Commentaries on *Senatus Consulta* and Imperial *Orationes*

Where only a single reference survives, it is cited (from *Digest* in each case). Otherwise, for the complete text of passages, see the relevant reference in O. Lenel, *Palingenesia iuris civilis*, Leipzig, 1889.

List no.	Gaius	
128	Ad SC Orphitianum liber singularis	*Dig.* 38.17.9
82	Ad SC Tertullianum lib. sing.	38.17.8
	Marcianus	
60	Ad SC Turpillianum lib. sing.	48.16.1
	Paulus	
	De senatus consultis lib. sing.	36.1.27

[27] *Ann.* 4.16.

44	Ad SC Claudianum lib. sing.	40.13.5
20	Ad SC Libonianum lib. sing.	48.10.22
128	Ad SC Orphitianum lib. sing.	Lenel I col. 1295
13	Ad SC Silanianum lib. sing.	Lenel I col. 1295
82	Ad SC Tertullianum lib. sing.	Lenel I col. 1296
60	Ad SC Turpillianum lib. sing.	Lenel I col. 1296
53	Ad SC Velleianum lib. sing.	16.1.23
130	Ad orationem divi Antonini et Commodi [or divi Marci?]	Lenel I col. 1145
134	Ad orationem divi Severi	Lenel I col. 1146

Pomponius
Senatusconsultorum libri quinque — Lenel II col. 148

3. *Senatus Consulta* Cited by Name in Legal Works

These are in addition to those listed in section 1. A single reference only to use of the name is given: for fuller information the list of SCC should be consulted.

List no.

63	Afinianum (correct reading?)	*CJ* 8.47.10.3
95	Apronianum	*Dig.* 36.1.27
156	Articuleianum	*Dig.* 40.5.51.7
144	Calvisianum	Ulpian, *Reg.* 16.4
50	Claudianum	Ulpian, *Reg.* 16.3
154	Dasumianum	*Dig.* 40.5.36 pr.
165	Gaetulicianum	*Frag. Berol.* 3 = *FIRA*[2] II p. 427
79	Iuncianum[1]	*Dig.* 40.5.51.8
36	Largianum	*CJ* 7.6.1.1a
65	Neronianum	*Sent. Paul.* 3.5.5
66	Neronianum	*Frag. Vat.* 85
72	Ninnianum	*CJ* 7.20.2
127	Orfitianum	*Sent. Paul.* 4.14.1
33	Pernicianum	Ulpian, *Reg.* 16.3
202	Pisonianum	*Dig.* 29.5.8 pr.
84	Plancianum	*Dig.* 35.2.59
85	Plancianum	*Dig.* 25.3.1.10
74	Rubrianum	*Dig.* 26.4.3.3
155	Vitrasianum	*Dig.* 40.5.30.6
162	Volusianum	*Dig.* 48.7.6

Note also "vetus senatus consultum Tiberianum" mentioned by Sidonius, *Ep.* 1.7.12 (no. 26).

[1] Alternatively named SC Aemilianum after the consul's *nomen* in a mediaeval source (*Script. Anecdot. Gloss.* I p. 174 Palmerius).

4. Imperial *Orationes* Cited in Legal Works

1. *Citations by jurists. Orationes* specifically stated to have been delivered in the senate are marked +. One instance where the speech was definitely not delivered there is noted. Otherwise the place of delivery is not mentioned, and the senate must remain only a reasonable assumption (secure enough in some cases—e.g. Gaius, *Inst.* 2.285; *Dig.* 23.2.16 pr.; 49.2.1.2).

(i) *Verbatim*:
Hadrian: +*Dig.* 5.3.22.
M. Aurelius: *Dig.* 49.4.1.7.
Septimius Severus: +*Frag. Vat.* 158; +*Dig.* 27.9.1.2.
Caracalla: *Dig.* 24.1.3 pr. and 32.2.

(ii) *Others*:
Hadrian: Gaius, *Inst.* 2.285; *Dig.* 5.3.40 pr.; 49.2.1.2; 50.15.1.1, "in quadam oratione."
M. Aurelius and L. Verus: *Frag. Vat.* 224; *Dig.* 26.2.19.1.
M. Aurelius: *Frag. Vat.* 195, "in castris praetoris"; 220; +*Dig.* 2.12.1 pr.-2 and 7; +2.15.8 pr.-20; +11.4.3; 17.2.52.10; 23.2.16 pr.; 23.2.67.3; 26.5.1.1; 27.1.1.4, ὁρατίων; 27.1.44 pr.; 28.3.6.9; 38.17.9; 40.15.1.3; 40.16.2.4; 42.1.56; 42.2.6.2; 47.19.1.
M. Aurelius and Commodus: +Ulpian, *Reg.* 26.7; *Dig.* 23.1.16; 23.2.20 and 60 pr.-8.
Pertinax: Just. *Inst.* 2.17.7-8.
Septimius Severus: *Sent. Paul.* 2.30; *Frag. Vat.* 213-214; 276; *Dig.* 24.1.23.
Severus and Caracalla: *Frag. Vat.* 294.2; *Dig.* +24.1.32 pr.-27 and 33.2; 27.9.14.
Unknown emperor: *Dig.* 40.14.4.

Discrepancies are apparently to be found in the attribution of *orationes* of emperors who shared their power with a colleague. Papinian attributes to M. Aurelius and L. Verus an *oratio* assigned to the former alone by Ulpian (*Frag. Vat.* 220, 224). In the same way Ulpian (*Dig.* 23.1.16) attributes to M. Aurelius and Commodus an *oratio* assigned to the former alone by Paulus (*Dig.* 23.2.16 pr.). Elsewhere Tryphoninus (*Dig.* 23.2.67.3) cites only M. Aurelius for an *oratio* attributed by Paulus (*Dig.* 23.2.60) to him and Commodus. A fourth *oratio* is erroneously assigned by Paulus (*Dig.* 27.9.14) to Severus and Caracalla (*divi principes*) instead of to the former alone (cf. *Dig.* 27.9.1.2).

2. *Orationes* cited by emperors (none verbatim) in Justinian, *Codex*:

Oratio of Antoninus Pius: 10.53.4
　　　　　　M. Aurelius: 5.62.17; 6.35.11; 7.2.15
　　　　　　Septimius Severus: 5.16.10; 5.70.2 and 71.9.
In Justinian, *Institutes*:
Oratio of Pertinax: 2.17.7-8.

Note *Cod.* 6.35.11 and 7.2.15, where measures by M. Aurelius can be referred to as both *constitutio* and *oratio* in the same paragraph (cf. Ulpian, *Frag. Vat.* 212-213).

5. *Senatus Consulta* and Imperial *Orationes*

Asterisk denotes survival of verbatim quotation.

A. DATABLE WITHIN A REIGN

Augustus (to A.D. 14)

1. *SC by which the month Sextilis was renamed Augustus, 27 B.C. (Macrobius, *Sat.* 1.12.35 = *FIRA²* I no. 42; for dating, see further chap. 11 sect. 3 above).

2. SC, passed early in 27 B.C., granted double pay to the Praetorian Guard (Dio 53.11.5).

3. *SC, introduced by the consul of 25 B.C. (May or June), concerning a treaty with Mytilene (Sherk, *Roman Documents*, no. 26 col. b lines 36-43 and col. c lines 1-8).

4. *SC, introduced by the consul of 25 B.C. (29 May or 29 June), concerning a treaty with Mytilene (Sherk, *Roman Documents*, no. 26 col. c lines 9-28).

5. *SC concerning the registration of *scribae quaestorii*, 23 B.C. (*CIL* VI. 32272).

6. *Three SCC, introduced by the consuls of 17 B.C., concerning *Ludi Saeculares* (*FIRA²* I no. 40 = G. B. Pighi, *De Ludis Saecularibus*, pp. 107ff.).

7. SC, introduced by Augustus in 13 B.C., laid down terms of service for soldiers (Dio 54.25.5-6).

8. SC, passed in 12 B.C., allowed bachelors and spinsters to attend shows and banquets in honor of the emperor's birthday (Dio 54.30.5).

9. SC, introduced by the consuls of 11 B.C., defining the legal status of the wife of the Flamen Dialis (Gaius, *Inst.* 1.136, with some restoration of text).

10. *Six SCC, introduced by the consuls of 11 B.C., concerning *curatores aquarum* and the management of aqueducts (Front. *Aqued.* 100-101, 104, 106-108, 125, 127).

11. *SC, introduced by the ordinary consuls of 4 B.C., making new arrangements for hearing cases of *repetundae* (*FIRA²* I no. 68 V).

12. *SC concerning ships and troops, A.D. 7 (*Inscr. Ital.* X. 1. no. 64; see above, chap. 14 sect. 3 note 6).

13. SC Silanianum [named after C. Iunius Silanus, cos. ord. A.D. 10?] was intended to act as a strong deterrent against the murder of masters by their slaves. In such an event most of the latter were to be tortured, and until the culprit was found the will (by which the slaves might benefit) was not to be opened. Titles in *Sent. Paul.* 3.5; *Dig.* 29.5; *CJ* 6.35. Commentary by Paulus. Cited by Gaius, *Dig.* 49.14.14.

14. SC, passed under the ordinary consuls of A.D. 11, prescribing that where a

will was alleged to have been opened contrary to the terms of SC Silanianum, any proceedings must be instituted within five years (Venuleius Saturninus, *Dig.* 29.5.13).

15. *(?)SC, introduced by the ordinary consuls of A.D. 11, regulating the appearance of freeborn young persons in shows (cited in no. 22 below; see refs. there).

16. SC, passed under Augustus, forbade *equites* to appear at shows and on stage (Suet. *Aug.* 43).

17. SC, passed under Augustus, reserved the first row of benches at every public spectacle for senators (Suet. *Aug.* 44).

18. *Oratio* of Augustus on the status of *municipia* (Frontinus, *de Controv.* p. 7 Thulin).

Tiberius (14-37)

19. SC, passed in 15, restrained actors and their fans (Tac. *Ann.* 1.77).

20. SC Libonianum punished under Lex Cornelia de falsis (81 B.C.) those who wrote themselves into another's will. The measure applied equally to soldiers' wills: cf. *Dig.* 29.1.15.3; 48.10.1.7. Title in *Dig.* 48.10. Commentary by Paulus. Cited by Papinian (*Dig.* 26.2.29), Julianus (ibid. 34.8.1), Caracalla, Sev. Alexander, and Diocletian and Maximian (*CJ* 9.23.2, 3 and 6); note also Marcellus, *Dig.* 37.4.8.6? If it precedes Claudius' edict on the same matter, it is most probably named after L. Scribonius Libo, cos. ord. 16; but another Libo was consul in 15 B.C.

21. SC, passed in 16, limited the use of luxury articles (Tac. *Ann.* 2.33). The question of curbing extravagance was raised again in 22, without result (ibid. 3.52-54).

22. *SC, introduced by the ordinary consuls of 19, forbidding members of the upper classes to take part in shows or to prostitute themselves, or to incur voluntary degradation for any such purpose (M. Malavolta, "A proposito del nuovo *S.C.* da Larino," *Sesta miscellanea greca e romana*, Studi pubblicati dall' Istituto Italiano per la storia antica, 27, Rome, 1978, pp. 347-382 = *AE* 1978. 145, with Tac. *Ann.* 2.85; Suet. *Tib.* 35; Tertullian, *De Spect.* 22; Papinian, *Dig.* 48.5.11.2; cf. no. 140 below).

23. SC, passed under the consuls of 20, punished under Lex Cornelia de falsis (81 B.C.) anyone party to bringing an accusation against an innocent person (*Coll.* 8.7.2; cf. Macer, *Dig.* 47.13.2; Ulpian, ibid. 48.10.1.1).

24. SC, passed either under the consuls of 20 or in 24, establishing that when an official was accompanied by his wife, he would be liable for any offense committed by her (Tac. *Ann.* 4.20 with later date; cf. 3.33-34; Ulpian, *Dig.* 1.16.4.2 with earlier date).

25. SC, passed under the consuls of 20, establishing that when a slave is accused, the same procedure and principles shall be followed as for a defendant who is free (Venuleius Saturninus, *Dig.* 48.2.12.3).

26. SC of 21 requiring an interval of ten days between the passage of a senatorial decree [or just a death sentence?] and its deposit in *aerarium Saturni* (Tac. *Ann.* 3.51, where the number of days must be restored; Dio 57.20.4; cf. Suet. *Tib.* 75). Interval later extended to thirty days? (cf. Quintilian, *Declam.* argum. 313; Sidonius, *Ep.* 1.7.12; Appendix 10 below).

27. SC(?), introduced by C. Sulpicius Galba (as consul in 22?), banned or restricted eating-houses (*popinae*) (Plin. *NH* 33.32).

28. SC(?), passed under the ordinary consuls of 23, defined eligibility to wear the gold ring of the equestrian order (Plin. *NH* 33.32).

29. SC, passed in 27, regulated the siting of amphitheaters and the mounting of gladiatorial exhibitions (Tac. *Ann.* 4.63).

30. SC, passed under the ordinary consuls of 29, extended Lex Cornelia de falsis (81 B.C.) to punish anyone who took bribes to arrange false testimony (*Coll.* 8.7.2; cf. Macer, *Dig.* 47.13.2; Ulpian, ibid. 47.15.7; Marcianus, ibid. 48.10.1.1; Papinian, ibid. 48.19.34.1).

31. SC, passed on the motion of Cossus Cornelius Lentulus (cf. R. S. Rogers, *Class. Phil.* 26. 1931. p. 40 n. 2) in the consulship of Faustus Cornelius Sulla and L. Fulcinius Trio (July-September 31), prohibiting accusation of an imperial legate (Venuleius Saturninus, *Dig.* 48.2.12 pr.).

32. SC, passed in the financial crisis of 33, requiring creditors to invest two-thirds of their capital in Italian land and debtors to repay the same proportion of what they owed (Tac. *Ann.* 6.17; Suet. *Tib.* 48).

33. SC Pernicianum ('Persicianum' after Paullus Fabius Persicus, cos. ord. 34, would be more accurate? In any event a date earlier than no. 50 below, of Claudius' time) laid down that when men had not conformed to Lex Papia Poppaea (A.D. 9) by 60, and women by 50, its penalties would continue to apply to them (Ulpian, *Reg.* 16.3; cf. Suet. *Claud.* 23; Sozomen, *Hist. Eccl.* 1.9.16).

34. SC, passed under Tiberius, arranged for the Praetorian Guard to be paid from "the public treasury" (Dio 58.18.3; see further above, chap. 14 sect. 3 note 14).

Claudius (41-54)

35. *SC, passed during the consulship of Suillius (rather than Velleus) Rufus and Ostorius Scapula (last two months of a year, probably 41. See P. A. Gallivan, *CQ* 28. 1978. p. 419), permitted a patron to assign a particular child or grandchild (by will or otherwise) the succession to a freedman (*Dig.* 38.4; Just. *Inst.* 3.8.3; cf. Terentius Clemens, *Dig.* 23.2.48.2).

36. SC Largianum, passed "Lupo et Largo consulibus" (latter months of 42), laid down an order of succession to the estates of Junian Latins (Gaius, *Inst.* 3.63-65; Just. *Inst.* 3.7.4; *Cod.* 7.6.1.1a and 12a).

37. *SC of 22 September 44 introduced by Claudius to prohibit demolition of

buildings for profit (*FIRA*² I no. 45 I, cf. II; cited by Paulus, *Dig.* 18.1.52; Sev. Alexander, *CJ* 8.10.2. For year, see P. A. Gallivan, *CQ* 28. 1978. p. 420).

38. SC, passed "Licinio V et Tauro conss." (a slip for "Vinicio II et Tauro," cos. ord. 45?), extended Lex Cornelia de falsis (81 B.C.) to punish forgery of wills or false testimony in connection with them (Ulpian, *Coll.* 8.7.1; cf. *Dig.* 48.10.9.3 and no. 143 below).

39. SCC of 45 and 46 authorized the emperor to handle all applications from senators to leave Italy (Suet. *Claud.* 23; Dio 60.25.6-7; see further chap. 4 sect. 2 note 42).

40. SC (or imperial edict?) of 47 set the maximum fee for an advocate at 10,000 HS (Tac. *Ann.* 11.5-7; cf. 13.42; see further below, no. 54).

41. *SC, introduced by the consuls of 47, concerning *Ludi Saeculares* (G. B. Pighi, *De Ludis Saecularibus*, pp. 131-132).

42. *Oratio* of Claudius and SC of 48 in some way eased the entry of Gallic chieftains to the senate (*FIRA*² I no. 43; Tac. *Ann.* 11.23-25; see further chap. 1 sect. 1 note 41).

43. SC of 49 permitted a man to marry his brother's daughter (Tac. *Ann.* 12.6-7; Suet. *Claud.* 26; Scholia on Juvenal 2.29 Valla; cf. Gaius, *Inst.* 1.62; Ulpian, *Reg.* 5.6).

(For SC Macedonianum, arguably datable to 51, see no. 70 below.)

44. SC Claudianum, passed in 52 or shortly before, imposed penalties upon a free woman who chose to cohabit with another person's slave; if she maintained the union in the face of the owner's disapproval, she became liable to enslavement herself. Commentary by Paulus. Titles in *Sent. Paul.* 2.21a; *Cod. Theod.* 4.12. See also Tac. *Ann.* 12.53; Gaius, *Inst.* 1.84, 91, 160; Ulpian, *Reg.* 11.11; *Sent. Paul.* 4.10.2; *Cod. Theod.* 10.20.10.4; 12.1.179; Just. *Inst.* 3.12.1; *Cod.* 7.24.

45. *SCC, passed on 23 January 52 and at a subsequent session, offering *praetoria insignia* and money to the imperial freedman Pallas (Plin. *NH* 35.201; *Ep.* 7.29; 8.6; Tac. *Ann.* 12.53).

46. SC of 53 conferred official status upon the judicial decisions of imperial procurators (Tac. *Ann.* 12.60; Suet. *Claud.* 12).

47. SC Claudianum (named after the emperor?) in some way reinforced SC Silanianum (no. 13 above). Title in *Dig.* 29.5. See further below, nos. 58 and 65.

48. SC, introduced by Claudius, forbade soldiers to attend a senator's *salutatio* (Suet. *Claud.* 25).

49. SC, passed under Claudius, declared the theft of one or more tillers from a wrecked vessel to render the culprit liable for everything (". . . omnium rerum nomine teneatur"; Ulpian, *Dig.* 47.9.3.8; cf. below, nos. 159 and 194).

50. SC Claudianum (named after the emperor?) permitted men over sixty to escape

the penalties of SC Pernicianum (above, no. 33) by marrying a woman under fifty (Ulpian, *Reg.* 16.3; cf. Suet. *Claud.* 23 and no. 144 below).

51. **Oratio* by unknown senator (Claudius? See further Appendix 4) on *decuriae iudicum* and the age of *reciperatores*. Datable between 37 (or 41) and 61 (*FIRA*² I no. 44 col. I).

52. **Oratio* by unknown senator (Claudius? See further Appendix 4) on curbing frauds by prosecutors (*FIRA*² I no. 44 cols. II, III).

53. **SC Velleianum or Vellaeanum, introduced by the consuls M. Silanus and Velleus Tutor (under Claudius or Nero? See M. Kaser, *Das römische Privatrecht* I p. 667 and refs. there), forbade women to assume liability for other persons. Titles in *Sent. Paul.* 2. 11; *Dig.* 16.1; *CJ* 4.29. Commentary by Paulus. Cited by Marcianus, *Dig.* 12.6.40 pr.; Diocletian and Maximian, *CJ* 4.12.1.

Nero (54-68)

54. **SC, passed in 54, required litigants to swear before their case was heard that they had neither paid, promised, nor guaranteed any sum to an advocate; afterwards, however, up to 10,000 HS might be paid (see above, no. 40; Tac. *Ann.* 13.5; Plin. *Ep.* 5.9.4; cf. ibid. 5.4.2 and 13.6-7; Suet. *Nero* 17).

55. **SC, introduced by the consuls on 2 March 56, granted an individual exemption from SC above, no. 37 (*FIRA*² I no. 45 II).

56. **SC Trebellianum, passed on 25 August 56, to regulate *fideicommissa*. In particular, it provided that whenever an heir did accept and hand over an estate to the beneficiary in accordance with the will, protection would be given to the heir against prosecution for recovery of debts by creditors of the dead person. Titles in *Sent. Paul.* 4.2; *Dig.* 36.1 (with quotation); *CJ* 6.49. Note also Gaius, *Inst.* 2.253-258; Just. *Inst.* 2.23.3ff.; *Cod.* 1.17.2.6a. Frequently cited by many jurists: see *Vocabularium iurisprudentiae romanae* I. col. 968.

57. SC, passed in 56, limiting the judicial prerogatives of tribunes and aediles (Tac. *Ann.* 13.28).

58. SC of 57 extended SC Silanianum (above, no. 13) by allowing that when a master had been killed by his slaves, even those manumitted under the will could be tortured and punished (Tac. *Ann.* 13.32; cf. *Sent. Paul.* 3.5.6; Ulpian, *Dig.* 29.5.3.16).

59. SC of 60 (or imperial constitution?) laid down that an appellant from a civil tribunal to the senate had to pay the same deposit as was required for an appeal to the emperor (Tac. *Ann.* 14.28; see further chap. 16 sect. 1 note 61).

60. SC Turpillianum (*sic*) after P. Petronius Turpilianus, cos. ord. 61, penalized accusers who withdrew from criminal proceedings without sound excuse. Titles in *Dig.* 48.16; *CJ* 9.45. Commentaries by Paulus and Marcianus; from the latter's discussion it is clear that Papinian, too, wrote on this SC at length somewhere. Note also Tacitus (*Ann.* 14.41), Ulpian (*Dig.* 3.1.1.6), Macer (47.15.3.3), Junius

Mauricianus (49.14.15 pr.). Citations in *Digest* by Tryphoninus (34.9.22), Papinian (50.2.6.3), Ulpian (38.2.14.2; 48.19.5.1); by Valerian and Gallienus, *CJ* 9.9.16.

61. SC, probably passed in 61, prescribed the manner in which documents should be drawn up (*Sent. Paul.* 5.25.6; cf. Suet. *Nero* 17; Just. *Inst.* 2.10.3). Date is deduced from the format of documents found at Pompeii, which changes around this time: see C. Zangemeister, *CIL* IV. Suppl. 1. p. 278; and further K. R. Bradley, *Suetonius*' Life of Nero: *An Historical Commentary, Collection Latomus* 157, Brussels, 1978, pp. 105-106.

62. SC of 62 provided that fictitious adoptions should render no advantage in competition for public office or in gaining inheritances (Tac. *Ann.* 15.19).

63. SC Afinianum (correct reading? If so, probably named after L. Afinius Gallus, cos. ord. 62) provided that a person who adopted one of three brothers must leave him no less than one quarter of his estate, even when he had emancipated him. See Just. *Cod.* 8.47.10.3; *Inst.* 3.1.14.

64. SC, introduced by Nero in 62 or soon afterwards, forbade votes of thanks to provincial governors (Tac. *Ann.* 15.22; cf. *Sent. Paul. Frag. Leidense* 2).

65. SC Neronianum extended SC Silanianum (above, no. 13) by providing that where a husband was killed by his slaves, those of his wife should be tortured, and vice versa (*Sent. Paul.* 3.5.5).

66. SC Neronianum, passed "auctore Nerone Caesare," provided that where a legacy was not made in the correct form, it should be interpreted in the manner most favorable to the intended beneficiary (Gaius, *Inst.* 2.197-198, 212-222; *Frag. Vat.* 85; Ulpian, *Reg.* 24.11a).

Vespasian (69-79)

67. *Lex/SC, passed in late 69, granting powers to Vespasian (*FIRA*[2] I no. 15).

68. SC Pegasianum, passed in the consulship of Pegasus and Pusio (early 70's: see P. A. Gallivan, *CQ* 31. 1981. p. 207), sought to resolve a difficulty left outstanding by SC Trebellianum (above, no. 56), namely, that an heir had no incentive to accept an estate and discharge *fideicommissa*. Pegasus' measure now gave him the right to retain one quarter of what he received under the will. Title in *Sent. Paul.* 4.3. See also ibid. 4.4.4; Gaius, *Inst.* 2.254-259, 286a; Ulpian, *Reg.* 25.14-16; *Dig.* 24.1.5.15; Just. *Inst.* 2.23.5ff.; *Cod.* 1.17.2.6a.

69. SC, passed in the consulship of Pegasus and Pusio (for date see above, no. 68), granted the right of obtaining Roman citizenship to slaves who became Latins on manumission over the age of thirty (Gaius, *Inst.* 1.31; cf. Ulpian, *Reg.* 3.4).

70. *SC Macedonianum forbade the loan of money to persons in the power of their *paterfamilias*. Titles in *Sent. Paul.* 2.10; *Codex Gregorianus* 3.10; *Dig.* 14.6 (with quotation); Just. *Cod.* 4.28 (cf. 2.22.1 and 4.13.1; *Inst.* 4.7.7). Frequently cited by many jurists: see *Vocabularium iurisprudentiae romanae* I. col. 967. The commonly accepted dating to Vespasian's reign depends upon Suetonius (*Vesp.*

11); but under 47 Tacitus (*Ann.* 11.13) mentions a law with similar provisions passed by Claudius. D. Daube (*ZSS* 65. 1947. pp. 308-310) may be too radical in suggesting a single measure put forward by Vespasian as consul at the end of 51, but his discussion of the problem is valuable.

71. **Oratio* of Vespasian proposing the award of *ornamenta triumphalia* to Tib. Plautius Silvanus Aelianus (*ILS* 986).

Domitian (81-96)

72. SC Ninnianum, passed in Domitian's reign and thus named after Q. Ninnius Hasta, cos. suff. May-August 88, penalized any collusion in an attempt to prove that a freedman was freeborn (Gaius, *Dig.* 40.16.1; Diocletian and Maximian, *CJ* 7.20.2).

Note: For an SC against Jews, arguably datable to the 90's and recorded only in the Midrash Rabbah, see Appendix 10.

Nerva (96-98)

73. SC, passed in the consulship of Neratius Priscus and Annius Verus (May-June 97), fined anyone who had a slave castrated (Venuleius Saturninus, *Dig.* 48.8.6; for dating see *Fast. Ost.* with F. Zevi, *List. Fil.* 96. 1973. pp. 125-137).

Trajan (98-117)

74. **SC Rubrianum*, passed in the consulship of Rubrius Gallus and Caepio Hispo (suffect pair in one of the early years of Trajan's reign: note discussion by F. Zevi, *La Parola del Passato* 34. 1979. pp. 198-199. See further below, nos. 154-157), provided that where fideicommissary manumission had been ordered in a will, and the beneficiary neither acted nor answered a praetorian summons, then the praetor may manumit. Discussed by Ulpian, *Dig.* 26.4.3.3; 40.5.26.7-11 (with quotation) and 28 pr.-3. Cited by Papinian, *Dig.* 40.5.22.2; Paulus, ibid. 40.5.33.1; Maecianus, ibid. 40.5.36 pr.

75. SC, passed c. 105, regulating the conduct of candidates for office (Plin. *Ep.* 6.19.1-4).

76. **SC of c. 113-116 concerning a request from Pergamum about the celebration of games (*IGRR* IV. 336).

77. SC, introduced by Trajan, provided that when the tenure of a guardian appointed by municipal magistrates ended, and he proved unable to restore all of his ward's property, then the latter could take out an action against the magistrates (Ulpian, *Dig.* 27.8.2; Diocletian and Maximian, *CJ* 5.75.5).

Hadrian (117-138)

78. SC, passed in the consulship of Aviola and Pansa (ord. 122), prohibiting the separate bequest of anything attached to a building and forming part of it. Discussed by Ulpian, *Dig.* 30.41 and 43; cf. *Sent. Paul.* 4.1.20 = *Dig.* 32.21.2.

79. **SC Iuncianum*, passed during the consulship of Aemilius Iuncus and Iulius

Severus (October-December 127), permitted the praetor to act in a case of fiduciary manumission where for any reason the person asked to manumit did not appear, and the slave did not belong to the testator (Ulpian, *Dig.* 40.5.28.4 with quotation; 40.5.51.8 and 10; cf. Julianus, ibid. 40.5.47.1).

80. SC, passed between 1 Jan. and at the latest 17 Feb. 129 (that is, during the consulship of P. Iuventius Celsus II and L. Neratius Marcellus II; the latter's successor is known to have been in office on 18 Feb.), extended to the provinces the *Lex Vetti Libici* (?), which apparently concerned the grant of Roman citizenship to *servi publici* on manumission (Diocletian and Maximian, *CJ* 7.9.3.1; cf. G. Rotondi, *Leges publicae populi Romani*, p. 471).

81. *Oratio* of Hadrian and *SC, introduced by the consuls on 14 March 129, dealing with claims of the *aerarium Saturni* against private individuals for the recovery of vacant inheritances. Discussed principally by Ulpian and Paulus, *Dig.* 5.3.20.6ff. passim. Cited by Paulus, *Dig.* 6.1.27.3; cf. M. Aurelius, *CJ* 3.31.1.

82. SC Tertullianum, passed under Hadrian, permitted a woman who had *ius liberorum* a right to succeed to those of her children who died intestate (though certain other relatives still took priority in succession). Commentaries by Gaius and Paulus. Titles in *Sent. Paul.* 4.9; *Dig.* 38.17; Just. *Inst.* 3.3; *Cod.* 6.56. See also Ulpian, *Reg.* 26.8; Just. *Cod.* 1.17.2.7. Named after Q. Flavius Tertullus, cos. suff. 133? (*PIR²* F 376).

83. SC of Hadrian's time granted the emperor authority to supplement the *edictum perpetuum* where necessary (*CJ* 1.17.2.18 = *Const. Tanta* 18). To be dated late in the reign? See H. F. Jolowicz and B. Nicholas, *Historical Introduction to the Study of Roman Law*, p. 356 n. 3 and literature cited there.

84. SC Plancianum, most probably named after C. Julius Plancius Varus Cornutus, legate of Cilicia under Hadrian, presumably as *praetorius* (R. Syme, *Historia* 18. 1969. pp. 365-366 = *Roman Papers* II. pp. 788-789; H. Halfmann, *Die Senatoren*, no. 31) and later consul in the same reign (cf. no. 86 below, known to be Hadrianic), penalized an heir who discharged *fideicommissa* fraudulently (Ulpian, *Reg.* 25.17; Papinian, *Dig.* 34.9.11; Gaius, ibid. 34.9.23; Modestinus, ibid. 35.2.59). For dating, note also that among penalties was loss of the quarter allowed by SC Pegasianum (above, no. 68), according to a rescript of Antoninus Pius.

85. SC Plancianum (for dating, see above, no. 84) dealt with the recognition of children born to a wife in the months after divorce. Rules were laid down to protect her rights against the former husband, as well as the latter's rights, if the child were not really his (*Dig.* 25.3 and 4.1).

86. SC, passed under Hadrian, extended to births during marriage the provisions concerning recognition laid down by SC Plancianum, above, no. 85 (Ulpian, *Dig.* 25.3.3.1).

87. SC, passed under Hadrian, established rules for the reporting (*delatio*) of *bona caduca* to the *aerarium Saturni* (Iunius Mauricianus, *Dig.* 49.14.15.3; cf. 5-6; Valens, ibid. 49.14.42.1).

88. SC, passed under Hadrian, established that in a case of fideicommissary manumission where the praetor has needed to act, the slave's liberty is not affected even if the heir dies without a successor (Paulus, *Dig.* 40.5.5).

89. SC, introduced by Hadrian, laid down that, as with legacies and inheritances, a *fideicommissum* could not be left in favor of an uncertain person or an afterborn stranger (Gaius, *Inst.* 2.287).

90. SC, introduced by Hadrian, permitted women to make wills without recourse to the procedure of *coemptio fiduciaria*, which had previously been necessary (Gaius, *Inst.* 1.115a; 2.112).

91. SC, passed under Hadrian, established the procedure required of an heir to an insolvent estate left to two or more slaves (Scaevola, *Dig.* 28.5.84.1).

92. SC, introduced by Hadrian, provided for revocation of *usucapio pro herede* (Gaius, *Inst.* 2.57).

93. SC, introduced by Hadrian, concerning how the father's will was affected in a case where a mistake had been proved under SC below, no. 158 (Gaius, *Inst.* 2.143; 3.5).

94. SC, introduced by Hadrian, following a constitution of Nerva, confirmed that legacies could be left to any city in the empire (Ulpian, *Reg.* 24.28).

95. SC Apronianum permitted *fideicommissa* to be awarded to all cities throughout the empire (Ulpian, *Reg.* 22.5; Paulus, *Dig.* 36.1.27). Attribution to a particular one of the Aproniani (or Apronii) who were consul is impossible, unless this SC was passed around the same time as no. 94 above, when it could be dated to 117, 123, or c. 145 (G. Alföldy, *Konsulat und Senatorenstand*, p. 150).

96. SC, introduced by Hadrian, established that a son born to a Latin father and a Roman citizen mother is a Roman citizen from birth (Gaius, *Inst.* 1.30, 80-81; Ulpian, *Reg.* 3.3).

97. SC, introduced by Hadrian, established that the son of a Roman citizen mother and a *peregrinus* is lawfully the latter's child even where *conubium* did not exist between the parents. The child is a Roman citizen only if citizenship is conferred on the father too (Gaius, *Inst.* 1.77 and 92).

98. SC, passed under Hadrian, extending to *peregrini* the provision of Lex Aelia Sentia (A.D. 4) nullifying manumissions in fraud of creditors (Gaius, *Inst.* 1.47; some editors would eliminate any reference to an SC).

99. SC, introduced by Hadrian, removed from those who had obtained Roman citizenship from the emperor without the knowledge or against the opposition of their patrons, the disability that they could never die as citizens (Gaius, *Inst.* 3.73).

100. *Oratio* of Hadrian and SC required that *fideicommissa* left to *peregrini* should be claimed for the *fiscus* (Gaius, *Inst.* 2.285).

101. *Oratio* of Hadrian forbade any appeal to the emperor from a sentence of the senate (Ulpian, *Dig.* 49.2.1.2).

102. *Oratio* of Hadrian about honors for Augustus (Charisius, *Art. Gramm*. II. p. 287 Barwick).

103. *Oratio* of Hadrian on an unspecified matter, in which he mentioned that Berytus was an Augustan colony enjoying *ius Italicum* (Ulpian, *Dig*. 50.15.1.1; cf. perhaps Gell. *Noct. Att*. 16.13.4).

Antoninus Pius (138-161)

104. *SC of 15 Oct. 138 licensing a market in *saltus Beguensis* (Africa) (*FIRA*² I no. 47).

105. *SC, passed under Antoninus Pius, recognizing a *collegium* of *neoi* at Cyzicus (*FIRA*² I no. 48).

106. *Oratio* of Antoninus Pius defining eligibility for exemption from *munera* (Diocletian and Maximian, *CJ* 10.53.4).

M. Aurelius and L. Verus (161-169)

107. *Oratio* of *divi fratres* extended to guardians appointed by magistrates the obligation to furnish security (Ulpian, *Dig*. 26.2.19.1).

108. *Oratio* of *divi fratres* (Papinian only) or M. Aurelius and SC ruled that even if a freedman enjoyed exemption from *tutelae*, he could still be appointed guardian of the children of his patron or patroness (Ulpian, *Frag. Vat*. 220; Papinian, ibid. 224; cf. *Dig*. 26.5.14; Sev. Alexander, *CJ* 5.62.5).

M. Aurelius (169-177)

109. SC, introduced by M. Aurelius, forbade a master to manumit at a show any slave among the performers belonging to himself or others (Sev. Alexander, *CJ* 7.11.3; cf. Dio 69.16.3; Paulus, *Dig*. 40.9.17 pr.).

110. SC in the reign of M. Aurelius permitted bequests to *collegia* (Paulus, *Dig*. 34.5.20).

111. *Oratio* of M. Aurelius and *SC laid down a ruling for cases where a governor consults the emperor about a sentence. Even though no appeal has been lodged, no penalty must be inflicted until the latter's reply is received. A sentence has effect only from the moment of its publication at Rome, so that the will of a defendant who died previously would always remain valid (Ulpian, *Dig*. 28.3.6.9; Macer, ibid. 48.21.2.1 with quotation of SC).

112. *Oratio* of M. Aurelius and SC defined the liabilities of creditors and debtors where a loan had been made for house repairs (Ulpian, *Dig*. 17.2.52.10; Papinian, ibid. 20.2.1; Gaius, ibid. 20.3.2; cf. Philippi, *CJ* 8.10.4).

113. *Oratio* of M. Aurelius and SC strengthened the rights of anyone searching for fugitive slaves, in particular allowing entry to others' property without prior permission. Penalties were also laid down for those who harbored fugitives (unless they relented, and handed them over within twenty days). (Ulpian, *Dig*. 11.4.1 and 3; cf. below, no. 161.)

114. *Oratio* of M. Aurelius strongly implied (though it did not specifically state) that after marriage a man who was assigned as guardian to his daughter-in-law should have valid reason for being excused on the grounds of propriety (Valerian and Gallienus, *CJ* 5.62.17).

115. *Oratio* of M. Aurelius prescribed punishment for plundering another's estate before the entry of the rightful heir (Marcianus, *Dig.* 47.19.1; cf. *CJ* 9.32. For the problem, cf. Fronto, *Ad M. Caes.* 1.6.2-5 = pp. 11-13 H).

116. *Oratio* of M. Aurelius permitted the legate of a proconsul to appoint a guardian (Ulpian, *Dig.* 26.5.1.1).

117. *Oratio* of M. Aurelius established that only freedmen from the same area should be assigned as guardians to wards of freedman status. Thus a freeborn man assigned as tutor to a freedman has a valid reason to decline (Modestinus, *Dig.* 27.1.1.4; Tryphoninus, ibid. 27.1.44 pr.).

118. *Oratio* of M. Aurelius laid down that as soon as a man declared to be *ingenuus* had died, his status could never be questioned thereafter, and that even an investigation pending at the time of death was to lapse automatically (Marcianus, *Dig.* 40.15.1.3).

119. *Oratio* of M. Aurelius permitted an *extraneus* to bring evidence of collusion to prove that a freedman was freeborn (Ulpian, *Dig.* 40.16.2.4; cf. SC Ninnianum above, no. 72).

120. *Oratio* of M. Aurelius laid down the general rule that no litigant could force the hearing of a case during the harvest or vintage. But where there was good cause, exceptions were allowed at these periods and on holidays (discussion by Ulpian, *Dig.* 2.12.1, 2 and 7).

121. *Oratio* of M. Aurelius, not clearly understood, equated a defendant *confessus in iure* with one *iudicatus* (Ulpian, *Dig.* 42.1.56 and 2.6.2, heavily interpolated).

122. *Oratio* of M. Aurelius laid down that no compromise could be made concerning provision of maintenance (*alimenta*) left by will unless the praetor had given authority (discussion by Ulpian, *Dig.* 2.15.8).

123. *Oratio* of M. Aurelius modified SC Silanianum (above, no. 13) to protect certain interests of slaves who after investigation were declared innocent of their master's murder, and were freed or otherwise benefited under his will. Children born to them during the investigation were to be considered freeborn, while they also took any profit which had accrued to legacies made in their favor (*CJ* 6.35.11).

124. **Oratio* of M. Aurelius laid down that the time within which an appeal was to be lodged should be calculated on the basis of *dies utiles* (Ulpian, *Dig.* 49.4.1.7).

M. Aurelius and Commodus (177-180)

125. **Oratio* of M. Aurelius and Commodus and SC, passed in late 177, concerning (among other matters) a request made by Miletus in connection with games. See P. Herrmann, "Eine Kaiserurkunde der Zeit Marc Aurels aus Milet," *Istanb. Mitt.* 25. 1975. pp. 149-166 = *AE* 1977. 801.

126. *Oratio* of M. Aurelius and Commodus and *sententia prima*, delivered c. 177/178 (in the earlier part of the year perhaps: see Appendix 3), concerning measures to reduce the cost of gladiatorial games. See J. H. Oliver and R.E.A. Palmer, "Minutes of an Act of the Roman Senate," *Hesperia* 24. 1955. pp. 320-349.

127. SC Orfitianum (named after Servius [Cornelius] Scipio [Salvidienus] Orfitus, cos. 178) modified Lex Fufia Caninia (2 B.C.) to allow testamentary manumission of slaves whose names had not been mentioned in the will, but whose identity had been clarified beyond doubt by other means (*Sent. Paul.* 4.14.1).

128. *Oratio* of the emperor and *SC Orfitianum or Orphitianum (A.D. 178; see above, no. 127 for name) gave a woman's children prior right of succession to her if she died intestate. Titles in *Dig.* 38.17 (with brief quotation of SC at 1.12 and citation of *oratio* at 9); Just. *Inst.* 3.4; *Cod.* 6.57. Commentaries by Gaius and Paulus. See also Ulpian, *Reg.* 26.7; *Dig.* 29.2.6.2; 38.7.2.4 and 8.1.9; HA, *Marcus* 11.8; Just. *Cod.* 1.17.2.7.

129. *Oratio* of M. Aurelius (and Commodus) and SC prohibited marriage between members of the senatorial class and certain other classes (Ulpian, *Dig.* 23.1.16; 24.1.3.1; Paulus, ibid. 23.2.16 pr.).

130. *Oratio* of M. Aurelius and Commodus and SC forbade a guardian to marry his ward or to give her in marriage to his son or grandson. Commentary by Paulus. Discussed by him, *Dig.* 23.2.59 and 60. See also Ulpian, *Frag. Vat.* 201; Callistratus, *Dig.* 23.2.64 pr.-1; Tryphoninus, ibid. 23.2.67.1, 3 (attributing the *oratio* to M. Aurelius alone), 4; Marcianus, ibid. 30.128; 48.5.7; Severus and Caracalla, *CJ* 5.6.1; Caracalla, ibid. 5.62.4; Philippus, ibid. 5.6.4.

Pertinax (193)

131. SC, requested by Pertinax, made senators elected praetor senior to those adlected into the rank (HA, *Pert.* 6.10; see further chap. 7 sect. 11 note 37).

132. *Oratio* of Pertinax concerning the validity of wills. He affirms that he will reject the inheritance of anyone who has instituted the emperor heir for purposes of litigation (HA, *Pert.* 7.2; Just. *Inst.* 2.17.7-8).

Septimius Severus (193-211) and Caracalla (198-217)

133. *SC concerning *Ludi Saeculares*, A.D. 204 (G. B. Pighi, *De Ludis Saecularibus*, pp. 140-144; for discussion of day, see chap. 6 sect. 4 note 71).

134. *Oratio* of Septimius Severus, delivered 13 June 195, and SC penalized fraudulent behavior by guardians towards minors in their care. In particular, restrictions were placed upon *nominatio potioris*, while property belonging to wards could only be sold with the permission of the praetor or the governor. Title in *Sent. Paul.* 2.30. Commentary by Paulus. Discussion in *Frag. Vat.* 158; *Dig.* 27.9 (both with quotations of *oratio*). See also *Frag. Vat.* 212-214; *CJ* 5.70.2; 71; 73.2-4.

135. *Oratio* of Severus and Caracalla and SC, passed in the ordinary consulship of Fulvius Aemilianus and Nummius Albinus (A.D. 206), recognized the validity of gifts between husband and wife in cases where the donor died first, and the couple were still married at the time of death. Discussion in *Frag. Vat.* 276; 294.2; *Dig.* 24.1 (with quotations of *oratio* at 3 pr. and 32.2); cf. Ulpian, *Dig.* 33.4.1.3; Gordian, *CJ* 5.16.10.

Severus Alexander (222-235)

136. SC, passed in 222 (allegedly the first one after Elagabalus' death), forbade any woman to enter the senate or to be introduced there (HA, *Elagab.* 18.3 and chap. 4 sect. 4 note 79).

Valerian (253-260)

137. *Oratio* of Valerian (also termed *rescriptum*), sent in summer 258, concerning measures to intensify persecution of Christians (Cyprian, *Ep.* 80.1.2-3).

B. MEASURES OF UNCERTAIN DATE

(i) *Senatus consulta* and *oratio* for which
there is some indication of date

138. *SC requiring all *collegia* except burial clubs to be licensed. Augustan date? (*FIRA*² I no. 46). Compare references to licensing of *collegia* by senate and emperor, and to the banning of *collegia illicita* by the same authorities (Tac. *Ann.* 14.17; Plin. *Paneg.* 54.4; Gaius, *Dig.* 3.4.1 pr.; Marcianus, ibid. 47.22.1.1 and 3 pr.-1. See further chap. 12 sect. 4 note 25).

139. SC (passed late in Augustus' reign?) penalized authors of defamatory publications. See *Sent. Paul.* 5.4.15; Ulpian, *Dig.* 28.1.18.1; 47.10.5.10-11; Paulus, ibid. 47.10.6. Discussion by R. A. Bauman, *Impietas in Principem, Münchener Beiträge* 67. 1974, chap. 2.

140. SC forbade senators to marry or keep wives who had been convicted of a criminal offense. Cited by Ulpian, *Dig.* 23.2.43.10. Possibly a provision in SC of A.D. 19 above, no. 22.

141. SC, passed early in the period (?), allowed the usufruct of all a person's possessions to be bequeathed, on condition that in certain instances security was furnished by the beneficiary. Discussion in *Dig.* 7.5. See also Ulpian, *Reg.* 24.27; *Dig.* 7.9.12; Paulus, ibid. 33.2.1 and 24 pr.; Pomponius, ibid. 35.2.69; Just. *Inst.* 2.4.2. Known to M. Cocceius Nerva (died 33), but apparently not to Cicero (*Pro Caecina* 11; *Topica* 17).

142. SC, or possibly two, likely to have been passed early in the period, affirmed that no asylum was offered by images of the emperor, regardless of whether the culprit fled to one or carried one. See Scaevola, *Dig.* 47.10.38 and Callistratus, ibid. 48.19.28.7 with discussion by R. A. Bauman, *Impietas in Principem*, pp. 85-92.

143. SC, passed "Statilio et Tauro consulibus," prescribed punishment under Lex Cornelia de falsis (81 B.C.) for forgery of any kind of document (*Coll.* 8.7.1; cf. Ulpian, *Dig.* 48.10.9.3). Dating is uncertain. Editors have proposed the emendation "Statilio Tauro et Scribonio Libone" to give a date of 16. But equally a Statilius Taurus is known to have been consul in 26 B.C., A.D. 11, 44, and 45 at least. Arguably the measure should follow no. 38 above, rather than precede it.

144. SC Calvisianum declared the marriage of a man under sixty to a woman over fifty to be *impar*, and severely limited the capacity of both partners to inherit (Ulpian, *Reg.* 16.4). Attribution to a particular one of the several Calvisii who were consul in the first and early second centuries is impossible. But if the measure were passed around the same time as two related ones (nos. 33 and 50 above), then it might belong to 44 or 53 (P. A. Gallivan, *CQ* 28. 1978. pp. 424-425).

145. Many SCC up to Vespasian's reign concerning monopolies (Plin. *NH* 8.135; cf. Suet. *Tib.* 30).

146. SC no later than Vespasian's reign (more likely to date from Republic than Principate?) excusing the Hirpi from military service and granting other *munera* in recognition of their service to Apollo (Plin. *NH* 7.19; Solinus 2.26, p. 38 Mommsen).

147. SC laid down that when a slave to be freed is bequeathed, the *Lex Falcidia* (40 B.C.) would apply only if he was left a legacy as well as his freedom. Cited by Paulus and Ulpian, *Dig.* 35.2.33 and 35 (possibly provisions of SC Pegasianum above, no. 68).

148. SC placed recipients of *donationes mortis causa* unlawfully awarded to them in the same position as persons bequeathed legacies which the law forbids them to accept. The measure apparently raised many questions, some of them discussed by Paulus, *Dig.* 39.6.35. For dating between the reigns of Vespasian and Hadrian, perhaps nearer the latter, see S. di Paola, *Donatio mortis causa*, Catania, 1950, pp. 193-197.

149. SC, passed no later than Domitian's reign, concerning the formal annulment of accusations (Papinian, *Dig.* 48.3.2.1).

150. SC concerning the acknowledgment of children and the grant of free-born rights to former slaves (not to be equated with SC Plancianum above, no. 85, which has more limited scope). Passed sufficiently before Trajan's time for his staff not to recall it (Plin. *Ep.* 10.72-73 with chap. 13 note 17).

151. SC confirmed the edict of Nerva which was the first measure to ban any investigation of the status of a deceased person more than five years after death (Sev. Alexander, *CJ* 7.21.4 pr.; Diocletian, ibid. 7; 8; cf. Suet. *Tit.* 8; *Dom.* 9; Plin. *Paneg.* 35.4; Callistratus, *Dig.* 40.15.4). Predates *oratio* of M. Aurelius above, no. 118?

152. *Oratio* of unknown emperor (presumably no earlier than Nerva: see above, no. 151) established that without exception any freedman's claim to free birth must

be lodged with consuls or governors within five years of manumission (Papinian, *Dig.* 40.14.4).

153. SC, passed no later than 100, obliging consuls to deliver a *gratiarum actio* to the emperor (Plin. *Paneg.* 4.1 with chap. 7 sect. 5 above).

154. SC Dasumianum provided that where fideicommissary manumission had been ordered in a will, and the beneficiary was either too young to act or absent for good cause, then the praetor may manumit (Maecianus, *Dig.* 40.5.36 pr.; Marcianus, ibid. 40.5.51.4-6; also perhaps, without name, *Sent. Paul.* 4.13.3; Ulpian, *Dig.* 40.5.30.4). If this measure were passed around the same time as others of similar purpose (above, no. 74; below, nos. 155-157), it could be named after one of the Dasumii who were consul in the 90's(?), 119, and 152 respectively.

155. SC Vitrasianum expedited fideicommissary manumission in cases where a child was among the co-heirs (Ulpian, *Dig.* 40.5.30.6). If this measure were passed around the same time as others of similar purpose (above, nos. 74, 154; below, nos. 156, 157), it could be named after one of the Vitrasii who were consul in 123, c. 137, and 151(?) respectively (G. Alföldy, *Konsulat und Senatorenstand unter den Antoninen*, pp. 151-152).

156. SC Articuleianum permitted a governor to hear cases of fideicommissary manumission even where the heir came from a different province (Marcianus, *Dig.* 40.5.51.7). If this measure were passed around the same time as others of similar purpose (above, nos. 74, 154, 155; below, no. 157), it could be named after Q. Articuleius Paetus, cos. ord. 101, or Q. Articuleius Paetinus, cos. ord. 123.

157. SC permitted the praetor to act in a case of fideicommissary manumission where there was nobody left eligible or willing to confer freedom (Ulpian, *Dig.* 40.5.30.9-14). This measure could date to the first half of the second century along with others of similar purpose (above, nos. 74, 154-156).

158. SC, passed not later than Hadrian's reign (see above, no. 93), offered help to a Roman citizen of either sex who married a partner of lower status under the false impression that he or she was of equal status. Where the mistake could be proved, children born of the marriage and (usually) the partner of lower status might gain Roman citizenship (Gaius, *Inst.* 1.67-75; 2.142; 3.73; cf. *Frag. Berol.* 2 = *FIRA²* II p. 427).

159. SC, possibly passed no later than Hadrian's reign, forbade interference in the collection of shipwrecked articles by any soldier, private person, or freedman or slave of the emperor (Callistratus, *Dig.* 47.9.7; cf. above, no. 49; below, no. 194).

160. SC, passed "iampridem" according to Papinian (*Dig.* 34.9.12), seems to have ruled that where a man had made two successive wills, in the latter of which he had instituted heirs who were in fact debarred from succession, the estate did not automatically revert to the heirs by the first will even though this had never been canceled. Dated to the reign of Antoninus Pius by M. Kaser, *Das römische Privatrecht* I, p. 692 n. 15 and p. 726 n. 49.

161. SC, passed in the consulship of Modestus, required local magistrates and all

property-owners, on pain of a fine, to help anyone who was searching for fugitive slaves and showed an official warrant (Ulpian, *Dig.* 11.4.1.2). The measure definitely precedes an *oratio* of M. Aurelius and SC relating to the same problem (above, no. 113), and the reference should be either to L. Claudius Modestus, cos. suff. mid 152, or to the man of the same name cos. suff. after c. 167 (*AE* 1958. 234), because no previous consul is known to have used that name.

162. SC Volusianum extended Lex Julia de vi privata (17 B.C.?) to punish those who conspired to collaborate in a case and to share any proceeds (Modestinus, *Dig.* 48.7.6). Attribution to a particular one of the several Volusii who were consul in the first and second centuries is impossible.

163. SC, no later than the reign of Commodus, ordering "that there be no Christians." See H. A. Musurillo, *The Acts of the Christian Martyrs*, no. 7 sects. 13-14 and 23; cf. Eusebius, *Hist. Eccl.* 5.21.4; and chap. 12 sect. 4 note 36 above.

164. SC exempting Roman senators from any compulsion to receive public guests. Cited in a letter of Severus and Caracalla, 31 May 204 (T. Drew-Bear, W. Eck, P. Herrmann, "Sacrae Litterae," *Chiron* 7. 1977. pp. 355-383; L. Robert, "Documents d'Asie Mineure, VIII. Règlement impérial gréco-latin sur les hôtes imposés," *BCH* 102. 1978. pp. 432-437 with *BE* 1978. 468; D. Knibbe, R. Merkelbach, "Allerhöchste Schelte," *ZPE* 31. 1978. pp. 229-232; and *AE* 1977. 807).

165. SC Gaetulicianum in some way limited the right of *uxor in manu* to succeed to her husband (*Frag. Berol.* 3 = *FIRA²* II p. 427). From its content E. Volterra (*Atti Accad. Lincei*, Memorie ser. 8 vol. 12.4. 1966. pp. 351-353) argues that this measure must be later than SC Orphitianum (above, no. 128). The style of reference by the jurist (Paulus?), "hodie autem . . . propter SC," may also be compared to that of Ulpian, *Dig.* 33.4.1.3, "hodie post SC," which definitely relates to a measure of the recent past (above, no. 135). If such dating for SC Gaetulicianum is correct, then the only known consular after whom it may be named is Iulius Gaetulicus, legate of Lower Moesia under Severus Alexander (perhaps early in the reign; *PIR²* I 332).

Note: Mention of an SC in Tacitus, *Histories* 4.42, arises purely from corruption of the text, and should be ignored (cf. H. Heubner ad loc.).

(ii) *Senatus consulta* for which the earliest citation occurs in second-century jurists

166. SC established that greater value was to be attached to the testimony of census registers and public records than to that of witnesses (Marcellus, *Dig.* 22.3.10).

167. SC established the procedure of *distractio bonorum*, principally for senators and their wives (Gaius and Neratius, *Dig.* 27.10.5 and 9; cf. Papirius Justus, *Dig.* 42.7.4).

168. SC prohibited those appointed envoys from attending to private business until their mission was completed (Scaevola, *Dig.* 50.7.13).

169. SC established that money bequeathed to a city for shows or wild beast hunts was not to be used thus, but was to be spent on whatever else the city most needed.

The donor's name was to be commemorated (Valens, *Dig.* 50.8.6; cf. Suet. *Tib.* 31; comment by R. Duncan-Jones, *Economy*, p. 137).

170. SC defined cases where a woman might bring an accusation (Papinian, *Dig.* 48.2.2 pr.; Sev. Alexander, *CJ* 9.1.5 and 46.2; cf. Gaius, *Dig.* 4.4.12).

171. SC concerning *substitutio* with reference to legacies (Celsus, *Dig.* 28.5.26).

172. SC affirmed that it was not treasonable to melt down rejected (that is, badly made?) statues of the emperor. Cited by Scaevola, *Dig.* 48.4.4.1 (otherwise such action was treasonable: cf. *Dig.* 48.4.6).

173. SC permitted relief to a prospective heir who in good faith had paid legacies which genuinely could not be recovered once it was shown that he was not the rightful successor. Cited by Gaius, *Dig.* 5.3.17 (interpolation?).

174. SC defined the circumstances in which *captatoriae institutiones* were admissible (Papinian and Paulus, *Dig.* 28.5.71-72.1). Volterra (op. cit. in introduction to this chapter, note 1, no. 169) noted that no such SC seemed to be known to M. Antistius Labeo (*Dig.* 28.7.20.2), who died in 21 (Tac. *Ann.* 3.75; W. Kunkel, *Herkunft und soziale Stellung der römischen Juristen*, p. 114), but suggested that by contrast a passage cited from Gaius, *Ad edictum provinciale* XV, did show awareness of restrictions (*Dig.* 30.64).

175. SC forbade the sale or purchase of a fugitive slave on pain of a fine (*Frag. de Iure Fisci* I. 9; *Sent. Paul.* 1.6a.2; *Dig.* 10.3.19.3). Volterra (op. cit. in introduction to this chapter, note 1, no. 170) reasonably suggests that this SC is cited by Gaius, *Ad edictum provinciale* X (*Dig.* 18.1.35.3).

176. SC modified Lex Visellia (A.D. 24) to grant Roman citizenship after three years, rather than six, to those Latins by manumission who served in the *Vigiles* (Gaius, *Inst.* 1.32[b]; Ulpian, *Reg.* 3.5; G. Rotondi, *Leges publicae populi Romani*, pp. 464-465).

177. "Specialia senatus consulta" which, along with Lex Fufia Caninia (2 B.C.), nullify attempts to evade the rules governing manumission as defined in Lex Aelia Sentia (A.D. 4) (Gaius, *Inst.* 1.46).

178. SC forbade a testator to free and institute as heir his slave aged under thirty (Gaius, *Inst.* 2.276).

179. SC prohibited the manumission of those who had deliberately allowed themselves to be sold into slavery (Pomponius, *Dig.* 40.13.3).

180. SC annulled any gift made by a person under twenty to an older one so that the latter would manumit a slave. Cited by Sev. Alexander, *CJ* 7.11.4. Cf. Marcellus, *Dig.* 18.7.4; Julianus, ibid. 40.9.7.1.

181. *SC concerning the property rights of slaves or freedmen whom a court declared *ingenui* (Paulus and Pomponius, *Dig.* 40.12.32 and 14.3, with quotation of three words by the latter; Sev. Alexander, *CJ* 7.14.1).

182. One or more SCC defined circumstances in which a woman might apply for

another guardian (Gaius, *Inst.* 1.173-183; Ulpian, *Reg.* 11.20-23; cf. below no. 217).

183. SC concerning cases where a husband deliberately furnished his wife with an adulterer in order to catch the pair of them and disgrace her (Scaevola, *Dig.* 48.5.15.1).

184. SC established that nobody against whom a claim was brought by the *fiscus* should be required to show the informer any documents other than those specifically relating to the case (Mauricianus, *Dig.* 2.13.3).

185. SCC concerning procedure to be followed when the same estate was claimed both by the *fiscus* and by private individuals. Cited by Pomponius from Iulianus, *Dig.* 49.14.35.

(iii) *Senatus consulta* for which the earliest citation
occurs in jurists and imperial constitutions of the third
century or later

186. SC ordered punishment according to Lex Julia peculatus (cf. G. Rotondi, *Leges publicae populi Romani*, pp. 453-454) of anyone who permitted inspection and copying of public records without the sanction of the official responsible (Paulus, *Dig.* 48.13.11.5).

187. SC prescribed that any person convicted under Lex Julia de vi privata (17 B.C.?) should be stripped of all his honors, as if *infamis* (Marcianus, *Dig.* 48.7.1 pr.).

188. SC punished with a fine and *infamia* anyone who sought a municipal magistracy or priesthood contrary to Lex Julia de ambitu (18 B.C.) (Modestinus, *Dig.* 48.14.1.1).

189. SC excused from *tutelae* those freedmen of senators who managed their patron's business (Papinian, *Dig.* 50.1.17; see further chap. 2 sect. 1 note 19 above).

190. SC prescribed punishment for anyone who instituted a new *vectigal* (Modestinus, *Dig.* 48.14.1.3).

191. SC prescribed punishment according to Lex Cornelia de sicariis et veneficiis (81 B.C.) for dealers who sold dangerous drugs irresponsibly (Marcianus, *Dig.* 48.8.3.3).

192. SC prescribed relegation as the penalty for a woman who in good faith administered a fertility drug which had a fatal effect (Marcianus, *Dig.* 48.8.3.2).

193. SC prescribed punishment according to Lex Cornelia de sicariis et veneficiis (81 B.C.) for anyone who castrated a person for sale or for sexual abuse (Marcianus, *Dig.* 48.8.3.4).

194. SC imposed the penalties of Lex Cornelia de sicariis et veneficiis (81 B.C.) on any attempts either to hinder aid to a wrecked ship, or to rob or defraud its

occupants (Ulpian, *Dig.* 47.9.3.8. Cf. above, nos. 49 and 159; and *Dig.* 48.7.1.1-2).

195. SC restricted gambling to athletic competitions mounted "for virtue" (*virtutis causa*) (Paulus, *Dig.* 11.5.2.1).

196. SC relaxed certain rules governing mourning by widows, but upheld the ban on remarriage until the customary interval had elapsed after the husband's death. Cited by Gordian in 239 (*CJ* 2.11.15).

197. SC laid down that a house erected illegally, and thus due for demolition, could not be left as a legacy or *fideicommissum*. But evidently there was no objection to bequeathing the materials of the house. See Marcianus, *Dig.* 30.114.9; Ulpian, ibid. 32.11.14.

198. SC required condemnation according to Lex Cornelia de sicariis et veneficiis (81 B.C.) of anyone who sacrificed with evil intent (Modestinus, *Dig.* 48.8.13).

199. SCC concerning the acknowledgment of children forbid a man to deny his own child. General reference by Diocletian and Maximian, *CJ* 8.46.9.

200. SC prohibited putting burial places to different use (Ulpian, *Dig.* 11.7.12.1).

201. SC related to Lex Petronia (date uncertain: see K.F.C. Rose, *The Date and Author of the Satyricon, Mnemosyne* Suppl. 16, Leiden, 1971, pp. 35-37) deprived masters of the power to send their slaves to fight in wild beast shows at their own whim. Such treatment could only be sanctioned by a court (Modestinus, *Dig.* 48.8.11.2; cf. Valerian and Gallienus, *CJ* 9.9.16.2).

202. SC Pisonianum required that where a slave still liable to punishment for a crime has been sold, the seller shall refund the purchase price to the buyer (Paulus, *Dig.* 29.5.8 pr.). Attribution to a particular one of the Pisones who were consul is impossible.

203. SC penalized masters who sold their slaves in flight. But it was permissible for an owner to give instructions for a fugitive to be caught and sold (Ulpian, *Dig.* 48.15.2.2-3).

204. SC instructed the consuls to hear certain applications to manumit slaves (Ulpian, *Dig.* 1.10.1.2, reading disputed).

205. SC permitted one consul to manumit slaves whose names had been referred to his colleague, in circumstances where the latter has unexpectedly proved unable to act (Ulpian, *Dig.* 1.10.1.1).

206. SC ruled that slaves manumitted with intent to defraud a city did not gain their liberty (Marcianus, *Dig.* 40.9.11 pr.).

207. SC offered Roman citizenship to a Latin woman who bore three children (Ulpian, *Reg.* 3.1; cf. *Sent. Paul.* 4.9.8).

208. SC permitted a master under the age of twenty to manumit a female slave

on condition that he first swore to marry her himself within six months (Ulpian and Modestinus, *Dig.* 40.2.13 and 9.21).

209. SC laid down with reference to a *causa liberalis* that where a number of people claimed ownership of a slave, they should all be sent before the same judge (Ulpian, *Dig.* 40.12.8).

210. SC granted freedom to any slave who avenged the murder of his master or denounced the culprit (Ulpian, *Dig.* 38.16.3.4; Diocletian and Maximian, *CJ* 7.13.1; cf. Paulus, *Dig.* 38.2.4 pr.).

211. SC required the praetor personally to hear charges that a master had been killed by his own slaves (Papinian, *Dig.* 1.21.1 pr.).

212. SC rendered defendants on a capital charge unable to manumit their slaves (Marcianus, *Dig.* 40.1.8.1).

213. SC laid down that when a *municipium* had been instituted heir by one of its freedmen, it could claim the estate (Ulpian, *Dig.* 38.3.1.1).

214. SC forbade a testator to prescribe whom his heir should institute in turn (Marcianus, *Dig.* 30.114.6).

215. SC concerning legacies and *fideicommissa* (Ulpian, *Dig.* 31.60).

216. SC forbade a man to be appointed guardian of the woman to whom he was betrothed (Modestinus, *Dig.* 27.1.1.5; cf. Ulpian, *Frag. Vat.* 201).

217. Several SCC arranged for the appointment of new guardians in place of ones who were insane, deaf, or dumb (Paulus, *Dig.* 26.1.17; cf. above, no. 182).

218. SC in some way regulated the appointment of guardians by will (Ulpian, *Dig.* 26.2.11.3).

219. SC prescribed the action to be taken by a court when neither the informer, nor the defendant against whom he laid charges, answered the summons (Callistratus, *Dig.* 49.14.2.3).

220. SC established the procedure to be followed when more than one plaintiff brought charges against the same defendant under Lex Julia de adulteriis coercendis (18 B.C.) (Ulpian, *Dig.* 48.5.30.8).

221. SC established that a praetor could be required to give evidence in an adultery case (Arcadius Charisius, *Dig.* 22.5.21.1).

222. SC laid down that where the same branch of the financial administration both pressed claims and had amounts outstanding, one item could be set off against another. Cited by Caracalla, *CJ* 4.31.1.

223. SC established that judicial proceedings concerning obligations contracted by governors and their staffs before entering their province should be instituted during their term of office only in special circumstances (Macer, *Dig.* 1.18.16).

224. SC allowed a criminal trial to be postponed if any interested party furnished the judges with sound reasons for their failure to appear (Papinian, *Dig.* 48.1.13.1).

225. SC confirmed Lex Julia de vi (17 B.C.?) in allowing a defendant to secure the formal abandonment of his case if death, or some other circumstance, prevented the plaintiff from pressing charges. But a fresh prosecutor could take up the case within thirty *dies utiles* (Paulus, *Dig.* 48.2.3.4).

226. SC laid down that when a person was summoned to court in connection with one case, he was not required to defend himself on the same occasion against charges concerning another crime committed previously (Papinian, *Dig.* 48.3.2.2).

227. SC forbade anyone to be accused of the same crime under several laws (Paulus, *Dig.* 48.2.14).

228. SC assigned to an heir any profit or yield of an estate from the moment of the testator's death (Papinian, *Dig.* 49.14.38 pr.).

229. SC concerning usufructs, otherwise unidentifiable. Cited in broken passage, *Frag. Vat.* 67.

230. SC forbade prior hearing of a claim for liberty under a will which had still to be proved (Ulpian, *Dig.* 5.3.7 pr.).

231. SCC relating to Lex Julia miscella (that is, Lex Julia de maritandis ordinibus: cf. G. Rotondi, *Leges publicae populi Romani*, p. 458), referred to generally by Justinian, *Cod.* 6.40.3.1.

232. SCC relating to Lex Papia (Poppaea) of A.D. 9 referred to generally by Justinian, *Cod.* 6.51.1.1c.

233. SCC concerning *operis novi nuntiatio* referred to generally, along with laws and imperial constitutions on the same matter, by Ulpian (*Dig.* 39.1.5.9), citing S. Pedius.

234. Unidentifiable SC referred to by Diocletian and Maximian, *CJ* 9.9.23.2.

Note: There can be no doubt that M. Guarducci, *Inscriptiones Creticae* III. IX. 10 is simply a conventional dedication to emperor and senate. Mariani (*Mon. Ant.* 6. 1895. p. 311) erred in conjecturing that a decree of the senate was mentioned. See further *Inscr. Cret.* I. VII. 9 and comment by A. M. Woodward, *JHS* 56. 1936. p. 95; L. Robert, *Rev. Phil.* 10. 1936. p. 169 = *Opera Min. Sel.* II p. 1248.

6. General Conclusions

For all their length, certain limitations of the lists above do need to be appreciated. First, it is plain that since only accident has preserved the evidence for these decrees, any conclusions from them concerning the general character, scope, and development of senatorial legislation should be drawn with the utmost caution. For all we know, the surviving material may be unrepresentative. Second, it cannot in itself contribute towards answering the important question of how *senatus consulta* relate to enactments by the emperor alone.[1] Beyond acknowledging that policy obviously varied among individual rulers (with the Julio-Claudians, Hadrian, and Marcus Aurelius in particular turning to the senate), we may only conjecture why it was that an emperor decided to settle this matter by constitution, and that matter through the senate. Yet the emperor's role in introducing business to the House is so crucial that until we can fathom this issue, the full significance of *senatus consulta* within the whole context of Roman law-making must remain hidden from us.

With these limitations understood, however, the lists may seem striking to the historian in a number of respects. The sheer quantity of enactments is immediately impressive, as is their continuation right into the early third century. Also, certain areas of lasting concern stand out: status (especially measures concerning slaves and freedmen); inheritance (measures relating to wills, bequests, heirs, guardians); and the maintenance of good public order by a variety of means. In the latter connection, as is argued in the following chapter, some decrees are likely to have been prompted by the senate's investigation of scandals and its sessions as a court. In sum, the senate emerges as a more serious and wide-ranging legislative body than has generally been assumed, and over a longer span. Thus reappraisal of its role in this sphere, as in others, is indeed justified. Finally, in consequence, members appointed as provincial governors or *legati*, for example, must regularly have found their experience of the legislative work of the House a useful preparation for the exercise of jurisdiction which formed a major part of these officials' duties.

---

[1] For imperial constitutions, see G. Gualandi, *Legislazione imperiale e giurisprudenza* I, with P. de Francisci, "Per la storia della legislazione imperiale durante il Principato," *Annali della storia del diritto* 12/13. 1968/9. pp. 1-41.

16

THE SENATORIAL COURT

1. Character and Scope of Senatorial Jurisdiction

In contrast to various other neglected functions, the origin, nature and development of the senate's work as a court have much occupied the attention of certain modern scholars, and this chapter must owe a special debt to them.[1]

No more than a few words will be said here about the origins of senatorial jurisdiction. It is plain enough that the senate did not sit regularly as a court during the Republic. Such little activity of a judicial nature as can be documented for Augustus' time seems to represent a transitional phase. As early as 43 and 40 B.C. respectively the senate is said to have taken a part in sentencing two men alleged to have conspired against Octavian, the praetor Q. Gallius,[2] and the consular Salvidienus Rufus[3]—the latter actually accused in the senate by Octavian himself, according to Dio. In 26 B.C. it passed condemnatory votes against the disgraced Prefect of Egypt, Cornelius Gallus, but specifically left his conviction to the courts, that is, to a regular *quaestio* presumably.[4] Likewise in 23 or 22 B.C. the charges of *maiestas* against Primus, Fannius Caepio, and Varro Murena were heard in a *quaestio*.[5] In 2 B.C., while Augustus reported the immoral behavior of his daughter Julia to the senate, he did not delegate to it her punishment or that of her lovers.[6] Having exiled Agrippa Postumus in A.D.

[1] Note in particular J. Bleicken, *Senatsgericht und Kaisergericht, Abhandlungen der Akademie der Wissenschaften in Göttingen*, phil.-hist. Klasse, 3rd series, no. 53, 1962; W. Kunkel, *Über die Entstehung des Senatsgerichts, Sitzungsberichte der Bayerischen Akademie der Wissenschaften*, phil.-hist. Klasse, Heft 2, Munich, 1969 = *Kleine Schriften*, pp. 267-323; P. Garnsey, *Social Status and Legal Privilege in the Roman Empire*, chaps. 1 and 2. This last work is especially valuable, even if the distinction it draws between the character of the senatorial court during the Julio-Claudian period and later may seem too sharp.

[2] Appian, *Bell. Civ.* 3.95; cf. Suet. *Aug.* 27.

[3] Suet. *Aug.* 66; Dio 48.33.3.

[4] Dio 53.23.7; cf. Suet. *Aug.* 66.

[5] Suet. *Tib.* 8; Dio 54.3.

[6] Vell. 2.100.3-5; Seneca, *De Clem.* 1.10.3; Tac. *Ann.* 3.24; Suet. *Aug.* 65; Dio 55.10.12-16.

7, however, he did ask it to ratify the sentence.[7] Yet the poet Ovid's complaint to Augustus about his banishment in the following year seems to assume a wider function for the corporate body: "You neither condemned my actions by decree of the senate, nor was my banishment ordered by a *iudex selectus* [that is, by a *quaestio*]."[8]

The implication here is that the House could hear a case and pass a sentence of exile. Under the same year (A.D. 8) too, Dio happens to make the general remark, upon which he omits to elaborate, that Augustus in old age "allowed the senate to try most cases without him."[9] It is indeed only from late in the reign that we can document such a development. In A.D. 8 or 12 the senate voted on oath that Cassius Severus be banished to Crete for defamation,[10] while about A.D. 13 it condemned Volesus Messalla, former governor of Asia, on charges of *repetundae, saevitia*, and possibly *maiestas*.[11] These two cases represent our earliest evidence for the senate sitting as a court in regular fashion. Even thereafter, some years elapse before the exercise of this function is regarded as normal. In 19, according to Tacitus,[12] Cn. Calpurnius Piso still expected that any charge brought against him for the murder of Germanicus would be heard in the *quaestio de veneficiis*. Later, when Piso is tried, Tacitus has Tiberius stress at the outset: "In this respect alone do we raise Germanicus above the laws, by investigating his death in the senate house rather than in the forum, before the senate rather than before *iudices* [in a *quaestio*]."[13]

Yet from the 20's the senatorial court was well established. Only just over a decade or so later, celebrated trials of mighty defendants here could fire Caligula's rhetorical imagination,[14] while a *senatus consultum* of 44 specifically stipulated that those who contravened its provisions should not only incur a fine, but also be reported to the House.[15] At the beginning of the second century Pliny's reply to a friend who has asked him to give a reading of a particular speech conveys the atmosphere at an important hearing:

I know very well that speeches read out lose all their warmth and spirit, almost

---

[7] Tac. *Ann.* 1.6; Suet. *Aug.* 65.

[8] *Tristia* 2.131-132, "Nec mea decreto damnasti facta senatus,
    Nec mea selecto iudice iussa fuga est."

[9] 55.34.2.

[10] Tac. *Ann.* 1.72; 4.21; cf. Suet. *Calig.* 16; Dio 56.27.1. For discussion of date, R. A. Bauman, *Impietas in Principem*, pp. 28-31.

[11] See Appendix 9, no. 1.

[12] *Ann.* 2.79.

[13] *Ann.* 3.12, "Id solum Germanico super leges praestiterimus, quod in curia potius quam in foro, apud senatum quam apud iudices de morte eius anquiritur." For earlier charges of murder against senators being heard in a *quaestio*, see Suet. *Aug.* 56; Dio 56.24.7.

[14] Suet. *Calig.* 53.

[15] *FIRA*[2] I no. 45 I lines 13-14.

their entire character, when they usually gain their spark and appeal from the assembly of judges, the throng of advocates, the suspense over the outcome, the reputation of the different counsel, and the divided inclinations of the listeners; and they gain, too, from the gestures of the speaker as he strides to and fro, the movements of his body corresponding to his changing passions.[16]

It is true that this description remains general, but almost certainly the speech which Pliny's friend had requested was that delivered against Marius Priscus in the senate in January 100; it would therefore be natural for Pliny to have senatorial trials in mind.[17] Matters of notable significance were frequently at issue, and proceedings were always likely to attract public interest—so much so that emperors are even heard of barring public access to certain trial hearings.[18] For the corporate body this role as a court was the most important and the most time-consuming new function which it gained under the Principate. Though the frequency of trials must have declined in the face of increasing jurisdiction by the emperor alone, there is no question that they did continue to be held in the House to the end of our period and even beyond.[19]

It is frustrating that we cannot trace the stages by which the senate came to emerge as a court, or the precise legal basis for this new function. But the evidence is lacking. Unsatisfying attempts have been made to claim that the origin of senatorial jurisdiction during the Principate lay with the passage of the *senatus consultum ultimum* in the last century or so of the Republic, and with the subsequent pronouncement of certain individuals as *hostes publici*. Yet the *SCU* was an exceptional expedient, its scope and legality both hotly contested. It could hardly have served as a basis for the regular, accepted institution which senatorial jurisdiction became during the Principate. As to the declaration of *hostes publici*, the one instance for which we have detailed information—that of the Catilinarian conspirators—looks equally unpromising as a basis for future practice. Here all the standard elements of a regular trial were missing, and again the execution of sentence by the presiding consul, Cicero, was to be bitterly disputed.

Jones[20] urged that capital jurisdiction could only have been assumed by the senate (and by the emperor) by virtue of a new law. But it may be that no systematic or formal explanation for the development of senatorial

---

[16] *Ep.* 2.19.2.

[17] See *Ep.* 2.19.8 with Sherwin-White ad loc.

[18] See chap. 6 sect. 3.

[19] Note how Dio (54.15.2) implies that emperors still refer *maiestas* cases to the senate in the early third century. For the fourth century cf. Firmicus Maternus, *Math.* 2.29.13 with comment by T. D. Barnes, *JRS* 65. 1975. p. 47; later, chap. 3 sect. 2 note 39 above.

[20] A.H.M. Jones, "Imperial and senatorial jurisdiction in the early Principate," *Historia* 3. 1955. pp. 464-488 = *Studies in Roman Government and Law*, pp. 67-98.

jurisdiction is appropriate. Other contributory factors should be taken into account. First, it is important to recall that no rigid distinction was ever drawn by contemporaries between the judicial and non-judicial business of the House. Then, both before it came to sit regularly as a court, and afterwards, matters of a semi-judicial nature continued to be brought before it, most notably by embassies and by private members. Hearings were sometimes required.[21] Without doubt, the regular, formal trial of individuals is a significant further step beyond such business, but given the right encouragement the development is an understandable one.

Augustus can be seen to have offered that encouragement. To be sure, he did not intend the senate to share in the ordinary routine of criminal jurisdiction. This was the function of the *quaestiones*, and he did not change it. Rather he overhauled their procedure, added a new *quaestio* for adultery, and enacted fresh statutes for other relevant offenses.[22] In A.D.4 he added a fourth *decuria* to the existing three from which jury members were drawn. Senators were to continue to sit on these juries, though in what numbers they were drafted we do not know.[23] Information on their participation thereafter, and how long it continued, is likewise lacking, except for the significant point that they were still liable for this service early in the second century.[24]

It was for needs and cases beyond the normal routine that Augustus turned to the senate. In addition to those other cases which we have already seen him draw to its attention, as early as 29 B.C. he is found bringing Antiochus of Commagene before the House on a charge of murder, and securing his condemnation.[25] Six years later he introduced Tiridates in person, together with envoys from Phraates, in an effort to achieve a settlement of the quarrel between the two men.[26] He is also said to have heard cases with his senatorial *consilium*,[27] and to have delegated the hearing of appeals by provincials to a number of *consulares*, one appointed

---

[21] For a brief review of such activity in the Republic, see C. Nicolet, *Rome et la conquête du monde Méditerranéen* I. pp. 377-378.

[22] See W. Kunkel, *PW* 24 s.v. quaestio IX, cols. 769-779.

[23] Together with *equites* and *tribuni aerarii* they were called upon to make up 3 *decuriae*, each comprising nearly 1,000 jurymen (Plin. *NH* 33.30). Magistrates, holders of most, if not all, official posts (for *curatores aquarum*, see Frontinus, *Aqued.* 101), and presumably the elderly, would be exempt, so that if the representation of senators was to be more than a token one, quite a substantial proportion of the remaining members eligible are likely to have been drafted. This conclusion is borne out by the stipulation of *Lex Julia de senatu habendo* that no court requiring the participation of senators should sit on days of stated meetings of the House, in case attendance at the latter be significantly affected (Dio 55.3.2).

[24] See A.H.M. Jones, *The Criminal Courts of the Roman Republic and Principate*, Oxford, 1972, pp. 88-90; Plin. *Ep.* 4.29 with Sherwin-White ad loc. Note also Dio 52.20.5.

[25] Dio 52.43.1.

[26] Dio 53.33.1-2.

[27] Dio 53.21.5.

for each province.[28] Neither of these claims can be documented further. But as we shall see in more detail shortly, he certainly did assign to the senate responsibility for a new procedure in *repetundae* cases to obviate embarrassing delays in the *quaestio*. This change is likely to have pleased members insofar as it meant that such charges against them would now be heard exclusively by fellow senators. More generally, it may well have been Augustus' unhappy experience in the *quaestio* at the trial of Primus which prompted him to have individual special cases referred to the senate, in particular those where his own prestige and interest were involved— above all, therefore, cases of *maiestas* broadly defined. In addition, he must have appreciated the problem posed by cases which a *quaestio* was unable to handle satisfactorily in any event, namely, those where charges were preferred under several heads,[29] or where there was seen to be a need for interpretation as to how the laws should be applied, as at the trials of Cassius Severus and Volesus Messalla. Once senatorial jurisdiction slowly began to emerge in such circumstances, contemporaries were not concerned to find a strict legal basis for it. Such lack of concern simply reflected the wider constitutional uncertainty of the age. Romans accepted this particular innovation for the same reason that they acknowledged the legislative force of *senatus consulta*: both developments enjoyed the approval and recognition of the emperor.

If we move next to the nature and scope of the senate's work as a court, the types of case heard by it may be considered first. Here the incompleteness of the surviving evidence again creates difficulties. The senate was only one among several courts before which an accuser might choose to bring his charge, and it is impossible to be certain whether most cases of a particular type were usually taken, say, to the senate, or whether accusers would approach other courts as well with such suits.

Uncertainty over this point is especially acute with reference to prosecutions brought by provincials against former Roman officials for the recovery of money extorted (*repetundae*). Though we can cite no specific instance, it can safely be assumed that all such cases continued to be heard by the long-established *quaestio de repetundis* until the introduction of a new procedure in a *senatus consultum* of 4 B.C. sponsored by Augustus himself.[30] In brief, under the new arrangements provincials seeking restitution (but not wishing to press capital charges) could approach the senate

---

[28] Suet. *Aug.* 33, "appellationes quot annis urbanorum quidem litigatorum praetori delegebat urbano, ac provincialium consularibus viris, quos singulos cuiusque provinciae negotiis praeposuisset." Strictly, the use of *litigatores* would indicate civil cases.

[29] Quintilian, *Inst. Or.* 3.10.1; cf. 7.2.20.

[30] *FIRA*[2] I no. 68 V, with bibliography and discussion in R. K. Sherk, *Roman Documents*, no. 31.

for the immediate appointment of a panel of five senators, who would hear the case and deliver judgment within thirty days. We do not know the procedure to be followed if a capital charge was laid, however. There are various possibilities. For example, it may be that the charge of *repetundae* was duly to go before the specially appointed panel of senators, while the capital charge would be heard by the appropriate *quaestio* for murder. Thus the former *quaestio de repetundis* would disappear. Alternatively, where a capital charge was laid in addition to extortion, the provincials may have had to take their whole case to the *quaestio de repetundis*. On this view, only if they were prepared to abandon the capital charge could they avail themselves of the new, speedier procedure for restitution through a panel of senators. Equally it might be that the senate reserved to itself the hearing of any capital charge in such circumstances.

For our purpose there is no value in further speculation on this point, because it is reasonably clear that the new arrangements under the *senatus consultum* of 4 B.C. were modified not long after their introduction. Yet a general reference by Pliny[31] and certain specific examples suggest that a panel of senators might still assess the compensation due to the injured provincials. We hear of this procedure in the cases of Granius Marcellus in 15 and Julius Bassus in 103.[32] It was perhaps requested, too, for a case of *repetundae* said to have been brought against an aedile by a tribune at Domitian's instigation.[33] In 100 the defendant Marius Priscus unsuccessfully asked for the immediate appointment of such a panel in order to avoid any hearing of the most serious charges against him,[34] and it may be that Pompeius Silvanus and Baebius Massa resorted to the same subterfuge in 58 and 93 respectively.[35] However it became increasingly common for charges to be associated with *repetundae*—cruelty (*saevitia*) and treason (*maiestas*) in particular. In all the instances known to us, dating from Tiberius' reign onwards, these charges, along with that of *repetundae*, were now heard by the full senate, without reference elsewhere.[36] What formal change was ever made in the law, if any, to sanction such a development is unknown.

While there can be no proof, the likelihood is that from Tiberius' reign, if not earlier, cases were no longer taken to the *quaestio de repetundis*, and that this court became a dead letter. Rather the convention arose that

[31] *Ep.* 3.20.9.
[32] Appendix 9, nos. 2 and 32.
[33] Suet. *Dom.* 8.
[34] Plin. *Ep.* 2.11.2-6.
[35] Tac. *Ann.* 13.52; Plin. *Ep.* 6.29.8.
[36] There is no parallel for the senate referring to a panel the murder charge against the praetor of 24, Plautius Silvanus (Tac. *Ann.* 4.22, where the interpretation of "datisque iudicibus" remains uncertain).

charges against ex-officials of senatorial rank were brought to the House, while those against imperial procurators and freedmen went to the emperor.[37] Exceptionally, one equestrian procurator was tried before the senate during the Julio-Claudian period, but at no stage do we hear of senators appearing before the emperor on charges of *repetundae*. It should be recognized, however, that our evidence up to Trajan's reign is incomplete, and hopelessly thin thereafter. For the former period we know of thirty or so cases heard before the senate where *repetundae* was more or less certainly among the charges; for the latter period we know of three at most.[38]

In our surviving sources *maiestas* appears as the charge most commonly laid before the senate, often in connection with other charges too.[39] Here again lack of relevant evidence makes it awkward to determine how far other courts were also taking such cases. Yet if the *quaestio de maiestate* were still operating, we never hear of it explicitly after A.D. 15, and some scholars have preferred to take such silence as a sign that this *quaestio*, like the *quaestio de repetundis*, soon became a dead letter.[40] Many emperors are known to have accepted cases of *maiestas* in their own court; thus, for example as Tacitus indicates,[41] it was the unusually embarrassing charge of having sold imperial appointments which prompted Nero to try Fabricius Veiento in 62. But emperors' reasons for reserving *maiestas* cases to themselves are not always so clear, nor is the extent to which they chose to do so.[42]

During the Julio-Claudian period we hear of a notable number of adultery cases being tried in the senate. In most, if not all of these, persons of high rank are implicated, and there might be associated charges as well as delicate political overtones. But again we do not know to what extent the *quaestio de adulteriis*, of which little is heard during this period, was taking other cases involving persons of high rank at the same date.[43] Beyond the Julio-Claudian period we know that the *quaestio* remained at work,[44] and that the emperor, too, came to hear cases of adultery.[45] But as it happens there is no further evidence for adultery trials in the senate.

[37] Note Tac. *Dial.* 7, and the discussion by P. Garnsey, *Social Status and Legal Privilege*, pp. 85-87.

[38] See Appendix 9.

[39] Cf. Tac. *Ann.* 3.38.

[40] In the exchange recorded by Tacitus (*Ann.* 1.72) under 15 it was presumably the praetor in charge of the *quaestio de maiestate* who approached Tiberius. It is conceivable, but no more, that the Macedonian Antistius Vetus was tried there in 21 (ibid. 3.38).

[41] *Ann.* 14.50.

[42] Most notably, our knowledge of Claudius' trials *intra cubiculum* is weak (rashly doubted by P. Garnsey, *Social Status and Legal Privilege*, p. 44).

[43] Tac. *Ann.* 3.38 and Dio 54.30.4 are the sole references. It was presumably from a mixed sense of tact and outrage that Tiberius himself took the scandalous case recounted by Josephus, *AJ* 18.65-80, instead of referring it elsewhere.

[44] See Dio 76.16.4.

[45] Plin. *Ep.* 6.31.4-6; Papinian, *Dig.* 48.18.17 pr.

If we turn to other offenses, the same uncertainty persists over how far charges were being brought to the senate, and how far to other courts. Tacitus' account of a *falsum* case in 61 is significant in this connection.[46] First, it indicates that the customary court for such a charge at this date was that of the Urban Prefect. In this instance it seems that the prosecutor, Valerius Ponticus, had deliberately chosen to approach the *quaestio de falsis* instead of the Prefect. Yet when he was caught negotiating with the defense, the case was transferred to the senate, which was competent to hear *falsum* charges (like the other two courts), but seems not to have done so normally at this date. Second, Tacitus' account indicates that both senators and others of lower rank were defendants in this case. There was evidently no difficulty in the former appearing before a *quaestio*, nor (when the case was transferred) in the latter appearing before the senate. We know for certain of only one other *falsum* case heard by the senate in the Julio-Claudian period, and none thereafter. It was laid in 20 against the highly exalted Aemilia Lepida, once betrothed to L. Caesar, and a whole range of further charges was then added.[47] Clearly, the involvement of individuals of the highest rank makes this case untypical. It hardly supports any notion that the senate regularly heard *falsum* cases. Instead perhaps, taken together with the other relevant evidence, it argues against it.[48]

Such information as we possess about other charges suggests that they, too, were only brought to the senate in certain circumstances which may be broadly defined: when individuals of high rank were involved; when the issue was especially serious or scandalous; or when an affair had attracted a special degree of public attention. Such reasons may explain adequately, for example, the senatorial trial of Vibius Serenus, proconsul of Hispania Ulterior (that is, Baetica), on a charge of *vis publica* in 23.[49] It is also understandable (though at the same time remarkable) that during the same year Tiberius wished to have his procurator in Asia, Lucilius Capito, tried in the senate for unauthorized use of force,[50] and at some unknown stage a *praefectus alae* likewise for *vis et rapinae*.[51] Naturally enough there were convictions for *calumnia* in the senatorial court arising out of prosecutions there.[52] The senatorial trial of the Cretan magnate,

[46] *Ann.* 14.40-41.

[47] Tac. *Ann.* 3.22-23; Suet. *Tib.* 49.

[48] The case involving a forged will to which Claudius was witness, brought during Gaius' reign, may have come to the senate, but the place of the trial remains obscure from Suetonius' account (*Claud.* 9).

[49] Tac. *Ann.* 4.13. It would be natural, too, to try Vibius in the same way as governors charged with *repetundae* and associated crimes.

[50] Tac. *Ann.* 4.15; Dio 57.23.4.

[51] Suet. *Tib.* 30.

[52] Note Tac. *Ann.* 3.37; 4.31; 6.7; 12.42; 13.33.

Claudius Timarchus, in 62 is explained by the contempt which his remarks had shown for the House.[53] In 21 the trial of Annia Rufilla for threatening abuse (if indeed there was much of a hearing) is accounted for by the senatorial status of her victim, and his ability to rouse members' sympathy.[54]

The case of Annia Rufilla leads on to a further range of instances where the senate took decisions of a judicial nature, or laid down sentences, even though sometimes there may never have been a formal hearing. In this broad category may be placed decrees against groups or communities considered a threat to public order. These have been cited elsewhere,[55] but a valuable illustration is the senate's investigation of the collapse of an unsafe amphitheater at Fidenae in 27, followed by the banishment of its freedman builder, Atilius, and the drafting of regulations to prevent the recurrence of such a disaster.[56] It is a fair guess that a number of *senatus consulta* which are cited without indication of the background to their passage followed similar investigation of scandals—for example, those penalizing attempts to hinder aid to a wrecked ship, or to rob or defraud its occupants, or to steal the tiller,[57] and also those concerning castration and the sale and administration of drugs.[58] Thus as a result of this function, and from its work as a court,[59] the senate can be thought to have made a significant contribution to the development of the law. By contrast, we know of two pleas discussed there—in 61 and 105—for waiving or reducing the existing harsh penalties prescribed for the slaves and freedmen of a murdered master.[60]

It is natural to ask next about the status of defendants in the senatorial court. In answer we should first note again the earlier conclusion from Tacitus' account of *falsum* proceedings in 61, which shows that there was no difficulty in senators being brought before a *quaestio*, nor in defendants of lower rank being brought before the senate. So members of the senatorial class might be prosecuted in other courts, although just how often this happened we cannot say. Equally, defendants of lower rank could be tried in the senate. But in practice we mostly find them there during the Julio-Claudian period, and under certain conditions: when senators are involved in the case (as prosecutors or accomplices); when senatorial interests are

[53] Tac. *Ann.* 15.20.
[54] Tac. *Ann.* 3.36.
[55] See chap. 12 sect. 4.
[56] Tac. *Ann.* 4.62-63.
[57] Nos. 49, 159, 194 in list, chap. 15 sect. 5.
[58] Nos. 191-193 in list.
[59] Note, for example, no. 64 in list. Further possible instances are put forward by F. de Marini Avonzo, *La funzione giurisdizionale del senato romano*, Milan, 1957, pp. 44-52.
[60] Tac. *Ann.* 14.42-45; Plin. *Ep.* 8.14.

specially affected; or when there had been a major scandal meriting investigation. As we have seen, it was for such reasons that Annia Rufilla, Claudius Timarchus, and Atilius (if he was actually tried) were brought before the House. In addition we may fairly guess that civil cases which came on appeal to the senate must sometimes have involved non-senatorial defendants. But only a single reference to such appeals survives, when Tacitus under 60 explains how Nero "increased the dignity of the House by laying down that those who appealed from *privati iudices* to the senate should be liable to a penalty of the same amount as those who appealed to the emperor."[61] The nature and frequency of such appeals to the senate, and how long they continued to be brought, are all a blank. We are quite unable to illuminate further the testimony of the *Historia Augusta* that M. Aurelius "gave the senate jurisdiction of appeals made from the consul."[62]

The virtual disappearance of non-senatorial defendants from the senatorial court after the Julio-Claudian period may largely be a reflection of the inadequacy of our evidence. Pliny[63] implies that some non-senators were tried there during the Flavian period, and more specifically we might reckon that there were some among the many defendants accused of violating Vestal Virgins under Domitian.[64] No doubt they did continue to appear later, too, for the same reasons as outlined above.[65] But more can hardly be said when our knowledge is so limited, and especially when we have no detailed reports of trials for *maiestas*, the occasions on which non-senatorial defendants appear most often earlier. Rather, now that the emperor practiced a regular criminal jurisdiction (as he had not done in the Julio-Claudian period), it may be that such people would be brought before him instead. Certainly M. Aurelius is said to have sent senatorial accomplices of Avidius Cassius for trial in the senate, while he decided the cases of those of lower rank in his own court.[66] As it is, almost the only cases we even simply hear of in the senate after the Julio-Claudian period are for *repetundae*, or *maiestas*, or against *delatores*. In all likelihood a wider range did continue, but it remains largely hidden from us.[67] Some

[61] *Ann.* 14.28, "auxitque patrum honorem statuendo ut, qui a privatis iudicibus ad senatum provocavissent, eiusdem pecuniae periculum facerent cuius si qui imperatorem appellarent." Cf. Suet. *Nero* 17. The penalty is otherwise known only from a letter of Titus to the town of Munigua, which had appealed to him from a decision in a civil case heard by the proconsul of Baetica. In this instance at least it was 50,000 HS (*AE* 1962. 288).

[62] *Marcus* 10.9, "senatum appellationibus a consule factis iudicem dedit."

[63] *Ep.* 9.13.21.

[64] Dio 67.3.3[2].

[65] It should be noted, however, that two hearings involving non-senators reported by Pliny (*Ep.* 4.12; 5.13) were not trials in the strict sense of the term.

[66] Dio 71.28.2-3.

[67] Hadrian's *oratio* banning appeals to the emperor from a verdict by the senate at least suggests an active court (*Dig.* 49.2.1.2). For assessment of the testimony for two trials allegedly heard there in Commodus' reign, see Extended Note L.

cases involving senators were now taken to the emperor, such as the unusual instance of unsavory mutual accusations between a governor and his *comes* heard by Trajan out of tact perhaps.[68] Others may still have gone to the *quaestiones*, such as the case of *calumnia* in Domitian's reign mentioned by Pliny.[69] Yet at least there is no reason to think that the emperor ever had the time or inclination to take all cases involving senators. Such a development would also have given needless offense to senatorial pride.

There was in fact a notable hardening of senatorial opinion over one issue, namely, the execution of members without trial before the House. The grievance had perhaps crystallized with executions ordered by Claudius, and although Nero undertook in his accession speech to end such autocratic behavior, and to abandon trials *intra cubiculum*,[70] he broke his promise after the Pisonian conspiracy of 65. The precise steps which the senate next took to safeguard its interests in this respect, and the circumstances in which they were taken, are hidden from us. Yet at least Vespasian and Titus must have reduced tension by rejecting charges of *maiestas*.[71] In Domitian's reign, either because members were already under attack, or because attack was feared, the senate is said to have shown uncharacteristically defiant initiative in passing repeated decrees which made it illegal for the emperor to put anyone of his own rank to death, prohibitions allegedly ignored by Domitian.[72] To point the contrast between himself and the "tyrant" he had succeeded, Nerva swore that he would execute no senator.[73] Among later emperors we know that a similar oath was taken by Trajan,[74] Hadrian,[75] Pertinax,[76] and Septimius Severus.[77] Further undertakings not to disfranchise senators, and not to confiscate their property, were said to have been included in the oaths of Trajan and Severus respectively. While no oath is recorded in surviving sources, it is clear that the same policy was respected by Antoninus Pius,[78] M. Aurelius,[79] Ma-

---

[68] Plin. *Ep*. 6.22. For other possible instances see Ulpian, *Dig*. 48.5.2.6; Marcianus, ibid. 48.13.12.1.

[69] *Ep*. 3.9.33.

[70] Tac. *Ann*. 13.4.

[71] Dio 66.9.1 and 19.1-2; cf. Suet. *Tit*. 9.

[72] Dio 67.2.4; cf. 11.3.

[73] Dio 68.2.3.

[74] Dio 68.5.2.

[75] Dio 69.2.4; HA, *Hadr*. 7.4.

[76] Dio 74.5.2.

[77] Dio 75.2.1-2; HA, *Sev*. 7.5; cf. Herod. 2.14.3. Garnsey (*Social Status and Legal Privilege*, pp. 44-45) is right to reject the suggestion of A. R. Birley that the oath may be traced back to Vespasian's time ("The oath not to put senators to death," *CR* 12. 1962. pp. 197-199).

[78] HA, *Antoninus* 7.3-4; cf. 8.10; *Fast. Ost.* A.D. 145. Unfortunately *Fast. Ost.* A.D. 151 is too fragmentary to reveal which court deported two or three senators (?) that year, and why: cf. *PIR²* E 104, I 717, L 2.

[79] Dio 71.28.2 and 30.1-3; HA, *Marcus* 25.6; 26.13; 29.4; *Avidius* 8.7.

crinus,[80] and Severus Alexander.[81] Among senators, Dio supports its continuation in the early third century. In the fictitious speech to Augustus he has Maecenas advocate that whenever charges involving the penalties of disfranchisement, exile, or death are brought against members of the senatorial class, the emperor should let the case be taken by the House, without any prior investigation on his part or any interference in the verdict.[82]

The value of the oath, and the degree to which it was observed by those emperors who swore it, may perhaps best be discussed in the context of a wider consideration of the treatment of defendants in the senatorial court, and of imperial interference there. Notionally the senate judged cases according to the laws, and was free of outside interference: it could decide as it pleased, Nero reminded members in 62.[83] Neither principle was adhered to in practice. First, unlike a *quaestio*, the senate as a law-making body itself claimed the right "both to reduce and to increase the severity of the law."[84] Astonishingly, even in 100 some members could uphold the contrary claim, that the senate was bound by the laws.[85] But it is no surprise that their plea was defeated, since as far back as Tiberius' reign the House had exercised its own discretion in the conduct of cases and in the fixing of penalties. It was natural enough for C. Laetorius, a young patrician on trial for adultery at some time in the first or early second centuries, to plead for a reduced penalty on the grounds of his age, rank, and ownership of Augustus' birthplace.[86] Second, the senate's theoretical independence was affected in the judicial sphere, as in every other, by the interest of the emperor. Nero's reminder mentioned above was heavily tinged with sarcasm.

How did the senate's discretion operate? Would it be valid to claim, for example, that the House was regularly biased against those non-senators it tried? Such a notion might gain general support from Pliny's remark about "the odium against the senate which raged among the other classes for showing severity to others while sparing its own members alone by a sort of mutual connivance."[87] If we turn to specific cases, instances can indeed be found where non-senatorial defendants were more brusquely

---

[80] Dio 78.12.2.

[81] HA, *Sev. Alex.* 52.2; cf. Herod. 6.1.7 and 9.8.

[82] Dio 52.31.3-4.

[83] Tac. *Ann.* 14.49; cf. *Agr.* 2.

[84] Plin. *Ep.* 4.9.17, "et mitigare leges et intendere"; for the senate exempting individuals from a law, see Gell. *Noct. Att.* 1.12.12; *FIRA²* I no. 45 II.

[85] Plin. *Ep.* 2.11.4; note also his defensiveness at 4.9.17.

[86] Suet. *Aug.* 5. Of course we do not know what response there was to the plea, if any, while possession of the house (the circumstance on which Laetorius seems to have placed most weight) was a point which any owner could have put forward in this situation, regardless of his social standing.

[87] *Ep.* 9.13.21.

treated than they may have deserved: Annia Rufilla, for example, for threatening abuse; Clutorius Priscus for bragging about a foolish composition; Norbanus Licinianus for collusion with the defendant in a *repetundae* case.[88] But then we have parallel instances of equally severe treatment for senators. The death sentence generally agreed for Antistius Sosianus, who had read out satirical verses against Nero at a dinner party, is one clear case,[89] and the venomous assault against C. Junius Silanus, former governor of Asia, on charges of *repetundae* and *maiestas*, may be considered another (even if he was guilty on the former count).[90] Tacitus[91] alleges that in 23 the House was dead set against C. Sempronius Gracchus also, and he must certainly be right in portraying it as bitterly hostile to P. Suillius Rufus in 58. Yet it is doubtful whether the treatment of any of these seven defendants cited was determined principally by their social standing. The sentences carried out on Clutorius, and first proposed for Silanus[92] and Antistius, were prompted mainly by fear of the emperor and eagerness to meet what were thought to be his wishes.[93] There was strong prejudice against Gracchus because his father had been exiled as one of Julia's lovers.[94] Suillius had been a notorious *delator* during Claudius' reign. Annia Rufilla's provocative behavior had aroused many members' fury on a sensitive issue, while the chief cause of Licinianus' downfall was his former association with Domitian. We must therefore be wary before suggesting bias on the part of the House against non-senatorial defendants simply because the latter were of lower class. Other factors could be just as important, or even more important, in influencing the senate's attitude. Unfortunately, the likelihood that non-senatorial defendants would only come to this court in the special circumstances outlined above perhaps made for a high proportion of convictions among this group.

We may be on safer ground in suggesting that where a senatorial defendant was prosecuted by someone of lower class, the House was biased in favor of the former against the latter. The non-senatorial advocate Tuscilius Nominatus possibly underestimated such bias when he agreed to speak for the Vicetians in opposition to the application of a *praetorius* who wished to hold a weekly market on his estate near the town. At the last minute Nominatus panicked because his friends, as he later explained, "had advised him not to be too persistent in opposing the wishes of a

[88] Tac. *Ann.* 3.36 and 49-51; Plin. *Ep.* 3.9.29-33.
[89] Tac. *Ann.* 14.48-49.
[90] Tac. *Ann.* 3.66-69.
[91] *Ann.* 4.13; 13.42-43.
[92] That is, exile to Gyaros.
[93] Cf. Dio's account (57.22.5) of the comparable case against Aelius Saturninus, whose rank is unknown.
[94] Tac. *Ann.* 1.53.

senator (and especially in the senate), who was no longer fighting the case on account of the proposed market, but because his influence, reputation, and position were at stake."[95]

The charge on which senators were most frequently brought before the House by prosecutors of lower class was that of *repetundae*. In these cases members' bias in favor of defendants of their own kind was notorious. This is not the place to discuss the topic in detail.[96] But, in brief, prejudice was shown, for example, in a willingness to let favorable testimony of a general nature outweigh specific proof of misconduct (as at the trial of Julius Bassus in 103), and in the tendency to inflict comparatively light penalties. Such bias is undeniable, but it should not be thought overwhelming. Even from our incomplete evidence it is clear that at least into the early second century a notable number of *repetundae* cases was brought, and a proportion of convictions obtained which may seem surprising. Then there was no attempt to spare the defendants the embarrassment of public attention. In fact these hearings, like all senatorial business, attracted widespread interest.[97] The penalties imposed on condemned officials personally may too often have been light, but at the same time the senate could offer provincials positive help by remedying damage done. Thus Julius Bassus suffered a lesser penalty than the law prescribed, but his acts in Bithynia-Pontus were also annulled, and any defendant sentenced by him could apply for a re-trial within two years.[98]

For the hearing of such a case the House undertook to furnish one or more members as advocates on the provincials' behalf, if they requested it. Naturally no senator relished the commission to attack one of his fellows, nor expected to gain popularity by it. Pliny[99] tells us as much. Yet again his testimony—that of the only such advocate whose attitude we can assess in any depth—should warn us against too ready an assumption that members appointed to this task regularly rendered provincials a halfhearted service.[100] Pliny has been criticized for apparent lack of enthusiasm in helping his fellow advocate Herennius Senecio to ensure that, after conviction at their hands in 93, Baebius Massa did not recover his property

[95] Plin. *Ep.* 5.13.2.

[96] See P. A. Brunt, "Charges of provincial maladministration under the early Principate," *Historia* 10. 1961. pp. 189-227; P. Garnsey, *Social Status and Legal Privilege*, p. 103.

[97] Note Plin. *Ep.* 4.9.22, and his remarks about the consequences of the adjournment in the case against Marius Priscus (ibid. 2.11.10-11).

[98] Plin. *Ep.* 10.56.4. Cf. Fronto, *Ad M. Caes.* 3.21.1 = p. 52 H.

[99] *Ep.* 3.4.7-8. For what may be the same sentiment on the part of Fronto, see *Ad Am.* 1.15.3 = p. 174H, with E. J. Champlin, *Fronto and Antonine Rome*, p. 68.

[100] Note also the special help given to the Cilicians by Thrasea Paetus (even if he was not officially appointed their advocate) to secure the condemnation of Cossutianus Capito in 57 (Tac. *Ann.* 13.33; 16.21).

until compensation had been duly paid to the Baeticans.[101] The real need
for an urgent approach to the consuls in this instance, and the propriety
of advocates appointed by the senate taking such a step, can no longer be
assessed accurately; but it is plain enough that both were open to doubt.
Pliny's hesitations may well have been justified, while Herennius' initiative
perhaps sprang as much from his special concern for fellow countrymen
as from a cool appraisal of the needs of the case.

In any event, judgment should certainly not be passed on the general
quality of Pliny's conduct as advocate appointed by the senate without
reviewing the relevant evidence more fully. First, it should be remembered
that he had been willing to gain for the Baeticans their right to an *inquisitio*,
which Massa had presumably wanted to have omitted, proceeding at once
to assessment of damages without any proper hearing of the charges against
him.[102] Then, much more important is the way in which Pliny and Tacitus
handled the Africans' case against Marius Priscus. They were commissioned to lead this in 98-100. Since Priscus pleaded guilty, and applied
for damages to be assessed at once, it would have been easy for indifferent
advocates simply to acquiesce. But, despite all the special difficulties which
were certain to arise, Pliny and Tacitus insisted that the more serious
charges be heard, and carried their point, even securing extra time in which
to speak.[103] A year or so later, too, when commissioned to lead the Baeticans' case against Caecilius Classicus (now dead) and his accomplices,
Pliny took the trouble to break down the plea of "superior orders" which
the defense had considered unassailable.[104] Altogether it might be fair to
conclude that while the senate could be expected to show a certain favor
towards its own members charged with *repetundae* by provincials, at the
same time it did make a genuine effort to ensure that the prosecution case
would be put forward satisfactorily, and it was not likely to be blindly
prejudiced in its assessment. The major obstacle for provincial prosecutors
was never really the nature of their reception in the senate. Rather their
greatest difficulties would come earlier, in gathering evidence, witnesses,
money, and support to launch a case in the first place.

The senate's work as a court, like all its other activities during the
Principate, was significantly affected by the emperor, so that it is important
to determine the character and depth of his involvement in this sphere.
Although differences of attitude among individual rulers must be allowed
for, a valid general distinction may arguably be drawn between imperial

---

[101] P. Garnsey, *Social Status and Legal Privilege*, pp. 50-52.
[102] Plin. *Ep.* 6.29.8.
[103] Plin. *Ep.* 2.11.2-6 and 14; cf. 2.19.8 with Sherwin-White ad loc.
[104] *Ep.* 3.9.15-16 with Sherwin-White ad loc.

attitudes towards the two main types of case heard by the senate, namely *repetundae* and *maiestas*.

While most emperors felt a responsibility for the welfare of their subjects to a greater or lesser degree, cases of *repetundae* were unlikely to threaten their personal interest. So, not least for this reason, imperial interference with the senate's handling of these trials seems to have been rare. Admittedly Tiberius was present, and expressed an opinion, on four occasions when charges of *repetundae* were brought before the senate, but in each instance there was an associated charge of *maiestas*, and it was the latter which principally concerned him. Indeed at the trial of Granius Marcellus in 15 he acquiesced in the arrangement whereby the matter of *repetundae* should be referred separately to a panel;[105] and in 21 he reduced the harsh sentence proposed for C. Junius Silanus.[106]

Nero is the next emperor known to have exercised any influence in *repetundae* cases, but it would be hard to sustain a claim that he did so improperly. Evidently he favored acquittal of two former proconsuls of Africa tried in 58.[107] This was during the period when relations between himself and the senate were considered to be excellent, and there is no suggestion from Tacitus that he acted other than on the merits of both cases. Likewise in 59, when the matter was referred to him, he acquitted Acilius Strabo, a special legate sent to Cyrene by Claudius for adjudicating the title to land bequeathed to Rome by Ptolemy Apion. Almost certainly this prosecution was malicious, arising from Acilius' decision not to find in favor of the provincials, so that again no suspicion attaches to Nero's verdict.[108] Three years earlier, while deliberately postponing any verdict on P. Celer, procurator of Asia (charged presumably in the emperor's court), Nero had made no effort to interfere with the senate's condemnation of Cossutianus Capito, legate of Cilicia. At the same time it was apparently only by his own intrigues, not through any imperial favor, that Eprius Marcellus, legate of Lycia, avoided the same fate.[109] It is true that Nero did subsequently restore Capito to the senate, but only five years or so later, and under pressure from the latter's relative, Tigellinus.[110] Such a restoration was by no means unusual anyway.[111]

---

[105] Tac. *Ann.* 1.74.

[106] Tac. *Ann.* 3.68-69. The other cases were those of Cn. Calpurnius Piso and C. Silius A. Caecina Largus: see Appendix 9, nos. 3 and 6.

[107] Tac. *Ann.* 13.52. We are not told whether Nero was present in the House to give this opinion, or whether he reversed a contrary verdict by the senate.

[108] Appendix 9, no. 21.

[109] Appendix 9, no. 16.

[110] Tac. *Ann.* 14.48.

[111] See chap. 1 sect. 3.

In describing reactions to his attack upon the *delator* Publicius Certus in 97 Pliny makes a statement which could reflect upon the senate's conduct of *repetundae* trials during the Flavian period: "I had in fact freed the senate from the odium against it which raged among the other classes for showing severity to others while sparing its own members alone by a sort of mutual connivance."[112] This remark can hardly relate to trials for *maiestas* either in the early part of Nerva's reign (when we know that senators were convicted),[113] or under Domitian, when again there were convictions and a keen interest shown by the emperor. Equally, while in one sense it might fit the sentences imposed upon the two men charged with violating the Vestal Virgin, Cornelia—exile for the senator, Licinianus, public flogging for the *eques*, Celer—there is no certainty that either or both were tried in the senate; nor would it be at all accurate to think of Licinianus as spared by the mutual connivance of his fellow members.[114] Rather it is fair to take the remark as a reference either to trials for *repetundae* or on other, less common charges. Though we lack the specific evidence on which to test the claim,[115] it stands as an astonishing tribute to the independence of the senatorial court during the Flavian period. In Domitian's reign, especially, we should hardly have expected such freedom, not least because of his known enthusiasm for strict regulation of provincial government.

From the instances recorded by Pliny it would seem that the senate continued to decide *repetundae* cases free from imperial intervention under Trajan. Though he did happen to be present as consul at the trial of Marius Priscus during January 100,[116] he is not said to have influenced the proceedings. The circumstances in which he came to discuss Julius Bassus' case with him are not known; yet if by any chance there was an attempt by the latter to enlist the emperor's help, it evidently failed.[117] Later, in 107, Trajan pointedly refused to be drawn into a conflict between prosecution and defense over summoning witnesses prior to the trial of Varenus Rufus, proconsul of Bithynia. He would only intervene eventually when a further dispute arose among the Bithynian delegates over whether or not the prosecution should be abandoned.[118]

[112] *Ep.* 9.13.21.

[113] See Plin. *Ep.* 9.13.4, where I take "minores" to mean "less dangerous," not "non-senatorial" as Sherwin-White does; cf. Tac. *Hist.* 2.10.

[114] Plin. *Ep.* 4.11; cf. Suet. *Dom.* 8.

[115] The trial of Baebius Massa for *repetundae* is no help because of course he was condemned. But Pliny never drops any hint that Domitian had influenced the verdict or the moves made later (*Ep.* 7.33).

[116] Plin. *Ep.* 2.11.10. For discussion of the possibility that he had never really intended to be there, see chap. 5 sect. 2 note 67.

[117] Plin. *Ep.* 4.9.7.

[118] Plin. *Ep.* 6.13; 7.6 and 10.

Even for the reigns cited above our knowledge of *repetundae* cases is likely to be incomplete, and this precludes a confident assessment of how far the senate could judge them free of imperial intervention. Important related questions cannot be tackled either. For example, were there cases where the senate's verdict was deliberately framed to meet what the emperor's wishes were imagined to be, even if he had not expressed any opinion? Were plans to prosecute imperial legates ever abandoned before any hearing, because would-be prosecutors expected the emperor to protect his own subordinate? In both instances it is impossible to say, whatever we may suspect. Yet these problems aside, we may conclude that the surviving evidence does consistently show that the senate enjoyed remarkable freedom from imperial interference in deciding cases where *repetundae* was the principal charge.

Maiestas trials in the senate, however, show a different pattern. Here much did depend on the attitude of the emperor, which could show wide variation. Thus Pliny can say of the former *delator*, M. Aquillius Regulus, after his death in Trajan's reign: "today he could certainly have been alive without being a public nuisance, now that we have an emperor who would prevent him from doing harm."[119] In all *maiestas* cases the emperor could feel his own safety and interest to be at risk, so that he considered it important to make his views known. And there was no exception to the principle which we have seen to apply to all other types of senatorial business, namely, that he expected his views to be adopted. If they were not, then of course he had the power to veto or override any verdict of the House. It was a major tragedy of Tiberius' reign that he valued concern for seeing his wishes met in politically sensitive cases above his desire to encourage senatorial independence.[120] His vigorous pursuit of certain defendants harmed his reputation irreparably. But such attitudes differed little from those of many of his successors, so that the senate was seldom left free to decide charges of *maiestas* laid before it. To be sure, the character and extent of intervention by the emperor might vary considerably, but some such involvement was almost inevitable when many charges of *maiestas* were brought to him in the first instance, and only referred to the senate on his initiative. The same applied to other serious charges heard there. The emperor was naturally seen, too, as a higher authority by those defendants who chose to address appeals to him from condemnation by the senate, until this practice was forbidden by Hadrian.[121]

At one extreme the House could find itself simply required to condemn

---

[119] *Ep.* 6.2.4 with Sherwin-White ad loc.
[120] His interest extended to the *quaestiones* as well of course: Tac. *Ann.* 1.75; cf. 3.38.
[121] Tac. *Ann.* 6.5 and 9; 16.8; Dio 59.18.2; Ulpian, *Dig.* 49.2.1.2.

victims on the instructions of the emperor; this was too often its plight in the latter years of Tiberius and Nero, for example.[122] It may be agreed that among later emperors Domitian, Trajan, and Septimius Severus at least came in person on occasion to speak against those whom they charged with *maiestas*. Such oaths as the latter two had taken not to execute senators without trial could thus have been formally observed. But as contemporaries realized, their fulfillment was a mockery when the House was left with no choice but to condemn,[123] and when the same emperors might equally well choose to ignore their pledges on other occasions. At the other extreme we hear of Titus, Antoninus, M. Aurelius, and Pertinax, who all refused to execute senators, acting to prevent the House condemning any of its members to death.[124] Nerva's decision to inflict no severer punishment than exile upon the rebel Calpurnius Crassus was made upon the same principles and apparently provoked senatorial protest.[125]

An emperor might seek to preserve an impartial position. Claudius' aim in sitting on the benches during trials, for example, rather than on the tribunal with the consuls, was presumably to give the impression that his part in the hearing was to be no more than that of a *privatus*.[126] Intervention, too, could be motivated by the fairest of intentions. In particular, emperors could render useful service in dismissing outright charges which were notably trivial[127] or vindictive.[128] Likewise, it was in the interests of justice that Tiberius introduced a statutory ten-day interval between condemnation and execution after the senate's over-hasty disposal of Clutorius Priscus in 21.[129]

Imperial intervention was frequently on the side of mercy. Understandably enough, when a defendant committed suicide before the verdict, and emperors protested that they would have pleaded for leniency, contemporaries remained unconvinced—perhaps rightly so.[130] But there are many instances where emperors were sufficiently impressed by the defense to

[122] Note Dio 58.21.3; cf. 58.3.3; 79.5.1-2.

[123] Tac. *Agr.* 45; Suet. *Dom.* 11; Dio 67.4.5; 68.16.2; HA, *Sev.* 8.3. For Trajan's attitude to *maiestas* charges laid by others, note Plin. *Ep.* 10.82.

[124] Aur. Vict. 10.3-4 with Suet. *Tit.* 9; HA, *Antoninus* 7.3; *Marcus* 25.6; Dio 74.8.5. If the *Historia Augusta* (*Marcus* 10.6) is to be believed, M. Aurelius' approach to capital charges against any senator was to examine the evidence in private first, and only later to bring the case to a public trial.

[125] *Epit. de Caes.* 12.6.

[126] Dio 60.16.3. Compare Velleius' praise of Tiberius for hearing the case against Libo Drusus "ut senator et iudex, non ut princeps" (2.129.2).

[127] Tac. *Ann.* 3.70; 4.29; Dio 57.24.8; cf. Suet. *Nero* 39.

[128] Tac. *Ann.* 13.43.

[129] See no. 26 in list, chap. 15 sect. 5.

[130] Tac. *Ann.* 2.31; 3.50; 15.35.

have a case abandoned,[131] or to reduce the penalty. Seneca[132] was very thankful for Claudius' notable benefit in once begging mercy for him from the senate after conviction on a charge of adultery. The grounds on which emperors were inclined to mercy are not always clear. High rank may often have swayed them, as it did Claudius and Nero in the cases of Lollia Paulina and Asinius Marcellus respectively, for example, and perhaps Tiberius likewise in that of Appuleia Varilla.[133] On the other hand, it should be remembered that high rank was itself to become the cause of Nero's attacks on certain individuals.[134]

It is no surprise that we seldom find signs of independence on the part of the senatorial court in trials where the emperor had expressed a view. While it had sometimes sought to adjourn cases referred by Tiberius in order to postpone condemnation,[135] the more decisive dismissal of certain defendants referred by him near the end of the reign is unexpected,[136] as is Dio's remark (in Zonaras) that the senate "had not condemned"[137] others charged by Gaius. Later a rational attitude was shown in the refusal to allow any vendetta against Seneca's brother after the Pisonian conspiracy,[138] and in the reluctance to endorse vicious pursuit of those who had been *delatores* under Nero after that emperor's fall.[139]

But in general the senate looked to the emperor's wishes in deciding cases of *maiestas* and other serious crimes—matters frequently referred by him in the first place of course. His attitude was therefore of paramount importance, and the senate seldom sought to exercise judgment independently. The frequency with which defendants committed suicide before the completion of their hearing indicates how they might feel doomed in such circumstances. It was an exceptional success on Thrasea Paetus' part to persuade the House not to inflict upon Antistius Sosianus the harsh penalty which it was thought that Nero would favor.[140] The instant execution of Clutorius Priscus for an equally trivial offense was much more characteristic senatorial behavior. Altogether, in hearing *maiestas* cases the corporate body was generally willing to acquiesce in the one role open to it, that of protecting the emperor's interests and endorsing his wishes. The

---

131 Dio 57.21.2; 59.19.3-6.

132 *Cons. Polyb.* 13.2 with M. Griffin, *Seneca: A Philosopher in Politics*, pp. 59-60.

133 Tac. *Ann.* 12.22; 14.40; 2.50. See further P. Garnsey, *Social Status and Legal Privilege*, pp. 37-38.

134 Tac. *Ann.* 13.1; 15.35; 16.7; cf. [Seneca], *Octavia* 495-498.

135 See sect. 2 below.

136 Suet. *Tib.* 73; cf. Dio 58.27.3.

137 59.26.1.

138 Tac. *Ann.* 15.73.

139 Tac. *Hist.* 2.10; 4.42.

140 Note the consuls' paralyzed reaction to the vote (Tac. *Ann.* 14.49).

pressure which senators endured on these occasions can perhaps help to account for their leniency towards fellow members at *repetundae* trials, where the emperor seldom took a part.

2. Court Procedure

It has been stressed above that no formal distinction was drawn between those sessions where the senate was summoned to hear a case, and those where it considered business of a non-judicial nature. Many relevant aspects of procedure have been examined already in chapter 7, and this section will therefore be confined to the special features of trials.[1]

Since Rome lacked a public prosecutor, an accusation had to be brought by a private individual or group. The House itself seems to have acted through the president only in special circumstances arising from accusations first made in the customary way. Thus in 100 there was approval for the *sententia* of the consul designate that Marius Priscus' legate, Hostilius Firminus, be summoned to account for his conduct in Africa. He had never been formally charged, though his close involvement in the crimes of his proconsul emerged at Priscus' trial.[2] In 103 the request by Valerius Paulinus for action to be taken against Theophanes, the leading accuser of Julius Bassus, met with such favorable reaction that the consuls' failure to respond came as a surprise.[3] Yet two years later they did respond to the *sententia* of the praetor Licinius Nepos that Tuscilius Nominatus be summoned to account for his failure to act on behalf of the Vicetians as he had agreed.[4] However, if Dio's account is accurate,[5] the trial of the *delator* L. Priscillianus in 217 may be an unusual example of the senate itself deciding to lay a charge in the first instance.

Magistrates were not permitted to bring accusations in their own right,[6] although emperors might authorize exceptions and even encourage them.[7] Otherwise in the normal way an accuser (*delator*) would first approach a magistrate with authority to summon the senate, and would make an application (*postulatio*)[8] for leave to bring a prosecution, naming the accused.

[1] The topic is treated extensively by F. de Marini Avonzo, *La funzione giurisdizionale del senato romano*; and briefly by A.H.M. Jones, *The Criminal Courts of the Roman Republic and Principate*, pp. 110-113.
[2] Plin. *Ep.* 2.11.23-24 and 12.1.
[3] Plin. *Ep.* 4.9.20.
[4] Plin. *Ep.* 5.4.2-4 and 13.1.
[5] 78.21.3-5.
[6] Note Hadrian's ruling, *Dig.* 5.1.48.
[7] Tac. *Ann.* 3.66; 4.19; Suet. *Dom.* 8.
[8] Cf. Tac. *Ann.* 13.44; Plin. *Ep.* 5.13.1.

An accuser might be joined by one or more supporters (*subscriptor*).[9] In practice it was the emperor who was approached, or one or both consuls— and in the case of *repetundae* charges, always the latter. All had authority to reject applications if they saw fit,[10] and the emperor had further to decide whether or not he wished to refer the matter to the senate. Strictly speaking, charges against magistrates and holders of official posts, or those designated to them, were inadmissible unless the accused could be persuaded or forced to resign first.[11] But again exceptional instances are known.[12]

When leave was given to bring a charge of *repetundae*, the next step would be for the consuls to introduce the prosecutors before the House. A period for gathering evidence and summoning witnesses (*inquisitio*) would normally then be requested, and also the assignment of one or more senators to lead the case. It seems that the law required the granting of an *inquisitio*,[13] but that in practice an accused governor might seek to have one refused by admitting his guilt at once, and requesting the immediate appointment of a panel to assess the damages due. As we have noted already, Pompeius Silvanus was evidently successful in such a plea in 58,[14] but Pliny[15] was able to block a similar one by Baebius Massa when the latter was charged by the Baetici in 93. No doubt it was to prevent any "misunderstandings" that a few years later prosecutors from the same province specifically asked for the *inquisitio* in their case against Caecilius Classicus to cover not only the proconsul himself, but also his accomplices.[16] We hear of as much as a whole year being allowed for an *inquisitio*.[17]

The assignment of one or more senators as advocates for the prosecution, if requested, was likewise obligatory. Pliny[18] speaks of the lot being used, but it is clear that there could also be direct appointment by the House, especially when provincials indicated a preference. Unless legally exempt, no senator could refuse this assignment. Exceptionally, for the Bithynians' case against Varenus Rufus Pliny was appointed defense counsel. So far as we are aware such aid is unique, though Pliny himself mentions his

[9] Tac. *Ann*. 1.74; cf. 2.29, "libellos et auctores recitat Caesar."

[10] Note Tac. *Ann*. 4.21; 13.10.

[11] Venuleius Saturninus, *Dig*. 48.2.12; Dio 58.8.3; 59.23.8; 60.15.4; cf. Tac. *Ann*. 13.44; Dio 55.10.15.

[12] Tac. *Ann*. 4.22; 14.48 (but note the proposal that the praetor accused be deprived of his office before execution); Suet. *Dom*. 8; Dio 56.24.7; 57.21.2; 76.8.1.

[13] Plin. *Ep*. 6.5.2.

[14] Tac. *Ann*. 13.52.

[15] *Ep*. 6.29.8.

[16] Plin. *Ep*. 3.9.6.

[17] Tac. *Ann*. 13.43. Note how the case laid against Caesius Cordus in 21 was not heard until the following year (ibid. 3.38 and 70).

[18] *Ep*. 10.3A.2; see further chap. 10 sect. 3 note 14.

assignment without further remark.[19] If he and Varenus were already friends, perhaps the commission is adequately explained.[20]

It was evidently unusual for defendants to be held in custody before their appearance in the senate, or during it. When the majority were persons of rank, this is not surprising of course. It is understandable enough perhaps that Vibius Serenus, summoned from exile to stand trial for plotting rebellion in 24, should have been kept in chains,[21] and that supporters of Sejanus were jailed after their patron's fall. But it is remarkable, and unexplained, that Asilius Sabinus was imprisoned at the same time, before standing trial for misconduct while accompanying a proconsul of Crete and Cyrene.[22] Tacitus[23] mentions two senators charged with support of Sejanus who were bailed by their brothers while awaiting trial.

Once an accusation had been accepted for hearing in the senate, the normal procedure was for a date to be fixed and for the defendant to be informed of the charges. We find the majority arguing for proper observance of these arrangements on an occasion in 69 when there was pressure to condemn out of hand a vicious *delator*.[24] But the House was not always so scrupulous. Not only did it agree to try the hated Baetican, Norbanus Licinianus, for collusion while the case against Caecilius Classicus and his accomplices was still to be completed, but it also refused him any advance notice, or a statement of charges.[25] In 66 it seems that Thrasea Paetus had to ask Nero for the charges laid against himself.[26] To arrange a hearing and to summon witnesses would take some days at least, so that a defendant could usually count on this amount of notice.[27] But no details of practice in individual cases are known, nor can we say whether there was a recognized minimum interval between notification of charges and the hearing itself. Republican *quaestiones* had allowed nine or ten days.[28]

Once an accuser, or his advocate, had embarked on a case, he was not permitted to abandon it. This issue, and related matters, came to be covered by the *SC Turpillianum* of 61.[29] A defendant, on the other hand, while

---

[19] *Ep.* 7.6.3.

[20] In writing of this episode Pliny certainly portrays Varenus as a friend (*Ep.* 6.13.1, "Varenus meus"; cf. 7.6.3). But whatever their earlier relationship, it cannot have been close enough either for Pliny to offer his services in the first place, or for Varenus to seek them direct with any success.

[21] Tac. *Ann.* 4.28.

[22] Seneca, *Controv.* 9.4.19-21; cf. Dio 58.15.2; Tac. *Ann.* 6.19.

[23] *Ann.* 5.8.

[24] Tac. *Hist.* 2.10.

[25] Plin. *Ep.* 3.9.29-33.

[26] Tac. *Ann.* 16.24.

[27] Cf. Tac. *Hist.* 2.10.

[28] Cf. Cic. *Ad Q. Fr.* 2.12.2 = SB 16; Asconius, *In Cornelian.* p. 59 C; Plut. *Cic.* 9.

[29] No. 60 in list, chap. 15 sect. 5. Cf. Tac. *Ann.* 4.29; *Hist.* 4.44; Plin. *Ep.* 5.4 and 13.

receiving a summons, did not necessarily have to be present for the hearing to go forward. Thus Thrasea Paetus and Paconius Agrippinus chose not to appear when their cases were heard in 66.[30] By contrast, when Marius Priscus failed to appear for trial in late 99, a consular's request that the case be adjourned to await his presence was upheld.[31] Other defendants left before a verdict was reached,[32] some of them to commit suicide. In certain exceptional instances the accused was not offered the opportunity to appear and make a defense.[33] Cases of *repetundae* and *maiestas* could even be brought against a dead man's estate.[34] So in 65, although Antistius Vetus had committed suicide when no more than notice to prosecute him for *maiestas* had been given, the case was heard all the same.[35] Similarly, Caecilius Classicus died while the case against him was still only in its preliminary stages; but the Baeticans persisted with their prosecution, a right not exercised in a *repetundae* case for a long time previously, according to Pliny.[36]

There never seems to have been any comprehensive statute which governed the conduct of hearings. In practice sundry legal provisions were often observed, but equally they might be overridden. The session would open with a reading of the charges.[37] The president or the emperor might then make some comments relating to the case, as Tiberius and Nero did at the trials of Piso and Thrasea Paetus respectively.[38] When more than one charge had been laid, at this opening stage a decision might next have to be taken on whether they were to be heard together or separately. At the trial of Appuleia Varilla in 17, for example, Tiberius asked that the charges of adultery and *maiestas* be given separate consideration.[39] For *repetundae* cases at least, observance of the legal limits upon time permitted to prosecution and defense might be expected, though there was no difficulty in setting them aside. We know that the time limit for the prosecution was extended in Marius Priscus' case, while it seems that for the trial of Julius Bassus each side received double the allowance which Pliny speaks of as prescribed by law.[40] The convention in other cases is obscure, but

[30] Tac. *Ann.* 16.34; Epictet. 1.1.28-31.
[31] Plin. *Ep.* 2.11.9.
[32] Note Dio 58.4.6.
[33] Dio 58.3.3; 67.4.5; 76.8.1.
[34] Modestinus, *Dig.* 48.2.20; Paulus and Marcianus, *CJ* 9.8.6 pr.-2; only within one year of death, according to Scaevola, *Dig.* 48.11.2.
[35] Tac. *Ann.* 16.11.
[36] *Ep.* 3.9.6.
[37] Note Tac. *Ann.* 2.29; Dio 60.16.3.
[38] Tac. *Ann.* 3.12; 16.27.
[39] Tac. *Ann.* 2.50.
[40] *Ep.* 2.11.14; 4.9.9; in general see further chap. 6 sects. 2 and 4, and Appendix 5.

we certainly find Tiberius as president arranging the limits for each side at the trial of Piso.[41]

The recognized manner in which cases were heard in the senate was taken over from the *quaestiones*: prosecution and defense in turn presented their complete cases, and only afterwards was evidence heard, both oral and written. Many prosecutions were of course conducted by the professional *delatores* who brought them. Otherwise it was normal for advocates to be engaged by either side, but not obligatory. It was an indication of Julius Bassus' concern that he went to the lengths of engaging three consulars, if not four, in his defense.[42] By contrast, Libo Drusus in 16 and C. Silanus in 22 were to be pitied since no one would defend them,[43] while Varenus Rufus, as we have seen, evidently gained a defense counsel only because the senate commissioned Pliny to act for him. Pliny[44] implies, too, that Hostilius Firminus spoke for himself when summoned to account for his conduct as Marius Priscus' legate. In Tacitus' substantial account there is no record of any attempt at defense on behalf of Thrasea Paetus (who did not even attend himself), while at the same time Barea Soranus and his daughter seem to do no more than interrupt the prosecution with passionate pleas.[45] At her trial in 20 Plancina was another defendant who deliberately chose to make no defense. But Cossutianus Capito, charged with *repetundae* in 57, only abandoned his plea in the face of determined accusers.[46]

On the prosecution side a number of Greeks among the provincial delegations bringing *repetundae* cases were eager to speak in person alongside the advocates assigned by the senate.[47] Magistrates in office might not wish to act as advocate, and they were exempt from compulsion in *repetundae* cases. But there was no formal ban on their advocacy. The reservations expressed by Pliny about this activity on the part of tribunes seem to spring from the special character of that magistracy's traditional

---

[41] Tac. *Ann.* 3.13.

[42] See Plin. *Ep.* 4.9 with Sherwin-White ad loc. The rank of Lucceius Albinus is not known, although it has been reasonably enough conjectured that he was consular by this date (*PIR*² L 355; F. Zevi, *La Parola del Passato* 34. 1979. p. 200).

[43] Tac. *Ann.* 2.29; 3.67.

[44] *Ep.* 2.12.1.

[45] *Ann.* 16.31-32.

[46] Tac. *Ann.* 3.17; 13.33.

[47] Quintilian, *Inst. Or.* 6.1.14; Plin. *Ep.* 4.9.3 and 14 (Theophanes); 5.20.4. H. Halfmann (*Die Senatoren*, no. 44) identifies Theophanes as the senator and ex-quaestor of Bithynia/Pontus, M. Pompeius Macrinus Neos Theophanes. But even allowing for prejudice, the contemptuous, hostile tone which Pliny adopts in writing of him makes the equation seem very dubious.

role. He himself almost certainly accepted the commission to prosecute Baebius Massa while still praetor in 93.[48]

From our meager evidence on the point, it seems that for the presentation of a case each side could divide up the time allotted as it chose. The initiative lay with the prosecution, which naturally opened the proceedings. If they so desired, its advocates could speak in turn, using up at a single stretch the whole time allotted to their side. Tacitus indicates that this was the pattern adopted in the case against Piso in 20.[49] There must have been a comparable arrangement at the trial of Julius Bassus in 103. Though Pliny never states the point, the president had evidently directed here that the major charge against Bassus, that of taking "presents,"[50] should be contested first, with consideration of the other charges to follow. At each stage two prosecution speeches in succession were followed by two for the defense. For their case against Caecilius Classicus and his accomplices, Pliny and Lucceius Albinus seem to have considered a similar plan, namely, that each would make one long speech encompassing all the defendants. But in view of the complications of the case, and the variety of defendants, they wisely abandoned any such scheme in favor of taking each defendant one by one.[51] More precise details of how they did this are not reported. Yet we do know that a similar method—of taking each charge separately— was resorted to for the prosecution of Libo Drusus after his accusers could not agree on which of them would otherwise lead at the trial.[52] The arrangements in the case against Marius Priscus were different again.[53] Here Pliny led off for the prosecution, to be followed by two speeches for the defense. Then Tacitus spoke for the prosecution, and there was a final speech for the defense. Speeches again alternated from each side in early 107 when the Bithynians objected to Varenus' unprecedented application for the extra-legal right to summon defense witnesses from the province, and the senate ordered an immediate hearing on the issue. Pliny led off for Varenus. There followed a speech for the Bithynians; then another for Varenus; and last came a second speech for the Bithynians.[54]

After each side had made its case, there followed the *probatio*, where

[48] See *Ep*. 1.23 and 7.33 with Sherwin-White ad locc., and his Appendix IV. In general, the claim by R. A. Bauman, "Tiberius and Murena," *Historia* 15. 1966. pp. 420-431, that no magistrate in office was permitted to act as accuser in any court is too rigid, as appreciated by S. Jameson, "22 or 23?" *Historia* 18. 1969. pp. 204-229.

[49] *Ann*. 3.13.

[50] *Ep*. 4.9.5.

[51] Plin. *Ep*. 3.9.9-11.

[52] Tac. *Ann*. 2.30.

[53] Plin. *Ep*. 2.11.14-18.

[54] Plin. *Ep*. 5.20; 6.29.11. It is important to appreciate that this *cognitio* concerned only whether or not Varenus be permitted to summon witnesses from the province.

evidence was produced.[55] Written documents were admissible, such as the
accounts and correspondence of Caecilius Classicus,[56] or the letters which
both Tiberius and Piso might have produced at the latter's trial, though
neither would do so.[57] Written statements made by absent witnesses were
equally admissible, even if the testimony was extracted by torture.[58] However, Livia's friend Urgulania was thought astonishingly presumptuous for
only testifying to a praetor sent to her home, when she could have attended
the senate in person.[59] No doubt she was nervous of the fact that witnesses
who testified in person were open to cross-questioning by either side.[60] In
repetundae cases the prosecution enjoyed the right to summon witnesses
from the province,[61] but the defense did not. Varenus Rufus broke entirely
new ground when he sought this privilege in 107, and it is no surprise that
his application proved such a bone of contention.[62]

It would be misleading to leave the impression that proceedings were
always completed without interruption, when our surviving evidence shows
clearly enough how they might be broken up by holidays[63] or by adjournments for one reason or another. Time could be requested to gather more
evidence,[64] for example, or for a harassed defendant to consider his position.[65] Marius Priscus' trial was adjourned while he was "informed" of
the need for him to make a defense.[66] The lengthy postponements in the
case against Julius Bassus heard during Vespasian's reign are unexplained.[67] The emperor himself might request a delay;[68] equally the president might introduce one in order to postpone an inevitable condemnation.[69]

After each side had put its case and evidence had been heard, the
president sought members' opinions in the customary fashion examined in

[55] Plin. *Ep.* 2.11.18; 4.9.15; cf. Tac. *Ann.* 16.32.
[56] Plin. *Ep.* 3.9.13.
[57] Tac. *Ann.* 3.14 and 16.
[58] Tac. *Ann.* 2.30; 3.14 and 67; 4.29; 6.47; cf. 3.22; Dio 76.8.2; and in general P. Garnsey, *Social Status and Legal Privilege*, pp. 213-216.
[59] Tac. *Ann.* 2.34.
[60] Note Plin. *Ep.* 3.9.24, "tam multi testes interrogandi sublevandi refutandi"; 7.19.5, where it remains obscure whether Fannia is being questioned as witness or accomplice.
[61] Cf. Plin. *Ep.* 2.11.5 and 8; 3.9.29.
[62] Plin. *Ep.* 5.20; 6.5 and 13; 6.29.11.
[63] Tac. *Ann.* 3.23; *Hist.* 4.10 and 40; Plin. *Ep.* 2.11.10.
[64] Perhaps Plin. *Ep.* 5.4.1.
[65] Tac. *Ann.* 3.67; cf. 6.48; Dio 57.18.10.
[66] Plin. *Ep.* 2.11.9-10. Sherwin-White (*Pliny*, p. 166) suggests that after condemnation by a panel Priscus could no longer attend the House without a summons. But one would surely have been issued for the hearing. It seems more likely that Priscus was deliberately absent.
[67] Plin. *Ep.* 4.9.1.
[68] Tac. *Ann.* 6.9.
[69] Tac. *Ann.* 4.66; perhaps 5.8; Suet. *Tib.* 61. Contrast Dio 58.27.3-5.

chapter 7. A single *sententia* would cover both verdict and sentence. Finally, in the light of the decisions reached, accusers were commonly rewarded or charged.[70] In Pliny's description of the case against Caecilius Classicus and his accomplices it remains uncertain whether judgment was passed in this way immediately after the hearing against each set of defendants was completed, or whether it was held over for all until the end. The former arrangement is suggested by Pliny's reference to verdict and sentence immediately after his descriptions of each of the first two hearings. But of course in correspondence this arrangement would be a natural choice to facilitate his readers' understanding of a complicated case. Later, by contrast, he refers,[71] not to a series, but to a single *senatus consultum*, in which a variety of sentences was passed, and the prosecution congratulated on its meritorious conduct of the case.

As Hadrian affirmed,[72] a verdict by the senate was final. There could be no appeal to the emperor.

In short, it is plain that trials were conducted before the House in accordance with many of the recognized conventions of Roman judicial practice. But the senate's wider powers and functions did offer the opportunity for flexibility in certain circumstances, and this was exercised, though it was by no means always to the advantage of defendants.

---

[70] While there were legal provisions for rewards (Tac. *Ann.* 4.20 and 30; Suet. *Nero* 10), these might not necessarily be followed of course: cf. Tac. *Ann.* 6.47; 16.33; *Hist.* 4.42.

[71] *Ep.* 3.9.22-23.

[72] *Dig.* 49.2.1.2.

17

CONCLUSION: THE CHANGING ROLE
OF THE SENATE

For all the value which can be attached to an examination of individual aspects of procedure and function such as has been attempted here, the need to see the senate's role and its general development in broader perspective will still be felt. A conclusion may undertake such a review in brief, thus drawing together some of the principal themes of this study.

Despite the efforts made by Augustus to restore dignity to the senate, and to elevate members and their relatives by forming them into a new, leading social class, it was reasonable enough for contemporaries to fear that his approach in other respects was certain all too soon to condemn the corporate body to insignificance. For the senate Augustus' reign may be represented as a period of painful, and in many ways unwelcome change, forming part of a wider constitutional transition. Not only were there three *lectiones senatus* to be endured; in addition the reign saw the codification of procedure in the *Lex Julia de senatu habendo*, and the institution of a *consilium* to prepare business. Above all, there encroached the influence of the emperor himself, "edging ahead step by step, drawing into his own hands the functions of senate, magistrates and the law," as Tacitus[1] summarized it. The senate was indeed permanently deprived of certain major functions, most notably oversight of foreign policy, together with military and financial affairs. Then the crowning blow fell in 13 when all decisions of the reformed senatorial *consilium* were granted authority equal to that of the corporate body itself.

The outlook for the latter could thus hardly have seemed more unpromising on Augustus' death. It would have been easy enough for the *consilium* to perpetuate indefinitely a temporary arrangement made in deference to a sick, aged emperor. Yet Augustus' successor, Tiberius, contrary to all expectation, introduced a decisive improvement in the senate's prospects, and for this he deserves the full recognition which Tacitus[2] in particular

[1] *Ann.* 1.2.
[2] His praise (*Ann.* 4.6) is confined to the earlier part of the reign.

would deny him. On his accession the *consilium* was soon abolished, and the primacy of the corporate body reasserted, despite discreet warnings against such openness from Augustus' confidant, C. Sallustius Crispus.[3] During the first twelve years of the reign—prior to Tiberius' retirement to Capri—no ruler could have proved more assiduous in attending the House and consulting it. It must have been with his approval, too, that within the same period elections to magistracies were transferred here, and regular judicial sessions were instituted. This is not to deny that supreme authority remained firmly in Tiberius' hands, or that the relationship between himself and the corporate body continued a tense one in many respects, with a marked deterioration caused by the emperor's absence from Rome after 26 and the crises of the final years of the reign. All this is incontrovertible. Nonetheless, the nature of the role which Tiberius had encouraged the senate to assume set a pattern for the future which was not to be radically modified by any of his successors for well over a century and a half. In particular, during that span there was never to be any question of the full House once again resigning prerogatives to a smaller group or council. Instead it continued to vote honors and to maintain its regular exercise of legislative, religious, diplomatic, and judicial functions broadly defined. Thereby the prospect of rapid decline into insignificance was averted. Even if much business was dull or uncontentious, the level of corporate activity still remained high, so that sessions could prove frequent and time-consuming. All the same, they were well attended. Imperial interest or interference might too often obtrude upon the senate's work, in some instances overwhelmingly, in others tragically, yet its involvement with the spheres outlined did persist throughout. It continued to be recognized everywhere as the symbol of the *respublica*, the major institution in the state which transcended individual rulers. Each emperor on his accession sought its approval and support. Moreover, the majority of his advisers continued to be senators, and all but a few of the highest official posts throughout the empire—legionary legateships, provincial governorships, the great administrative prefectures—were likewise assigned exclusively to them. As individuals, therefore, senators' supremacy and importance were assured.

It may be claimed, then, that Tiberius reversed the prospect of a damaging decline in the scope and nature of business to be handled by the corporate body. Thus it was all the more unfortunate that at the same time there should be developing a different threat to its vigor, in the form of a fall in the hereditary element among the membership. In a disturbing number of families fathers were not followed into the House by sons. The mere number of members was kept up by introducing not only further

---

[3] Tac. *Ann.* 1.6.

Italians, but also provincials. Claudius specially encouraged Westerners, the Flavians Easterners. Thereafter the proportion of provincial senators continued to climb. For the future of the corporate body, however, the attitude which all such new entrants adopted towards their status and obligations was of greater concern than mere numbers. Carelessness or indifference could do serious harm. In fact such fears proved ungrounded, and as it turned out, the new entrants served to strengthen the corporate body rather than weaken it. They became proud upholders of senatorial dignity, tradition, and procedure. It could well be claimed that their enthusiastic contribution in significant measure enabled the House to maintain the vigor which during the first half of the first century it had seemed in danger of losing.

A marked decline in the activities of the corporate body is discernible only during the second century. Even then the impact of change is uneven, and attempts to trace just how or why it came to occur when it did in any particular area are persistently baffled by lack of evidence. But diplomatic approaches do seem to falter from around the middle of the century, and a reduction in judicial activity apparently sets in too. By contrast, some detailed civil legislation continues to be passed right into the early third century. In general, less business appears to be brought forward by anyone except the emperor. The jurists' citation of imperial *orationes* from Hadrian's reign onwards as law in their own right is possibly a reflection of that trend, though the significance of this particular practice may not in itself warrant undue stress, when the wishes of all emperors had regularly been accepted, and when full *senatus consulta* did continue to be drawn up on at least some such occasions. Much more disturbing perhaps were occasions of a different character, when discussion of imperial proposals was now severely curtailed, or when a series of them came to be ratified merely by a single, brief decree. In addition, while the emperor did thus continue to put forward business, two more developments served to set him further apart than ever from the corporate body. First, his increasing absence from Rome for long stretches demanded that he communicate by letter rather than in person. Then, more generally, the contemporary tendency to exalt the figure of the emperor into a lofty, godlike being affected the senate no less than other institutions, so that the obstacles to rational consideration of his business became stronger than ever.

The quest to identify a single "turning point" in the development of a state or institution may rightly be considered a futile undertaking in many instances, calculated to mask the slowness and complexity of change. The caution applies with full force to the history of the senate's decline during the Principate. But with hindsight the death of Marcus Aurelius in 180 does stand out as a crucial event in this connection. For beyond that date, as time came to show, the senate could never again resume the role which it had more or less consistently followed ever since the reign of Tiberius over a century and a half before. During the latter part of that span in particular, every emperor had striven to gain the respect of the House and its partnership in rule. Yet Marcus' son and successor, Commodus, proved careless of government and hostile to the corporate body and its members, showing none of his father's special concern to consult them.[4] Later Septimius Severus, secure only after four years of unrest in which many senators had opposed him, had neither reason nor inclination to re-create the old pattern. To be sure, he and his successors did bring certain business before the House, informed it of their doings, and looked for its support. But altogether its activities remained notably diminished. Individual members in their turn, like the rest of society, suffered from the military and economic pressures of an unstable period, while at the same time they had to witness an increasingly important part in the administration of the empire being entrusted to *equites*. As it was, for senators to have been assigned the substantial number of newly created posts would in any event have required first an increase in the total membership of the corporate body, unchanged since Augustus' day. Not surprisingly, the Severan emperors seemed averse to contemplating an initiative of that nature. It is true that the events of 238 did show that the senate could still display courage and high ideals in a crisis, despite all it had suffered. But this year marks the end of an era. Ahead lay a new, obscure age of unprecedented strife, where the dignified civil assembly of the Roman senate would be of small account.

[4] Compare no. 125 in list, chap. 15 sect. 5, with J. Reynolds, *Aphrodisias and Rome*, no. 16, the latter being the decision of Commodus alone about a request which his father could well have been expected to bring before the senate.

APPENDICES

Appendix 1. Latin and Greek Terms
for the Senate and Senators

In Latin a senator is usually termed *senator*, and the corporate body *senatus*. The senatorial order may simply be *ordo senatorius*, but it also came to be indicated specifically by the superlative *amplissimus ordo*.[1] The latter term was used further as an alternative to *senatus*; both are even written by Trajan with the same meaning within a single sentence.[2] Tacitus uses *ordo senatorius*,[3] but never *amplissimus ordo*; yet in a speech which he puts into the mouth of C. Cassius Longinus in 61 he has the latter refer to his presence "in hoc ordine" (that is, in the House).[4]

Of course various complimentary superlatives might always be used of senators, and it is impossible to determine when the choice of one in particular ceased to be accidental, and became deliberate and standardized instead. But by the early second century, if not before, *clarissimus/clarissima* (*vir, femina, puer*, etc.) was commonly reserved to denote a member of the senatorial class, male or female, of any age.[5] The title, which was not invariably used, might be written in full or abbreviated.

In the course of the second century *consularis* (ὑπατικός) came to be used as a title in its own right for consular governors of imperial provinces.[6]

---

[1] For example, Plin. *Ep.* 10.4.2; exceptionally Suetonius (*Vesp.* 9) speaks of senators and *equites* as "amplissimi ordines."

[2] Plin. *Ep.* 10.95; note also 8.6.13 (*senatus consultum* of 52); 10.3A and B; Suet. *Vesp.* 2.

[3] For example, *Ann.* 13.25.

[4] *Ann.* 14.43.

[5] For early instances in our period, note *FIRA*² I no. 45 II line 24 (A.D. 56); ibid. no. 59 lines 13-14 (A.D. 69); *ILS* 6106 lines 9 and 18-19 (A.D. 101); ibid. 2487 end; 9134 line 7 (A.D. 128); Martial, Book 9 pref.; Plin. *Paneg.* 90.3; *Ep.* 3.8.1; 7.33.8; 9.13.19; 10.56.2, 61.5, 77.1, 87.3; Vindolanda tablet inventory nos. 29 + 31 quoted in A. R. Birley, *The Fasti of Roman Britain*, p. 87. In a speech attributed to Asinius Gallus under 16, Tacitus (*Ann.* 2.33) uses "clarissimus quisque" of senators and *equites*. For discussion, O. Hirschfeld, "Die Rangtitel der römischen Kaiserzeit," in *Kleine Schriften*, pp. 646-681; M. Bang, Appendix 8 in L. Friedländer, *Darstellungen aus der Sittengeschichte Roms*, Vol. 4, 9/10 ed., Leipzig, 1921; H. U. Instinsky, "Formalien im Briefwechsel des Plinius mit Kaiser Trajan," Akad. der Wiss. und Lit., Mainz, *Abhandlungen geistes- und sozialwiss. Klasse*, 1969, no. 12, pp. 12-22 (limited value); A. Chastagnol, "Les femmes dans l' ordre sénatorial: titulature et rang social à Rome," *Rev. Hist.* 262. 1979. pp. 3-28.

[6] See H. J. Mason, *Greek Terms for Roman Institutions*, pp. 169-171; A. R. Birley, loc. cit. in previous note.

More generally, at the same time snobbery led to wives of men who attained the consulship being specially styled *consularis femina* (ὑπατική). Not surprisingly, grave offense was taken when the slave mother of Elagabalus' bedfellow, Hierocles, was brought to Rome and accorded this rank[7]—all the more so because, according to Ulpian,[8] while wives of consulars enjoyed it, general opinion was that the distinction did *not* extend to their mothers. As we might expect,[9] the title is rare on inscriptions found in the West,[10] but common enough on those from Asia Minor.[11] There would seem to be no cases of the relatives of less senior senators following this practice. Problems of precedence might still remain. Ulpian could raise the delicate question of whether a *vir praefectorius* outranked a *consularis femina* or vice versa.[12] Elsewhere he explains how it had occasionally been known for a woman previously married to a *consularis*, yet later to a man of lesser dignity, to petition the emperor to retain her former rank: Caracalla allowed Julia Mamaea to do this.[13] In other cases apparently a consular couple would not end their marriage, even when they had lived apart for a long time;[14] possibly the wife was loath to lose her rank. At the end of our period we find Severus Alexander reassuring Severiana, a lady otherwise unknown, that because her grandfather had been *consularis*, her father *praetorius*, and she herself had married into the senatorial class, there was no question that she did remain *clarissima*.[15]

At sessions the president addressed individual senators by name, as did senators each other.[16] Otherwise a speech was addressed, not to the president alone (as we could have expected), but to the whole House. The ancient title *patres conscripti* was regularly used (abbreviated *p.c.*),[17] except possibly by an occasional foreigner.[18] Tacitus[19] comments on the untimely formality of the title when used by the town council of Mutina

---

[7] Dio 79.15.2.

[8] *Dig.* 1.9.1.1.

[9] See further chap. 2 sect. 6 note 96.

[10] See *ILS* 1166 (Asculum, Italy); 1200 (Taksebt, Mauretania); *CIL* II. 1174 (Hispalis, Baetica); II. 4129 = G. Alföldy, *Die römischen Inschriften von Tarraco*, Berlin, 1975, no. 137.

[11] See, for example, *IGRR*, indices, s.v. ὑπατική.

[12] *Dig.* 1.9.1 pr. The man was superior, he thought.

[13] *Dig.* 1.9.12 pr.

[14] Ulpian, *Dig.* 24.1.32.13.

[15] *CJ* 12.1.1.

[16] Plin. *Ep.* 9.13.9 and 19. Note that both members here are addressed only by their *cognomen*, not *praenomen* and *cognomen*, which was formal Republican usage: on the latter see further J. N. Adams, "Conventions of naming in Cicero," *CQ* 28. 1978. pp. 145-166, esp. 154 and 157-158.

[17] Note Quintilian's disapproval of a witty play on the title (*Inst. Or.* 8.5.20).

[18] Note how Josephus (*AJ* 19.242) has Herod address the House as ὦ βουλή in 41.

[19] *Hist.* 2.52.

towards the group of Othonian senators who were stranded and fearful of the future after that emperor's suicide in April 69. In his *Metamorphoses*[20] Apuleius pointedly recalls a session of the senate, among other ways by having the president Jupiter address the assembled gods as "dei conscripti." Authors, and poets in particular, may term senators *patres*. But the singular *pater conscriptus* does not seem to have been in use.

In Greek the formal, official translation of *senatus* is σύγκλητος.[21] Though the word is in origin an adjective, it is commonly used alone, except in second- and third-century authors (Herodian in particular), who may choose to use σύγκλητος βουλή.[22] Other terms for the senate in use among authors of our period are βουλή, συνέδριον, γερουσία. These especially appealed to authors who sought to reproduce pure Attic style and vocabulary.[23] Most notably, Dio uses all three indiscriminately, while rigidly eschewing σύγκλητος.[24] In the sections where his text is fully preserved, the latter term occurs just once in the form σύγκλητος βουλή, though συγκλητικός is also used once in a passage which (as he tells us) is specifically meant to be verbatim translation of a remark made in Latin.[25]

The noun *senator* and adjective *senatorius* are most commonly translated συγκλητικός.[26] As an alternative, derivatives from the other Greek nouns mentioned were in use. Josephus is simply inaccurate when he uses εὐπατρίδαι to denote all senators, rather than just patricians.[27]

Appendix 2. The Appropriate Capital for a Senator

In Duncan-Jones' view, eight million HS is the sum which "contemporary sources sometimes indicate as an appropriate capital for a senator."[1] Though most probably sheer accident, it is true that the fortune of Voconius Ro-

---

[20] 6.23.

[21] On this term and all others cited here, see more fully D. Magie, *De vocabulis sollemnibus*, pp. 4-6 and 43ff.; H. J. Mason, *Greek Terms for Roman Institutions*, pp. 121-124.

[22] For its occasional occurrence in documents too, note *AE* 1977. 801 line 13 (M. Aurelius and Commodus); Ulpian, *Dig.* 16.1.2.3 (Septimius Severus); J. Reynolds, *Aphrodisias and Rome*, no. 22 line 5 (Gordian III).

[23] Note, for example, the choice of γερουσία in Ael. Aristid., *To Rome* 90.

[24] See G. Vrind, *De Cassii Dionis vocabulis quae ad ius publicum pertinent*, The Hague, 1923, esp. p. 5; on Dio's style in general, F. Millar, *A Study of Cassius Dio*, pp. 40-46.

[25] 78.16.5; 63.15.1. Among Dio's epitomators, however, Xiphilinus was not so fastidious: note σύγκλητος in 77.3.3, where by contrast Petrus Patricius uses βουλευτήριον.

[26] In the bilingual regulations concerning the provision of transport for official use by Sagalassus in Pisidia early in Tiberius' reign the Greek text omits phrases contained in the Latin on a number of occasions. Among these it is interesting that τοῖς συνκλητικοῖς is considered adequate rendering of "senatori populi Romani" (S. Mitchell, *JRS* 66. 1976. pp. 107-108 = *SEG* 26. 1976/7. no. 1392 lines 17 and 41).

[27] For example, *BJ* 2.212-213.

[1] *Economy*, p. 18; cf. p. 242.

manus, for whom Pliny[2] sought the *latus clavus*, might be in this range: he had been given four million HS by his mother, had inherited his father's estate and had been adopted by his stepfather. But to estimate the capital appropriate for any senator from the grants of annual income made by Nero and Vespasian, as Duncan-Jones does, may be an unsound procedure. The figure of 500,000 HS for such grants is indeed mentioned, which would imply capital of around eight million HS at 6%—a reasonable enough expectation. Yet 500,000 HS was perhaps a maximum reserved for the most distinguished, rather than the modest sufficiency which Duncan-Jones takes it to be. It approaches the annual income of 600,000 HS which in Cicero's view would permit a life of luxury.[3] Suetonius says that Nero ". . . granted to the most distinguished of the senators who were without means an annual salary, to some as much as 500,000 HS."[4] More specifically, Tacitus[5] cites an annual grant of 500,000 HS made by Nero to his colleague as *consul ordinarius* in 58, Valerius Messalla, of illustrious family. By contrast, no figure is cited for the grants likewise made to the less distinguished pair, Aurelius Cotta and Haterius Antoninus, at the same time. Of Vespasian's generosity Suetonius says that "he made up the census of senators, supporting needy ex-consuls with 500,000 HS annually."[6]

From the figures known, the gifts made by Augustus and Tiberius would have yielded nowhere near so high an income. Augustus merely made up to the minimum census, and gave 200,000 HS extra when he was feeling generous.[7] He bestowed one million HS upon young M. Hortalus;[8] the same amount was granted by Tiberius to a *praetorius* in 15.[9] According to Velleius, Tiberius' policy was "to raise the census of senators . . . but in such a way as not to encourage luxurious living, nor yet to allow senators to lose their rank because of honest poverty."[10]

Unquestionably a senator with capital of eight million HS would have been comfortably off, and it may be that this level of wealth was needed for a *consularis* to live in style. But there is no reason to think that capital of the same order was a suitable "minimum" for any senator. A variety of evidence cited in chapter 2 section 3 shows how many members in fact could not meet obligations which should hardly have bothered anyone with

[2] *Ep*. 10.4.
[3] *Stoic Paradoxes* 49.
[4] *Nero* 10.
[5] *Ann*. 13.34.
[6] *Vesp*. 17.
[7] Suet. *Aug*. 41; Dio 54.17.3; 55.13.6.
[8] Tac. *Ann*. 2.37.
[9] Tac. *Ann*. 1.75.
[10] 2.129.3.

that sum. Furthermore, if the capital required to support any senator really was eight million HS, most members with families would have been faced with a crushing burden, and the number of sons following their fathers into the House would have been even lower than it actually was. A father's modest hope of retaining his own membership of the senate, preparing for, say, one son to follow him,[11] and endowing one daughter might then cost a minimum of eighteen million HS, if the dowry were a mere two million HS.[12] Even for the highest class in the empire, these figures are unrealistic as minima. While many members were indeed very wealthy by any standard, others lived close to the census qualification. Unfortunately our sources never indicate what "adequate" capital for a senator might be, not least perhaps because so much would depend upon personal taste and circumstances. We may only note that the seven million HS gained by Aquillius Regulus from his activities as *delator* during the last years of Nero's reign are implied to be an ample fortune for a *quaestorius* who had inherited next to nothing from his father.[13]

Appendix 3. The Date on Which Proconsuls Began Their Year of Office

Pliny[1] tells of a quaestor returned from abroad and present in the senate during the third quarter of 105. Likewise, as Sherwin-White comments, Pliny's own absence from Rome and the news that a quaestor has died on his way home both point to, though do not prove, a date in late summer for *Ep*. 5.21—and thus a midsummer changeover of proconsuls. Otherwise further clear evidence relating to the time when they took up their posts is lacking. We do not even know whether there was a standard time throughout the senatorial provinces, or whether practice varied, say, according to the length of the journey. The former alternative is implied by the speaker of the *sententia prima* about reducing the cost of gladiatorial games c. 177 in a passage which might be used to argue that it was delivered at a meeting in the earlier, rather than the later, part of the year. Here he advocates: "Let the *viri clarissimi* who went out as proconsuls a short

[11] Of course a son would frequently be entering the House while his father was still active as a member: see, for example, Plin. *Ep*. 6.26.1; 7.24.3; *ILS* 1061 lines 10-13. For a father helping his son with the expenses of being a senator, note Scaevola, *Dig*. 5.3.58.

[12] We lack information on the amount of dowry brought by senators' daughters; but note how Tiberius contributed one million HS to the dowry of Domitius Pollio's daughter (Tac. *Ann*. 2.86). Likewise Martial (11.23.3-4; 12.75.8) and Juvenal (*Sat*. 6.137; 10.335-336) expect a wealthy bride to bring her husband this sum.

[13] Tac. *Hist*. 4.42.

[1] *Ep*. 4.12 with Sherwin-White ad loc.

while ago be informed. . . ."[2] At the same time, given ancient traveling conditions, a smooth changeover every twelve months would be hard to achieve with clockwork precision, at least for the more distant areas. From time to time there were bound to be delays. No doubt men like C. Salvius Liberalis[3] and Fronto caused them by seeking to abandon or defer their governorship of Asia after election to it, while more generally Venuleius[4] indicates the many factors which could affect the time taken upon a voyage, say, from Rome to Ephesus. We should remember, too, that proconsuls would not invariably go to or from their provinces in what we might consider the shortest time or by the shortest route. Thus we know that in 107 Calestrius Tiro, proceeding to his proconsulship of Baetica, made visits to Ticinum and Mediolanum on the way, evidently taking a round-about land route at his own convenience.[5] So clearly he would have been away from Rome longer than absolutely necessary.

T. D. Barnes[6] rightly casts doubt upon the view of C. A. Behr[7] that 1 September was the date at which the governor of Asia would enter office in the second century. Logic alone makes a time so late in the year unlikely, when it would regularly leave the retiring governor with a hazardous journey back to Rome at the end of the sailing season. Yet as G. W. Clarke[8] indicates in turn, Barnes' own attempt to fix July as the start of the proconsular year in Africa remains insecure, since to generalize, as he does, from c. 193 of all times is risky. Equally, no conclusion can be drawn from Pliny's arrival in Bithynia on 17 September, since his was a special governorship.[9] It is a fair guess that by this date the previous governor had left, exceptional though this may seem; Pliny, at least, makes no mention whatsoever in *Letters*, Book 10 of his immediate predecessor, or of when he had gone.

Altogether it does appear justifiable to conclude that proconsuls began their year of office around midsummer, the most convenient season of the year for both incoming and outgoing staffs. But let it be stressed that the evidence for this conclusion remains thin as yet, and that we lack all knowledge of practice in detail.[10]

[2] *Hesperia* 24. 1955. p. 333 lines 53-54.
[3] *ILS* 1011.
[4] *Dig.* 45.1.137.2.
[5] Plin. *Ep.* 7. 16, 23, 32.
[6] *Tertullian: A Historical and Literary Study*, pp. 260-261.
[7] *Aelius Aristides and the Sacred Tales*, p. 79 note 2.
[8] *Latomus* 31. 1972. p. 1053 note 3.
[9] *Ep.* 10.17A. 2.
[10] The fact that Agricola arrived in Britain to take up his imperial governorship there "media iam aestate" can indicate no more than the convenience of this season. See Tac. *Agr.* 9.6 and 18.1; on the date (probably 78, after a suffect consulship at the end of 77), R. M. Ogilvie and I. Richmond, *Cornelii Taciti de Vita Agricolae*, Oxford, 1967, Appendix I; A. R. Birley, *The* Fasti *of Roman Britain*, pp. 73-81; and P. A. Gallivan, *CQ* 31. 1981. p. 189 note 23.

Appendix 4. The Attribution of Two Anonymous Speeches to the Senate Preserved on Papyrus

Millar[1] has questioned the attribution to Claudius of two speeches to the senate preserved on papyrus, and datable by their subject matter between 37 (or 41) and 61.[2] Neither speaker is identified in the document. But if, as has been persuasively suggested, he was a single individual and an emperor, then Claudius does remain the best choice for this period. Yet it is unusually awkward to attribute or deny any speech to him of all people on grounds of (say) style or tone, when we know how these could vary so erratically in his case. Among members, it is possible that Thrasea Paetus, for example, would lecture his fellow senators with the vigor which certain passages reveal.[3] Yet a copy of an emperor's speeches is more likely to have been preserved.[4] Unfortunately we do not know who took this copy, nor why, nor can we fix the stage in the debate at which either piece came.

In the latter connection interest naturally centers around the second, more fully preserved speech. It could have come after the *sententia prima*, with the crowning rebuke referring to the lack of originality already displayed on this occasion: "For, Conscript Fathers, it is most unbecoming to the high dignity of this order here that one member only, the consul designate, should deliver a *sententia*, and that drawn word for word from the *relatio* of the consuls."[5] On this reading these remarks would clearly gain point. Yet equally the speech could be either the explanation after the *relatio*, or the *sententia prima* itself, with the same rebuke referring to no more than general practice in the senate at the time.[6]

To learn the stage at which the speech came would indeed be interesting, although this detail still might hardly help towards identification of the speaker, since an emperor or magistrate could intervene at any stage in debate.[7] However, due weight has perhaps not been attached to the offer of extra time to consider the proposals;[8] etiquette would hardly have permitted anyone other than the emperor, or a president himself delivering the explanation after the *relatio*, to make such a striking concession. Al-

---

[1] *Emperor*, p. 350 note 59.

[2] R. Cavenaile, *Corp. Pap. Lat.* 236 = *FIRA*[2] I no. 44 (with bibliography).

[3] Cf. especially col. II lines 11-18; col. III lines 10-22.

[4] See chap. 9 sect. 3.

[5] Col. III lines 18-21, "Mini[me] enim dec[o]r[um] est, p.c., ma[iestati] huius or[di]nis hic un[um ta]ntummodo consule[m] designatum [de]scriptam ex relatio[n]e consulum a[d ver]bum dicere senten[tia]m."

[6] Note Tac. *Ann.* 6.2 (A.D. 32).

[7] See chap. 7 sect. 19.

[8] Col. III lines 13-14.

together Millar has rightly warned that attribution of the speech to Claudius cannot automatically be assumed. On the other hand, the identification perhaps has more to commend it than he allows, and it remains plausible.

Appendix 5. The Duration of Hearings in the Cases of Marius Priscus and Julius Bassus

We know from Pliny[1] that the trial of Marius Priscus, begun during autumn 99, resumed the following January, and in all likelihood during the latter part of that month, when there would have been approximately 9½ to 10 hours of daylight.[2] At least this notion does fit with Pliny's account, from which it would seem that on both days members may have been spared having to continue sitting up to the absolute limit of time available. On the first day he opened himself with a prosecution speech of about five hours,[3] which included one extra hour specially permitted to him. This amount of time was gained by first combining half the prosecution's allowance of six hours with the one extra hour, and then arranging that the water clocks either be filled especially full, or be allowed to run a little slower than normal.[4] Next followed a speech by the first of the three defense counsel. We are not told its length, but Pliny does explain that there was still time left free afterwards, though not enough to make it possible for another advocate to complete a speech before nightfall. Three hours would thus be a reasonable conjecture for the length of the speech (so that the House sat for 9 to 9½ hours altogether), and would also square with the likelihood that the nine hours allotted to the defense were divided equally between its three advocates. On this basis we may envisage the two remaining defense counsel taking up six hours altogether on the following day, with a three-hour speech by Tacitus (completing the prosecution's six hours) in between. Certainly the suggestion that the House again sat

[1] *Ep.* 2.11; see further in general chap. 16.

[2] See Appendix 6.

[3] He writes consistently in terms of "hours" measured by water clocks. I have taken these to be standard periods of effectively the same length as our hour today, not the Roman hours which varied in length according to season. See J. Marquardt, *Das Privatleben de Römer* (ed. 2), Leipzig, 1886, p. 257; in general O. Neugebauer, *A History of Ancient Mathematical Astronomy*, Berlin/Heidelberg/New York, 1975, Part 3 Book VIA.

[4] While Pliny's adjective "spatiosissimus" (*Ep.* 2.11.14) might be interpreted in either sense, the result is the same. I have assumed that there were four water clocks to the hour, not three. The latter possibility will hardly serve. Pliny's "12 water clocks" must then represent four of the six hours allowed to the prosecution, with the "4 water clocks" amounting to 1 hour 20 minutes specially granted yet not fully used. In addition, it is unlikely that the time allowance for the prosecution would have been arranged to give Pliny four hours and his senior Tacitus only two. For their relationship, see R. Syme, *Tacitus*, pp. 112-114.

for something over nine hours on this second day matches Pliny's points that none of the speakers had to cut short his words, but that it did not seem worth beginning the examination of witnesses until the third day.

After the case against Julius Bassus had been presented,[5] Baebius Macer, who took up a suffect consulship on 1 April 103,[6] spoke as consul designate, and since he is not likely to have been elected earlier than January of the same year,[7] the hearing must have taken place within those limits. In fact we should be able to fix it with greater accuracy. There were evidently two sets of charges against Bassus, and it seems to have been arranged that prosecution and defense should both be allowed the standard amount of time—six hours for the former, nine for the latter—for each charge. On the first day two prosecution advocates put their full case for the first set of charges. Pliny then started to reply for the defense, but was interrupted by nightfall after 3½ hours. Allowing for preliminaries therefore, and an interval between successive speakers, there would seem to have been, say, 10 to 10½ hours of daylight. The next day we know that Pliny and a fellow defense advocate opened with speeches of 1½ and 4 hours respectively, thus rounding off the defense's allowance for the first set of charges. They were followed by two prosecution advocates who evidently used up their side's entire allowance of six hours for the second set of charges that day, though only by gaining permission to continue after sunset—perhaps by an hour or more if there were 10 to 10½ hours of daylight at this season. Then on the third day the defense's full allowance of nine hours for the second set of charges must have been used up, leaving only 1 to 1½ hours of daylight. At least on such a view it is easy to see why the examination of witnesses was held over until the fourth day. Altogether, therefore, this hearing required the House to sit for approximately 10 to 10½, 11½, and 9 hours on three successive days, with one, or possibly two, further days to hear witnesses and reach a verdict. No wonder that Pliny was pleased by the freshness of members' attention at the start of the second day! The supposition that there were 10 to 10½ hours of daylight must put the trial in late January or the first three weeks of February.

Appendix 6. Times of Sunrise and Sunset at Rome[1] and Hours of Daylight

These figures are the same for antiquity as for today. The times for sunrise

---

[5] Plin. *Ep.* 4.9.
[6] *Fast. Ost.*
[7] See chap. 6 sect. 4 note 58.
[1] Latitude 41 degrees 55 minutes and 19.2 seconds North.

and sunset refer respectively to the first and last rays of sunlight. Local geography can cause a few minutes' variation, and allowance must be made for this.

The Gregorian calendar is used here. During the first century A.D. the Julian calendar is two days ahead (thus, for example, 21 March Julian = 19 March Gregorian); during the second century one day ahead; in the third century there is no difference between the two calendars. Calendar differences have been ignored in making the calculations in chapter 6 and appendix 5.

Date		Sunrise	Sunset	Daylight (hours and minutes)
Jan.	5	7:28	16:43	9:15
Jan.	10	7:28	16:48	9:20
Jan.	15	7:26	16:53	9:27
Jan.	20	7:23	16:59	9:36
Jan.	25	7:20	17:05	9:45
Jan.	30	7:16	17:11	9:55
Feb.	4	7:10	17:18	10:08
Feb.	9	7:04	17:25	10:21
Feb.	14	6:58	17:31	10:33
Feb.	19	6:51	17:37	10:36
Feb.	24	6:44	17:44	11:00
March	1	6:36	17:49	11:13
March	6	6:28	17:55	11:27
March	11	6:20	18:01	11:41
March	16	6:11	18:07	11:56
March	21	6:03	18:13	12:10
March	26	5:54	18:18	12:24
March	31	5:46	18:24	12:38
April	5	5:37	18:30	12:53
April	10	5:29	18:35	13:06
April	15	5:20	18:41	13:21
April	20	5:13	18:46	13:33
April	25	5:06	18:51	13:45
April	30	4:58	18:57	13:59
May	5	4:51	19:03	14:12
May	10	4:45	19:08	14:23
May	15	4:40	19:13	14:33
May	20	4:35	19:18	14:43
May	25	4:31	19:23	14:52
May	30	4:28	19:27	14:59
June	4	4:25	19:31	15:06

Date		Sunrise	Sunset	Daylight (hours and minutes)
June	9	4:24	19:34	15:10
June	14	4:23	19:37	15:14
June	19	4:23	19:39	15:16
June	24	4:25	19:40	15:15
June	29	4:27	19:40	15:13
July	4	4:29	19:39	15:10
July	9	4:32	19:38	15:06
July	14	4:36	19:35	14:59
July	19	4:40	19:32	14:52
July	24	4:45	19:27	14:42
July	29	4:50	19:22	14:32
Aug.	3	4:54	19:17	14:23
Aug.	8	5:00	19:11	14:11
Aug.	13	5:05	19:04	13:59
Aug.	18	5:10	18:56	13:46
Aug.	23	5:16	18:49	13:33
Aug.	28	5:20	18:41	13:21
Sept.	2	5:26	18:33	13:07
Sept.	7	5:31	18:25	12:54
Sept.	12	5:36	18:16	12:40
Sept.	17	5:41	18:07	12:26
Sept.	22	5:47	17:58	12:12
Sept.	27	5:52	17:50	11:50
Oct.	2	5:58	17:41	11:43
Oct.	7	6:03	17:32	11:29
Oct.	12	6:09	17:24	11:15
Oct.	17	6:14	17:16	11:02
Oct.	22	6:20	17:08	10:48
Oct.	27	6:26	17:02	10:36
Nov.	1	6:32	16:55	10:23
Nov.	6	6:38	16:49	10:11
Nov.	11	6:44	16:43	9:59
Nov.	16	6:51	16:38	9:47
Nov.	21	6:56	16:35	9:39
Nov.	26	7:02	16:32	9:30
Dec.	1	7:08	16:29	9:21
Dec.	6	7:13	16:29	9:16
Dec.	11	7:18	16:28	9:10
Dec.	16	7:22	16:29	9:07
Dec.	21	7:25	16:31	9:06
Dec.	26	7:27	16:34	9:07
Dec.	31	7:28	16:38	9:10

Appendix 7. The Behavior of M. Aquillius Regulus at the Trial of Marius Priscus

An incident in the *interrogatio* at the trial of Marius Priscus is puzzling:[1] the consular Pompeius Collega[2] delivered a *sententia* along lines suggested to him by a number of members, principally M. Aquillius Regulus, and then was disgruntled afterwards when these associates did not support him in the vote. Why did Regulus seek to have his opinion conveyed through another, rather than deliver it himself? A definite answer cannot easily be given, especially when his status is uncertain, and the identity and motives of the other associates are altogether unknown. Regulus is never securely attested as more than *quaestorius*, in 70.[3] If he really had never proceeded further by 100,[4] sense may be made of his behavior at the trial. Assuming that we can trust Pliny's assurance in *Panegyricus* 76.2, even as a junior senator Regulus would definitely have been asked for his *sententia* on this occasion. But it was natural to reckon that a fresh proposal made towards the end of the *interrogatio* would come too late to make an impact on the House. To achieve their end therefore, Regulus, Pompeius, and their associates possibly felt that the best course would be for the proposal to be put by the highest-ranking member of their group—Pompeius, as it happened (cos. ord. 93). This notion offers a sound explanation of why he agreed to voice Regulus' opinion for him, and may illustrate a tactic otherwise never mentioned for our period, whereby a junior senator could secure a better hearing for his views than he could achieve himself.

Unfortunately, however, our earlier examination of the senatorial career and of all members known to have eschewed advancement[5] makes it impossible to credit that a man of Regulus' talent, ambition, and distinguished ancestry[6] had not climbed to the consulship—and no doubt well ahead of Pompeius too.[7] If Regulus would thus have been called to speak earlier of the two, it seems a mystery that he asked Pompeius to make his proposal for him, and that the latter accepted. Regulus may conceivably have been

---

[1] Plin. *Ep.* 2.11.20-22.

[2] M. Lambertz, *PW* 21 s.v. Pompeius no. 73, col. 2269.

[3] Tac. *Hist.* 4.42.

[4] As Sherwin-White, *Pliny*, p. 171, believes.

[5] Chap. 1 sect. 2.

[6] For the possibility, see R. Syme, *Tacitus*, p. 101.

[7] Syme (*Tacitus*, p. 102) places great weight on the question put by Regulus' attacker in 70 as prophetic: "et quem adhuc quaestorium offendere non audemus, praetorium et consularem ausuri sumus?" (Tac. *Hist.* 4.42). But there is no need. For judicious rejection of the specific conjecture that Regulus was consul in 93, see R. Syme, *Roman Papers* I. p. 259.

concerned at the offense he might give personally, though such worries evidently did not hold him back on other occasions, and in any case the proposal here was less severe than that of the consul designate. So the puzzle remains. While it is worth stressing again that of course Pliny's account does not give us the full story, at least we can still appreciate how Regulus' contemporaries so often found him an enigma.

Appendix 8. Proconsuls Known to Have Served Extended Terms

DURING THE REIGNS OF AUGUSTUS AND TIBERIUS

Africa:

Cossus Cornelius Lentulus, procos.	II (A.D. 5-7 or 6-8)
L. Nonius Asprenas	III (12-15 or 13-16)
L. Apronius	III (18-21)
Q. Iunius Blaesus	II (21-23)
C. Vibius Marsus	III (27-30)

Asia:

Potitus Valerius Messalla	II (20's B.C.?)
C. Vibius Postumus	III (about A.D. 13-16?)
M. Aemilius Lepidus	II (26-28)
P. Petronius	VI (28-34 or 29-35)

Crete with Cyrene:

P. Viriasius Naso	III (in Tiberius' reign, after the fall of Sejanus: *ILS* 158)

Unknown province:

Fulvius (?)	III (probably under Tiberius: *AE* 1976. 121)

LATER IN THE FIRST CENTURY

Africa:

Q. Marcius Barea Soranus, procos.	II (41-43)
Ser. Sulpicius Galba	II (44-46 or 45-47)
M. Pompeius Silvanus Staberius Flavinus	III (53-56: *AE* 1968. 549)

Asia:

T. Clodius Eprius Marcellus	III (70-73)

If M. Griffin (*Seneca: A Philosopher in Politics*, p. 91 n. 2) is correct in doubting the attribution to Eprius of acephalous *CIL* XIV. 2612, then we would have another contemporary of Claudius who governed Asia for three years.

Bithynia/Pontus:
M. Plancius Varus   II (under Vespasian: H. Halfmann, *Die Senatoren*, no. 80)

Crete with Cyrene:
C. Arinius Modestus   II (73-75?)
possibly also Caesernius Veiento   II (46-47: see W. Eck, *Zephyrus* 23/24. 1972/3. p. 246, conjecturing from *AE* 1951. 207)

For further documentation, see the lists of proconsuls cited in Bibliography 2.

Appendix 9. Table of *Repetundae* Cases

The table starting on p. 507 presents a summary of cases heard in the senate where *repetundae* was among the charges (though not necessarily the most important one). Whenever the court is not specified by the sources, it has been assumed that senators would be tried before the House, officials of lower rank before the emperor. For earlier lists of similar type, see P. A. Brunt, *Historia* 10. 1961. pp. 224-227; J. Bleicken, *Senatsgericht und Kaisergericht*, pp. 158-166.

Appendix 9

No.	Province from which charge was made	Defendant(s)	His office	Date of trial	Source	Verdict on charge of repetundae	Notes	On defendant see further
1	Asia	L. Valerius Messalla Volesus	Proconsul	c. 13	Tac. Ann. 3.68; cf. Seneca, De Ira 2.5.5	Condemned		R. Hanslik, PW 7A s.v. Valerius no. 270 cols. 170-171
2	Bithynia	M. Granius Marcellus	Proconsul	15	Tac. Ann. 1.74	Unknown		PIR² G 211
3a	Tarraconensis	Cn. Calpurnius Piso	Legate	20	ibid. 3.13	Committed suicide before sentence	"Ancient, pointless" charge, says Tacitus	PIR² C 287
b	Syria	Cn. Calpurnius Piso	Legate	20	ibid. 3.14		Uncertain whether repetundae relating to Syria was made one of the charges	
4	Asia	C. Junius Silanus	Proconsul	22	ibid. 3.66-69	Condemned		PIR² I 825
5	Crete/Cyrene	Caesius Cordus	Proconsul	22	ibid. 3.38 and 70	Condemned		PIR² C 193
6	Upper Germany	C. Silius A. Caecina Largus and wife	Legate	24	ibid. 4.18-20	Condemned		A. Nagl, PW 5A s.v. Silius no. 12 cols. 74-77
7	Asia	C. Fonteius Capito	Proconsul	25	ibid. 4.36	Acquitted	Charge uncertain	PIR² F 470
8	Moesia	Pomponius Labeo and wife	Legate	34	ibid. 6.29; Dio 58.24.3	Committed suicide before trial		R. Hanslik, PW 21 s.v. Pomponius no. 51 col. 2340
9	Crete/Cyrene	Asilius Sabinus and Turdus	Comites proconsulis	In Tiberius' reign, after fall of Sejanus	Seneca, Controv. 9.4.19-21	Unknown	Charge uncertain	PIR² A 1213

No.	Province from which charge was made	Defendant(s)	His office	Date of trial	Source	Verdict on charge of repetundae	Notes	On defendant see further
10	Pannonia	C. Calvisius Sabinus	Legate	39	Dio 59.18.4	Committed suicide before trial	Charge uncertain	PIR² C 354
11	Bithynia	C. Cadius Rufus	Proconsul	49	Tac. Ann. 12.22; Hist. 1.77	Condemned		PIR² C 6
12	Africa	T. Statilius Taurus	Proconsul	53	Tac. Ann. 12.59	Committed suicide before verdict		A. Nagl, PW 6A s.v. Statilius no. 37 cols. 2205-2207
13	Unknown	Lurius Varus	Consular post	Well before 57	ibid. 13.32; perhaps Suet. Otho 2	Condemned	Charge uncertain	PIR² L 428
14	Crete/Cyrene	Cestius Proculus	Proconsul	56	Tac. Ann. 13.30	Acquitted		PIR² C 695
15	Cilicia	Cossutianus Capito and Numitor (or Tutor?)	Legate	57	Tac. Ann. 13.33; 14.48; 16.21; Quintil. Inst. Or. 6.1.14; Juvenal, Sat. 8.92–94	Condemned		PIR² C 1543
16	Lycia	T. Clodius Eprius Marcellus	Legate	57	Tac. Ann. 13.33	Acquitted		PIR² E 84 with AE 1956. 186
17	Asia	P. Suillius Rufus.	Proconsul	58	ibid. 13.43	Condemned		M. Fluss, PW 7A s.v. Suillius no. 4 cols. 719-722
	A subsequent attempt to prosecute Suillius' son on the same charge was vetoed by Nero.)							
18	Africa	Q. Sulpicius Camerinus	Proconsul	58	ibid. 13.52	Acquitted	Charge uncertain	F. Miltner, PW 7A s.v. Sulpicius no. 30 cols. 745-746

No.	Province	Name	Charge	Date	Source	Outcome	Note	Reference
19	Africa	M. Pompeius Silvanus Staberius Flavinus	Proconsul	58	ibid. 13.52	Acquitted		B. E. Thomasson, *PW* Suppl. 9, s.v. Pompeius no. 116a cols. 862-863, and W. Eck, Suppl. 14 cols. 437-438
20	Crete/Cyrene	Pedius Blaesus	Proconsul	59	ibid. 14.18; *Hist.* 1.77	Condemned		W. Eck, *PW* Suppl. 14, s.v. Pedius no. 3a col. 375
21	Cyrene	L. Acilius Strabo	Special legate	59	Tac. *Ann.* 14.18	Acquitted	Charge uncertain	*PIR*² A 82
22	Bithynia	M. Tarquitius Priscus	Proconsul	61	ibid. 14.46	Condemned		M. Fluss, *PW* 8A s.v. Tarquitius no. 9 cols. 2394-2395
23	Unknown	Paquius Scaevinus	Unknown	Before 69	Tac. *Hist.* 1.77	Condemned	Name uncertain	
24	Crete/Cyrene	(M.?) Antonius Flamma	Proconsul	70	ibid. 4.45	Condemned		H. Halfmann, *Die Senatoren*, no. 7
25	Bithynia	C. Julius Bassus	Quaestor	Under Vespasian	Plin. *Ep.* 4.9.1	Acquitted	Charge uncertain	*PIR*² I 205 = H. Halfmann, *Die Senatoren*, no. 19
26	—	Aedile charged by tribune		Under Domitian	Suet. *Dom.* 8	Unknown		
27	Baetica	Baebius Massa	Proconsul	93	Plin. *Ep.* 6.29.8; 7.33	Condemned		*PIR*² B 26
28	Baetica	Gallus?	?	97-98?	ibid. 1.7 with Sherwin-White ad loc.	Unknown	Name and charge uncertain	Cf. *PIR*² G 59

No.	Province from which charge was made	Defendant(s)	His office	Date of trial	Source	Verdict on charge of repetundae	Notes	On defendant see further
29	Africa	Marius Priscus	Proconsul	100	ibid. 2.11 and 19.8; 6.29.9; 10.3A.2	Condemned		F. Miltner, *PW* 14 s.v. Marius no. 59 cols. 1836-1837
30	Africa	Hostilius Firminus	Legate of proconsul	100	ibid. 2.11. 23-24 and 12	Condemned		*PIR*² H 225
31	Baetica	Caecilius Classicus and accomplices	Proconsul	100 or 101	ibid. 3.4 and 9; 6.29.8	Condemned posthumously; accomplices variously treated		*PIR*² C 32
32	Bithynia	C. Julius Bassus	Proconsul	103	ibid. 4.9; 6.29.10; 10.56.4	Condemned	Charged with *repetundae* and other crime(s) not clarified by Pliny (see esp. *Ep.* 4.9.5 and chap. 16 sect. 2 note 50 above)	No. 25 above
33	Bithynia	Varenus Rufus	Proconsul	107	ibid. 5.20; 6.5, 13 and 29.11; 7.6 and 10	Uncertain whether case ever proceeded beyond preliminary stages		R. Hanslik, *PW* 7A s.v. Varenus no. 7 cols. 375-376
34	Spanish province	Cornelius Priscianus	Governor	145	*Fast. Ost.*	Unknown	Charge uncertain	*PIR*² C 1418
35	Bithynia	Unknown	Proconsul?	Under Antoninus Pius	Fronto, *Ad Am.* 1.14. 2-1.15 = pp. 173-174 H	Condemned?		E. J. Champlin, *Fronto and Antonine Rome*, pp. 67-68
36	Noricum	Pollenius Sebennus	Legate	c. 205	Dio 76.9.2-3	Condemned		C. Wolff, *PW* 21 s.v. Pollenius no. 5

Appendix 10. The Roman Senate in Rabbinic Literature

Not only is Rabbinic literature vast; its value and reliability are often difficult to estimate. Yet it does contain a variety of references to the Roman senate. These need to be assessed with caution. On inspection, some seem to reflect no more than a pedantic desire to exhibit knowledge of the technical term σύγκλητος, while others are merely a play upon words.[1] In at least one instance in the Babylonian Talmud[2] specific mention of the senate turns out to be no more than a modern gloss. Thus the unexplained "it" which the emperor "Antoninus" was to ask to appoint his son "Asverus" to reign in his place may conceivably mean the senate, but there can be no certainty.

Though it does still raise some difficulties, the most valuable Rabbinic reference of all to the senate occurs in the *Midrash Rabbah*[3] and merits quotation:

Once our Rabbis R. Eliezer, R. Joshua and R. Gamaliel were in Rome when the senate issued a decree that within thirty days no Jew should be found in the world. Now one of the emperor's senators was a God-fearing man, and he came to R. Gamaliel and disclosed to him the decree. Our Rabbis were in great distress, but that God-fearing man said to them: "Do not be distressed; within thirty days the God of the Jews will arise to help them." At the end of twenty-five days he revealed the decree to his wife, and she said to him: "Look, twenty-five days have already gone." He replied to her: "There are still five days left." Now his wife was even more righteous than he, and she said to him: "Have you not a ring?[4] Suck it and die, and the sitting of the senate will be suspended for thirty days, and the decree will not come into force." He followed her advice and sucked his ring and died.

The visit to Rome of the four rabbis, all of whom are known to have been active in the late first and early second centuries, is frequently alluded to in Rabbinic literature, and it seems reasonable enough to follow those modern authorities who date it more precisely to the period of Domitian's hostility towards Jews during the 90's.[5] Though senatorial activity against them is never cited elsewhere, it is still credible. To be sure, the senate would hardly have gone to the extreme of decreeing the wholesale expulsion of Jews from the Roman world, as the hostile tradition represents;[6] but the

---

[1] For example, the equation of "senators" with "enemies" in Midrash Rabbah, *Genesis* 67.8.

[2] *'Abodah Zarah* 10a. For discussion of the identification of this emperor and his son, see E. M. Smallwood, *The Jews under Roman Rule*, pp. 485-486 and 490 note 14.

[3] *Deuteronomy* II. 24. The Soncino translation is followed both here and below.

[4] Sc. containing poison.

[5] See E. M. Smallwood, *The Jews under Roman Rule*, pp. 383-384.

[6] Compare in the Christian tradition the alleged decree no. 163 in list, chap. 15 sect. 5.

imposition, say, of some ban upon Jewish practices would be by no means unprecedented.[7]

The belief that the death of a senator would lead to automatic suspension of senatorial activity for thirty days, followed by deferment or even abrogation of a decree due to come into effect, is a curious one. It is amplified somewhat in the Babylonian Talmud:[8]

> It has been taught: When Turnus Rufus[9] the wicked destroyed the Temple, R. Gamaliel was condemned to death. A high officer came and stood up in the Beth-Hamidrash and called out: "The Nose-man is wanted, the Nose-man is wanted." When R. Gamaliel heard this, he hid himself. Then the officer went up secretly to him and said: "If I save you, will you bring me into the world to come?" He replied: "Yes." He then asked him: "Will you swear it to me?" And the latter took an oath. The officer then mounted the roof and threw himself down and died. Now there was a tradition [among the Romans][10] that when a decree is made and one of their own [leaders] dies, then that decree is annulled.[11]

The fact is that this practice as represented by the two Rabbinic passages was no part of Roman senatorial procedure, and it is difficult to see how it ever came to be imagined. Just possibly, however, there has been confusion with the obligatory interval of at least ten days imposed between the passage of some or all senatorial decrees and their deposit in the *aerarium Saturni* (and thus their enforcement). Pseudo-Quintilian does indeed record the interval as thirty days, rather than ten. Whatever the precise range of measures to which this compulsory delay applied, death sentences were certainly among them,[12] so that the rabbinic writers' confusion may arise thus. Yet no matter how that point is explained, the credibility of an anti-Jewish *senatus consultum* is unaffected, and it is the latter which stands out as the most valuable material in the passages cited.[13]

[7] Cf. chap. 12 sect. 4 note 12.

[8] *Ta 'anith* 29a.

[9] That is, Q. Tineius Rufus, legate of Judaea during Bar Cochba's revolt in the 130's: see E. M. Smallwood, *The Jews under Roman Rule*, pp. 449 and 550.

[10] A modern gloss, but entirely in keeping with the context.

[11] Glossed by the celebrated mediaeval commentator Rashi: "They regard the death as a punishment for the evil decree."

[12] See further chap. 9 sect. 1 note 4 and no. 26 in list, chap. 15 sect. 5.

[13] I should like to thank my colleagues D.R.G. Beattie and D. W. Gooding for their expert advice in connection with this Appendix.

EXTENDED NOTES

A (chap. 1 sect. 1)

I have broadly accepted here the account of Augustus' restriction upon the wearing of the *latus clavus* put forward by A. Chastagnol, *Rev. Hist. Droit* 53. 1975. pp. 375-394, which rests upon Dio 59.9.5 and Suet. *Aug.* 38. In seeking to dismiss Chastagnol's view, R. P. Saller, *Patronage under the Early Empire*, p. 51 note 58 has rightly drawn attention to Dio's hint of uncertainty and the possibility of interpreting Suetonius' reference more loosely. It may be, too, as he suggests, that Dio has misunderstood his source in some way. All the same, I am not fully persuaded to reject out of hand his testimony on this aspect of the senatorial career, a topic by no means obscure or uninteresting to him. As it is, a restriction upon the wearing of the *latus clavus* could fit well enough with Augustus' wider attempts to define and exalt a senatorial class, and to encourage sons of senators to follow their fathers into the House. This particular method may have turned out short-lived, a fate comparable with the failed attempt to impose fines upon members who missed meetings, for example, or the abandoned plan to reduce the senate to 300 members: yet the restriction might be one of the experiments and changes which we know Augustus to have been making. There remains the point—on which both A. Chastagnol, *Historia* 25. 1976. pp. 253-256 and Saller are agreed—that Suetonius' account (*Vesp.* 2) of Vespasian's early career reads anachronistically. But this need not be taken to show that there was never any restriction imposed by Augustus. Conceivably it had already long been ignored in practice by the 30's, even if its abandonment was only taken to be indisputably sealed by Gaius' grant of the *latus clavus* to a whole group of *equites* in 38.

B (chap. 3 sect. 2)

The claim has been made by F. Dvornik that in their arrangements for seating and procedure, among other matters, church councils followed the practice of the Roman senate. Thus where the latter's practice is unknown, as in the matter of seating, some light might conceivably be shed by later ecclesiastical practice. This opens up a large topic which it would not be appropriate to treat here. But a note of caution must be struck on a number of points. First, it is unfortunate that Dvornik omits to support all his arguments with detailed evidence. Then, while church practice certainly did reflect general Roman influence, the degree of imitation in detail is to be doubted, and the many significant differences between church councils and the senate borne in mind. Finally, even if the records of church councils do reveal their exact seating arrangements, the validity of deducing the Roman senate's practice from such later evidence would still seem highly questionable. See F. Dvornik, "The authority of the state in the oecumenical councils," *The Christian East* 14. 1933. pp. 95-108, sect. III; idem, "Emperors, popes, and general councils," *Dumbarton Oaks Papers* 6. 1951. pp. 3-23, esp. pp. 4 and 18 = *Photian and Byzantine Ecclesiastical Studies*, London, 1974, XV.

C (chap. 3 sect. 2)

In his description of a meeting in 238 Herodian (7.11.3) puzzlingly states that the altar of Victory was inside the door round which the populace was crowding; only those brave spirits who crept beyond the altar could gain a clear impression of the proceedings. If it had always been situated thus, it is curious that no earlier writer should ever have mentioned it as an obstacle to spectators on the threshold of the House, especially when tradition had always required that they be permitted to observe sessions from there. Are the doors referred to by Herodian here actually the rear ones, if these were a feature of the Curia Julia, as they are of Diocletian's reconstruction? (They would doubtless prove convenient, but they cannot have been essential. As we gather from the alterations ordered by Agrippina at Tac. *Ann.* 13.5, there were none in the chamber on the Palatine where the senate met often enough during the Julio-Claudian period.) Non-members at any rear doors can be imagined creeping round the altar under the statue of Victory. But here a spectator is already close to the tribunal as the focus of proceedings, and the view is not actually blocked by the altar. Though no ancient source does ever distinguish between front and rear doors of the House, it is still more natural to assume that Herodian refers to the front door, facing on to the Comitium. This is where a crowd would gather, rather than at the rear doors, which seem to have opened on to the Chalcidicum. In general Herodian is not a historian in whom special trust should be placed on matters of detail, and thus there seems all the more reason to discount his testimony on the location of the altar as well as the statue of Victory. On the wider issue of his uncertain social class, it is hard to know how far this altogether dubious grasp of the layout of the Curia Julia might justifiably be used in support of the argument that he had at least never been a member of the senate. See further C. R. Whittaker,

Loeb ed. vol. 1 pp. xix-xxiv; G. Alföldy, "Herodians Person," *Ancient Society* 2. 1971. pp. 204-233, esp. pp. 231-233.

D (chap. 4 sect. 2)

Sherwin-White, *Pliny*, p. 378, takes the view (generally supported by A. Chastagnol in *Mélanges offerts à Léopold S. Senghor*, Dakar, 1977, p. 48) that the regulations governing the movements of senators "evidently were neglected in practice," but hardly strengthens the conjecture by citing Dio's ownership of a villa in Campania and estates in Bithynia. With his property so divided, Dio was typical of the substantial number of senators of non-Italian origin. From our knowledge of his career it is in fact hard to see when he might have returned to Bithynia for a long stretch. After his second consulship in 229 he did retire there permanently, it is true, but by then, in his mid-sixties at least, he had exceeded the age at which senators were still summoned to meetings (see chap. 4 sect. 3), and anyway had a valid excuse in his illness (see F. Millar, *A Study of Cassius Dio*, pp. 13-27 with Dio 80.5.2-3). His remarks about events he had witnessed himself, and his claim not to have seen Claudius Pompeianus in the senate before or after the reign of Pertinax, all suggest that he did attend regularly when he could (cf. 72.4.2; 74.3.2 and 12.2-3; 75.1.4; 80.1.2). Indeed his career might even be used to argue for the exact opposite of what Sherwin-White sought to show, namely, a conscientious senator with some ambition for advancement *did* feel compelled to attend regularly at tedious sessions, in which he took no individual part of note, and where he was frequently terrified. Yet when all this is said, it must be understood that Dio's career (however interpreted) reflects the experience and attitude of only a single member. It would be wrong to generalize too much from it.

E (chap. 7 sect. 11)

The fact that quaestors designate did not sit in the House must undermine the suggestion of G. Alföldy and H. Halfmann ("Iunius Maximus und die Victoria Parthica," *ZPE* 35. 1979. pp. 195-212 = C. Börker and R. Merkelbach, *Die Inschriften von Ephesos* III. no. 811) that Iunius Maximus was, according to an inscription from Ephesus, "quaestor(em) extr[a] s[e]n[t]entias des[i]gnatum, suscipien[tem] munus laureatar[um] victoriae Parthicae" for the specific purpose of communicating to the House news of victory in Parthia in 166. In fact designation would give him no immediate right to attend a session, and he could just as well have been introduced by the consuls, like any envoy. Moreover, if Fronto wrote his letter *Ad Amicos* 1.6 (= pp. 168-169 H) *after* Iunius had delivered his despatches (as seems likely), it might appear a little superfluous for him to say to Avidius Cassius "dignus est quem diligas et suffragiis tuis ornes." The significance of "extra sententias" remains a puzzle. It may be intended to convey that Iunius was offered accelerated promotion as was C. Vesnius Vindex, for example (*CIL* XI. 6053 with W. Eck, *PW* Suppl. 15 s.v. Vesnius, cols. 901-902), though clearly that is not what the phrase itself should mean. But a misunderstanding of terminology on the part of the Greek responsible for the dedication is possible (cf. C. Habicht, *Istanb. Mitt.* 9/10. 1959/60. p. 110 lines 10-12, discussed above, chap. 1 sect. 2 note 35; *SIG*³ 858. The possibility of misunderstanding in each of these instances is overlooked by A. B. Bosworth, *ZPE* 39. 1980. p. 269).

F (chap. 7 sect. 12)

Tacitus and Frontinus, both of them senators writing in the late first and early second centuries, use *pedarius* quite unaffectedly to denote members who had not yet reached the praetorship—as seems clear enough from the context at *Ann.* 3.65 and *Aqued.* 99 respectively. But apart from the single instances in each author the term occurs elsewhere in our period only in Aulus Gellius (3.18) later in the second century, and he is plainly not familiar with it. See further L. R. Taylor and R. T. Scott, *TAPA* 100. 1969. pp. 548-557. Elsewhere Tacitus speaks of *consulares, praetorii,* and "the rest of the senate" (*Ann.* 3.28; cf. *FIRA*² I no. 68 V lines 107-111).

There can be no support for A. Chastagnol's view (*Miscellanea in onore di Eugenio Manni* II, pp. 473-475), following L. Cantarelli, of *pedarii* as *equites* with the right to attend and vote, but not speak, who continued to be introduced simply to make up a fixed total of members until Claudius began the practice of adlection instead. Quite apart from other objections, this interpretation presupposes an altogether implausible concern for the maintenance of a precise number of members; it takes Frontinus and Tacitus to use the term in a highly technical sense, rather than just informally; and it entirely overlooks the latter's explicit indication that *pedarii did* speak.

This final point again seems to be overlooked by J. Korpanty, "Przyczynek do problemu tzw. 'senatores pedarii,' " *Meander* 34. 1979. pp. 415-418, who according to the Latin summary on p. 418 argues that *pedarii* could vote, but not speak. An earlier Polish discussion by L. T. Błaszczyk, *Ze studiów nad senatem rzymskim w okresie schyłku republiki,* Łódź, 1965, chap. 2 with French summary pp. 94-96, is helpfully reviewed by A. Deman, *Latomus* 26. 1967. p. 271.

G (chap. 7 sect. 12)

There is a need to consider claims of like nature made by two long-lived consuls of the Julio-Claudian period—by L. Volusius Saturninus (cos. A.D. 3, who died in 56 aged 93: R. Hanslik, *PW* Suppl. 9 cols. 1861-1862; W. Eck, *PW* Suppl. 14 col. 963) that he had outlived all the persons whose opinions in debate he had asked as consul, and by L. Calpurnius Piso (cos. 27: *PIR*² C 293) that none of those he had called on to speak when he was consul could still be seen in the senate (Plin. *NH* 7. 156; Plin. *Ep.* 3.7.12). Neither claim will necessarily help to prove that junior senators were called upon for their opinions, yet equally neither need argue against it. The most junior *quaestorius* in A.D. 3 (that is, one who had held the magistracy in A.D. 2 at the minimum age of 25) would be 79 in A.D. 56 and so could plausibly have been outlived by Volusius. Piso presumably must have lived at least till Vespasian's reign: in a letter written no earlier than mid-99, Pliny said that he used to make his claim "lately" ("nuper"), but we have no further clue to when he died. It is impossible to know, too, whether there is significance in the phrasing of his claim. Perhaps some contemporaries of 27 survived but no longer attended the senate. We know that C. Cassius Longinus (cos. 30: *PIR*² C 501), for example, spent most of his latter years in exile.

H (chap. 8)

Imperial references to *SC* rather than *oratio* (all in *CJ*):

M. Aurelius citing no. 81 in list, chap. 15 sect. 5, passed under Hadrian (3.31.1).

Sev. Alexander citing no. 108 in list, passed under M. Aurelius and L. Verus (5.62.5).

Sev. Alexander citing no. 128 in list, passed under M. Aurelius and Commodus (6.57.1). (*SC Orphitianum* was of course the usual form of citation in this case, but the *oratio* was also available.)

Severus and Caracalla (5.6.1), Caracalla (5.62.4), and Philippus (5.6.4) all citing no. 130 in list, passed under M. Aurelius and Commodus.

Caracalla (5.71.1), Gordian (5.73.2), Valerian and Gallienus (5.71.5), Carus, Carinus, and Numerian (5.71.7), and Diocletian and Maximian (5.71.8, 11, 15-17; 73.3-4) all citing no. 134 in list, passed under Severus.

Imperial references to *oratio* rather than *SC* (all in *CJ*):

Gordian (5.70.2), and Diocletian and Maximian (5.71.9) citing no. 134 in list, passed under Severus.

Gordian (5.16.10) citing no. 135 in list, passed under Severus and Caracalla.

J (chap. 11 sect. 4)

For triumphs and ovations specifically known to have been voted to emperors and their close relatives by the senate, see:

RG 4.1; Dio 51.25.2 (M. Crassus and Octavian); 53.26.5 (Augustus); 54.11.6 and 24.7 (Agrippa); 54.31.4 (Tiberius); 56.17.1-2 (Augustus and Tiberius).

Tac. *Ann.* 2.64, cf. 3.11 (Germanicus and Drusus); ibid. 3.47 (abortive proposal in honor of Tiberius).

Dio 59.16.11 and 23.2 (Gaius); note also Suet. *Calig.* 48.

Dio 60.22.1 (Claudius).

Tac. *Ann.* 13.8 (Nero).

Josephus, *BJ* 7.121 (Vespasian and Titus); cf. Dio 66.7.2.

Dio 68.28.3 and 29.2 (Trajan).

HA, *Hadr.* 6.3 (Hadrian's celebration for Trajan).

HA, *Commod.* 2.4-5 (Marcus and Commodus).

HA, *Sev.* 9.10 (Severus); 16.6-7 (Severus and Caracalla).

K (chap. 12 sect. 5)

Votes by the senate:

Games:
RG 22.2; Tac. *Ann.* 3.64; Suet. *Vesp.* 2; Dio 58.12.4-5; HA, *Antonin.* 5.2; *ILS* 88, 95, 8894.

Festivals:
Tac. *Ann.* 15.74; Suet. *Calig.* 16; Dio 51.19; 54.10.3 and 34.2; 59.26.3; 60.23.6; cf. G. K. Boyce, *Corpus of the Lararia of Pompeii, MAAR* 14. 1937. no. 466.

Feriae ex s.c.: see *Inscr. Ital.* XIII. 2. pp. 559-560; note in general Ulpian, *Dig.* 4.6.26.7.

Priesthoods:
Tac. *Ann.* 3.29; 4.4; 13.2; Dio 56.46.1.

Sacrifices:
Martial 8.15; Tac. *Ann.* 6.25; Dio 51.20.3; 57.6.4; 59.4.4 and 16.10; 61.16.4; 77.1.4.

Altars and other dedications:
RG 11; 12.2; 34; 35; Tac. *Ann.* 4.74; Suet. *Claud.* 11; Dio 54.10.3; 25.3; 27.2.

Epigraphic evidence for dedications *ex s.c.* (from Rome unless otherwise stated):

Octavian/Augustus: *ILS* 81, 82 (Potentia), 83, 84 (Ariminum); *CIL* V. 7817 (Alps);

X. 1619 (Naples); *AE* 1952. 165 (Arles); for honors voted on 13 January 27 B.C., see *Inscr. Ital.* XIII. 2. p. 396.

Livia: *ILS* 202.

C. and/or L. Caesar: *ILS* 136(?); *CIL* VI. 3748(?), 36908; *AE* 1973. 34.

Germanicus: *CIL* VI. 894 = 31194(?).

Drusus: *CIL* VI. 31200.

Nero Caesar: *ILS* 182.

Claudius: *ILS* 216.

Vespasian: *ILS* 245.

Titus: *ILS* 264, 265.

Nerva: *ILS* 274.

Trajan: *ILS* 282 (Tarracina), 283, 292, 294, 296 (Beneventum), 302 (Alba Fucens); *CIL* VI. 30958, 31215; *NSc* 1. 1947. p. 98.

Trajan, Plotina and diva Marciana: *ILS* 298 (Ancona).

Hadrian: *ILS* 309; *CIL* VI. 974, 36915.

Antoninus: *ILS* 341.

M. Aurelius: *ILS* 374.

Septimius Severus and Caracalla: *ILS* 425.

L (chap. 16 sect. 1)

Any notion of senatorial involvement in two cases during Commodus' reign is best regarded with skepticism:

(1) According to Eusebius (*Hist. Eccl.* 5.21), an educated Christian, Apollonius, was first brought before Perennis (Praetorian Prefect, 183-185) and then required to defend himself in the senate, which passed the death sentence. A later, badly confused version of this affair has survived among Christian martyr acts: see H. A. Musurillo, *The Acts of the Christian Martyrs*, no. 7. Perennis' marked hostility to the senate makes it most unlikely that he would have referred such a matter to it (unless out of mockery), while senatorial involvement with the trials of Christians is otherwise unknown (cf. chap. 12 sect. 4 note 37). Jerome (*De viris illust.* 42) actually terms Apollonius a senator, but perhaps that was merely in order to account for the alleged place of his trial. For further discussion, see *PIR*² A 931; T. D. Barnes, *JRS* 58. 1968. pp. 46-48; and R. Freudenberger, "Die Überlieferung vom Martyrium des römischen Christen Apollonius," *ZNTW* 60. 1969. pp. 111-130.

(2) In a pair of papyrus fragments, Appian, a gymnasiarch from Alexandria, has been sentenced to death for having made accusations that

Commodus was sharing in the profits on the sale of Egyptian grain. As he is led away from the emperor's presence, however, he is recalled, and then asks who is responsible for this order—the senate, or Commodus himself. Naturally this question raises the possibility that the senate had taken some part in deciding the case. But altogether it seems unlikely, and it would be unheard-of for the senate to grant a stay of execution independently of the emperor. More probably Appian is just citing "the senate" in a loose fashion as another authority in Rome beside the emperor. See H. A. Musurillo, *The Acts of the Pagan Martyrs*, no. 11; J. Crook, *Consilium Principis*, pp. 77-78.

INFORMATION FOR NON-SPECIALIST READERS

1. The Roman emperors from Augustus to Gordian III

The names given are those officially assumed by each emperor after his accession. The name by which each is usually known is in italics. Unofficial names are in parentheses.

Julio-Claudians

Imperator Caesar *Augustus*	died A.D. 14
Tiberius Julius Caesar Augustus	14-37
Gaius Caesar Augustus Germanicus (Caligula)	37-41
Tiberius *Claudius* Caesar Augustus Germanicus	41-54
Imperator *Nero* Claudius Caesar Augustus Germanicus	54-68
Servius *Galba* Imp. Caesar Augustus	68-69
Imp. Marcus *Otho* Caesar Augustus	69
Aulus *Vitellius* Imp. Germanicus Augustus	69

Flavians

Imp. Caesar *Vespasianus* Augustus	69-79
Imp. *Titus* Caesar Vespasianus Augustus	79-81
Imp. Caesar *Domitianus* Augustus Germanicus	81-96
Imp. *Nerva* Caesar Augustus Germanicus	96-98
Imp. Caesar Nerva *Traianus* Optimus Augustus Germanicus Dacicus	98-117
Imp. Caesar Traianus *Hadrianus* Augustus	117-138

Antonines

Imp. Caesar Titus Aelius Hadrianus *Antoninus* Augustus *Pius*	138-161
Imp. Caesar *Marcus Aurelius* Antoninus Augustus	161-180 ⎫
Imp. Caesar *Lucius* Aurelius *Verus* Augustus	161-169 ⎬
Imp. Caesar Marcus Aurelius *Commodus* Antoninus Augustus	177-192 ⎭
Imp. Caesar Publius Helvius *Pertinax* Augustus	193
Imp. Caesar Marcus *Didius* Severus *Julianus* Augustus	193

Severans

Imp. Caesar Lucius *Septimius Severus* Pertinax Augustus	193-211 ⎫
Imp. Caesar Marcus Aurelius Antoninus Augustus (*Caracalla*)	198-217 ⎬
Imp. Caesar Publius Septimius *Geta* Augustus	209-212 ⎭
Imp. Caesar Marcus Opellius *Macrinus* Augustus	217-218
Imp. Caesar Marcus Aurelius Antoninus Augustus (*Elagabalus*)	218-222
Imp. Caesar Marcus Aurelius *Severus Alexander* Augustus	222-235

Imp. Caesar Gaius Julius Verus *Maximinus* Augustus	235-238
Imp. Caesar Marcus Antonius *Gordianus* (I) Sempronianus Romanus Africanus Senior Augustus Imp. Caesar Marcus Antonius *Gordianus* (II) Sempronianus Africanus Iunior Augustus	238
Imp. Caesar Decimus Caelius Calvinus *Balbinus* Augustus Imp. Caesar Marcus Clodius *Pupienus* Augustus	238
Imp. Caesar Marcus Antonius *Gordianus* (III) Augustus	238-244

2. The senatorial magistracies (cursus honorum): *a simplified summary*

Grant of *latus clavus* from the emperor (for those not already members of the senatorial class).

✧

Vigintivirate (20 posts annually). Service as *tribunus militum* in a legion might either precede or follow, though (unlike the Vigintivirate) it remained optional.

✧

Quaestorship (20 posts), tenable no earlier than twenty-fifth year. Election gave entry to the senate and conferred lifelong membership.

✧

Tribunate (10 posts) *or* Aedileship (6 posts). Patricians were excused this stage.

✧

Praetorship (variable number of posts until late first century, 18 thereafter), tenable no earlier than thirtieth year.

✧

Consulship (always two consuls in office simultaneously, otherwise number per year, and hence length of tenure, both variable). A distinguished senator might be elected a second, or even a third, time.

In the Republic the censorship outranked the consulship, but this office was practically defunct under the Principate.

3. Glossary of technical terms

Brief definitions of the principal terms which recur in the text are intended. There is no attempt at exhaustive coverage, nor any attention to terms used only in the notes. The definitions relate to the way in which terms are used in this book, and are not to be taken as necessarily comprehensive.

Acta senatus (pl.), the official record of senatorial proceedings.

Adlectus (sing.), *-ti* (pl.), non-member introduced, or "adlected," to the senate by the emperor at a specified rank (*inter quaestorios, tribunicios*, qq.vv., etc.); equally a member promoted from a lower rank to a higher one in the same way.

Adventus, an emperor's formal arrival in Rome.

Aedilicius, *-cii*, senator who had held the aedileship (see sect. 2 above), but no higher magistracy.

Aerarium militare, the "military" treasury at Rome, established by Augustus in A.D. 6 to furnish bounties payable to soldiers on discharge.

Aerarium Saturni, the state treasury and official depository in Rome, housed in a temple of Saturn, and under the general supervision of the senate. See map, p. 99.

Album senatorium, the list of members of the senate in order of seniority, publicly displayed, and updated each year.

Alimenta (pl.), child support schemes in Italy. Those established by the Roman government were funded by a combination of its capital and payments by local landowners.

Altercatio, at meetings of the senate a series of speeches and counter-speeches on a controversial issue delivered by two or more members (often out of the normal order).

Apocolocyntosis, a satiric skit attributed to Seneca, in which the emperor Claudius' attempt to join the gods on his death leads, not to deification, but instead—after a debate in the heavenly senate—to "pumpkinification" (the Greek title).

Arval Acta (pl.), the detailed record on stone (of which much, uniquely, survives) of the meetings of the Fratres Arvales, a priestly college in Rome. The dozen members were all senators, and included the emperor. Much light is shed on their careers and movements.

Auctoritas, (1) the informal influence (as opposed to legal authority) possessed by any person: understandably, the auctoritas of the emperor was especially strong; (2) a resolution of the senate which was passed, but for some reason remained invalid (because it was later vetoed, for example, or the relevant meeting was only informal).

Auxilia (pl.), the auxiliary forces of the Roman army, mostly non-citizens.

Clarissimus, honorific adjective (literally "most distinguished") reserved to describe or address any member of the senatorial class.

Codicillus, *-li*, a communication from the emperor (thus amounting to instructions).

Collegium, *-ia*, general term for any club, society, association.

Colonia, */-iae*, community enjoying the most privileged status granted by Rome, in particular considerable local independence and significant tax benefits.

Comitia (pl.), general term for a popular assembly at Rome.

Concilium, */-ia* (in Greek-speaking provinces *koinon*, */-na*), a representative assembly in each province, established primarily to supervise celebration of the imperial cult, though it might extend its activities further, in particular to thank certain retiring governors and to prosecute others.

Consilium, an advisory council, such as any individual or magistrate might assemble for guidance; most notably the emperor's advisory council (consilium principis).

Consularis, */-res*, senator who had held the consulship: see sect. 2 above.

Corrector, */-res, curator, /-res*, an official sent from Rome to set in order the affairs of one or more communities, in particular their finances.

Curator, */-res*, (1) = *corrector*, q.v.; (2) senatorial official(s) charged with supervision of a public service, for example aqueducts in Rome (*aquarum*), main roads in Italy (*viarum*).

Curia, the senate's principal meeting place, the Curia Julia; but the term could also be used for any other place where the senate met. See map, p. 99.

Delator, */-res*, an accuser, informer.

Designatus, */-ti*, in the senate the status of a member who had been elected to a magistracy, but had not yet taken it up.

Discessio, at meetings of the senate strictly the stage when a vote was taken about a matter on which members had not been asked for opinions individually; but also used loosely of votes taken after opinions *had* been sought thus.

Discessus senatus, s.v. *Res prolatae*.

Ab epistulis, court official who coordinated the presentation of correspondence to the emperor and the issuing of replies.

Eques, */equites*, literally horseman. The second of the two upper classes of Rome. While still a very exclusive group by any general standard, it was considerably larger and more varied than the senatorial class. Admission was mostly informal, and no commitment to public life was expected, although certain senior posts in the emperor's service, together with some army officerships, were reserved for members of the class.

EX S(enatus) C(onsulto), "by resolution of the senate."

Falsum, forgery, fraud.

Fasti (pl.) (1) an annual calendar of notable events; (2) a year-by-year list of the holders of one or more offices.

Fideicommissum, */-sa*, literally "trust". A request to carry out an action made by a testator to one or more beneficiaries of the will.

Fiscus, abstract general term used to denote the finances claimed by the emperor.

Gratiarum actio, a speech of thanks, in particular that addressed to the emperor in the senate by consuls entering office.

Historia Augusta, a collection of biographies of emperors from Hadrian to the late third century. Their quality and reliability vary considerably. Authorship and date of composition are hotly disputed: however, the latter must at least be well after the reigns treated.

Horti (pl.), literally gardens. Country estate.

Hostis, */-tes*, an enemy; notably the senate might declare any individual hostis, or enemy of the state, and thus liable to summary execution.

Imperator, literally general. Originally an honorific title conferred upon outstandingly successful commanders. During the Principate this practice continued, but the award quickly came to be reserved for the emperor and members of his family. *In addition*, the custom developed whereby emperors used the title as a name: see sect. 1 above.

Imperium, the power and authority (administrative, judicial, military) conferred upon senior Roman magistrates.

Infamia, disgrace; notably a variety of disabilities imposed upon convicted defendants in certain cases.

Interrogatio, at meetings of the senate the stage where the president sought members' opinions in order on a matter raised by him.

Ius trium liberorum, a set of legal and fiscal privileges granted to the parent(s) of three or more children, and to others at the emperor's pleasure.

Iustitium, a suspension of public business (especially court sittings) in an emergency. Though the senate had authority to declare a iustitium, its own meetings could continue during one.

Koinon (Greek), s.v. *concilium*.

Latus clavus, the broad purple stripe on the tunic, which denoted a member of the senatorial class; hence the adjective laticlavius. See also sect. 2 above.

Lectio senatus, a review of the senatorial roll (carried out by the emperor).

Legatus, */-ti*, an administrative assistant to a provincial governor.

Legatus Augusti propraetore, a governor of one of the emperor's provinces, appointed by him.

Legatus legionis, a legionary commander.

Legitimus, */-mi, senatus, /-tūs*, a stated meeting of the senate (in contrast to one summoned at short notice).

Lex, */leges*, a law passed by a popular assembly, normally after the senate had been consulted and had given its approval.

Lex de imperio Vespasiani, a law passed on Vespasian's accession at the end of 69 conferring a range of imperial prerogatives. A portion of the text survives.

Lex Julia de senatu habendo, a law passed in 9 B.C. regulating senatorial procedure.

Lex Papia Poppaea, a law passed in A.D. 9 with the purpose of encouraging marriage and the production of children by offering a variety of incentives, while at the same time imposing certain disabilities upon those who failed to respond.

A libellis, court official who coordinated the presentation of petitions (*libellus, /-li*) to the emperor and the issuing of his replies.

Ludi Saeculares, special games to celebrate the end of one century or saeculum and the start of the next, arranged by the *Quindecimviri sacris faciundis* (q.v.) under general supervision of the senate. In fact during the Principate the games were held in 17 B.C., A.D. 47, 88, and 204.

Maiestas, treason. During the Principate any act which could be seen as damaging to the emperor or his interests might lead to a charge on this ground.

Mandata (pl.), instructions from the emperor to an official.

Munus, /-nera, general term for any duty or obligation, private or public.

Notarius, /-ii, shorthand writer.

Novus, /-vi, homo, -/mines, literally "new man," the first member of a family to enter the senate.

Oratio, /-ones, literally a speech. In a senatorial context, above all a communication by the emperor, however delivered, which came to be considered to possess the force of law.

Ordinarius, /-rii (consul, /-les), consul (see sect. 2 above) whose term of office began on 1 January, and thus carried greater prestige than that of *suffecti* (q.v.) who followed.

Ornamenta (pl.), literally ornaments, decorations, a term used in particular to denote the award of an honorary triumph (ornamenta triumphalia), or of honorary senatorial rank (ornamenta quaestoria, praetoria, etc.).

Ovatio, a lesser form of triumph, q.v.

Panegyricus, the title usually given to the surviving speech of thanks to the emperor delivered by Pliny on his entry to the consulship in September 100.

Pater patriae, literally "father of his country"; during the Principate a special title bestowed upon the emperor alone.

Patricians, originally the privileged class of Roman citizens in contrast to the general body, the plebeians. There were almost no practical differences between the two groups by the imperial period, but for reasons of religion and tradition emperors did seek to maintain and exalt a tiny group of patricians.

Pedarius, /-ii (senator, /-res), informal term for senators below praetorian rank.

Peregrinus, /-*ni*, a foreigner; strictly any person who did not have Roman citizenship.

Plebeians, s.v. *patricians*.

Pomerium, the religious boundary line of the city of Rome (see map, p. 99). The senate could only meet within it or up to one mile beyond.

Pontifex Maximus, the office of chief priest of the Roman state religion, invariably occupied by the emperor.

Populi diurna acta (pl.), literally "the daily doings of the people," an official gazette established in 59 B.C. Copies were sent from Rome all over the empire. The range of subject matter was varied, and did include senatorial business.

Praefectus frumenti dandi, senatorial official responsible for distributing free corn in Rome (4 posts).

Praefectus Urbi, senior senatorial official responsible for maintaining law and order in Rome.

Praefectus Vigilum, equestrian official who commanded the force of night watchmen and fire fighters in Rome.

Praetorian Guard, the privileged force of soldiers which comprised the emperor's bodyguard. It was normally commanded by a pair of equestrian prefects, and came to be housed in barracks on the edge of Rome. See map, p. 99.

Praetorius, /-*rii*, senator who had held the praetorship (see sect. 2 above), but no higher magistracy.

Prima sententia, at meetings of the senate the opinion expressed by the first member called upon by the president, to which special weight was attached.

Princeps, /*principes*, literally "chief man," a description applied loosely to leading figures in the late Republic. Thereafter, however, it became an informal title of the emperor alone. See also following entry.

Princeps senatus (to be distinguished from Princeps alone), in the Republic the title of the senator placed at the head of the senatorial roll by the censors. Later, although each emperor must have headed the roll during his reign, only a few assumed the actual title.

Privatus, /-*ti* (*senator*, /-*res*), senator not currently holding a magistracy.

Proconsul, governor of one of the provinces entrusted to the senate, chosen by lot for a one-year term.

Procurator, /-*res*, equestrian official in the emperor's service.

Profectio, an emperor's formal departure from Rome.

Quaestio, /-*ones*, at Rome a jury court presided over by a praetor and established to hear charges of a particular type (adultery, for example, or poisoning).

Quaestorius, /-*rii*, senator who had held the quaestorship (see sect. 2 above), but no higher magistracy.

Quindecimviri sacris faciundis (pl.), one of the great Roman priestly colleges; its duties included custody of the oracular Sibylline books, and celebration of the *Ludi Saeculares* (q.v.).

A rationibus, court official with oversight of the emperor's finances.

Relatio, /-*ones*, at meetings of the senate the stage where the president raised one or more matters on which he sought guidance.

Relegatio, one of the categories of exile which a Roman court might impose. A variety of restrictions was laid down by law, but these were not notably severe.

Repetundae (pl.), charges of misgovernment brought against an official, in particular any allegation of extortion.

Res Gestae (*divi Augusti*), a document (which survives) published after Augustus' death, in which he had summarized his achievements together with the expenses borne by himself on the state's behalf.

Res prolatae (pl.) = *Discessus senatus* (sing.), an annual recess of the senate for most of April and early May.

Saevitia, harshness, cruelty.

Salutatio, the formal ceremony held early in the morning at which a distinguished person was greeted by his dependents and associates.

Senatus consultum, /-*ta* (abbreviated SC, SCC), resolution of the senate.

Sententia, /-*ae*, at meetings of the senate an opinion expressed by a member; alternatively, in other contexts, a decision.

Suffectus, /-*ti* (*consul*, /-*les*), consul (see sect. 2 above) whose term of office was second, or later, in the year, and was thus less esteemed than that of the *ordinarii* (q.v.).

Supplicatio, /-*ones*, a special approach to some or all the gods at a time of notable success or disaster.

Tribunicia potestas, one of the powers granted to Augustus and later emperors, not notably strong in itself, but paraded by them because of tribunes' popular image as protectors of the people.

Tribunicius, /-*cii*, senator who had held the tribunate (see sect. 2 above), but no higher magistracy.

Tribunus, /-*ni militum*, officer in a legion, of senatorial or equestrian status (6 per legion); see sect. 2 above.

Triumph, celebratory procession in Rome awarded as a great honor to victorious generals.

Tutor, /-*res*, guardian.

Vectigal, /-lia, general term for indirect taxes.

Verba facere, clause used (in the absence of any noun) to describe the stage at meetings of the senate where the president explained or discussed a matter raised by him.

Vigintivir, /-ri, junior magistrate taking his first compulsory step in the senatorial career (see sect. 2 above).

BIBLIOGRAPHY

1. Senators

Investigation of the background of individual senators, their families, careers, and other allied topics has for long engaged the attention of many scholars. No more than a very limited selection of studies is cited here, with the emphasis upon the most recent works to attempt a conspectus of the senate's membership at different dates. For all their value, older works, now mostly superseded, have been omitted—those by Stech, Lambrechts, and Garzetti, for example. For further investigation *PW* (especially the later *Supplementbande*) and *PIR*[2] are indispensable; for new developments see *AE* in particular. Many other relevant titles appear in the general bibliography below.

G. Alföldy, "Senatoren in der römischen Provinz Dalmatia," *Epig. Stud.* 5. 1968. pp. 99-144.

G. Alföldy, "Septimius Severus und der Senat," *Bonn. Jahrb.* 168. 1968. pp. 112-160.

G. Alföldy, *Konsulat und Senatorenstand unter den Antoninen: prosopographische Untersuchungen zur senatorischen Führungsschicht*, Antiquitas 1. 27, Bonn, 1977.

G. Barbieri, *L' albo senatorio da Settimio Severo a Carino (193-285)*, Rome, 1952.

A. Chastagnol, "Les sénateurs d' origine provinciale sous le règne d'Auguste," in *Mélanges de philosophie, de littérature et d' histoire ancienne offerts à Pierre Boyancé, Collection de l' Ecole Française de Rome* 22. 1974. pp. 163-171.

J.-P. Coriat, "Les hommes nouveaux à l'époque des Sévères," *Rev. Hist. Droit* 56. 1978. pp. 5-27.

K. Dietz, *Senatus contra principem: Untersuchungen zur senatorischen Opposition gegen Kaiser Maximinus Thrax*, Vestigia 29, Munich, 1980.

W. Eck, *Senatoren von Vespasian bis Hadrian. Prosopographische Untersuchungen mit Einschluss der Jahres- und Provinzialfasten der Statthalter*, Vestigia 13, Munich, 1970.

W. Eck, "Die Präsenz senatorischer Familien in den Städten des Imperium Romanum bis zum späten 3. Jahrhundert," in *Studien zur antiken Sozialgeschichte: Festschrift F. Vittinghoff*, ed. W. Eck, H. Galsterer, H. Wolff, Cologne/Vienna, 1980. pp. 283-322.

H. Halfmann, *Die Senatoren aus dem östlichen Teil des Imperium Romanum bis zum Ende des 2. Jahrhunderts n. Chr.*, Hypomnemata 58, Göttingen, 1979.

B. W. Jones, *Domitian and the Senatorial Order: A Prosopographical Study of Domitian's Relationship with the Senate, A.D. 81-96*, Memoirs of the American Philosophical Society 132. 1979.

S. J. de Laet, *De Samenstelling van den romeinschen Senaat gedurende de eerste Eeuw van het Principaat (28 vóór Chr.-68 na Chr.)*, Antwerp, 1941.

M.W.H. Lewis, *The Official Priests of Rome under the Julio-Claudians, Papers and Monographs of the American Academy in Rome* 16. 1955.

H.-H. Pistor, "Prinzeps und Patriziat in der Zeit von Augustus bis Commodus," diss. Freiburg, 1965.

L. Schumacher, "Prosopographische Untersuchungen zur Besetzung der vier hohen römischen Priesterkollegien im Zeitalter der Antonine und der Severer (96-235 n. Chr.)," diss. Mainz, 1973.

2. Proconsuls and Proconsular Legates

The most recently published lists are cited here. New discoveries demand constant updating, however: see especially *AE*. Most provinces have now been adequately treated, although a comprehensive study of proconsuls of Asia would be very welcome.

Proconsuls

Achaea: E. Groag, *Die römische Reichsbeamten von Achaia bis auf Diokletian*, Vienna and Leipzig, 1939, with W. Eck, "Über die prätorischen Prokonsulate in der Kaiserzeit. Eine quellenkritische Überlegung," *Zephyrus* 23/24. 1972/3. pp. 233-260 at pp. 244-245.

Africa: B. E. Thomasson, *PW* Suppl. 13 s.v. Africa (2), cols. 1-11.

Asia: D. Magie, *Roman Rule in Asia Minor*, Princeton, 1950, pp. 1580-1585; W. Eck, "Prokonsuln von Asia in der Flavisch-Traianischen Zeit," *ZPE* 45. 1982. pp. 139-153.

Baetica: G. Alföldy, *Fasti Hispanienses*, Wiesbaden, 1969 (summary on pp. 308-309).

Bithynia/Pontus: D. Magie, op. cit. p. 1591.

Crete with Cyrene: W. Eck, *Zephyrus* 23/24. 1972/3. pp. 244-251; I. F. Sandars, *Roman Crete*, Warminster, 1982, Appendix I.

Cyprus: W. Eck, loc. cit. pp. 250-253.

Lycia with Pamphylia: D. Magie, op. cit. p. 1600.

Macedonia: (27 B.C.-A.D. 15) R. Szramkiewicz, *Les gouverneurs de province à l'époque augustéenne*, Paris, 1976, vol. 2 p. 514; (A.D. 44 onwards) W. Eck, loc. cit. pp. 240-243.

Narbonensis: H.-G. Pflaum, *Les fastes de la province de Narbonnaise (Gallia*, Supplement 30, Paris, 1978), chap. 1.

Sardinia with Corsica: P. Meloni, *L' amministrazione della Sardegna da Augusto all' invasione Vandalica*, Rome, 1958.

Sicily: W. Eck, loc. cit. pp. 238-241.

For all provinces in the period 69-138, see also W. Eck, *Senatoren von Vespasian bis Hadrian*, pp. 112ff.; and (to 96) B. Kreiler, "Die Statthalter Kleinasiens unter den Flaviern," diss. Munich, 1975.

Synchronized tables of proconsuls and other governors are set out by B. E. Thomasson, *Laterculi Praesidum*, Lund, 1972-

Proconsular Legates

For all provinces, see W. Eck, "Zu den prokonsularen Legationen in der Kaiserzeit," *Epig. Stud.* 9. 1972. pp. 24-36 at pp. 32-36.

3. General

This section does no more than list those works cited in the text and footnotes. All encyclopedia articles are omitted, together with a few peripheral items. Works already cited under "Abbreviations" and in sections 1 and 2 of the bibliography do not appear again here. The latest material of which it was possible to take full account dates to mid 1981; however there was an opportunity a few months later to incorporate limited reference to certain more recent publications.

J. N. Adams, "Conventions of naming in Cicero," *CQ* 28. 1978. pp. 145-166.

G. Alföldy, "Ein senatorischer Cursus Honorum aus Bracara Augusta," *Madrider Mitteilungen* 8. 1967. pp. 185-195.

G. Alföldy, "Die Legionslegaten der römischen Rheinarmeen," *Epig. Stud.* 3. 1967.

G. Alföldy, "Herodians Person," *Ancient Society* 2. 1971. pp. 204-233.

G. Alföldy, *Noricum*, London, 1974.

G. Alföldy, *Die römischen Inschriften von Tarraco*, Berlin, 1975.

G. Alföldy, "Consuls and Consulars under the Antonines: Prosopography and History," *Ancient Society* 7. 1976. pp. 263-299.

G. Alföldy, review of P. Setälä, *Private domini*, cited below, *Erasmvs* 30. 1978. cols. 297-302.

G. Alföldy and H. Halfmann, "Iunius Maximus und die Victoria Parthica," *ZPE* 35. 1979. pp. 195-212.

G. Alföldy, "Ein Senator aus Vicetia," *ZPE* 39. 1980. pp. 255-266.

J. E. Allison and J. D. Cloud, "The Lex Julia maiestatis," *Latomus* 21. 1962. pp. 711-731.

J. M. Alvarez Martínez, "Una escultura en bronce del *genius senatus*, hallada en Merida," *Archivo Español de Arqueologia* 48. 1975. pp. 141-151.

M. Amelotti, "La posizione degli atleti di fronte al diritto romano," *SDHI* 21. 1955. pp. 123-156.

J. C. Anderson, Jr., "Domitian, the Argiletum and the Temple of Peace," *AJA* 86. 1982. pp. 101-110.

J. H. d'Arms, *Romans on the Bay of Naples*, Harvard, 1970.

J. H. d'Arms, "Senators' involvement in commerce in the late Republic: some Ciceronian evidence," *MAAR* 36. 1980. pp. 77-89.

J. H. d'Arms, *Commerce and Social Standing in Ancient Rome*, Harvard, 1981.

T. Ashby, *The Aqueducts of Ancient Rome*, Oxford, 1935.

B. Ashmole, "A lost statue once in Thasos," in *Fritz Saxl 1890-1948: A Volume of Memorial Essays*, ed. D. J. Gordon, London, 1957, pp. 195-198.

A. E. Astin, "The status of Sardinia in the second century A.D.," *Latomus* 18. 1959. pp. 150-153.

A. E. Astin, "Augustus and 'Censoria Potestas,' " *Latomus* 22. 1963. pp. 226-235.

A. E. Astin, " 'Nominare' in accounts of elections in the early Principate," *Latomus* 28. 1969. pp. 863-874.

H. R. Baldus, *Uranius Antoninus: Münzprägung und Geschichte, Antiquitas* 11, Bonn, 1971.

H. R. Baldus, "Zum Rechtsstatus syrischer Prägungen der 1. Hälfte des 3. Jahrhunderts n. Chr.," *Chiron* 3. 1973. pp. 441-450.

B. Baldwin, "The *acta diurna*," *Chiron* 9. 1979. pp. 189-203.

B. Baldwin, "Acclamations in the *Historia Augusta*," *Athenaeum* 59. 1981. pp. 138-149.

J.P.V.D. Balsdon, "Roman History, 58-56 B.C.: three Ciceronian problems," *JRS* 47. 1957. pp. 15-20.

J.P.V.D. Balsdon, *Life and Leisure in Ancient Rome*, London, 1969.

T. D. Barnes, "Legislation against the Christians," *JRS* 58. 1968. pp. 32-50.

T. D. Barnes, "A senator from Hadrumetum, and three others," *BHAC* 1968/9. pp. 47-58.

T. D. Barnes, "The first African consul," *CR* 21. 1971. p. 332.

T. D. Barnes, *Tertullian: A Historical and Literary Study*, Oxford, 1971.

T. D. Barnes, "Who were the nobility of the Roman empire?" *Phoenix* 28. 1974. pp. 444-449.

T. D. Barnes, "Two senators under Constantine," *JRS* 65. 1975. pp. 40-49.

A. A. Barrett, "The career of Tiberius Claudius Cogidubnus," *Britannia* 10. 1979. pp. 227-242.

A. Bartoli, "La statua porfiretica della curia (Roma)," *NSc* 1. 1947. pp. 85-100.

A. Bartoli, "Il monumento della perpetuità del senato," *Studi Romani* 2. 1954. pp. 129-137.

A. Bartoli, *Curia Senatus, lo scavo e il restauro*, Rome, 1963.

R. A. Bauman, "Tiberius and Murena," *Historia* 15. 1966. pp. 420-431.

R. A. Bauman, *Impietas in Principem, Münchener Beiträge* 67. 1974.

A. Bay, "The letters *SC* on Augustan *aes* coinage," *JRS* 62. 1972. pp. 111-122.

C. A. Behr, *Aelius Aristides and the Sacred Tales*, Amsterdam, 1968.

F. Benoit, "Le sanctuaire d'Auguste et les cryptoportiques d'Arles," *Rev. Arch.* 39. 1952. pp. 31-67.

D. van Berchem, "Un banquier chez les Helvètes," *Ktema* 3. 1978. pp. 267-274.

A. Beschaouch, "Éléments celtiques dans la population du pays de Carthage," *CRAI* 1979. pp. 394-409.

A. R. Birley, "The oath not to put senators to death," *CR* 12. 1962. pp. 197-199.

A. R. Birley, "The duration of military commands under Antoninus Pius," in *Corolla memoriae Erich Swoboda dedicata, Römische Forschungen in Niederösterreich* 5. 1966. pp. 43-53.

A. R. Birley, *Septimius Severus*, London, 1971.

A. R. Birley, *The* Fasti *of Roman Britain*, Oxford, 1981.

E. Birley, "Senators in the emperors' service," *Proc. Brit. Acad.* 39. 1953. pp. 197-214.

B. Bischoff, "Der Fronto-Palimpsest der Mauriner," *Sitzungsberichte der Bayerischen Akademie der Wissenschaften*, phil.-hist. Klasse, Heft 2, Munich, 1958.

L. T. Błaszczyk, *Ze studiów nad senatem rzymskim w okresie schyłku republiki*, Łódź, 1965 (with review by A. Deman, *Latomus* 26. 1967. p. 271).

J. M. Blázquez, "Hispania desde el año 138 al 235," *Hispania* 132. 1976. pp. 5-87.

J. Bleicken, *Senatsgericht und Kaisergericht, Abhandlungen der Akademie der Wissenschaften in Göttingen*, phil.-hist. Klasse, 3rd series, no. 53, 1962.

C. Börker and R. Merkelbach, *Die Inschriften von Ephesos*, Bonn, 1979-

H. Boge, *Griechische Tachygraphie und Tironische Noten*, Berlin, 1973.

R. Bonini, *I "Libri de Cognitionibus" di Callistrato*, Milan, 1964.

A. B. Bosworth, *A Historical Commentary on Arrian's History of Alexander* I, Oxford, 1980.

A. B. Bosworth, "Firmus of Arretium," *ZPE* 39. 1980. pp. 267-277.

E. Bourguet, *De rebus Delphicis imperatoriae aetatis capita duo*, Montpellier, 1905.

G. W. Bowersock, *Augustus and the Greek World*, Oxford, 1965.

G. W. Bowersock, "Suetonius and Trajan," in *Hommages à Marcel Renard*, ed. J. Bibauw, *Collection Latomus* 101, Brussels, 1969, vol. 1 pp. 119-125.

G. W. Bowersock, *Greek Sophists in the Roman Empire*, Oxford, 1969.

G. W. Bowersock, "Syria under Vespasian," *JRS* 63. 1973. pp. 133-140.

A. A. Boyce, "The origin of *ornamenta triumphalia*," *Class. Phil.* 37. 1942. pp. 130-141.

G. K. Boyce, *Corpus of the Lararia of Pompeii, MAAR* 14. 1937.

K. R. Bradley, *Suetonius' Life of Nero: An Historical Commentary, Collection Latomus* 157, Brussels, 1978.

H. Braunert, "Das Athenaeum zu Rom bei den Scriptores Historiae Augustae," *BHAC* 2. 1963. pp. 9-41.

R. Brilliant, *Gesture and Rank in Roman Art, Memoirs of the Connecticut Academy of Arts and Sciences* 14. 1963.

P. A. Brunt, "Charges of provincial maladministration under the early Principate," *Historia* 10. 1961. pp. 189-227.

P. A. Brunt, "The Lex Valeria Cornelia," *JRS* 51. 1961. pp. 71-83.

P. A. Brunt, "The 'fiscus' and its development," *JRS* 56. 1966. pp. 75-91.

P. A. Brunt, "Conscription and volunteering in the Roman imperial army," *Scripta Classica Israelica* 1. 1974. pp. 90-115.

P. A. Brunt, "C. Fabricius Tuscus and an Augustan dilectus," *ZPE* 13. 1974. pp. 161-185.

P. A. Brunt, "Stoicism and the Principate," *PBSR* 43. 1975. pp. 7-35.

P. A. Brunt, "Lex de imperio Vespasiani," *JRS* 67. 1977. pp. 95-116.

P. A. Brunt, "From Epictetus to Arrian," *Athenaeum* 55. 1977. pp. 19-48.

W. H. Buckler and D. M. Robinson (eds.), *Sardis* VII.1, *Greek and Latin Inscriptions*, Leiden, 1932.

536   BIBLIOGRAPHY

T. Büttner-Wobst, *De legationibus reipublicae liberae temporibus Romam missis,* Leipzig, 1876.

A. M. Burnett, "The authority to coin in the late Republic and early Empire," *NC* 17. 1977. pp. 37-63.

G. P. Burton, "Proconsuls, assizes and the administration of justice under the empire," *JRS* 65. 1975. pp. 92-106.

G. P. Burton, "The issuing of *mandata* to proconsuls and a new inscription from Cos," *ZPE* 21. 1976. pp. 63-68.

G. P. Burton, "The Curator Rei Publicae: towards a reappraisal," *Chiron* 9. 1979. pp. 465-487.

G. Calza, "Una statua di porfido trovata nel foro," *Atti della Pontificia Accademia Romana di Archeologia* (serie III) Rendiconti 22. 1946/7. pp. 185-191.

A. Cameron, *Circus Factions: Blues and Greens at Rome and Byzantium,* Oxford, 1976.

G. Camodeca, "La carriera di L. Publilius Probatus e un inesistente proconsole d' Africa, Q. Volateius," *Atti dell' Accademia di scienze morali e politiche, Napoli,* 85. 1974. pp. 250-268.

B. Campbell, "Who were the 'viri militares'?" *JRS* 65. 1975. pp. 11-31.

G. P. Carratelli, "Tabulae Herculanenses," *La Parola del Passato* 3. 1948. pp. 165-184.

F. Castagnoli, "Sulla biblioteca del tempio di Apollo Palatino," *Accademia dei Lincei* (Classe di scienze morali), *Rendiconti* Ser. 8. 4. 1949. pp. 380-382.

F. Castagnoli, "Note sulla topografia del Palatino e del Foro Romano," *Arch. Class.* 16. 1964. pp. 173-199.

R. Cavenaile, *Corpus papyrorum latinarum,* Wiesbaden, 1958.

M. Cébeillac, *Les 'Quaestores Principis et Candidati' aux Ier et IIème Siècles de l'Empire,* Milan, 1972.

E. J. Champlin, "The chronology of Fronto," *JRS* 64. 1974. pp. 136-159.

E. J. Champlin, "The life and times of Calpurnius Siculus," *JRS* 68. 1978. pp. 95-110.

E. J. Champlin, "Notes on the heirs of Commodus," *AJP* 100. 1979. pp. 288-306.

E. J. Champlin, *Fronto and Antonine Rome,* Harvard, 1980.

N. Charbonnel, "A propos de l'inscription de Kymé et des pouvoirs d'Auguste dans les provinces au lendemain du règlement de 27 av. n. è.," *Rev. Int. Droits Ant.* 1979. pp. 177-225.

A. Chastagnol, "Les modes d'accèss au sénat romain au début de l'empire: remarques à propos de la table Claudienne de Lyon," *Bulletin de la société nationale des antiquaires de France* 1971. pp. 282-310.

A. Chastagnol, "La naissance de l'*Ordo Senatorius,*" *MEFR* 85. 1973. pp. 583-607.

A. Chastagnol, " 'Latus Clavus' et 'Adlectio': l'accès des hommes nouveaux au sénat romain sous le haut-empire," *Rev. Hist. Droit* 53. 1975. pp. 375-394.

A. Chastagnol, "*Latus clavus* et *Adlectio* dans l'Histoire Auguste," *BHAC* 1975/6. pp. 107-131.

A. Chastagnol, "Le laticlave de Vespasien," *Historia* 25. 1976. pp. 253-256.

A. Chastagnol, "Le problème du domicile légal des sénateurs romains à l'époque impériale," in *Mélanges offerts à Léopold S. Senghor*, Dakar, 1977, pp. 43-54.

A. Chastagnol, "Les femmes dans l'ordre sénatorial: titulature et rang social à Rome," *Rev. Hist.* 262. 1979. pp. 3-28.

A. Chastagnol, "La crise de recrutement sénatorial des années 16-11 av. J.-C.," in *Miscellanea di studi classici in onore di Eugenio Manni* II, Rome, 1979, pp. 465-476.

A. Chastagnol, "Les homines novi entrés au sénat sous le règne de Domitien," in *Studien zur antiken Sozialgeschichte: Festschrift F. Vittinghoff*, ed. W. Eck, H. Galsterer, H. Wolff, Cologne/Vienna, 1980, pp. 269-281.

G.E.F. Chilver, *A Historical Commentary on Tacitus' Histories I and II*, Oxford, 1979.

G. W. Clarke, "Prosopographical notes on the Epistles of Cyprian, II. The Proconsul of Africa in 250 A.D.," *Latomus* 31. 1972. pp. 1053-1057.

G. Clemente, "La presunta politica di scambio dei governi provinciali fra imperatore e senato nel I e II secolo," *Parola del Passato* 20. 1965. pp. 195-206.

G. Clemente, "Il patronato nei collegia dell' impero romano," *Studi classici e orientali* 21. 1972. pp. 142-229.

R. A. Coles, *Reports of Proceedings in Papyri (Papyrologica Bruxellensia* 4), Brussels, 1966.

G. Colonna, "Viterbo—Calendari romani dai Bagni Communali e da Riello," *NSc* 29. 1975. pp. 37-42.

M. Corbier, *L' Aerarium Saturni et l'Aerarium Militare: administration et prosopographie sénatoriale*, Rome, 1974.

E. Courtney, *A Commentary on the Satires of Juvenal*, London, 1980.

F. H. Cramer, *Astrology in Roman Law and Politics*, American Philosophical Society, Philadelphia, 1954.

G. Crifò, "Attività normativa del senato in età repubblicana," *Boll. Ist. Dir. Rom.* 71. 1968. pp. 31-115.

J. Crook, *Consilium Principis*, Cambridge, 1955.

J. Crook, *Law and Life of Rome*, London, 1967.

D. Daube, "Did Macedo murder his father?" *ZSS* 65. 1947. pp. 261-311.

D. Daube, *Forms of Roman Legislation*, Oxford, 1956.

A. Degrassi, *I fasti consolari dell' impero romano (30 a.c.-613 d.c.)*, Rome, 1952.

A. Degrassi, *Il confine nord-orientale dell' Italia romana*, Berne, 1954.

N. Degrassi, "La dimora di Augusto sul Palatino e la base di Sorrento," *Atti della Pontificia Accademia Romana di Archeologia* (serie III) Rendiconti 39. 1966/7. pp. 77-116.

J. Desanges, "Un drame africain sous Auguste," in *Hommages à Marcel Renard*, Collection Latomus 102, Brussels, 1969, vol. 2 pp. 197-213.

J. DesGagniers and others, *Laodicée du Lycos. Le nymphée: campagnes 1961-1963*, Université Laval, Recherches Archéologiques, série I: fouilles, Québec and Paris, 1969.

538   BIBLIOGRAPHY

J. Devreker, "L'*adlectio in senatum* de Vespasien," *Latomus* 39. 1980. pp. 70-87.

F. K. Dörner, "Der Erlass des Statthalters von Asia Paullus Fabius Persicus," diss. Greifswald, 1935.

M. A. de Dominicis, "Il 'ius sententiae' nel senato romano," *Annali*, Facoltà di giurisprudenza, Perugia, 44. 1932. pp. 243-300.

M. Dondin, "Une anomalie du *cursus* sénatorial sous l'empire: les legations provinciales préquestoriennes," *Latomus* 37. 1978. pp. 148-172.

G. Dossin, "La 'lunule' des sénateurs romains," in *Hommages à Marcel Renard, Collection Latomus* 102, Brussels, 1969, vol. 2 pp. 240-243.

T. Drew-Bear, W. Eck, P. Herrmann, "Sacrae Litterae," *Chiron* 7. 1977. pp. 355-383.

R. Duncan-Jones, *The Economy of the Roman Empire: Quantitative Studies*, Cambridge, 1974.

F. Dvornik, "The authority of the state in the oecumenical councils," *The Christian East* 14. 1933. pp. 95-108.

F. Dvornik, "Emperors, popes and general councils," *Dumbarton Oaks Papers* 6. 1951. pp. 3-23.

F. Dvornik, *Photian and Byzantine Ecclesiastical Studies*, London, 1974.

W. Eck, "Zum Rechtsstatus von Sardinien im 2 Jh. n. Chr.," *Historia* 20. 1971. pp. 510-512.

W. Eck, "Die Familie der Volusii Saturnini in neuen Inschriften aus Lucus Feroniae," *Hermes* 100. 1972. pp. 461-484.

W. Eck, "Bemerkungen zum Militärkommando in den Senatsprovinzen der Kaiserzeit," *Chiron* 2. 1972. pp. 429-436.

W. Eck, "Sozialstruktur des römischen Senatorenstandes der hohen Kaiserzeit und statistische Methode," *Chiron* 3. 1973. pp. 375-394.

W. Eck, "Beförderungskriterien innerhalb der senatorischen Laufbahn, dargestellt an der Zeit von 69 bis 138 n. Chr.," *ANRW* II.i. 1974. pp. 158-228.

W. Eck, *Die staatliche Organisation Italiens in der hohen Kaiserzeit, Vestigia* 28, Munich, 1979.

W. Eck, "Traian als Stifter der Alimenta auf einer Basis aus Terracina," *Archäologischer Anzeiger* 1980. pp. 266-270.

W. Eck, "Miscellanea prosopographica," *ZPE* 42. 1981. pp. 227-256.

D. E. Eichholz, "How long did Vespasian serve in Britain?" *Britannia* 3. 1972. pp. 149-163.

H. Engelmann and D. Knibbe, "Aus ephesichen Skizzenbüchern," *JÖAI* 1978-80 Hauptblatt 52. pp. 19-61.

P. Fabia, *Les sources de Tacite dans les Histoires et les Annales*, Paris, 1893.

J.-C. Faur, "Un discours de l'empereur Caligula au Sénat (Dion, Hist. rom. LIX, 16)," *Klio* 60. 1978. pp. 439-447.

E.W.B. Fentress, *Numidia and the Roman Army: Social, Military and Economic Aspects of the Frontier Zone (B.A.R.*, International Series 53), Oxford, 1979.

J. Fitz, "Prosopographica Pannonica," *Epigraphica* 23. 1961. pp. 66-94.

G. Forni, "ΙΕΡΑ e ΘΕΟΣ ΣΥΝΚΛΗΤΟΣ: un capitolo dimenticato nella storia del

Senato Romano," *Atti Accad. Naz. Lincei*, Memorie (Classe sc. mor., stor., fil.) VIII. V. 3 (1953).

P. de Francisci, "Per la storia della legislazione imperiale durante il Principato," *Annali della storia del diritto* 12/13. 1968/9. pp. 1-41.

R. Frei-Stolba, *Untersuchungen zu den Wahlen in der römischen Kaiserzeit*, Zurich, 1967.

R. Freudenberger, "Die Überlieferung vom Martyrium des römischen Christen Apollonius," *ZNTW* 60. 1969. pp. 111-130.

G. Freyburger, "La supplication d'action de grâces sous le Haut-Empire," *ANRW* 16.2. 1978. pp. 1418-1439.

L. Friedländer, *Darstellungen aus der Sittengeschichte Roms* (ed. 9/10), Leipzig, 1921.

B. W. Frier, *Landlords and Tenants in Imperial Rome*, Princeton, 1980.

H. Furneaux, *The Annals of Tacitus* (ed. 2), Oxford, 1896.

E. Gabba, *Appiano e la storia delle guerre civili*, Florence, 1956.

E. Gabba, "Senati in esilio," *Boll. Ist. Dir. Rom.* 63. 1960. pp. 221-232.

M. J. le Gall, *Le Tibre, fleuve de Rome dans l'antiquité*, Paris, 1953.

P. A. Gallivan, "Some comments on the *Fasti* for the reign of Nero," *CQ* 24. 1974. pp. 290-311.

P. A. Gallivan, "The *Fasti* for the reign of Claudius," *CQ* 28. 1978. pp. 407-426.

P. A. Gallivan, "The Fasti for the reign of Gaius," *Antichthon* 13. 1979. pp. 66-69.

P. A. Gallivan, "The Fasti for A.D. 70-96," *CQ* 31. 1981. pp. 186-220.

P.D.A. Garnsey, *Social Status and Legal Privilege in the Roman Empire*, Oxford, 1970.

P.D.A. Garnsey, "Rome's African empire under the Principate," in *Imperialism in the Ancient World*, ed. P.D.A. Garnsey and C. R. Whittaker, Cambridge, 1978, pp. 223-254.

J. Gascou, "Le décret municipal de Tergeste en l'honneur de Lucius Fabius Severus," *Annuaire de l'école pratique des hautes études* (IVe section, sciences historiques et philologiques) 99. 1966/7. pp. 511-520.

J. Geiger, "M. Hortensius M. f. Q. n. Hortalus," *CR* 20. 1970. pp. 132-134.

H. Gerstinger, "Neue Texte aus der Sammlung Papyrus Erzherzog Rainer in Wien," *Anzeiger der phil.-hist. Kl. d. öst. Akad. d. Wiss.* 1958. no. 15.

F.R.D. Goodyear, *The Annals of Tacitus*, Cambridge, 1972-

F.R.D. Goodyear, "Tacitus," in *The Cambridge History of Latin Literature* 2, ed. E. J. Kenney, Cambridge, 1982, pp. 642-655.

A. E. Gordon, *Quintus Veranius Consul A.D. 49*, California, 1952.

O. Gradenwitz, *Vocabularium iurisprudentiae romanae*, Berlin, 1903-

M. Griffin, "The Elder Seneca and Spain," *JRS* 62. 1972. pp. 1-19.

M. Griffin, *Seneca: A Philosopher in Politics*, Oxford, 1976.

A. Grilli, *Il problema della vita contemplativa nel mondo greco-romano*, Milan and Rome, 1953.

P. Groebe, "Die Obstruktion im römischen Senat," *Klio* 5. 1905. pp. 229-235.

G. Gualandi, *Legislazione imperiale e giurisprudenza*, Milan, 1963.

M. Guarducci, *Inscriptiones Creticae*, 4 vols., Rome, 1935-1950.

A. Guarino, "Il mestiere di senatore," *Labeo* 24. 1978. pp. 20-36.

A. Gudeman, *P. Cornelii Taciti Dialogus de Oratoribus*, Leipzig and Berlin, 1914.

R. Güngerich, *Kommentar zum Dialogus des Tacitus*, Göttingen, 1980.

C. Habicht, "Zwei neue Inschriften aus Pergamon," *Istanb. Mitt.* 9/10. 1959/60. pp. 109-127.

C. Habicht, *Altertümer von Pergamon, VIII. 3: Die Inschriften des Asklepieions* (Deutsches Archäologisches Institut, Berlin, 1969).

C. Habicht, "Zwei römische Senatoren aus Kleinasien," *ZPE* 13. 1974. pp. 1-6.

M. Hammond, "Curatores Tabularum Publicarum," in *Classical and Mediaeval Studies in Honor of E. K. Rand*, ed. L. W. Jones, New York, 1938, pp. 123-131.

M. Hammond, "A statue of Trajan represented on the 'Anaglypha Traiani,' " *MAAR* 21. 1953. pp. 127-183.

M. Hammond, "The transmission of the powers of the Roman emperor from the death of Nero in A.D. 68 to that of Alexander Severus in A.D. 235," *MAAR* 24. 1956. pp. 61-133.

M. Hammond, "Composition of the senate A.D. 68-235," *JRS* 47. 1957. pp. 74-81.

M. Hammond, *The Antonine Monarchy, Papers and Monographs of the American Academy in Rome* 19. 1959.

R. Harder, *Didyma* II, Berlin, 1958.

L. Harmand, *Le patronat sur les collectivités publiques des origines au bas-empire*, Paris, 1957.

W. V. Harris, *War and Imperialism in Republican Rome, 327-70 B.C.*, Oxford, 1979.

A. Henrichs, "Vespasian's visit to Alexandria," *ZPE* 3. 1968. pp. 51-80.

P. Herrmann, "Die Inschriften römischer Zeit aus dem Heraion von Samos," *Ath. Mitt.* 75. 1960. pp. 68-183.

P. Herrmann, *Der römische Kaisereid, Hypomnemata* 20, Göttingen, 1968.

P. Herrmann, "Eine Kaiserurkunde der Zeit Marc Aurels aus Milet," *Istanb. Mitt.* 25. 1975. pp. 149-166.

H. Heubner, *P. Cornelius Tacitus, Die Historien*, 4 vols., Heidelberg, 1963-1976.

G. F. Hill, "Some coins of southern Asia Minor," in *Anatolian Studies presented to Sir William Mitchell Ramsay*, ed. W. H. Buckler and W. M. Calder, Manchester, 1923, pp. 207-224.

O. Hirschfeld, "Die Rangtitel der römischen Kaiserzeit," in *Kleine Schriften*, Berlin, 1913, pp. 646-681.

O. Hirschfeld, "Die römische Staatszeitung und die Akklamationen im Senat," ibid. pp. 682-702.

O. Hirschfeld, "Die Abfassungszeit der MAKPOBIOI," ibid. pp. 881-884.

R. Hodot, "La grande inscription de M. Pompeius Macrinus a Mytilène," *ZPE* 34. 1979. pp. 221-237.

T. Hölscher, *Victoria Romana*, Mainz, 1967.

A. J. Holladay, "The election of magistrates in the early Principate," *Latomus* 37. 1978. pp. 874-893.

A. M. Honoré, *Gaius*, Oxford, 1962.

A. M. Honoré, "The Severan lawyers: a preliminary survey," *SDHI* 28. 1962. pp. 162-232.

A. M. Honoré, " 'Imperial' rescripts A.D. 193-305: authorship and authenticity," *JRS* 69. 1979. pp. 51-64.

A. M. Honoré and J. Menner, *Concordance to the Digest Jurists*, Oxford, 1980 (microfiche).

K. Hopkins, "Economic growth and towns in classical antiquity," in *Towns in Societies*, ed. P. Abrams and E. A. Wrigley, Cambridge, 1978, pp. 35-77.

K. Hopkins, *Conquerors and Slaves*, Cambridge, 1978.

N. Horsfall, "The Ides of March: some new problems," *Greece and Rome* 21. 1974. pp. 191-199.

G. W. Houston, "Notes on some documents pertaining to Flavian administrative personnel," *ZPE* 20. 1976. pp. 25-34.

G. W. Houston, "Vespasian's adlection of men *in senatum*," *AJP* 98. 1977. pp. 35-63.

M.P.J. van den Hout, *M. Cornelii Frontonis Epistulae*, Leiden, 1954.

H. U. Instinsky, "Formalien im Briefwechsel des Plinius mit Kaiser Trajan," Akad. der Wiss. und Lit., Mainz, *Abhandlungen geistes- und sozialwiss. Klasse*, 1969. no. 12.

S. Jameson, "22 or 23?" *Historia* 18. 1969. pp. 204-229.

A. C. Johnson, P. R. Coleman-Norton, F. C. Bourne, *Ancient Roman Statutes*, Austin, 1961.

H. F. Jolowicz and B. Nicholas, *Historical Introduction to the Study of Roman Law* (ed. 3), Cambridge, 1972.

A.H.M. Jones, "Imperial and senatorial jurisdiction in the early Principate," *Historia* 3. 1955. pp. 464-488.

A.H.M. Jones, *Studies in Roman Government and Law*, Oxford, 1960.

A.H.M. Jones, *The Later Roman Empire*, Oxford, 1964.

A.H.M. Jones, *The Criminal Courts of the Roman Republic and Principate*, Oxford, 1972.

C. P. Jones, "Towards a chronology of Plutarch's works," *JRS* 56. 1966. pp. 61-74.

C. P. Jones, *Plutarch and Rome*, Oxford, 1971.

C. P. Jones, "The date of Dio of Prusa's Alexandrian oration," *Historia* 22. 1973. pp. 302-309.

J. R. Jones, "Mint magistrates in the early Roman empire," *BICS* 17. 1970. pp. 70-77.

U. Kahrstedt, *Das wirtschaftliche Gesicht Griechenlands in der Kaiserzeit*, Berne, 1954.

M. Kaser, *Das römische Zivilprozessrecht*, Munich, 1966.

M. Kaser, *Das römische Privatrecht* I (ed. 2), Munich, 1971.

J. Keil and A. von Premerstein, *Bericht über eine dritte Reise in Lydien*, Vienna, 1914.

J. Keil, "Die dritte Neokorie von Ephesos," *Num. Zeitschr.* 48. 1915. pp. 125-130.

J. Keil, "Die erste Kaiserneokorie von Ephesos," *Num. Zeitschr.* 52. 1919. pp. 115-120.

P. Kneissl, *Die Siegestitulatur der römischen Kaiser, Hypomnemata* 23, Göttingen, 1969.

D. Knibbe, R. Merkelbach, "Allerhöchste Schelte," *ZPE* 31. 1978. pp. 229-232.

L. Koenen, "Die 'Laudatio Funebris' des Augustus für Agrippa auf einem neuen Papyrus," *ZPE* 5. 1970. pp. 217-283.

G. Koeppel, "Profectio und Adventus," *Bonn. Jahrb.* 169. 1969. pp. 139-194.

E. Koestermann, *Cornelius Tacitus, Annalen,* 4 vols., Heidelberg, 1963-1968.

J. Korpanty, "Przyczynek do problemu tzw. 'senatores pedarii,' " *Meander* 34. 1979. pp. 415-418.

K. Kraft, "S(enatus) C(onsulto)," *JNG* 12. 1962. pp. 7-49.

K. Kraft, *Das System der kaiserzeitlichen Münzprägung in Kleinasien, Istanbuler Forschungen* 29, Berlin, 1972.

H. Kramolisch, *Die Strategen des Thessalischen Bundes vom Jahr 196 v. Chr. bis zum Ausgang der römischen Republik,* Bonn, 1978.

H. Kunckel, *Der römische Genius, Mitteilungen des deutschen Archaeologischen Instituts,* Roemische Abteilung, Ergänzungsheft 20, Heidelberg, 1974.

A. Kunisz, *Recherches sur le monnayage et la circulation monétaire sous le règne d'Auguste,* Wrocław, 1976.

W. Kunkel, *Herkunft und soziale Stellung der römischen Juristen* (ed. 2), Graz, Vienna, Cologne, 1967.

W. Kunkel, *Über die Entstehung des Senatsgerichts, Sitzungsberichte der Bayerischen Akademie der Wissenschaften,* phil.-hist. Klasse, Heft 2, Munich, 1969.

W. Kunkel, *Kleine Schriften,* Weimar, 1974.

W. K. Lacey, "Octavian in the senate, January 27 B.C.," *JRS* 64. 1974. pp. 176-184.

P. Lambrechts, *La composition du sénat romain de l'accession au trône d'Hadrien à la mort de Commode,* Antwerp, 1936.

S. Lancel, *Actes de la conférence de Carthage en 411,* vol. 1 (Sources Chrétiennes no. 194, Paris, 1972).

O. Lenel, *Palingenesia iuris civilis,* Leipzig, 1889.

B. M. Levick and S. Jameson, "C. Crepereius Gallus and his *gens*," *JRS* 54. 1964. pp. 98-106.

B. M. Levick, "The coinage of Pisidian Antioch in the third century A.D.," *NC* 6. 1966. pp. 47-59.

B. M. Levick, *Roman Colonies in Southern Asia Minor,* Oxford, 1967.

B. M. Levick, "Imperial control of the elections under the early Principate: commendatio, suffragatio and 'nominatio,' " *Historia* 16. 1967. pp. 207-230.

B. M. Levick, "The beginning of Tiberius' career," *CQ* 21. 1971. pp. 478-486.

B. M. Levick, *Tiberius the Politician,* London, 1976.

B. M. Levick, "Antiquarian or Revolutionary? Claudius Caesar's Conception of his Principate," *AJP* 99. 1978. pp. 79-105.

N. Lewis and M. Reinhold, *Roman Civilization* II, New York, 1955.

A. W. Lintott, "Popular justice in a letter of Cicero to Quintus," *Rhein. Mus.* 110. 1967. pp. 65-69.

G. Lugli (ed.), *Fontes ad topographiam veteris urbis Romae pertinentes*, Rome, 1952-

S. MacCormack, "Latin Prose Panegyrics," in *Empire and Aftermath: Silver Latin II*, ed. T. A. Dorey, London, 1975, pp. 143-205.

D. Mack, *Senatsreden und Volksreden bei Cicero*, Würzburg, 1937.

R. Macmullen, "Romans in tears," *Class. Phil.* 75. 1980. pp. 254-255.

F. Magi, *I rilievi Flavi del Palazzo della Cancellaria*, Rome, 1945.

F. Magi, "Il calendario dipinto sotto Santa Maria Maggiore," *Pontificia Accademia Romana di Archeologia: Memorie* 11. 1972.

D. Magie, *De Romanorum iuris publici sacrique vocabulis sollemnibus in Graecum sermonem conversis*, Leipzig, 1905.

A. Maiuri, *Nuova silloge epigrafica di Rodi e di Cos*, Florence, 1925.

M. Malavolta, "A proposito del nuovo *S.C.* da Larino," *Sesta miscellanea greca e romana* (Studi pubblicati dall' Istituto Italiano per la storia antica, 27, Rome, 1978), pp. 347-382.

F. de Marini Avonzo, *La funzione giurisdizionale del senato romano*, Milan, 1957.

J. Marquardt, *Das Privatleben der Römer* (ed. 2), Leipzig, 1886.

F. B. Marsh, *The Reign of Tiberius*, Oxford, 1931.

H. J. Mason, *Greek Terms for Roman Institutions: A Lexicon and Analysis* (American Studies in Papyrology 13), Toronto, 1974.

V. A. Maxfield, *The Military Decorations of the Roman Army*, London, 1981.

R. Mayer, "Calpurnius Siculus: technique and date," *JRS* 70. 1980. pp. 175-176.

R. Mayr, *Vocabularium codicis Iustiniani*, Prague, 1923-1925.

D. McAlindon, "The senator's retiring age: 65 or 60?" *CR* 7. 1957. p. 108.

R. Meiggs, *Roman Ostia* (ed. 2), Oxford, 1973.

R. Mellor, ΘΕΑ ΡΩΜΗ, *The worship of the goddess Roma in the Greek world*, Hypomnemata 42, Göttingen, 1975.

A. Mentz, "Die Entstehungsgeschichte der römischen Stenographie," *Hermes* 66. 1931. pp. 369-386.

M. Meslin, *La Fête des kalendes de janvier dans l'empire romain*, Collection Latomus 115, Brussels, 1970.

P. M. Meyer, *Griechische Papyri im Museum der oberhessischen Geschichtsvereins zu Giessen*, Leipzig and Berlin, 1910.

J. Meyshan, "The coinage of Agrippa the First," *Israel Exploration Journal* 4. 1954. pp. 186-200.

A. K. Michels, *The Calendar of the Roman Republic*, Princeton, 1967.

F. Millar, *A Study of Cassius Dio*, Oxford, 1964.

F. Millar, "The aerarium and its officials under the Empire," *JRS* 54. 1964. pp. 33-40.

F. Millar, "Epictetus and the imperial court," *JRS* 55. 1965. pp. 141-148.

F. Millar, "The emperor, the senate and the provinces," *JRS* 56. 1966. pp. 156-166.

F. Millar, "Triumvirate and Principate," *JRS* 63. 1973. pp. 50-67.

F. Millar, *The Emperor in the Roman World*, London, 1977.

S. Mitchell, "Requisitioned transport in the Roman empire: a new inscription from Pisidia," *JRS* 66. 1976. pp. 106-131.

T. B. Mitford and I. K. Nicolaou, *Salamis* vol. 6, Nicosia, 1974.

L. Mitteis and U. Wilcken, *Grundzüge und Chrestomathie der Papyruskunde*, Leipzig/Berlin, 1912.

A. Mocsy, "Tampius Flavianus Pannoniában," *Archaeologiai Értesitö* 93. 1966. pp. 203-207.

G. Molisani, "Un nuovo curator operum publicorum in un' iscrizione inedita dei Musei Capitolini," *ZPE* 13. 1974. pp. 7-17.

G. Molisani, "Il governo della Licia-Panfilia nell' età di Marco Aurelio," *Rivista di Filologia* 105. 1977. pp. 166-178.

A. D. Momigliano, "Historiography on written tradition and historiography on oral tradition," in *Studies in Historiography*, London, 1966, pp. 211-220.

T. Mommsen, "Sui modi usati da' Romani nel conservare e pubblicare le leggi ed i senatusconsulti," in *Gesammelte Schriften* (8 vols., Berlin, 1904-1913), III. pp. 290-313.

T. Mommsen, "Das Verhältniss des Tacitus zu den Acten des Senates," ibid. VII. pp. 253-263.

T. Mommsen, "Senatus consultum de sumptibus ludorum gladiatorum minuendis factum a. p. c. 176/7," ibid. VIII. pp. 499-531.

T. Mommsen, "Commentaria ludorum saecularium quintorum et septimorum," ibid. VIII. pp. 567-626.

J. Morris, "The Roman Senate 69-193 A. D.," unpublished Ph.D. thesis (London, 1953).

J. Morris, "Senate and Emperor," in *Geras, Studies Presented to George Thomson on the Occasion of His 60th Birthday*, Prague, 1963, pp. 149-161.

J. Morris, "Leges Annales under the Principate, I. Legal and Constitutional," *List. Fil.* 87. 1964. pp. 316-337; "II. Political Effects," ibid. 88. 1965. pp. 22-31.

H. A. Musurillo, *The Acts of the Pagan Martyrs*: Acta Alexandrinorum, Oxford, 1954.

H. A. Musurillo, *The Acts of the Christian Martyrs*, Oxford, 1972.

O. Neugebauer, *A History of Ancient Mathematical Astronomy*, Berlin/Heidelberg/New York, 1975.

R. F. Newbold, "The spectacles as an issue between Gaius and the senate," *Proceedings of the African Classical Associations* 13. 1975. pp. 30-35.

C. Nicolet, "Le cens senatorial sous la République et sous Auguste," *JRS* 66. 1976. pp. 20-38.

C. Nicolet, *Rome et la conquête du monde Méditerranéen 264-27 avant J.-C., 1. Les structures de l' Italie romaine* (ed. 2), Paris, 1979.

J. Nicols, "Pliny and the patronage of communities," *Hermes* 108. 1980. pp. 365-385.

K. L. Nipperdey, *Tacitus*, Annals I-VI, ed. 11, revised G. Andresen, Berlin, 1915.

D. Nörr, "Drei Miszellen zur Lebensgeschichte des Juristen Salvius Julianus," in *Daube Noster: Essays in Legal History for David Daube*, ed. A. Watson, Edinburgh and London, 1974, pp. 233-252.

A. F. Norman, "The book trade in fourth-century Antioch," *JHS* 80. 1960. pp. 122-126.

R. M. Ogilvie and I. Richmond, *Cornelii Taciti de Vita Agricolae*, Oxford, 1967.

J. H. Oliver and R.E.A. Palmer, "Minutes of an Act of the Roman Senate," *Hesperia* 24. 1955. pp. 329-349.

J. H. Oliver, "The epistle of Claudius which mentions the proconsul Iunius Gallio," *Hesperia* 40. 1971. pp. 239-240.

J. H. Oliver, "Imperial commissioners in Achaia," *GRBS* 14. 1973. pp. 389-405.

J. H. Oliver, "Minutes of a trial conducted by Caracalla at Antioch in A.D. 216," in *Mélanges Helléniques offerts à Georges Daux*, Paris, 1974, pp. 289-294.

A. Ormanni, *Saggi sul "regolamento interno" del senato romano*, Milan, 1971.

W. Orth, "Ein vernachlässigtes Zeugnis zur Geschichte der römischen Provinz Creta et Cyrenae," *Chiron* 3. 1973. pp. 255-263.

M. L. Paladini, "Le votazioni del senato romano nell' età di Traiano," *Athenaeum* 37. 1959. pp. 3-133.

M. L. Paladini, "La 'gratiarum actio' dei consoli in Roma attraverso la testimonianza di Plinio il Giovane," *Historia* 10. 1961. pp. 356-374.

S. Panciera, "L. Pomponius L. F. Horatia Bassus Cascus Scribonianus," *Atti della Pontificia Accademia Romana di Archeologia*, Rendiconti 45. 1972/3. pp. 105-131.

S. di Paola, *Donatio mortis causa*, Catania, 1950.

B. Parsi, *Désignation et investiture de l'empereur romain*, Paris, 1963.

H. Pavis d'Escurac, *La préfecture de l'annone: service administratif impérial d'Auguste à Constantin*, Rome, 1976.

H. Pavis d'Escurac, "Aristocratie sénatoriale et profits commerciaux," *Ktema* 2. 1977. pp. 339-355.

T.E.V. Pearce, "Notes on Cicero, In Pisonem," *CQ* 20. 1970. pp. 309-321.

H.-G. Pflaum, *Le Marbre de Thorigny*, Paris, 1948.

H.-G. Pflaum, "Légats impériaux à l'intérieur de provinces sénatoriales," in *Hommages à Albert Grenier, Collection Latomus* 58, Brussels, 1962, pp. 1232-1242.

H.-G. Pflaum, "De nouveau sur les *agri decumates* à la lumière d'un fragment de Capoue, CIL X. 3872," *Bonn. Jahrb.* 163. 1963. pp. 224-237.

H.-G. Pflaum, "Augustanius Alpinus Bellicus Sollers, membres de la gens Cassia," *Archivo Español de Arqueologia* 39. 1966. pp. 3-23.

H.-G. Pflaum, "Epigraphie latine impériale," *Ecole Pratique des Hautes Etudes (IVe section): Annuaire* 1973/4. pp. 269-277.

H.-G. Pflaum, "Les progrès des recherches prosopographiques concernant l'époque du Haut-Empire durant le dernier quart de siècle (1945-1970)," *ANRW* II.i. 1974. pp. 113-135.

H.-G. Pflaum, *Abrégé des procurateurs équestres*, Paris, 1974.

H.-G. Pflaum, "La carrière de C. Iulius Avitus Alexianus, grand'père de deux empereurs," *Rev. Et. Lat.* 57. 1979. pp. 298-314.

H.-G. Pflaum, *Gaule et l'empire romain: scripta varia* II, Paris, 1981.

B. Pick, "Die tempeltragenden Gottheiten und die Darstellung der Neokorie auf den Münzen," *JÖAI* 7. 1904. pp. 1-41.

A. Piganiol, "Les *trinci* Gaulois, gladiateurs consacrés," *Rev. Et. Anc.* 22. 1920. pp. 283-290.

G. B. Pighi, *De Ludis Saecularibus Populi Romani Quiritium* (ed. 2), Amsterdam, 1965.

A. Plassart, *Fouilles de Delphes* III. 4, Paris, 1970.

S. B. Platner and T. Ashby, *A Topographical Dictionary of Ancient Rome*, Oxford, 1929.

H. A. Pohlsander, "Victory: the story of a statue," *Historia* 18. 1969. pp. 588-597.

F. Preisigke and others (eds.), *Sammelbuch griechischer Urkunden aus Ägypten*, Stuttgart and elsewhere, 1915-   .

M. Rachet, *Rome et les berbères, Collection Latomus* 110, Brussels, 1970.

B. Radice, "Pliny and the *Panegyricus*," *Greece and Rome* 15. 1968. pp. 166-172.

P. Ramondetti, "La terminologia relativa alla procedura del *senatum habere* in Svetonio," *Atti Accad. Sc. di Torino*, Classe Sc. Mor., Stor. e Filol. 111. 1977. pp. 135-168.

W. M. Ramsay, "Inscriptions de la Galatie et du Pont," *BCH* 7. 1883. pp. 15-28.

E. Rawson, "Caesar's heritage," *JRS* 65. 1975. pp. 148-159.

E. Rawson, "The Ciceronian aristocracy and its properties," in *Studies in Roman Property*, ed. M. I. Finley, Cambridge, 1976, pp. 85-102.

M. Reinhold, "Usurpation of status and status symbols in the Roman Empire," *Historia* 20. 1971. pp. 275-302.

B. Rémy, "Ornati et ornamenta quaestoria praetoria et consularia sous le haut empire romain," *Rev. Et. Anc.* 78-79. 1976/7. pp. 160-198.

J. M. Reynolds, "Notes on Cyrenaican inscriptions," *PBSR* 20. 1965. pp. 52-54.

J. M. Reynolds, "Inscriptions from south Etruria," *PBSR* 21. 1966. pp. 56-67.

J. M. Reynolds, "Hadrian, Antoninus Pius and the Cyrenaican Cities," *JRS* 68. 1978. pp. 111-121.

J. M. Reynolds, *Aphrodisias and Rome*, London, 1982.

L. Richardson, Jr., "The Curia Julia and the Janus Geminus," *Röm. Mitt.* 85. 1978. pp. 359-369.

G. E. Rickman, *The Corn Supply of Ancient Rome*, Oxford, 1980.

E. Ritterling, "Ein Offizier des Rheinheeres aus der Zeit des Caligula," *Germania* 1. 1917. pp. 170-173.

E. Ritterling, "Military forces in the senatorial provinces," *JRS* 17. 1927. pp. 28-32.

L. Robert, *Etudes anatoliennes*, Paris, 1937.

L. Robert, *Monnaies grecques*, Geneva and Paris, 1967.

L. Robert, "Sur des inscriptions d'Éphèse: fêtes, athlètes, empereurs, épigrammes," *Rev. Phil.* 41. 1967. pp. 7-84.

L. Robert, *Opera Minora Selecta*, 4 vols., Amsterdam, 1969-1974.

L. Robert, "La titulature de Nicée et de Nicomédie: la gloire et la haine," *HSCP* 81. 1977. pp. 1-39.

L. Robert, "Documents d'Asie Mineure, VIII. Règlement impérial gréco-latin sur les hôtes imposés," *BCH* 102. 1978. pp. 432-437.

C. Rodewald, *Money in the Age of Tiberius*, Manchester, 1976.

A. Rodger, "A note on A. Cascellius," *CQ* 22. 1972. pp. 135-138.

R. S. Rogers, "Lucius Arruntius," *Class. Phil.* 26. 1931. pp. 31-45.

R. S. Rogers, "The emperor's displeasure—*amicitiam renuntiare*," *TAPA* 90. 1959. pp. 224-237.

K.F.C. Rose, *The Date and Author of the Satyricon, Mnemosyne* Suppl. 16, Leiden, 1971.

G. Rotondi, *Leges publicae populi Romani*, Milan, 1912.

I. S. Ryberg, *Rites of the State Religion in Roman Art, MAAR* 22. 1955.

S. Şahin, *Bithynische Studien (Inschriften griechischer Städte aus Kleinasien* 7, Bonn, 1978).

R. P. Saller, *Personal Patronage Under the Early Empire*, Cambridge, 1982.

P. Salway, *Roman Britain*, Oxford, 1981.

J. Scheid and H. Broise, "Deux nouveaux fragments des actes des frères Arvales de l'année 38 ap. J.-C.," *MEFR* 92. 1980. pp. 215-248.

A. Schenk Graf von Stauffenberg, *Die römische Geschichte bei Malalas*, Stuttgart, 1931.

A. A. Schiller, "Senatus consulta in the Principate," *Tulane Law Review* 33. 1958/9. pp. 491-508.

A. A. Schiller, *An American Experience in Roman Law*, Göttingen, 1971.

L. Schumacher, "Das Ehrendekret für M. Nonius Balbus aus Herculaneum (AE 1947, 53)," *Chiron* 6. 1976. pp. 165-184.

E. Schwartz, *Acta Conciliorum Oecumenicorum* I and II, Berlin and Leipzig.

K. Scott, "Greek and Roman honorific months," *Yale Class. Stud.* 2. 1931. pp. 201-278.

P. Setälä, "Private Domini in Roman Brick Stamps of the Empire: A Historical and Prosopographical Study of Landowners in the District of Rome," Ann. Acad. Scient. Fenn., Diss. Hum. Litt. 10, Helsinki, 1977.

J. N. Settle, "The trial of Milo and the other *Pro Milone*," *TAPA* 94. 1963. pp. 268-280.

D. R. Shackleton Bailey, *Cicero's Letters to Atticus*, 6 vols. and indices, Cambridge, 1965-1970; *Epistulae ad Familiares*, 2 vols., ibid. 1977; *Epistulae ad Quintum Fratrem et M. Brutum*, ibid. 1980.

I. Shatzman, *Senatorial Wealth and Roman Politics, Collection Latomus* 142, Brussels, 1975.

R. K. Sherk, "The *inermes provinciae* of Asia Minor," *AJP* 76. 1955. pp. 400-413.

R. K. Sherk, "Roman imperial troops in Macedonia and Achaea," *AJP* 78. 1957. pp. 52-62.

R. K. Sherk, *Roman Documents from the Greek East*: Senatus Consulta *and* Epistulae *to the Age of Augustus*, Baltimore, 1969.

R. K. Sherk, *The Municipal Decrees of the Roman West* (Arethusa Monographs II), Buffalo, 1970.

A. N. Sherwin-White, *The Letters of Pliny: A Historical and Social Commentary*, Oxford, 1966.

S. M. Sherwin-White, *Ancient Cos, Hypomnemata* 51, Göttingen, 1978.

C. E. van Sickle, "Headings of rescripts of the Severi," *Class. Phil.* 23. 1928. pp. 270-277.

E. M. Smallwood, *Documents Illustrating the Principates of Gaius, Claudius and Nero*, Cambridge, 1967.

E. M. Smallwood, *The Jews under Roman Rule* (corrected ed.), Leiden, 1981.

P. A. Stadter, *Arrian of Nicomedia*, Chapel Hill, 1980.

C. G. Starr, Jr., "Epictetus and the tyrant," *Class. Phil.* 44. 1949. pp. 20-29.

A. Stein, "Die Protokolle des römischen Senates und ihre Bedeutung als Geschichtsquelle für Tacitus," *Jahresberichte der I. deutschen Staatsrealschule in Prag* 43. 1904. pp. 5-33.

A. Stein, "Die Stenographie im römischen Senat," *Archiv für Stenographie* 56. 1905. pp. 177-186.

A. Stein, *Der römische Ritterstand*, Munich, 1927.

P. Stein, "Die Senatssitzungen der Ciceronischen Zeit (68-43)," diss. Münster, 1930.

H. Stern, "Le calendrier de Sainte-Marie-Majeure," *Rev. Et. Lat.* 51. 1973. pp. 41-48.

J. Straub, "Senaculum, id est mulierum senatus," *BHAC* 1964/5. pp. 221-240.

G. V. Sumner, "Germanicus and Drusus Caesar," *Latomus* 26. 1967. pp. 413-435.

J. Suolahti, "Princeps Senatus," *Arctos* 7. 1972. pp. 207-218.

L. A. Sussman, *The Elder Seneca*, Leiden, 1978.

C.H.V. Sutherland, *The Emperor and the Coinage: Julio-Claudian Studies*, London, 1976.

R. Syme, "The colony of Cornelius Fuscus: an episode in the *Bellum Neronis*," *AJP* 58. 1937. pp. 7-18.

R. Syme, "Tacfarinas, the Musulamii and Thubursicu," in *Studies in Roman Economic and Social History in Honor of A. C. Johnson*, ed. P. R. Coleman-Norton, Princeton, 1951, pp. 113-130.

R. Syme, "Marcus Lepidus, *Capax Imperii*," *JRS* 45. 1955. pp. 22-33.

R. Syme, "The senator as historian," Fondation Hardt, *Entretiens*, Geneva, 1956, pp. 187-201.

R. Syme, "Some Pisones in Tacitus," *JRS* 46. 1956. pp. 17-21.

R. Syme, *Tacitus*, Oxford, 1958.

R. Syme, "Consulates in absence," *JRS* 48. 1958. pp. 1-9.

R. Syme, "Pliny's less successful friends," *Historia* 9. 1960. pp. 362-379.

R. Syme, *Sallust*, California, 1964.

R. Syme, "The historian Servilius Nonianus," *Hermes* 92. 1964. pp. 408-414.

R. Syme, "People in Pliny," *JRS* 58. 1968. pp. 135-151.

R. Syme, "Pliny the Procurator," *HSCP* 73. 1969. pp. 201-236.

R. Syme, "Legates of Cilicia under Trajan," *Historia* 18. 1969. pp. 352-366.

R. Syme, *Ten Studies in Tacitus*, Oxford, 1970.

R. Syme, *Danubian Papers*, Bucharest, 1971.

R. Syme, "The enigmatic Sospes," *JRS* 67. 1977. pp. 38-49.

R. Syme, "How Tacitus wrote *Annals* I-III," in *Historiographia Antiqua, Symb. Fac. Lit. Phil. Lovaniensis* Ser. A Vol. 6, 1977, pp. 231-263.

R. Syme, "Antonius Saturninus," *JRS* 68. 1978. pp. 12-21.

R. Syme, *Roman Papers*, Oxford, 1979.

R. Syme, "Juvenal, Pliny, Tacitus," *AJP* 100. 1979. pp. 250-278.

R. Syme, "An eccentric patrician," *Chiron* 10. 1980. pp. 427-448.

R.J.A. Talbert, "Some causes of disorder in 68-69 A.D.," *AJAH* 2. 1977. pp. 69-85.

R.J.A. Talbert, "Pliny the Younger as governor of Bithynia-Pontus," in *Studies in Latin Literature and Roman History* II, ed. C. Deroux, *Collection Latomus* 168, Brussels, 1980, pp. 412-435.

L. R. Taylor, *Roman Voting Assemblies*, Ann Arbor, 1966.

L. R. Taylor and R. T. Scott, "Seating space in the Roman senate and the *senatores pedarii*," *TAPA* 100. 1969. pp. 529-582.

E. Tengström, *Die Protokollierung der Collatio Carthaginiensis*, Göteborg, 1962.

B. E. Thomasson, *Die Statthalter der römischen Provinzen Nordafrikas von Augustus bis Diocletianus*, Lund, 1960.

B. E. Thomasson, "Zur Verwaltungsgeschichte der Provinz Sardinia," *Eranos* 70. 1972. pp. 72-81.

D. L. Thompson, "The meetings of the Roman senate on the Palatine," *AJA* 85. 1981. pp. 335-339.

G. B. Townend, "The consuls of A.D. 69/70," *AJP* 83. 1962. pp. 113-129.

G. B. Townend, "Calpurnius Siculus and the *Munus Neronis*," *JRS* 70. 1980. pp. 166-174.

J.M.C. Toynbee, *Roman Medallions*, A.N.S. Numismatic Studies 5, New York, 1944.

J.M.C. Toynbee, "The Ara Pacis re-considered and historical art in Roman Italy," *Proc. Brit. Acad.* 39. 1953. pp. 67-95.

J.M.C. Toynbee, *The Flavian Reliefs from the Palazzo della Cancellaria in Rome*, Oxford, 1957.

S. Treggiari, *Roman Freedmen During the Late Republic*, Oxford, 1969.

S. Treggiari, "Jobs in the household of Livia," *PBSR* 43. 1975. pp. 48-77.

B. L. Trell and M. J. Price, *Coins and Their Cities*, London, 1972.

B. L. Trell, "Architectura Numismatica," *NC* 12. 1972. pp. 45-59.

P. Veyne, "Un gouverneur impérial en Asie," in *Mélanges d'archéologie et d'histoire offerts à A. Piganiol*, ed. R. Chevallier, Paris, 1966, III. pp. 1395-1396.

F. Vittinghoff, *Der Staatsfeind in der römischen Kaiserzeit: Untersuchungen zur "damnatio memoriae,"* Berlin, 1936.

A. Voirol, "Die Darstellung eines Keltentempels auf einem Denar von Kaiser Augustus," *Jahrbuch der Schweizerischen Gesellschaft für Urgeschichte* 31. 1939. pp. 150-157.

E. Volterra, "Nuove ricerche sulla conventio in manum," *Atti Accad. Lincei*, Memorie ser. 8 vol. 12.4. 1966. pp. 251-355.

G. Vrind, *De Cassii Dionis vocabulis quae ad ius publicum pertinent*, The Hague, 1923.

J.-P. Waltzing, *Etude historique sur les corporations professionnelles chez les Romains*, Louvain, 1895.

K. H. Waters, "Traianus Domitiani Continuator," *AJP* 90. 1969. pp. 385-405.

A. Watson, *Law Making in the Later Roman Republic*, Oxford, 1974.

K. Wellesley, "The *dies imperii* of Tiberius," *JRS* 57. 1967. pp. 23-30.

A. B. West (ed.), *Corinth* VIII.2, Harvard, 1931.

C. R. Whittaker, *Herodian* (Loeb edition), 2 vols., 1969-1970.

T. Wiegand and others, *Milet*, Berlin, 1906- .

W. Williams, "Individuality in the imperial constitutions: Hadrian and the Antonines," *JRS* 66. 1976. pp. 67-83.

W. Williams, "Caracalla and the authorship of imperial edicts and epistles," *Latomus* 38. 1979. pp. 67-89.

L. M. Wilson, *The Clothing of the Ancient Romans*, Baltimore, 1938.

T. N. Winter, "The publication of Apuleius' *Apology*," *TAPA* 100. 1969. pp. 607-612.

T. P. Wiseman, *New Men in the Roman Senate 139 B.C.-A.D. 14*, Oxford, 1971.

Z. Yavetz, *Plebs and Princeps*, Oxford, 1969.

F. Zevi, "Il calcidico della *Curia Julia*," *Atti Accad. Lincei* (Classe sc. mor., storiche e filologiche) 26. 1971. pp. 237-251.

F. Zevi, "I consoli del 97 d. Cr. in due framenti già editi dei Fasti Ostienses," *List. Fil.* 96. 1973. pp. 125-137.

F. Zevi, "Un frammento dei *Fasti Ostienses* e i consolati dei primi anni di Traiano," *La Parola del Passato* 34. 1979. pp. 179-201.

INDEX OF ANCIENT SOURCES

For the most part this index is limited to passages quoted, discussed, or highlighted in the text and notes. In the case of major authors (Dio and Tacitus, for example) a severely selective approach has been taken. By contrast, in the case of inscriptions and legal sources, the diffuseness of relevant references has prompted a more comprehensive listing. However, all citations in chap. 15 sects. 1-4 and Extended Notes H-K, have been excluded from this index.

LITERARY SOURCES

Acts of the Christian Martyrs (Musurillo)
  7: 453, 519
Acts of Pagan Martyrs (Musurillo)
  4: 73, 161
  8: 34, 161
  11: 520
Aelian
  Frag. 112 Hercher: 86
  Hist. Anim. 15.19: 89
Aelius Aristides
  Orationes 19.13 Keil: 149
Appian
  Bell. Civ. 2.5: 245
    2.7: 355
    2.30: 151
    2.116: 225
Apuleius
  Florida
    8: 35
    16: 88
  Metam. 6.23: 17, 122,
    139, 495
Asconius (Clark)
  42 (p.): 317
  43: 199, 282
Aurelius Victor
  13.11: 411
Ausonius
  Grat. Act. 7: 370
Calpurnius Siculus
  Buc. (Verdière)
    1.69-71: 141
    1.71: 137
Carthage, *Acts of Conference*(A.D. 411)
  I.219: 320

Charisius
  Art. Gramm. (Barwick) II
    p. 287: 127, 326,
    447
Chronog. 354 (T. Mommsen, *MGH* IX)
  pp. 146, 148: 115
Cicero
  Ad Att. 1.14.5: 151
  Ad Fam. 8.11.4: 309
  Ad Q. Fr.
    2.1.1: 151
    2.11.1: 126
  De Domo 8: 134
  De Legibus 3.40: 135
  Pro Sulla 41-42: 316
  Red. Sen. 26: 151
Columella
  De re rust.
    I praef. 9-10: 12
    I praef. 10: 55
    1.1.19: 58, 152
Cyprian
  Ep. 80.1.2-3: 450
Dio
  40.46.1: 218
  44.16.1: 319
  46.46.3-4: 367
  51.19.2: 408
  51.22.1: 115
  52.19.2: 53
  52.20.1-2: 18
  52.31.1: 424
  52.31.3-4: 471
  52.32.2-3: 282
  52.42.6: 140
  52.43.1: 463
  53.1.3: 164

  53.11.5: 438
  53.12.4: 395
  53.12.9: 392
  53.13.2: 348
  53.14.1: 151
  53.14.2: 349
  53.14.3: 353, 403
  53.15.6: 376
  53.17.5: 428
  53.18.4: 355
  53.21.3: 434
  53.21.5: 463
  53.21.6: 412
  53.23.7: 460
  53.27.6: 90
  53.32.5: 165
  53.33.1-2: 463
  54.1.3: 197
  54.3: 404, 460
  54.4.1: 395
  54.10.2: 409
  54.14.1: 131
  54.14.3: 270
  54.14.4-5: 29
  54.15.2: 462
  54.15.5-6: 241
  54.16.2: 44
  54.17.3: 10
  54.18.3: 138, 277
  54.24.7: 427
  54.25.5-6: 438
  54.26.3-5: 10
  54.26.8: 132
  54.27.4: 278
  54.30.1: 224
  54.30.4: 466
  54.30.5: 438
  54.35.1: 132, 137

GENERAL INDEX

Most Romans are indexed under their *nomen* (that is, in many cases, the *second* of their names). However, emperors, authors, and a few others appear under the name by which they are commonly known.

Plautius, *see* Aelius
Plautius, A., 362
Plautius Lateranus, 29, 52
Plautius Silvanus, M., 465
Plautius Silvanus Aelianus, Tib., 326, 444
Plebeii, ludi, 60-62
Pliny (Elder), 193, 333
Pliny (Younger), consul, 227-28; governor, 400, 403, 498; lifestyle, 49, 58, 62, 74-75; priest, 346;
    and senate: as advocate, 65, 156, 376, 473-74; attacks Publicius Certus, 238, 252; canvasses, 55; describes sessions, 248, 251-52, 264-65, 461-62, 500-501; enters, 12; estimate, 84-85, 87, 269; references to "acclamation," 299-301; seeks guidance on procedure, 198-99, 223, 281-82; speaks first, 232; view of procedure, 221, 223-24
Plotina, 161, 519
Plotinus, 25
Plotius Sabinus, L., 69
Plutarch, 326, 370
Pola, 426
Pollenius Sebennus, 510
Pollentia, 384
Polybius, 156
pomerium, 99, 114, 119-20, 390, 527
Pompeii, 384-85, 443
Pompeius, Sex., 48, 57, 228, 247, 258, 271, 350
Pompeius Collega, 282, 504
Pompeius Hermippus, Cn., 424
Pompeius Macrinus Neos Theophanes, M., 143, 484
Pompeius Pennus, 229
Pompeius Secundus, Q., 274
Pompeius Silvanus Staberius Flavinus, M., 465, 481, 505, 509
Pompeius Sosius Falco, Q., 160-62, 181
Pomponius, Q., 189
Pomponius Bassus, T., 153
Pomponius Flaccus, L., 204, 246
Pomponius Gallus Didius Rufus, C., 402
Pomponius Graecinus, C., 201, 237
Pomponius Labeo, 507
pontifex maximus, 355, 527
Pontius Allifanus, L., 211
Pontius Laelianus Larcius Sabinus, M., 335
Pontius Paulinus, C., 62
Pontus, *see* Bithynia
Popilius Pedo Apronianus, 183, 325
Poppaea, 24, 358, 387
Poppaea Sabina, 252

populi diurna acta, 195, 199, 306, 308-10, 317, 323, 326, 333, 527
Porcius Optatus Flamma, P., 411
Porcius Priscus Longinus, C., 335
Postumus Romulus, P., 36
Praeneste, 58
praetor, 18-20, 90, 130, 151, 167, 243, 522; election, 204-207; expenses, 61-64; games, 59-62, 347;
    and senate: powers, 185-87, 235, 237; seating, 123
Praetorian camp, 99, 120, 191
Praetorian guard, 81-82, 377, 384, 426-27, 438, 440, 527
Praetorian prefect, 11, 160-61, 367-68
praetorius, 147-48, 246-47, 348-49, 393, 396, 527
priest (of senate), 96
priesthood (Roman), 23, 60, 355; games, 60; nominations, 208, 345-46; role in senate, 237; voted by senate, 388, 518
Primus, M., 404, 460, 464
princeps senatus, 164-65, 240, 527
Priscillianus, L., 480
privatus: attendance of emperor as, 175-76, 180, 184; position of, 166, 237-38, 278, 527
proconsul, 145, 392-407, 527, 532-33; date of entry to office, 497-98; extended terms, 505-506; selection, 348-53
Proculus, 405
procurator, 78, 527
profectio, 70-72, 409, 527
Propertius Postumus, C., 20, 373
Protogenes, 156
provinces: administration, 392-407; character, 352
Pteleon, 418
Ptolemy (king of Mauretania), 411
Ptolemy Apion (king of Cyrene), 400, 475
publica acta, *see* populi diurna acta
Publicius Certus, 91, 130, 143, 238, 252, 266, 272, 300, 476
Pupienus, 165, 197, 245, 409, 522
Pusio, *see* Cornelius
Puteolia, 384, 417

quaestio, 74, 139, 211, 287, 460-68, 482, 484
quaestor, 13-14, 24, 131-33, 155, 187, 313, 348-49, 522; ages, 17-18; designate, 243, 515-16; duties, 17, 130, 145, 151, 208, 303, 398, 497; expenses, 58-61; salary, 64; timing of election, 204-207, 214; voting rights in senate, 150

211, 262, 276, 409; relationship with emperor, 68-73, 136, 152, 163-64, 171-72; residence, 40, 56-58, 67-68, 141, 152, 188, 441; respect for age, 153; restrictions on movement, 139-40, 515; retirement age, 150, 515; salaries, 64-65, 79; salutatio, 74, 441; seating at shows, 43, 72, 439; shoes, 219-20; snobbery, 34-35, 494; suburban property, 58; wealth, 47-53, 495-97

senatus consultum, 162, 212, 431-59; emperors' references, 517; form, 304; identification, 304-305; passed by acclamation, 301-302; publication, 306-308; registration, 170, 285, 303, 308, 313, 315, 440; relationship to oratio, 294-97; "writing," 247, 285, 303, 312, 315, 319

Seneca (Elder), 12, 323-24

Seneca (Younger), 32, 37, 75, 135, 326; career, 77; estimate of senate, 82-83; houses, 58

sententiae, 233, 308, 331, 528; assent, 255; decision deferred, 198, 275, 280-81, 292-93, 499; delivery, 253-57, 261-62, 268-70, 504; division, 282; extra sententias, 515-16; "off the question," 257-60; order, 222, 240-49; prima, 244, 281, 292, 317, 321, 499, 527; pugnantes, 281; put to the vote, 281-83; scope, 256-57; sworn, 223; variae, 254; vetoed, 170-71; withdrawal, 260-61, 282

Sentius Saturninus, C., 383

Sentius Saturninus, Cn., 274

Septimius Severus (addressed by Statius), 32

Septimius Severus (emperor), 71, 359, 521; accent, 268; career, 12, 16, 344, 352; deifies Commodus, 170, 358, 387; honors, 360, 410, 518-19; legislation under, 449-50; measures, 41-42, 143, 294, 394, 399; offers Numerianus senatorial rank, 90; routine, 189, 193-95; senatorial embassy to, 411; verdicts, 62, 152; wealth, 52, 57
　　and senate: attends, 158, 160, 181, 183, 478; communicates, 230, 296; condemned, 356; elevated, 120; reads acta senatus, 310, 323; relationship, 47, 470, 491; speaks, 169, 325; summons secret session, 199

Septimius Severus, C., 12

Septizonium, 57, 99

Servaeus, Q., 328

Servilia, 270

Servilius Fabianus Maximus, M., 335

Servilius Nonianus, M., 333

Severiana, 494

Severus Alexander, 345, 399, 522; legislation under, 450;
　　and senate: attends, 183, 389; designated consul, 204; ius relationis, 166; reltionship, 471

Sextilis, 361, 433, 438

Sextius Africanus, T., 203

shorthand: development of, 316-17, 320; writer (notarius), 125, 129, 314-17, 320-21, 526

Sibylline books/oracles, 168-69, 391

Sicily, 133, 140, 351-52, 395, 532

Side, 97

Silanianum, SC, 435-36, 438-39, 441-43, 448

Silanus, *see* Iunius

Silius, C. (cos. A.D. 48), 232-33

Silius A. Caecina Largus, C. (cos. A.D. 13), 189, 259, 357, 475, 507

Silius Italicus, 70, 74, 154

Silvius, 205

Smyrna, 41, 97, 108, 149, 281, 348, 400, 421-22

sodales, Antoniniani, 345

sodales Augustales, 345

Sollers, 87

Solon, J., 54

Sosia Falconilla, 95

Sparta, 329, 390, 413, 418

Statilius Maximus, T., 335

Statilius Taurus, T., 183, 413, 508. *See also* 451

Statilius Taurus Corvinus T. (cos. 45), 441

Stoic beliefs, influence of, 25

Strabo Aemilianus, 88

Stratonicea-Hadrianopolis, 414

Suetonius, use of acta senatus by, 310, 313-14, 324-25

suffectus, consul, 21, 201-207, 242-43, 528

Suillius Rufus, P., 48, 170, 177, 232-33, 261, 440, 472, 508

Sulla, L. (praetorius), 10

Sulla, L. (noble), 83, 329-30

Sulpicia Praetextata, 157

Sulpicius Camerinus, Q., 508

Sulpicius Galba, C., 144, 239, 350, 440

Sulpicius Quirinius, P., 50, 364, 370

sunrise (at Rome), 502-503

sunset (at Rome), 502-503

supplicatio, 388-89, 528

Library of Congress Cataloging
in Publication Data

Talbert, Richard J. A., 1947-
The Senate of Imperial Rome.
Bibliography: p.
Includes index.
1. Rome. Senate. 2. Rome—Politics and
government—30 B.C.-284 A.D. I. Title.
JC85.S4T17   1984   328′.3′0937   83-42580

ISBN 0-691-05400-2